The J. Paul Getty Museum
Handbook of the Collection

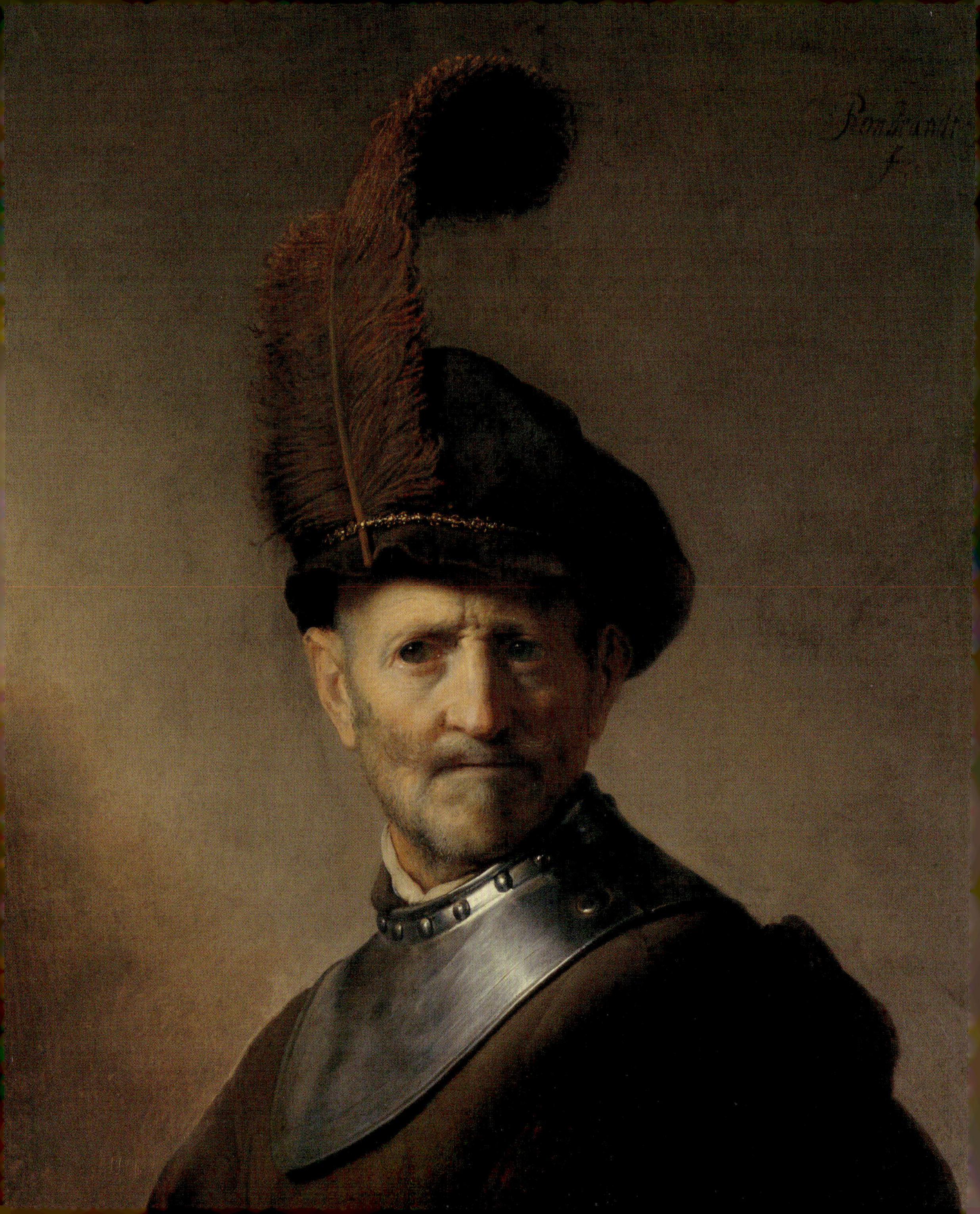
Rembrandt
f.

The J. Paul Getty Museum

Handbook of the Collection

Los Angeles

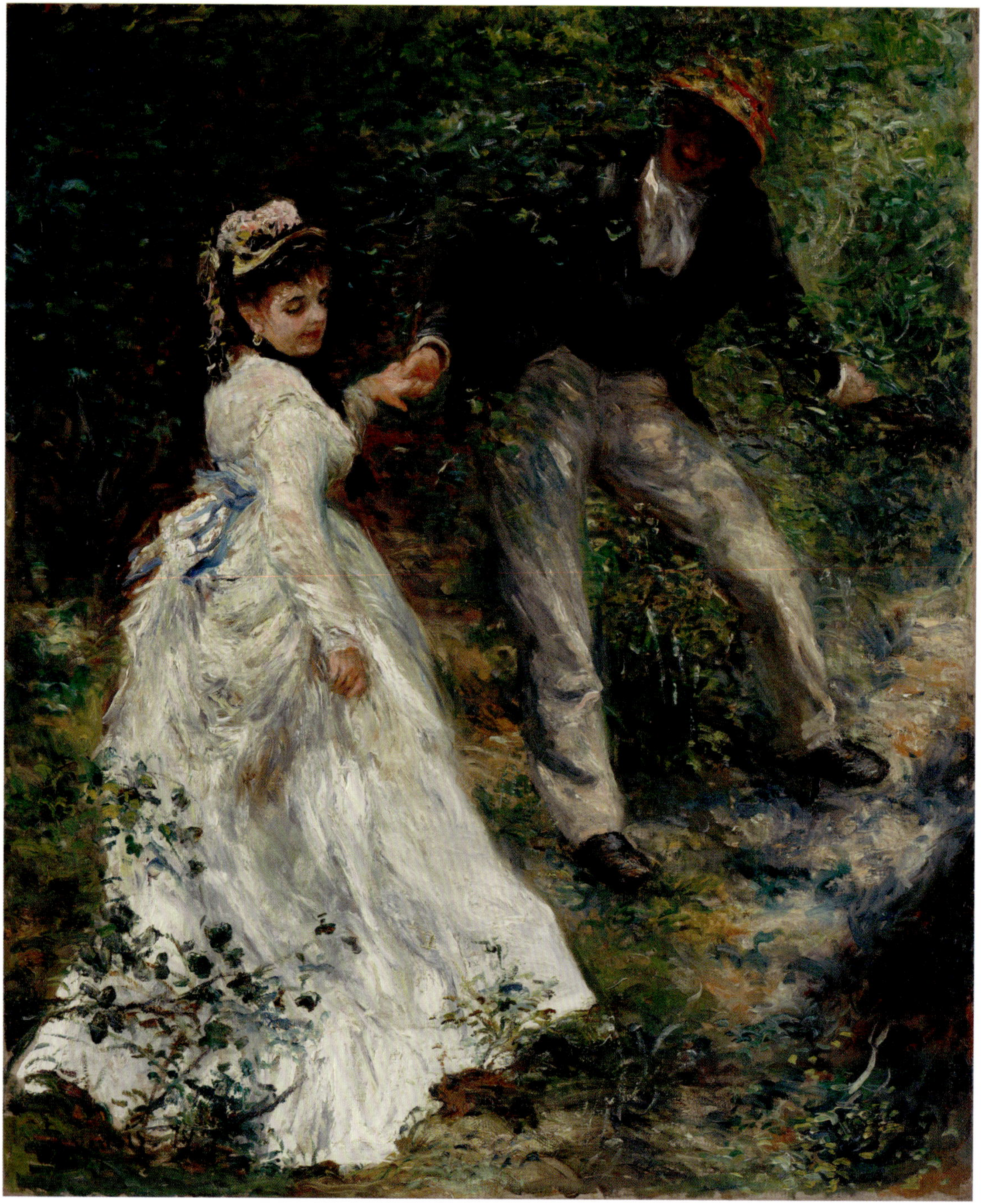

Contents

Foreword

Of the many great museums in the United States and around the world, none is quite like the Getty. Its eponymous founder was the oil magnate J. Paul Getty, and the ambition that underpinned his business success can be seen also in his decision to direct the bulk of his estate to the creation of an institution devoted to the visual arts. Today, some five decades later, the museum he made possible contains one of the most distinguished collections of ancient through nineteenth-century European art in the world, displayed in twin buildings that have themselves become architectural icons of Roman classicism and late-twentieth-century modernism, surrounded by celebrated gardens and landscaping, all giving way onto some of the most spectacular views over the cityscape of Los Angeles. As nearly two million visitors per year can testify, once visited, the Getty Museum is never forgotten.

This is a remarkable achievement for what is still a young institution. When Mr. Getty started collecting for his private residences in the 1930s, his focus was on Greek and Roman antiquities, French furniture and decorative arts of the seventeenth and eighteenth centuries, and a smaller assemblage of old master paintings. He opened the most important of these treasures to public view in 1954 with the conversion of his Malibu ranch house (on the site of the current Villa) into a museum. However, it was only with the settlement of Getty's estate in 1982, which left his fortune to support a trust that would "maintain and perpetuate ... a museum, gallery of art and library for the diffusion of artistic and general knowledge," that collecting began in earnest for what was clearly going to be a trailblazing newcomer among the world's leading museums. Thanks to the appointment of some of the most distinguished directors, curators, and conservators of their generations, the decades that followed saw the Getty's collection grow in scope and quality to become the finest west of Chicago, making the Museum the must-see cultural attraction of California.

From this rebirth as a fully professional institution, it was clear that the narrow scope of the founder's collecting was too arbitrary and constraining for a museum of the Getty's newfound ambition and broad educational mission. In 1983–84, new departments of Manuscripts, Drawings, and Photographs were created, and the department of Decorative Arts was broadened to include all such media and sculpture. The temporal range of the collection also was extended by the trustees from Mr. Getty's terminus of around 1800 to the early 1900s, thus making possible the more rounded representation of European art from ancient Greece to the birth of modernism that today's visitor enjoys.

Even this expanded remit has been interpreted liberally, with the result that the collection now embraces works of art from as far afield as Egypt, Iraq, Persia, Ethiopia, and Armenia. As the understanding of art history becomes increasingly global and intercultural, this broader context of artistic and cultural traditions that interacted with Europe will continue to be reflected in our exhibitions and acquisitions. The commissioning of a sculpture by Martin Puryear in 1999 and the generous gift in 2005 of the Fran and Ray Stark collection of twentieth-century sculpture, installed in prominent positions around the Getty Center, have allowed us to extend our presentation of the history of this medium even closer to the present day.

Research on the history, materiality, and appreciation of art not only informs how we build the collection but is critical also to the lectures, workshops, theatrical performances, and many other educational programs that complement the Museum's displays. In this we are uniquely fortunate to have as collaborators our sister programs, the Getty Research Institute, the Getty Conservation Institute, and the Getty Foundation. As well as a great museum, this broader Getty is effectively a university of the arts, convening programs of research, conservation, training, and education that have a global impact on the preservation and understanding of the world's artistic heritage and, in the process, attracts into our midst many of the greatest and most innovative minds.

If a collection is defined by what it *is*, a museum as a whole is defined by what it *does*. Our core mission is educational: to make the works of art come alive, both by explaining the meanings that their makers intended them to convey and by connecting these to the interests of today's visitors of all ages and backgrounds. Beyond the walls of the Museum, the means of engaging with the Getty and other museums are rapidly expanding through web-based access and mobile devices, technologies that we continue to expand and enhance. That said, the visual, emotional, and even spiritual power of the face-to-face encounter with great works of art has in no way diminished—as is confirmed, happily, by the multitude of visitors who come to the Getty to experience our collection directly and unmediated. It is our hope that the *Handbook* will provide both a memento of such a visit and an inspiration to those who have yet to enjoy the delights in store at the Getty Villa and the Getty Center.

Timothy Potts
Maria Hummer-Tuttle and Robert Tuttle Director

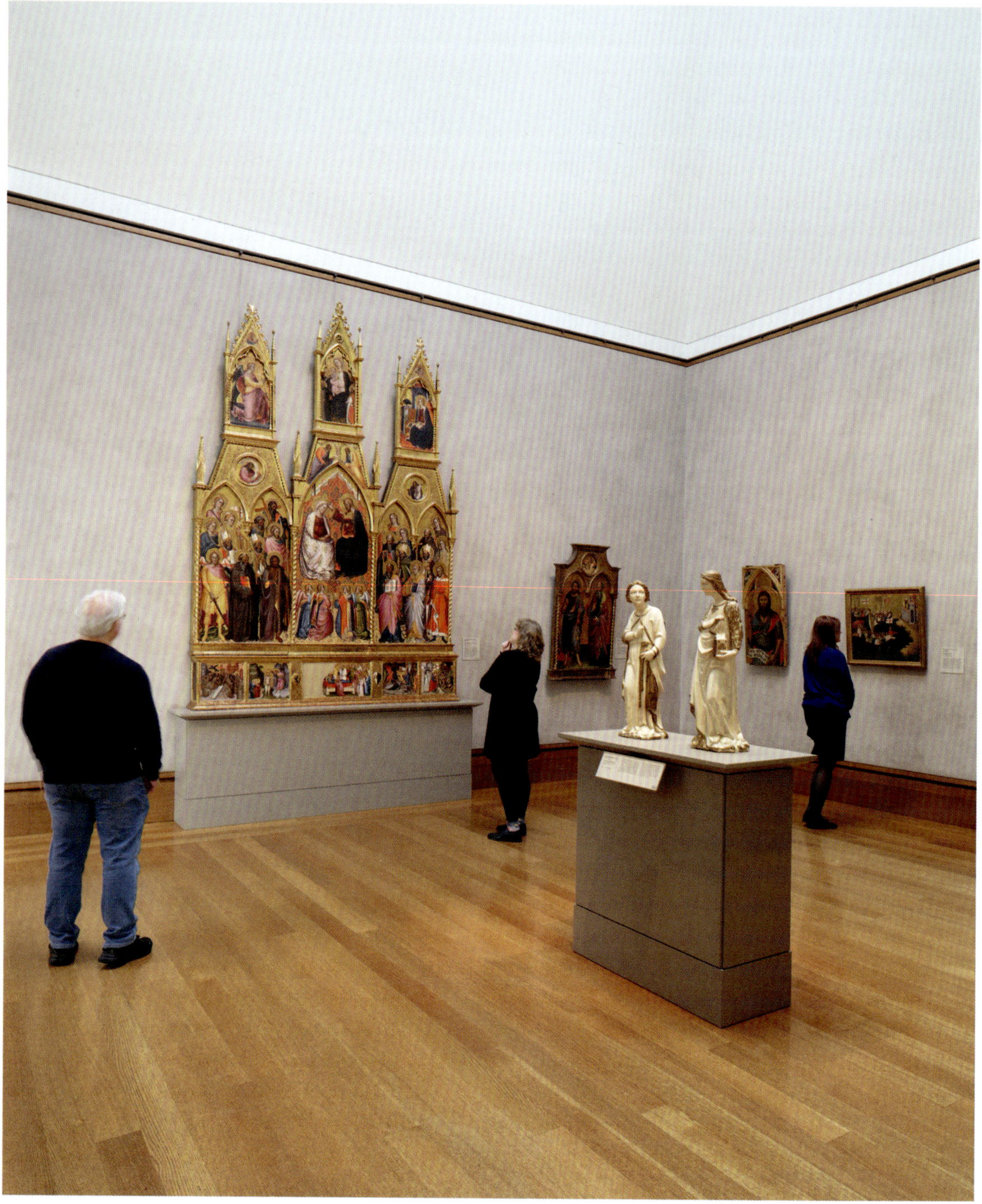

Introduction

Each year the J. Paul Getty Museum welcomes nearly two million visitors from all over the world to its two spectacular locations in Los Angeles: the "original" Getty Villa in Malibu (opened 1974) and its much larger sister, the Getty Center, in the Santa Monica Mountains (opened 1997). Both renowned for their enticing combination of magnificent art, vibrant gardens, and iconic architecture, the two sites offer an overview of European art history, from antiquity through the Middle Ages and the Renaissance, up to nineteenth-century Impressionism and photography from its inception to the present day.

The Getty Museum began as the personal endeavor of Jean Paul Getty (1892–1976), a bold, wealthy, and eccentric individual. Known as Paul to family and friends, he was an oil prospector, businessman, writer, and art collector whose life was marked by both personal tribulation and astonishing financial success. Born in Minneapolis in 1892, Paul was the only surviving child of Sarah Risher Getty and George Franklin Getty, an attorney-turned-oilman who moved his family first to the Oklahoma Territory in 1904 and shortly later to Los Angeles. There, Paul attended high school, returning to work in the Oklahoma oil fields during summer vacations. After briefly attending the University of Southern California and the University of California, Berkeley, Paul studied political science and economics at the University of Oxford in England. Acceding to his father's wish that he devote one year to the oil business, in the fall of 1915 the young Getty struck oil near Stone Bluff, Oklahoma, and by the age of twenty-three was able to declare himself a millionaire. After his father's death in 1930, Paul prevailed in a bitter battle with his mother for control of his father's company and quickly built a reputation as a shrewd and audacious businessman. Though keenly focused on his oil investments, Getty used his growing wealth to pursue other passions—one of which was art.

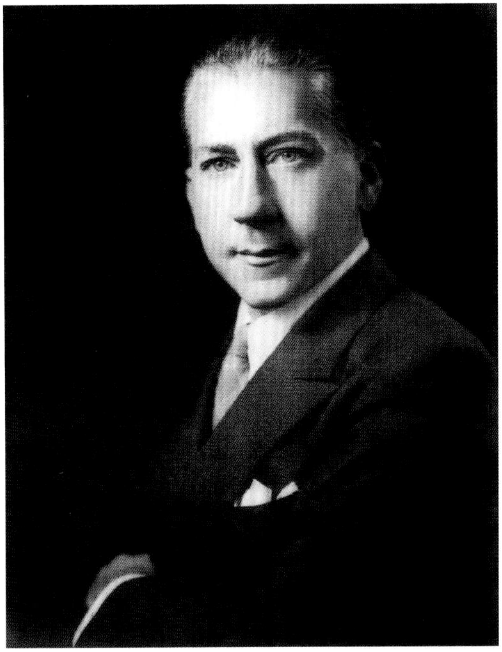
J. Paul Getty

Getty traveled widely, read voraciously, and visited museums across Europe and the Middle East. Ever the smart investor, he recognized the economic depression of 1929 as an opportunity to begin collecting art, purchasing his first object of value, a landscape by the seventeenth-century Dutch painter Jan van Goyen, at auction in Berlin for about $1,100. It was his first taste of what he later described as "the romance and zest—the excitement, suspense, thrills, and triumphs—that make art collecting one of the most exhilarating and satisfying of all human endeavors."

As a collector, Getty prided himself on following his own tastes. He initially focused on Italian Renaissance and Baroque paintings, as well as works by Rembrandt van Rijn and other Dutch masters. A 1936 stay in a New York penthouse containing furniture from the era of Louis XV inspired him to collect French decorative

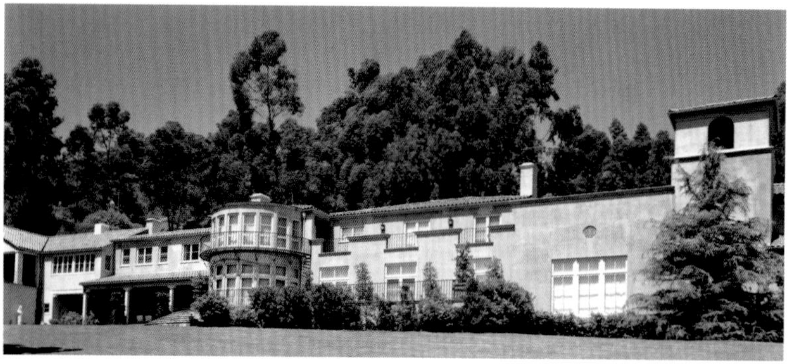

The Museum at the ranch house, circa 1965

arts, and at one sale in 1938 he acquired, among other items, a Savonnerie carpet and a rolltop desk by Bernard Molitor—rare and prized objects of a quality not often seen on the market. A visit to the Vatican Museums in 1939 reinforced his early interest in antiquities, especially sculpture, and shortly thereafter he acquired the marble portrait heads of two Roman empresses.

World War II temporarily curtailed Getty's collecting activities. His oil companies, however, performed well throughout the war, providing capital for expansion into the European oil market and exploration in North Africa and the Middle East. Getty's instincts and timing paid off again when oil was discovered in a concession he had acquired along the Kuwait–Saudi Arabia border, and his personal wealth soared. In 1951 Getty took up residence in England at Sutton Place, a sprawling Tudor estate outside London, where he was closer to his burgeoning businesses. He never again set foot on American soil.

Over the following decades, Getty continued very actively to collect, now with an increasing awareness of art's value to the public. Though he would later earn a reputation for parsimony—illustrated most famously by the pay phone he had installed in the seventy-two-room mansion—he acquired a number of major works of art that are still considered among the most important in the Museum's collection, including the monumental Roman Lansdowne Herakles, Rembrandt's *Saint Bartholomew*, and a double desk by Bernard II van Risenburgh. Getty also made several generous donations to museums in the years before establishing his own institution, including three of his most valuable works—Rembrandt's *Portrait of Marten Looten* and two spectacular Persian carpets—which he gave to the Los Angeles County Museum of Art. His stated desire "to make fine art freely available for viewing by the greatest possible number of people" seems to have been genuine. In response to suggestions that he owned enough art to open his own collection to the public, in 1954 he made part of a ranch house he owned in Malibu accessible to visitors on selected days.

Three years later, in 1957, *Fortune* magazine named Getty the richest living American. The article made him a celebrity, a status he did not always enjoy. The press would thereafter report every turn in his private life, which ultimately included five marriages, five divorces, and the births of five sons, one of whom died during childhood.

Although Getty never returned to Los Angeles, at Sutton Place one evening in 1968 he made the

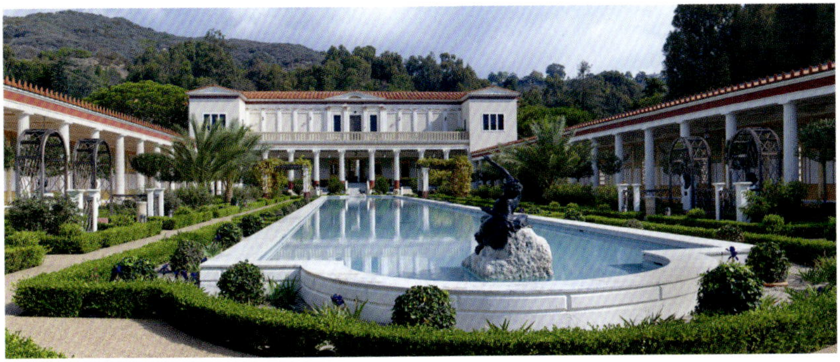

The Outer Peristyle at the Getty Villa

surprising announcement that he wished to build a purpose-designed museum on the grounds of his Malibu property. It would be a near replica of the Villa dei Papiri, a partially excavated ancient Roman villa in Herculaneum, overlooking the Bay of Naples, Italy, which had been buried by the eruption of Mount Vesuvius in 79 CE that had also destroyed nearby Pompeii. Ground was broken on its construction in December 1970; additional staff members were hired; and over subsequent years numerous works of art were purchased to fill the new galleries. Getty supervised all aspects of the architecture and design from England, approving acquisitions and proudly displaying an architectural model of the Villa to his friends. The new J. Paul Getty Museum opened its doors in January 1974. Getty did not attend the opening and died two years later, in 1976, at the age of eighty-three, never having seen the museum that bore his name.

Upon his death Getty left four million shares of Getty Oil stock, worth about $700 million, to his Museum. By the time the estate was settled in 1982, the value of the shares had grown to $1.2 billion. Faced with the responsibility of allocating these exceptional resources, the J. Paul Getty Trust's board of trustees decided, in accordance with Getty's wishes, to strengthen the Museum and support the advancement of art scholarship, education, conservation, and related philanthropic initiatives. The Museum would continue to acquire in Getty's three major areas of interest—European antiquities, decorative arts, and pre-twentieth-century paintings—but it would also expand the scope of its collecting to include new departments of illuminated manuscripts and drawings, a wider range of decorative arts and sculpture, and, in a more radical extension into contemporary art, photography from its inception to the present day.

It was clear that this ambitious acquisition program would require more space for the display of art and associated programming. The trustees envisioned a complex similar to a university campus, a place where the many approaches to understanding art—display, scholarship, conservation, and education—could flourish. A dramatic 742-acre spur of the Santa Monica Mountains in west Los Angeles was purchased in 1983, and plans for the Getty Center were set in motion.

In 1984 Richard Meier was appointed architect of the new Getty Center. Inspired by the location, which overlooks the urban landscape of Los Angeles and the Pacific Ocean, Meier designed the complex to highlight both nature and culture. The celebrated American artist Robert

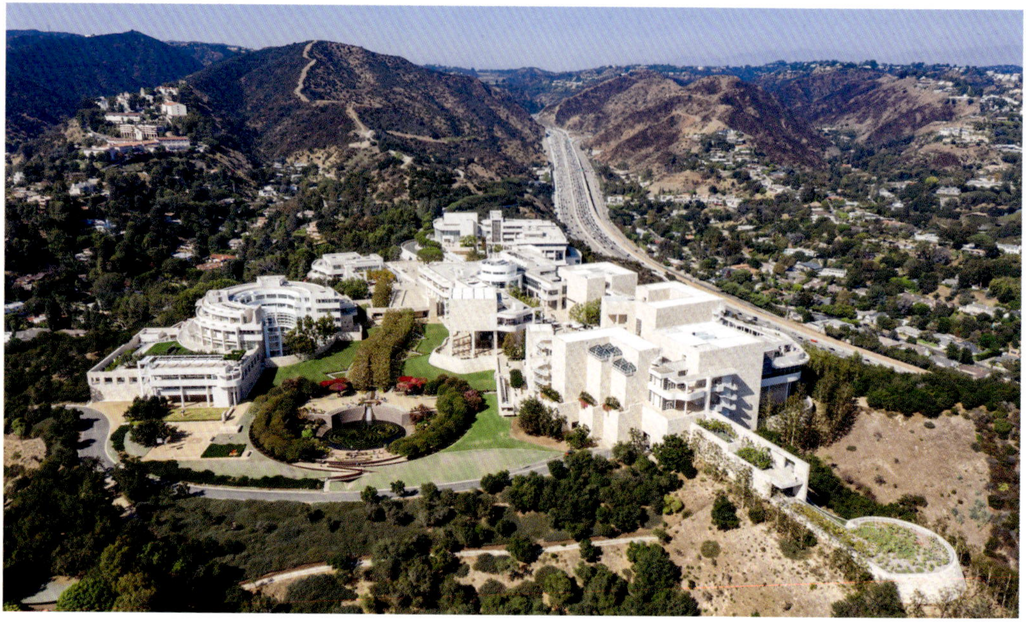

Aerial view of the Getty Center and Central Garden

Irwin was commissioned to design the Central Garden, an evolving work of art with tree-lined walkways that lead visitors through a sensual variety of sights, sounds, and scents. Construction began in 1989, and the Getty Center opened in 1997. Today the site houses four Getty programs: the J. Paul Getty Museum, the Getty Conservation Institute, the Getty Research Institute, and the Getty Foundation.

The Museum's collection is arranged in historical sequence across four pavilions, starting in the Middle Ages and ending with photography of the twenty-first century; a fifth pavilion is reserved for major international loan exhibitions. The plaza level includes several galleries dedicated to the display of light-sensitive works, including drawings and manuscripts, as well as the collection of decorative arts, while the second floor of each pavilion showcases paintings and sculpture that benefit from controlled natural light.

In 2005 the Museum was enhanced by the gift of twenty-eight modern and contemporary outdoor sculptures, from the collection of Ray and Fran Stark. The following year, the Center for Photographs opened in the West Pavilion, giving the Museum one of the largest gallery spaces devoted to photography in the country.

Following the opening of the Getty Center, the original museum in Malibu underwent a major renovation, designed by the firm Machado Silvetti. The expanded and enhanced Getty Villa reopened in 2006, dedicated exclusively to the arts of ancient Greece, Rome, and Etruria. A reinstallation, completed in 2018, created a broadly historical presentation of the collection that allows visitors to follow the development of Greek and Roman art over some five thousand years, from the Bronze Age through the late Roman Empire. The Villa remains the only museum in the United States devoted solely to the arts of the classical world.

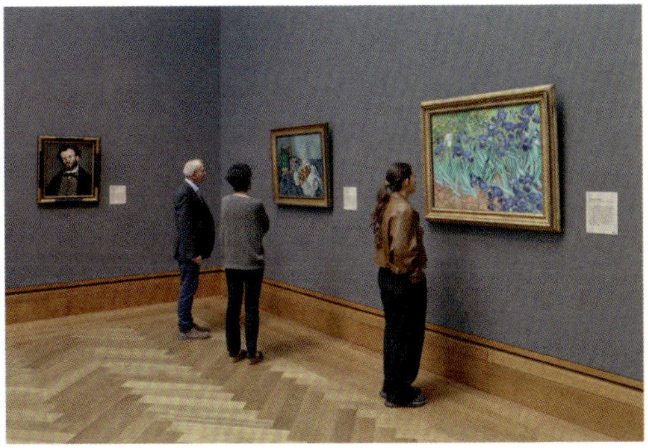

Interior view of a West Pavilion gallery at the Getty Center

Its gardens are integral to its coastal setting and include herbs and shrubs inspired by those grown in ancient Roman homes for food and ceremony.

In recent years the deployment of digital technologies has helped make the Museum's collection available to a much broader audience. In 2013, with the adoption of its Open Content policy, Getty became one of the first cultural institutions to offer full digital access to its holdings, making high-resolution downloads of color images of thousands of artworks available free of charge. Getty's website now also features comprehensive records of its holdings, including provenance history and other scholarly information. Virtual programming and Getty's social media channels offer further ways to access the collections and engage with the visual arts across local and global communities.

To remain dynamic and engaging, the Getty Museum, like other museums, needs to embrace new approaches and perspectives. In recent years this has included temporary interventions and installations of contemporary art within the permanent displays at both Getty Museum sites; the Classical Worlds in Context series of exhibitions at the Getty Villa; and the introduction of bilingual English and Spanish labels and narratives. Reflecting Getty's philanthropic mission, every five years the Getty-sponsored initiative PST ART brings dozens of cultural institutions across Southern California together in exploring a single theme through exhibitions and public programs. Additionally, considerations of environmental and climate sustainability increasingly influence all our activities, displays, and outreach.

Seventy years have elapsed since J. Paul Getty first opened his collection to the public. Today, in addition to showcasing its remarkable collection, the Getty Museum each year presents a rich schedule of visiting exhibitions from around the world; hosts nearly a hundred thousand schoolchildren on guided tours; restores and conserves important artworks from major museums and institutions; publishes books on the arts and culture for scholars, art enthusiasts, and young readers; and offers a wide selection of free public programs, from tours, classes, concerts, and plays to family festivals, films, lectures, and scholarly symposia. A heightened emphasis on providing memorable and inspiring experiences of the visual arts to visitors of all ages and backgrounds will continue to ground our mission in the years ahead.

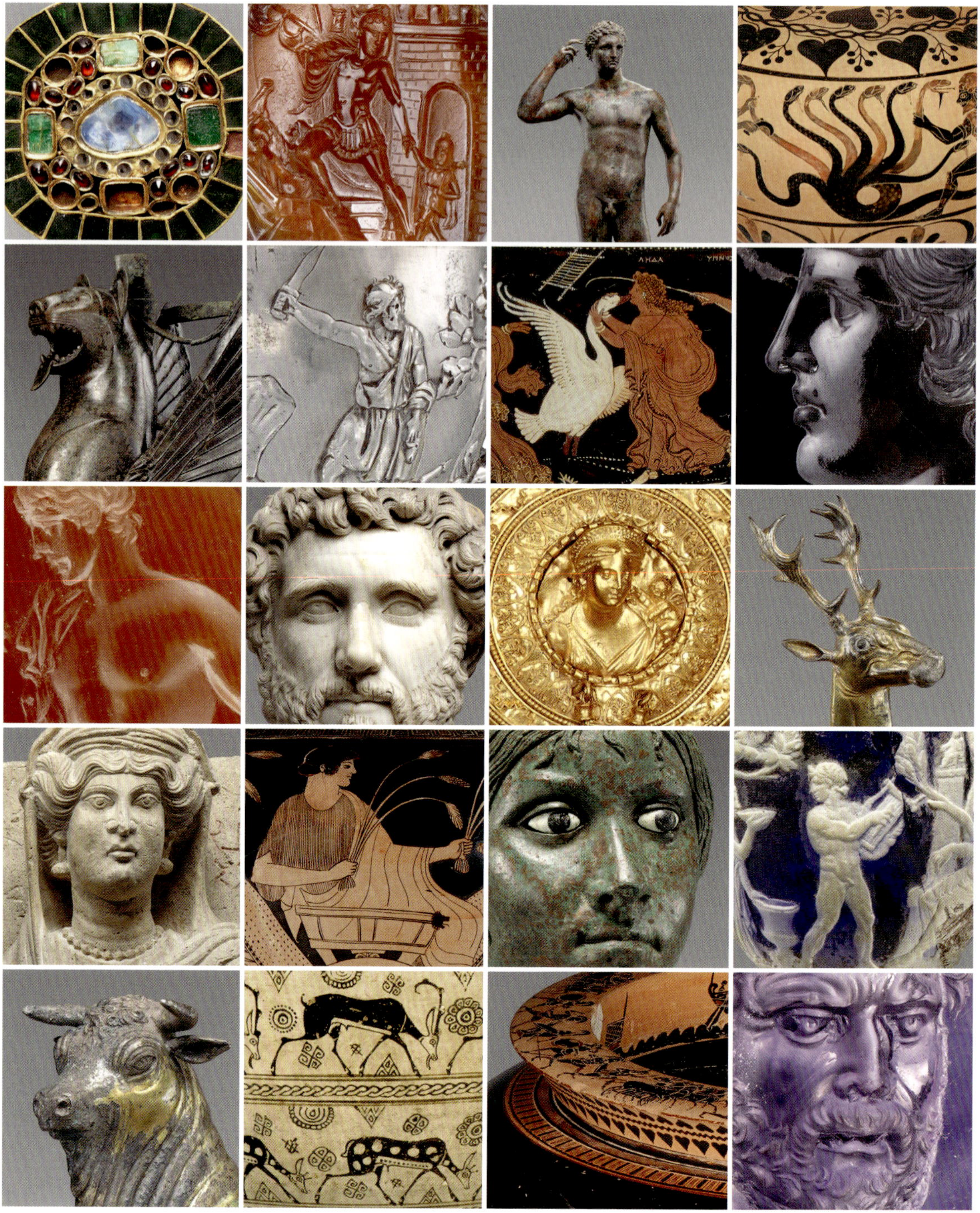
ΛΗΔΑ

Antiquities

J. Paul Getty traveled widely throughout his life, visiting museums and archaeological sites across Europe, along the shores of the Mediterranean Sea, and in the Middle East. He first explored the ancient cities of Pompeii and Herculaneum in 1912 and later traced his interest in classical art to his earliest visits to Italy and Greece, where, as he later wrote, he "saw the crumbled and fragmentary remnants of the architectural marvels that these long dead civilizations have produced." Getty began collecting antiquities in Rome in the summer of 1939, some years after his first purchases of old master paintings and European decorative arts, and eventually bought two seaside villas in Italy, both built on ancient Roman ruins. In his diary for August 28, 1939, he wrote, "Decided to concentrate on Greco-Roman things as I like them best; and an occasional painting, new or old." From then until his final acquisition, in 1976, his collection of Greek, Roman, and Etruscan art grew to become one of the most important in North America. Indeed, Getty's love for classical art inspired him to model the Getty Villa Museum on the ancient Villa dei Papiri at Herculaneum, which was buried by the eruption of Mount Vesuvius in 79 CE.

Sculpture formed the heart of Getty's holdings, and he favored works associated with aristocratic British collectors. Many of the Museum's finest statues, including the Lansdowne Herakles (p. 76) and the portrait head of Alexander the Great (p. 46), were obtained under his personal direction. Since his death in 1976, acquisitions have ranged more broadly in time and place from early Bronze Age marble figures from Anatolia and the Cyclades that illustrate the prehistoric origins of stone carving in and around the Aegean (pp. 16–17), to the Hellenistic bronze statue of a victorious youth (p. 47), which is now an icon of the Villa. Together with works in other media and period styles, these attest to the outstanding achievements of the Greek artistic tradition throughout the Archaic, Classical, Hellenistic, and Roman periods. Greek vase painting is a strength of the Museum's holdings. More recently, important acquisitions of Greek and Roman engraved gems, gold jewelry, and silver luxury wares exemplify other artistic genres that were highly prized in elite circles in antiquity. And more than four hundred striking examples of glass collected by Erwin Oppenländer provide a comprehensive survey of ancient glassmaking techniques.

In scope, the antiquities collection reflects the geographic extent of the Roman Empire, including Parthian metalwork, Romano-Egyptian funerary portraits, and mosaics from Gaul, Tunisia, and Syria. Complementing the core collection, a small number of objects represent other cultures, from Persia to the Iberian Peninsula, demonstrating how the classical world interacted with, and was influenced by, the visual arts of neighboring peoples.

Female Figure of the Kilia Type

Anatolian, 4500–3500 BCE

Marble, H: 14.3 cm (5⅝ in.); W: 5.4 cm (2⅛ in.); D: 3.6 cm (1⁷⁄₁₆ in.), 88.AA.122

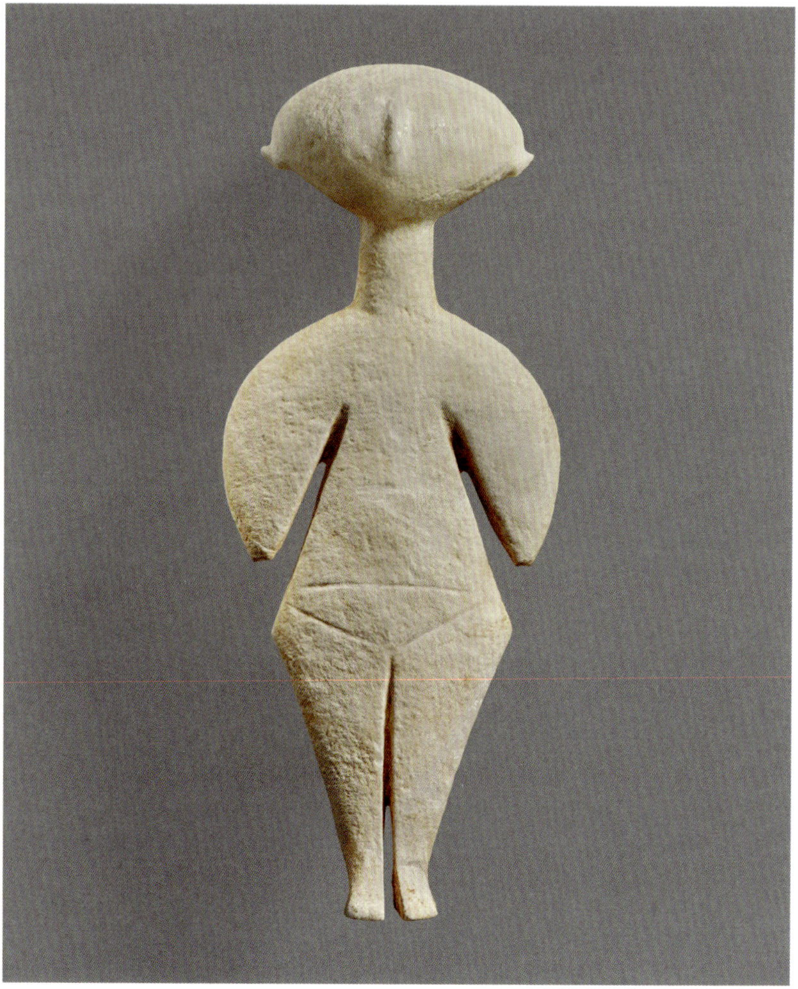

Female figures were produced throughout the Aegean basin during the prehistoric period, including in ancient Anatolia (present-day Turkey). This figure represents a highly stylized standing nude female. Her bulbous head, long neck, and flat body are characteristic of the so-called Kilia type, named after the village in northwest Turkey where the first examples were found. Carved from translucent white marble, these figures typically have carefully detailed ears, noses, and eyes, the last of which were likely originally painted. An incised triangle emphasizing the pubic area confirms that this statuette depicts a female. Kilia-type statuettes are considerably earlier than related marble figures produced in the Cyclades (p. 17). They are also likely associated with fertility and the cycle of life, central spiritual concerns in the ancient Mediterranean.

Statuette of a Harpist

Cycladic, circa 2500 BCE

Marble, H: 35.8 cm (14⅛ in.); W: 9.5 cm (3¾ in.); D: 28 cm (11 in.), 85.AA.103

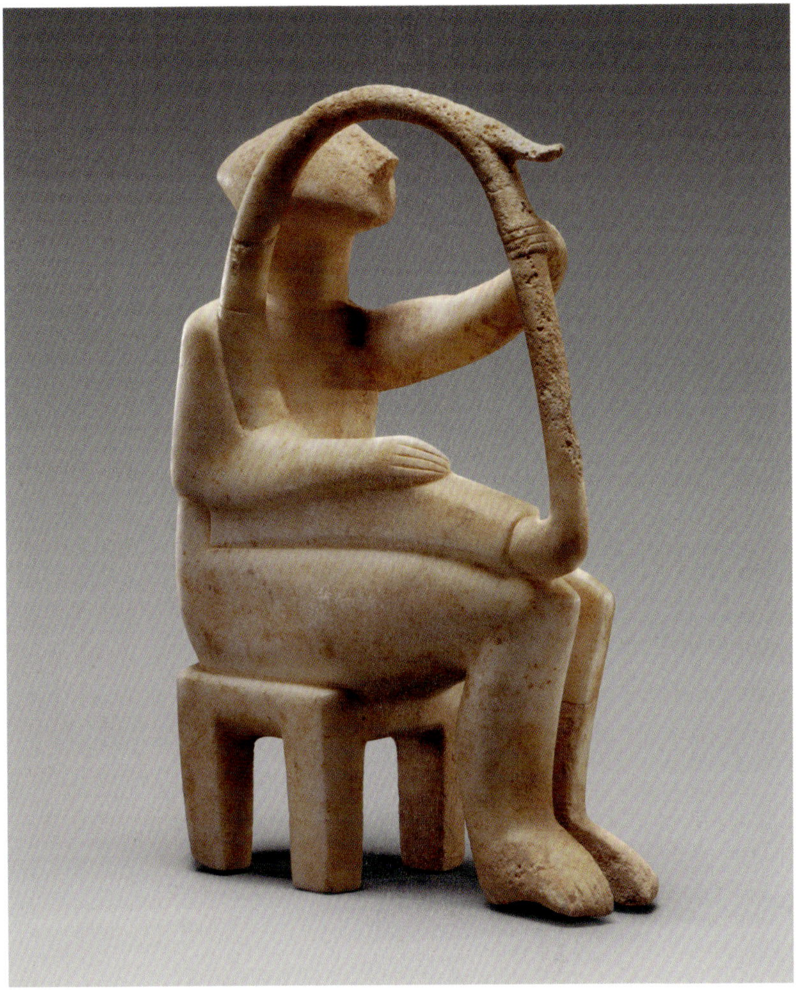

Head raised as if singing, this seated musician is one of only ten such figures known. Most Cycladic sculptures from the Early Bronze Age (ca. 3600–2070 BCE) represent standing or reclining females. Only five percent of them depict men, which, unlike the women, are frequently shown playing a musical instrument. The simplified forms reflect a taste for abstraction, but the figures' eyes and hair were once highlighted with added pigments, creating a considerably bolder visual impact for the ancient viewer. Musicians were important individuals in preliterate societies. They provided entertainment and transmitted common history, mythology, and folklore through their stories and songs. The instrument depicted here is a frame harp, which originated in the Near East and is the ancestor of the modern harp.

Gem Depicting a Bull Leaper

Minoan (made in Crete),

1450–1300 BCE

Blue-gray hematite lentoid, Diam: 1.9 cm (¾ in.); D: .7 cm (¼ in.), 2001.14.1

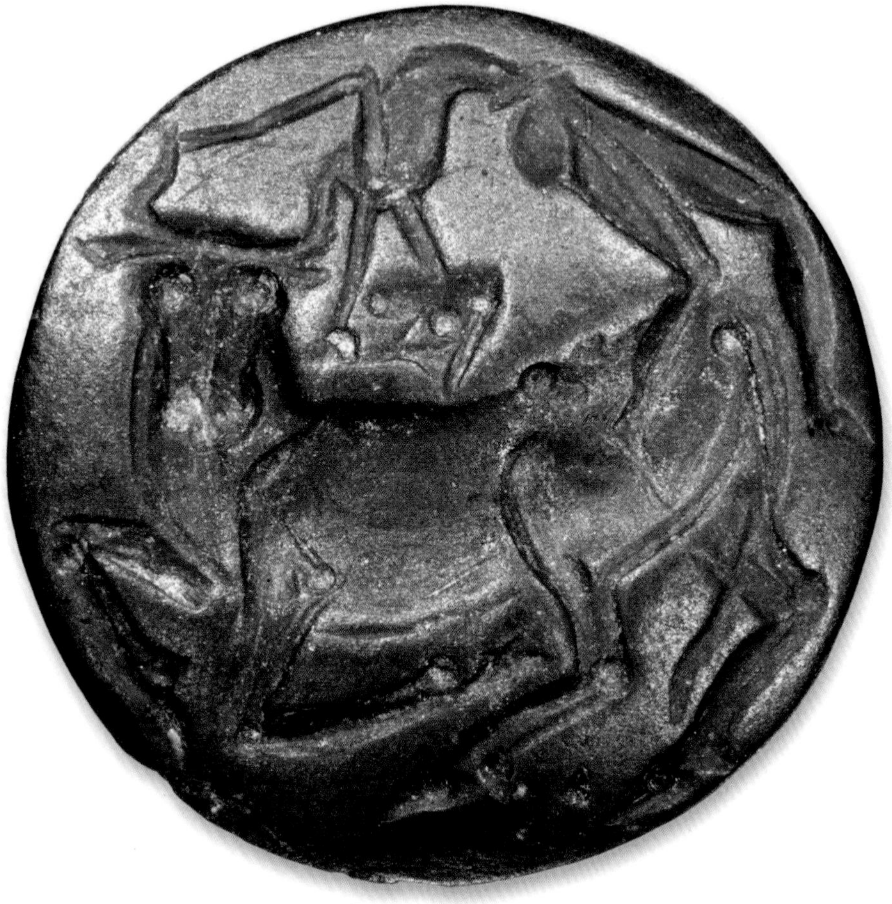

A male acrobat leaps over a bull, grabbing hold of one of its horns. The engraver has arranged the figures on this tabloid (lens-shaped) gem to accommodate the implied motion of the scene: the man's body arcs along the top edge, over the bull, which is forward facing and in profile. *Taurokathapsia* (bull leaping) scenes appear often in the art of Late Bronze Age Crete (ca. 1600–1200 BCE), not only on gems, but also in frescoes and as statuettes. Minoan craftspeople carved seals like this in stone, ivory, and other precious materials. When pressed into soft clay or wax, the engraved designs left relief impressions that served as a type of signature on documents or, when applied to pots and other containers, labeled or guaranteed their contents.

Furniture Support Representing a Winged Feline

Tartessian, 700–575 BCE

Bronze, H: 61 cm (24 in.); W: 19.4 cm ($7\frac{5}{8}$ in.); D: 33 cm (13 in.), 79.AC.140

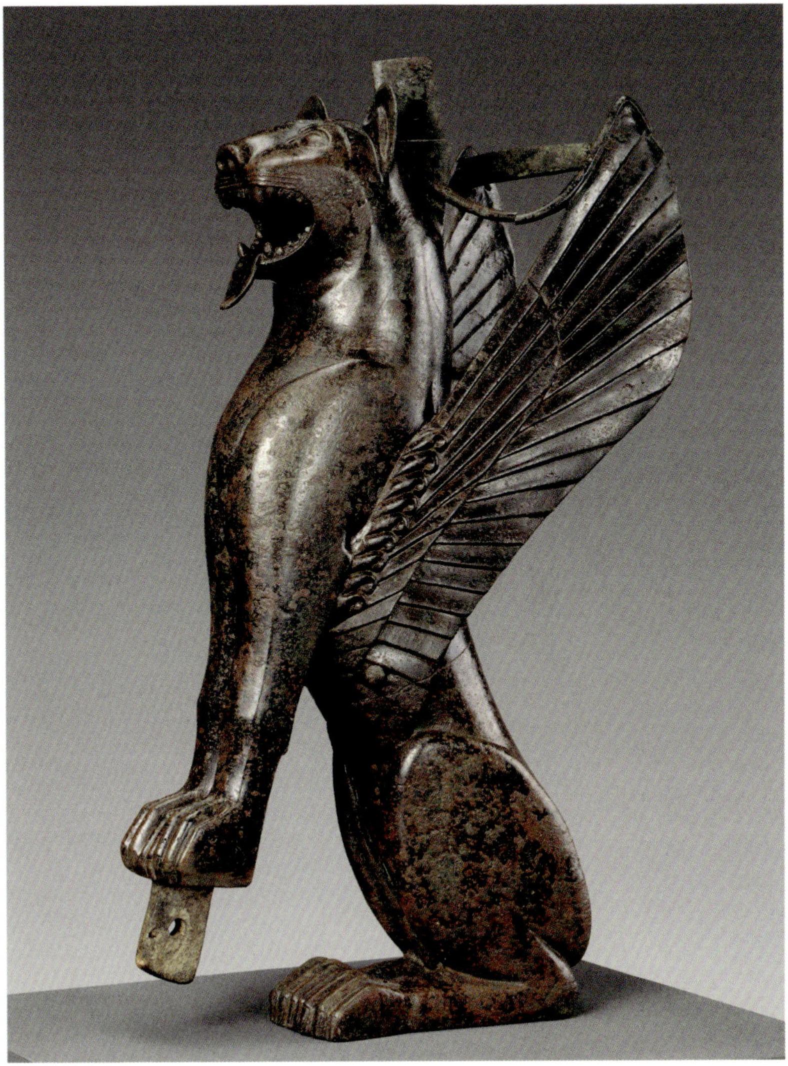

Details of the feathered wings and head of this imaginary lynxlike creature, as well as particularities of its manufacturing technique, suggest that it was made in Tartessos, an ancient kingdom on the southern Atlantic coast of present-day Spain. Rich in metal ores, particularly gold, silver, and tin, Tartessos was a key port of call on Greek, Phoenician, and Etruscan trade routes in the western Mediterranean. Tartessian art forms favored by local elites combine native Iberian elements with Eastern influences introduced by foreign merchants and colonists. This fearsome figure was cast in two pieces, which are joined with rivets just below the wings. Pierced projections behind the head and beneath the front paws indicate that it was part of a larger structure, probably a tripod-based candelabrum or incense burner.

Wine Jug (*Oinochoe*) with Animals

East Greek (made in Miletos), circa 625 BCE

Terracotta, H: 35.7 cm (14 in.); Diam (body): 26.5 cm (10⅜ in.), 81.AE.83

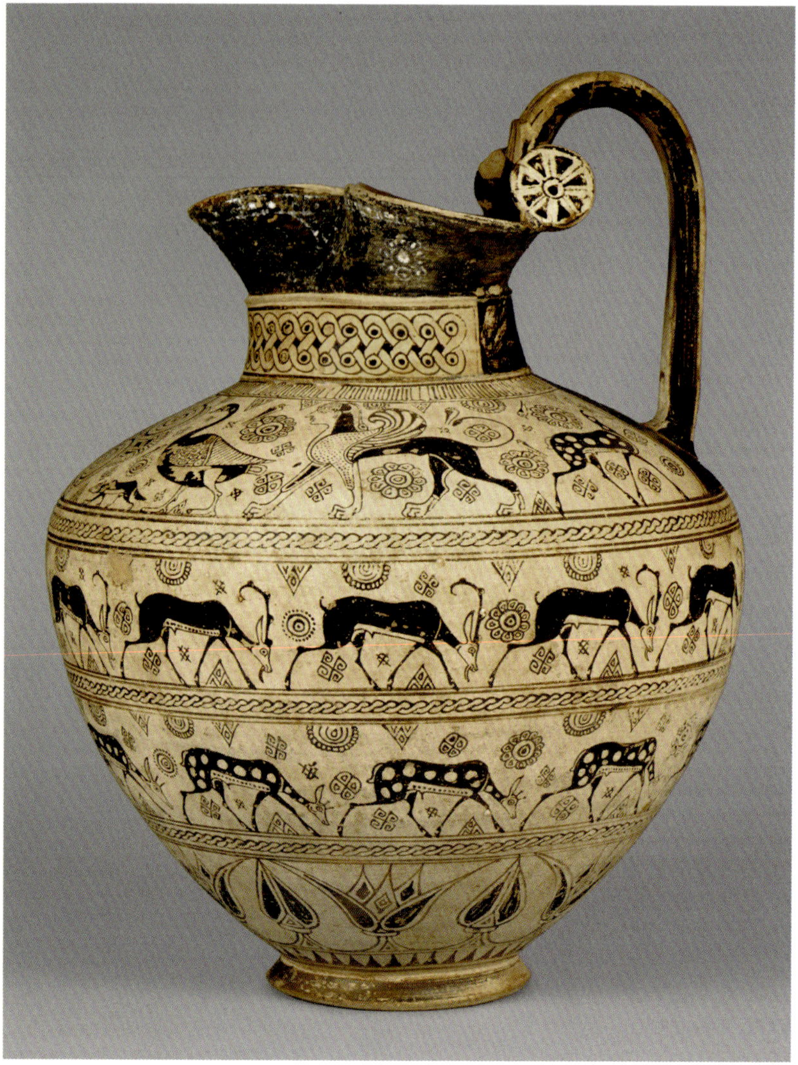

Arranged single file in discrete registers, wild goats and spotted deer prance around the belly of this wine vessel. On the shoulder, pairs of dogs, enormous waterbirds, and sphinxes flank an elaborate central floral ornament just below the trefoil mouth. The cream-colored background is filled neatly with geometric and floral patterns, including rosettes, some of which are enlivened by small birds perched on the petals. This "Wild Goat–style" pottery, as it is now known, was produced in the Greek settlements on the coast and offshore islands of Ionia (present-day western Turkey and eastern Greece) during the seventh and sixth centuries BCE. Textile patterns may have inspired the friezes of repeated figures, while the pair of disks applied at the join of the handle and rim derive from metalwork.

Shield-Strap Fragment with Mythological Scenes

Greek (made in Argos), circa 575 BCE
Signed by Aristodamos of Argos
(active 590–570 BCE). Bronze, H: 16.2 cm
(6 3/8 in.); W: 8 cm (3 1/8 in.), 84.AC.11

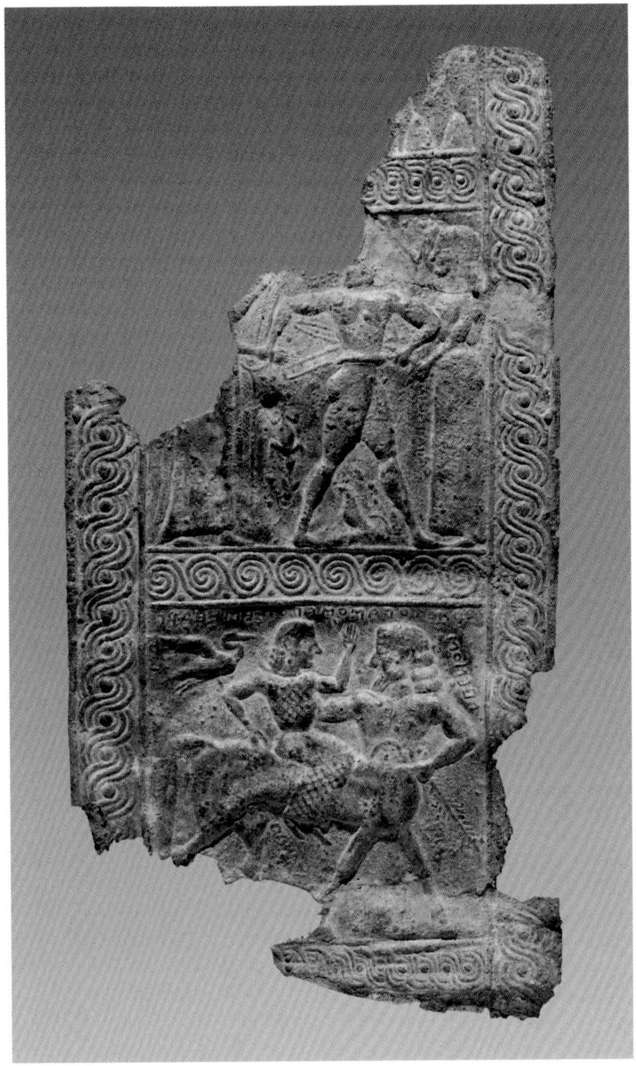

The leather straps on the inside of Archaic-period (ca. 700–480 BCE) Greek shields were often covered with strips of bronze decorated with scenes from mythological narratives. The lower square on this example shows the centaur (human-horse hybrid) Nessos abducting Deianeira, wife of the hero Herakles. The scene above it depicts the recovery of Helen of Troy by her husband, Menelaos, king of Sparta. The goddess Athena, identified by her inscribed name, stands at right. Similar straps have been found at religious sites, for example, the Sanctuary of Zeus at Olympia, where worshippers offered elaborate shields as dedications to the gods. Of significance here is the inscription along the top edge of the lower square: "Aristodamos of Argos made [this]," which represents the earliest surviving signature of an ancient Greek metalworker.

Statuette of Apollo

Greek (made in Lakonia), 550–530 BCE

Bronze, H: 18.3 cm (7$^{3}/_{16}$ in.); W: 5.4 cm (2$^{1}/_{8}$ in.); D: 4.6 cm (1$^{13}/_{16}$ in.), 2019.127

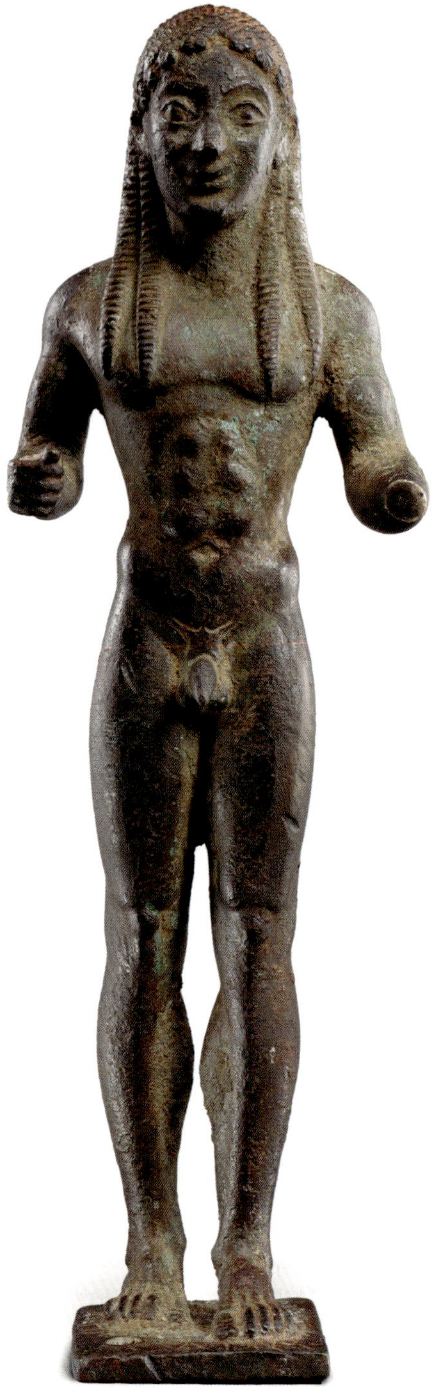

In the sixth century BCE, Greek sculptors adapted into their own repertoire Egyptian representations of standing males. With weight balanced evenly between the advanced left and withdrawn right foot, these idealized figures, conventionally called kouroi (youths), commemorated the dead in cemeteries and were offered to the gods in sanctuaries. Unlike many funerary kouroi who held their arms straight along the sides of the torso, the arms of this solid cast bronze statuette are bent sharply at the elbow and project horizontally from the body. The left hand is lost, but the clenched right hand once held a separately fashioned object, likely a bow, for an inscription on the base identifies the figure as Apollo (*Apelon* in Lakonian dialect), apparently the recipient of this offering. The second word is *Hyamos*, which, according to ancient authors, is the name of a grandson of Apollo, the founder of the city of Hyameia, and one of the early kings of Messenia, the region adjacent to Lakonia in the southern Peloponnesos. Like other kouroi in diverse media, this highly idealized figure displays well-developed musculature, long hair gathered by a fillet, large, open eyes, and an up-turned mouth. Two holes in the base served to fasten the statuette as an offering.

Chalcidian Black-Figure Storage Jar (Neck Amphora)

Greek (made in Rhegion, South Italy), circa 540 BCE

Attributed to the Inscription Painter (active 570–530 BCE). Terracotta, H: 39.6 cm (15 5/8 in); Diam: 24.9 cm (9 3/4 in.), 96.AE.1

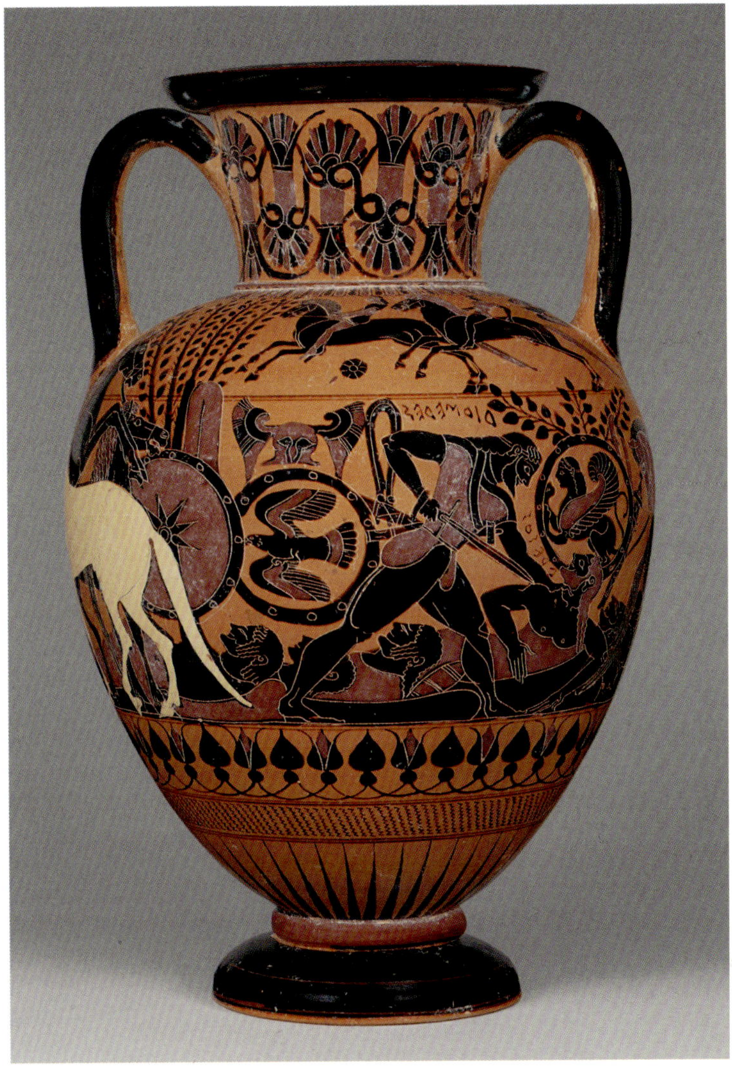

During the legendary Trojan War, King Rhesos of Thrace fought on the side of Troy. One night, while camped in a field, the Thracians removed their armor to sleep. The Greek heroes Odysseus and Diomedes massacred the disarmed soldiers to steal their immortal horses. Details of this episode as recounted in Homer's epic poem the *Iliad*, including a stallion as "white as snow," appear here with remarkable, though not exact, fidelity. On one side, Diomedes slays the Thracian commander; on the other, Odysseus murders a soldier as he sleeps. Odysseus, Diomedes, and Rhesos are identified by inscriptions. This vase has been attributed to an artist known as the Inscription Painter, so named because his work frequently features written labels, as well as a bold use of red and white paint.

Black-Figure Mixing Bowl (*Dinos*) with Ships and Battle Scenes

Greek (made in Athens), 520–510 BCE
Attributed to the circle of the Antimenes Painter (active 530–510 BCE). Terracotta, H (with stand): 58 cm (22 13/16 in.); Diam (rim): 33.5 cm (13 3/16 in.), 92.AE.88

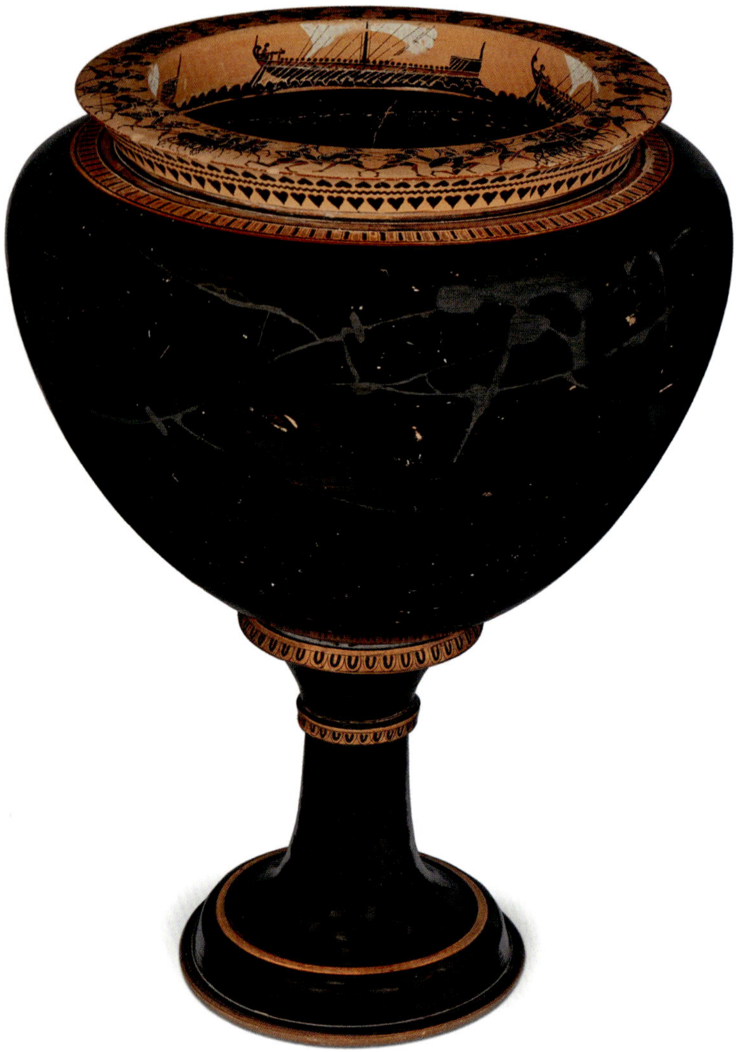

The centerpiece of the Greek wine-drinking ritual known as a *symposion* was a large bowl (*dinos*) for mixing wine with water. The battle scenes painted along the rim of this example evoke tales of bravery and glory—apt subjects for the drinkers' spirited conversations. When the vessel was full, the four ships painted on the interior would have appeared to be afloat. The motif is playful but also instructive: just as boats might be shipwrecked in stormy seas, so too might symposiasts be "wrecked" by drinking too much wine. This bowl was discovered in 1873 in a grave at Capua, an Etruscan settlement north of Naples, where it had been repurposed as a burial urn.

Black-Figure Water Jar (Hydria) with Herakles and Hydra

Etruscan (made in Caere), 520–510 BCE
Attributed to the Eagle Painter (active 530–500 BCE); lotus palmette and neck ornament by the Busiris Painter (active 530–500 BCE).
Terracotta, H: 44.6 cm (17 9/16 in.); Diam (with handles): 38 cm (14 15/16 in.),
83.AE.346

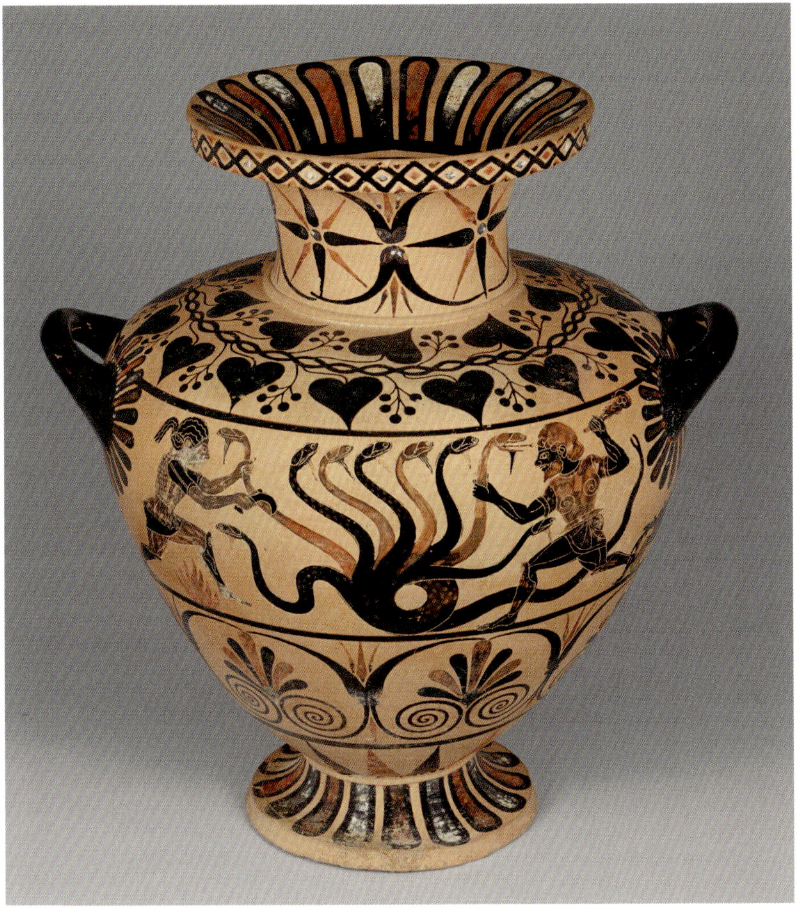

Between 600 and 400 BCE, ancient Etruria was a prime market for imported Greek pottery, and several immigrant potters and painters established workshops there. At Caere, two artists from East Greece—known today as the Eagle Painter and the Busiris Painter—created vividly decorated water jars with two horizontal handles for carrying and a vertical one for pouring. On this example, the hero Herakles (right) clubs the Hydra of Lerna, a monster with multiple snaky heads, while a crab nips at his heel. Herakles's nephew and charioteer Iolaos (left) decapitates the dreadful creature with a sickle. This favorite episode from the Labors of Herakles was an allegory of skill, bravery in combat, and ingenuity.

Red-Figure Cup (Kylix) with Man and Youth Kissing

Greek (made in Athens), 510–500 BCE
Attributed to the Carpenter Painter
(active 515–500 BCE). Terracotta, H: 11 cm
(4 3/8 in.); Diam: 33.5 cm (13 1/8 in.), 85.AE.25

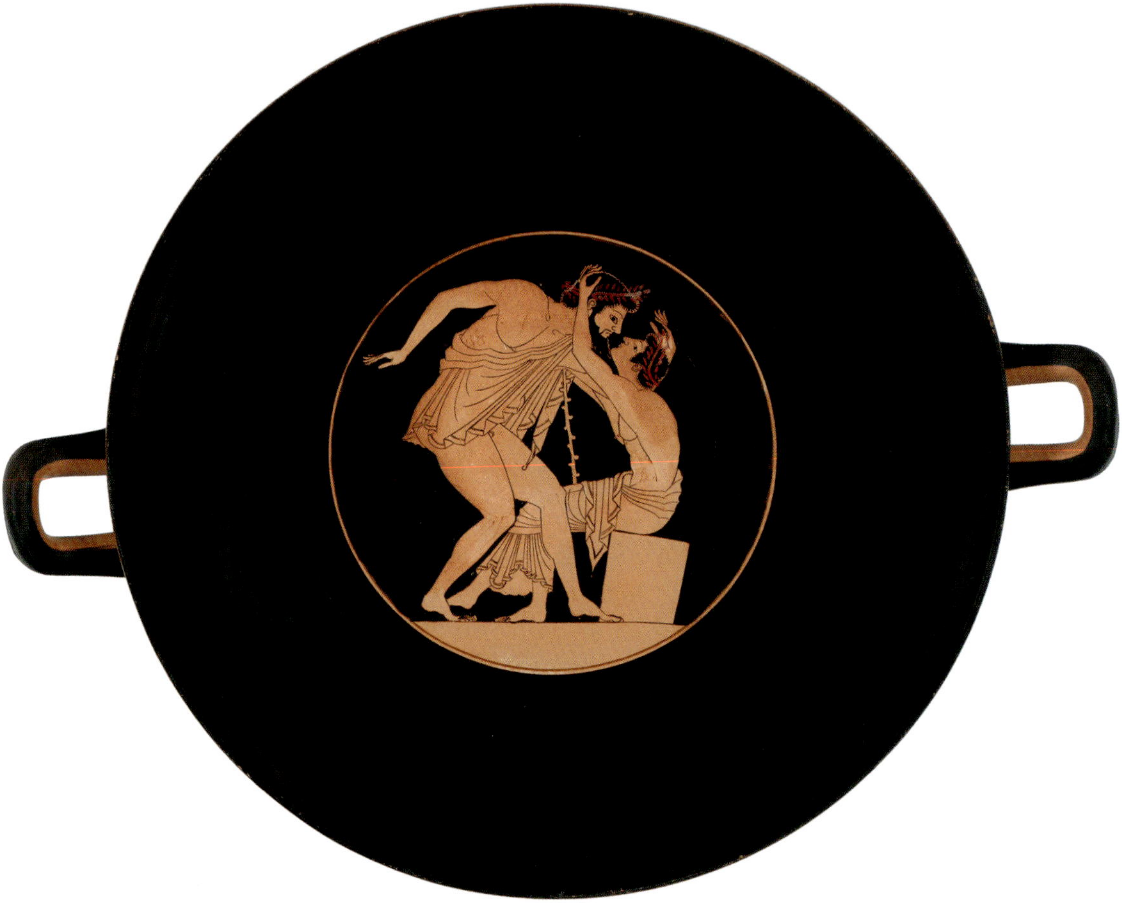

Relationships between adult male citizens and freeborn youths were a fundamental part of elite Greek society. Conventionally, it was proper for the older lover (*erastes*) to be the active partner, but in the scene painted on this cup's interior, it is the adolescent beloved (*eromenos*) who reaches up for an embrace, showing that the affection could be mutual. In ancient Greece same-sex relationships between men might involve not only physical intimacy but also education and training. A primary context for male interaction and the display of bodily prowess was the gymnasium, and the exterior of this cup is decorated with athletes practicing the discus, javelin, and long jump to the musical accompaniment of a flute player.

White-Ground Oil Jar (Lekythos) with Warriors Donning Armor

Greek (made in Athens), 500–490 BCE
Painting attributed to Douris (active ca. 500–475 BCE). Terracotta, H: 33.4 cm (13⅛ in.); Diam (shoulder): 12.6 cm (5 in.), 84.AE.770

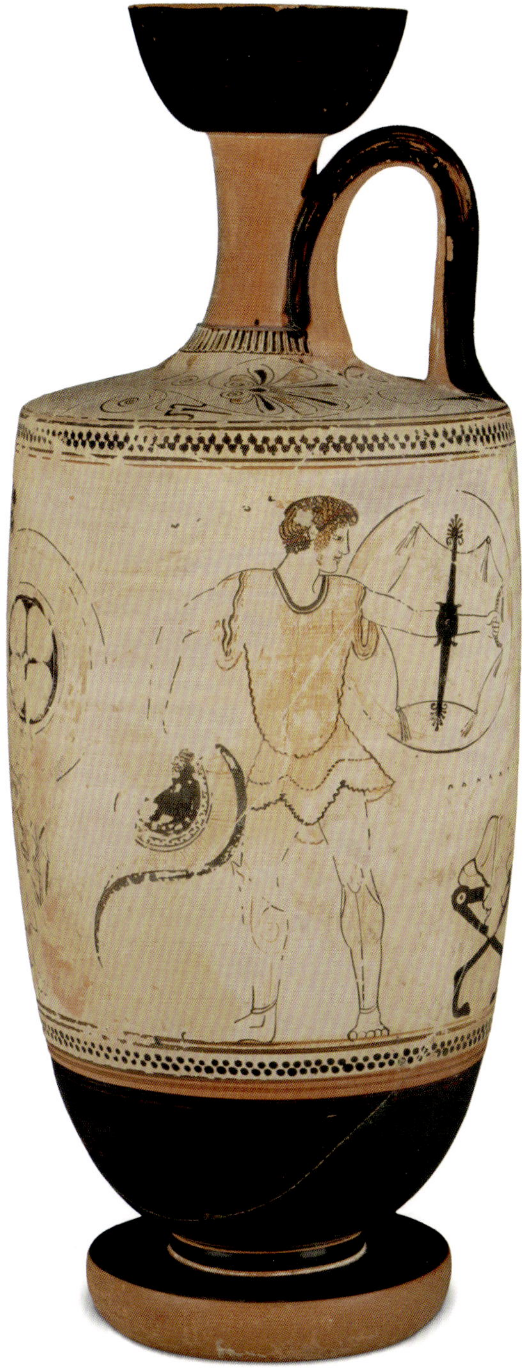

On the body of this lekythos (a vase used for storing oil or perfume), two young men arm themselves in the presence of a boy and a woman. One of the youths, rendered in fine outline, holds his helmet and shield. A honey-colored dilute wash adds volume to his short tunic and hair. The second youth, standing before a household altar, lifts his leg to fit a shin guard. In the field between the figures, inscriptions praise the beauty of two male contemporaries, Nikodromos and Panaitios. These names help date the vase to early in the career of Douris, one of the most skilled and productive vase painters in Athens during the Late Archaic period (about 510–480 BCE).

Appliqué Depicting the Sun God Usil

Etruscan, 500–475 BCE
Bronze, H: 20.7 cm (8 1/8 in.); max. W: 18 cm (7 1/16 in.), 2017.126

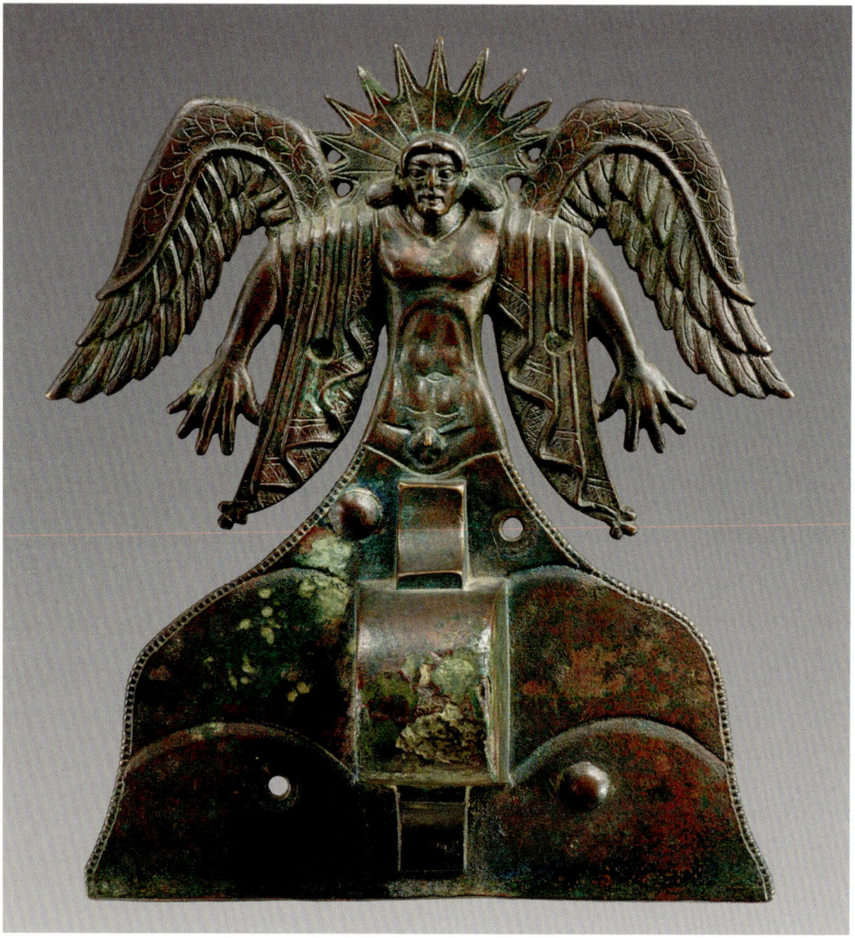

The widespread wings and nimbus of rays identify this figure as the solar deity Usil. His nude torso merges into a broad plate, which would have been attached to a cart or chariot as an ornamental tenon cover. The wavy lines on the plate represent the ocean, into which the sun god sinks at dusk, reemerging at daybreak in a cyclical orbit of death and rebirth. The Etruscans were early adopters of the conception of the sun god as a charioteer, which has precedents in both Near Eastern religion and Greek myths of the god Helios. Usil was thus an appropriate symbol for wheeled vehicles, which were used by wealthy landowners to manage their rural estates and in processions to transport the dead, which is why many carts and chariots are found in tombs.

Statuette of a Bearded Man, Probably Tinia

Etruscan, circa 480 BCE

Bronze, H: 17.2 cm (6 3/4 in.); W: 9 cm (3 9/16 in.); D: 4 cm (1 9/16 in.), 55.AB.12

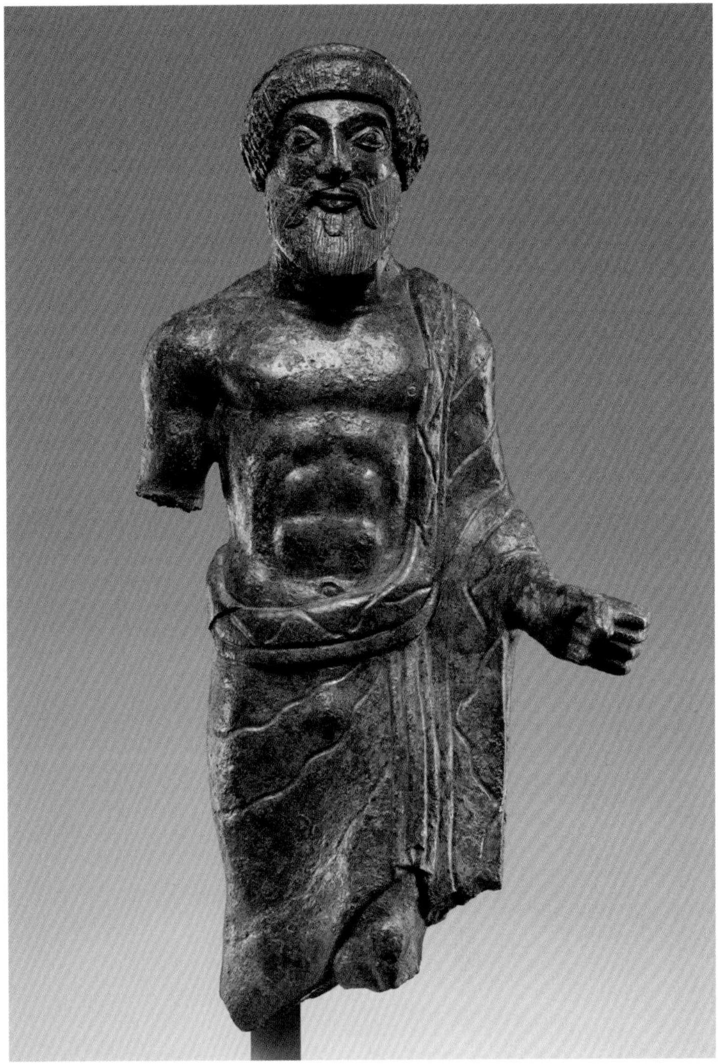

Wearing a *tebenna*, the Etruscan precursor of the Roman toga, this commanding bearded figure originally held an object in his clenched left hand. It was likely a thunderbolt or scepter, which would confirm his identity as Tinia, supreme god in the Etruscan pantheon, analogous to the Greek Zeus or Roman Jupiter. Tinia, a deity of the sky and mountains, was believed to hurl thunder and lightning to communicate warnings and other omens. Bronze figurines such as this one were offered as votive dedications at altars and in religious sanctuaries, in fulfillment of a vow or in gratitude for an answered prayer. This statuette is related stylistically to a group of masterful bronzes made in a workshop in northern Etruria, probably located at Populonia.

Red-Figure Mixing Bowl (*Dinos*) with Triptolemos, Demeter, and Persephone

Greek (made in Athens), circa 470 BCE
Attributed to the Syleus Painter (active 490–470 BCE). Terracotta, H: 36.8 cm (14½ in.); Diam (body): 35.7 cm (14 in.), 89.AE.73

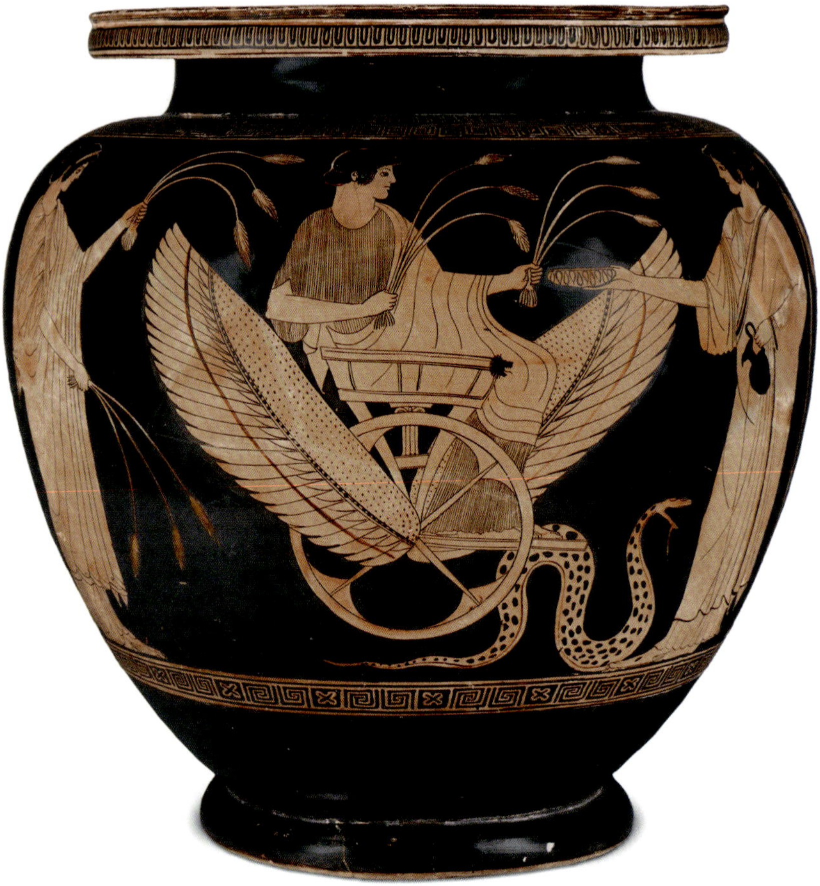

Demeter and Persephone flank Triptolemos on this wine-mixing bowl from the early Classical period (480–450 BCE). The scene illustrates the heroes and deities of Eleusis, a city outside Athens that was home to the secretive cult ("mysteries") of Demeter, goddess of agriculture. Demeter, shown here standing with stalks of grain in both hands, gave Triptolemos a winged chariot so as to spread the knowledge of agriculture across the world. As he sets off on that journey, the goddess's daughter (here inscribed "Pheraphata," an alternative form of her usual name, Persephone) wishes him good fortune by offering a libation bowl, which she has just filled from a jug. Looking on is "Theos" (Hades), god of the Underworld. Also named by inscriptions are the heroes Hippothon and Kalamites and the female personification of Eleusis.

Statuette of a Fallen Youth

Greek, 480–460 BCE

Bronze with copper inlays, L: 13.5 cm (5¼ in.); W: 7.3 cm (2⅞ in.), 86.AB.530

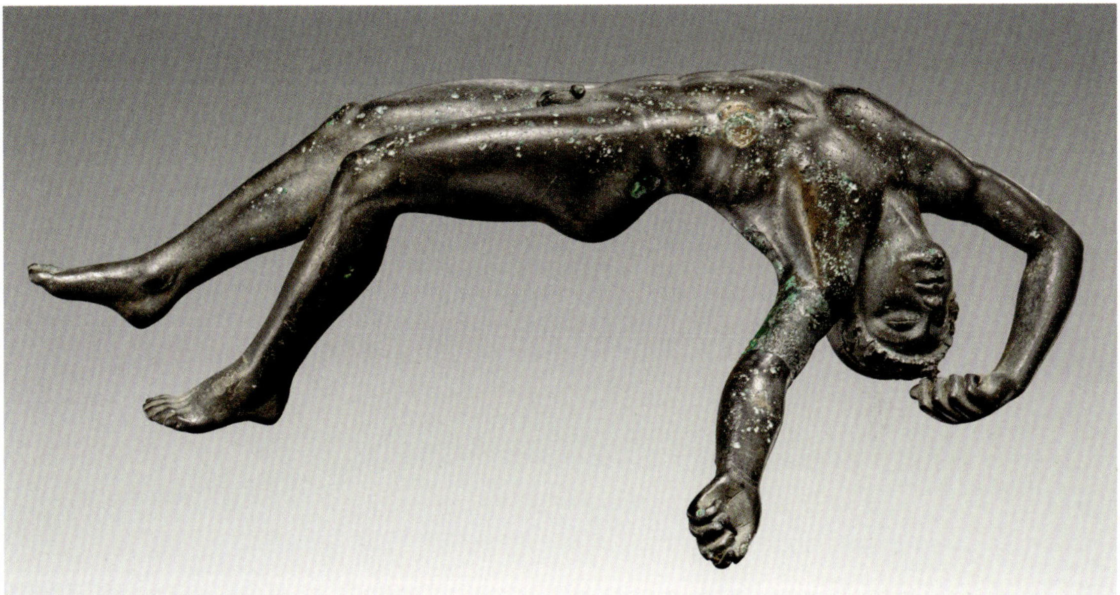

With eyes closed and legs dangling, this depiction of a prostrate youth is unparalleled among surviving bronzes of the early Classical period (ca. 480–450 BCE) for its vivid naturalism. Reddish-copper inlays were used for the nipples and, uniquely, for the curls around the youth's face. Now lost or altered by oxidation and burial, these inlays once created a rich contrast with the golden polished-bronze flesh. No attachment marks remain to indicate how this figure was joined to a larger composition. He may be a fallen warrior in a battle scene or one of the murdered Niobids, lying in an uneven, rocky landscape. In Greek myth the gods Apollo and Artemis slaughtered the fourteen children of Niobe, a mortal, when she foolishly boasted that she had more offspring than the deities' mother, the goddess Leto.

Gem with a Persian King Fighting a Hoplite

Achaemenid (probably made in Anatolia), circa 450 BCE
Banded agate scaraboid, H: 1.7 cm (11/16 in.); W: 1.2 cm (1/2 in.); D: 0.7 cm (1/4 in.), 2019.13.9

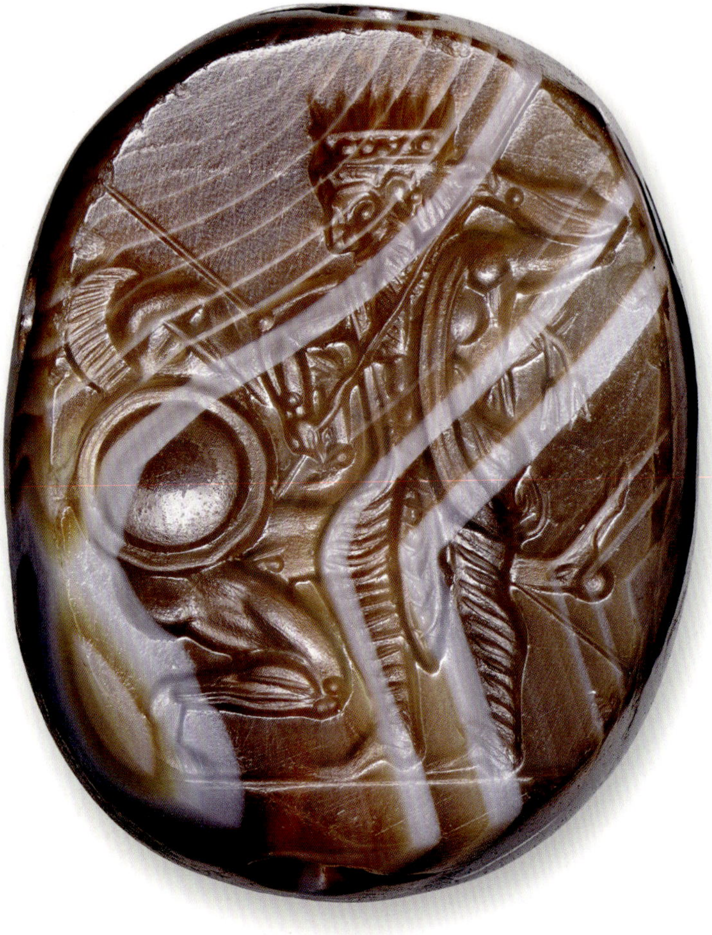

On this seal, carved from naturally banded agate, the Great King of Persia drives a spear into a collapsing Greek hoplite, or foot soldier, who is nude except for a crested Corinthian helmet and carries a shield and spear. The crown and long robe of the Persian king are carefully detailed, and a bow and quiver are slung over his left shoulder. The style of engraving suggests an origin in western Anatolia (present-day Turkey), perhaps Sardis. The king and other Persians are often shown on seals as victors over various enemies, including Greeks, and the scene may allude to ongoing conflict between Greeks and Persians in the fifth century BCE.

Gem with a Grasshopper

Greek, 425–400 BCE

Mottled yellow jasper scaraboid,

H: 2.1 cm (13/16 in.); W: 1.8 cm (11/16 in.);

D: 0.8 cm (5/16 in.), 2019.13.4

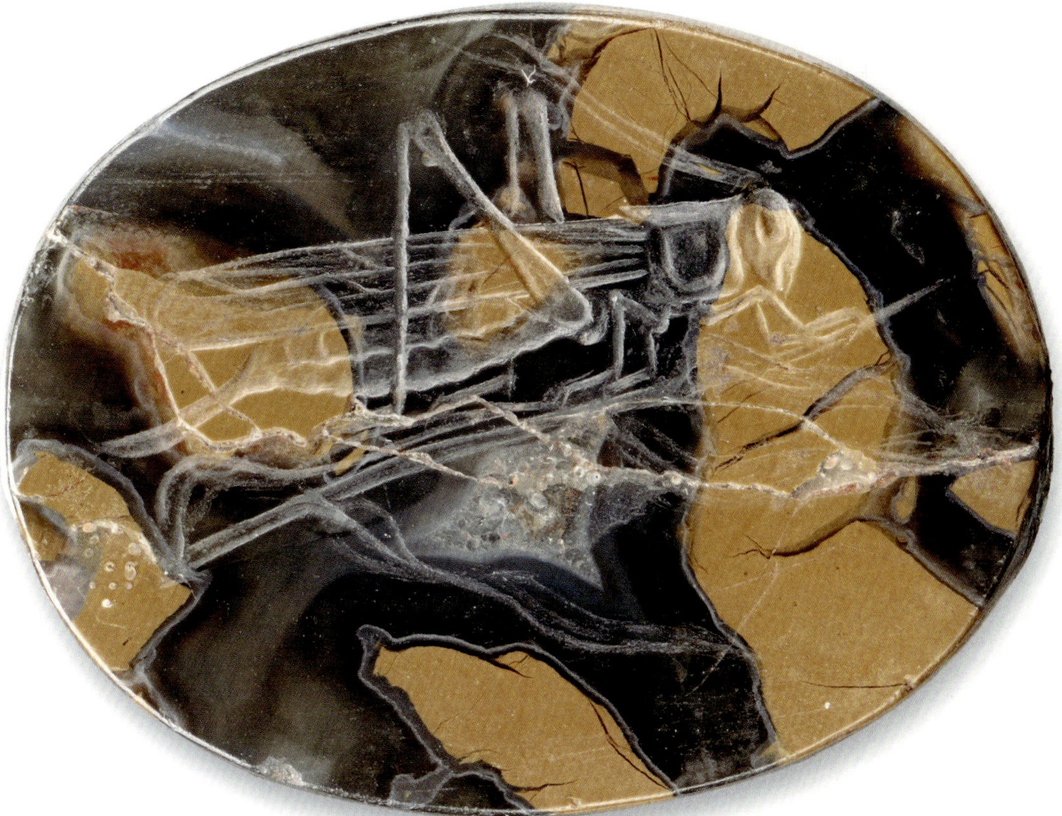

The insect perched here on a blade of grass is likely a locust, a kind of grasshopper. In the ancient Mediterranean, brightly colored hardstones were believed to have magical properties, such as the ability to repel evil, and one bearing the image of a locust might have been meant to ward off crop-eating insects. Grasshoppers, meanwhile, were thought to protect against scorpions. Ancient Greek words for the insect (*akris, bruokhos, mastikos*) might have functioned as puns on the name of a gem's owner. (Another word used to describe grasshoppers, *mantis*, means "seer.") The distinctive material of this gem, mottled jasper, and the quality of its carving has led to its association with Dexamenos of Chios, a master engraver who signed other gems cut from similar stones, some of them also featuring grasshoppers.

Gem with Perseus

Greek, 400–350 BCE

Mottled red jasper scaraboid, H: 3 cm (1 3/16 in.); W: 2.2 cm (7/8 in.); D: 1.2 cm (1/2 in.), 2019.13.6

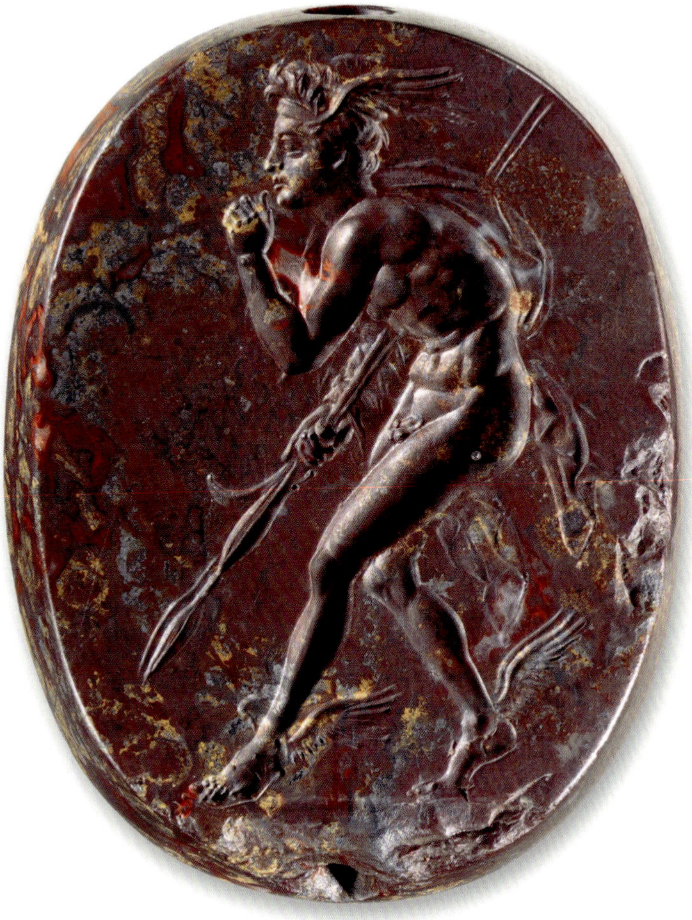

The hero Perseus tiptoes forward on the groundline of this gem, raising his left hand toward his mouth. He wears a winged diadem and matching sandals with a cloak draped over his right shoulder. One of the two spears he carries has a *dorydepanon* (sickle blade) attached to the shaft. According to legend, Perseus used such a weapon to behead the Gorgon Medusa, after whom he may be depicted in pursuit. The carving of the hero's musculature and the careful depiction of his implied movement through space are exceptional. The mottled red stone may have been selected by the carver to allude to the blood that eventually flowed from the monster's severed neck.

Engraved Ring with Herakles Pouring a Libation

Greek, circa 400 BCE

Gold, H of bezel: 2.1 cm (13/16 in.); W: 1.6 cm (5/8 in.), 2019.13.5

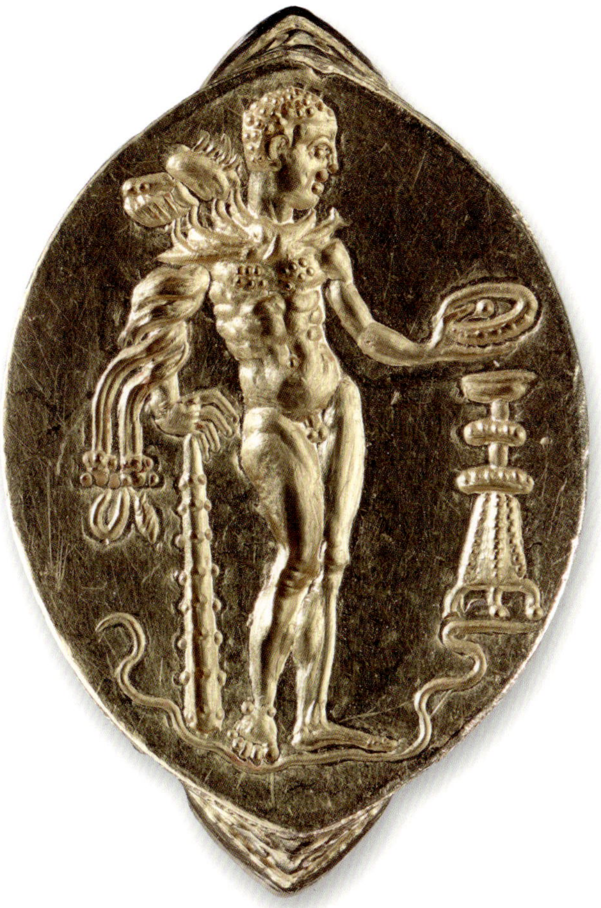

On the bezel of this elaborate ring, a youthful Herakles stands leaning on his club, a lion skin knotted around his neck and twisted around his right arm. With his left hand he holds a fluted offering dish (*phiale*) over a tripod incense burner (*thymiaterion*). Both the muscular hero and the incense burner stand on a wavy groundline. The hoop of the ring is ridged, and the two shoulders below the bezel take the form of stylized griffin heads.

Red-Figure Jug (*Chous*) with Three Boys Playing Knucklebones

Greek (made in Athens), circa 420 BCE
Painting attributed to the Group of Boston 10.190 (active 440–420 BCE).
Terracotta, H: 17.3 cm (6 13/16 in.); Diam (of body): 13.7 cm (5 3/8 in.), 96.AE.28

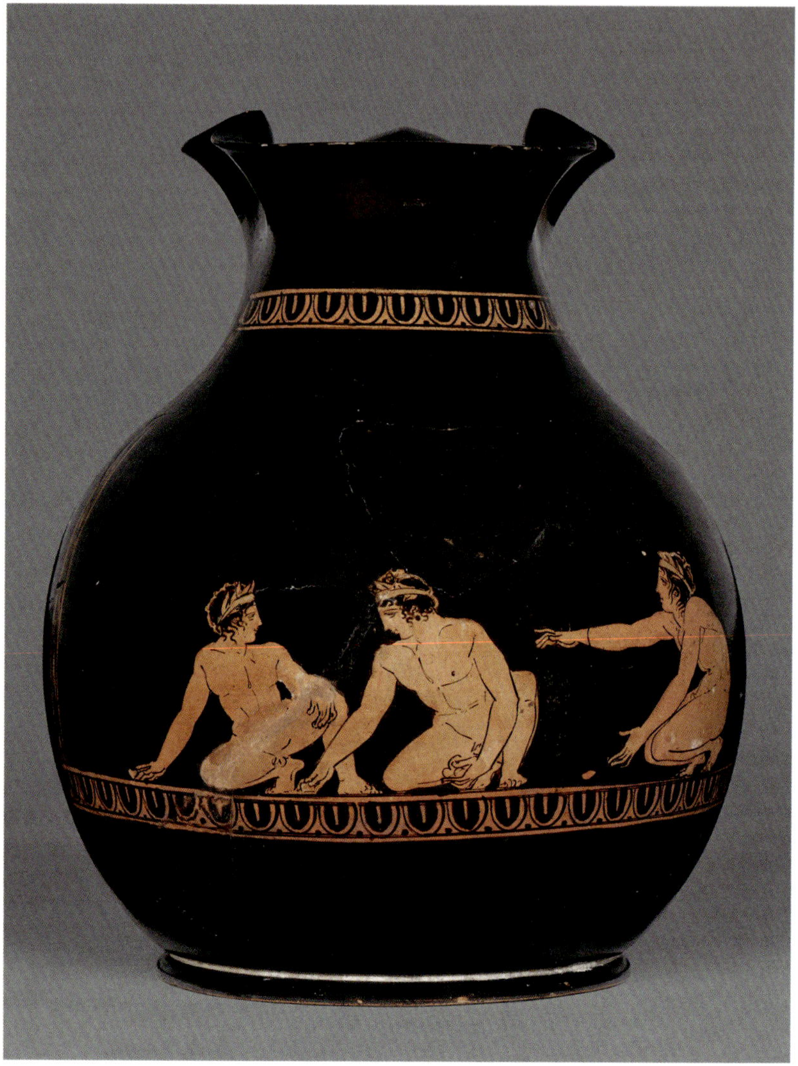

Jugs of this form, known as *choes*, were used during the Anthesteria, a three-day Athenian festival honoring the wine god Dionysos. On the first day of celebrations, the new vintage was opened; on the second, drinkers competed to consume a standard volume of wine from *choes*; and on the third, offerings were made to the dead. The festival also marked the formal acceptance of three-year-old boys into their fathers' kinship groups, which may explain the frequent depiction of children on *choes*, as seen here. This example was found at the Etruscan site of Vulci, suggesting that it had been exported from Greece during antiquity. It was later acquired by Martine de Béhague, comtesse de Béarn (1870–1939), who traveled the world to build her eclectic collection.

Grave Stele of Philoxenos and Philoumene

Greek (made in Athens), circa 400 BCE
Marble, H: 102 cm (40¼ in.); W: 44.5 cm (17½ in.); D: 16.5 cm (6½ in.), 83.AA.378

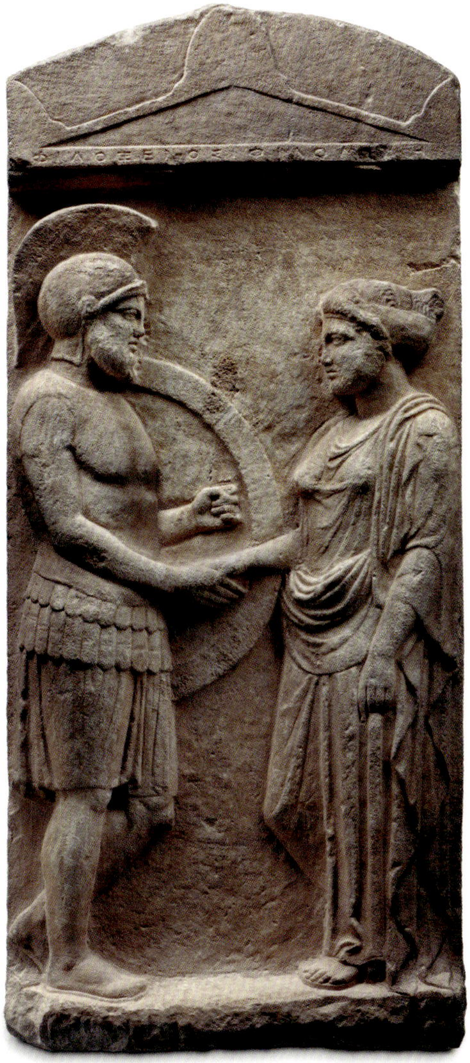

Bearing the armor and shield of a warrior, Philoxenos solemnly shakes hands with Philoumene, the two identified by the names inscribed on the pediment above their heads. The couple are likely husband and wife but may depict another familial pairing. The handshake, or *dexiosis*, was a common motif on reliefs of the Classical period (480–323 BCE). It could represent a simple farewell, a reunion in the afterlife, or the lasting bond between the deceased and the living. The couple's faces have idealized features and convey the calm detachment that prevailed in the sculptural style of Athens and the surrounding region, Attika. Now colorless, the scene might once have been enhanced by pigments, most notably to depict the warrior's shield strap, an element that was typically painted rather than carved.

Pair of Altars

Greek (probably made in Taras, South Italy), 400–375 BCE
Terracotta, altar 1: H: 41.8 cm (16½ in.), W (top): 31.5 cm (12⅜ in.), D (top): 27 cm (10⅝ in.); altar 2: H: 41.8 cm (16½ in.), W (top): 31.5 cm (12⅜ in.), D (top): 27.8 cm (11 in.), 86.AD.598.1, .2

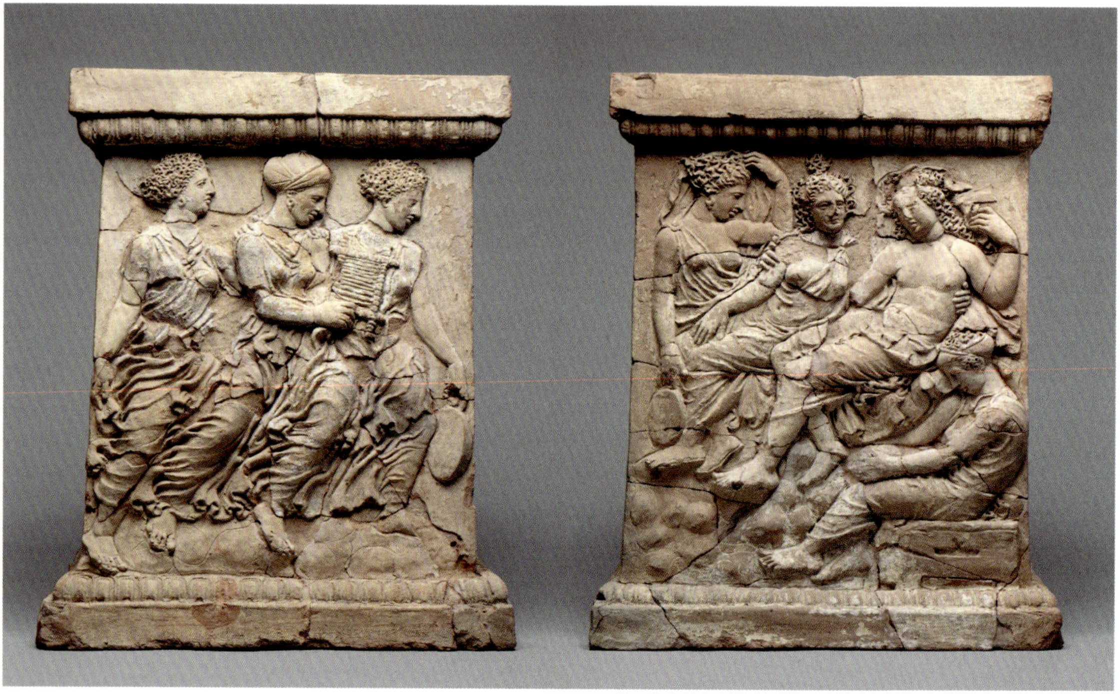

Seven figures represented across two altars form a single composition. On the right altar (.2), Aphrodite, goddess of love, and her lover Adonis sit in a rocky landscape, attended by two women. On the left altar (.1), three women dance toward the pair. These reliefs celebrate the myth of Adonis, a beautiful young hunter who was also beloved by Persephone, consort of Hades in the Underworld. To appease both deities, Zeus, king of the gods, decreed that Adonis spend half the year with one goddess and half with the other. Persephone may be the mourning seated female on the right altar. Fated to die and be resurrected annually, Adonis was associated with the seasonal regrowth of nature. Small altars for burning offerings or incense were common in domestic shrines and sanctuaries.

Red-Figure Mixing Bowl (Volute Krater) and Stand

Greek (made in Athens), 390–380 BCE
Attributed to the Meleager Painter (active 400–370 BCE). Terracotta, H (krater): 54 cm (21¼ in.); Diam (krater): 40 cm (15¾ in.); H (stand): 16.5 cm (6½ in.), 87.AE.93

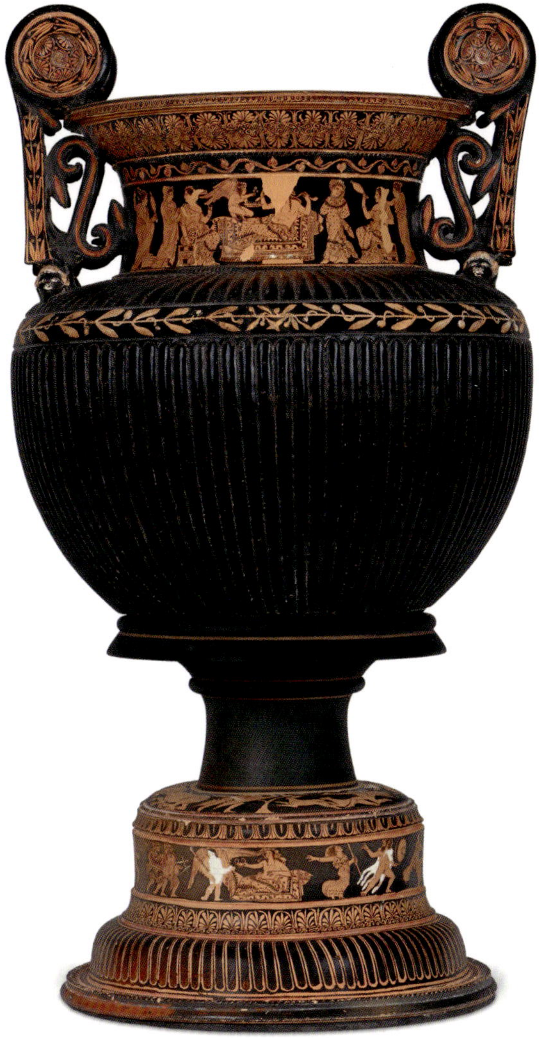

Vertical ribbing on the black-glazed body of this superbly crafted krater intentionally imitates the appearance of precious-metal vessels, as do the openwork volute handles, here supported by molded heads of Black Africans (called Aithiopians by the ancients). The combination of relief elements, painted floral patterns, mythological scenes, and copious gilding mark this vessel as a tour de force of ceramic art. On the front of the neck, Adonis relaxes on a couch between his rival lovers, Aphrodite and Persephone. Echoing this vignette, the stand below shows a reclining Dionysos attended by the gods Apollo and Sabazios, as well as a company of his acolytes, the satyrs and maenads. Hunting motifs decorate the shoulder of the stand, which was at some point cut down and has been restored following ancient parallels.

Red-Figure Storage Jar (Pelike) with the Judgment of Paris

Greek (made in Athens), circa 360 BCE
Attributed to the Painter of the Wedding Procession (active 360s BCE). Terracotta with polychromy and gilding, H: 48.3 cm (19 in.); Diam (body): 27.2 cm (10¾ in.), 83.AE.10

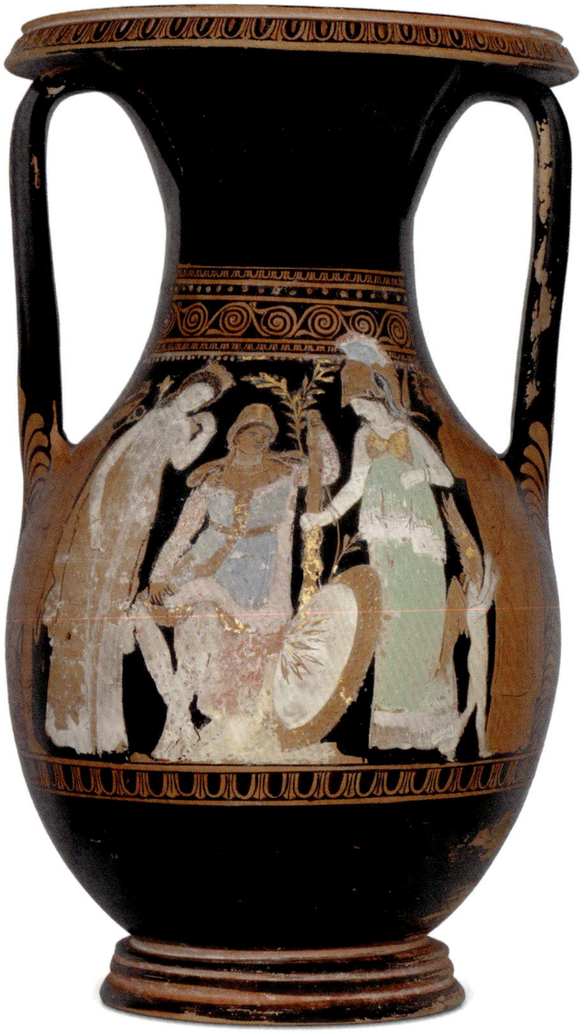

Outstanding for its relatively well-preserved pastel pigments and gilding, which may reflect monumental wall painting, this tall pelike (storage jar) depicts the mythical Judgment of Paris. Dressed in rich attire, Paris, the shepherd-prince of Troy, sits on a rock and looks toward Athena, goddess of war. Behind her, Aphrodite, goddess of love, is entirely veiled, while her son Eros tugs at her cloak. To Paris's right stands Hera, queen of the Olympian deities, followed by the messenger god Hermes. He served as escort to the goddesses, whose beauty Paris must now judge. Bribed by all three contestants, Paris chooses Aphrodite after she promises him the love of the world's most beautiful woman, Helen. Paris later abducts Helen, precipitating the Trojan War.

Fragment of a Gnathian Bell Krater

South Italian (made in Apulia), circa 350 BCE
Attributed to the Konnakis Painter (active 375–350 BCE). Terracotta, H: 10.7 cm (4 3/16 in.); W: 11 cm (4 5/16 in.). Gift of Suzanne A. Rosenborg, 83.AE.431

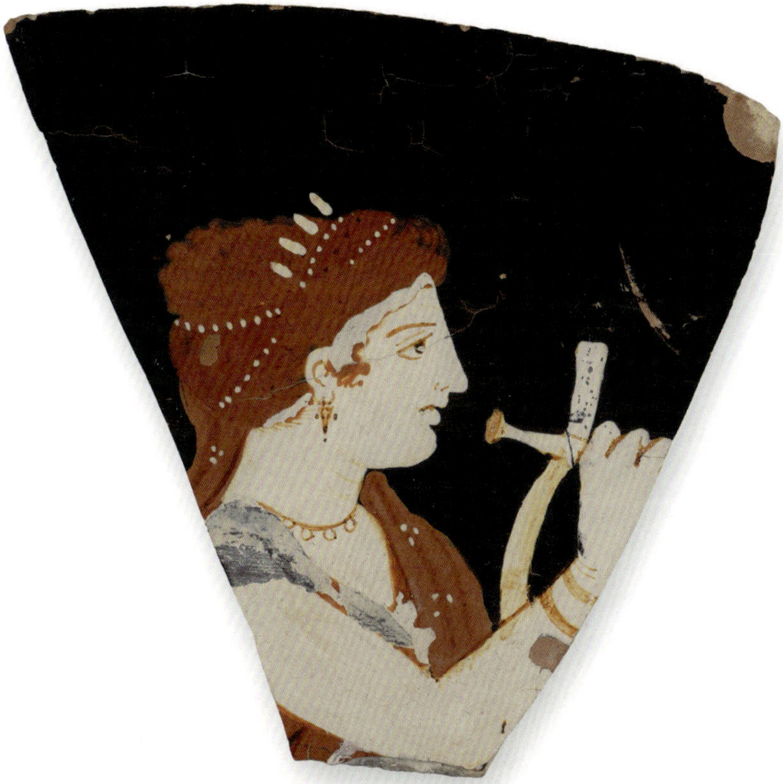

The woman depicted on this small fragment probably represents one of the Muses, the goddesses of learning and the arts. She holds a lyre (a kind of harp) and wears several items of jewelry: a diadem (crown), earrings, a necklace, and bracelets. The fragment comes from a mixing bowl decorated in the so-called Gnathia technique, named after modern Egnazia, a site in southern Italy where examples were first found. Rather than leaving the figures in reserve and painting the background black—as was typical in the red-figure vase-painting technique—the artist painted the entire vase black and then added the figure in white, along with a range of reddish brown, orange, and yellow hues. The painterly technique extends to the golden shading along the upper side of the Muse's forearm.

Core-Formed Perfume Jar (Alabastron)

Greek, 350–250 BCE

Glass, H: 16.5 cm (6½ in.); Diam: 5 cm (1 15/16 in.), 2003.193

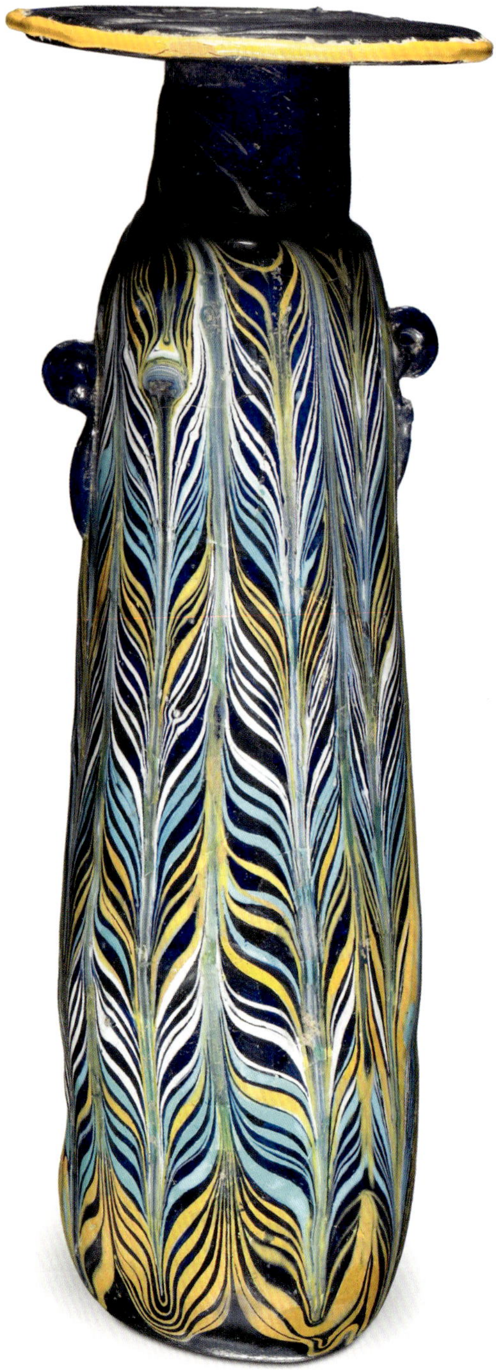

Elongated glass vessels were used to hold perfume or cosmetics, much like their counterparts in clay, stone, and metal. This alabastron was constructed by encasing a dried core of some composite material, probably a mixture of clay and an organic binder, in a dark blue glass. Trails of molten white, yellow, and turquoise glass were wound around the vessel's body and then dragged with a pointed tool to create a featherlike pattern. Still visible are the tool marks left by the pincers used to shape the pinched neck and flattened rim. Small handles added to the shoulder allowed for the attachment of a leather suspension cord or bronze chain. According to illustrations on Athenian vases, vessels like this example were hung from the wrist or a belt.

Box-Bezel Ring with Bellerophon, Pegasos, and Chimaera

Greek (made in South Italy), 340–320 BCE

Attributed to the Santa Eufemia Master (active 340–320 BCE). Gold, H (bezel): 2.04 cm (13/16 in.); W (bezel): 1.42 cm (9/16 in.); D (bezel): 0.77 cm (5/16 in.); Diam (hoop): 2.31 cm (15/16 in.), 88.AM.104

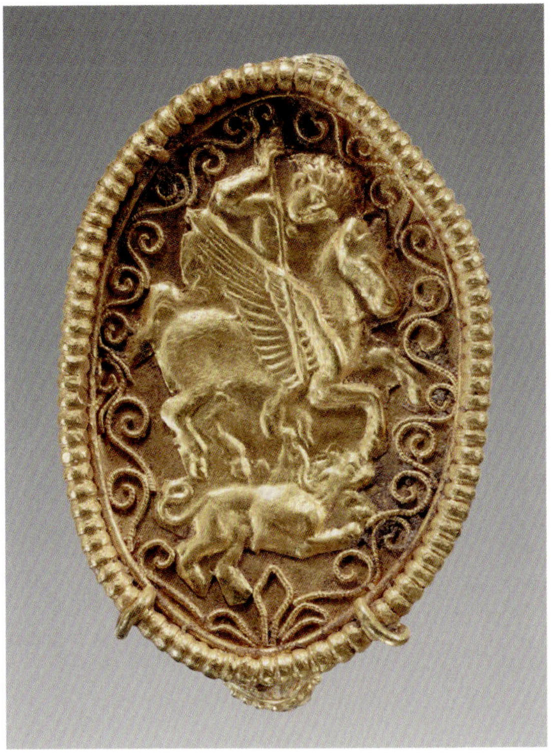

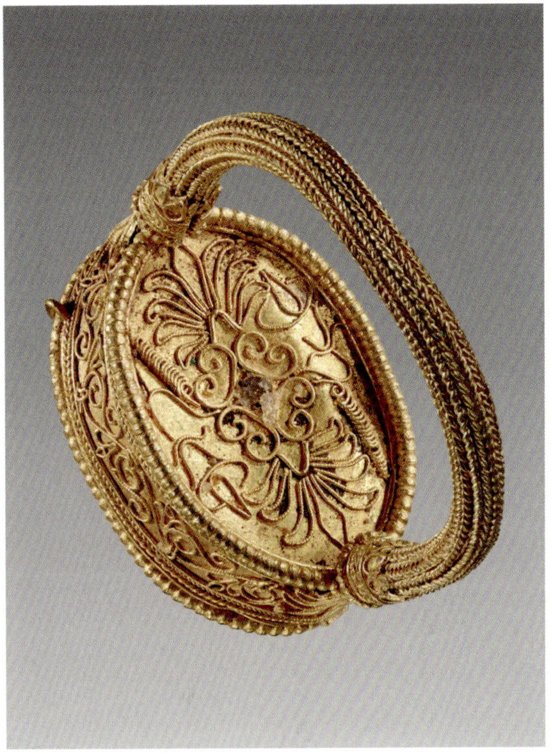

Elaborate ornamentation distinguishes this ring, one of few from antiquity that can be attributed to a particular goldsmith. On top of the oval, box-shaped bezel, surrounded by filigree spirals and florals, is a thin, embossed gold sheet. It depicts the hero Bellerophon, mounted on his winged horse Pegasos, slaying the Chimaera, a monstrous lion-goat hybrid with a serpent-headed tail. Although not visible when the ring was worn, the underside of the box is decorated with filigreed palmettes, a tendril spiral, and a bellflower. The technique of these motifs seems particular to the craftsperson, who used corkscrew coils of gold wire lying flat on the surface. He is called the Santa Eufemia Master after similar pieces of jewelry found in a female burial cache in the town of that name in southern Italy.

Panathenaic Prize Amphora

Greek (made in Athens), 340/339 BCE
Attributed to the Marsyas Painter (active 370–330 BCE). Terracotta, H (with lid): 99.5 cm (39⅛ in.); Diam (body): 39.2 cm (15⅜ in.), 79.AE.147

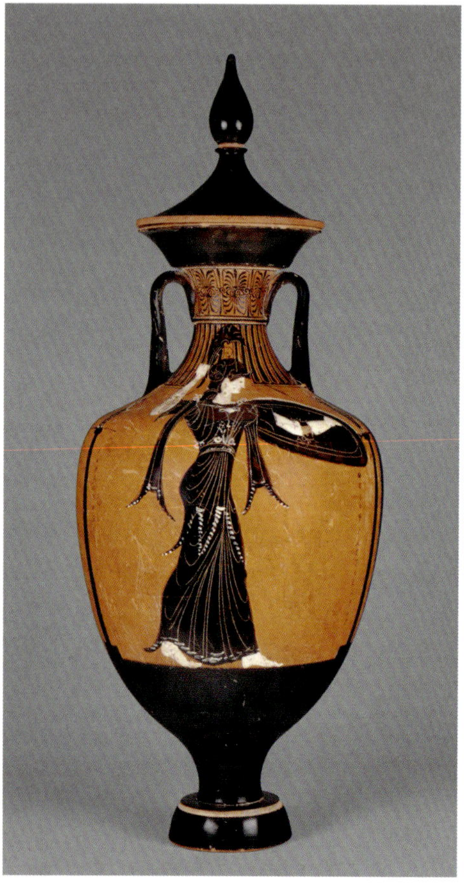

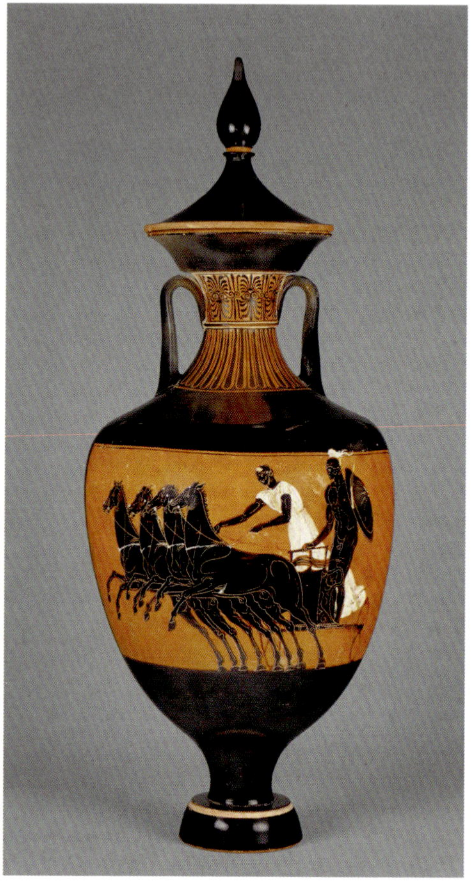

This amphora was made as a container for high-quality olive oil from Athens, to be awarded to winners of the Panathenaic Games. The goddess Athena is depicted on the front of the vase, while the back (right) shows the contest for which it was awarded. A charioteer wearing a long white garment stands in his vehicle; next to him is a naked man with a helmet and a shield. This scene depicts the race of the *apobates*, literally, the "dismounter": the warrior is about to leap from the chariot and continue running on foot. The inscription "Theophrastos was *archon*" on the front names the magistrate responsible for collecting the oil. Because that official was appointed annually, we can date this amphora precisely to the year 340/339 BCE.

Red-Figure Water Jar (Loutrophoros) with Zeus and Leda

South Italian (made in Apulia),
circa 330 BCE
Attributed to the Painter of Louvre MNB 1148 (active 350–330 BCE). Terracotta,
H: 90.1 cm (35½ in.); Diam (body):
35.5 cm (14 in.), 86.AE.680

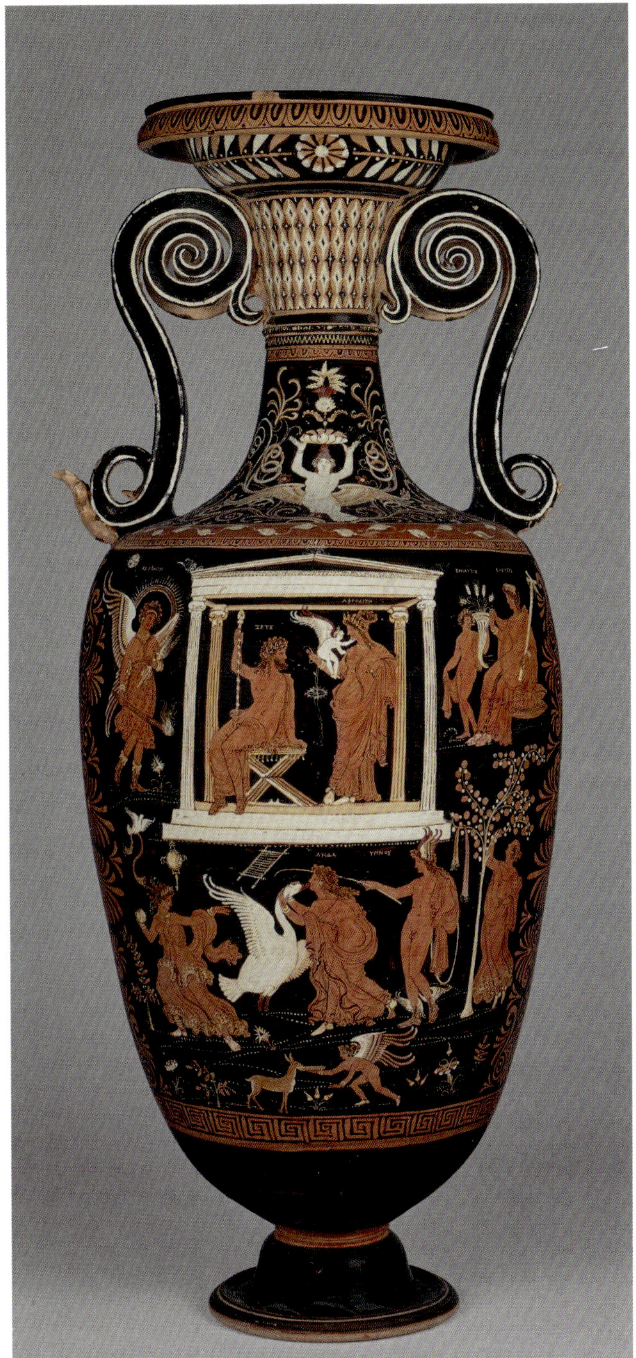

This elaborate vessel has a hole at the bottom, so it could not have served as a container. It was instead a showpiece, to be seen by mourners at a grave. The central scene depicts Zeus, king of the gods, meeting Aphrodite, goddess of love. Below, he reappears as a swan, kissing the Spartan queen Leda, whom he intends to seduce. Hypnos, the personification of Sleep, assists Zeus's trickery by stretching out his staff to lull Leda to sleep. Images of mortals seduced or carried off by gods may have been consolatory metaphors for death. Here, the funerary aspect is further suggested by Eleusis, who sits to the right of Zeus's palace. She personifies the Greek town that was home to the Eleusinian Mysteries, an annual festival promoting good harvests and a happy afterlife.

Head of Alexander the Great

Greek, circa 320 BCE

Marble, H: 29.1 cm (11½ in.), 73.AA.27

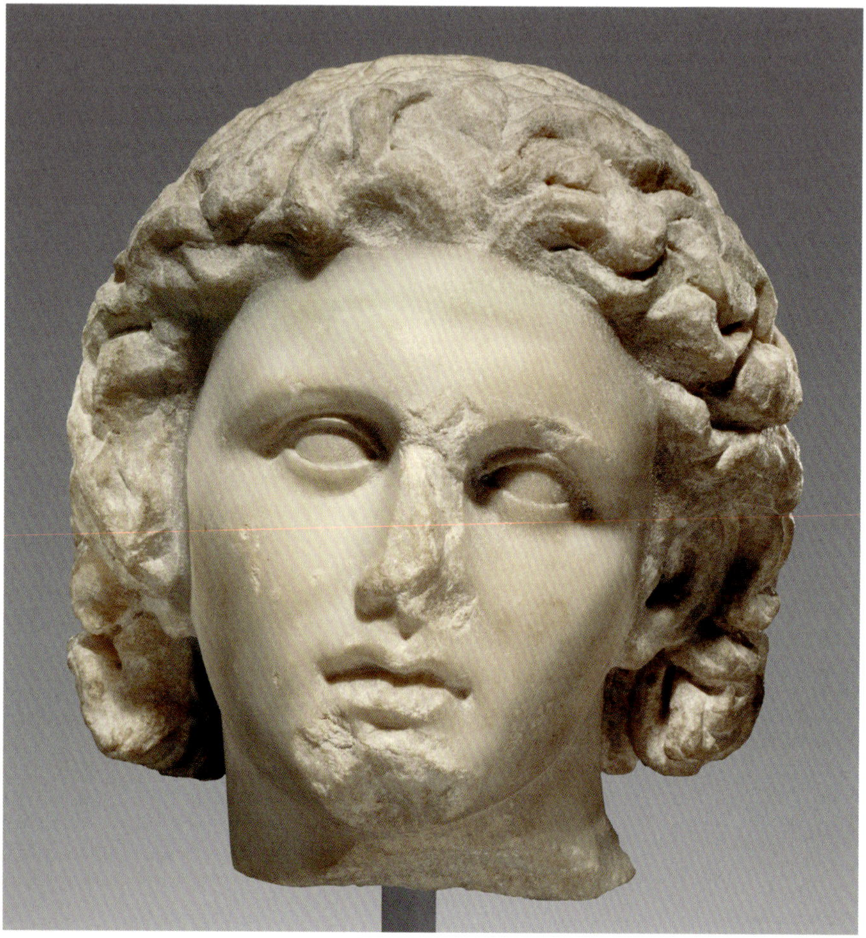

Alexander the Great, king of Macedon (r. 336–323 BCE), was the first Greek ruler to exploit the propagandistic power of portraiture. According to ancient literary sources, the only sculptor Alexander permitted to carve his likeness was Lysippos from Sikyon (active ca. 370–300 BCE), who created this standard portrait type. This head is one of the earliest portraits of Alexander to survive, combining the conqueror's youthful appearance with the idealized characteristics used to portray gods and heroes. The soft, smooth skin contrasts strikingly with the roughly textured hair, tousled with Alexander's trademark upswept *anastolé*, or cowlick. The sculpture's dynamism and level of expression would become hallmarks of the Hellenistic style, particularly in images of rulers.

Statue of a Victorious Youth

Greek, 300–100 BCE

Bronze with copper inlays, H: 151.5 cm (59⅝ in.), 77.AB.30

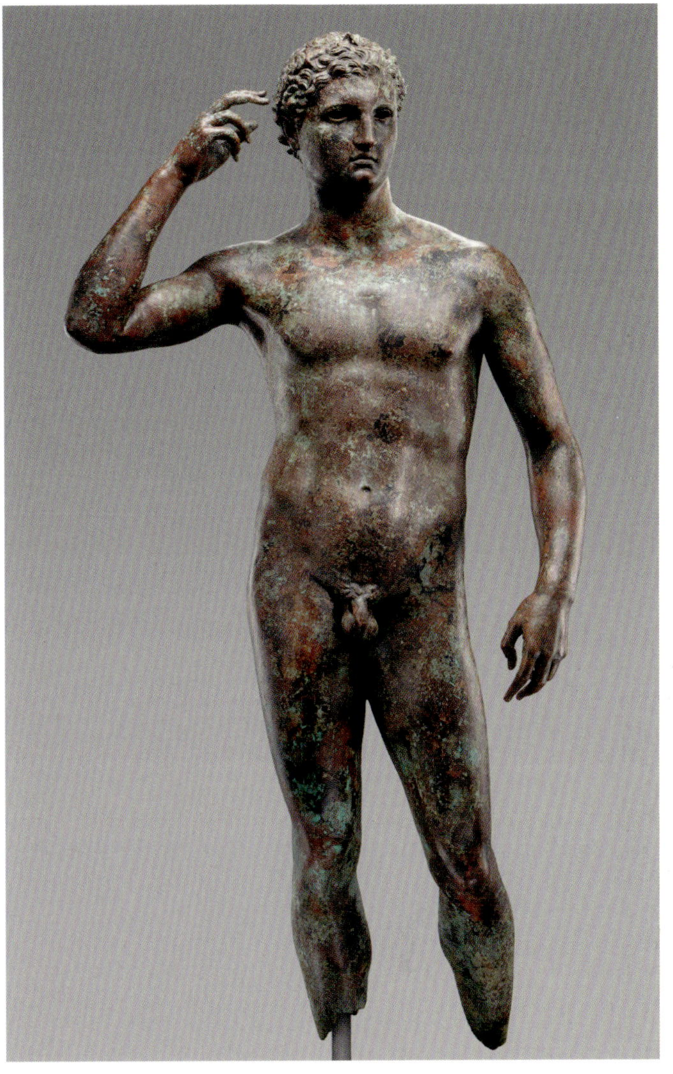

Reaching for an olive wreath on his head, this nude youth is presented as a victorious athlete. Netted by fisherman in the Adriatic Sea in 1964, the statue was found encrusted with shells, corals, and other marine organisms, and its original surface is now discolored. The eyes, once made of colored stones or glass paste, are lost, as is the object, probably a palm brunch, once held in the right hand, but the red-copper inlays at the nipples survive. They would have contrasted naturalistically with the golden-bronze skin. The youth's identity and the circumstances of his victory, and perhaps also the name of the artist responsible for the sculpture, would have been inscribed on the base, which, like the feet, does not survive. The proportions and style of the statue, combining realism and idealism, date the work to the Hellenistic period (323–31 BCE).

Assemblage of Ptolemaic Jewelry

Greek (possibly made in Alexandria, Egypt), 220–100 BCE
Gold with various inlaid and attached stones, including garnet, cornelian, pearl, and glass paste; various dimensions, 92.AM.8.1–.11

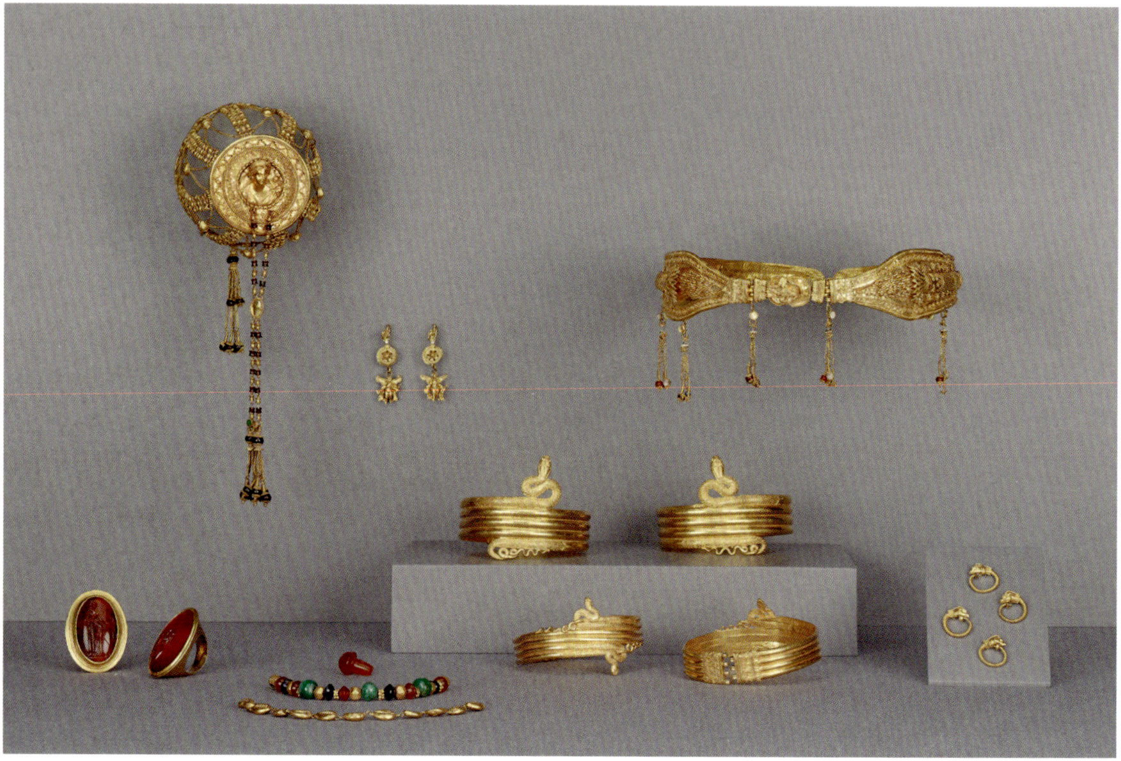

This spectacular collection of gold jewelry was likely the prized possession of a woman of high social rank. Signs of ancient repair indicate that the jewelry was worn. The style and imagery of the pieces suggest the work of Greek goldsmiths active during the reign of the Ptolemies, a succession of rulers of Egypt descended from Ptolemy I Soter (r. 305/304–282 BCE) a general in the army of the Macedonian conqueror Alexander the Great (r. 336–323 BCE). The group includes a hairnet (upper left) with an image of Aphrodite and Eros; an elaborate diadem (center right); four snake bracelets (a custom imported to Egypt); two pairs of antelope-head earrings and one pair featuring Erotes; two cornelian seal rings, one engraved with an image of Tyche, goddess of good fortune, and the other representing the Ptolemaic queen Arsinoe II (316–270 BCE) as Artemis; and a necklace of multicolored gems.

Gem with Youth Feeding a Dog

Italic, 200–100 BCE

Cornelian set in a gold ring, H (gem): 1.81 cm (11/16 in.); W (gem): 1.32 cm (1/2 in.); Diam (ring): 2.8 cm (1 1/8 in.), 85.AN.165

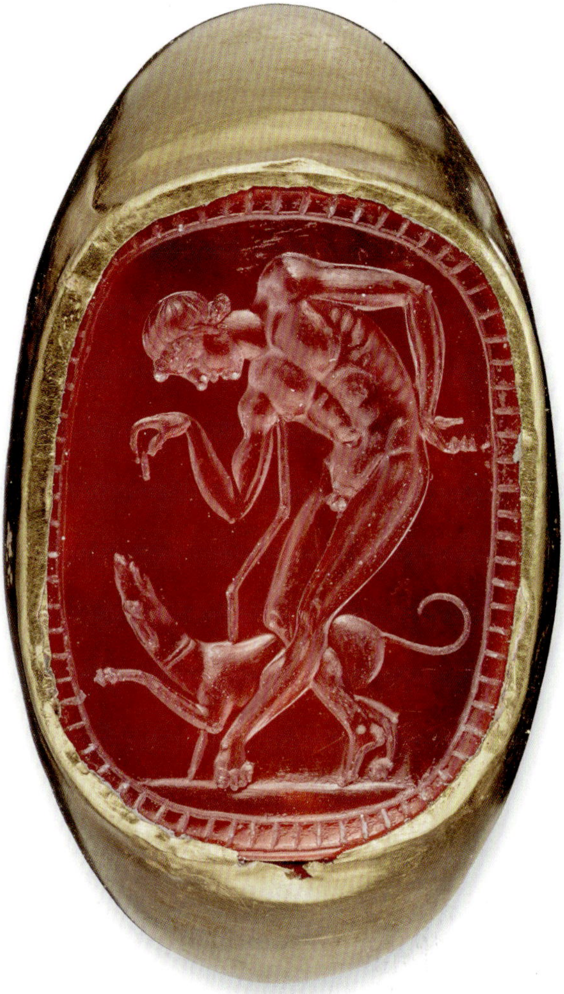

In addition to the practical function of sealing documents when pressed into hot wax or soft clay, engraved gems set into rings demonstrated their owners' social status. Carved on the surface are a nude youth and a dog, popular motifs on both Greek and Etruscan gems. The youth leans on a crooked staff, delicately balanced on the balls of his crossed feet, as the dog lifts its head toward a scrap of food in his hand. The dog's lean body, smooth coat, and elongated snout are characteristic of the Lakonian hound, a breed favored in antiquity for hunting and herding. Even on this miniature scale, the unknown carver has carefully modeled both figures' musculature in a naturalistic manner.

Cameo with Bust of the Goddess Isis

Greek (made in Egypt), 200–30 BCE
Banded agate, H: 4.2 cm (1⅝ in.);
W: 2.9 cm (1⅛ in.), 2019.13.16.1

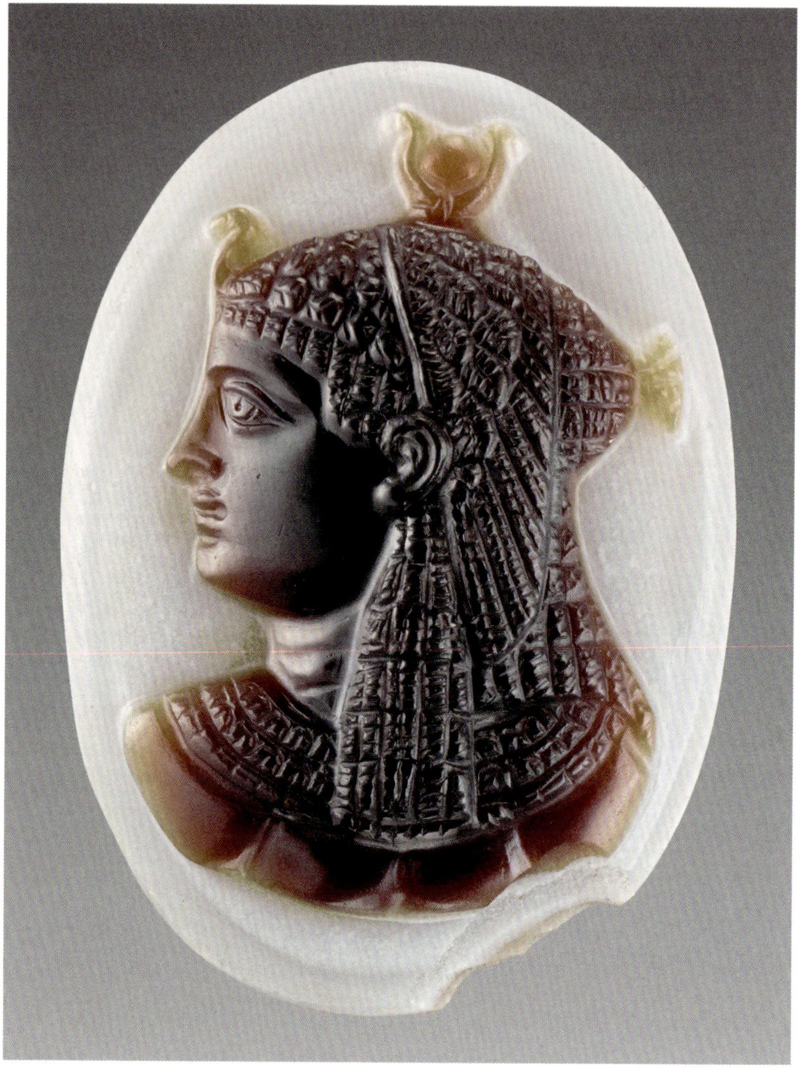

The Egyptian goddess Isis was the wife of Osiris, god of the dead, and the mother of Horus, god of kingship. She was popular in the cross-cultural milieu of Ptolemaic Egypt (305/304–31 BCE), and her cult subsequently spread across the Mediterranean. On this fine cameo, the goddess appears with a vulture headdress, a horned crown with a solar disk, and an elaborately beaded collar. Isis was frequently assimilated with the Hellenistic queens of Egypt, and here she displays the exaggerated neck folds, called "Venus rings," that often appear in their portraits.

Head of a Bearded Man

Greek, 160–150 BCE

Marble, H: 40.7 cm (16 in.), 91.AA.14

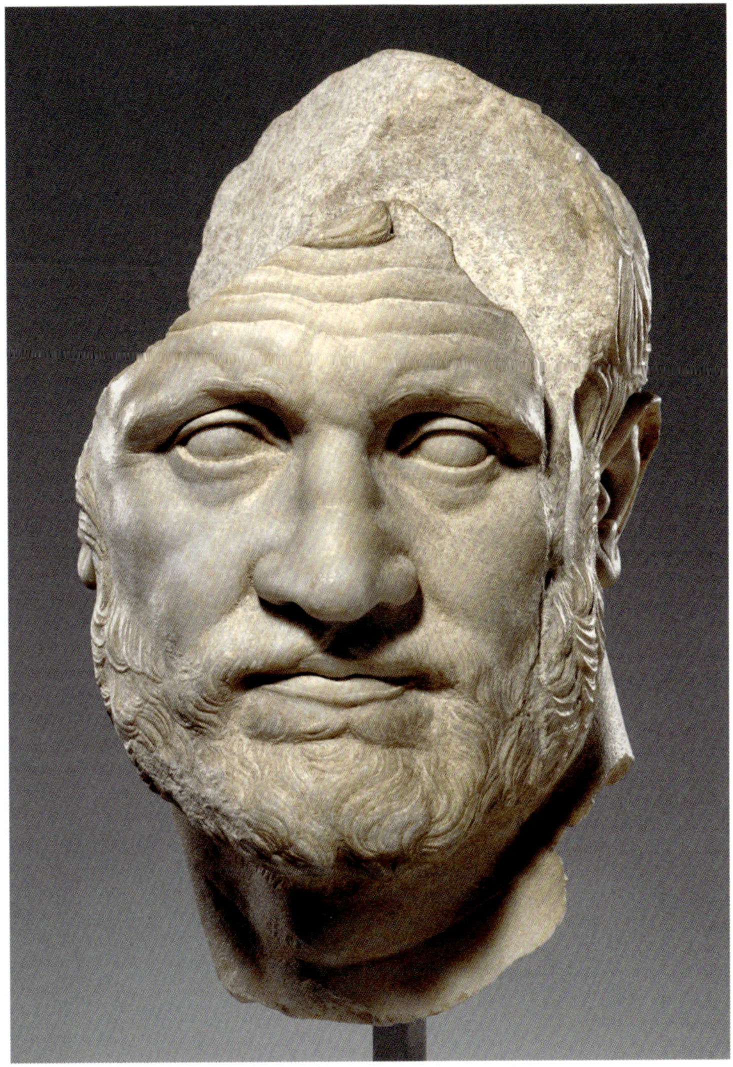

The scale of this powerful, over-life-size head suggests that its subject was a high-ranking individual worthy of an expensive portrait statue, perhaps a hero or a statesman. It is meticulously carved, with an exceptional degree of expressive detail. Blending features such as exaggerated facial muscles with a lined forehead and a bumpy nose, the man's face looks experienced but not exhausted. This vigorous style of royal portraiture, first adopted by the successors of Alexander the Great (356–323 BCE), was employed by sculptors working at Pergamon, a Hellenistic kingdom on the western coast of present-day Turkey. The resemblance to portraits of Pergamene kings, especially those of Attalos II (r. 158–138 BCE), may have been intended to link this unidentified man to the Attalid court.

Stag Rhyton

Parthian (made in present-day Iran),
circa 100 BCE
Silver with gilding and glass inlays,
H: 27.4 cm (10¾ in.); L: 46 cm (18⅛ in.);
Diam (rim): 12.6 cm (5 in.), 86.AM.753

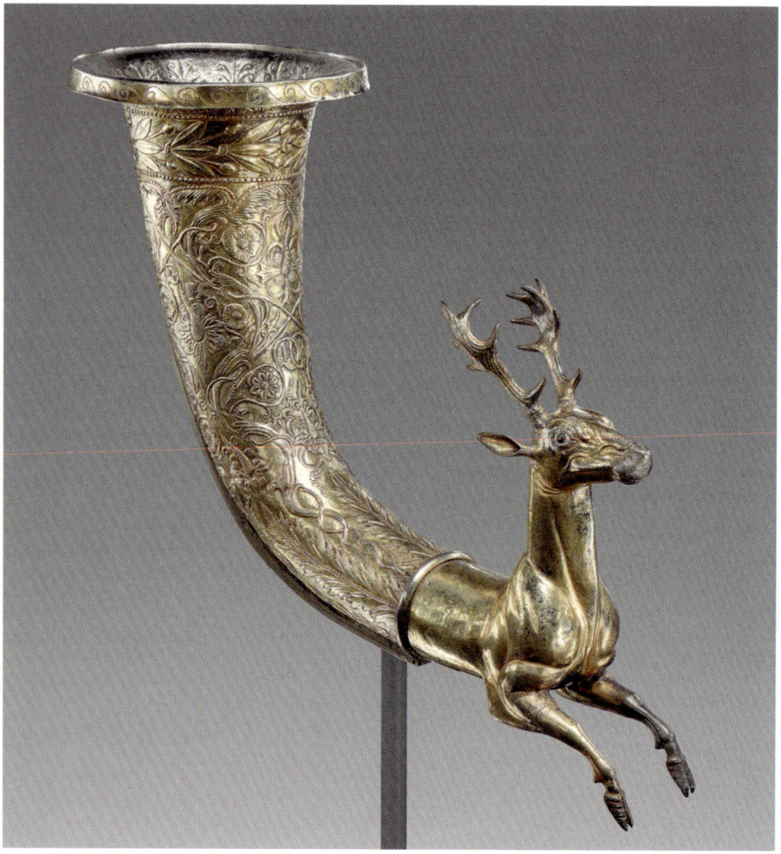

This extensively gilded silver vessel is one of the finest to survive from the Parthian Empire, which had its origins in Iran. The ornate decoration includes alternating acanthus leaves and tendrils, ascending in an elaborate floral pattern. The stag's horns, ears, and legs were cast separately and soldered to the body; its eyes were made of glass. A spout, now lost, was once attached to the hole between the legs. Wine could be poured through the spout into a cup or directly into the mouth of the drinker. Two inscriptions in Aramaic are preserved. A name scratched into the top of the rim may read either Fradāt or Frahāt, both common Parthian male names. A longer inscription on the stag's belly suggests that this rhyton may have been used as a dedication or to pay a debt.

Herm of Dionysos

Greek, 100–50 BCE
Attributed to the workshop of Boëthos of Kalchedon (active second century BCE).
Bronze with calcite inlays,
H: 103.5 cm (40⅜ in.); W (base): 23.5 cm (9¼ in.), 79.AB.138

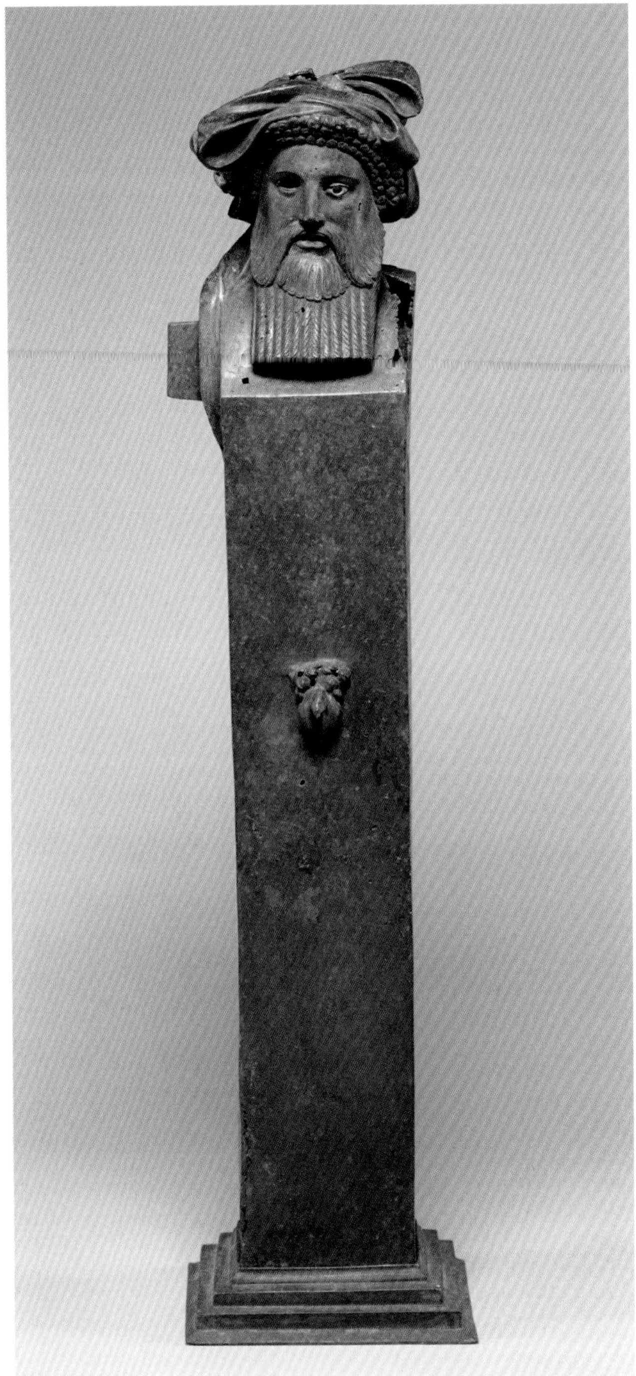

Statues in the form of a rectangular pillar surmounted by a head or bust are known as herms. Originally, herms represented Hermes, god of travelers and commerce, from whom they got their name. Later, heads of other gods and mythical figures, and eventually those of athletes, philosophers, and other prominent citizens, appeared. Equipped with a phallus, perhaps to avert evil, herms often stood at crossroads (to protect travelers) and at the entrances of homes. This example features Dionysos, god of wine, his eyes originally inlaid with stone. In style and size it is remarkably similar to a herm recovered from a Roman shipwreck near the town of Mahdia, Tunisia. That herm was signed by Boëthos of Kalchedon (in present-day Turkey), and this twin probably came from the same workshop.

Statue of Jupiter (The Marbury Hall Zeus)

Roman (found in Tivoli), 100–1 BCE

Marble, H: 207 cm (81½ in.), 73.AA.32

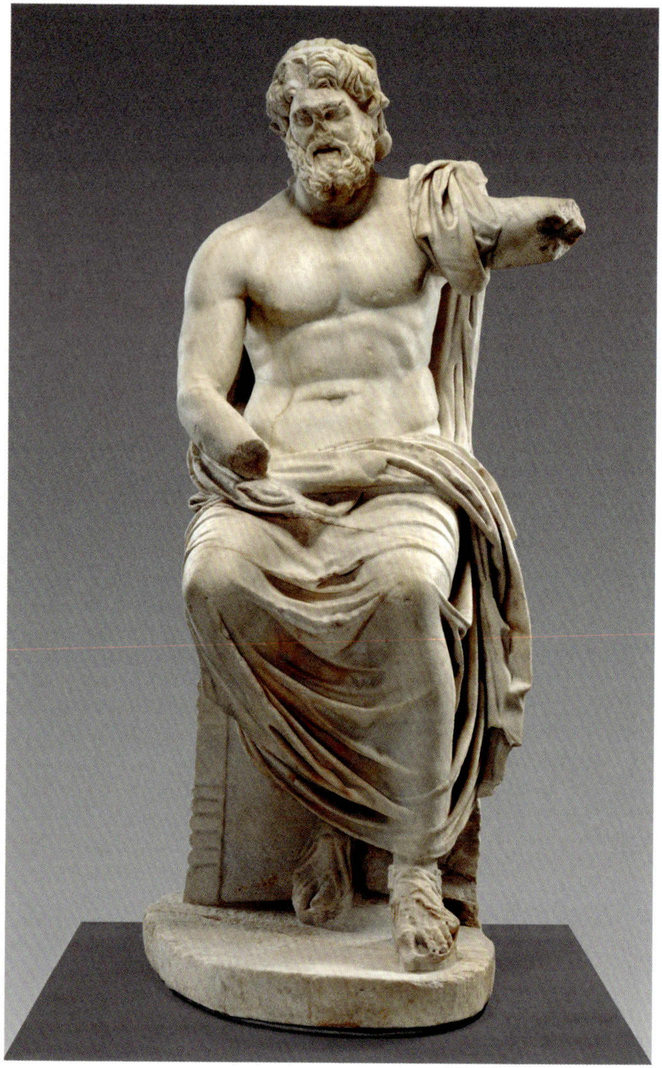

Among the largest Roman sculptures in the United States, this imposing statue depicts Jupiter—known to the Greeks as Zeus—enthroned as king of the gods, originally holding a scepter and a thunderbolt. Likely created for a public setting in early imperial Rome, the sculpture updates the god's paternal image, reimagining the ancient Greek statue of Zeus of Olympia, sculpted by Pheidias in the 430s BCE, as a more dynamic, muscular protector befitting the self-perception of the expanding Roman Empire. The statue boasts an extensive provenance going back to 1572, when it decorated a fountain in the villa of Cardinal Ippolito d'Este at Tivoli, outside Rome. Its modern nickname reflects its 1781 purchase for Marbury Hall, the British estate of James Hugh Smith Barry, whose family owned the work until 1932.

Mixing Bowl (*Lebes*) with Drunken Satyr

Greek, 50–1 BCE

Bronze with silver and copper inlays,
H: 58 cm (22 7/8 in.), 96.AC.51

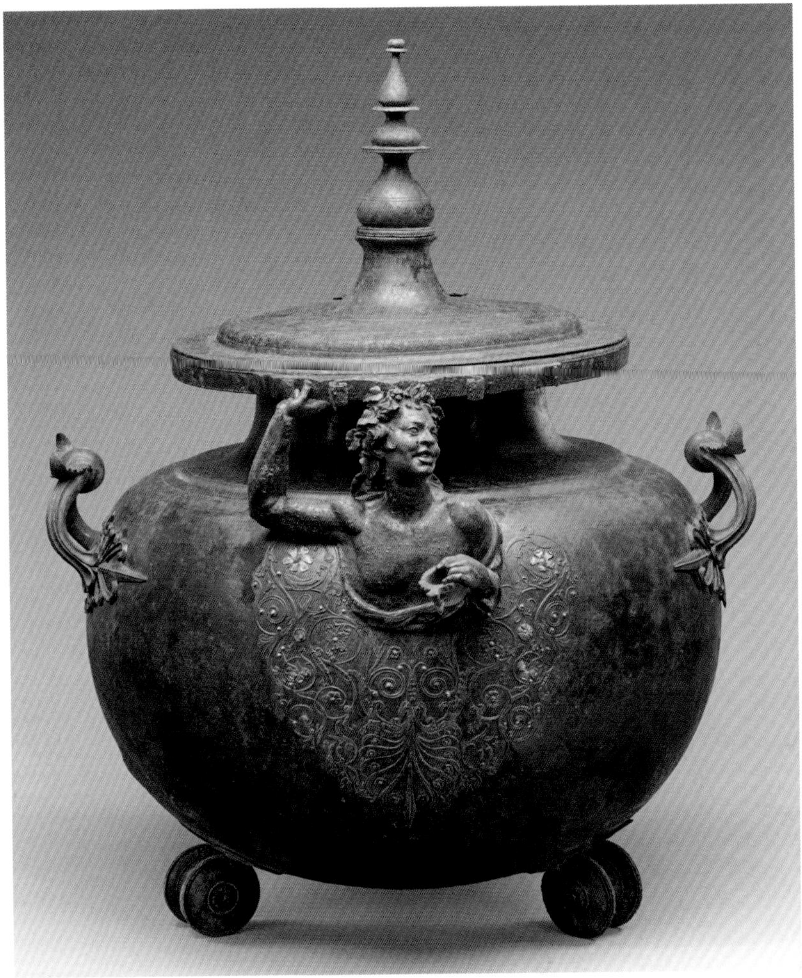

The half-length figure of a young satyr, a follower of Dionysos, god of wine, adorns the front of this *lebes* (cauldron). Holding a drinking cup in one hand, apparently about to fling the dregs of his wine in the ancient game of *kottabos*, the handsome rustic snaps his fingers and bares his silvered teeth in an impudent grin, encouraging the viewer to share the pleasures of wine. His eyes are silvered, as are the exuberant flowers, grape leaves, and spiraling tendrils surrounding him. These vegetal motifs represent the regenerative forces of nature that the god oversaw, and this vessel may have been used to serve wine mixed with water at festivals and during religious rituals performed in his honor.

Statuette of a Bull

Roman, 25 BCE–75 CE

Silver with gilding, H: 14 cm (5½ in.),

2001.7

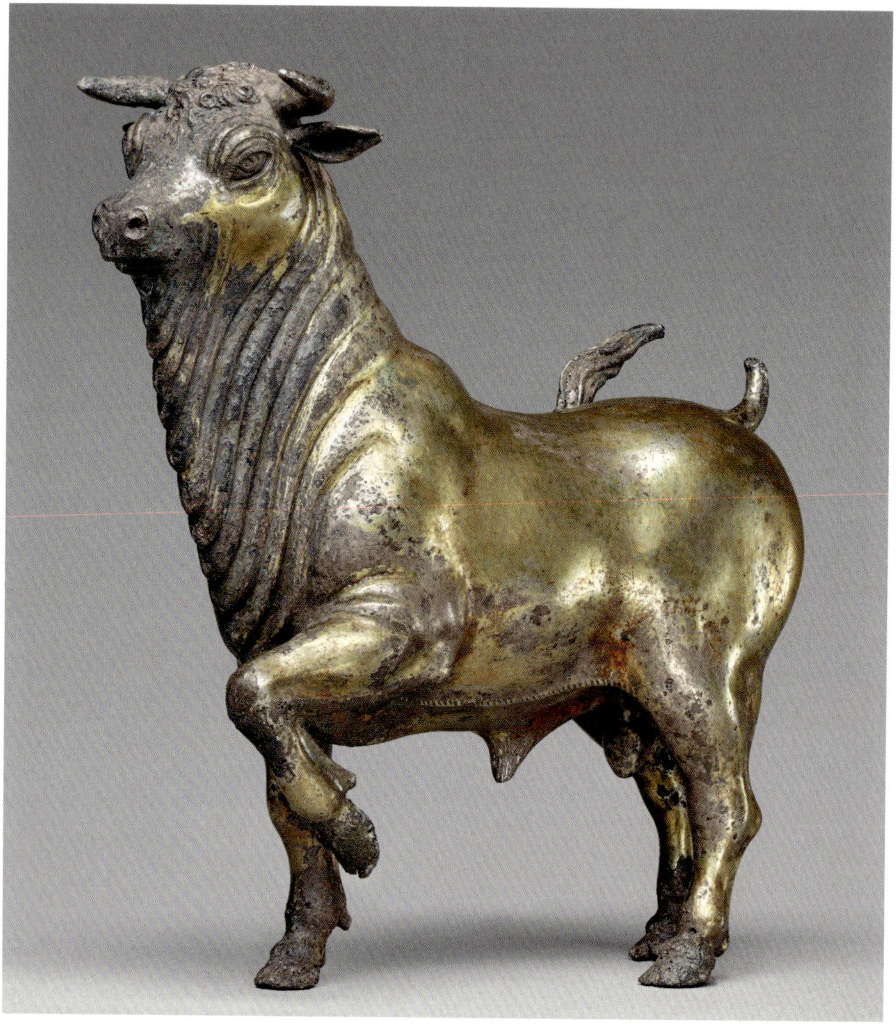

This fine statuette likely joined other figurines of divinities and their familiars in a *lararium* (domestic shrine) dedicated to the gods who protected the Roman household. Standing erect with its tail curled up onto its flank and its head raised proudly, the bull probably represents Jupiter, king of the gods, who often assumed the guise of this mighty animal.

Cameo Glass Cup (Skyphos)

Roman, 25 BCE–25 CE

Glass, H (preserved): 10.5 cm (4⅛ in.);

Diam: 10.6 cm (4⅛ in.), 84.AF.85

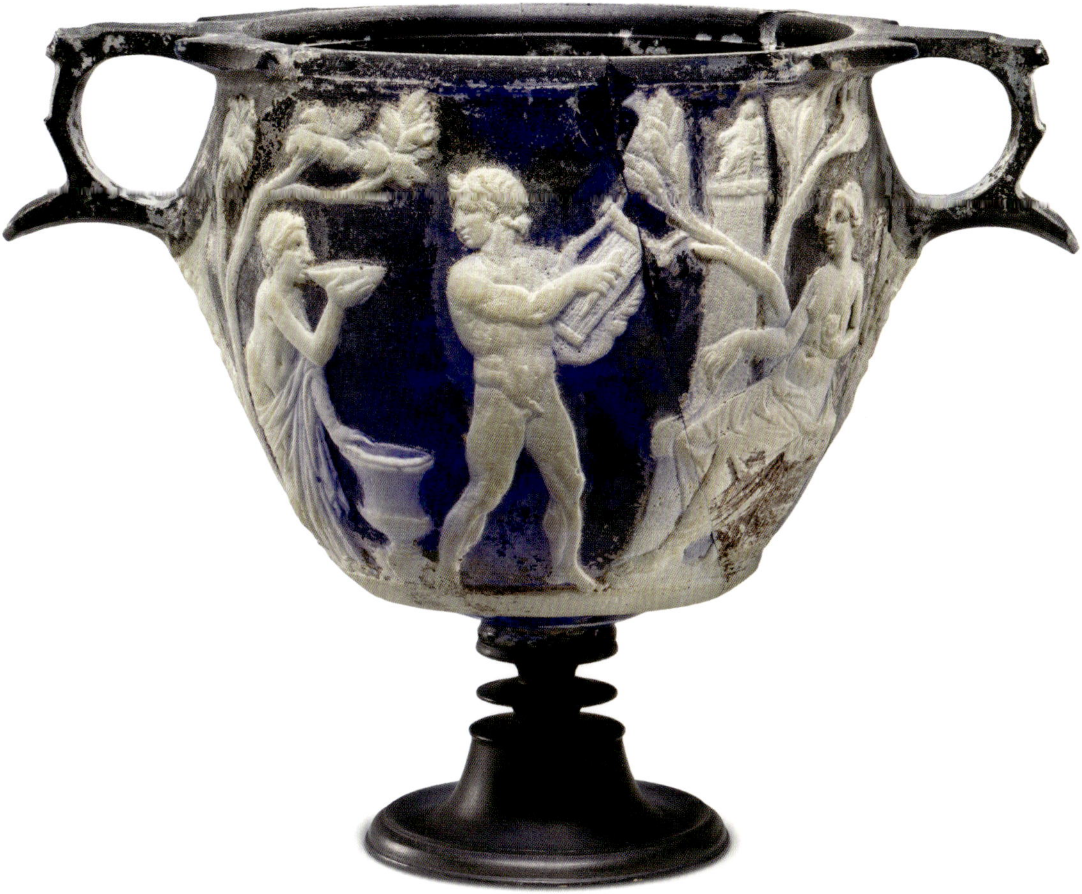

Images of the wine god Bacchus (Greek Dionysos) and his followers decorate several Roman cameo glass vessels, which are exceptionally rare: fewer than twenty complete examples survive. On one side of this drinking cup, a woman, perhaps the god's consort Ariadne, leans against a krater, a large vessel used for mixing wine and water, and sips from a bowl. Bacchus himself sits by a stele topped with an image of the Phrygian mother goddess Cybele. He places an offering, probably incense, on a flaming altar. On the opposite side, a seated woman looks back at a female attendant holding a covered *cista*, a shallow box for sacred objects used in mystery cults. Satyrs, acolytes of Bacchus, holding musical instruments accompany each scene—one plays a harp; the other, panpipes.

Head of Augustus

Roman, 25–1 BCE

Marble, H: 39 cm (15 3/8 in.), 78.AA.261

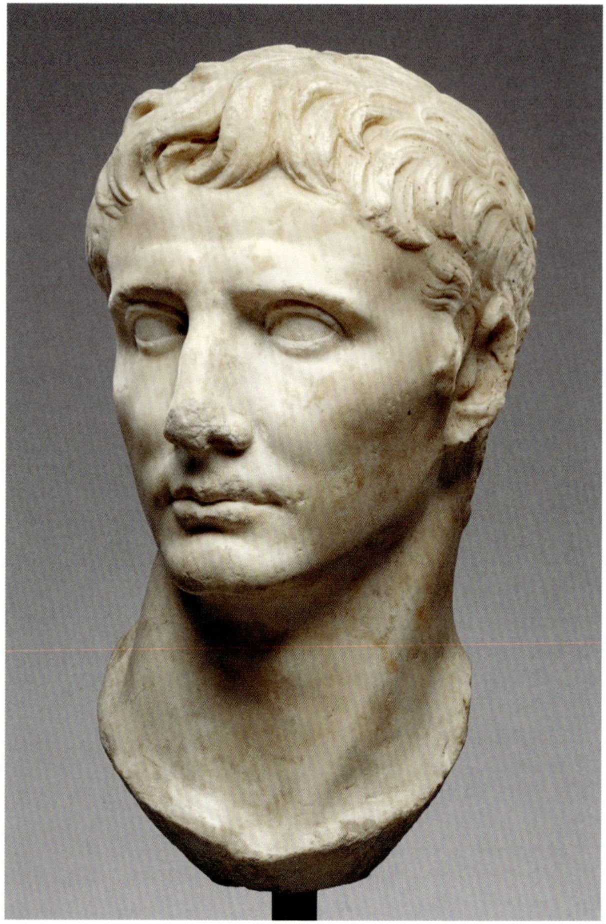

Augustus was Rome's first emperor, or *princeps*, ruling from 27 BCE to 14 CE. He consolidated power and restored peace after a period of civil war while expanding the empire through military conquest. Designed to be iconic, his image served as a symbol of his political agenda of stability and prosperity. As in this head—originally inserted into a separately carved body—Augustus is always shown in an idealized fashion, echoing Classical Greek sculpture from the fifth century BCE, and in a state of seemingly eternal youth. One constant feature is his hairstyle, with its distinctive arrangement of locks in the form of forks and pincers on his forehead. Such reliably recurring visual motifs allowed ruler portraits in diverse media to be recognized across the vast empire.

Gem with Bust of Demosthenes

Roman, circa 25 BCE
Signed by Dioskourides (active late first century BCE). Amethyst intaglio,
H: 2.0 cm (13/16 in.); W: 1.4 cm (9/16 in.);
D: 0.5 cm (3/16 in.), 2019.13.15

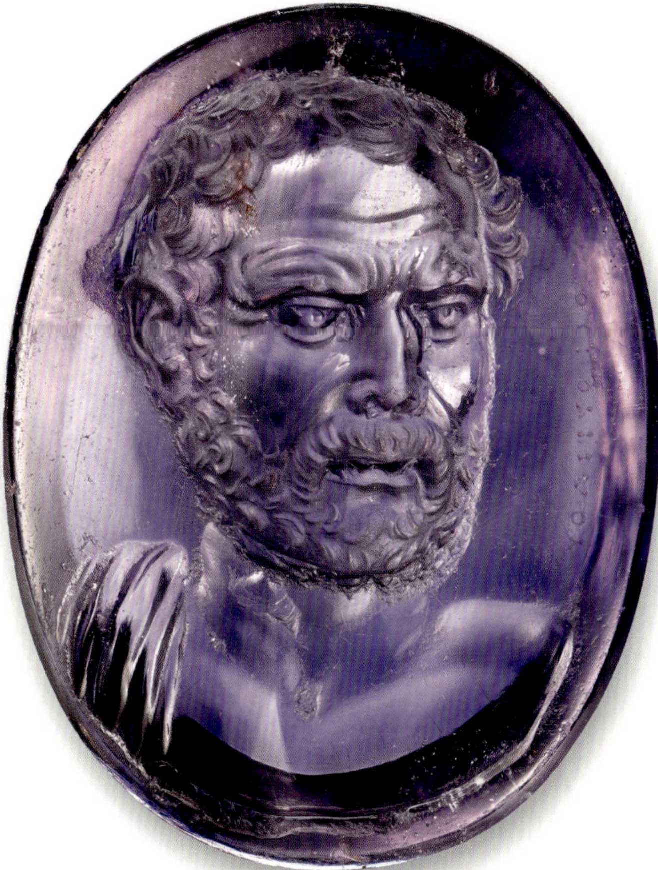

This deeply engraved intaglio features a bust of Demosthenes, an Athenian orator and pro-democracy statesman of the fourth century BCE. His compelling likeness is modeled on an honorific statue commissioned by the citizens of Athens from the sculptor Polyeuktos in the early third century BCE. Several life-size ancient replicas in marble survive. The type was also popular on gems, allowing adherents of democracy to carry his image on their fingers. This fine example is signed in tiny letters by the master gem engraver Dioskourides, who also carved the sealstone of the emperor Augustus (r. 27 BCE–14 CE). Known since at least 1602, this gem was formerly owned by such eminent collectors as the Italian humanist Lelio Pasqualini, the princes of the Boncampagni-Ludovisi family, the Polish count Michel Tyszkiewicz, and the British archaeologist Sir Arthur Evans.

Gem with Venus and Anchises

Roman, circa 25 BCE

Cornelian intaglio with modern gold and enamel mount, H (gem): 3.3 cm (1 5/16 in.); H (with mount): 4.9 cm (1 15/16 in.), 2017.2

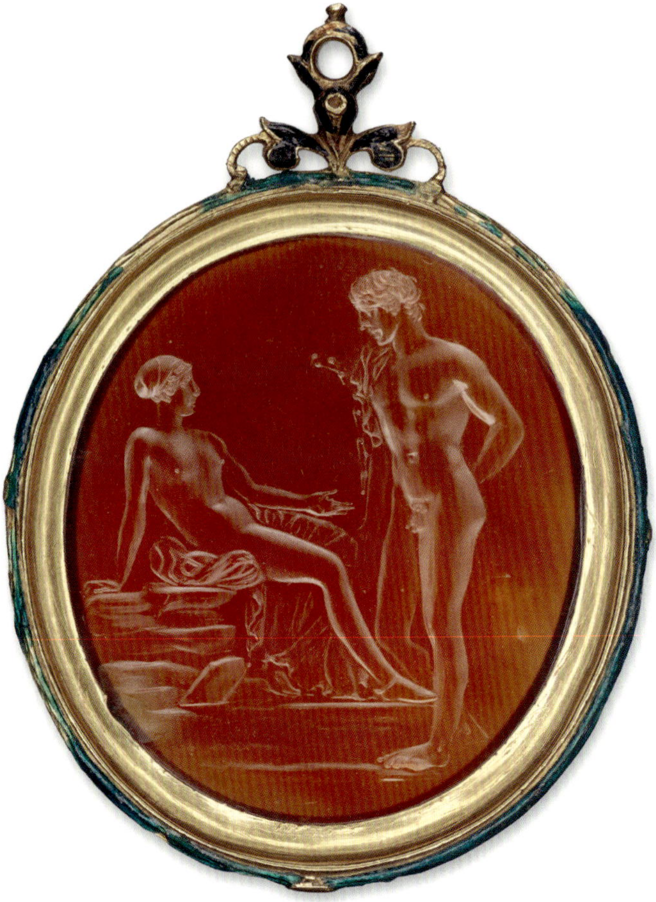

The identity of the couple carved into this gem has long been the subject of debate. The *pedum* (hunter's throwing stick) near the man's shoulder suggests that he is the Trojan Anchises, appearing here alongside his lover, the goddess Venus. The Roman statesman Julius Caesar traced his lineage to the couple's son, Aeneas, mythological fore-father of the Roman people, and Caesar's heir, the emperor Augustus (r. 27 BCE–14 CE), used images of the couple to reinforce his dynastic aspirations. The gem was previously owned by the 4th Duke of Marlborough (1739–1817) and later by Kurt Walter Bachstitz (1882–1949), who was forced to sell it to one of Adolf Hitler's art buyers during World War II. After it was returned to Bachstitz's descendants, Getty purchased the gem.

Gem with Aeneas and His Family Escaping Troy

Roman, circa 20 BCE

Cornelian intaglio, H: 2.2 cm (7/8 in.); W: 1.8 cm (11/16 in.); D: 0.6 cm (1/4 in.), 2019.13.14

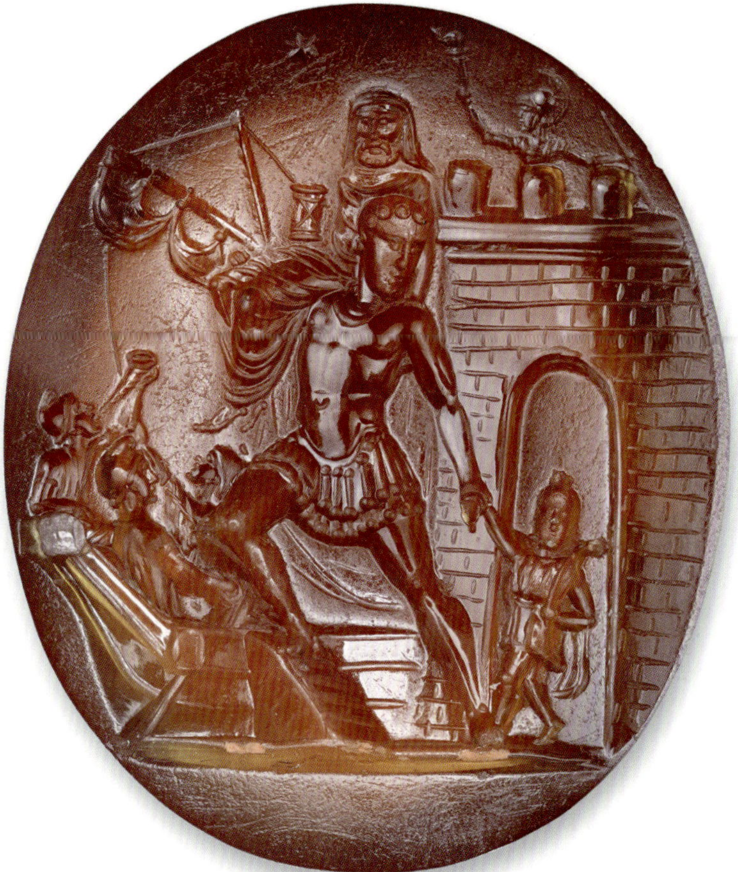

In a dramatic episode at the end of the Trojan War, Aeneas, son of the Trojan prince Anchises and the goddess Venus, flees the doomed city carrying his father on one shoulder while holding the hand of his young son, Ascanius. Three sailors prepare their ship—one mans the rudder, one blows a horn, and a third hoists the sails—while a victorious Greek soldier on the battlements holds a torch and a spear. Minute details further enhance the scene: the engraver carved individual blocks of stone inside the city gate, creating the impression of depth when the fiery gem is turned. Writing at the end of the first century BCE, the Roman poet Vergil transformed Aeneas's escape into the founding myth of Rome, tracing his long journey from Troy to Italy.

Miniature Portrait Bust of a Young Woman

Roman, 25 BCE–25 CE
Bronze with glass-paste inlays,
H: 16.5 cm (6½ in.), 84.AB.59

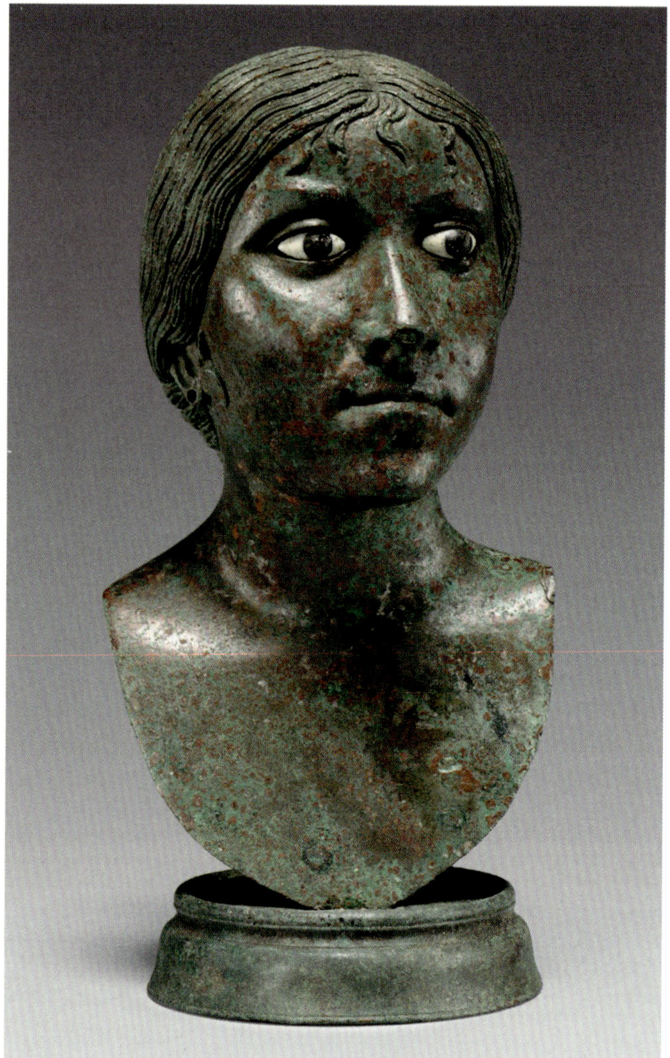

After this smaller-than-life-size bust of a Roman lady was cast in bronze, its skilled maker engraved it with delicate details, capturing her pensive demeanor. The complicated braided and knotted coiffure was fashionable during the reign of the emperor Augustus (27 BCE–14 CE), a period that favored Greek classicism. The earrings that originally hung from her pierced earlobes are now lost, but the eyes preserve their glass-paste inlays, adding to the head's strikingly realistic expression. Small-scale portraits of the imperial family and ordinary citizens were produced in various media throughout the Roman Empire. Most were intended for niches or shrines that commemorated the genealogy and notable deeds of family members in semiprivate, domestic settings.

Portrait Bust of Menander

Roman, 1–25 CE

Bronze, H: 17 cm (6¾ in.), 72.AB.108

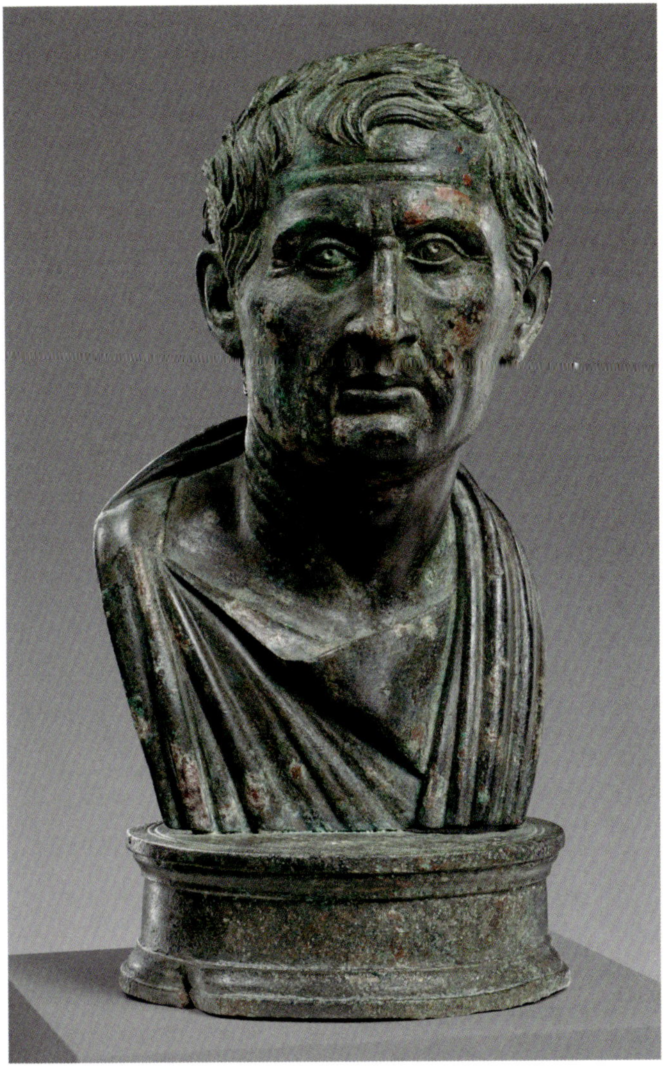

This small bronze portrait bust is identified by a Greek inscription as the famous Athenian playwright Menander (342–291 BCE), who wrote more than one hundred comedies. His plays remained popular among Romans, and playwrights such as Plautus (ca. 244–184 BCE) and Terence (ca. 190–159 BCE) imitated them. About seventy Roman portraits of Menander survive, with identifying features derived from a famous bronze statue of him commissioned after his death by the people of Athens for the Theater of Dionysos. This portrayal was so influential that later artists copied it for more than six centuries. The Getty bust is, however, the only inscribed version, confirming the identity of the sitter. Roman homeowners bought decorative figures like this one to showcase their erudition and taste for comedy.

Grave Relief of a Silversmith

Roman, 1–25 CE

Marble, H: 79.9 cm (31½ in.); W: 58.5 cm (23 in.); D: 31.7 cm (12½ in.), 96.AA.40

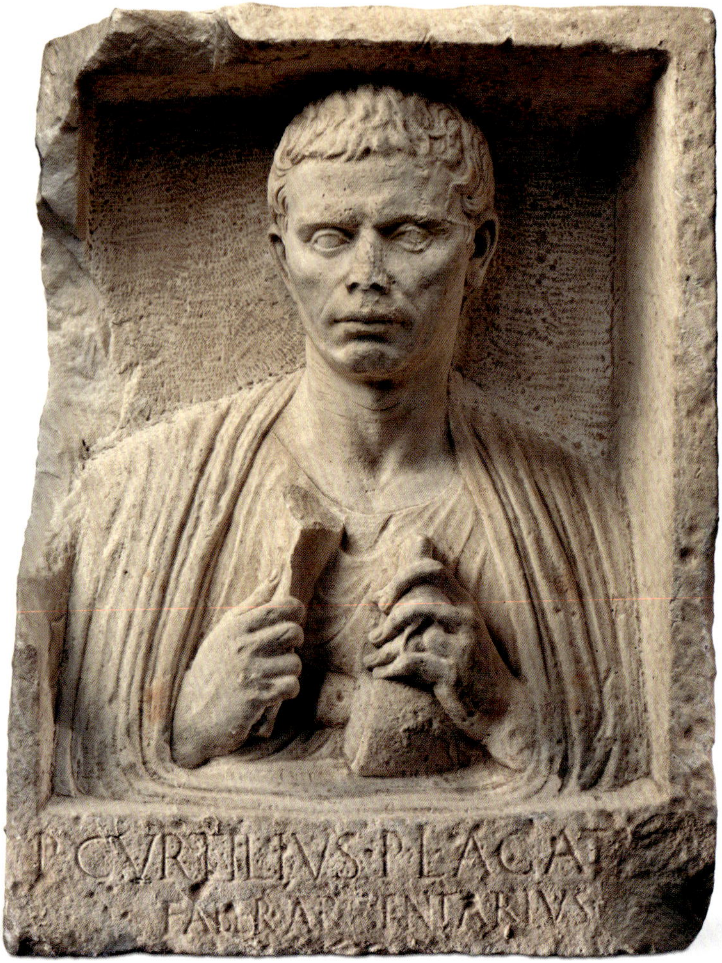

This funerary relief, once part of a larger grave monument, depicts a serious-looking man with a hairstyle emulating that of Emperor Augustus (r. 27 BCE–14 CE; see p. 58). The Latin inscription at the bottom reads "Publius Curtilius Agatho, freedman of Publius, silversmith." That he is referred to as a "freedman" (*libertus*) means that Agatho, probably a Greek, counted among the formerly enslaved people who were brought to Rome as captives and later freed. Many were educated or had skills they could exchange for their freedom, after which they often worked for their former enslavers. Although *liberti* were still subject to certain legal exclusions, some were able to amass large fortunes. Agatho wears a toga, a symbol of Roman citizenship, and a ring. He also wields a silversmith's tools as he embosses the figure of a dancing satyr on a cup filled with a wooden plug.

Head of the Young Bacchus

Roman, 1–50 CE

Bronze with silver inlays, H: 21.6 cm

(8½ in.), 96.AB.52

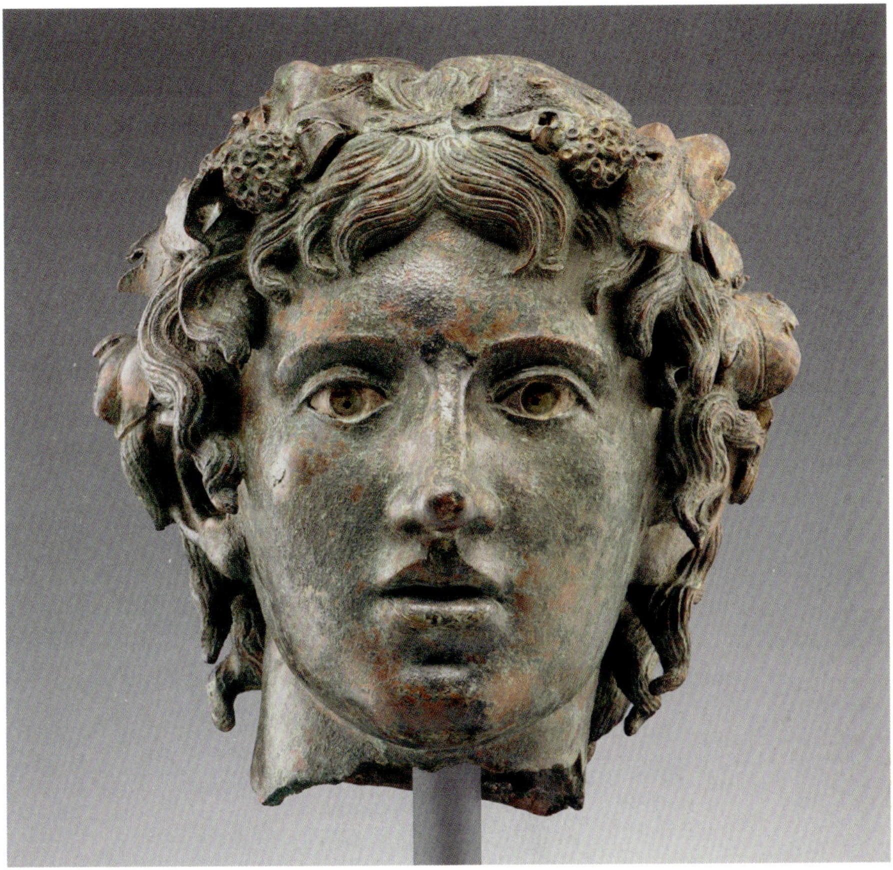

A wreath of twisted vines intertwined with leaves and berries identifies this beautifully wrought head as the Roman god of wine and fertility, Bacchus (known to the Greeks as Dionysos). Silver inlays denote the whites of his eyes, and the pupils and irises (now missing) were made of colored stone or glass paste to create a lifelike image with an intense gaze. Long, curling locks of hair, cast separately, hang down the neck. The head was probably originally attached to a full-length statue of the young god, which may have served as an ornate figural lamp, tray bearer, or other household furnishing.

Statue of an Infant, Perhaps Cupid

Roman, 1–50 CE

Bronze with silver and copper inlays, H: 64 cm (25¼ in.), 96.AB.53

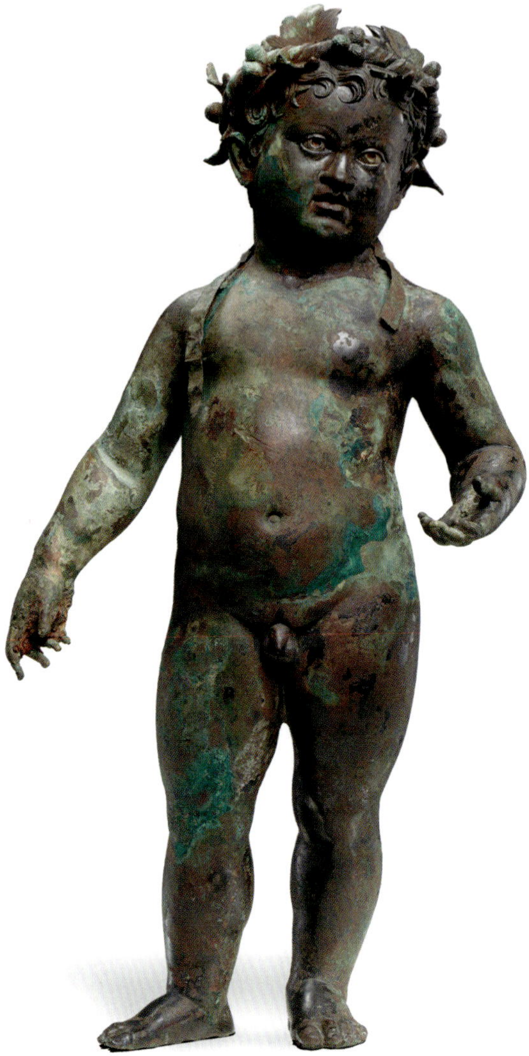

The attributes of this large bronze statue of an infant, once assumed to be Cupid, god of love, suggest that he is rather the young Bacchus, god of wine and revelry. The wreath resting on his soft curls is woven of vine leaves and ribbons that fall over his shoulders, like those worn by athletes and the hero Hercules. He may have held a drinking vessel in his outstretched left hand. Silver irises once encircled pupils with inlays of stone or glass. Despite his pudgy, childlike features, his contrapposto pose seems remarkably adult, and although he stands upright, his head tilts lazily with a dreamy upward gaze. Bronze statues such as this one were popular decorative elements in the gardens and courtyards of wealthy Roman households.

Bust of Germanicus

Roman, 20–40 CE

Marble, H: 51.4 cm (20¼ in.); W: 38 cm (14 15/16 in.); D: 22.9 cm (9 in.), 2021.66

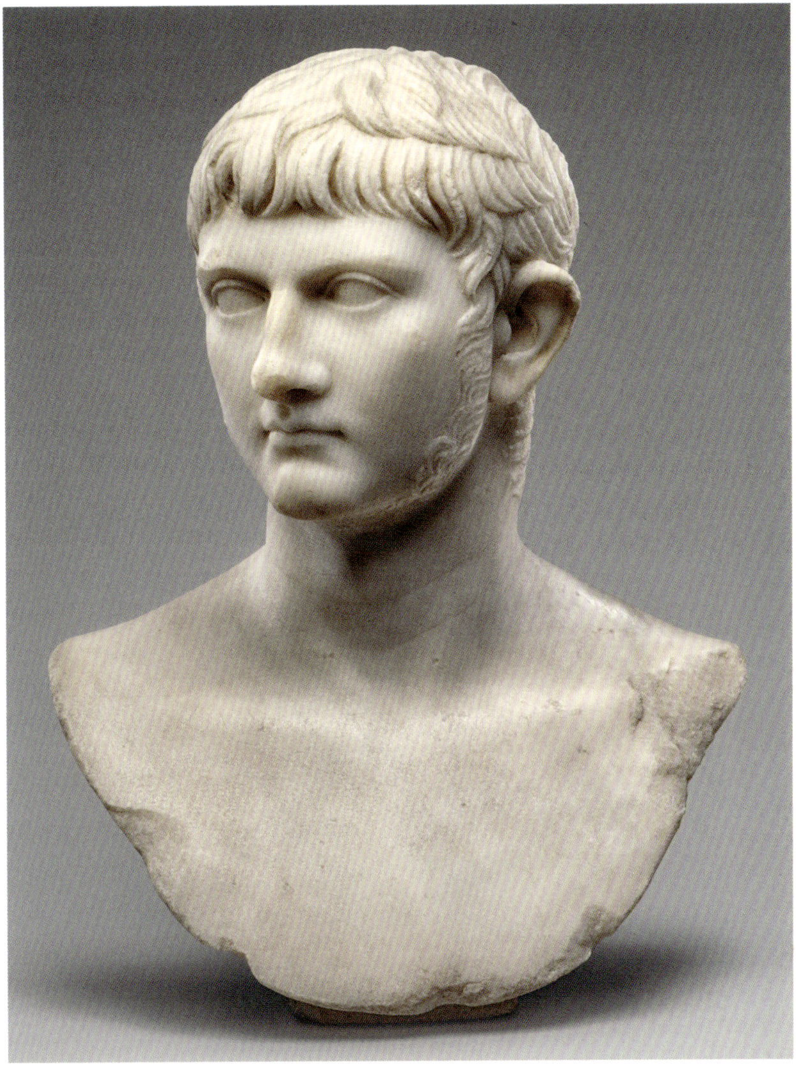

This stately bust depicts the young Germanicus Julius Caesar (15 BCE–19 CE) before his *depositio barbae*, or ritual first shaving of the beard. While this portrait type was created at the time of Germanicus's adoption by the Roman emperor Tiberius in 4 CE, this likeness was made after his death. Germanicus was a successful general who was immensely popular with both the military and the Roman citizenry. Though groomed to be emperor, he died young and never acceded to the throne, but he did receive extensive posthumous honors and was venerated as Rome's version of Alexander the Great (see p. 46). This portrait may have been acquired in Rome in 1798 by Thomas Bruce, 7th Earl of Elgin (1766–1841), and was long part of the collection of the earls of Elgin and Kincardine in Scotland.

Two-Handled Cup with Mythological Scenes

Roman, 1–100 CE

Silver, H: 12.5 cm (4⁷/₈ in.); Diam: 16.3 cm (6³/₈ in.), 96.AM.57

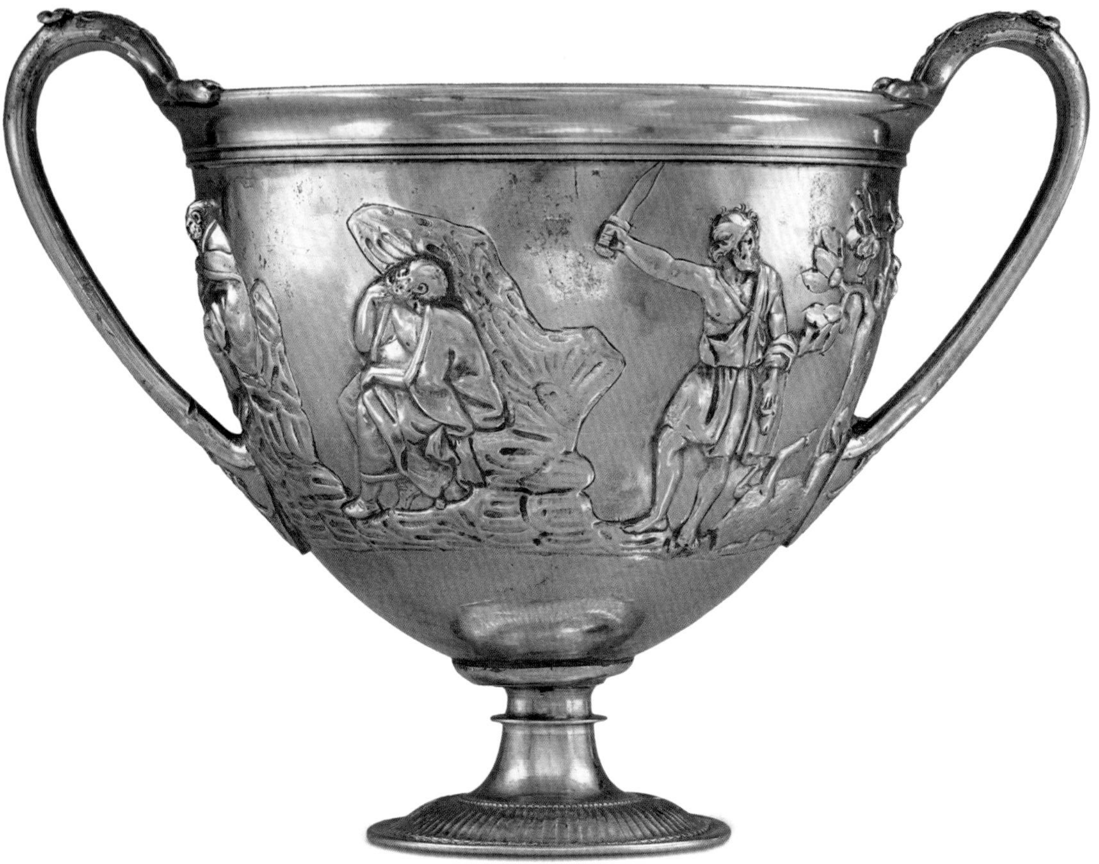

Encircling this drinking cup is a narrative scene from Book 11 of Homer's *Odyssey*. When Odysseus (known to the Romans as Ulysses) left the island of the sorceress Circe after a yearlong stay, she directed him to sail west to the entrance of the Underworld, to ask the blind seer Teiresias about the route home to Ithaka. Here, we see Odysseus, his sword upraised, after he has sacrificed a ram, spilling its blood to summon the ghost of the seer, who sits on a rocky outcrop. On the opposite side, five figures, perhaps representing philosophers or sages, engage in conversation. The relief decoration was produced by repoussé, the technique of hammering and punching motifs from behind before sharpening surface details.

Statue of Leda and the Swan

Roman (found in Rome), 1–100 CE

Marble, H: 132.1 cm (52 in.), 70.AA.110

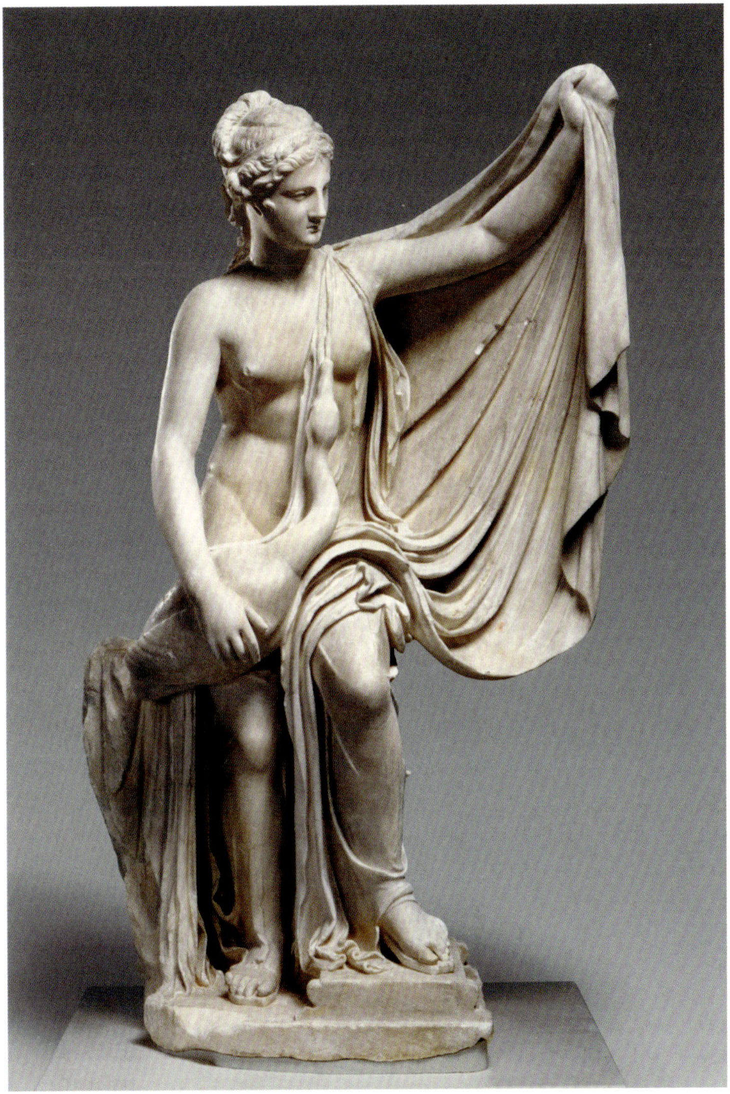

In Greek mythology, the Spartan queen Leda attracted the attention of Zeus, king of the gods, who often assumed animal disguises to seduce mortal women. Here, the god in the guise of a swan, seeking refuge from a pursuing eagle, lands in the queen's lap, raising its beak toward her face as she lifts her sheer drapery to protect it. The theme of Leda and the swan was popular among the Romans, and this sculpture is one of several Roman replicas of an earlier Greek version, sculpted by Timotheos in the 300s BCE. The Getty Villa's marble has been heavily restored, including the addition of Leda's head from an ancient statue of Venus, soon after its discovery on Rome's Palatine Hill in 1775.

Relief with Theater Masks

Roman, 1–100 CE

Marble, H: 24 cm (9 7/16 in.); W: 31 cm (12 3/16 in.), 2018.8

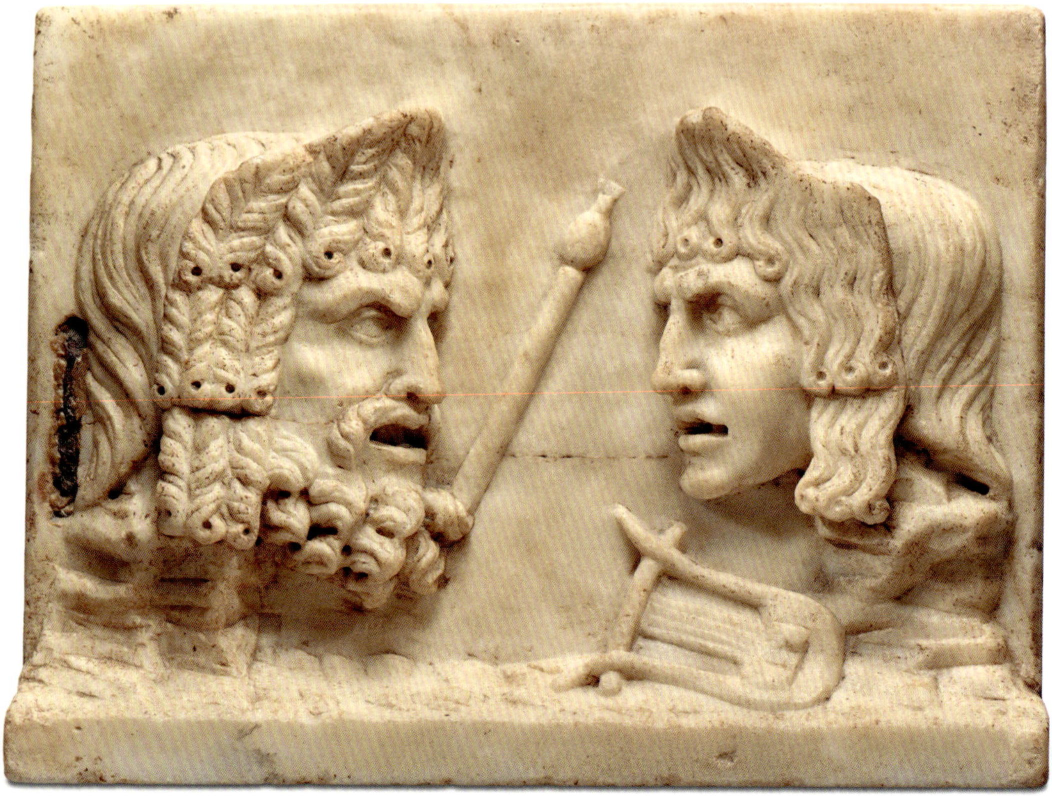

Double-sided reliefs with theatrical masks were standard elements of elite domestic decoration in Italy of the first century CE. Their imagery closely adheres to themes typical of the theater and its patron god, Bacchus. This example juxtaposes a bearded and a youthful mask on one side with a balding satyr (a follower of Bacchus) on the other. The compositions, however, also function as skillful optical illusions: carved in high relief with lifelike features, the masks at first resemble a confrontation between living figures rather than inanimate objects placed on the ground. Displayed in homes alongside illusionistic wall paintings and floor mosaics, such reliefs transformed everyday residential areas into dramatic spaces, imbuing them with a playful irreverence.

Fresco Fragment with a Nilotic Landscape

Roman, circa 70 CE

Plaster with pigment, H: 45.7 cm (18 in.); W: 38 cm (15 in.), 72.AG.86

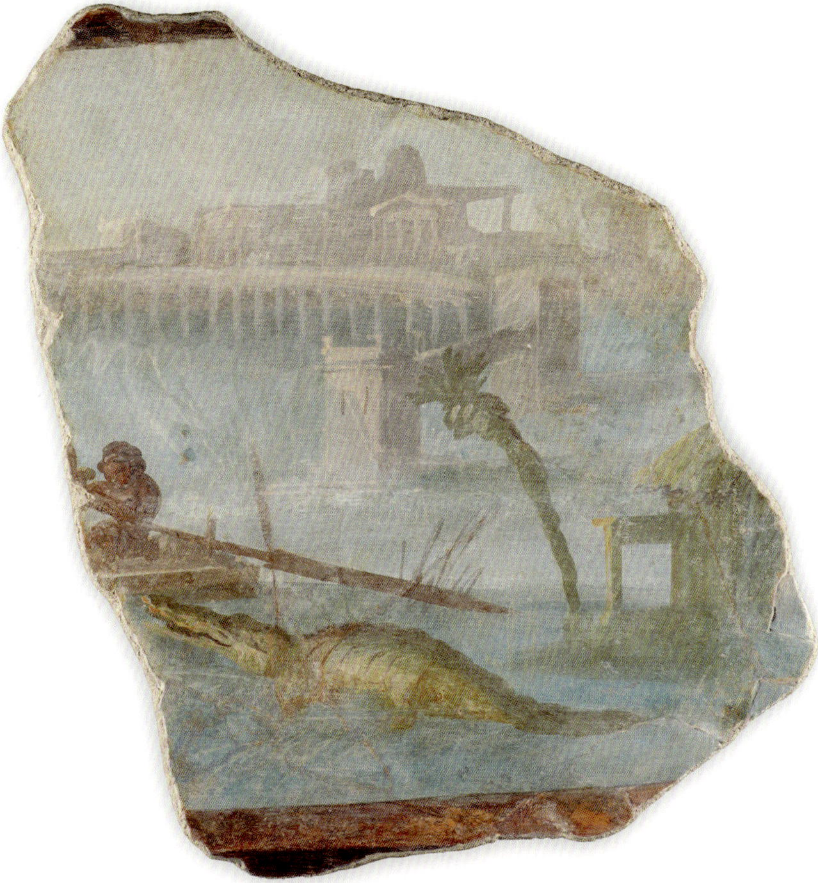

In a scene set on the banks of the Nile River in Egypt, a crocodile moves through a stand of rushes toward a small figure rowing a boat beside a thatched hut and a scraggly palm tree. In the background is an impressionistic rendering of a bridge and a colonnaded portico supporting various buildings of Greco-Roman architectural style. During the first and second centuries CE, Nilotic scenes appear often in Roman frescoes and mosaics, primarily in domestic settings. These landscapes sometimes portray Egypt's inhabitants as the dwarf-like *pygmaioi* (pygmies) of Greek myth, believed to live in faraway lands. It is possible that the figure rowing the boat is one such individual, lending the scene a wondrous quality and representing Egypt as a land of mystery.

Statue of Venus

Roman (from Rome), 100–200 CE

Marble, H: 184 cm (72 7/16 in.), 54.AA.11

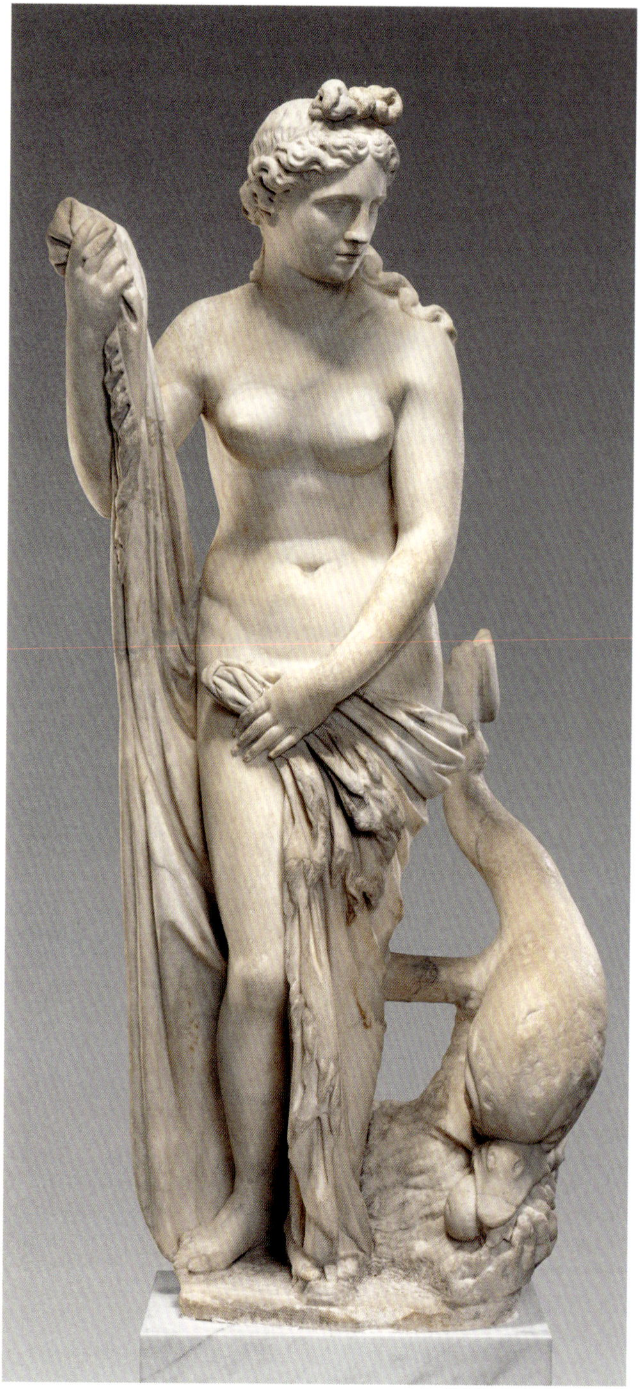

Venus, the Roman goddess of love, wraps her nude body in a fringed mantle. At her side, a large dolphin engages with a cuttlefish, symbolizing the goddess's marine origins while also aiding the statue's stability. The head, breasts, and right arm are restorations—some of them centuries old. The modern history of the statue can be traced to a 1509 engraving depicting a matching Venus, described as "recently found in Rome." By the nineteenth century, the statue's pedigree had stirred excitement and debate, including a longstanding misattribution to the collection of Cardinal Mazarin, adviser to the French king Louis XIV (r. 1643–1715). Damage on Venus's back was even rumored to be from cannon fire sustained during the French Revolution.

Head of Julia Titi

Roman, circa 90 CE

Marble with pigment, H: 33 cm (13 in.); W: 22.5 cm (8⅞ in.); D: 24.4 cm (9⅝ in.), 58.AA.1

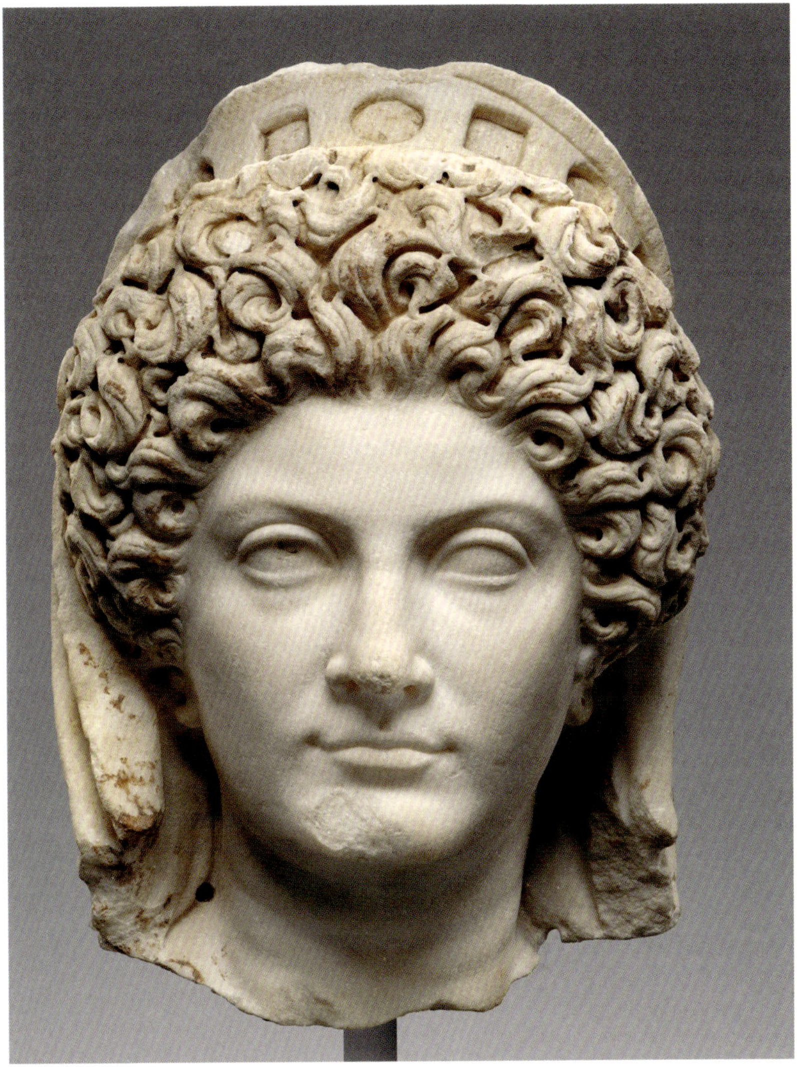

This portrait originally was quite colorful. Traces of pigment in the hair attest to the application of paint, and depressions in the diadem (crown) were once inlaid with glass or precious stones. Drill holes in the earlobes and on either side of the neck indicate the presence of real jewelry. The mantle over her head is an attribute of either a Roman matron or a priestess. Small curls typical of women in the Flavian period (69–96 CE) have led to her possible identification as Julia Titi (63/64–89 CE), daughter of the emperor Titus (r. 79–81 CE), or perhaps his second wife, Marcia Furnilla. If Julia Titi, she may be represented here as a *diva*, or consecrated goddess, a status awarded to her after she died.

Mummy Portrait of Isidora

Romano-Egyptian (from Egypt),
circa 100 CE
Encaustic on linden wood, linen, and gold: H: 48 cm (18⅞ in.); W: 36 cm (14¹³⁄₁₆ in.); D: 12.8 cm (5¹⁄₁₆ in.), 81.AP.42

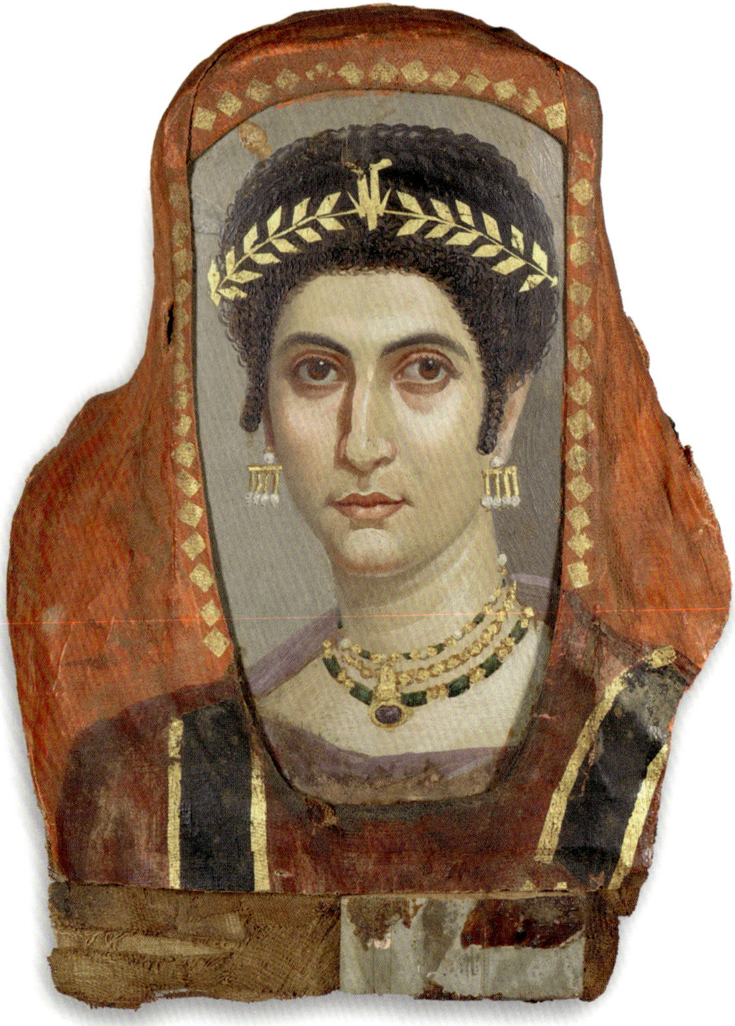

Mummification burials from Roman Egypt sometimes combined individualized portraiture in Greco-Roman style with traditional Egyptian burial practices. This portrait of a refined woman bears remnants of a linen shroud, indicating that its subject was buried in a similar manner to Herakleides (see p. 75). The name Isidora is painted on the shroud above the right shoulder. She wears a purple tunic with dark *clavi* (stripes). Her upper torso, or perhaps her full body, was painted onto the shroud in which the mummified body was originally wrapped. A gold wreath and gold and silver hairpins adorn her intricately curled hair. Her elaborate jewelry also includes pearls and emeralds. The portrait was painted in the encaustic technique, in which the pigment was mixed with hot beeswax, creating a luminous and three-dimensional quality.

Mummified Body of Herakleides

Romano-Egyptian (from Egypt), 120–140 CE
Human and bird remains, linen, pigment, beeswax, gold, and wood, L: 175.3 cm (69 in.); W: 44 cm (17 5/16 in.); D: 33 cm (13 in.), 91.AP.6

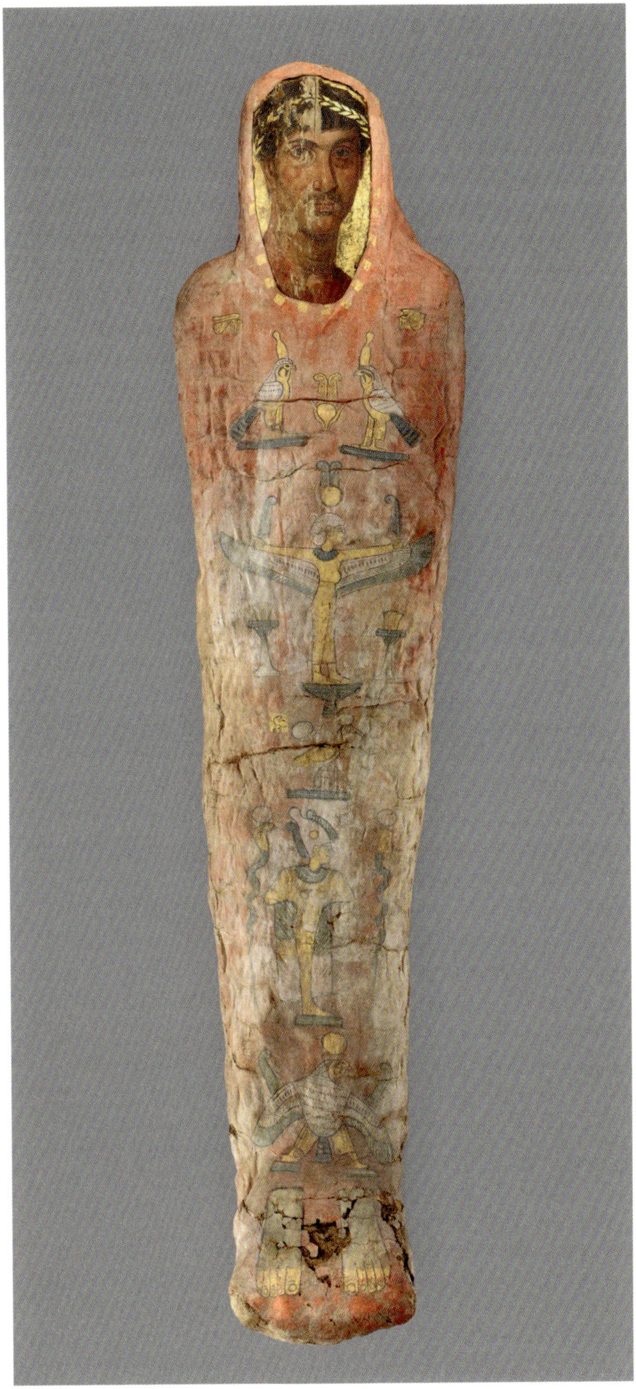

The name of this mummified young man, Herakleides, is written in Greek letters along the top of the footcase. Depicted with a light moustache and curly hair, he likely belonged to the blended Greco-Egyptian communities that had emerged in Egypt during the preceding Ptolemaic period (305/304–31 BCE). Herakleides's body is wrapped in a linen shroud painted with red-lead pigment from Spain's Rio Tinto Valley, testifying to the wide-ranging trade networks of the era. Extensive gilding enhances the background and wreath of his portrait, which is surrounded by decorative gilded squares. His shroud features Egyptian motifs, including an ibis. CT scans revealed a mummified ibis inside the wrappings, suggesting that Herakleides may have been a priest, scribe, or devotee of the Egyptian god Thoth, one of whose manifestations was an ibis.

Statue of Hercules (The Lansdowne Herakles)

Roman (found near Tivoli), circa 125 CE

Marble, H: 193.5 cm (76 1/8 in.), 70.AA.109

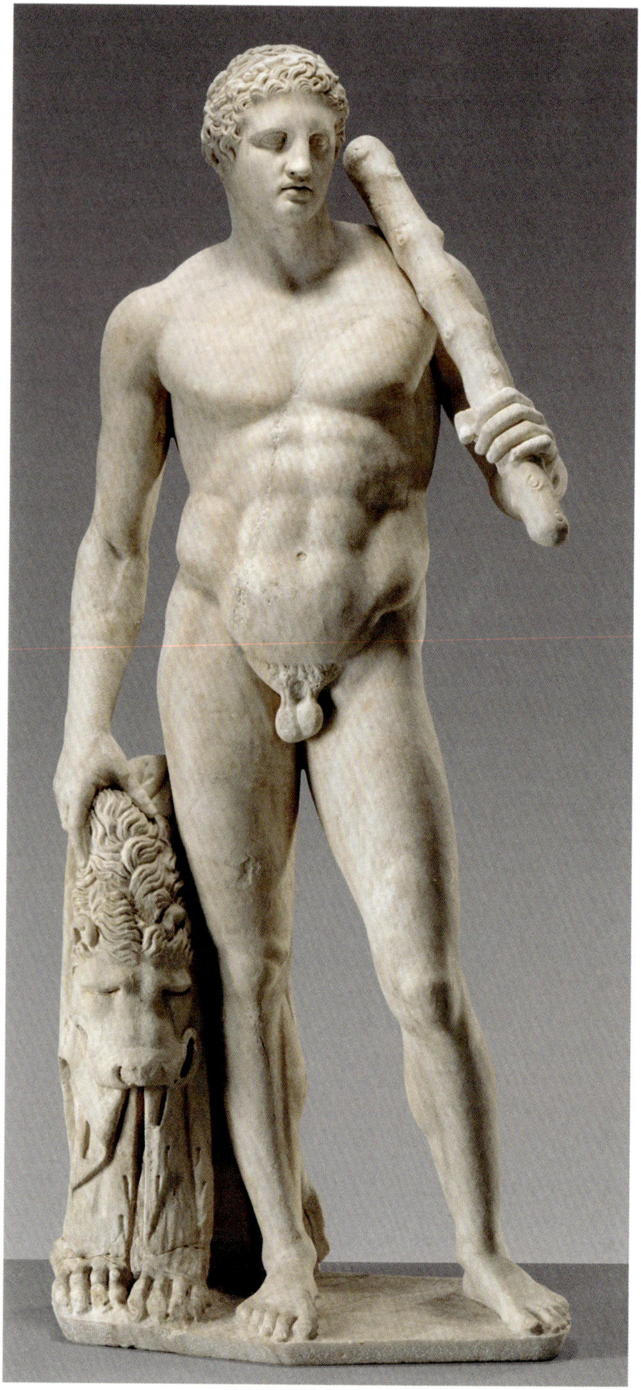

The Greek hero Herakles—son of Alkmene, a mortal woman, and Zeus, king of the gods—achieved fame by completing twelve labors for King Eurystheus of Argos. In ancient art he is often depicted with the adversaries vanquished and weapons used during those feats. As his first labor, he killed the Nemean Lion and here holds its pelt and a club. Though carved in a Roman workshop, this statue of Herakles (known as Hercules to the Romans) derives from an earlier Greek version. Found in 1790 in the villa of the emperor Hadrian (r. 117–138 CE) at Tivoli, the sculpture was restored in Rome and sold in 1792 to Henry Thomas Petty-Fitzmaurice, 4th Marquess of Lansdowne (1816–1866), from whose family J. Paul Getty acquired it in 1951. Getty considered it his most prized possession and created an opulent gallery for its display.

Gem with Bust of Antinous

Roman, 131–138 CE

Dark brown chalcedony intaglio set in a modern gold mount, H: 3.5 cm ($1\frac{3}{8}$ in.); W: 2.9 cm ($1\frac{1}{8}$ in.), 2019.13.17

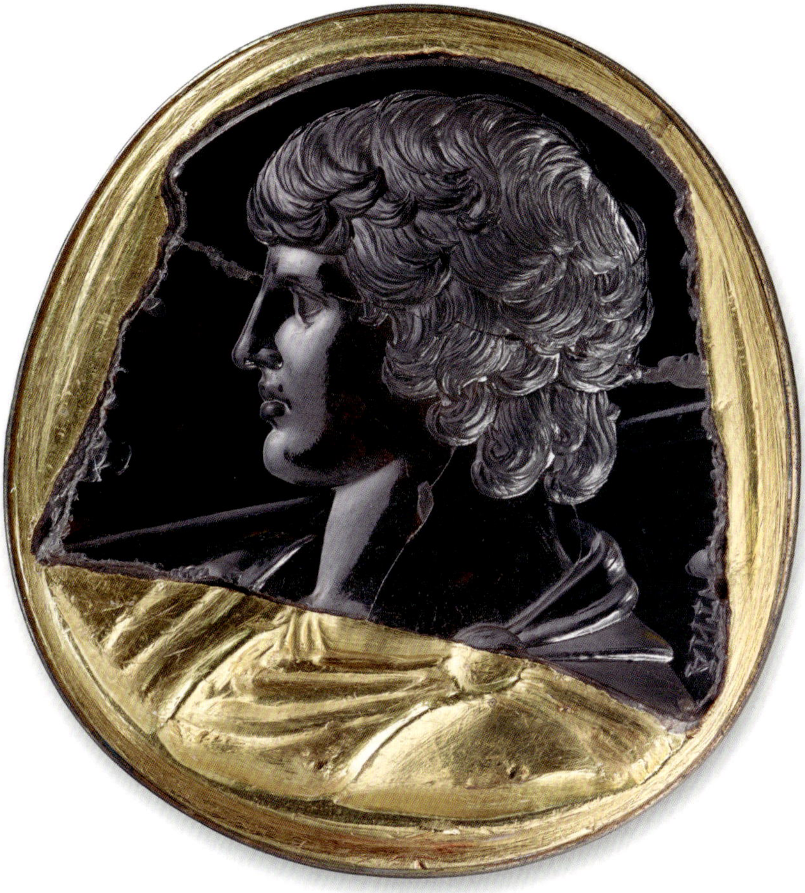

Intricately carved in dark chalcedony, this gem portrays Antinous, beloved companion of the Roman emperor Hadrian (r. 117–138 CE). His early death by drowning in the Nile River in 130 CE led the grief-stricken emperor to honor him with a cult, in which Antinous was revered as a semidivine hero. Across the empire, idealized portraits of Antinous were fashioned in different media, from the monumental to the intimate, like this gem. Shown in profile, Antinous carries a hunting spear over one shoulder; a fragmentary Greek inscription appears near the other. First documented in the eighteenth century in the collection of the Venetian aristocrat Anton Maria Zanetti (1679–1767), this gem and its mount, customized to compensate for damage, later became a highlight of the famed gem cabinet of the British dukes of Marlborough.

Bust of Antoninus Pius

Roman, circa 140 CE

Marble, H: 96 cm (37¾ in.), 2023.13

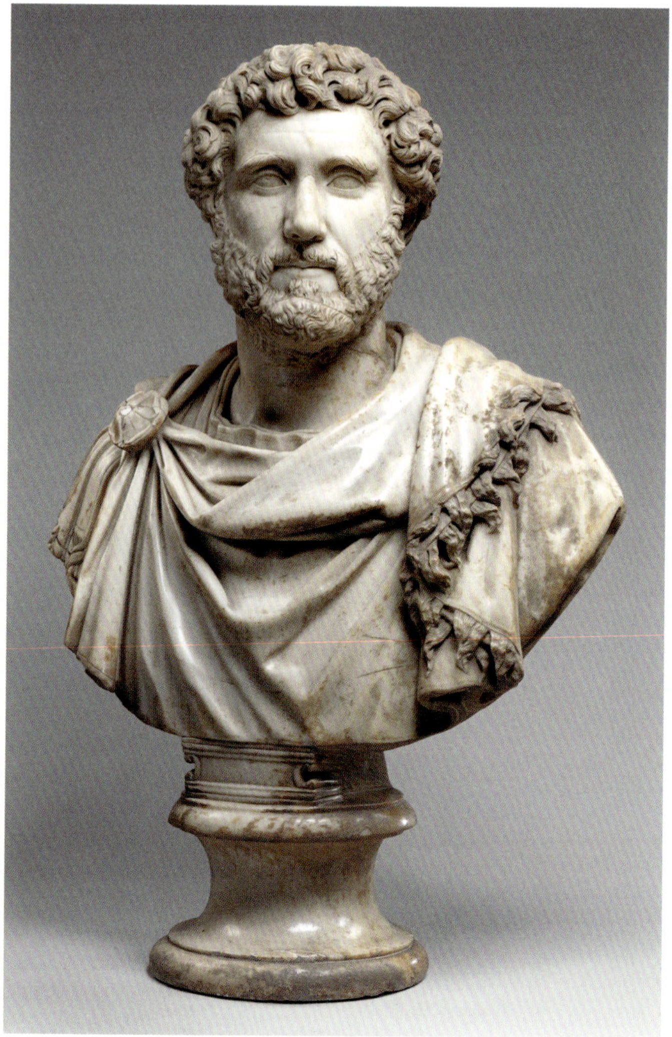

The Roman emperor Antoninus Pius (r. 138–161 CE) is here shown as a mature man with a full, neatly trimmed beard and a dense mass of curly hair. The bust presents him wearing three garments—a tunic, a cuirass, and a fringed military cloak (paludamentum) that functioned as an imperial attribute. The emperor's unmistakable physiognomy is well known from his coinage. Today, some one hundred sculpted portraits of him are known, a relatively small number, given that he was in power for twenty-three years and imperial images were distributed widely across the vast empire. The prototype for this official portrait was created when Antoninus acceded to the throne, at the advanced age of fifty-two, and remained current throughout his reign. The image's longevity exemplifies the stability the Roman Empire experienced under his benign rule.

Bust of Commodus

Roman, 180–185 CE

Marble, H: 92.5 cm (36 7/16 in.), 92.SA.48

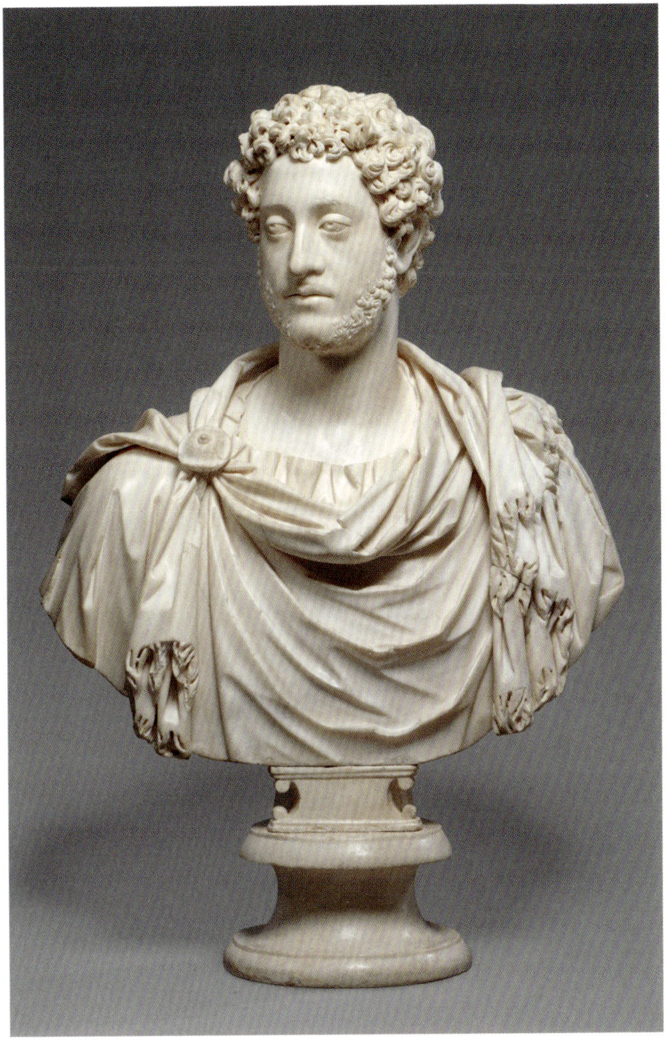

Wearing the imperial military cloak (paludamentum), Commodus (161–192 CE), the last emperor of the Antonine dynasty, is represented here in a portrait type created when he became sole ruler in 180 CE. This bust was long considered an Italian work of the late 1500s, but recent scholarship supports its status as an ancient sculpture made during the emperor's lifetime. Uncertainty over the bust's date was a consequence of its modern history. In the 1800s, when the sculpture was at Castle Howard in Yorkshire, England, abrasive cleaning and recarving significantly altered its appearance. The Getty Commodus is now counted among the most striking ancient portraits of the emperor.

Head of a Young Woman

Roman, 170–190 CE

Marble, H: 32.5 cm (12¾ in.), 2022.14

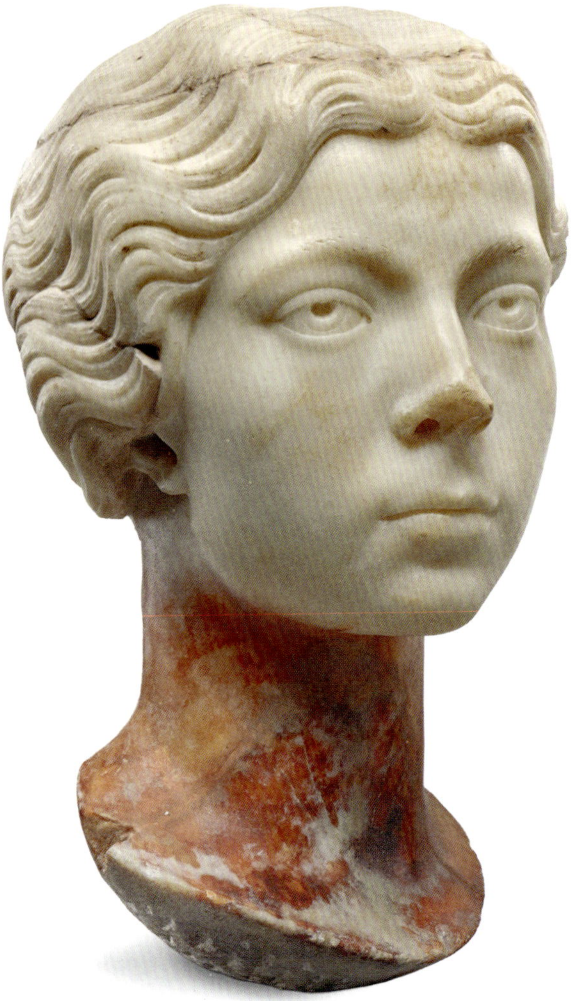

Carved to be inserted into the body of a full-length statue, this head portrays a young, perhaps teen-aged, woman. The discoloration of her long, slender neck may be the result of the marble's exposure to metallic mineral compounds. She wears her hair simply: parted in the center, with long, wavy strands converging in a bun (now missing) at the back of the head. Whereas other female portraits might dazzle with their elaborate hairstyles, here, the sculptor's focus is on the face. Its subtle features come together in a sensitive depiction of a nonimperial woman. Her ambivalent expression, which seems to oscillate between alertness, reservation, pride, and anticipation, makes this portrait an observant study of a yet-unidentified individual of the Antonine period (138–192 CE).

Sarcophagus with Scenes from the Life of Achilles

Roman (made in Athens), 180–220 CE

Marble, H (box): 134 cm (53 in.); W (box): 147 cm (58 in.); L (box): 211 cm (83⅛ in.); H (lid): 100 cm (39½ in.); W (lid): 95 cm (37½ in.); L (lid): 218 cm (86 in.), 95.AA.80

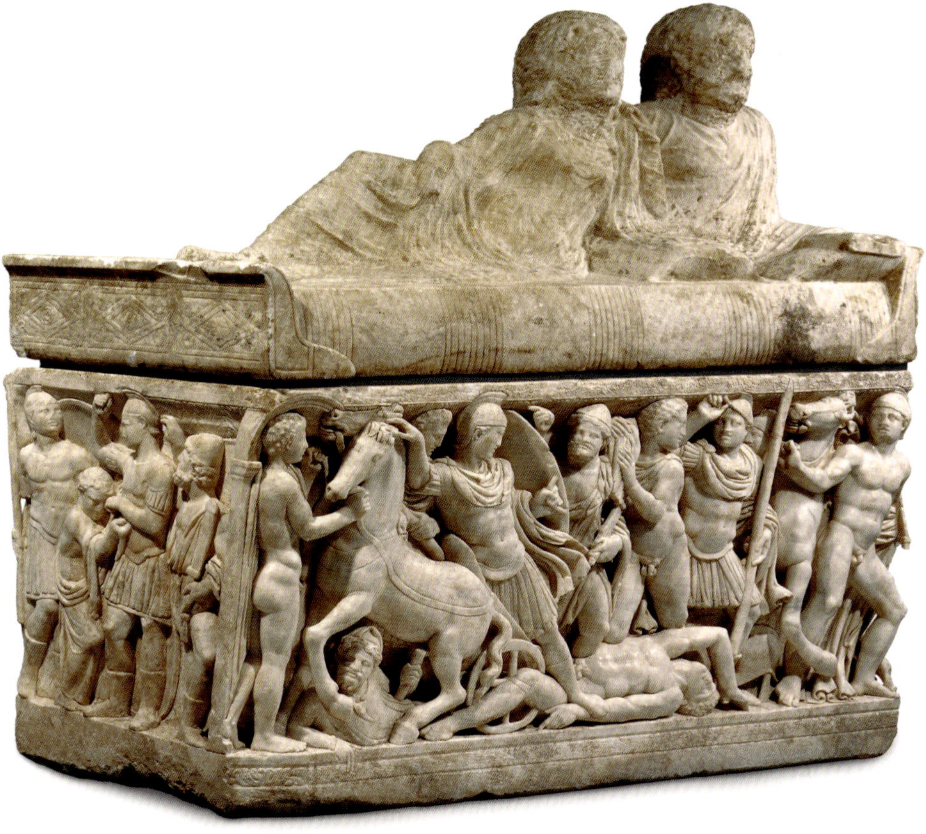

Sarcophagus burials were prevalent in Rome from about 150 to 250 CE. The lid of this example takes the form of a *kline* (couch-bed), on which a couple reclines, holding book rolls. Their heads are only roughed out, never completed with individualized portraits. Episodes from the life of the Greek hero Achilles decorate three sides of the sarcophagus. On the right, he is discovered evading military service on the island of Skyros; on the left, he arms for battle; and on the front, he stands triumphant over the slain Trojan hero Hector, whose corpse he prepares to drag behind his chariot. Carved in low relief on the rear is a scene of the Lapiths fighting the centaurs (human-horse hybrids), a possible reference to Achilles's teacher, the centaur Chiron. These mythological scenes, together with the book rolls, allude to the deceased couple's pretensions to high culture.

Assemblage of Gold Jewelry

Roman, 250–400 CE

Gold with various inlaid and attached stones, including sapphire, emerald, garnet, and glass paste; various dimensions, 83.AM.224, .225, .227, .228

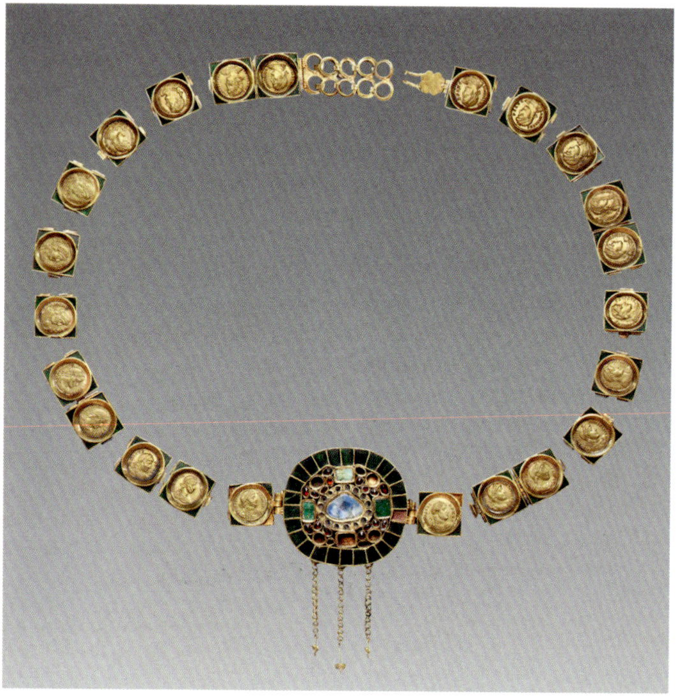

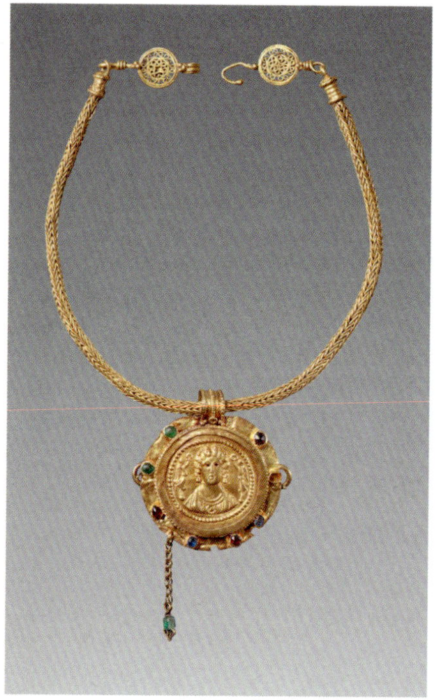

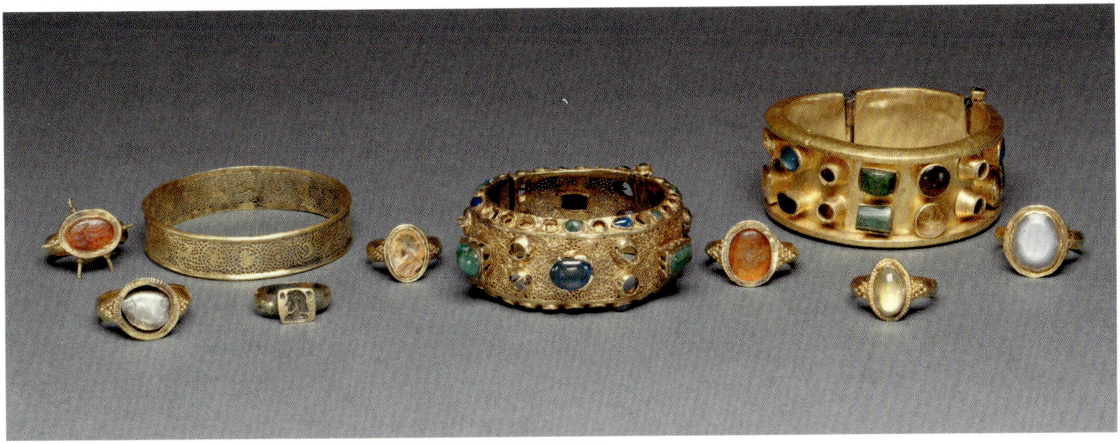

Boasting a fascinating mix of materials and techniques, this magnificent hoard of jewelry may have been buried in a time of war or insecurity by owners who were never able to retrieve it. The centerpiece of the assemblage is an elaborate gold *cingulum*, or belt (far left), that features a large central medallion set with a sapphire, surrounded by stone and glass inlays. Gold coins fill the twenty-three surviving squares and span the reigns of the Roman emperors Constans I (r. 337–350 CE) to Theodosius I (r. 379–395 CE). One necklace (left) has a gold repoussé (hammered) medallion depicting the bust of a woman, perhaps an empress. Two openwork gold bracelets, one decorated with animals within floral scrolls and the other encrusted with vibrantly colored gems, were found with a solid cuff inlaid with glass and precious stones. One ring has a gold intaglio; three are set with engraved gems; and three others are mounted with semiprecious stones. The large size of the rings suggests that they may have been worn by a man, but the small dimensions of the belt and bracelets indicate that they were sized for a woman.

Funerary Relief of Hadirat Katthina, Daughter of Sha'ad

Palmyran, 200–220 CE
Limestone with polychromy and gilding,
H: 50.8 cm (20 in.); W: 40.6 cm (16 in.);
D: 20.3 cm (8 in.), 2019.12

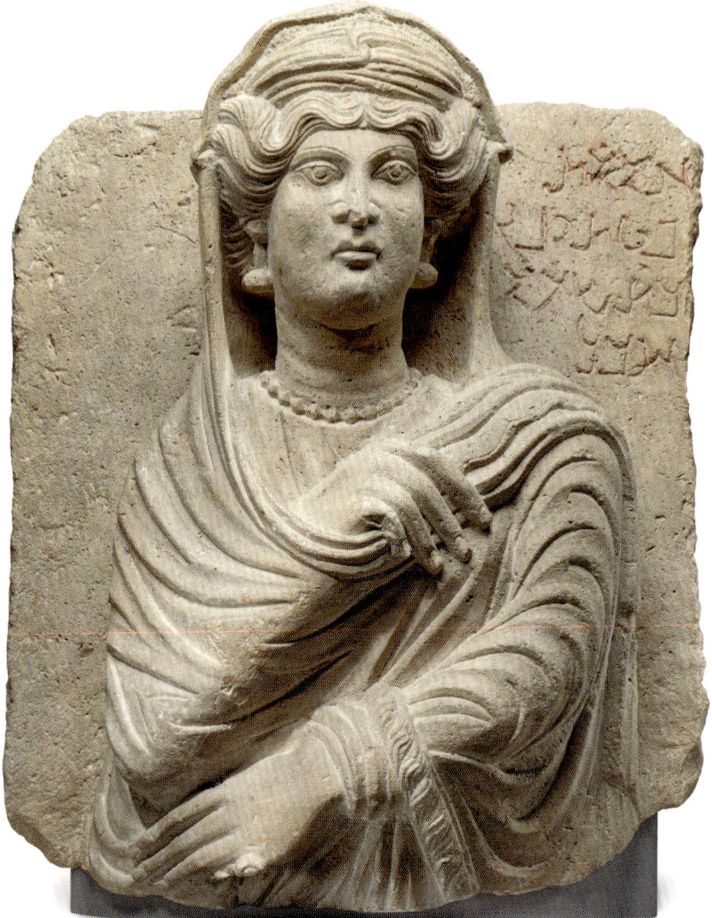

Carved in high relief, this portrait shares many features with the approximately four thousand surviving funerary reliefs from Palmyra, a rich oasis city in the Syrian Desert near the border between the Roman and Parthian Empires. The slab originally closed a small chamber in a larger communal tomb. The sitter, named in the Aramaic inscription, turns slightly to her left, eyes open and alert. A veil and tightly bound "turban" cover her head, but her long hair nonetheless flows out in abundant waves. She wears a long-sleeved tunic and pulls a heavier fringed mantle around her, grasping the edge of her garment in a gesture associated with modesty. Her beaded necklace, pendant earrings, and jeweled ring signal the wealth and status of her family.

Plate with Disputation Scene

Late Antique (from the Eastern Mediterranean), 500–600 CE

Silver, H: 45 cm (17¾ in.); W: 28 cm (11 in.), 83.AM.342

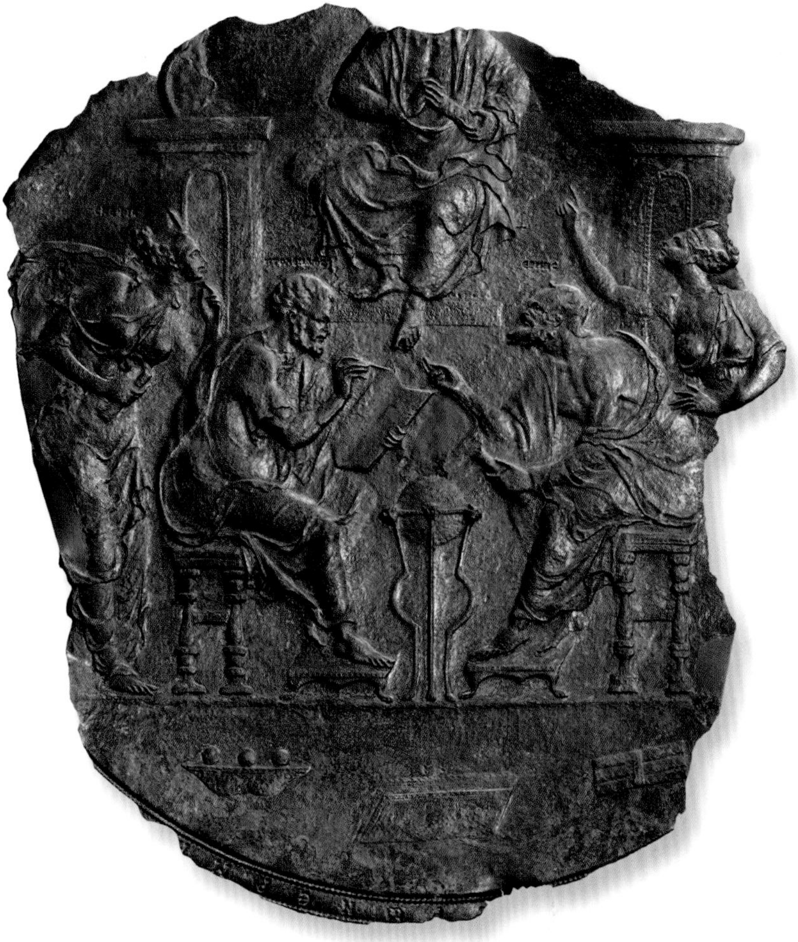

This large but fragmentary plate allegorizes the philosophical dispute between science and magic. Such "picture-dishes," plates in which figural scenes fill the surface, first became popular in the second century CE. Here, Greek inscriptions identify three of the five figures. Ptolemy (left), the founder of the Alexandrian school of scientific thought, debates Hermes Trismegistos ("the thrice greatest," right), a syncretic deity supporting the side of magic. Behind Ptolemy is a woman labeled Skepsis, the personification of speculation or doubt. The figure behind Hermes may be Pistis (faith), but neither she nor the central figure, seated above the group as if in judgment, can be definitively identified. Although some scholars have suggested on stylistic grounds that the plate may date to the 1500s, technical study has confirmed its origins in antiquity.

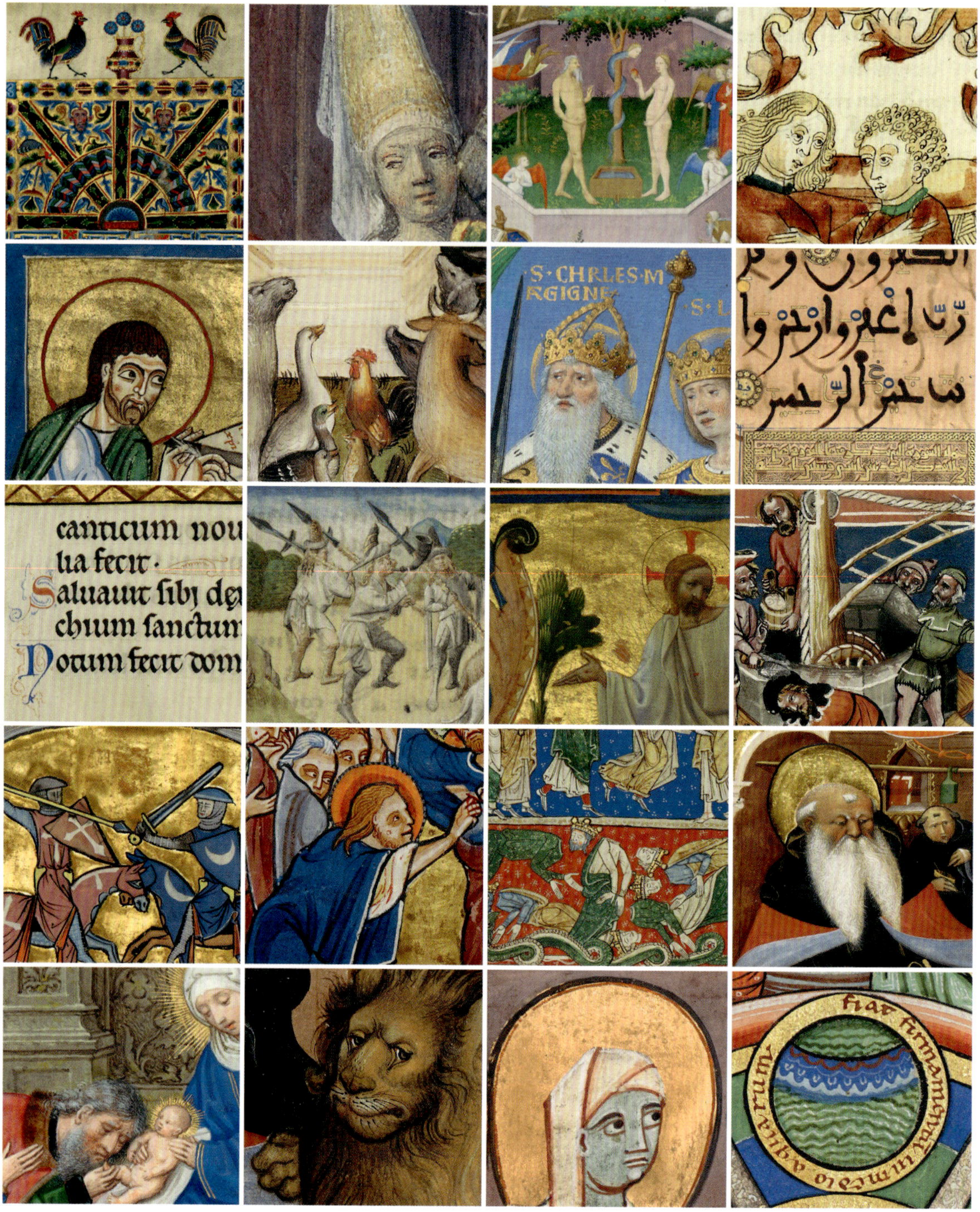
S·CHRLES·M
RGIGNE
canticum nou
lia fecit·
Saluauit sibi dex
chium sanctum
Notum fecit dom

Manuscripts

In Europe between about 500 and 1500 CE, manuscripts—books written and produced by hand—not only represented the most important means of recording knowledge, but also could be objects of great beauty and luxury. The most impressive examples contain illuminations (painted decorations) that together constitute the most comprehensive record of painting in this period. J. Paul Getty did not collect medieval art, but in 1983 the trustees of the Museum decided to bridge the gap between antiquities and Italian Renaissance panel painting by acquiring one of the most important private collections of illuminated manuscripts in the world, assembled by Dr. Peter and Irene Ludwig of Germany. Since then, Getty has acquired more than 125 additional works of this kind, from entire books to cuttings or groups of leaves from individual manuscripts.

The collection largely comprises illuminated manuscripts created in Europe between the ninth and sixteenth centuries but also includes examples from the eastern Mediterranean region, such as Byzantium (the successor state of the Eastern Roman Empire), Armenian communities, North Africa, and Ethiopia. Although many of these manuscripts contain texts and images related to Christianity for use in church services or for private prayer, others concern history, literature, law, philosophy, science, and even romance. The Getty Museum's holdings have, moreover, expanded to include manuscripts representing all the Abrahamic faiths—Christianity, Judaism, and Islam—providing a better reflection of the varied religious traditions practiced throughout the period, as well as their interconnectedness. The department continues to add works that reflect a diversity of authors, artists, imagery, and types of books in order to create a more balanced representation of voices and subjects across the vast chronological and geographical extent of the era.

The Getty Museum has one of the most ambitious programs in the world for the display of illuminated manuscripts, showing works from the collection on a rotating basis year-round and in special exhibitions augmented with loans from other institutions. The aim is to make manuscripts—seldom seen in American museums—understandable and engaging to contemporary audiences, who are invited to explore the appealing visual narratives created by illuminators and to uncover historical context for issues of current interest. Much of what we know about the preoccupations, intellectual pursuits, and daily activities of those living in the period from 500 to 1500 can be gleaned from the pages of manuscripts. Collecting and displaying these precious objects enables visitors to discover, both in the galleries and online, the artistic and cultural complexity of the Middle Ages and the Renaissance in Europe and beyond.

The Women Approach the Empty Tomb of Christ

Irmengard Codex (in Latin); German (Reichenau), shortly after 1053. Tempera, gold, and ink on parchment, 254 leaves, 22.2 × 18.7 cm (8¾ × 7⅜ in.). Ms. 125, fol. 117v; 2023.6

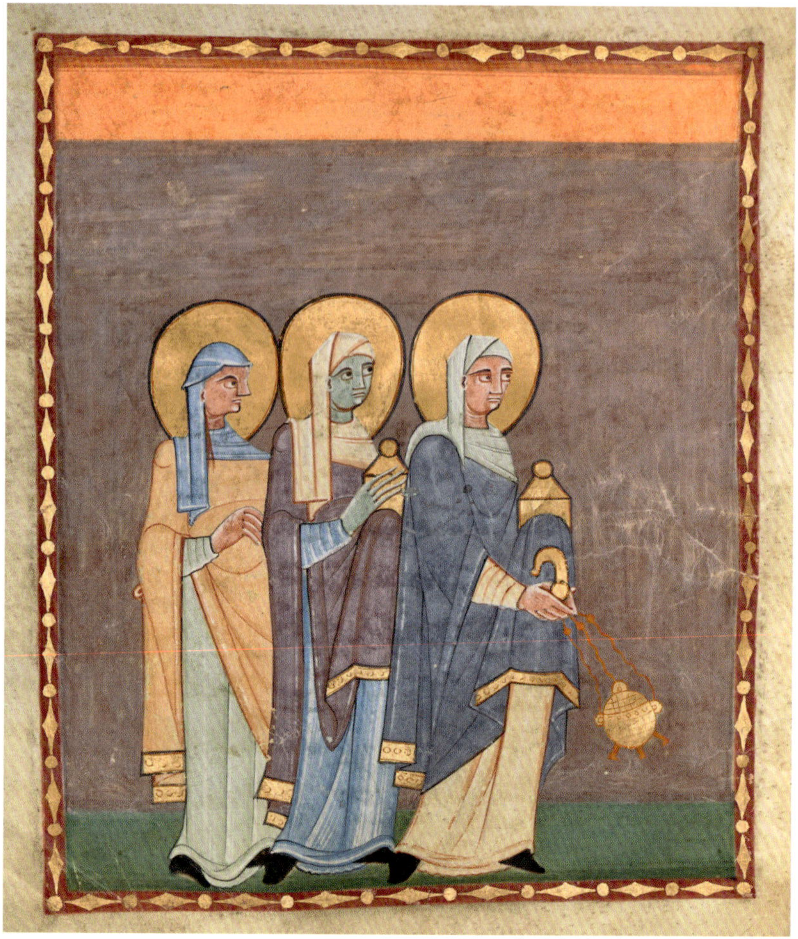

This manuscript containing a series of readings for use during the celebration of Christian Mass features a portrait of its patron, Irmengard of Nellenburg, who donated the manuscript to a monastery to memorialize the death of her husband in 1053. Its fifteen large images include portrayals of the four evangelists, who wrote the Gospels, as well as a series of narrative images highlighting important Christian holidays. Some of the illuminations were conceived as a single composition spanning both pages. Here, three women approach Christ's tomb (depicted in the manuscript on the opposite page) to anoint his body after his death. They are stately figures, ageless and immutable, standing out against a simple background composed of pastel green, lavender, and orange.

The Nativity

Sacramentary (in Latin); German (Mainz or Fulda), circa 1025–50. Tempera, gold, and ink on parchment, 180 leaves, 26.7 × 18.9 cm (10½ × 7⁷⁄₁₆ in.). Ms. Ludwig V 2, fol. 18v; 83.MF.77

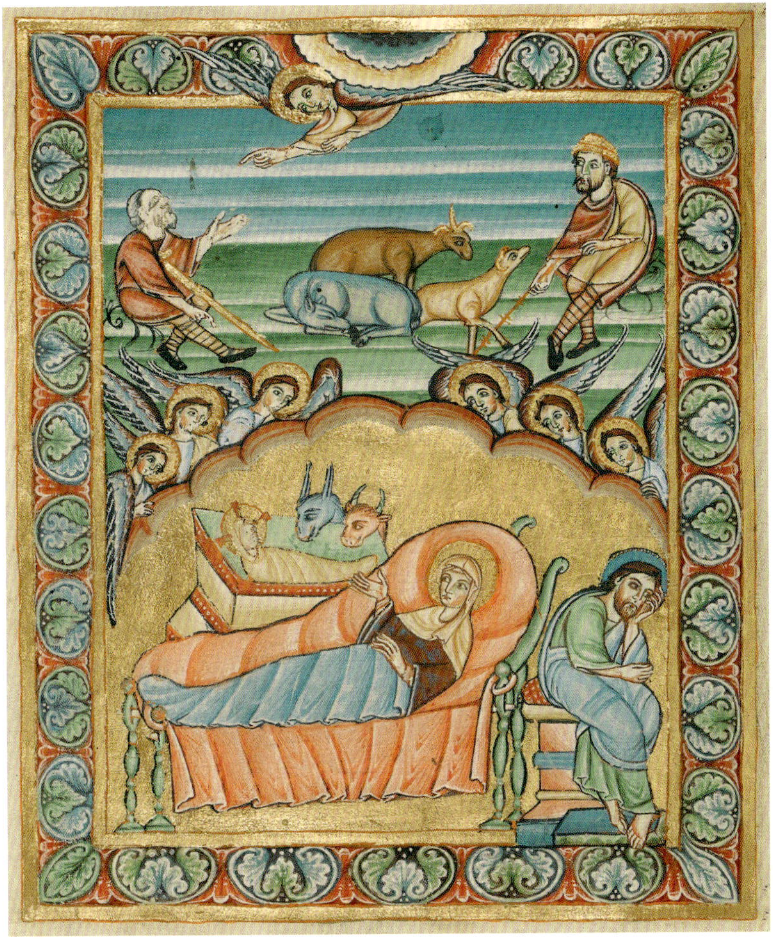

The most important type of liturgical book in the early medieval Christian Church, the sacramentary contains the prayers recited by the priest at Mass. This splendid eleventh-century example also includes a set of images devoted to the life of Christ, unusual in this type of book. In the foreground of this Nativity scene, the newborn Christ child lies in a crib, attended by his mother, the Virgin Mary; an ox and an ass; and six angels. His earthly father, Joseph, sits on the right, lost in thought. Set in a sparkling golden cave, the scene evokes the holy site in Bethlehem that pilgrims revered as Jesus's birthplace. In the background, an angel announces the birth to shepherds tending animals in a field, rendered in muted stripes of green under the pastel blue bands of the sky.

Saint Matthew

Gospel book (in Latin); German (Helmarshausen), circa 1120–40. Tempera, gold, silver, and ink on parchment, 168 leaves, 22.9 × 16.5 cm (9 × 6½ in.). Ms. Ludwig II 3, fol. 9v; 83.MB.67

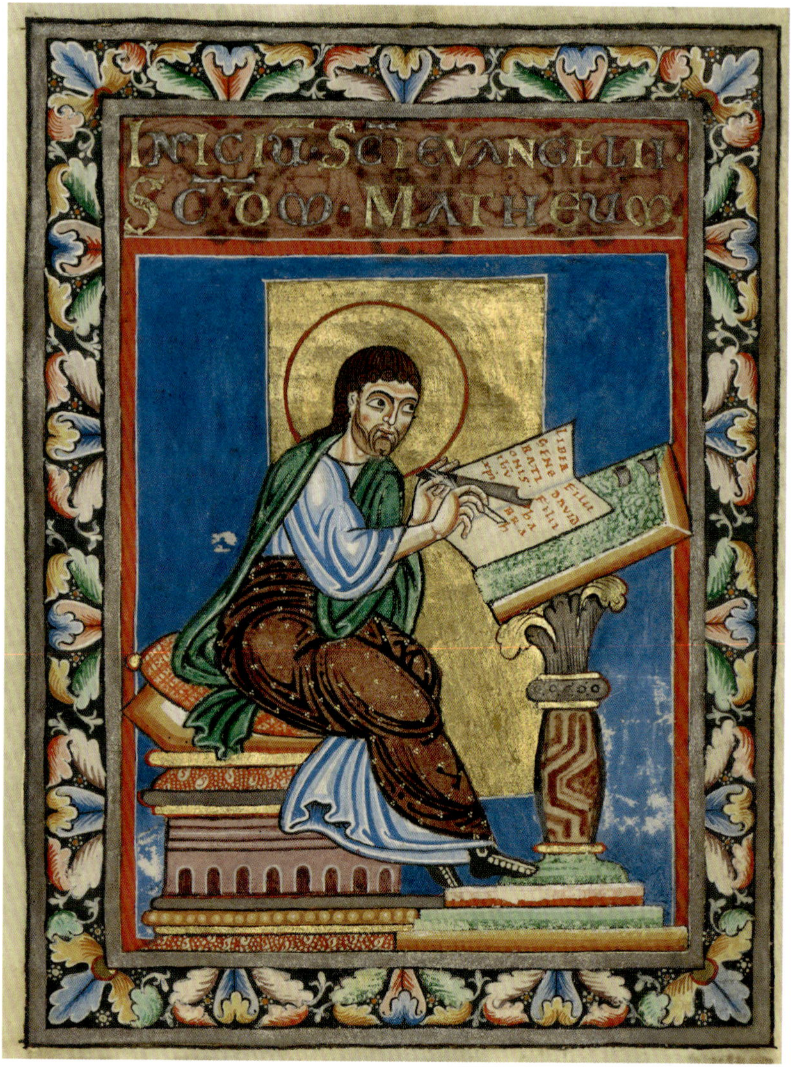

Portraits of the four evangelists (Saints Matthew, Mark, Luke, and John) adorn this Christian Gospel book, which was made at Helmarshausen Abbey, an important North German center for intellectual and artistic pursuits in the twelfth century. Lively patterns built up from vibrant, saturated colors characterize the compositions. Set against a golden panel, Saint Matthew is shown writing the very text that starts on the opposite page of the manuscript. For his divinely inspired work, he uses the instruments of a medieval scribe: leaves of parchment, a quill pen, and a knife, to scrape away any mistakes.

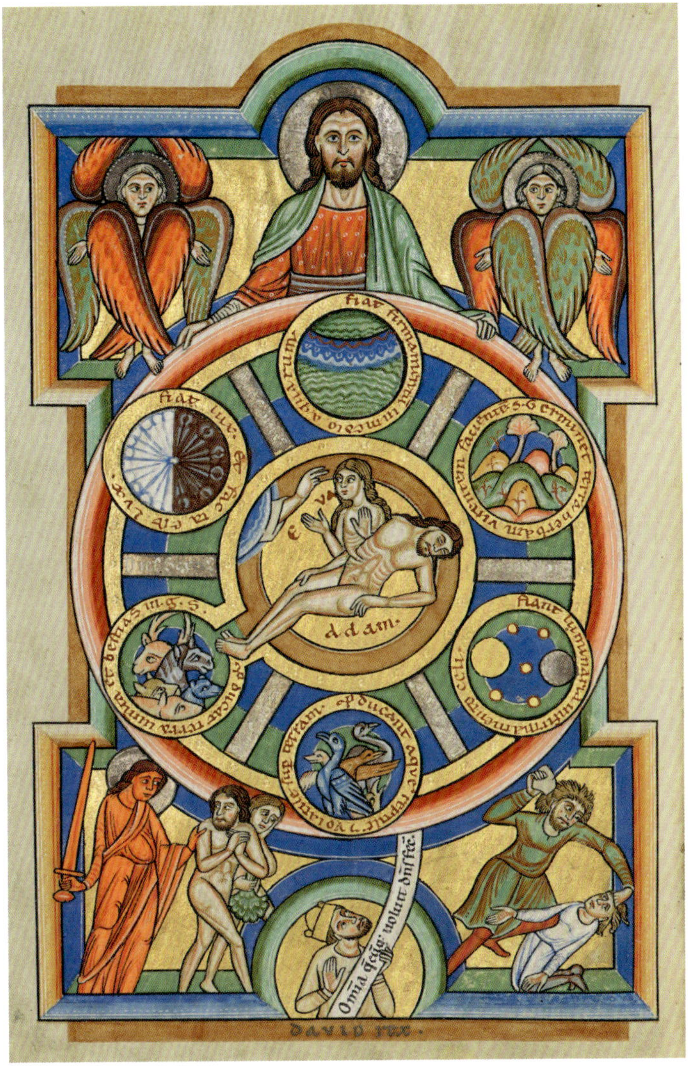

The Creation of the World

Stammheim Missal (in Latin); German (Hildesheim), circa 1170s. Tempera, gold, silver, and ink on parchment, 184 leaves, 28.2 × 18.9 cm ($11\frac{1}{8} \times 7\frac{7}{16}$ in.). Ms. 64, fol. 10v; 97.MG.21

Hundreds of decorated initials and a series of large, stunning images are the hallmark of this profusely illuminated twelfth-century missal, a book containing the texts necessary for the performance of the Christian Mass. Painted in saturated colors and adorned with glowing gold and silver leaf, the compositions are organized geometrically to convey complex theological concepts. This image features God, flanked by two angels, solemnly presiding over the Creation of the World. Inside a disk, six small roundels depicting the six days of Creation surround a central image of Eve emerging from Adam's side. Below, between two scenes showing the story's aftermath (the expulsion of Adam and Eve from Paradise and Cain's killing of Abel), King David praises God's act of creation with the psalm "All that pleased the Lord, he did."

Doubting Thomas

Life of Christ with devotional supplements (in Latin); English (possibly York), circa 1190; (East Anglia), circa 1490.

Tempera, gold, and ink on parchment, 107 leaves, 17.6 × 12.8 cm (6 15/16 × 5 1/16 in.).
Ms. 101, fol. 89; 2008.3

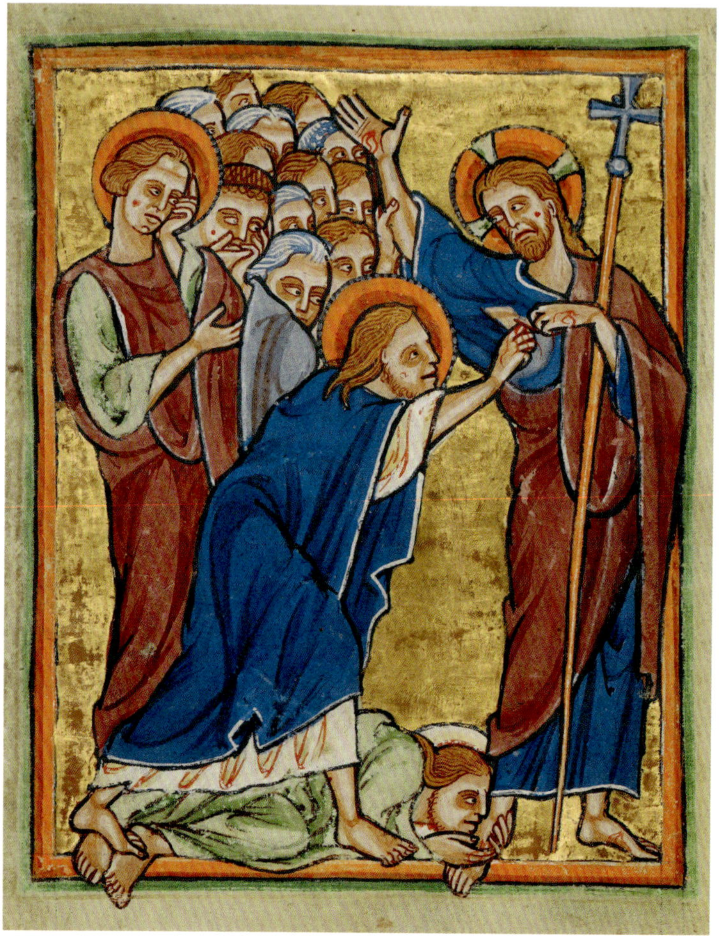

This elaborately illuminated Christian manuscript contains more than one hundred scenes from the life of Christ accompanied by devotional texts and other images. Created in the late twelfth century, the manuscript was repurposed several hundred years later, when more pictures and prayers were added. In this image from the late 1100s, Jesus invites the skeptical apostle Thomas to inspect the wounds he suffered on the cross, thus proving his identity as the risen Savior. The faithful apostles react in horror as Christ flings an arm wide to allow Thomas to lunge forward and press his fingers into the wound in his side. The boldly outlined, sculptural figures enact moments of high drama that embody a sense of expressiveness and theatricality.

Initial C: David Playing Bells

Master of the Ingeborg Psalter (active ca. 1195–ca. 1210). Psalter (in Latin); French (probably Noyon), after 1205.

Tempera, gold, and ink on parchment, 176 leaves, 31 × 21.9 cm (12 3/16 × 8 5/8 in.). Ms. 66, fol. 105v; 99.MK.48

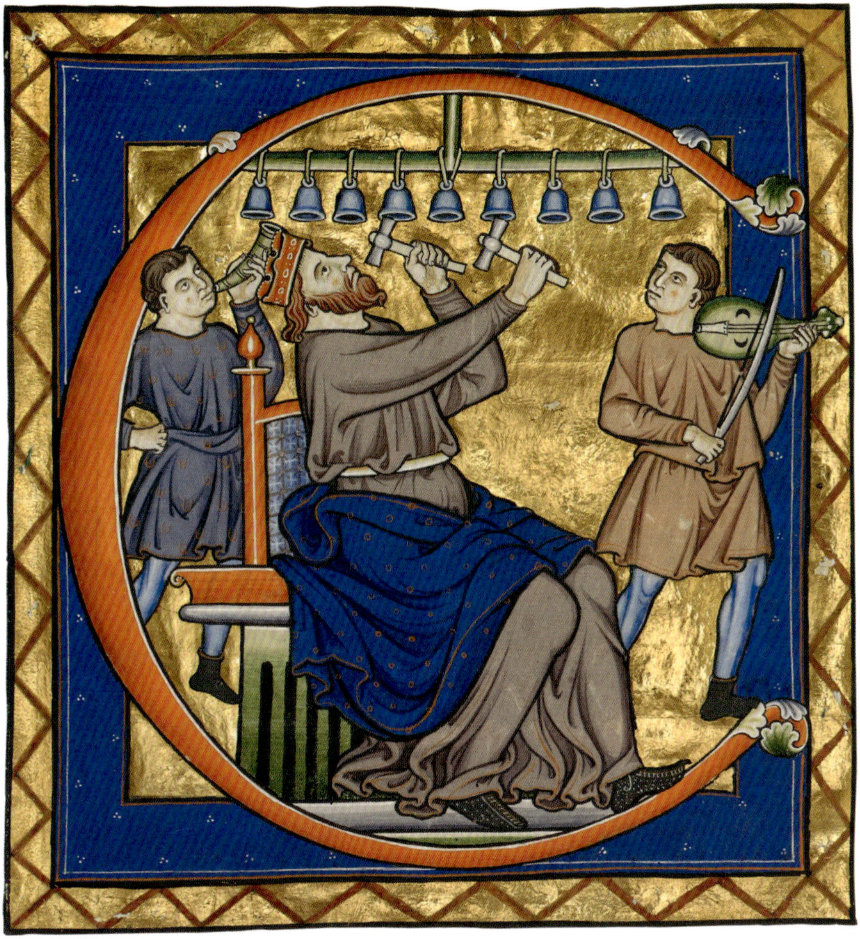

King David, traditionally thought to have composed the biblical Psalms, plays a carillon of bells, accompanied by two musicians. All three figures are set against a background of shimmering gold leaf and enclosed within an initial *C*, which begins the phrase "Cantate domino" (Sing to the Lord). The king's form suggests a convincing weight and monumentality as he reaches up to strike the bells above him, while his left foot braces against the bottom portion of the initial *C*, as if the letter's curved shape were a real part of the scene. The manuscript was almost certainly made for a wealthy Christian layperson for use in private prayer and contains all 150 Psalms, divided into ten sections by large, decorated initials such as this one.

Inhabited Initial *C*

Breviary (in Latin); Italian (Montecassino), 1153. Tempera, gold, and ink on parchment, 428 leaves, 19.2 × 13.2 cm (7 9/16 × 5 3/16 in.). Ms. Ludwig IX 1, fol. 138v; 83.ML.97

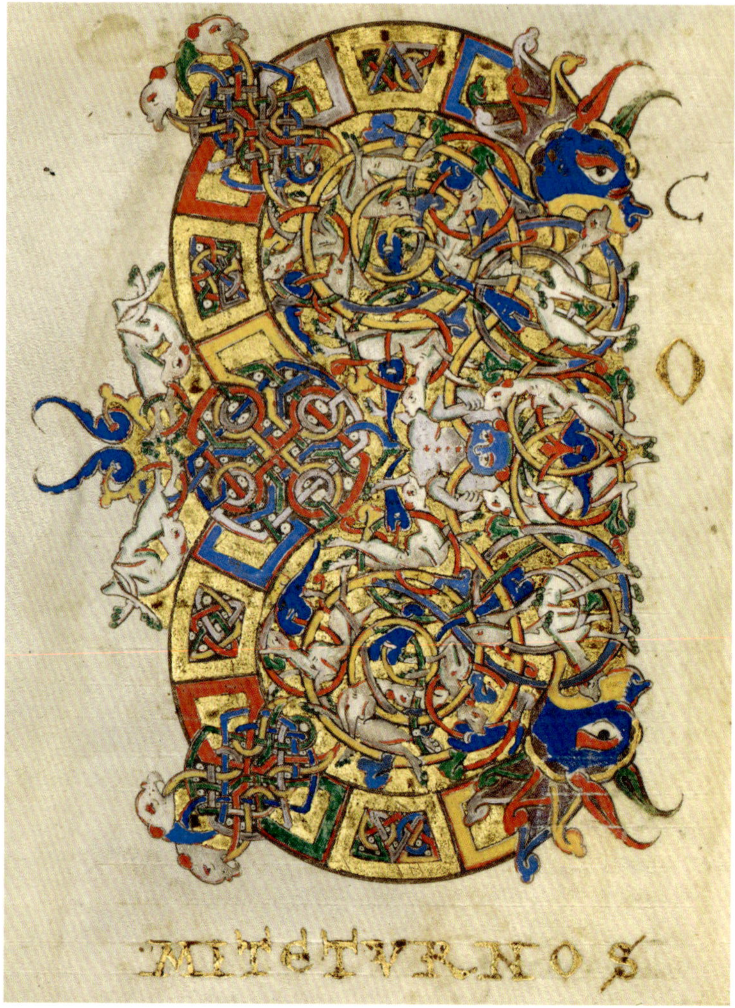

Christian priests, monks, and nuns use a specific prayer book called a breviary to celebrate the divine office, a series of prayers, hymns, and psalms read at eight times throughout the day. This twelfth-century example was made at the monastery of Montecassino in southern Italy, an important center for learning and book production at the time. A prayer in the manuscript mentions the scribe Sigenulfus, who may also have executed the book's decoration. Painted in bright colors and sparkling gold, the convoluted initial here represents a capital *C*, the first letter of the prayer "Comitetur nos" (Look after us). In this whimsical and dynamic design, biting dogs inhabit the raucous mass of spiraling tendrils, while the ends of the initial itself terminate in dragon heads.

Decorated Text Page

Leaf from the Pink Qur'an (in Arabic); Spanish (Granada or Valencia), thirteenth century. Tempera colors, gold, silver, and ink on pink paper, leaf: 31.8 × 25.1 cm (12½ × 9⅞ in.). Ms. 122, leaf 1v; 2021.44.1

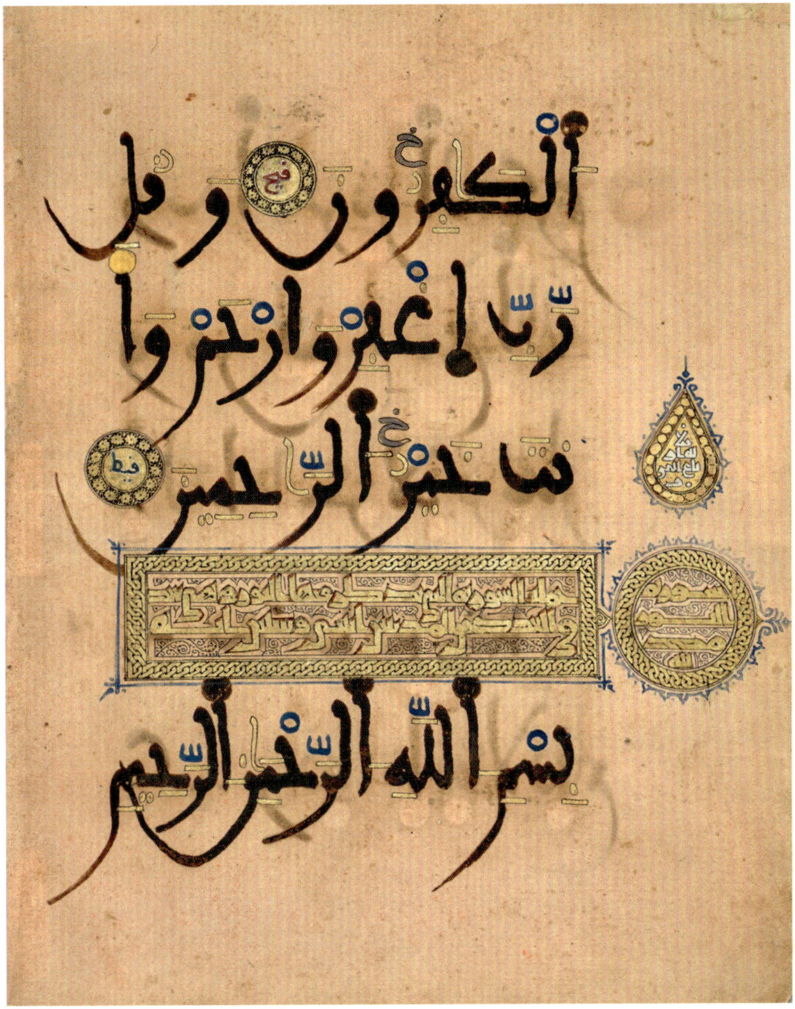

Probably produced for a noble patron from either Granada or Valencia, in southern Spain, this leaf originally belonged to a thirteenth-century Islamic manuscript known as the Pink Qur'an on account of its distinctive pastel-tinted paper. The manuscript features five lines on each folio in Maghribi, a cursive script developed in northern Africa, Iberia, and the West African Sahel. Because figural imagery was prohibited in the Qur'an, calligraphy as well as organic and geometric decorative elements were considered the highest form of artistic expression for religious works in the medieval Islamic world. The ornamental headpiece, executed in brilliant gold leaf with other features in green, red, blue, and silver, help direct the reader to the correct uses of both the spoken and the written word of the Qur'an.

Adam Naming the Animals

Northumberland Bestiary (in Latin); English (London), circa 1250–60. Colored washes and ink on parchment, 75 leaves, 21 × 15.7 cm (8¼ × 6³⁄₁₆ in.). Ms. 100, fol. 5v; 2007.16

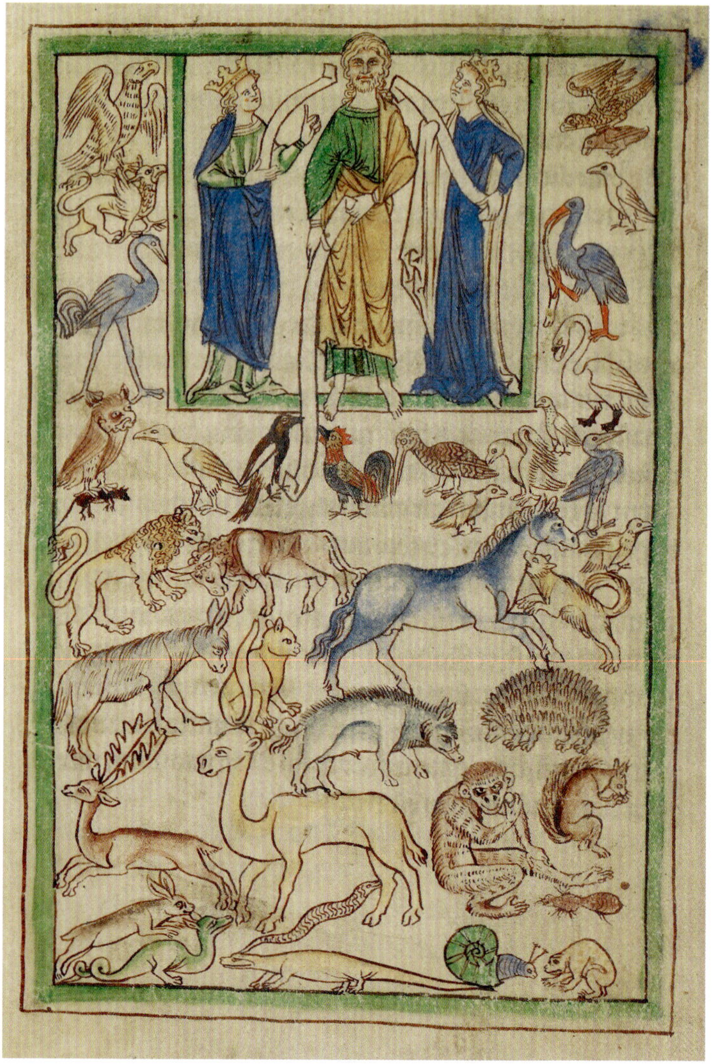

The bestiary—a collection of descriptions and images of real and imaginary animals intended to provide readers with moral lessons—was a kind of medieval encyclopedia that explored the world of animals primarily to explain their significance within the Christian worldview. Each of the more than one hundred animals featured in this manuscript has a unique story, visualized in lively and colorful terms. The manuscript opens with an image of the biblical figure of Adam presiding over an impressive array of the earth's creatures, arranged so that birds, some in flight, appear at the top; land animals occupy the middle of the page; and, finally, crawling insects and serpents populate the bottom. The colored drawing technique lends immediacy to the animals, which leap, caper, and scramble across the page.

The Battle between Angels and Dragons

Getty Apocalypse (in Latin); English (probably London), circa 1255–60.

Tempera, gold, colored washes, and ink on parchment, 41 leaves, 31.9 × 22.5 cm ($12^{9}/_{16}$ × $8^{7}/_{8}$ in.). Ms. Ludwig III 1, fol. 20v; 83.MC.72

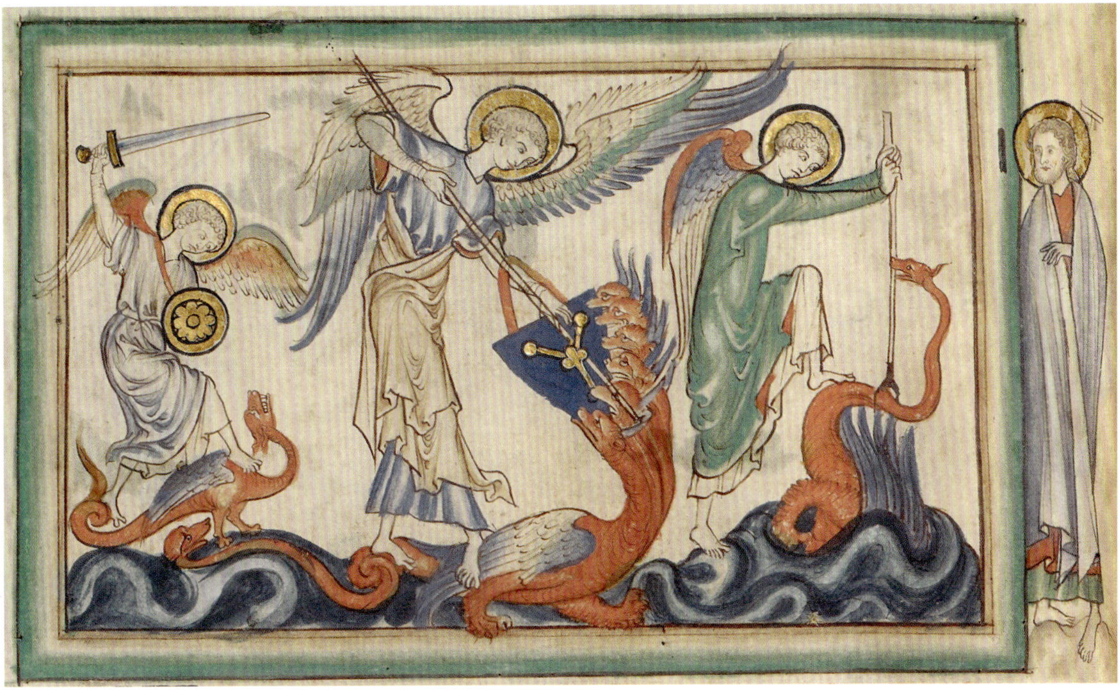

Containing the biblical book of Revelation—Saint John's vision of the end of the world—this manuscript foretells the calamitous events awaiting humankind in eighty-two half-page images. Remarkable for their dynamic interpretation of the saint's prophecies, the visual narratives show John witnessing the extraordinary episodes as they occur. Here, he safely watches from outside the frame as three dragons writhe beneath a trio of attacking angels. The elegance of the angels, with their fluttering tunics and carefully coiffed curls, finds balance in the naturalism of their physical forms. The combination of crisp details emphasized by inked outlines and augmented by modeling in thin colored washes lends a sense of vitality to the scene.

The Lamb Defeating the Ten Kings

Leaf from a commentary on the Apocalypse (in Latin) by Beatus of Liébana (ca. 730–ca. 800); Spanish, circa 1220–35. Tempera, gold, and ink on parchment, 29.4 × 23.5 cm ($11\frac{9}{16} \times 9\frac{1}{4}$ in.). Ms. 77, recto; 2003.103

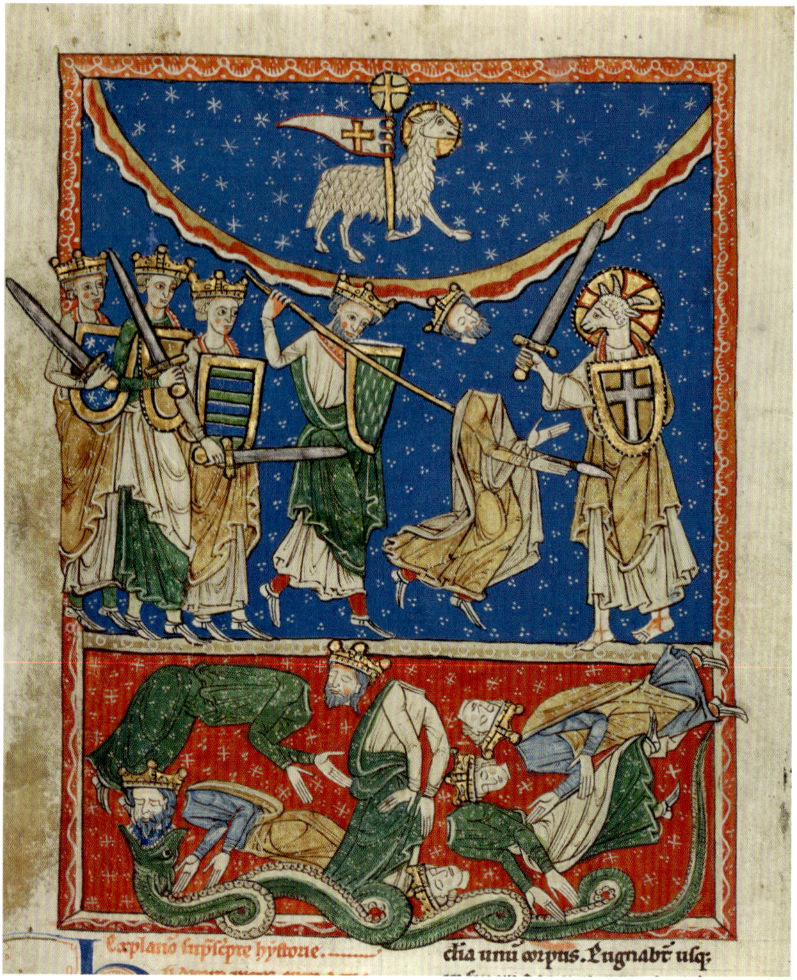

This detached leaf is from a manuscript containing a commentary on the Apocalypse, the Christian Bible's account of the events leading to the end of the world. Skillfully wielding a sword in the guise of a medieval knight, Christ as the Lamb of God slays his foes, while in the scene below a monstrous serpent swallows their remains. The illumination is unusual for its balanced combination of elegant forms and gruesome subject matter. The dancelike movements of the kings and the evenly spaced, almost decorative coils of the dragon belie the ruthless determination of the lamb and the violence inherent in the severed heads. Illustrated Apocalypses produced in Spain between 900 and 1300 are famed for their vibrant colors, original imagery, and powerful visionary quality.

Initial *I*: Scenes from the Creation and the Life of Christ

Abbey Bible (in Latin); Italian (Bologna), circa 1250–62. Tempera, gold, and ink on parchment, 514 leaves, 27 × 19.7 cm (10⅝ × 7¾ in.). Ms. 107, fol. 4; 2011.23

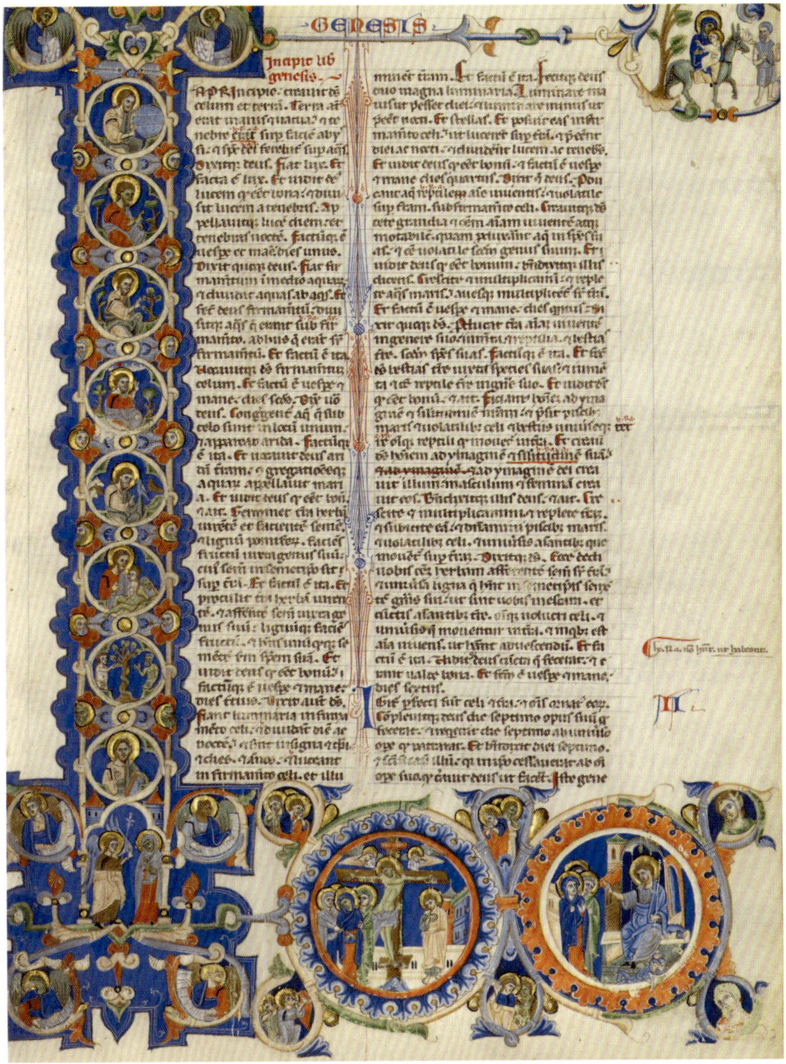

Saints, angels, musicians, and animals cavort amid scrolling vines in the margins of this copiously illuminated Christian Bible, probably made for a community of friars in Bologna, Italy, in the mid-1200s. The opening of Genesis, the first book of the Bible, is the most lavishly decorated page in the volume, capturing the major events in the story of Christian salvation, starting with the Creation of the World and culminating in Jesus's death and miraculous resurrection. Stretching the entire length of the page, the initial *I* recounts the seven days of Creation and the Fall of Adam and Eve. In the top right corner, a tendril encircles the Holy Family, and two ornate disks toward the bottom depict, respectively, the Crucifixion and an angel at the empty tomb of the risen Christ.

Canon Table Page

T'oros Roslin (active 1256–68). Canon Tables from the Zeyt'un Gospels (in Armenian); Armenian (Hromklay), 1256. Tempera, gold, and ink on parchment, 8 leaves, 26.5 × 19 cm (10 7/16 × 7 1/2 in.). Gift of the Catholicosate of the Great House of Cilicia, Ms. 59, fol. 6; 94.MB.71

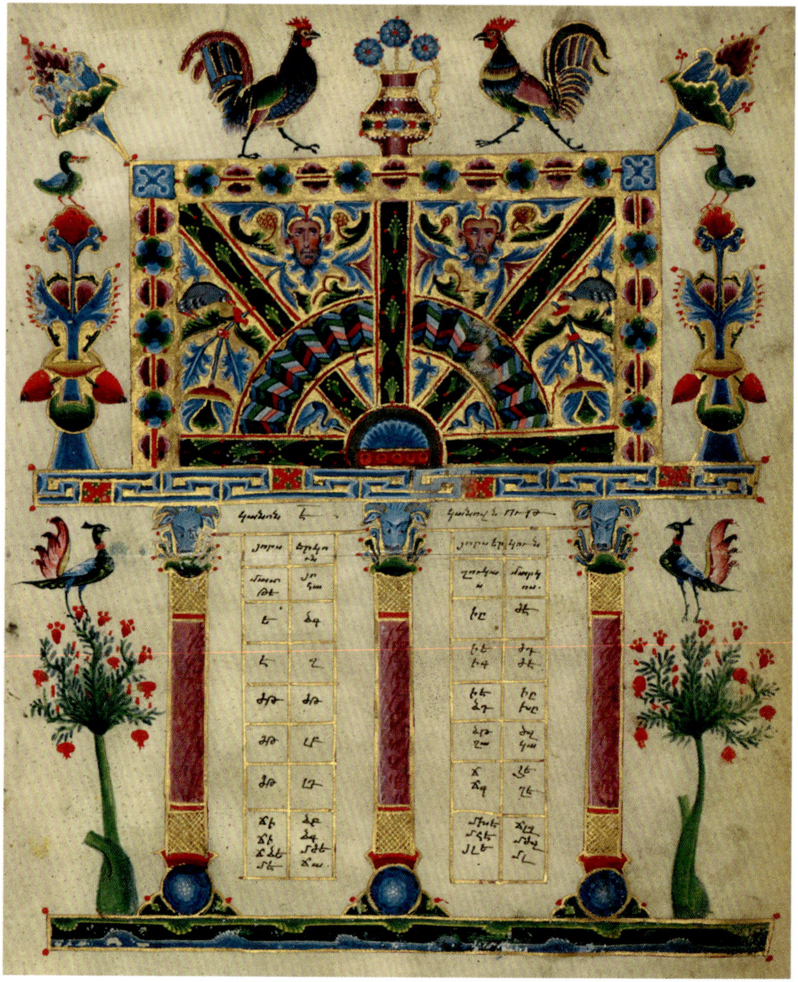

Canon tables present a concordance of passages relating the same events in the four Gospels of the Christian Bible. This detached set of eight canon tables was originally found at the beginning of a Gospel book made for Constantine I, catholicos of the Armenian Apostolic Church from 1221 to 1267. The manuscript is the earliest signed work by T'oros Roslin, the most celebrated Armenian illuminator and scribe of the Middle Ages. The columns of numbers are enclosed within a monumental and brilliantly colored architectural structure enlivened by symmetrically arranged geometric and naturalistic forms. Two roosters painted in gemlike tones of blue, green, and pink highlighted with gold strut across the top, imparting both vibrancy and majesty to the page.

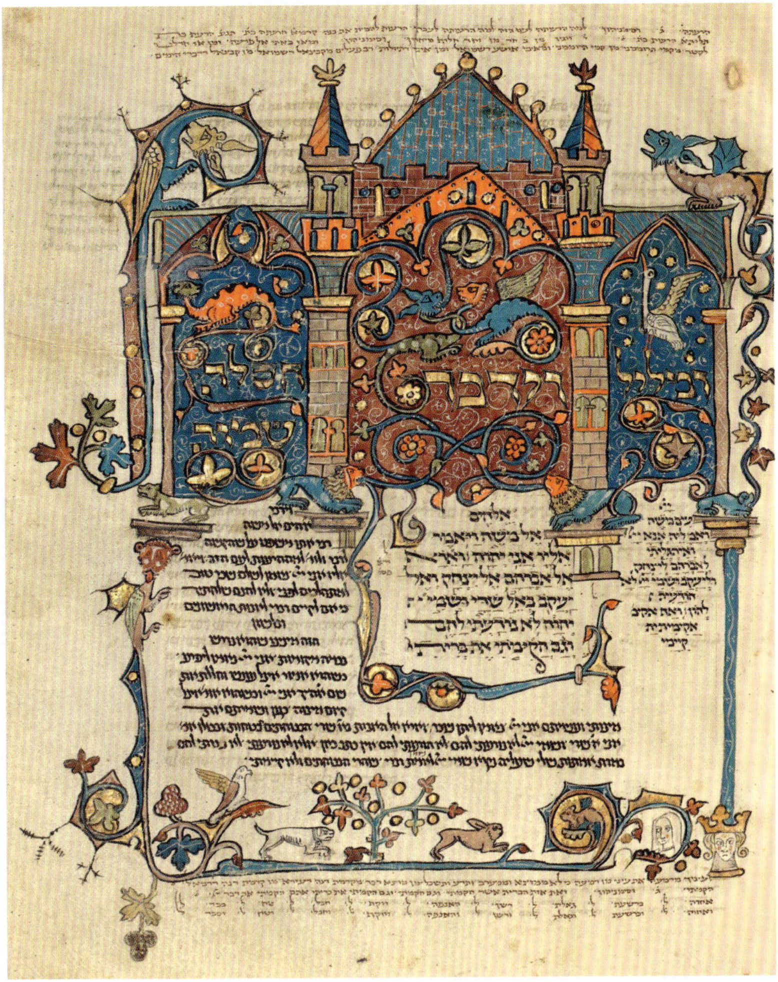

Decorated Text Page

Rothschild Pentateuch (in Hebrew and Aramaic); French or German, 1296. Tempera, gold, and ink on parchment, 584 leaves, 27.5 × 21 cm (10 13/16 × 8 1/4 in.). Acquired with the generous support of Jo Carole and Ronald S. Lauder, Ms. 116, fol. 130; 2018.43

Teeming with renderings of real and imaginary animals, intertwined plant forms, and spectacular displays of calligraphic virtuosity, the Rothschild Pentateuch features hundreds of illuminated folios among its more than one thousand pages. The manuscript contains the central sacred text of Judaism, the Pentateuch (the Torah in the strictest sense), divided into sections to be read over the course of a year. The decoration of this page from the book of Genesis resembles a vibrantly colored medieval tapestry, with large, gold Hebrew letters occupying the center, while a rabbit-chasing dog and ferocious dragons enliven the margins. With its seemingly endless variety of illuminated motifs ranging from the imposing to the whimsical, the Rothschild Pentateuch is one of the most elaborate illuminated copies of the Hebrew Pentateuch to survive from the Middle Ages.

Initial *E*: An Equestrian Duel between a Creditor and a Debtor

Feudal Customs of Aragon
(in Navarro-Aragonese); Spanish (northeastern Spain), circa 1290–1310.
Tempera, gold, and ink on parchment, 277 leaves, 36.5 × 24 cm ($14\frac{3}{8} \times 9\frac{7}{16}$ in.).
Ms. Ludwig XIV 6, fol. 169v; 83.MQ.165

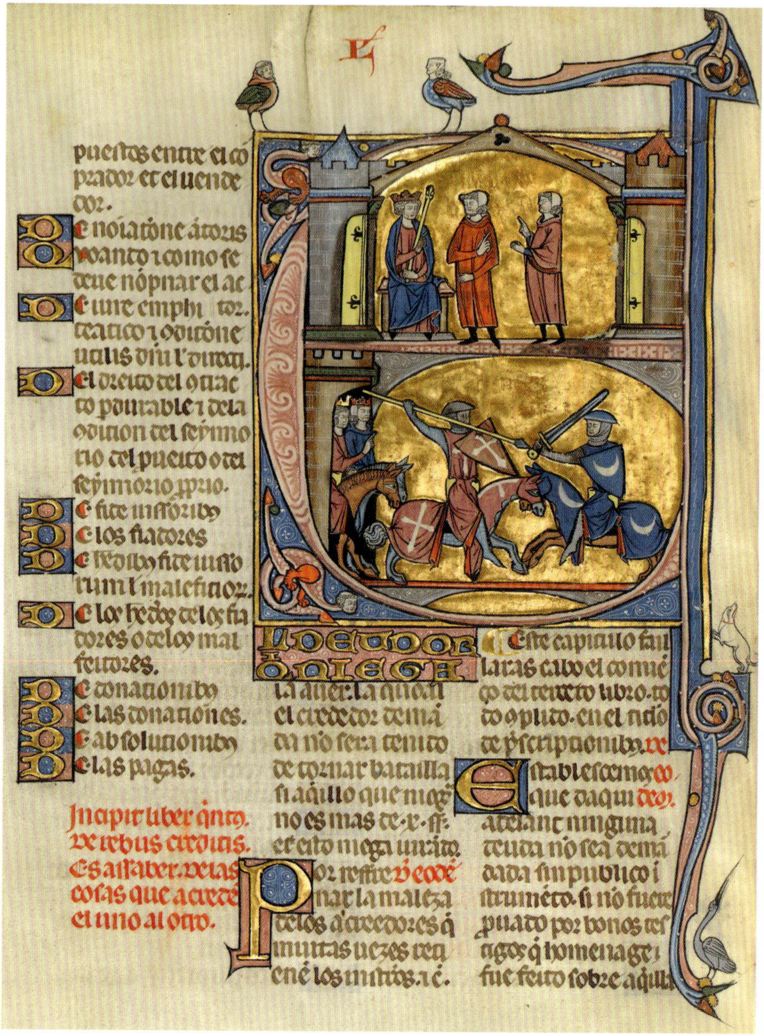

This sumptuous volume is the only known copy of the law code of Aragon, which King James I of Aragon (r. 1214–76) ordered Vidal de Canellas, the Christian bishop of Huesca, to compile in 1247. It is illustrated with ten large scenes and more than one hundred smaller scenes set into initials. Here, in the upper register of the image, an enthroned king listens to a dispute between a creditor and debtor, settled in the scene below by a combat on horseback. The crosses emblazoned on the shield and saddlecloth of one combatant identify him as a Christian, while the crescent-moon shapes on the other suggest that he is Muslim. The battle may demonstrate what would happen if there were no rule of law, implying that the implementation of a legal system prevents bloodshed.

The Agony in the Garden

Gospel book (in Greek); Byzantine (Nicaea or Nicomedia), early thirteenth century, with additions in the late thirteenth century. Tempera, gold, and ink on parchment, 241 leaves, 20.6 × 14.9 cm ($8\frac{1}{8} \times 5\frac{7}{8}$ in.). Ms. Ludwig II 5, fol. 68; 83.MB.69

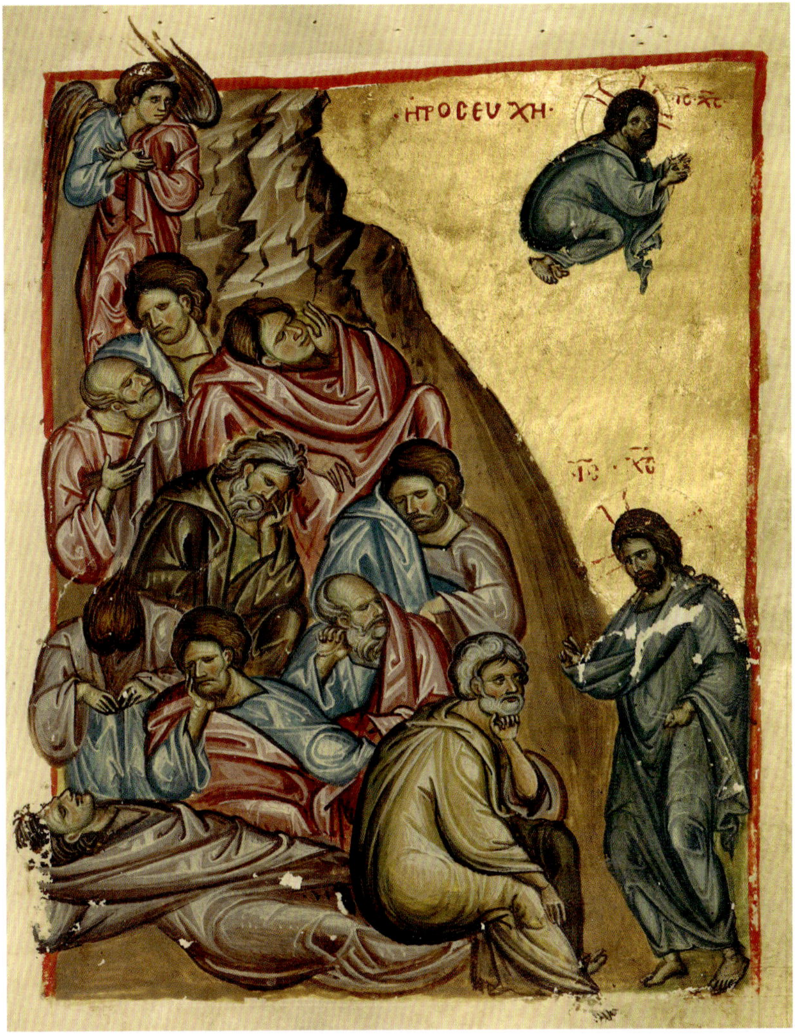

Likely made in the thirteenth century in Byzantium, the Christian successor state of the Eastern Roman Empire, this lavishly illuminated Gospel book contains the four accounts of Christ's life, as told by each of the evangelists. In addition to the ornate opening page of each Gospel, fifteen large scenes from the life of Christ and the life of the Virgin appear throughout the text. This page shows Jesus and his apostles in the Garden of Gethsemane, where Jesus went on the night before his arrest to meditate on his impending Passion. He asks his disciples to stay awake with him to pray, but they fall asleep. They huddle together, mimicking the mountain behind them, while Jesus kneels in prayer, isolated from them both psychologically and spatially by the golden background.

Saint Hedwig of Silesia with Duke Ludwig and Duchess Agnes

Life of the Blessed Hedwig (in Latin); Silesian, 1353. Tempera, colored washes, and ink on parchment, 204 leaves, 34.1 × 24.8 cm (13 7/16 × 9 3/4 in.). Ms. Ludwig XI 7, fol. 12v; 83.MN.126

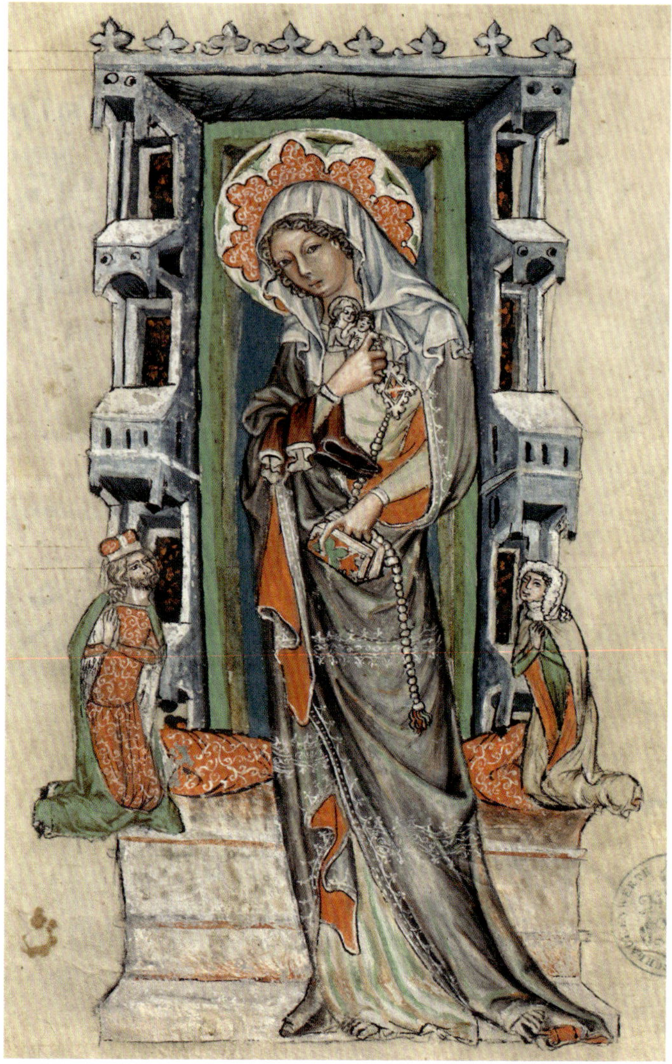

This manuscript, the earliest known example of the *Life of the Blessed Hedwig*, is adorned with a profuse set of images devoted to Saint Hedwig (1174–1243). She was a duchess of Silesia (on the border of modern-day Poland and Germany) who, after her husband's death, retired to a convent and lived an austere life dedicated to helping the poor. This striking image portrays Hedwig standing gracefully before an elaborate throne. The radiant halo encircling her head and the inclusion of objects emphasizing her personal devotion—a prayer book, prayer beads, and a small ivory statue of the Virgin and Child—signal her sanctity. Kneeling to either side of Hedwig are her descendants, Duke Ludwig and his wife, Agnes, who commissioned the magnificent manuscript.

Saint Anthony Abbot Blessing the Animals, the Poor, and the Sick

Master of Saint Veronica (ca. 1395–1415). Illuminated leaf; German (Cologne), circa 1400–1410. Tempera and gold on parchment, one of a pair of leaves, each: 23.7 × 12.4 cm (9 5/16 × 4 7/8 in.). Ms. Ludwig Folia 2, leaf 2; 83.MS.49

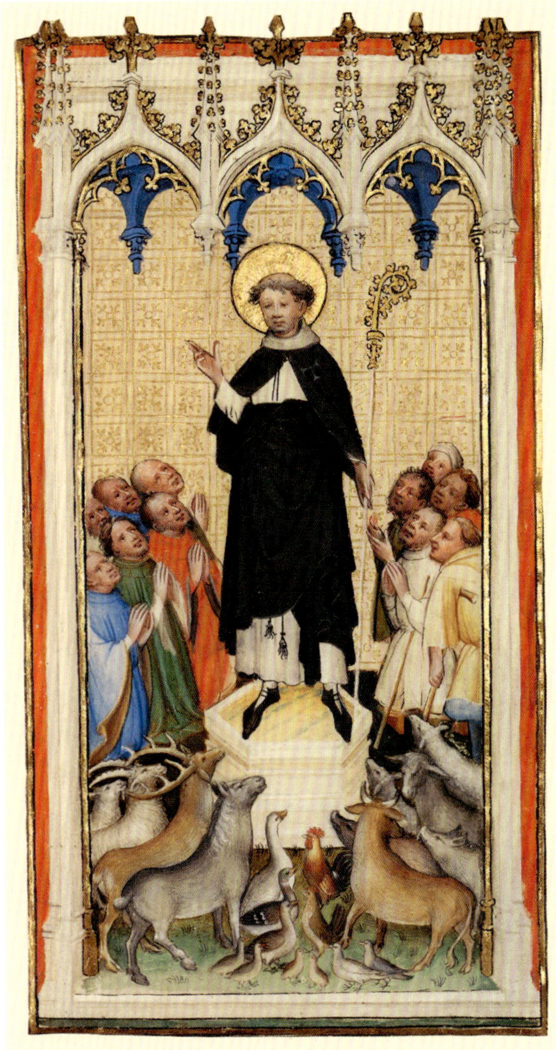

Under finely rendered pointed arches, Saint Anthony stands calmly on a pedestal like a living statue, blessing the people and animals gathered around him. Anthony was a fourth-century Christian hermit who lived in the Egyptian desert, but he enjoyed great popularity as the patron saint of the sick, animals, and farmers. Here, at right, several men on crutches approach the saint in the hope of being healed, while a group of wild and domesticated animals clusters at his feet. Single-leaf illuminations like this one and its companion (a Crucifixion scene, also in the Getty collection), were popular in fifteenth-century Europe. The faithful used them variably according to their needs, for instance, by pinning them to walls or inserting them into a bound manuscript to suit their preferred form of devotion.

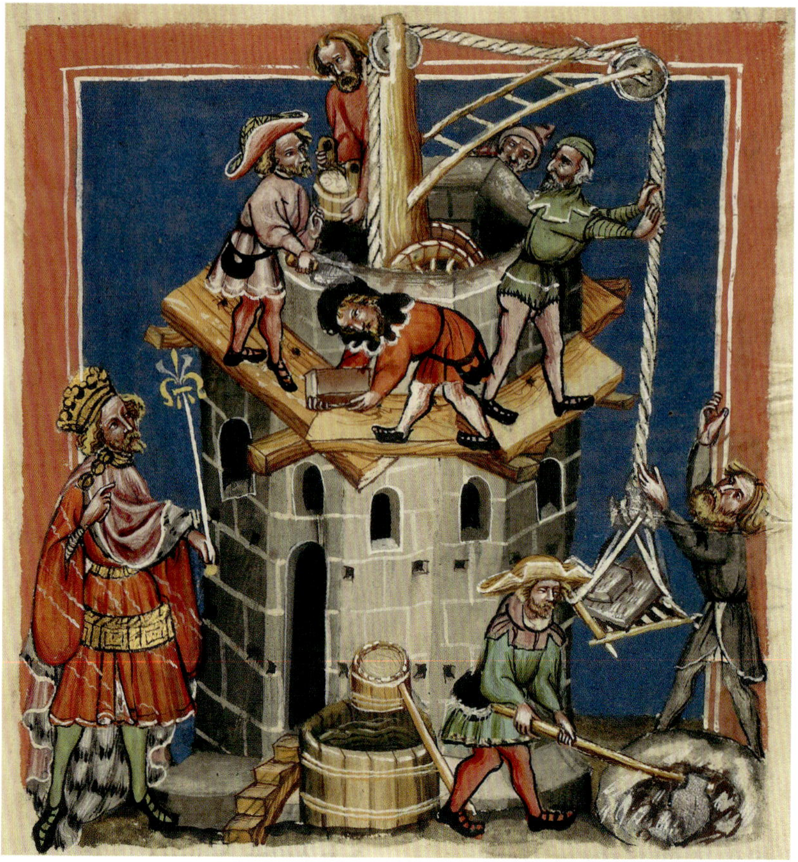

The Construction of the Tower of Babel

World Chronicle (in German) by Rudolf von Ems (ca. 1200–1254); German (Regensburg), circa 1400–1410, with an addition in 1487. Tempera, gold, silver, and ink on parchment, 309 leaves, 33.5 × 23.5 cm (13³⁄₁₆ × 9¼ in.). Ms. 33, fol. 13; 88.MP.70

Composed in rhyming couplets by Rudolf von Ems in the mid-thirteenth century, the *World Chronicle* weaves biblical, classical, and other secular texts into an encyclopedic history, beginning with the Creation of the World. The book's overarching theme is the revelation over time of God's plan for Christian salvation. Of the many surviving versions of this important German text, this copy from the 1400s is the most lavishly decorated, containing more than 380 individual scenes across six hundred pages. This image portrays the building of the Tower of Babel as a medieval construction site. Overseen by a king, master masons diligently lay the finely carved stones with the help of a crane. They hope to use this monumental structure to reach God in heaven but never realize their ambition.

The Story of Adam and Eve

Boucicaut Master and workshop (active ca. 1400–1430). *Concerning the Fates of Illustrious Men and Women* (in French) by Giovanni Boccaccio (1313–1375); French, Paris, circa 1415. Tempera, gold, and ink on parchment, 318 leaves, 42 × 29.6 cm (16 9/16 × 11 5/8 in.). Ms. 63, fol. 3; 96.MR.17

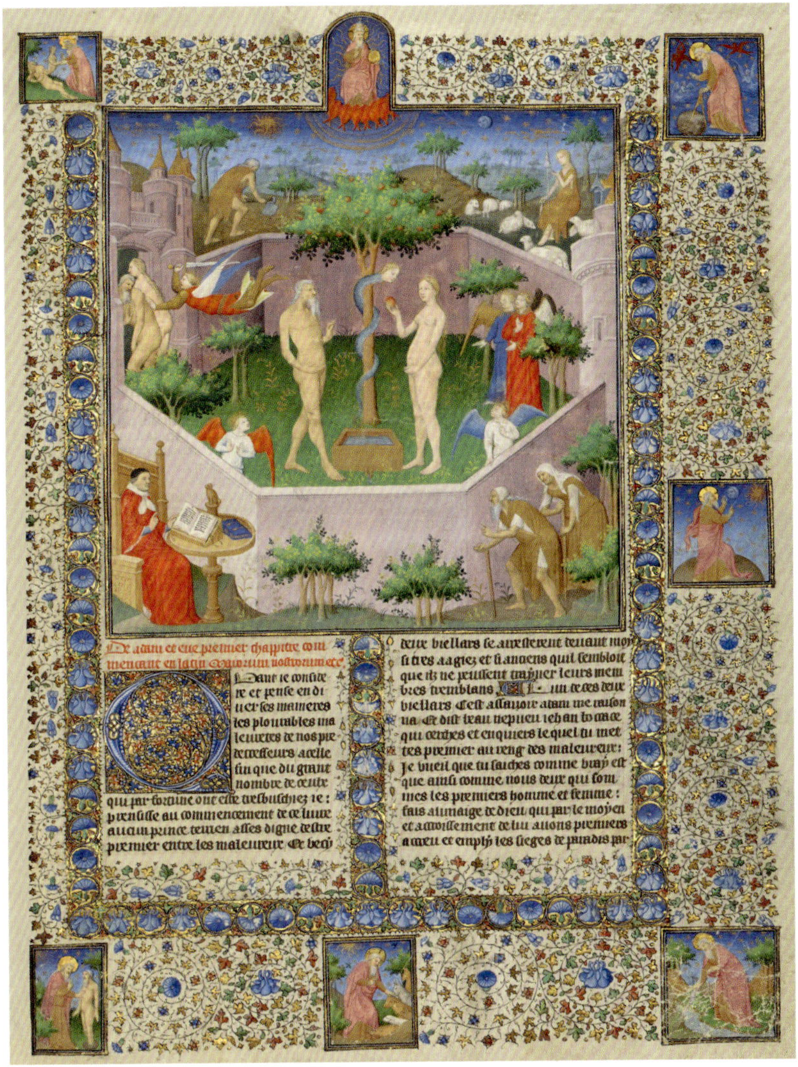

Recounting the stories of notable individuals from biblical, classical, and medieval history, *Concerning the Fates of Illustrious Men and Women* was written by the Italian poet Giovanni Boccaccio. This copy of the text (translated into French) opens with an elaborate page depicting episodes from the story of Adam and Eve, the biblical first couple. The artist skillfully structured the page around the wall encircling the Garden of Eden. The pivotal event is the Temptation—when Adam and Eve eat fruit from the Tree of Knowledge—which takes place at center. In the foreground, the aged couple approaches Boccaccio, who sits to the left, to tell their tale, while around the edges of the page are small squares showing the seven days of the Creation of the World.

Saint Jerome Extracting a Thorn from a Lion's Paw

Master of the Murano Gradual (active ca. 1430–1460). Cutting from a gradual; Italian (Venice), second quarter of the fifteenth century. Tempera and gold on parchment, 21 × 16.5 cm (8¼ × 6½ in.). Ms. 106, recto; 2010.21

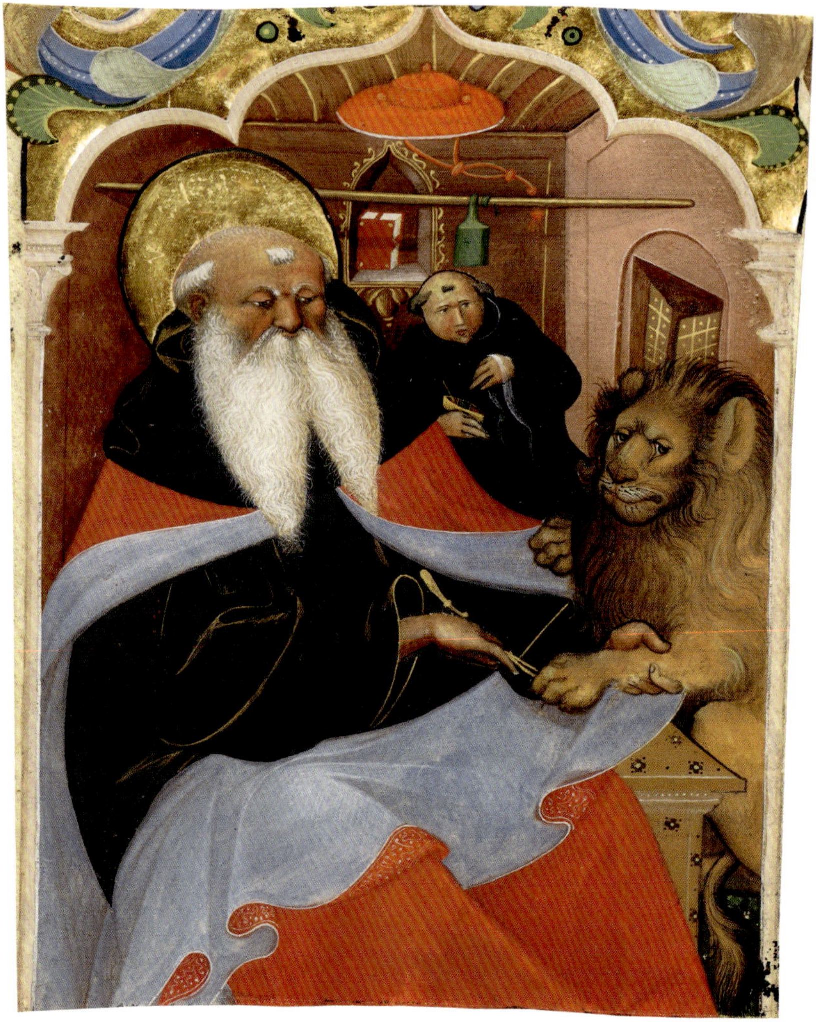

This charming scene depicts a story from the life of the Christian saint Jerome (ca. 341–420). When an injured lion enters the monastery where Jerome resides, his fellow monks flee, but he cures the animal by removing a thorn from its paw. The artist eloquently captures this touching encounter between man and beast, showing the moment when the lion submits to the saint. Jerome exudes concentration as he removes the thorn, while an apprehensive monk hovers in the background. This image comes from a mid-fifteenth-century Italian gradual, a type of choir book, probably belonging to a monastery in Murano, Venice. This once splendid book exists today only as a series of elaborately illuminated detached leaves and cuttings.

Initial *A*: Pentecost

Attributed to Stefano da Verona (ca. 1375–1438). Cutting from an antiphonal; Italian (Lombardy), circa 1430–35.

Tempera and gold on parchment, 11.9 × 12.5 cm (4 11/16 × 4 15/16 in.). Ms. 95, recto; 2005.28

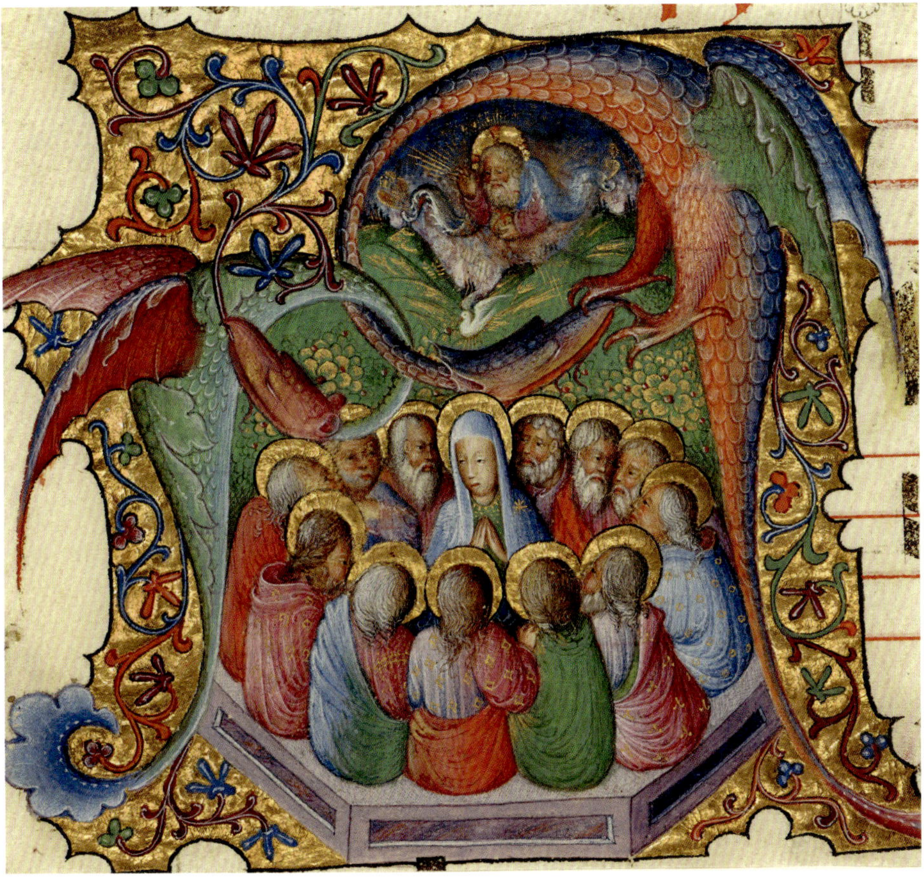

In a verdant, hilly landscape, Christ's apostles gather in a tight circle around the Virgin Mary, ready to receive the Holy Spirit descending in the form of a white dove from God the Father above. Painted in luminous pastels with fluid brushstrokes, the scene takes place within an initial *A*, formed by the curved bodies of two sleepy dragons entwined at their necks. The initial once decorated the page in an antiphonal—a large choir book of chants sung during church services—marking the opening of the feast day of Pentecost, a Christian holiday that commemorates the descent of the Holy Spirit as recorded in the New Testament.

Initial *V*: The Ascension

Designed by Lorenzo Monaco (active ca. 1394–1422); completed by Zanobi di Benedetto Strozzi (1412–1468) and Battista di Biagio Sanguini (1393–1451). Cutting from a gradual; Italian (Florence), designed circa 1410; completed circa 1431. Tempera and gold on parchment, 40.2 × 32.4 cm ($15^{13}/_{16}$ × $12^{7}/_{8}$ in.). Ms. 78, recto; 2003.104

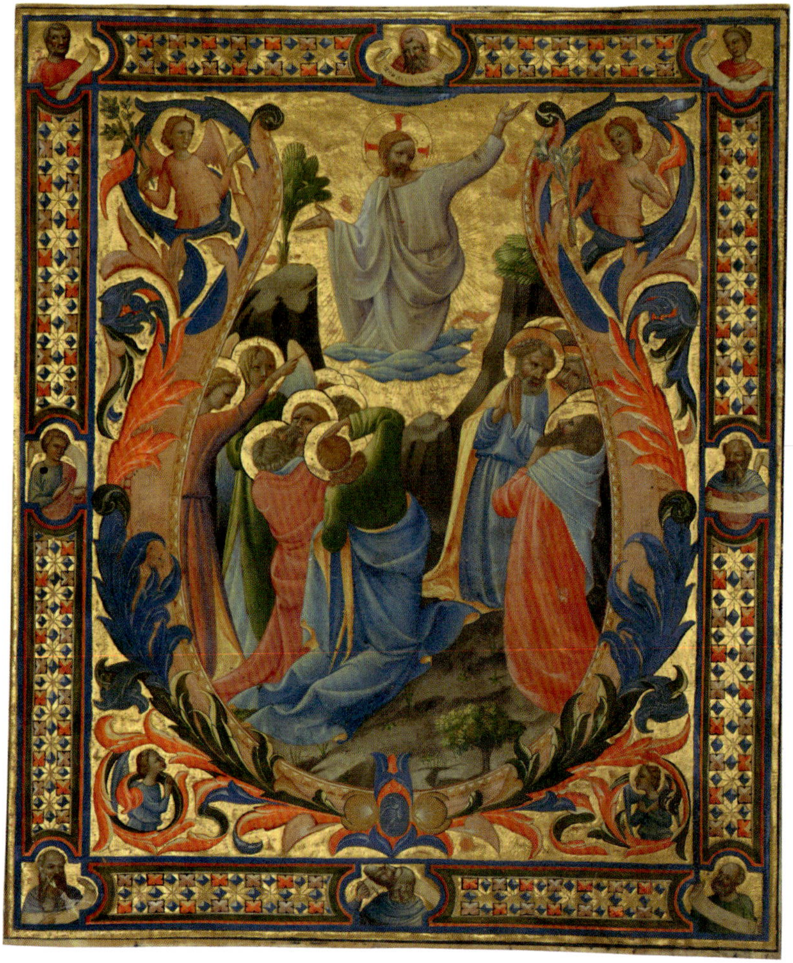

This monumental illuminated initial *V* depicts Christ's last appearance on earth to his apostles after his Resurrection. The apostles gaze up in amazement at Christ, who ascends into heaven on a blue cloud. The upward-sweeping motion of the colorful acanthus leaves that climb the letter form reflects and enhances Christ's own movement. While the figures' gestures and drapery are portrayed naturalistically, the scene is set against a highly polished gold background, which lends it an otherworldly feeling. The initial originally graced a large gradual (choir book) designed by Lorenzo Monaco, Florence's most celebrated late medieval painter, for his own monastery, Santa Maria degli Angeli, but it was finished by his students long after his death.

Saint Catherine of Alexandria

Taddeo Crivelli (active ca. 1451–79). Gualenghi-d'Este Hours (in Latin); Italian (Ferrara), circa 1469. Tempera, gold, and ink on parchment, 211 leaves, 10.8 × 7.9 cm (4¼ × 3⅛ in.). Ms. Ludwig IX 13, fol. 187v; 83.ML.109

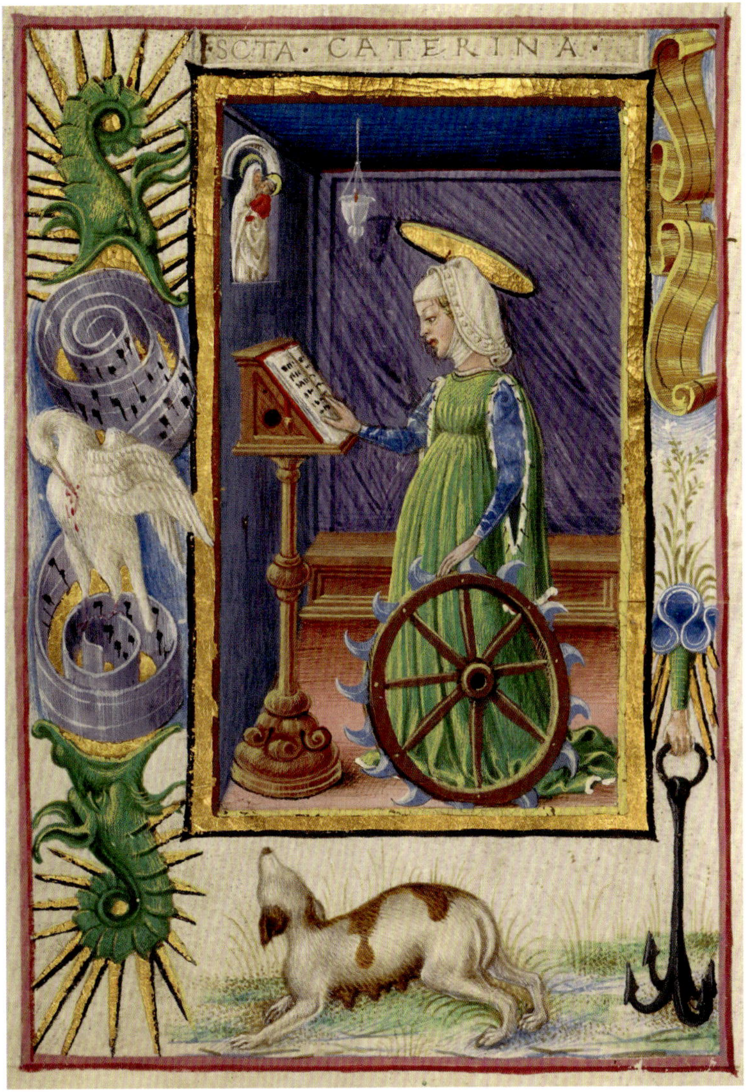

This exquisitely illuminated Christian prayer book likely once belonged to Andrea Gualengo and his wife, Orsina d'Este, members of the ruling family of Ferrara, one of the most important artistic centers of fifteenth-century Italy. The refined images in this tiny manuscript mainly portray saints of significance to the book's noble patrons, including Saint Catherine of Alexandria. Catherine is here identified by her attribute, the spiked wheel upon which she was tortured after refusing to renounce her faith. Dressed as a late medieval aristocratic lady, she prays from a book resting on a lectern in the privacy of a small room. Her focused devotional immersion would have served as a model of piety for the reader of this book.

An Emperor at Court

Letters and *The Story of Two Lovers* (in Latin) by Aeneas Silvius Piccolomini (1405–1464); French, circa 1460–70. Tempera, gold, and ink on parchment, 46 leaves, 17.6 × 11.4 cm ($6\frac{15}{16} \times 4\frac{1}{2}$ in.). Ms. 68, fol. 14v; 2001.45

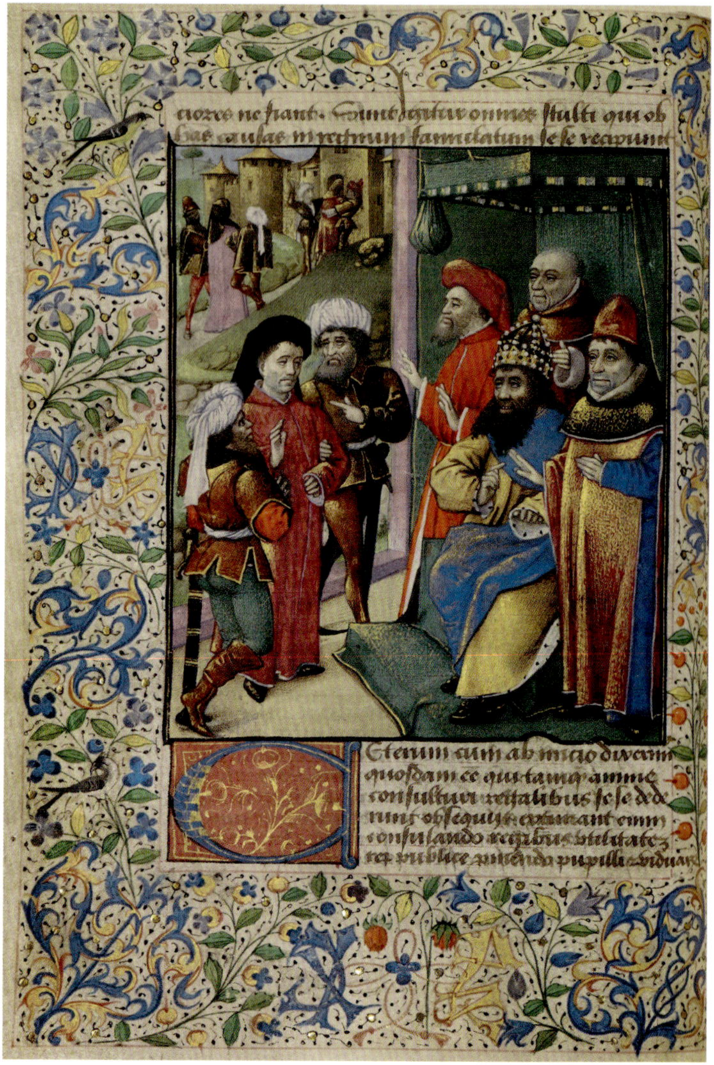

Aeneas Silvius Piccolomini, later Pope Pius II, authored the texts in this manuscript while working at the court of the Holy Roman Emperor. This image accompanies a letter he wrote to a friend describing in frank terms the dangers of life at court. The unpleasant fate of a prisoner standing trial before the emperor is revealed in the background: he is hauled off to the city gate, presumably to meet an unpleasant fate. The artist imparts psychological complexity to the scene by portraying a series of distinctive individuals whose interactions and responses contribute to the flow of the narrative. The figures are painted in jewel-like tones and with a light touch, giving the images an unusual luminosity.

Simon de Varie Kneeling in Prayer

Jean Fouquet (ca. 1415–before 1481). Hours of Simon de Varie (in Latin); French (Tours and perhaps Paris), 1455. Tempera, gold, and ink on parchment, 97 leaves, 11.4 × 8.3 cm (4½ × 3¼ in.). Partial gift of Gerald F. Borrmann, Ms. 7, fol. 2; 85.ML.27

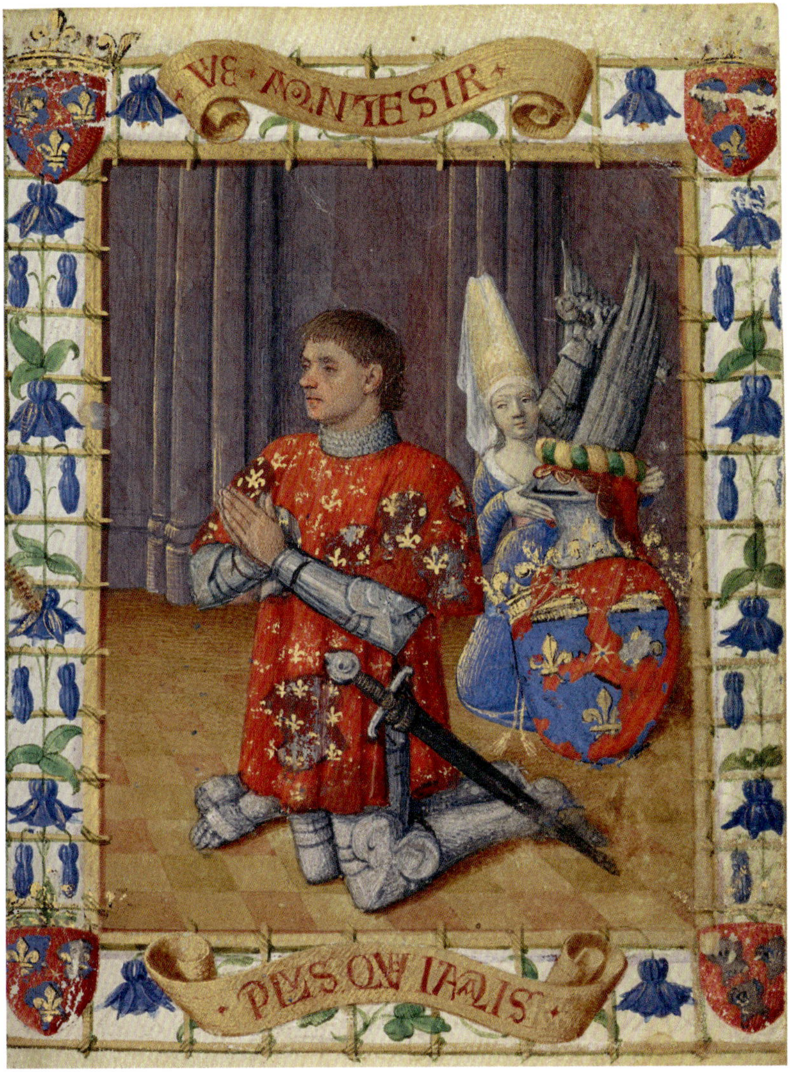

Jean Fouquet, who worked at the court of the French king, is famous for the geometric simplicity and monumentality of his imagery. This Christian prayer book was commissioned from the renowned illuminator by Simon de Varie, an official in the French royal treasury whom the king had recently ennobled. In the volume's introductory portrait, Varie wears armor and a surcoat decorated with the fleur-de-lis, a symbol of French royal power, while behind him a female attendant supports a shield crowned with his family crest. The coat of arms, like the ones in the borders that appear along with Varie's chosen mottos, is now partially overpainted. Varie signaled his newly gained noble status by engaging the most celebrated artist of his day, who was no doubt instructed to emphasize Varie's personal emblems.

A Naval Battle

Lieven van Lathem (ca. 1430–1493).
Romance of Gillion de Trazegnies (in French); Flemish (Antwerp), after 1464.
Tempera, gold, and ink on parchment, 237 leaves, 37 × 25.5 cm ($14\frac{9}{16} \times 10\frac{1}{16}$ in.).
Ms. 111, fol. 21; 2013.46

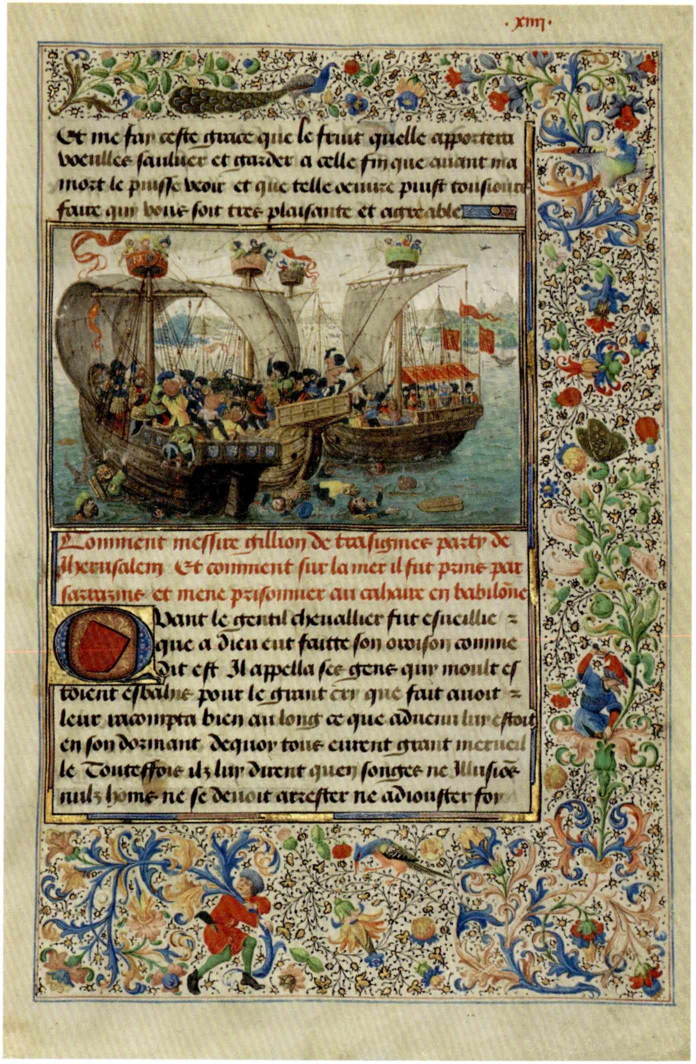

This lavishly illuminated text recounts the adventurous and romantic exploits of the medieval Christian nobleman Gillion de Trazegnies, who journeyed to Egypt on pilgrimage, mistakenly became a bigamist, and died in battle as a glorious hero. The tale encompasses all the most thrilling elements of the romance genre: faithful love, nefarious villainy, family loyalty, and violent battle. The book was commissioned by Louis de Gruuthuse (1422–1492), trusted adviser of Philip the Good, duke of Burgundy, and one of the great book collectors of the fifteenth century. Here, at left, two ships carrying the army of the sultan of Egypt attack Gillion's galleon. Several dead and dying combatants appear in the swirling water, itself alive with a sense of movement as blood colors the waves.

Sri Lanka (Traponee)

Master of the Geneva Boccaccio (active ca. 1445–1470). *Book of the Marvels of the World* (in French); French, circa 1460–65. Colored washes, gold, and ink on parchment, 60 leaves, 30.2 × 22.5 cm (11⅞ × 8⅞ in.). Ms. 124, fol. 32; 2022.15

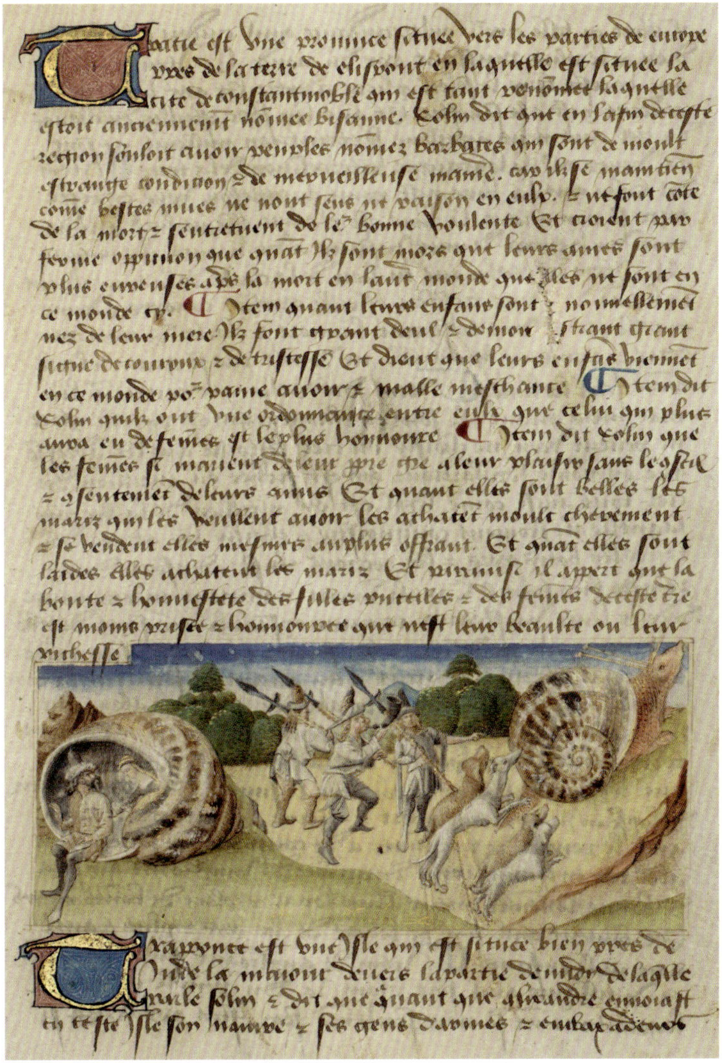

Based on ancient sources, medieval folklore, and supposed eyewitness accounts of travelers, the *Book of the Marvels of the World* weaves together tales of lands both near to and far from its place of creation in France. Organized alphabetically, the book serves as a compendium of medieval views of various locales, ranging from Asia to Africa to Europe. For an "armchair traveler" of the era, the book's descriptions and images of diverse peoples, customs, and environments, including the house-sized snails depicted here, supposedly found in Sri Lanka, no doubt seemed wondrous or bizarre. The colored drawing technique used in the book's images allows for dynamic and fluid compositions that capture the sense of a traveler moving quickly from place to place around the known globe.

Josaphat and Barlaam Embracing

Follower of Hans Schilling (active 1459–67). *Barlaam and Josaphat* (in German) by Rudolf von Ems (ca. 1200–1254); German (Hagenau), 1469. Colored washes, tempera, and ink on paper, 370 leaves, 28.6 × 20.3 cm (11¼ × 8 in.). Ms. Ludwig XV 9, fol. 79v; 83.MR.179

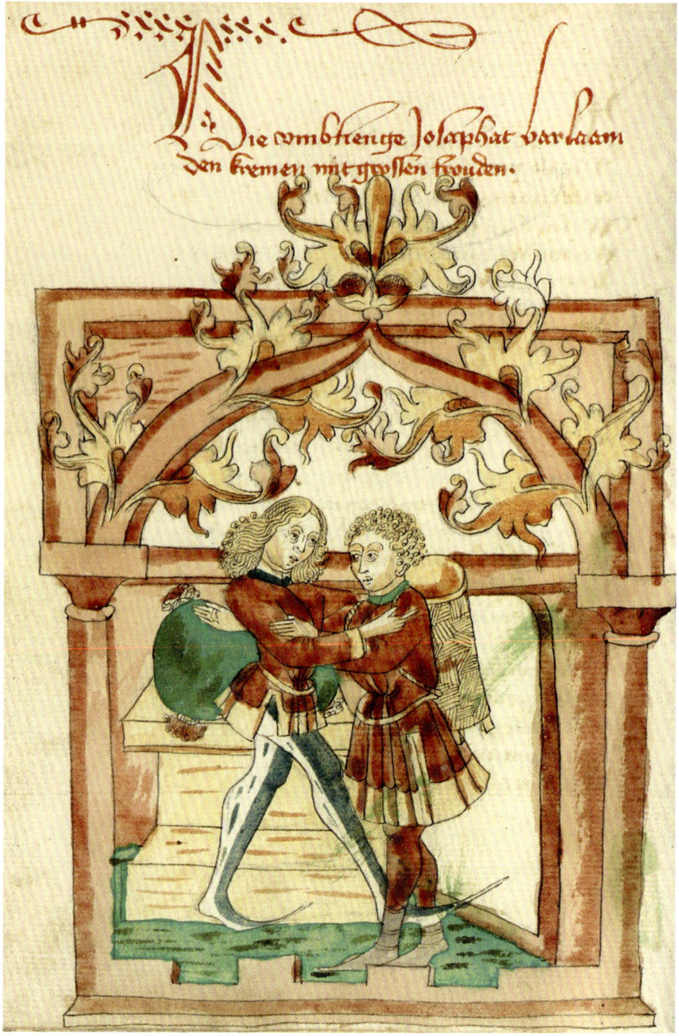

Barlaam and Josaphat recounts a Christianized version of the story of Siddhartha Gautama's conversion from worldly prince to enlightened Buddha. In it, the Indian prince Josaphat serves as a surrogate for the Buddha. He converts to Christianity under the influence of the holy teacher Barlaam and, after many tribulations, became a saintly hermit. This image captures the moment of Josaphat's revelation upon learning about Jesus's life. Overjoyed, the prince embraces his teacher under a flamboyant architectural framework, but his elegant, long hair and luxurious attire (note his exaggeratedly pointed shoes) allude to his lingering worldly attachments. Made for a noble patron in 1469, the Museum's manuscript contains a German version of the story, composed by Rudolf von Ems. It features 138 lively images of Josaphat's life.

The Beast Acheron

Simon Marmion (ca. 1425–1489). *The Visions of the Knight Tondal* (in French); Franco-Flemish (Valenciennes and Ghent), 1475. Tempera, gold, and ink on parchment, 45 leaves, 36.3 × 26.2 cm ($14\frac{5}{16} \times 10\frac{5}{16}$ in.). Ms. 30, fol. 17; 87.MN.141

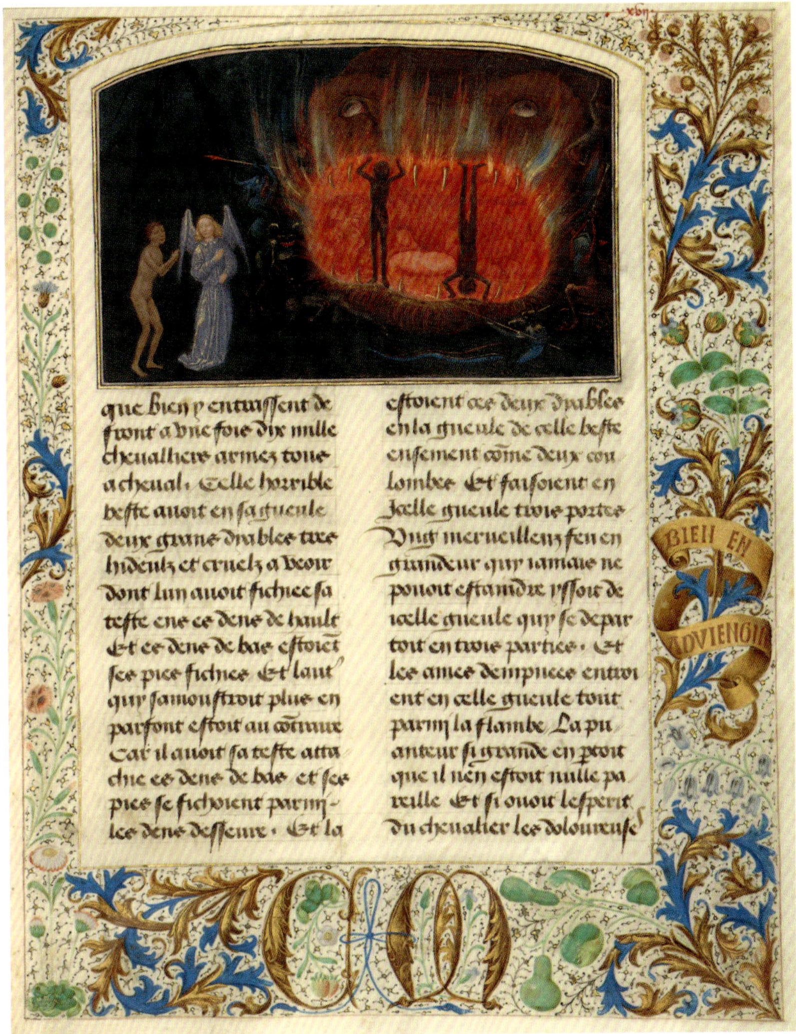

The Visions of the Knight Tondal is a medieval Christian tale about a wealthy Irish knight whose soul embarks on a journey through Hell, Purgatory, and Heaven, during which he learns the wages of sin and the value of penitence. Written in Latin in the mid-twelfth century, the popular story was translated into fifteen European languages over the next three centuries. This sumptuous manuscript, commissioned by Margaret of York, duchess of Burgundy (1446–1503), is the only known illustrated copy of the text, containing twenty large images. In the scene illustrated here, Tondal's guardian angel shows the knight's soul the punishments meted out to the greedy, with the entrance to Hell depicted as the gaping maw of a horrific beast.

Anne of Brittany Enthroned and Accompanied by Her Ladies-in-Waiting

Master of the *Chronique scandaleuse* (active ca. 1493–1510). Excerpts from *Heroides* (in French) by Ovid (43 BCE–17 CE) and letters (in French) by Octavien de Saint-Gelais (1468–1502); French (Paris), circa 1493. Tempera, gold, and ink on parchment, 59 leaves, 25.3 × 18.7 cm ($9^{15}/_{16}$ × $7^{3}/_{8}$ in.). Ms. 121, fol. 55; 2021.7

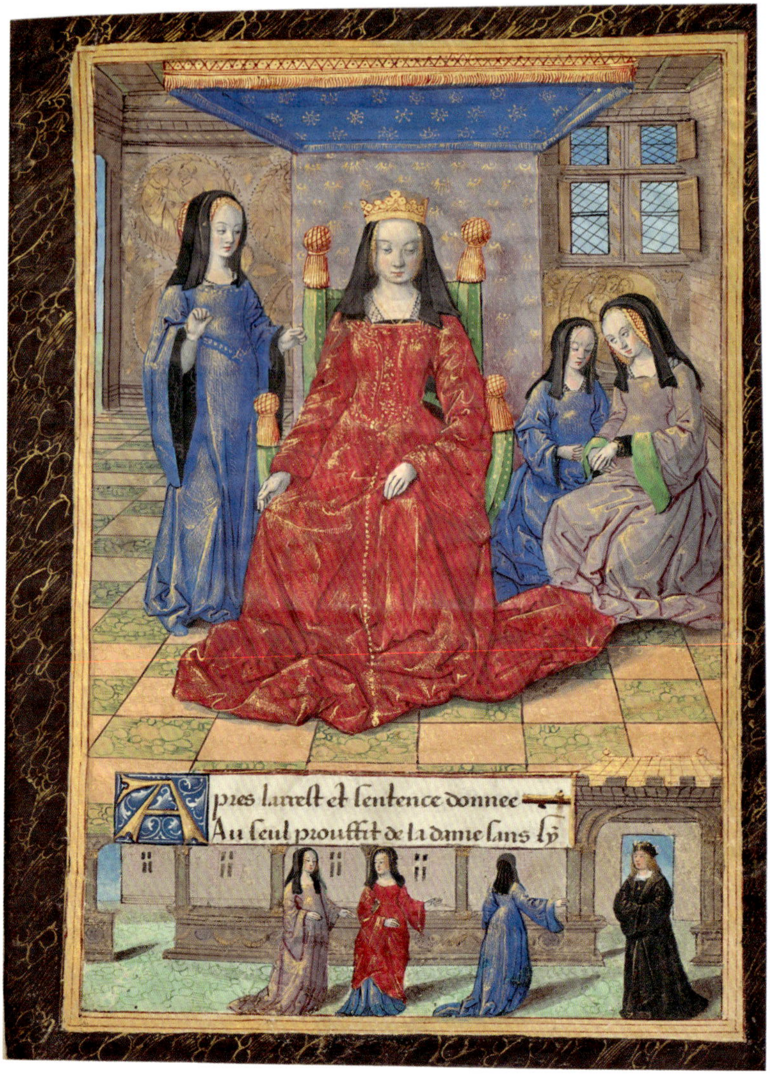

Executed for Anne of Brittany, queen of France (1477–1514), this luxurious manuscript begins with a compendium of letters, supposedly authored by mourning heroines of antiquity to their unfaithful husbands or lovers. The accompanying illuminations comprise a series of large images that culminates with an image of Queen Anne seated under a cloth of honor with her ladies-in-waiting. According to the text, the queen and her companions are debating whether men have the right to judge the female ideal, and they cast aspersions on the general ability of male authors to tell the truth. This portrait is likely the earliest image of Anne as queen, and the manuscript may have been formative for the young ruler as she navigated the politics of the French court.

Louis XII of France Kneeling in Prayer, Accompanied by Saints Michael, Charlemagne, Louis, and Denis

Jean Bourdichon (1457–1521). Leaf from the Hours of Louis XII (in French and Latin); French (Tours), 1498/99. Tempera and gold on parchment, 24.3 × 15.7 cm (9 9/16 × 6 3/16 in.). Ms. 79a, recto; 2004.1

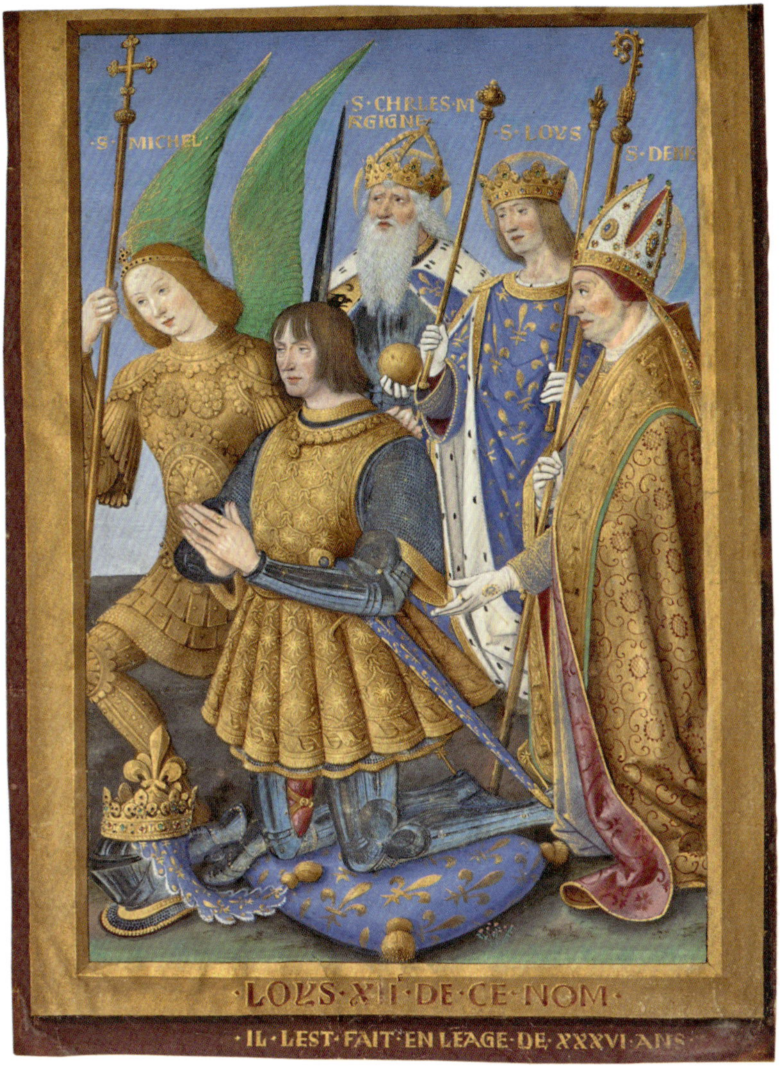

This imposing portrait of the French king once opened a lavish Christian prayer book, called the Hours of Louis XII after its royal owner. Jean Bourdichon, the artist, served as court painter to four successive French kings, including Louis XII (r. 1498–1515). In this frontispiece to the manuscript, the king is shown surrounded by the most important saints associated with the French monarchy: Denis, Louis, Charlemagne, and Michael. The depiction of the king in his parade armor probably celebrates his coronation in 1498. The manuscript was dispersed in the 1800s, and only seventeen of its original images have since come to light. The Getty Museum has acquired four of them, including a moving scene of the Lamentation of Christ that would have originally faced this portrait of the king.

The Virgin and Child with Archangels

Gospel book (in Ge'ez); Ethiopian, circa 1504–5. Tempera on parchment, 269 leaves, 34.4 × 26.5 cm (13 9/16 × 10 7/16 in.). Ms. 102, fol. 19v; 2008.15

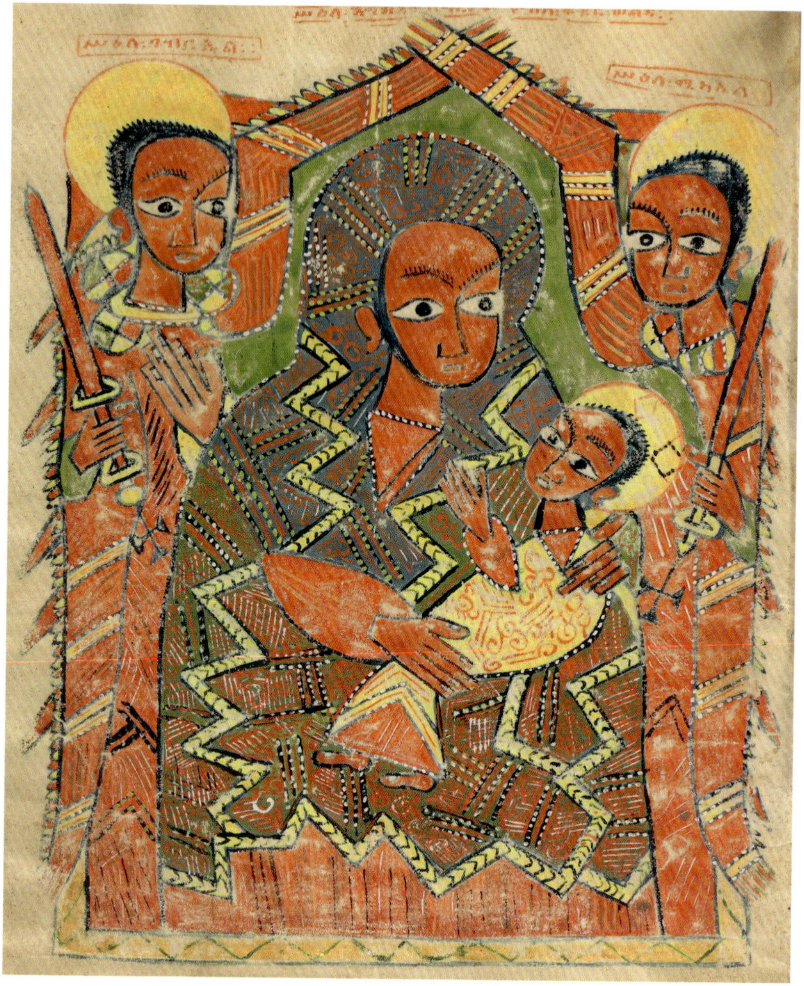

This Gospel book from the sixteenth-century Christian kingdom of Ethiopia is illuminated in the distinctive and profoundly expressive style that characterizes manuscripts painted at Gunda Gundé monastery, a key center of learning and book production. The book is adorned with intricately decorated headpieces (called *haräg*), a set of canon tables (a concordance of passages relating the same events in the four Gospels of the Christian Bible), and five large images. The introductory painting depicts the Virgin Mary holding her newborn child under the protecting wings of the archangels Michael and Gabriel. The almond-shaped eyes framed with pronounced eyebrows add a sense of alertness to the figures' demeanor, while the vibrating dots and zigzagging lines lend dynamism to the scene, painted in vivid reds, greens, and yellows.

The Annunciation

Master of James IV of Scotland (active ca. 1485–ca. 1530). Spinola Hours (in Latin); Flemish (Bruges and Ghent), circa 1510–20. Tempera, gold, and ink on parchment, 312 leaves, 23.2 × 16.7 cm (9 1/8 × 6 9/16 in.). Ms. Ludwig IX 18, fol. 92v; 83.ML.114

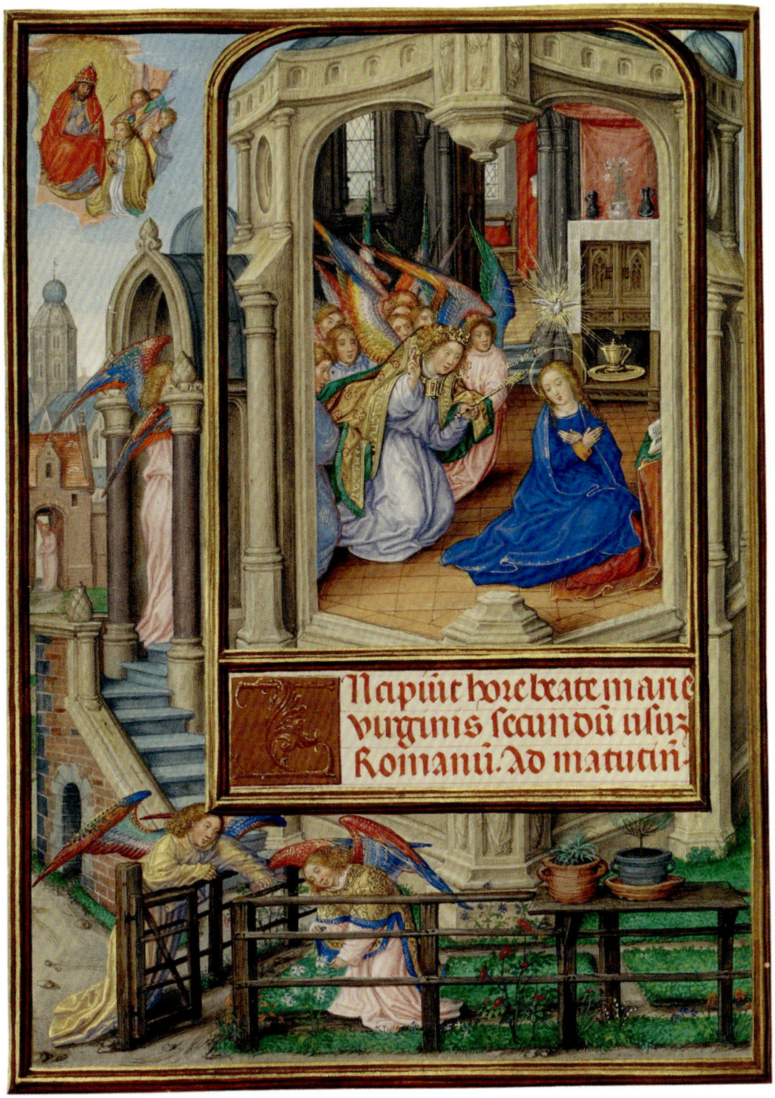

The Spinola Hours, a Christian prayer book, is one of the greatest surviving examples of Flemish illumination. In this inventive page design, the anonymous artist known as the Master of James IV of Scotland unified the traditionally separate zones of the main image and the decorated border. The central scene of the Annunciation—when the angel Gabriel arrives to tell the Virgin Mary that she will become Jesus's mother—takes place inside the Virgin's chamber. The exterior of the same building, where angels joyously pick flowers, is depicted in the surrounding border. Thus the setting of the composition has expanded beyond its traditional boundaries to fill the page and provide the viewer with a playful interaction of illusion and reality.

The Adoration of the Magi

Simon Bening (ca. 1483–1561). Prayer book of Cardinal Albrecht of Brandenburg (in German); Flemish (Bruges), circa 1525–30. Tempera, gold, and ink on parchment, 337 leaves, 16.8 × 11.4 cm ($6^5/_8 \times 4^1/_2$ in.). Ms. Ludwig IX 19, fol. 36v; 83.ML.115

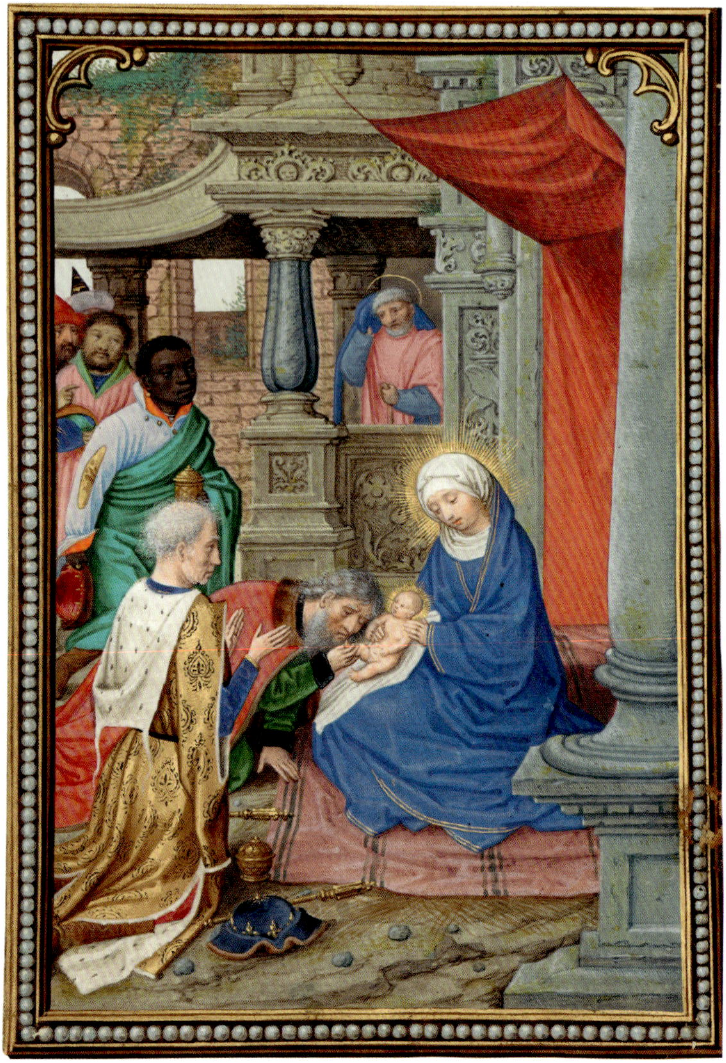

The esteemed Flemish artist Simon Bening illuminated this Christian prayer book for Cardinal Albrecht of Brandenburg (1490–1545), an ambitious patron of the arts. Its forty-one large images dramatically recount events from the life of Christ, inspiring the reader's compassion by emphasizing Christ's humanity. In this scene of the Adoration of the Magi, Jesus is just a tiny baby, but the three magi pay him homage, recognizing his future role as an even mightier king. The oldest magus, representing Europe, kneels to kiss Christ's foot; the king from Asia wears sumptuous golden robes; and the youngest ruler, standing, is identified in medieval legends as coming from Africa. The cardinal selected Bening as the artist for his ability to bring out the rich narrative and subtle psychological elements of Christ's story.

Initial *A*: King David

Matteo da Milano (active ca. 1492–1523). Missal (in Latin); Italian (Rome), circa 1520. Tempera, gold, and ink on parchment, 98 leaves, 33.6 × 23.4 cm (13¼ × 9³⁄₁₆ in.). Ms. 87, fol. 52v; 2004.65

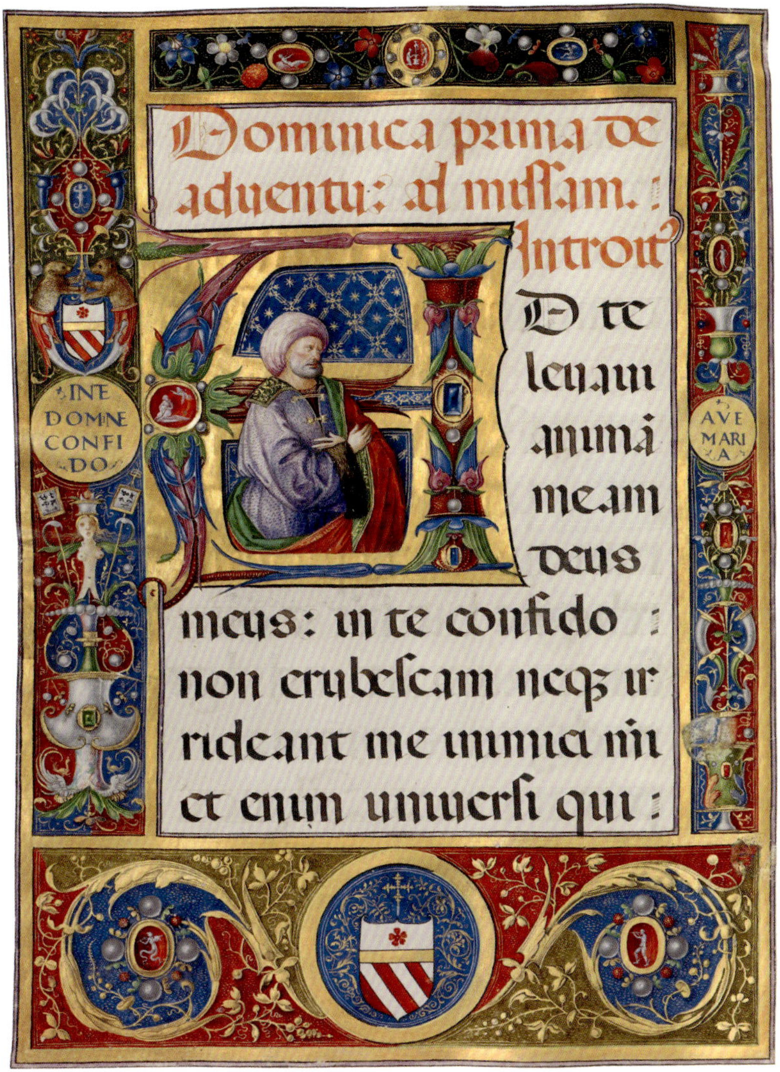

This missal, a book containing the texts recited during Christian Mass, was commissioned by a member of the powerful Orsini family in Rome in the early sixteenth century. It is illuminated with four large historiated initials (letters containing a narrative scene) surrounded by lavishly decorated borders filled with cameos, gems, flowers, and hybrid creatures. The opening page for the Mass of the first Sunday of Advent (the four weeks preceding the Birth of Christ) depicts the biblical King David inhabiting a fanciful initial *A*. He lifts his eyes piously toward heaven as if enacting the psalm next to him, "To thee, have I lifted up my soul." The king's cape, robe, and turban emulate attire worn by Ottoman noblemen at the time the book was made.

Carnation, Walnut, Marine Mollusk, and Insects

Joris Hoefnagel (1542–1601). *Model Book of Calligraphy* (in various languages); Flemish and Hungarian, written 1561–62; illuminated circa 1591–96. Tempera, watercolor, gold, silver, and ink on parchment and paper, 150 leaves, 16.6 × 12.4 cm (6⁹⁄₁₆ × 4⁷⁄₈ in.). Ms. 20, fol. 74; 86.MV.527

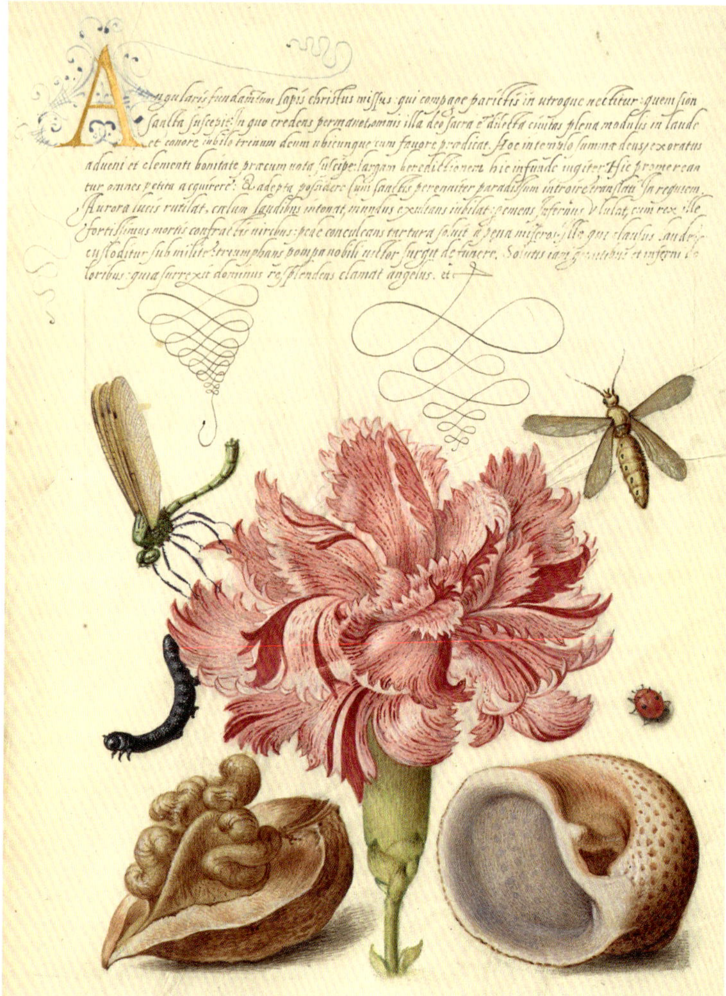

Originally written for Holy Roman Emperor Ferdinand I (r. 1558–64), the *Model Book of Calligraphy* is a compendium of display scripts by one of the great scribes of the day, Georg Bocskay (d. 1575). The calligraphy on each page represents a different style of writing, inventively arranged. Thirty years later, Emperor Rudolf II (r. 1576–1612), Ferdinand I's grandson, commissioned Joris Hoefnagel to add illuminations to the pages. Hoefnagel's exuberant depictions of flowers, shells, insects, and fruit often echo the forms of Bocskay's imaginative script. On this page, the ruffled petals of the carnation and the curling forms of the walnut and mollusk mimic the fine edges of the italic script above, as well as the curvilinear forms of the penwork ribbons that descend from the last line.

Saint John the Evangelist

Mesrop of Khizan (active 1605–51). Gospel book (in Armenian); Armenian (Isfahan), 1615. Tempera, gold paint, and gold leaf on glazed paper, 246 leaves, 23 × 17.1 cm (9 1/16 × 6 3/4 in.). Ms. Ludwig II 7, fol. 193v; 83.MB.71

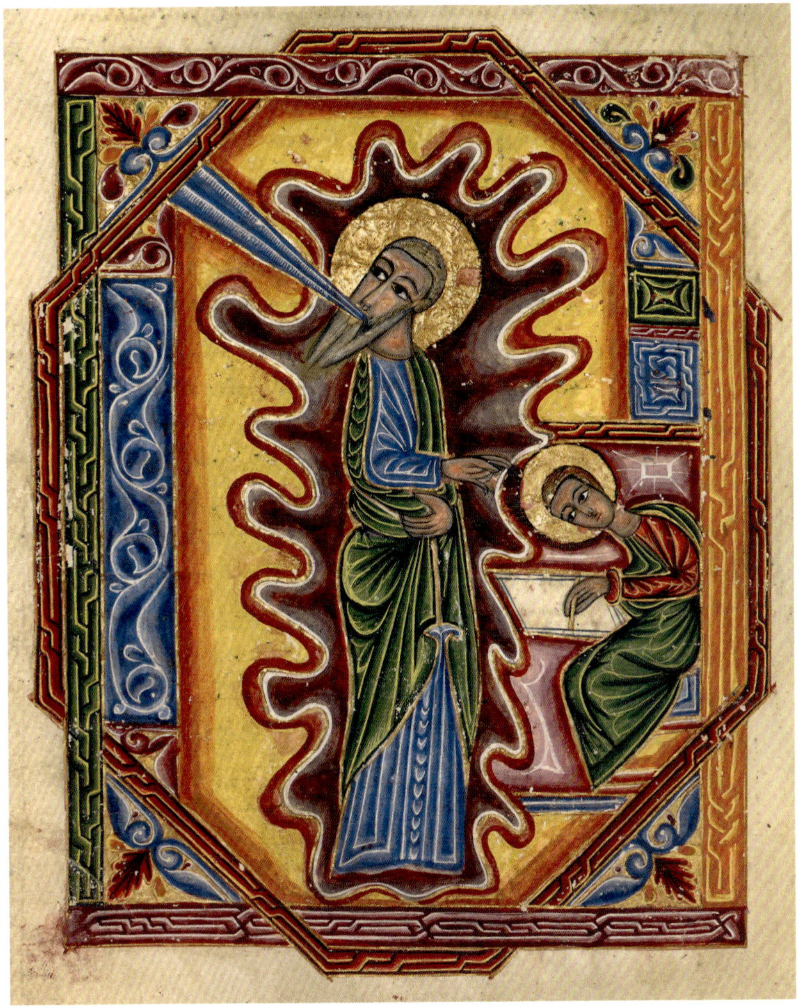

This lavish Christian Gospel book with portraits of the four evangelists (the authors of the four biblical accounts of Christ's life) was illustrated by the famous seventeenth-century Armenian painter Mesrop of Khizan. Created in the tradition of medieval Armenian art, its imagery is characterized by rhythmic geometric patterning rendered in bold, vibrant colors. In this image, blue rays signifying divine inspiration shoot directly from heaven to the lips of Saint John as he is surrounded by pulsating purple swells of energy. At some point in the early twentieth century, sixteen images showing scenes from Christian sacred history were removed from the manuscript and dispersed. The Getty Museum acquired the main portion of the manuscript in 1983, and three additional leaves from the original cycle since then.

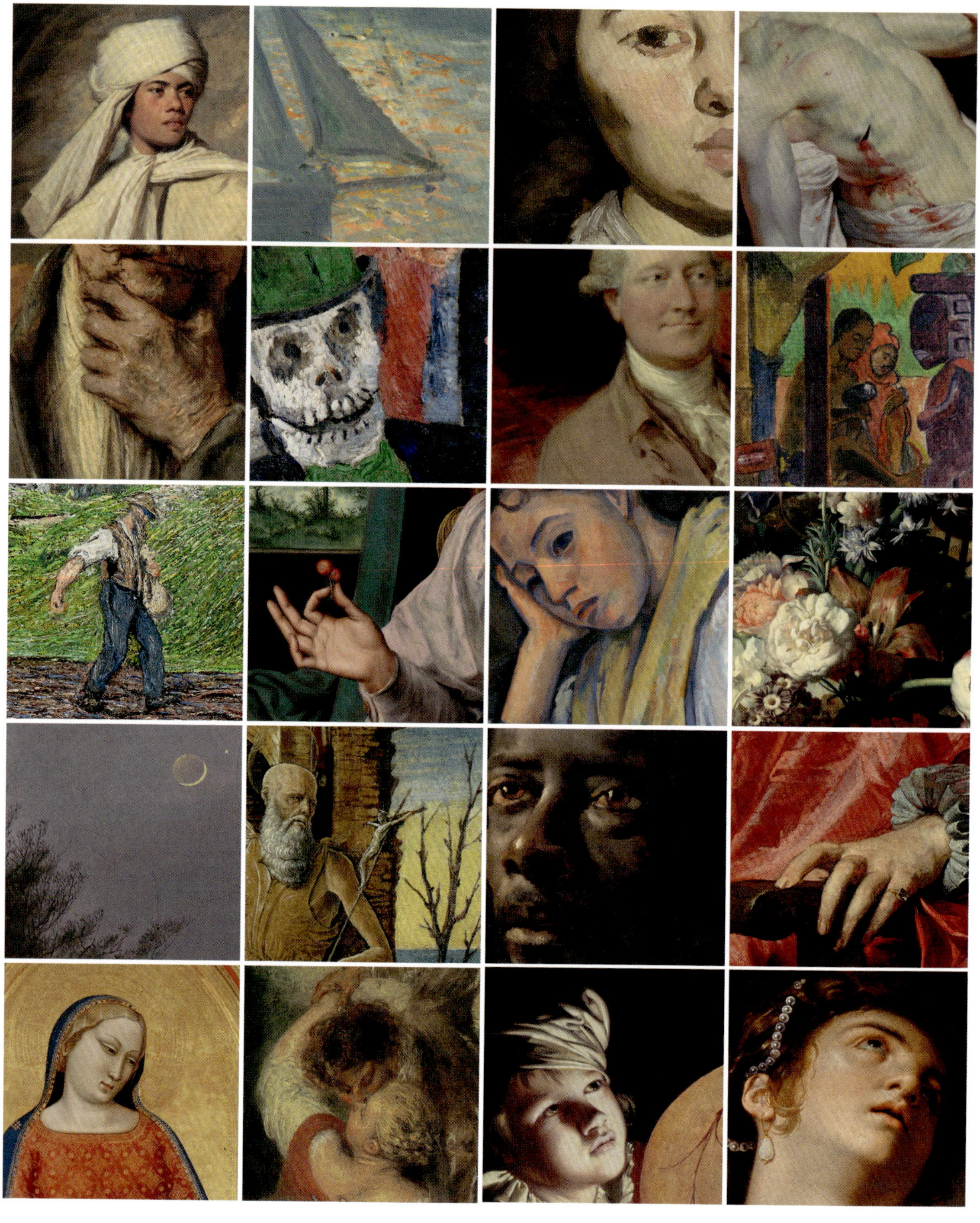

Paintings

J. Paul Getty began collecting European paintings in the 1930s. By World War II he owned two major pictures—Thomas Gainsborough's *Portrait of James Christie* (p. 192) and Rembrandt van Rijn's *Portrait of Marten Looten* (given to the Los Angeles County Museum of Art in 1953)—as well as several other paintings, mostly by seventeenth-century Dutch artists. It was not until the mid-1960s that he sought to buy pictures equal in stature to his finer holdings of decorative arts, such as Rembrandt's magnificent *Saint Bartholomew* in 1962 (p. 178), Anthony van Dyck's majestic *Portrait of Agostino Pallavicini* in 1968 (p. 164), and Georges de La Tour's *The Musicians' Brawl* in 1972 (p. 179).

Since Getty's death in 1976, the Museum has continued to acquire major paintings, greatly enhancing the scope and quality of the collection. Today, its holdings include some of the finest examples of European painting from the Middle Ages through the nineteenth century, distinguished by their importance and excellent state of preservation. The Italian Renaissance, one of Getty's preferred periods, is represented by masters including Andrea Mantegna, Pontormo (Jacopo Carucci), Agnolo Bronzino, Titian (Tiziano Vecellio), Jacopo Bassano, and Parmigianino (Francesco Mazzola). Recent acquisitions have also expanded the collection into new areas not previously represented, such as the Netherlandish and German Renaissance, with works by renowned artists Dieric Bouts, Gerard David, Quentin Metsys, Lucas Cranach the Elder, and others. Prominent additions to the seventeenth-century French and Dutch schools include three early works by Rembrandt, among them *The Abduction of Europa* (p. 177), one of his first major history paintings. The work of the Flemish Baroque artist Peter Paul Rubens also represents a notable area of depth. The number of eighteenth-century French paintings—an area that, curiously, Getty never pursued to complement the French decorative arts he collected with such enthusiasm—has grown significantly and today includes celebrated masterpieces such as *The Surprise* by Jean-Antoine Watteau (p. 184) and *The Fountain of Love* by Jean-Honoré Fragonard (p. 195). *The Portrait of Mai (Omai)* by Joshua Reynolds (p. 193), jointly purchased with the National Portrait Gallery, London, marks a notable recent addition to the collection's eighteenth-century British paintings and grants public access to a masterwork that was until recently (2023) kept in private collections. Getty's French Impressionist pictures, assembled almost entirely since 1982, today include major works by Édouard Manet, Claude Monet, Pierre-Auguste Renoir, and Edgar Degas, as well as what is perhaps the Museum's most beloved picture, *Irises*, by the Dutch-born artist Vincent van Gogh (p. 217). The late nineteenth century outside France is also well represented in outstanding works by James Ensor (Belgium; p. 219), Edvard Munch (Norway; p. 220), Giovanni Segantini (Italy; p. 218), and Vilhelm Hammershøi (Denmark; p. 221), among others. The acquisition of pictures of exceptional quality by Lavinia Fontana (p. 151), Artemisia Gentileschi (p. 154), and other female practitioners reflects the Getty Museum's ongoing commitment to highlighting the contributions of underrepresented artists and subjects in the history of art.

Bernardo Daddi
Italian, circa 1280–1348
The Virgin Mary with Saints Thomas Aquinas and Paul, circa 1330
Tempera on panel,
central panel: 120.7 × 55.9 cm (47½ × 22 in.); left panel: 105.5 × 28 cm (41½ × 11 in.); right panel: 105.5 × 27.6 cm (41½ × 10⅞ in.), 93.PB.16

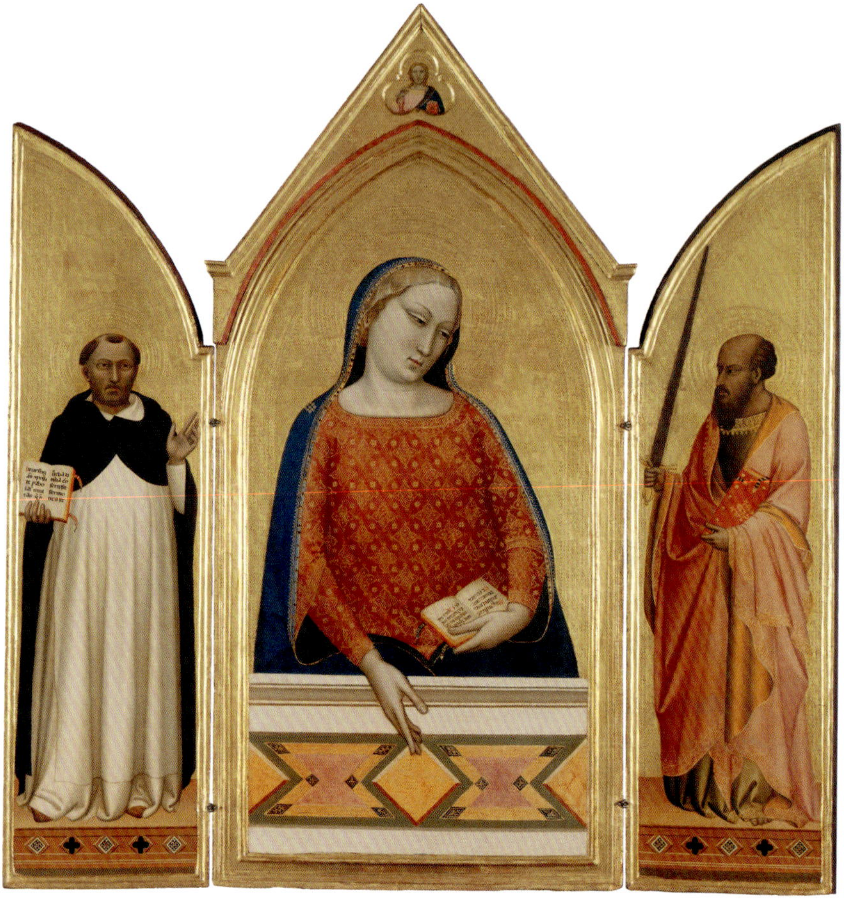

Triptychs with a central image of the Madonna flanked by one or more standing saints became a popular form of devotional imagery in fourteenth-century Italy, reflecting the growing veneration of the Virgin Mary. Here, Daddi, one of the leading Florentine painters of his generation, depicted a serene yet majestic Mother of God, reading the Magnificat (Luke 1:46–48) and extending her hand across a ledge toward the viewer. At left is Saint Thomas Aquinas, dressed in the black-and-white habit of the Dominican order and displaying the text of Ecclesiastes 12:9–10. Saint Paul, at right, holds a book of his epistles and the sword by which he was martyred. The solid, elegantly rendered figures, resonant colors, and exquisitely tooled gold all contribute to the painting's ethereal effect.

Simone Martini

Italian, circa 1284–1344

Saint Luke, early 1330s?

Tempera and gold leaf on panel,
with engaged frame, 67.5 × 48.3 × 3.8 cm
(26 9/16 × 19 × 1 1/2 in.), 82.PB.72

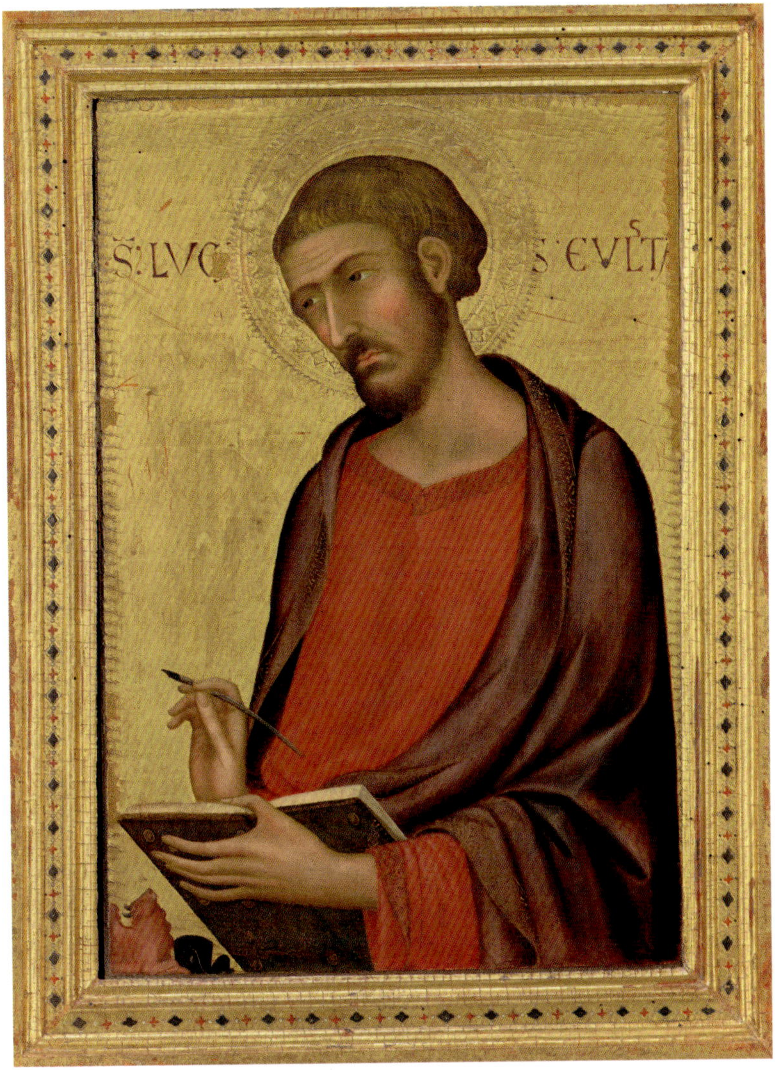

Saint Luke, one of the four evangelists, is shown in the act of writing his Gospel. His serene face is rendered in minute detail, each hair of his beard carefully described. The modeled folds of his cloak, achieved through subtle gradations of finely brushed pigments, lend a rhythmic elegance. Such features contribute to the overall refinement that characterizes Martini's figures. Also typical of the artist is the flair with which he depicts Luke's traditional attribute, the winged ox, which appears in miniature at bottom left, acting as proud custodian of the inkpot. This panel originally was one of five sections of a polyptych, or multipart painting, made for the Palazzo Pubblico in Siena, the seat of the city government. The gilded and painted frame is original.

Gentile da Fabriano

Italian, circa 1370–1427

Coronation of the Virgin, circa 1420

Tempera and gold leaf on panel,

93 × 64.1 cm (36⅝ × 25¼ in.), 77.PB.92

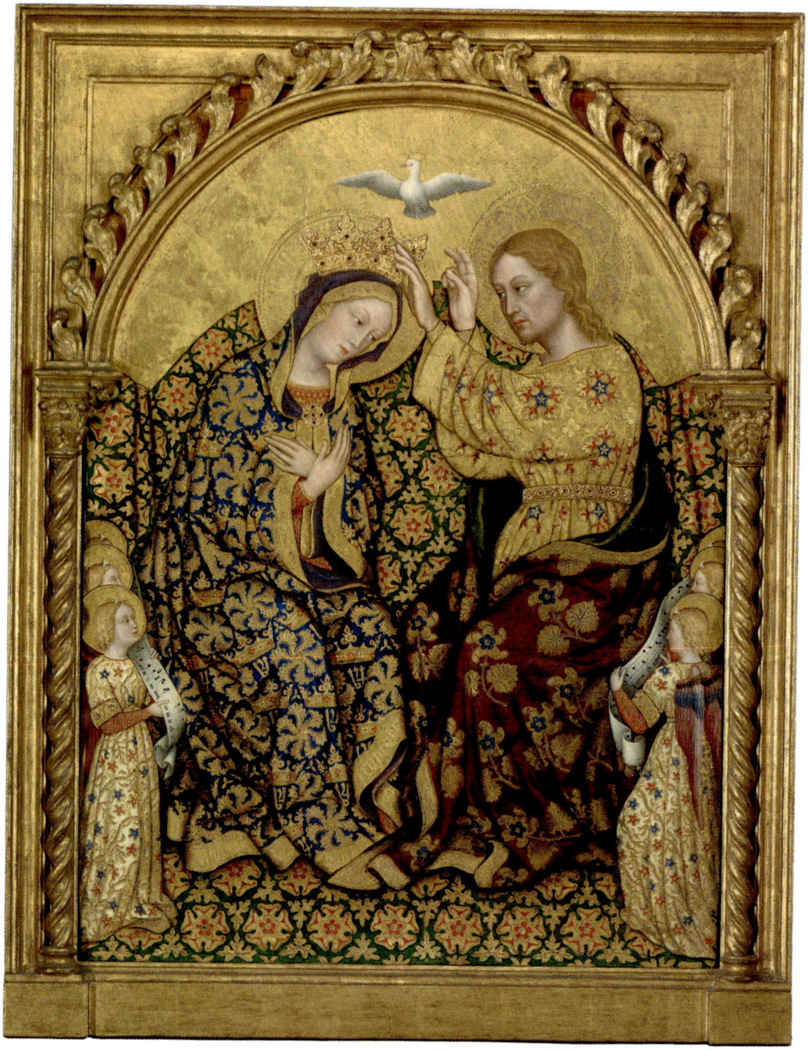

The mood in this scene is one of lavish ceremony as Christ places an ornate gold crown on the Virgin Mary's slightly bowed head. Groups of singing angels holding sheet music look on from either side. The artist used extensive tooling and *pastiglia* (areas of raised gesso that is molded and gilded) layered with richly pigmented glazes to create a sumptuous surface resembling a tapestry. The work was painted for a religious confraternity associated with the Church of San Francesco in Gentile's hometown, Fabriano, in the Marche region of Italy. The panel originally was double-sided and served as a processional standard, held aloft in ceremonies honoring the Virgin. The reverse, depicting the *Stigmatization of Saint Francis*, is now in the collection of the Fondazione Magnani Rocca in Parma, Italy.

Masaccio (Tommaso di Giovanni Guidi)
Italian, 1401–1428
Saint Andrew, 1426
Tempera on panel, 52.4 × 32.1 cm
(20⅝ × 12⅝ in.), 79.PB.61

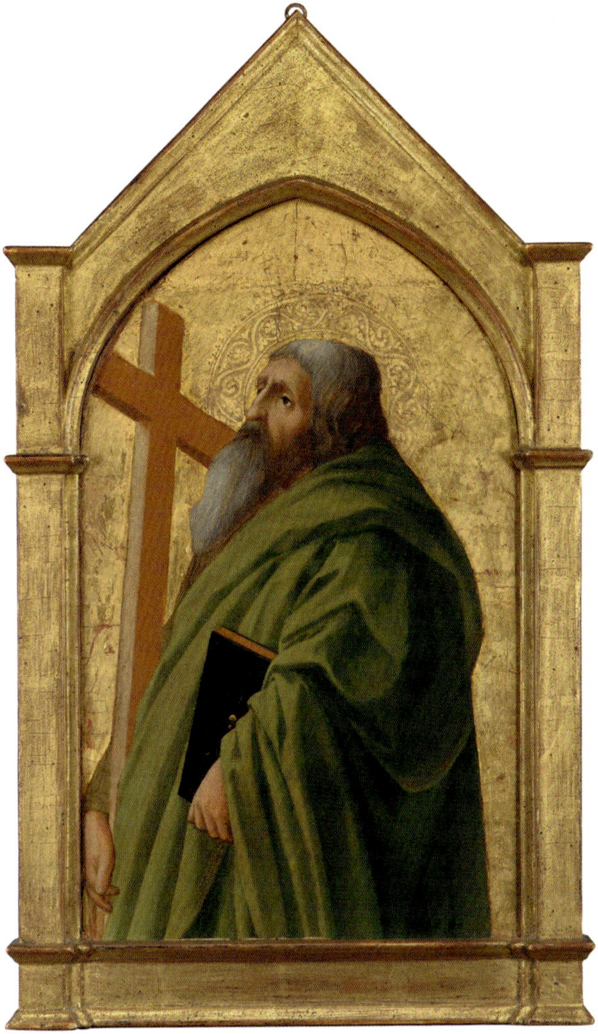

This image of Saint Andrew comes from the only securely documented altarpiece by Masaccio, a polyptych (multipart painting) made in 1426 for the private chapel of Giuliano da San Giusto, a wealthy notary, in the Church of the Carmine in Pisa, Italy. The panel was positioned at the upper right of the polyptych, so that Andrew gazed sadly down toward the central panel, depicting the Crucifixion. Since the panel stood high above the ground, the figure is slightly foreshortened, to accommodate viewing from below. The single figure endowed with volume and solidity, and the simplified draperies falling in sculptural folds, exemplifies Masaccio's contribution to the early Renaissance painting style, as does the more naturalistic treatment of emotion. It was this powerful combination of form and expression that so impressed his contemporaries.

Ercole de' Roberti

Italian, circa 1450–1496

Saint Jerome in the Wilderness,

circa 1470

Tempera on panel, 34 × 21.9 cm

(13 3/8 × 8 5/8 in.), 96.PB.14

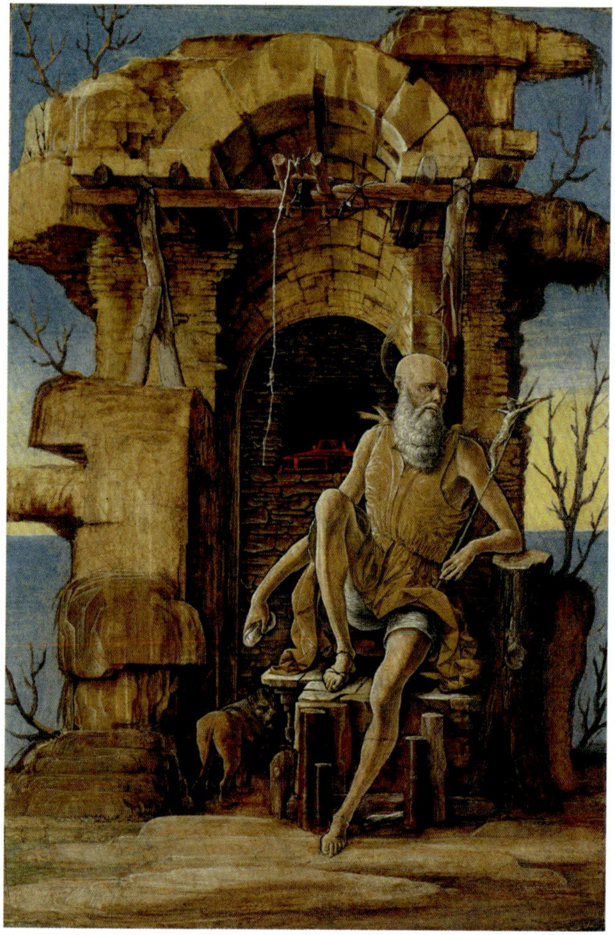

Sheltered by vaulted ruins reminiscent of a church, the emaciated Saint Jerome contemplates a crucifix as he clasps a rock with which to beat his breast. The intensity of his gaze suggests his religious and intellectual fervor. In the nook behind Jerome are his most prominent attributes: a book, alluding to his translation of the Bible into Latin, and a cardinal's hat. The small lion, a species apparently known to the artist only from a book illustration, refers to an episode in which Jerome won the animal's friendship by pulling a thorn from its paw. Roberti worked principally in the northern Italian city of Ferrara, where he produced exquisite, expressive paintings marked by elongated forms, a refined palette, and meticulous, gold-flecked details.

Vittore Carpaccio

Italian, circa 1460–circa 1526

Hunting on the Lagoon, circa 1490–95

Oil on panel, 75.6 × 63.8 cm

(29¾ × 25⅛ in.), 79.PB.72

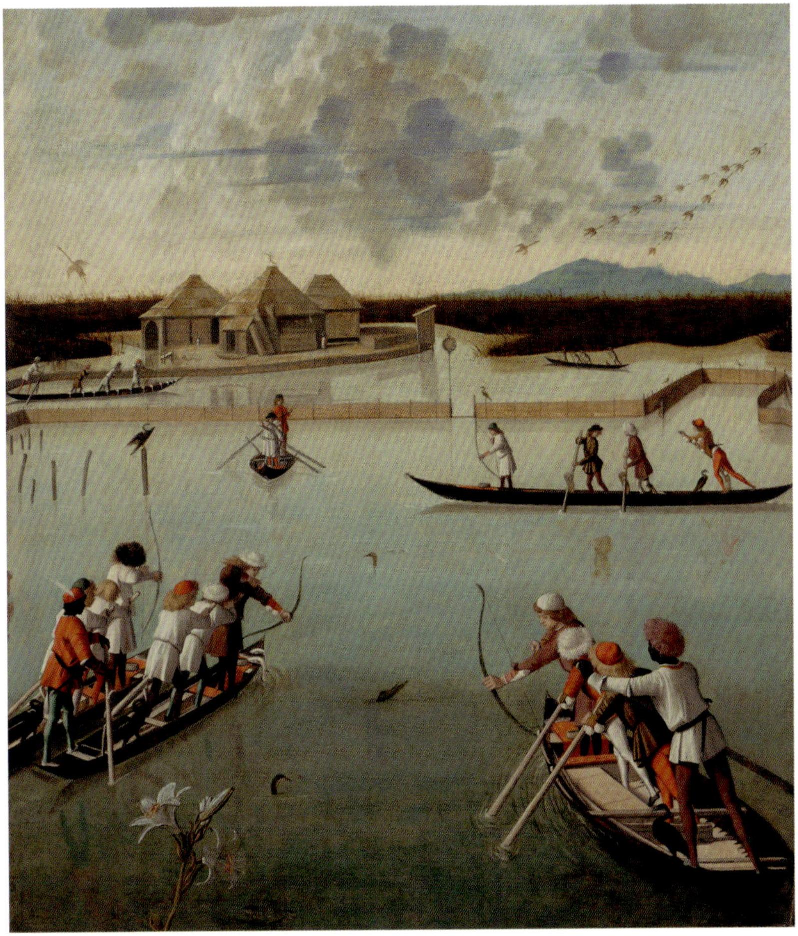

Archers in shallow-bottomed rowboats hunt cormorants on the Venetian lagoon. They use clay pellets rather than arrows to avoid damaging the birds' valuable plumage. The lily in the bottom left corner is out of scale and seemingly out of place with the rest of the painting. That is because this scene was originally the upper portion of a larger composition in which two women sit on a balcony overlooking the lagoon. That part of the painting, today in the Correr Museum in Venice, Italy, features a blossomless stem in a vase that corresponds to the bloom in the Getty Museum's painting. Hinge marks indicate that this panel once functioned as a decorative shutter or cabinet door, the reverse of which is painted with a trompe-l'oeil (illusionistic) letter rack.

Andrea Mantegna

Italian, circa 1431–1506

The Adoration of the Magi,

circa 1495–1505

Distemper on linen, 54.6 × 69.2 cm

(21½ × 27⅜ in.), 85.PA.417

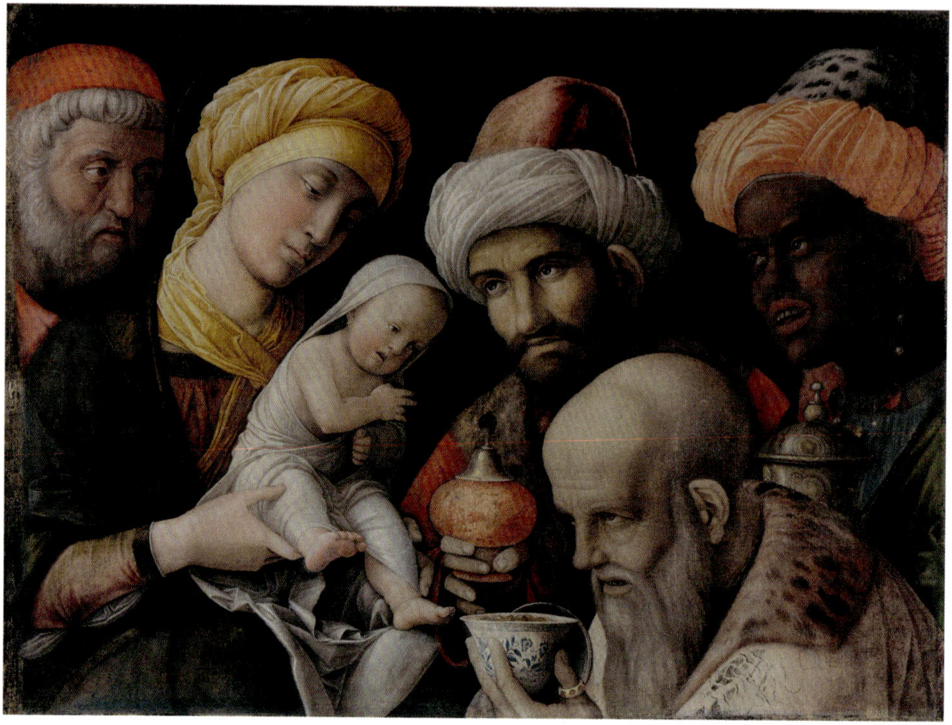

This private devotional painting depicting the Adoration of the Magi takes as its focus the psychological interactions among characters. The compositional scheme of close-up, half-length figures compressed within a shallow space and set before a neutral background was influenced by the artist's study of ancient Roman reliefs and reflected the Renaissance interest in classical antiquity. The magi, or kings, represent the three parts of the then-known world—Europe, Asia, and Africa—and personify royal recognition of Christ's superior kingship. They offer their gifts in vessels of carved agate, Turkish metalware, and Chinese porcelain. The painting's probable patrons, the Gonzaga family, rulers of Mantua, employed Mantegna as court painter. His unusual technique—thin washes of pigment in animal glue—resulted in a matte surface, emphasizing his refined draftsmanship and brushwork.

Dieric Bouts

Netherlandish, circa 1415–1475

The Annunciation, circa 1450–55

Distemper on linen, 90 × 74.5 cm

(35 7/16 × 29 3/8 in.), 85.PA.24

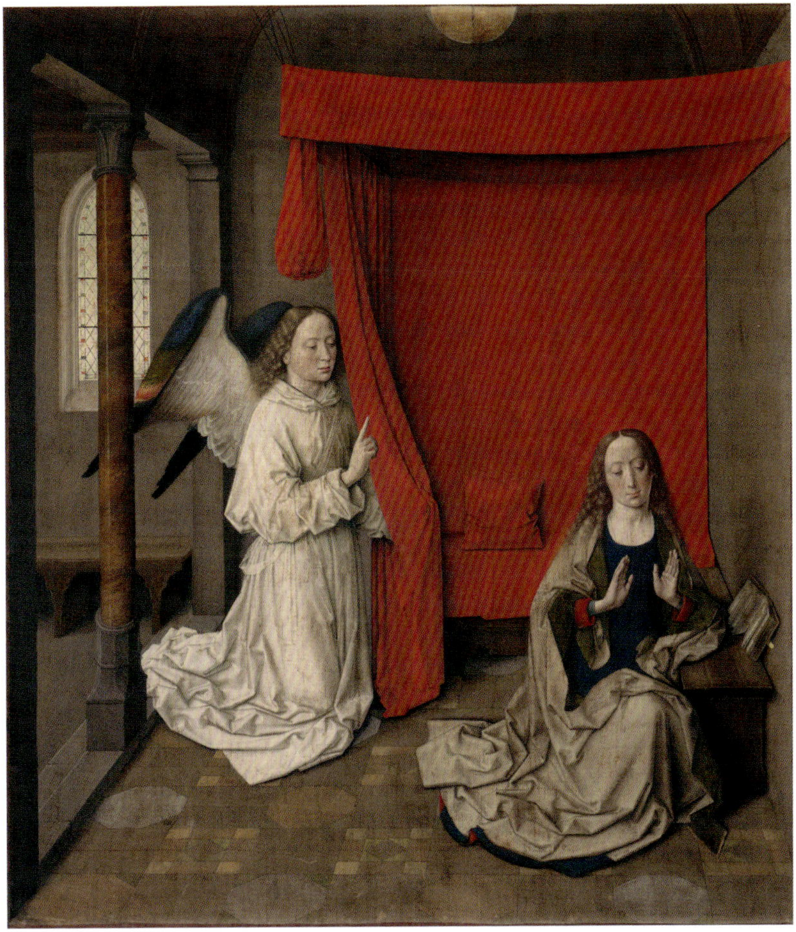

This portrayal of the Incarnation, or conception of Christ, was probably part of a movable polyptych (multipart painting) featuring scenes from the Life of Christ. The archangel Gabriel alights within the Virgin Mary's chamber, where she sits humbly beside a bench. He pulls aside the rich red drapery of her sanctuary to announce that she will bear a son (Luke 1:31). Mary turns away from her book of prayers at the sound of Gabriel's arrival, acknowledging both the miracle and her acceptance of God's will with a solemn gesture. Through a technique of applying thin washes of pigment mixed with animal glue to a fine linen support, Bouts achieved remarkably delicate, luminous effects that convey the joy and importance of the subject.

Gerard David

Netherlandish, circa 1460–1523

The Holy Family, circa 1520

Oil on panel, 40.9 × 33 cm (16⅛ × 13 in.),

2023.104

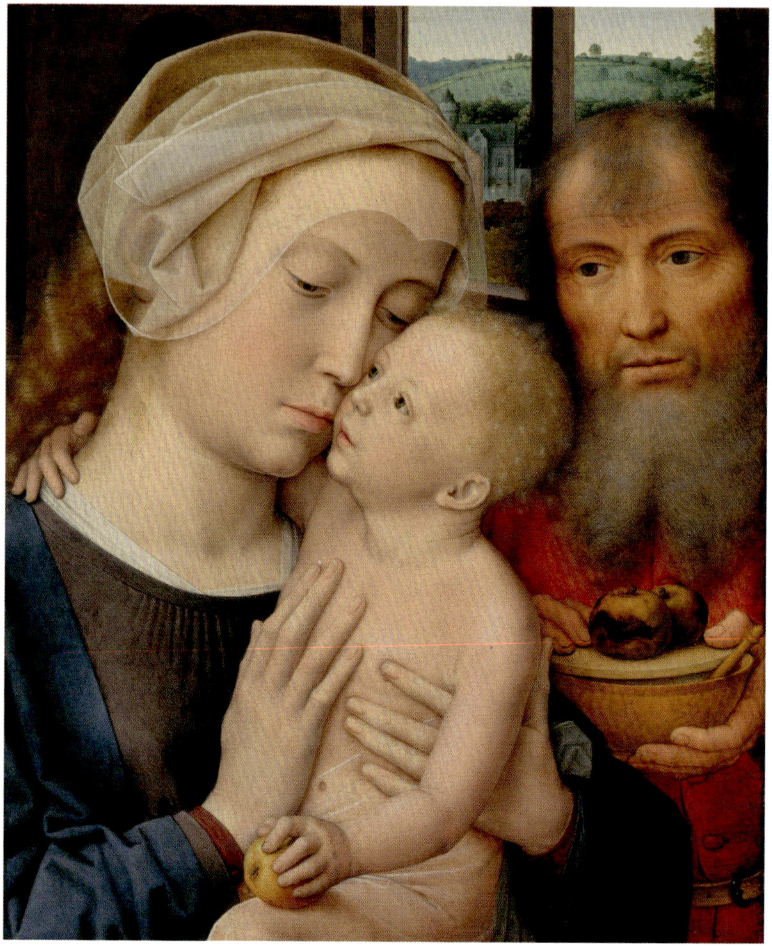

This tender scene offers an intimate view of human relationships while also making stark references to Christ's future suffering and sacrifice. The Virgin and Child embrace cheek to cheek, her fingers pressing into the soft flesh of her son's torso. Christ holds an unblemished apple, a symbol of his role as the new Adam, the biblical progenitor of humankind. By boldly cropping the figures to half-length and placing Christ's left arm and leg at an angle, David dissolves the boundary between viewer and subject, as though allowing us to join the Holy Family at home. Joseph stands protectively close by, holding a bowl of porridge kept warm by a lid that supports two decaying apples—an exquisite still life and allusion to the Passion of Christ.

Quentin Metsys

Netherlandish, 1465/66–1530

Madonna of the Cherries, circa 1520–25

Oil on panel, 75.3 × 62.9 cm

(25 5/8 × 23 3/4 in.), 2024.56

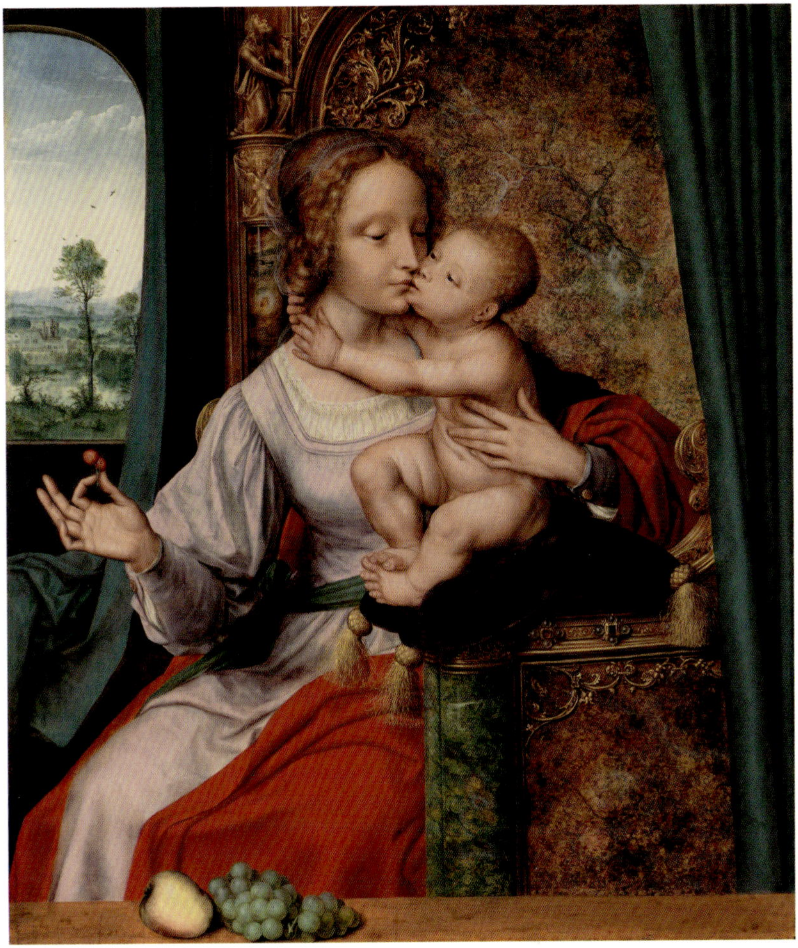

In this striking painting, one of the artist's most celebrated works, Metsys situates a tender portrayal of mother and son in a splendid setting to celebrate the essential human bond at the center of the Christian devotional tradition. Christ, portrayed as a robust infant, lovingly kisses the Virgin, who squeezes him tightly. They are seated on an immense throne comprised of precious stones, adorned with gold tracery and jewels, enclosed by velvet curtains. The precisely rendered still life in the foreground signifies Christ's role as the new Adam (apple) and the Eucharist (grapes). The Virgin delicately flourishes a stem of red cherries, the fruit of paradise whose rich color alludes to future holy blood of Christ's passion and sacrifice on the cross.

Martin Schongauer

German, circa 1450/53–1491

Madonna and Child in a Window,

circa 1485–90

Oil on panel, 16.5 × 11 cm (6½ × 4⁵⁄₁₆ in.),

97.PB.23

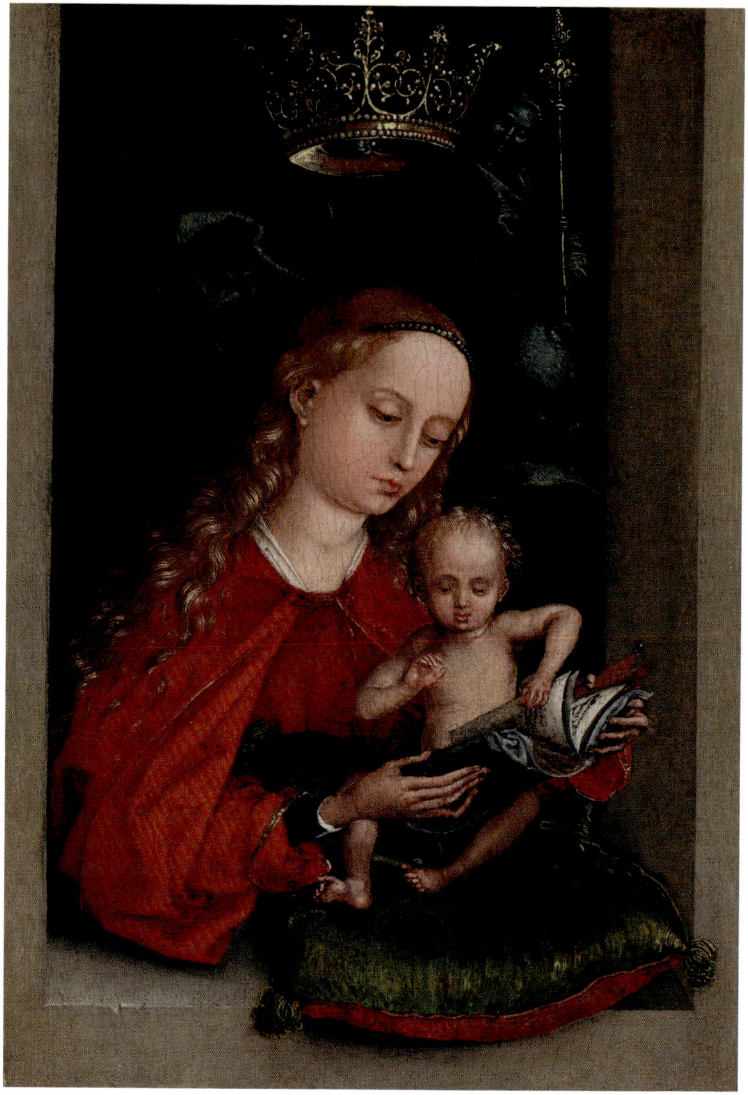

In a scene that symbolizes the Virgin's role as the tutor of Jesus Christ, she lovingly restrains the Christ child as she reads to him from a book by the light of the open window. Seated on a plush, tasseled cushion, Jesus rifles through the pages, the taut angles of his feet and elbows revealing his excitement. This tiny panel, intended for private devotion, showcases Schongauer's astonishingly skillful rendering of materials and visual effects, such as the glittering jeweled crown and scepter held by the diaphanous angel. *Madonna and Child in a Window* is one of only seven paintings by Schongauer, who is more widely known as an influential printmaker.

Lucas Cranach the Elder

German, 1472–1553

A Faun and His Family with a Slain Lion,

circa 1526

Oil on panel, 82.9 × 56.2 cm

(32⅝ × 22⅛ in.), 2003.100

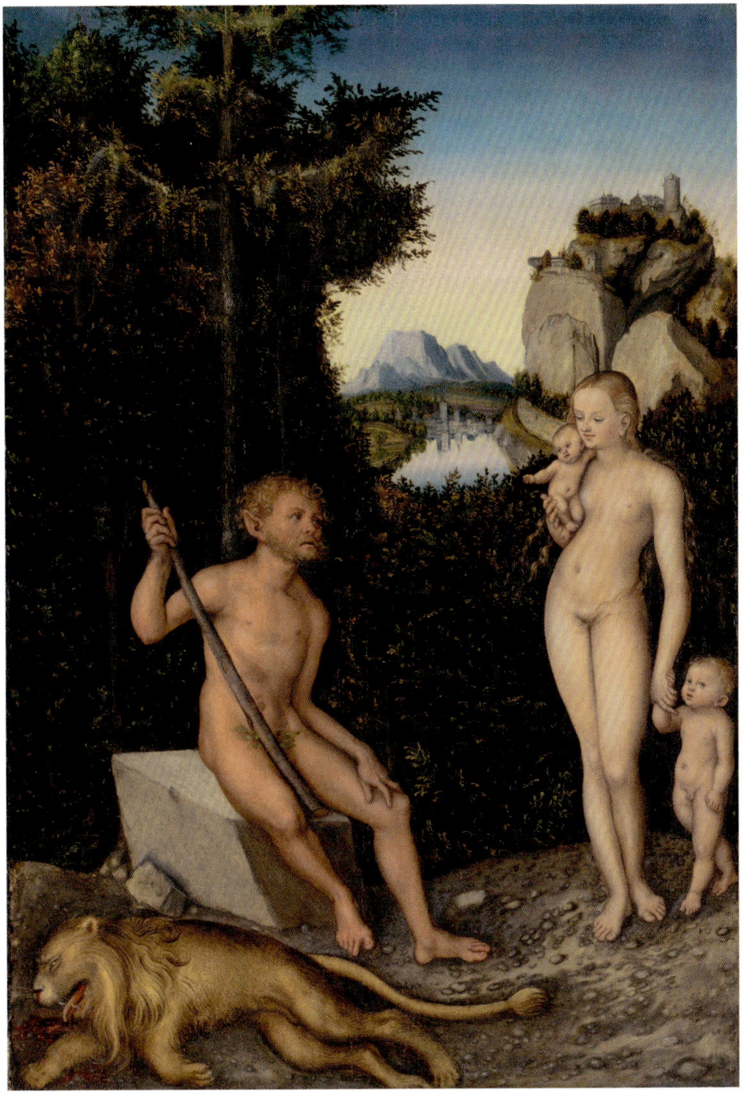

As court painter to the electors of Saxony in Wittenberg, Germany, Cranach devised highly original imagery for his sophisticated patrons. His mythological scenes of the late 1520s blend native German and classical literary sources and feature his signature sinuous female nudes. While the precise subject of this panel remains elusive, it conveys the essence of beloved characters from local lore—forest dwellers who reside beyond civilization and live a simple, heroic existence in the wilderness. Here, a faun, identified by his distinctively shaped ears, sits on a hewn block, marking the boundary between his idyllic native environment and the town visible in the distance.

Fra Bartolommeo (Baccio della Porta)

Italian, 1472–1517

The Rest on the Flight into Egypt with Saint John the Baptist, circa 1509

Oil on panel, 130.8 × 105.7 cm (51½ × 42⅝ in.), 96.PB.15

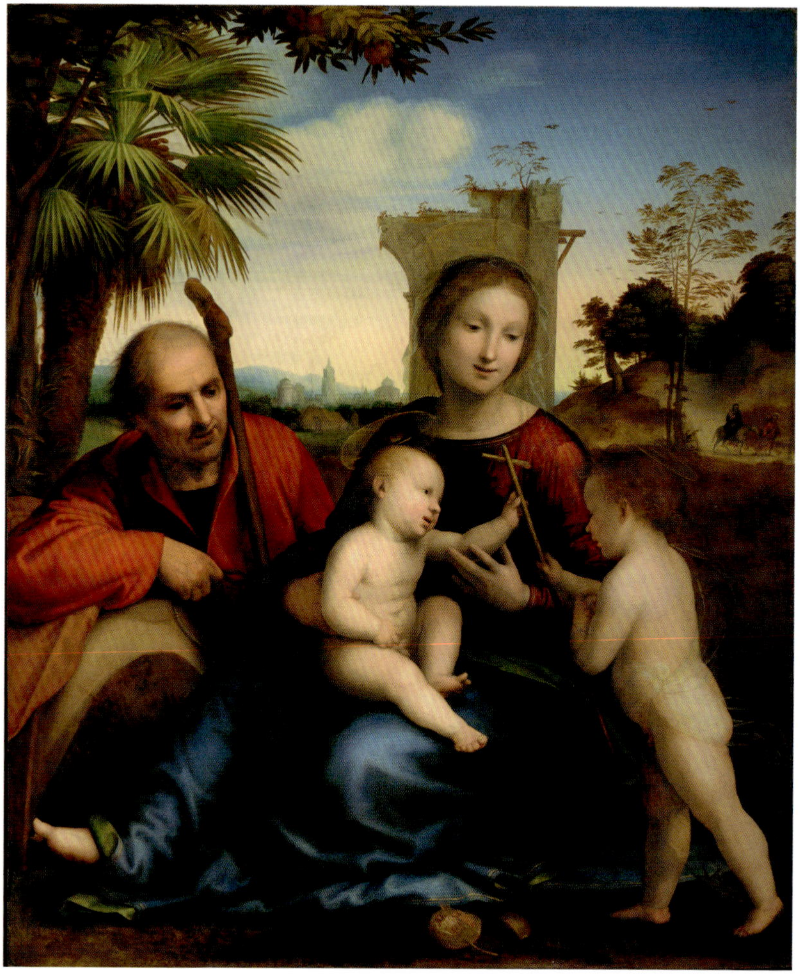

The Holy Family stops to rest during their flight into Egypt, having safely escaped Bethlehem and the massacre of male children ordered by King Herod. The Christ child, cradled in his mother's lap, reaches out to accept a small cross proffered by the young Saint John the Baptist—a premonition of Christ's future sacrifice. Other hints at what lies ahead include the date palm and pomegranate trees, traditional iconographic symbols that prefigure Christ's death and rebirth, while the crumbling building in the background signifies the pagan order, to be rebuilt as the Christian Church, personified by the Virgin Mary. Fra Bartolommeo, a Dominican friar whose harmonious style led him to become one of the foremost Florentine painters of his time, carried out this image at the height of his career.

Giulio Romano (Giulio Pippi)

Italian, before 1499–1546

The Holy Family, circa 1520–23

Oil (and tempera?) on panel,
77.5 × 61.9 cm (30½ × 24⅜ in.), 95.PB.64

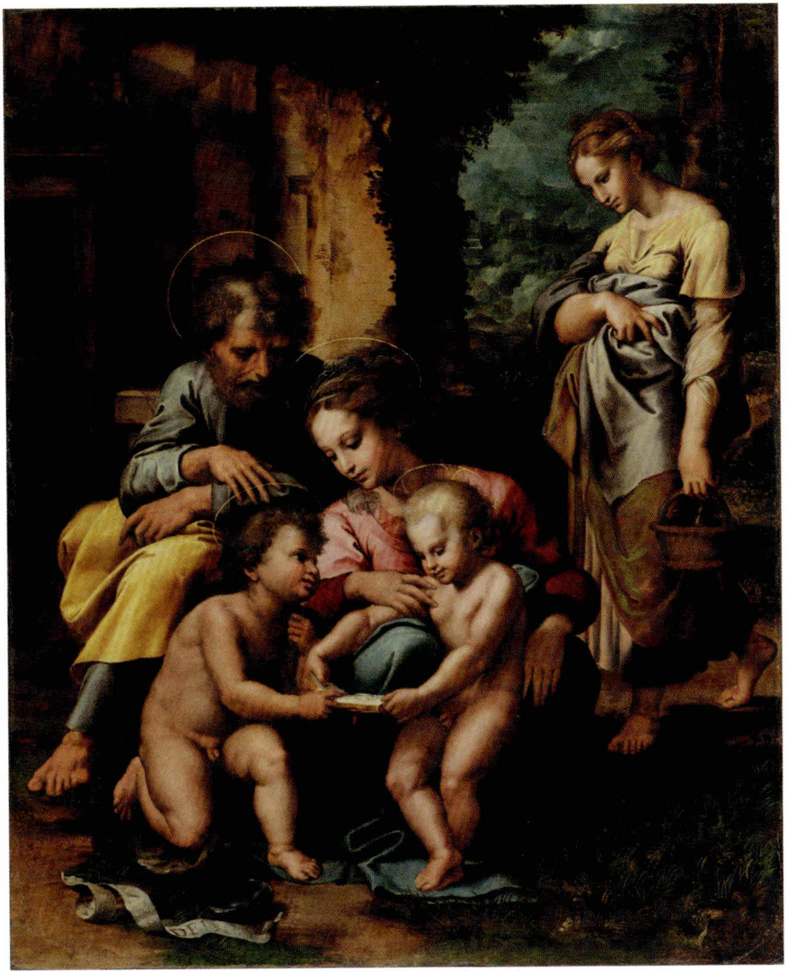

Enigmatic and engaging, this painting depicts the Christ child meeting the young Saint John the Baptist. Giulio positioned the two boys in the foreground, precociously handling a book, while Mary and Joseph look on. A woman approaches the group from the right; she holds a basket with two turtledoves, a detail related to a post-childbirth ritual of purification not usually found in such scenes. The metallic colors and brawny bodies are characteristic of Giulio's works, while the tightly interlocked figures and idealized female faces show his conscious adaptation of the late style of his teacher, Raphael (1483–1520).

Jacopo Pontormo (Jacopo Carucci)

Italian, 1494–1557

Portrait of a Halberdier (Francesco Guardi?), 1529–30

Oil (and tempera?) on panel, transferred to canvas, 95.3 × 73 cm (37½ × 28¾ in.), 89.PA.49

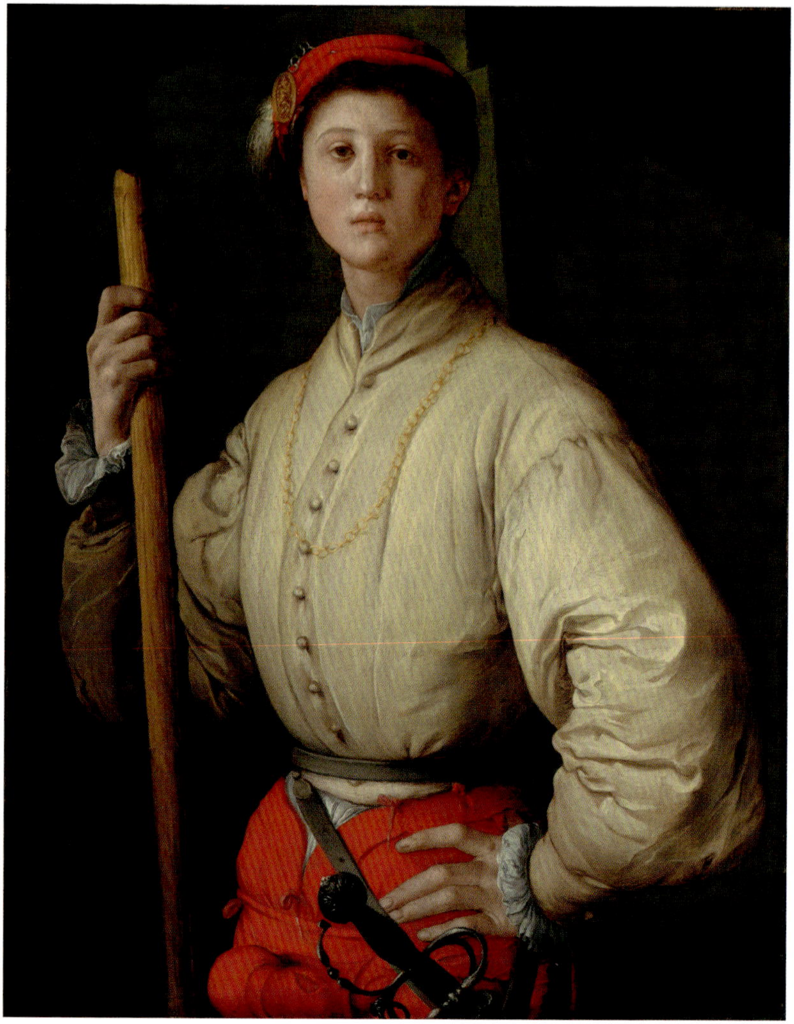

In this masterpiece of Renaissance portraiture, Pontormo depicts an armed youth standing before a fortification. His elegant pose exudes confidence, but his wide eyes suggest unease. Pontormo was highly sought after as a portraitist by the sixteenth-century Florentine elite, and this painting was long thought to represent the young Cosimo I de' Medici (1519–1574), the future Grand Duke of Tuscany. A different interpretation, based on an account by Pontormo's contemporary Giorgio Vasari, a chronicler of artists' lives, suggests that the subject may be a young man named Francesco Guardi (1514–1554), whom Pontormo is said to have painted during the 1529–30 siege of Florence. The age and presentation of the halberdier align well with Guardi at that time, and the dating accords with what we know of Pontormo's own biography and style.

Jan Gossaert

Netherlandish, circa 1478–1532

Francisco de los Cobos y Molina, circa 1530–32

Oil on panel, 43.8 × 33.7 cm (17¼ × 13¼ in.), 88.PB.43

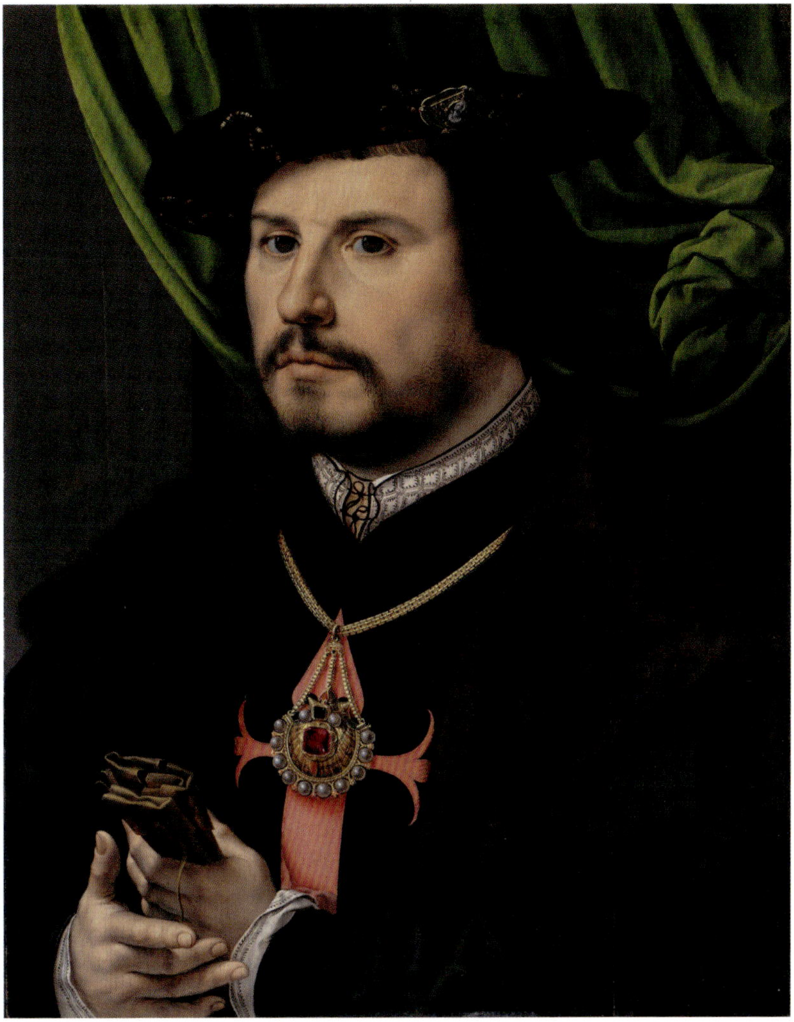

Working in the last year of his life, Gossaert captured the robust features and dignified character of his subject during a sojourn at the imperial Habsburg court in Brussels. The sitter is probably Francisco de los Cobos (1477–1547), a Spanish nobleman, art collector, and powerful secretary and chief financial adviser to Holy Roman Emperor Charles V (r. 1519–56). Gossaert's smooth and descriptive brushwork portrays the sitter's elegant attire in detail, from his leather gloves to the intricate jewel on his cap and the splendid scallop pendant of the chivalric Order of Santiago, of which Cobos was Comendador Mayor. Cobos elegantly acknowledges the viewer with an inviting gesture of his right hand.

Agnolo Bronzino

Italian, 1503–1572

Virgin and Child with Saint Elizabeth and Saint John the Baptist, circa 1540–45

Oil on panel, 102.7 × 83.4 cm

(40 7/16 × 32 13/16 in.), 2019.116

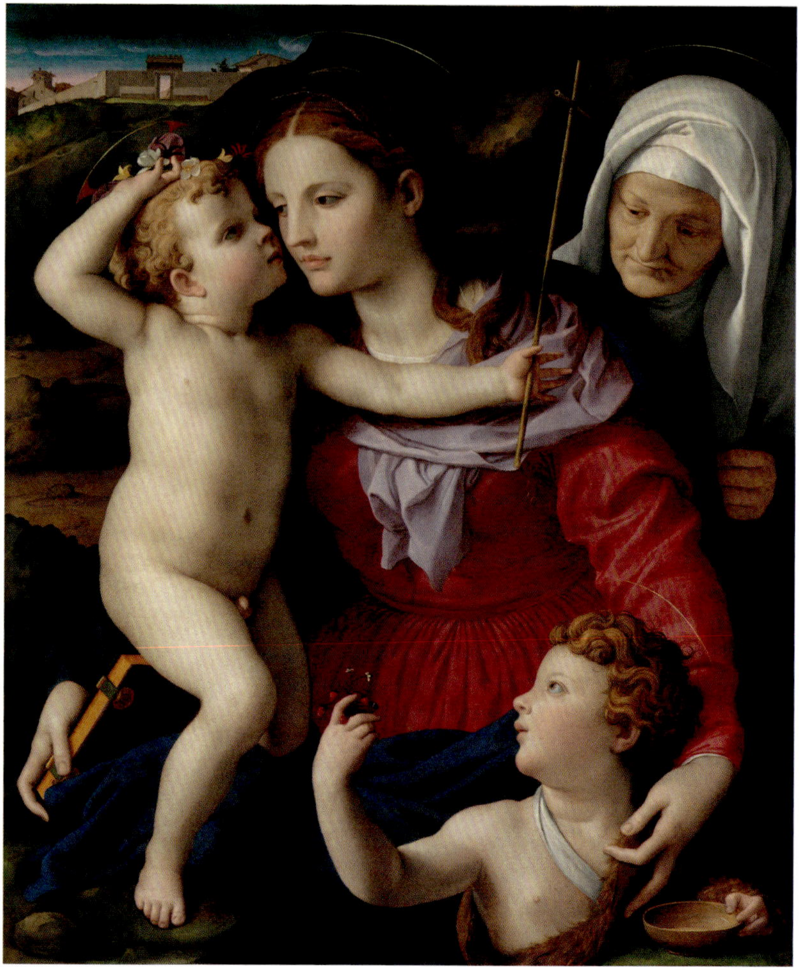

An infant Christ, leaning against his mother, holds a small cross in one hand and raises flowers to his head with the other. Below, the young Saint John the Baptist, only partially visible, offers him wild strawberries, a portent of Christ's Crucifixion. John's elderly mother, Elizabeth, peers over the Virgin Mary's shoulder. Bronzino represents the figures closely entwined, their graceful forms filling the composition. Their gazes, however, do not meet, and their expressions are detached, if not—in the case of the Virgin—inscrutable. Painted with crisp outlines and a surprising combination of subtly contrasting tones, Bronzino's image feels lavishly decorative, with a luminous surface intended to appeal to the refined taste of his patrons at the noble Medici court in Florence.

Parmigianino (Francesco Mazzola)

Italian, 1503–1540

Virgin and Child with Saint John the Baptist and Mary Magdalene, circa 1535–40

Oil on paper, laid down on panel, 75.9 × 59.7 cm (29 7/8 × 23 1/2 in.), 2017.22

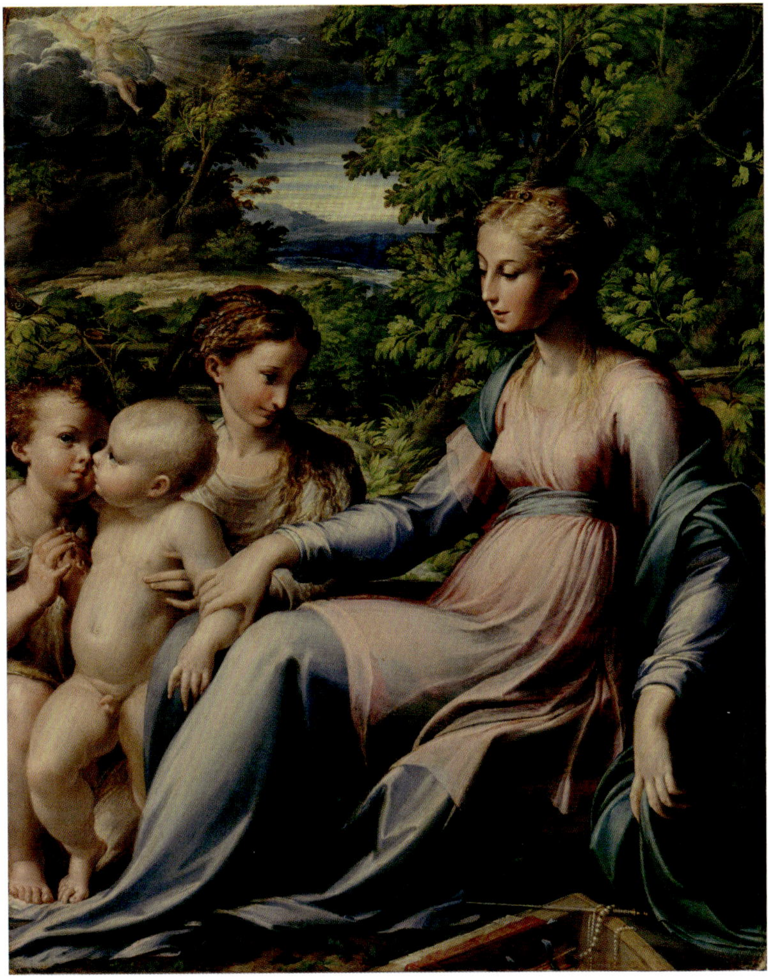

This charming work is unconventional in both support and iconography. It was painted on several sheets of paper, which had been carefully laid down and smoothed onto a wood panel. Extremely well preserved, it exhibits Parmigianino's characteristic enamel-like paint surface and meticulous attention to detail. The unusual scene shows the Virgin seated in a landscape, admiring her son as he embraces the young Saint John the Baptist. Both children are supported by Mary Magdalene—who appears a second time in the background, ascending to heaven. Parmigianino imbues the flowing drapery, glistening hair, and vibrant landscape with a sense of subtle yet pervasive movement. The painting, probably intended for private devotion, presents a superlative example of the artist's mature style.

Dosso Dossi (Giovanni di Niccolò de Lutero)
Italian, circa 1490–1542

An Allegory of Fortune, circa 1530
Oil on canvas, 181.3 × 194.9 cm
(71³/₈ × 76³/₄ in.), 89.PA.32

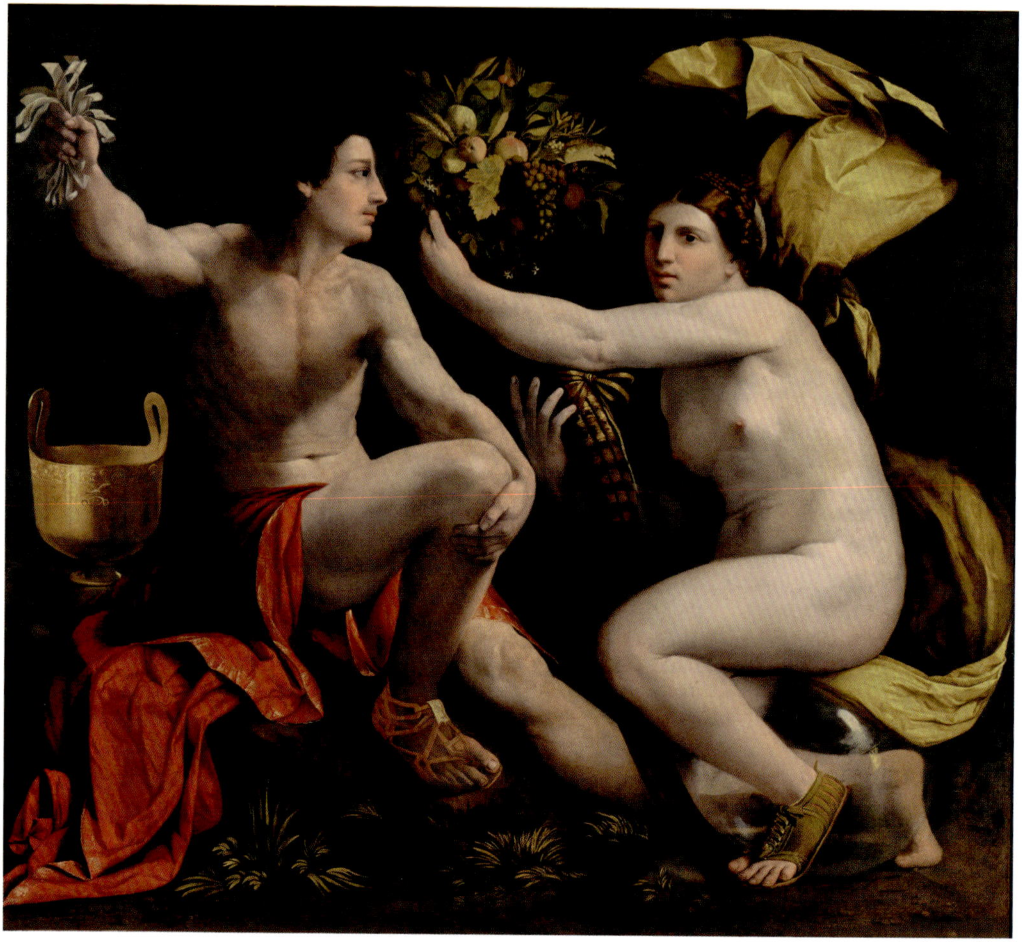

Dosso's strange, sophisticated painting shows a personification of Fortune kneeling beside her seated consort, Chance. The allegory captures the idea that Fortune, the indifferent force that determines fate, is capable of bestowing not only good luck but also bad. She rests on a bubble, symbolic of the fleeting nature of her favors, while her billowing drapery implies that she is as changeable as the wind. Chance, holding up lots, or lottery tickets, looks to her to decide the outcome of his wager. Dosso probably produced the allegory for Isabella d'Este (1474–1539), marchioness of Mantua, whose personal emblems included a bundle of lots.

Giovanni Girolamo Savoldo
Italian, active 1506–circa 1548

Saint Mary Magdalene at the Sepulchre,
circa 1530s
Oil on canvas, 92.7 × 79.4 cm
(36½ × 31¼ in.), 97.PA.55

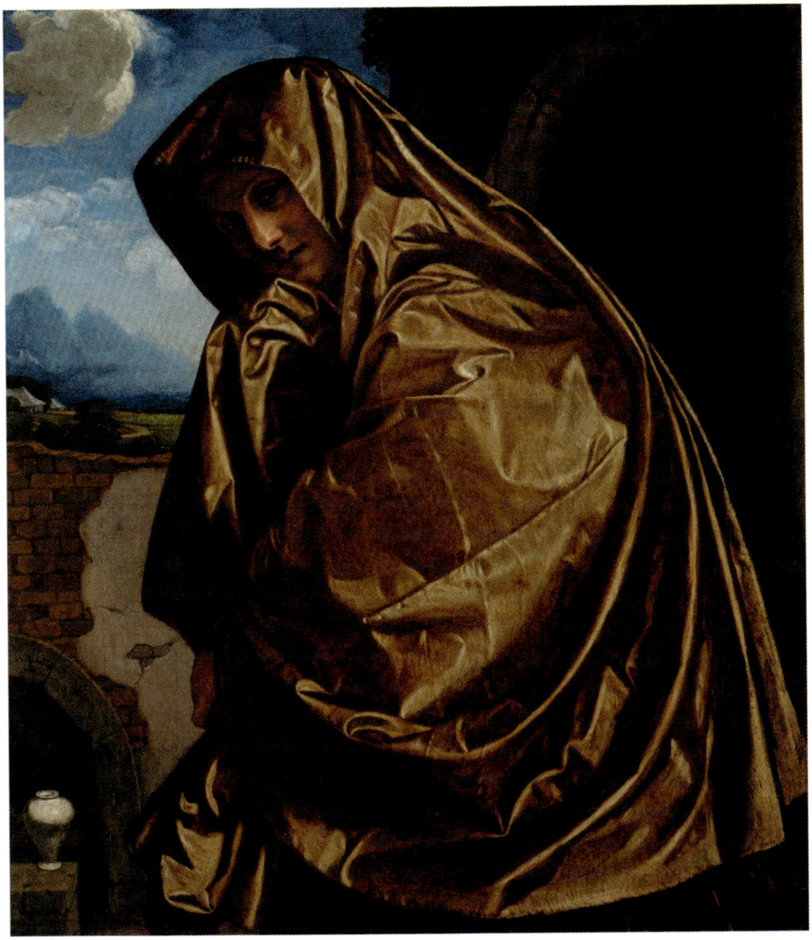

Celebrated for his mastery of light effects, Savoldo here uses illumination to further enrich a miraculous story. According to the New Testament, on the third day after Christ's Crucifixion, Mary Magdalene visited his tomb at dawn, to anoint his body with oil. Finding it empty, she encountered a man whom she did not at first recognize, but who was in fact the risen Christ. Savoldo depicts Mary Magdalene in the moments before she realizes Christ's identity. She turns and looks out from under her glistening shawl, her impassive face partially hidden in shadow. Her iridescent drapery, meanwhile, fills the canvas, reflecting the glow of divine presence. Savoldo painted four slightly different versions of this scene, each defined by a singular attention to light.

Jacopo Bassano

Italian, circa 1510–1592

The Miracle of the Quails, 1554

Oil on canvas, 150 × 235 cm

(59 1/16 × 92 1/2 in.), 2021.60

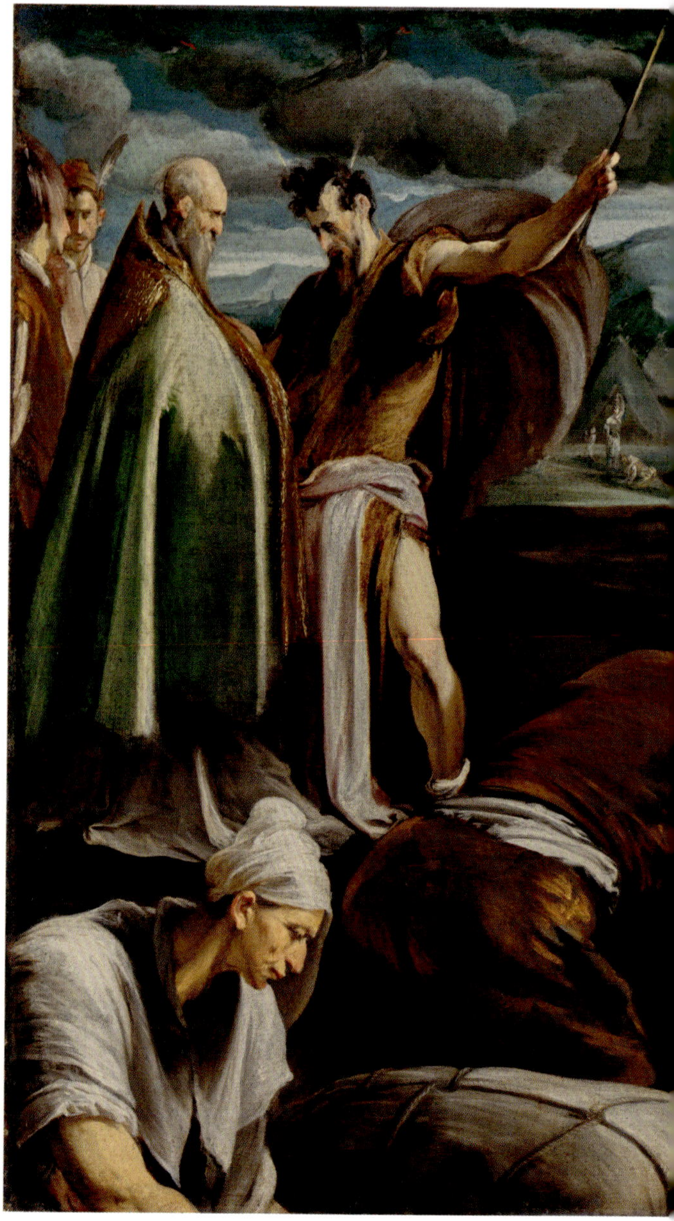

Jacopo's monumental *Miracle of the Quails* elevates an obscure story into a grand narrative. In the biblical tale, Israelites in the wilderness are saved from starvation by God's provision of quails falling from the sky. The artist animates the subject through his figures' dynamic poses and his attention to naturalistic details. The background landscape evokes the mountainous region overlooking Bassano del Grappa, Jacopo's hometown, in the Veneto region of northern Italy. Commissioned by a Venetian nobleman, the large-scale painting is probably one of a pair: another biblical picture of comparable size and format (*Lazarus and the Rich Man*, now at the Cleveland Museum of Art) is thought to have been its pendant.

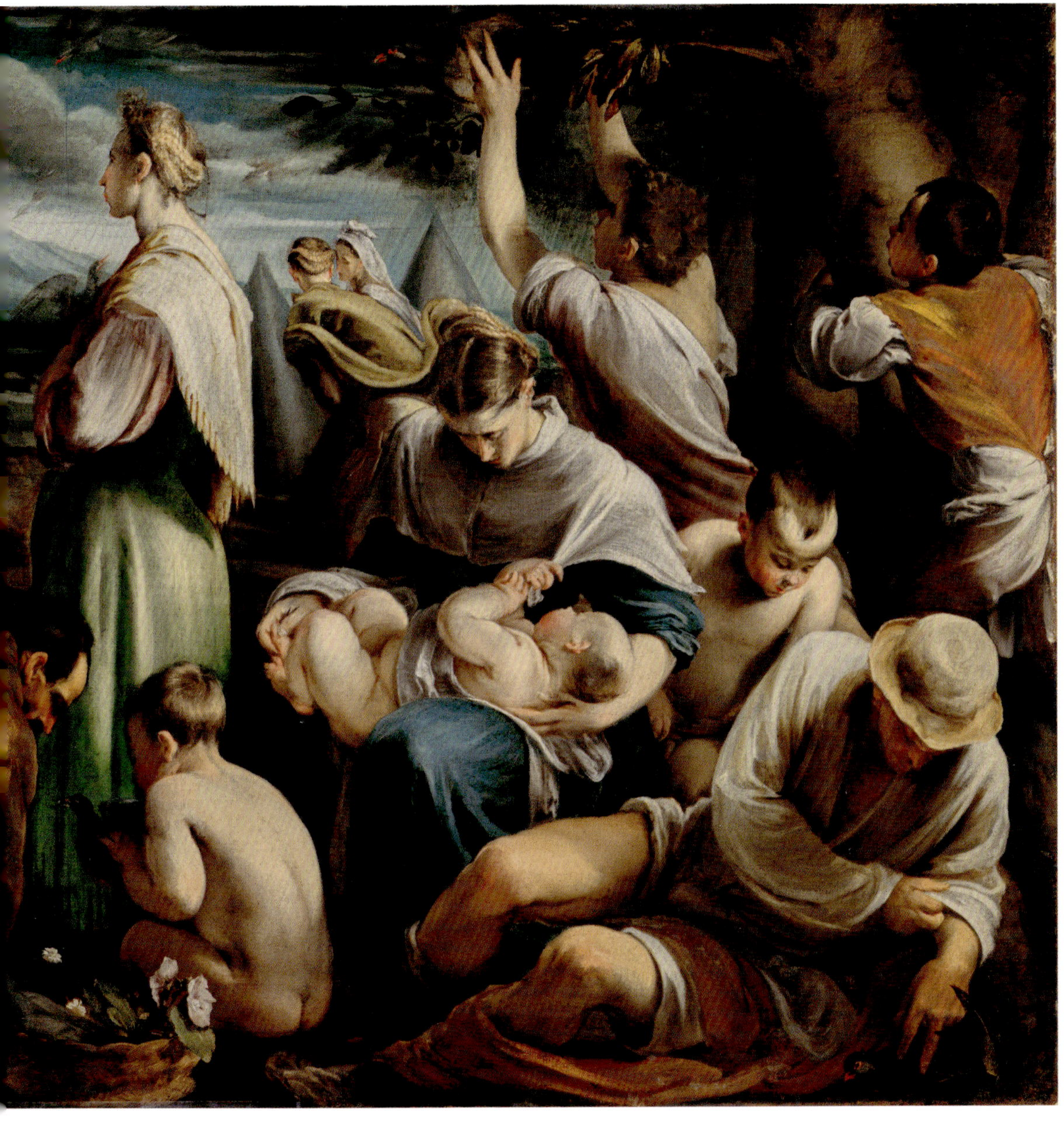

Titian (Tiziano Vecellio)

Italian, circa 1487–1576

Venus and Adonis, circa 1555–60

Oil on canvas, 160 × 196.5 cm

(63 × 77⅜ in.), 92.PA.42

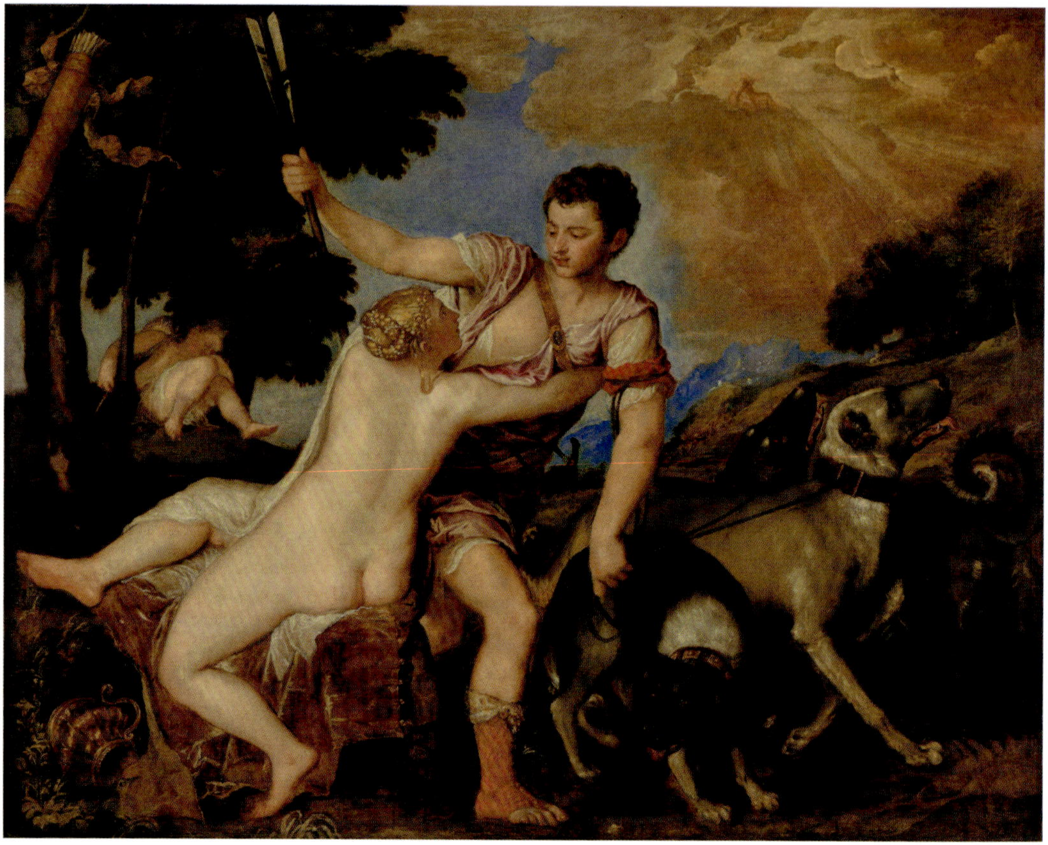

Originally designed for King Philip II of Spain, *Venus and Adonis* is among Titian's most famous mythological compositions. In the story, as told by the ancient Roman poet Ovid in the *Metamorphoses*, the goddess Venus implores Adonis, her mortal lover, not to go hunting. Afraid for his life, she clings to him as his dogs strain at their leashes, echoing his impatience. Cupid sleeps in the lush landscape beyond, symbolizing Adonis's obliviousness to his own danger. The hunt ends tragically when Adonis is fatally wounded by a wild boar. Titian captured the scene's poignancy through a combination of rich colors and shimmering highlights, applied with loose, energetic strokes of paint.

Lavinia Fontana

Italian, 1552–1614

The Wedding Feast at Cana,

circa 1575–80

Oil on copper, 47.3 × 36.2 cm

(18⅝ × 14¹/₁₄ in.), 2022.28

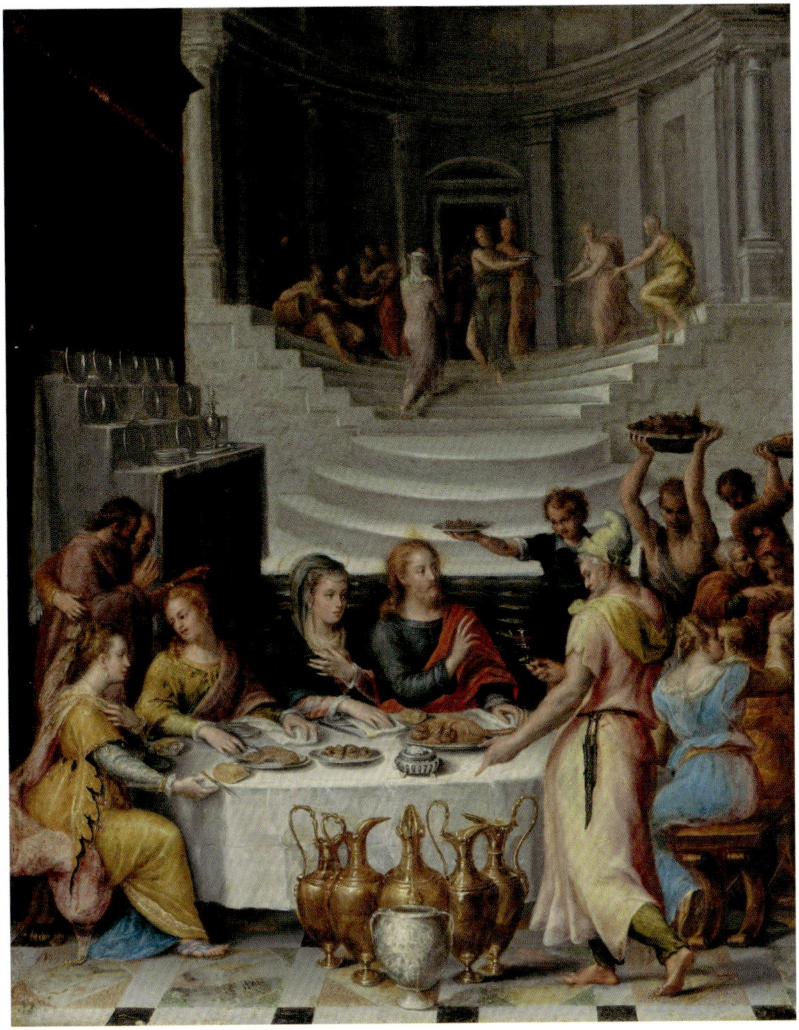

One of the first female painters to attain widespread fame in Renaissance Italy, Lavinia Fontana pioneered the use of copper as a support for small paintings meant for private devotion. This work, for example, depicts the biblical episode in which Jesus and his mother, the Virgin Mary, are guests at a wedding. When Mary notices that the wine has run out, Jesus demonstrates his divinity by turning water into wine. Fontana set the scene against a rich architectural backdrop, highlighting the golden jugs—evidence of the miracle—in the foreground. She applied the paint in painstakingly thin layers supplemented with rich glazes, resulting in a polished, luminous composition brimming with intricate detail.

Ludger tom Ring the Younger

German, 1522–1584

Bouquet of Flowers in a Two-Handled Vase, early 1560s

Oil on panel, 38 × 29 cm (14 15/16 × 11 7/16 in.), 2023.101

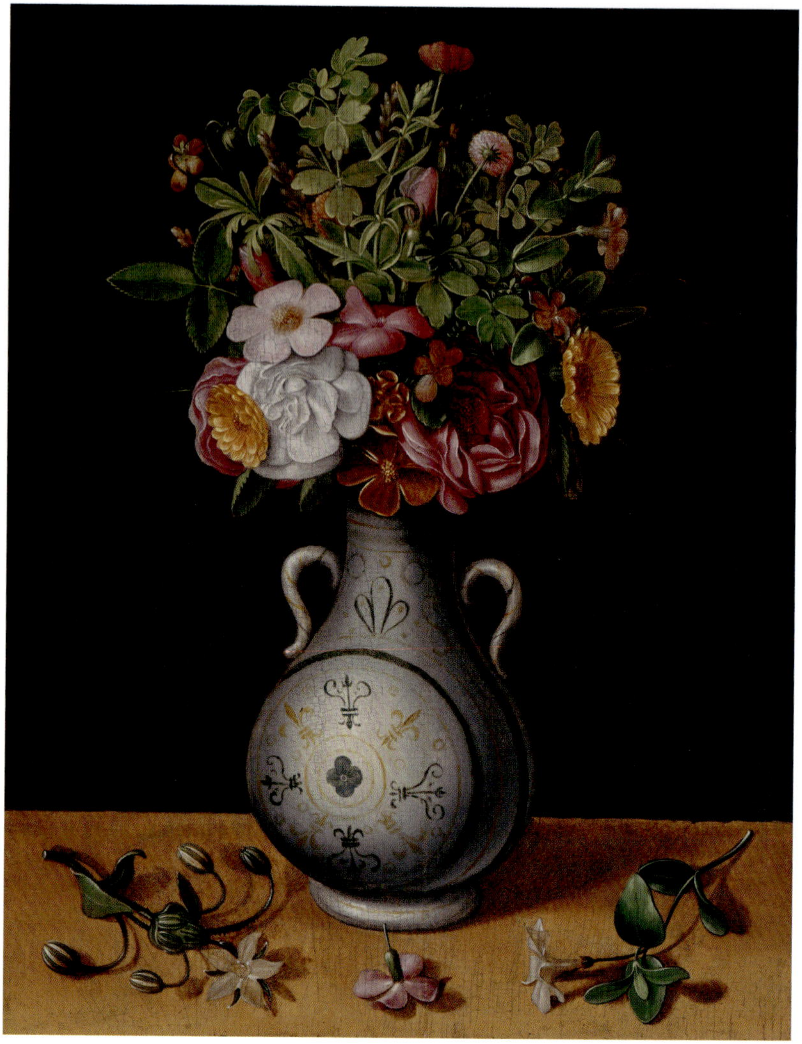

Tom Ring the Younger, a German painter originally from Westphalia who worked briefly in Antwerp before pursuing a career as a portraitist in Braunschweig, created some of the earliest paintings in Northern Europe depicting flowers as an independent subject. Here, he combines cultivated blooms such as roses with bright field flowers and verdant foliage into a dense arrangement, placed on a table. A luxurious enameled opaque-glass vase displays the stems to advantage. By adopting visual strategies from German portraiture—situating the vase against an inky black background and illuminating it with strong light from the left side—Tom Ring imbues the bouquet with a sense of monumentality.

Hans Hoffmann

German, 1545/50–1591/92

A Hare in the Forest, circa 1585

Oil on panel, 62.2 × 78.4 cm

(24½ × 30⅞ in.), 2001.12

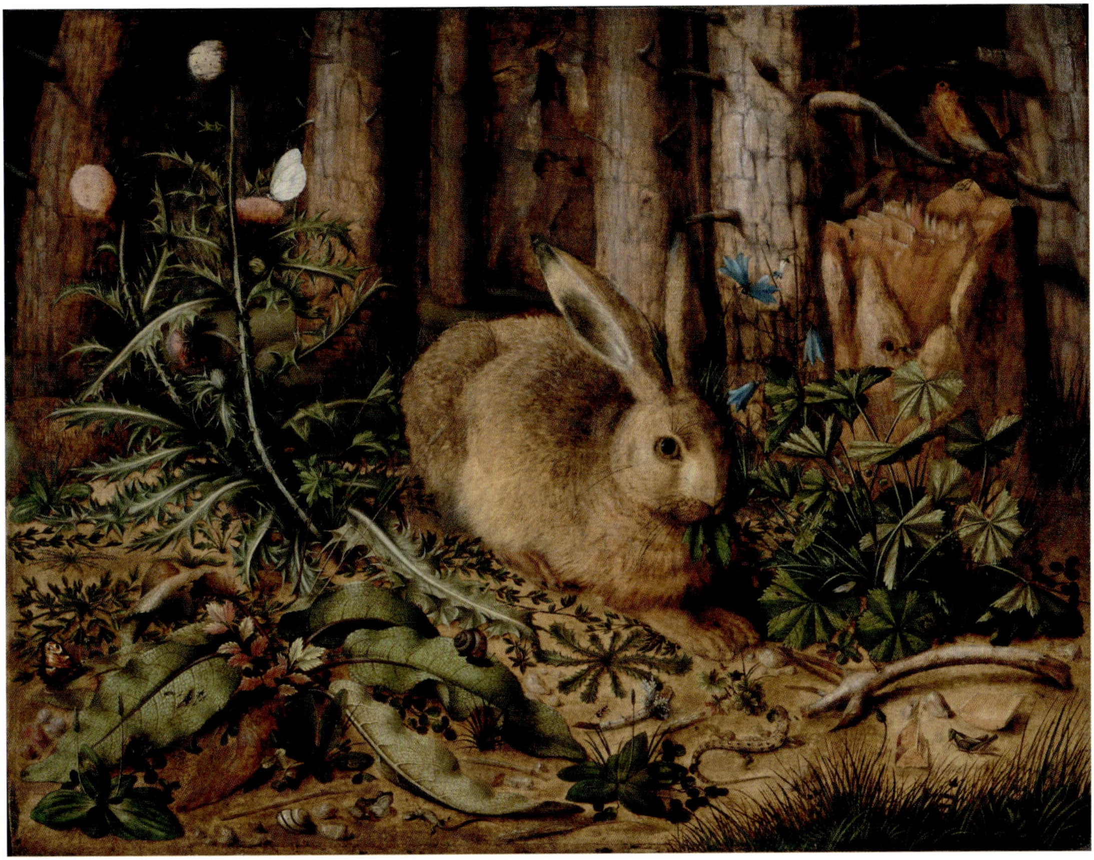

Hoffmann was among the most inventive artists to take inspiration from the animal studies made a generation earlier by the influential German painter and printmaker Albrecht Dürer (1471–1528). The subject of this innovative scene is a hare grazing in a meadow on the edge of a coniferous forest. Hoffmann assembled a variety of plants, small animals, insects, and even a robin—first drawn in separate watercolor studies—to complete what is one of the first narratives of everyday nature. The artist's crisp, precise brushwork allows for the identification of all elements, most of which are not typically found together. Holy Roman Emperor Rudolf II (1552–1612), who avidly collected wonders of art and of nature at his court in Prague, acquired this scene directly from the artist.

Artemisia Gentileschi

Italian, 1593–after 1654

Lucretia, circa 1627

Oil on canvas, 92.9 × 72.7 cm

(36 9/16 × 28 5/8 in.), 2021.14

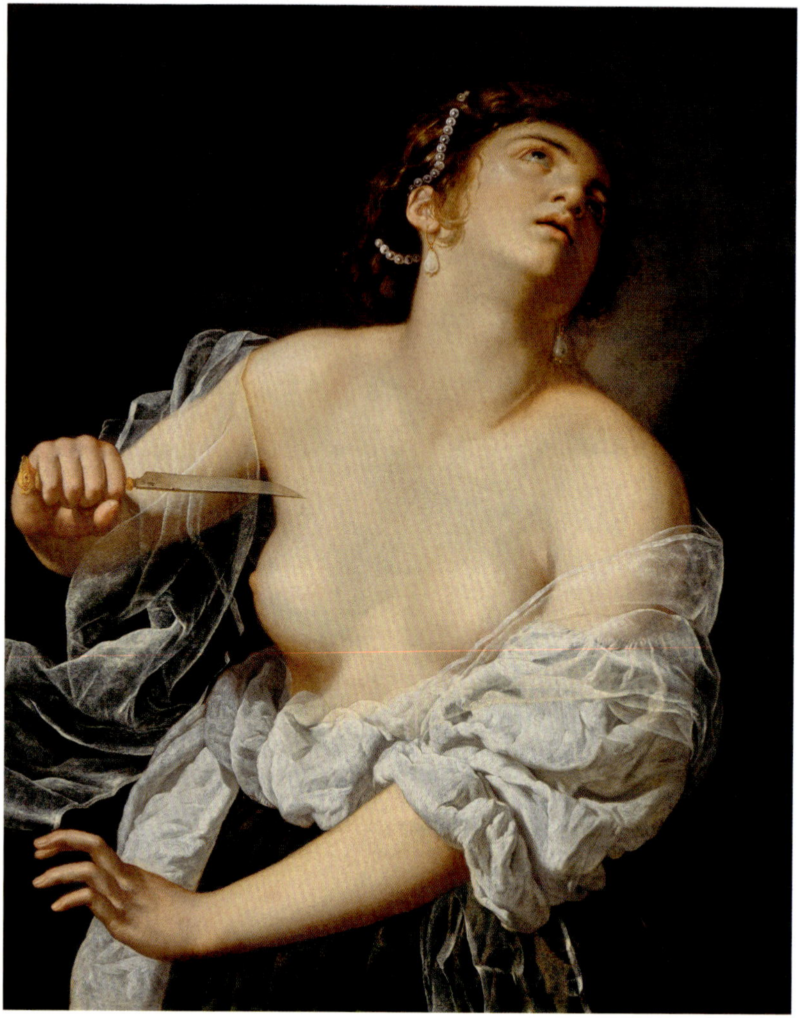

Lucretia, an ancient Roman noblewoman, emerges from the shadows with a dagger in hand, poised to pierce her chest. The beauty of her translucent skin, the pearls in her hair, and the luxurious fabrics all stand in contrast to the horror of what is about to unfold—and that which preceded. According to legend, after being raped by a prince of Rome, Lucretia called for vengeance before taking her own life, eliciting widespread anger and grief and sparking a rebellion that turned her into a martyr for freedom. Artemisia Gentileschi painted many female heroes known for their strength and passion, approaching her subjects with empathy and translating their experiences into emotionally complex paintings. Lucretia's story likely resonated with the artist, for she, too, had experienced sexual violence as a young woman.

Annibale Carracci

Italian, 1560–1609

Madonna and Child with Saints Lucy, Dominic, and Louis of France, about 1596–98

Oil on copper, 43.5 × 33.7 cm (17⅛ × 13¼ in.), 2023.3

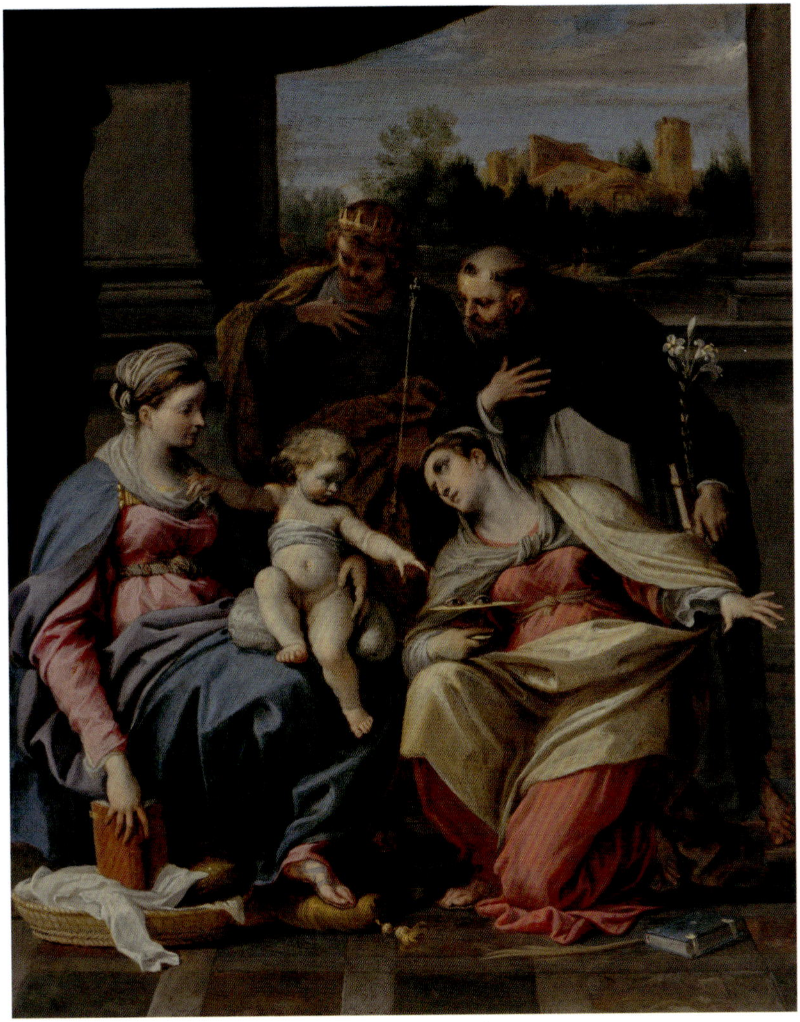

Executed on a small copper plate, Annibale's composition is simultaneously intimate and monumental, almost an altarpiece in miniature. The Christ child sits at center on a pillow in the Virgin Mary's lap. With his outstretched left hand he points to the plate on which Saint Lucy's eyes, the symbol of her martyrdom, rest. Behind this principal grouping, two additional saints—Louis of France, with scepter and crown, and Dominic, holding a lily and a book—look on with intensity. Annibale imagined his figures, bathed in golden sunlight, within a classical loggia opening onto a landscape. We do not know who commissioned the work, but the three saints likely had relevance to the original patron.

Orazio Gentileschi

Italian, 1563–1639

Lot and His Daughters, circa 1622

Oil on canvas, 151.8 × 189.2 cm

(59¾ × 74½ in.), 98.PA.10

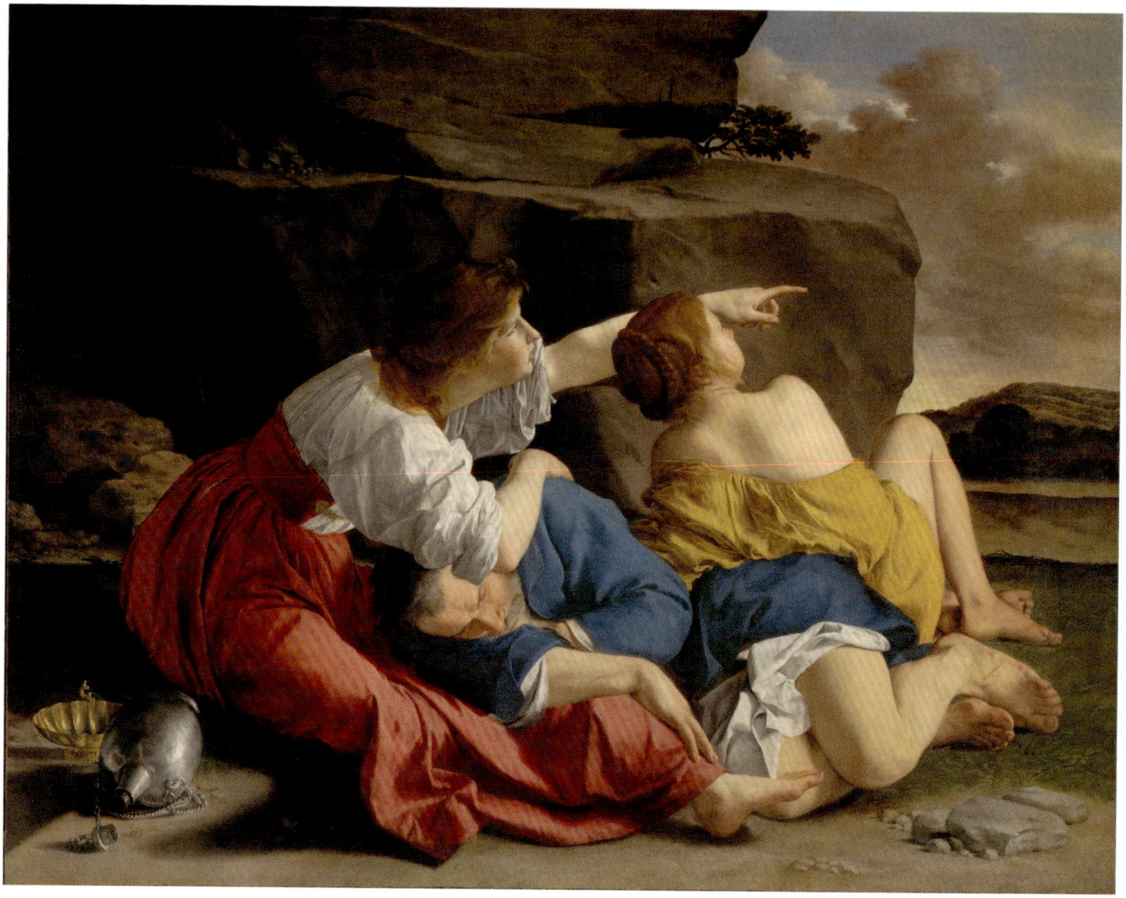

In this scene recounting an oft-told episode from the Bible, Lot's daughters, sheltering safely in the cave where they have taken refuge, are absorbed by an event taking place beyond the painting's borders: God's annihilation of the city of Sodom, burning in the distance. Believing that they alone survived to perpetuate the human race, the daughters have plied their father with alcohol, to aid their incestuous seduction of him. The elegant composition of the three interlocking figures, along with the luminous harmony of colors and the rich play of textures, characterizes the sophisticated and poetic style that made Orazio Gentileschi's works popular at royal courts across Europe.

Guercino
(Giovanni Francesco Barbieri)

Italian, 1591–1666

Pope Gregory XV, circa 1622–23

Oil on canvas, 133.4 × 97.8 cm

(52½ × 38½ in.), 87.PA.38

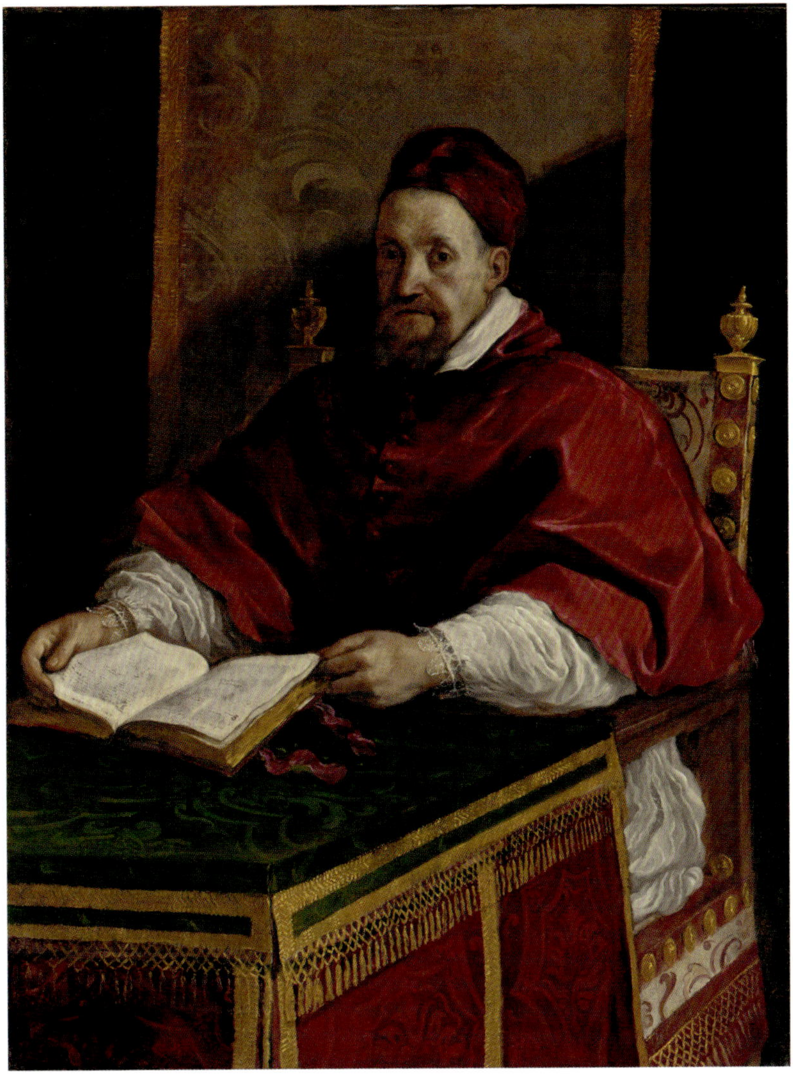

Though using a format that had become standard for papal portraiture since its adoption during the Renaissance, about a century before this painting was made, the artist deviated from tradition by placing less emphasis on the trappings of power and more on his subject's character. In 1621 Guercino was called to Rome from his hometown of Cento, in northern Italy, to work for the newly elected Pope Gregory XV (1554–1623). Instead of merely portraying the pontiff in his official capacity as head of the Roman Catholic Church, Guercino depicted him sympathetically in the last months of his life, worn down by the burdens of his role and in failing health.

Jusepe de Ribera
Spanish, 1591–1652
Euclid, circa 1630–35
Oil on canvas, 125.1 × 92.4 cm
(49¼ × 36⅜ in.), 2001.26

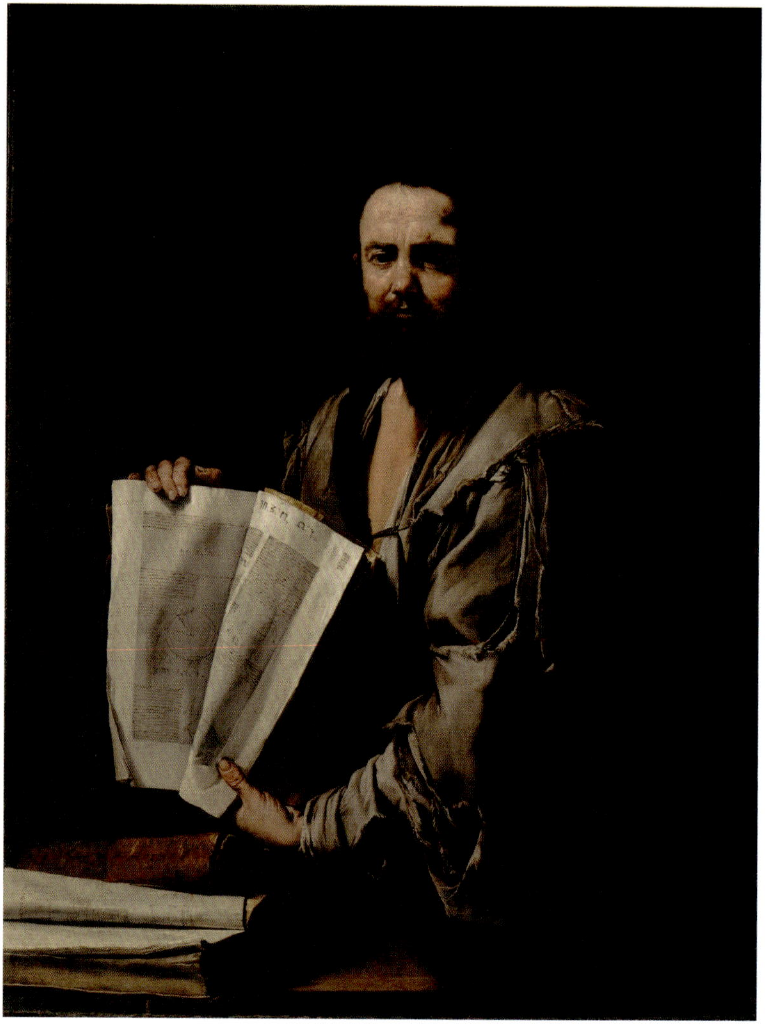

Although the subject of the ragged philosopher dates back to antiquity, the type gained popularity in the early seventeenth century with a revival of interest in the ancient Stoics. In this painting, Ribera depicts the moral ideal of stoicism: the neglect of outward appearance in devotion to intellectual pursuits. The figure's penetrating gaze and the mathematical diagrams in his book suggest that he represents the ancient Greek scholar and mathematician Euclid (active third century BCE). Characteristics of Ribera's early works are the strong contrasts of light and dark; the realistic depiction of his blackened fingers; and the torn garb and tattered book, which give the painting a visceral presence and emotional immediacy.

Valentin de Boulogne

French, 1591–1632

Christ and the Adulteress, circa 1620s

Oil on canvas, 167 × 221.3 cm

(65¾ × 87⅛ in.), 83.PA.259

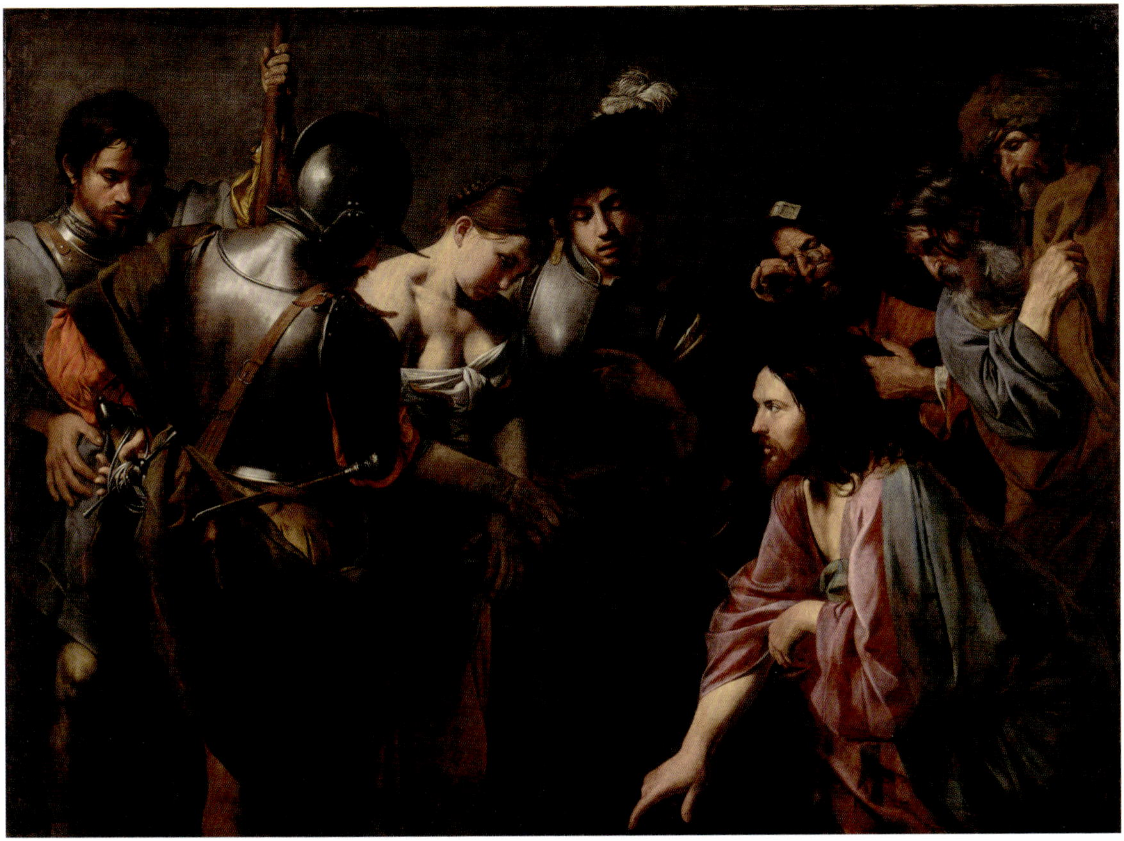

This painting recounts a story from the New Testament, that of the Pharisees asking Christ whether a woman who has committed adultery should be stoned, to which Christ replies, "He that is without sin among you, let him first cast a stone at her." Profoundly influenced by the stark realism and dramatic chiaroscuro (balance of light and shadow) pioneered by the Italian artist Caravaggio (1571–1610), Valentin applied variations of these techniques within a shallow, friezelike composition to convey the scene's emotion. The figures are highly individualized, especially the grizzled man with the weathered face who clasps his cape against his shoulder (right) and the elderly man nearby who holds his glasses to his nose and peers down at Christ. Valentin used contemporary working-class people as models, a practice initiated by Caravaggio.

Hendrick ter Brugghen

Dutch, 1588–1629

Bacchante with an Ape (Allegory of Taste), 1627

Oil on canvas, 102.9 × 89.2 cm (40½ × 35⅛ in.), 84.PA.5

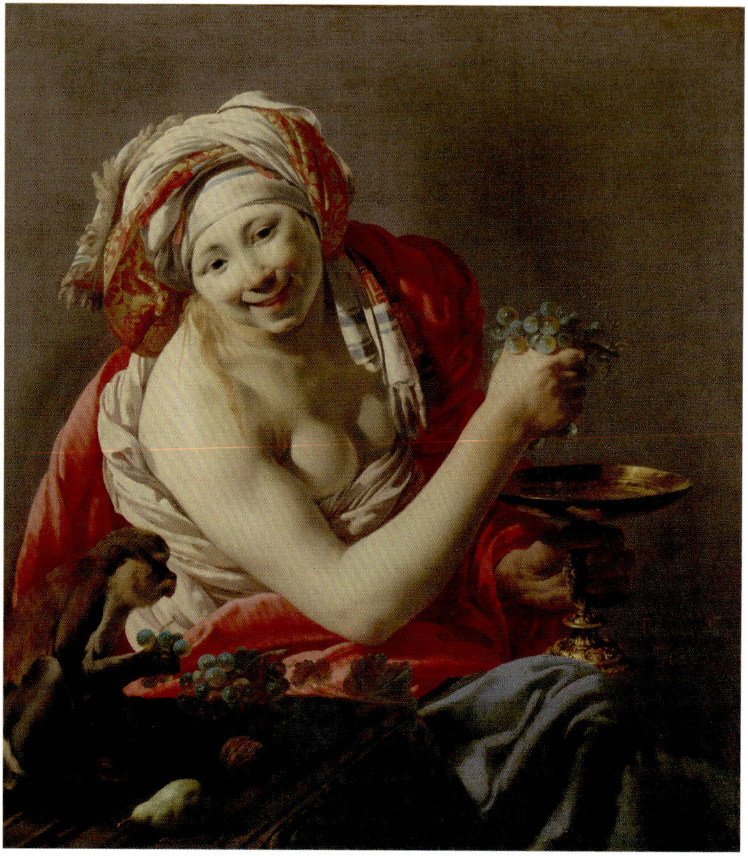

A grinning female devotee of the Roman wine god Bacchus, fancifully attired and somewhat disheveled, leans forward and squeezes a fistful of grapes into a large gilt tazza (footed cup). Catching the viewer's eye, she invites them to join in the drunken carousing. The monkey beside her emulates the gesture, thereby mocking the human tendency to thoughtlessly follow the actions of others. The personification of the sense of taste as a female figure drinking wine had a long history in the Netherlands. Ter Brugghen may have been inspired by the "portraits" of Bacchus he saw while in Rome from 1604 to 1614, and the marblelike flesh and brilliant textiles in this work exemplify his exuberant translation of these models upon his return to his native Utrecht.

Bartolomeo Manfredi

Italian, 1582–1622

A Drinking and Musical Party, circa 1615–20

Oil on canvas, 129.5 × 190.5 cm (51 × 75 in.), 2024.24

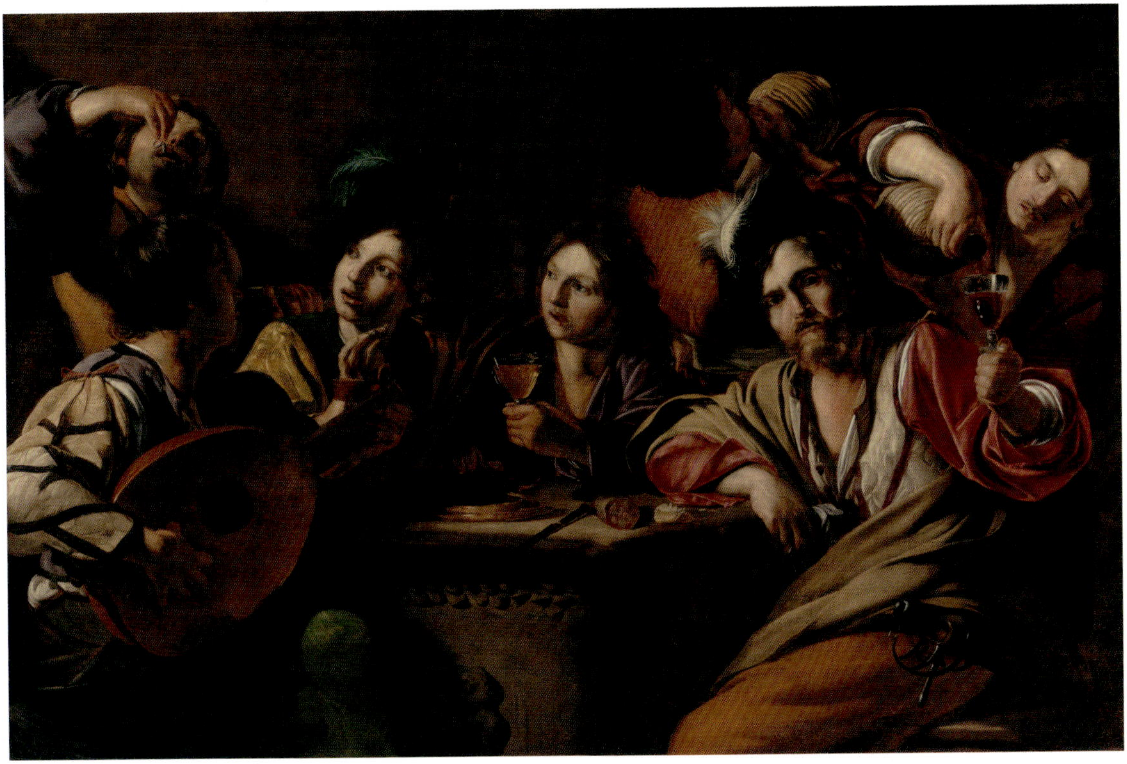

Seven young men gather around a table to eat and drink; an elegantly dressed man at the bottom left entertains them by playing a lute. In early seventeenth-century Italy, Manfredi was instrumental in popularizing such images of lively gatherings of half-length figures painted from life. The artist's strikingly realistic depictions of everyday scenes, characterized by a sumptuous color palette and stark contrasts of light and shadow, made him the first and most significant follower of the immensely influential style initiated by the Italian artist Caravaggio (1571–1610). Such pictures, often executed on large horizontal canvases like this one, were made for a lucrative market of exacting private collectors.

Peter Paul Rubens

Flemish, 1577–1640

The Calydonian Boar Hunt, circa 1611–12

Oil on panel, 59.2 × 89.7 cm

(23 5/16 × 35 5/16 in.), 2006.4

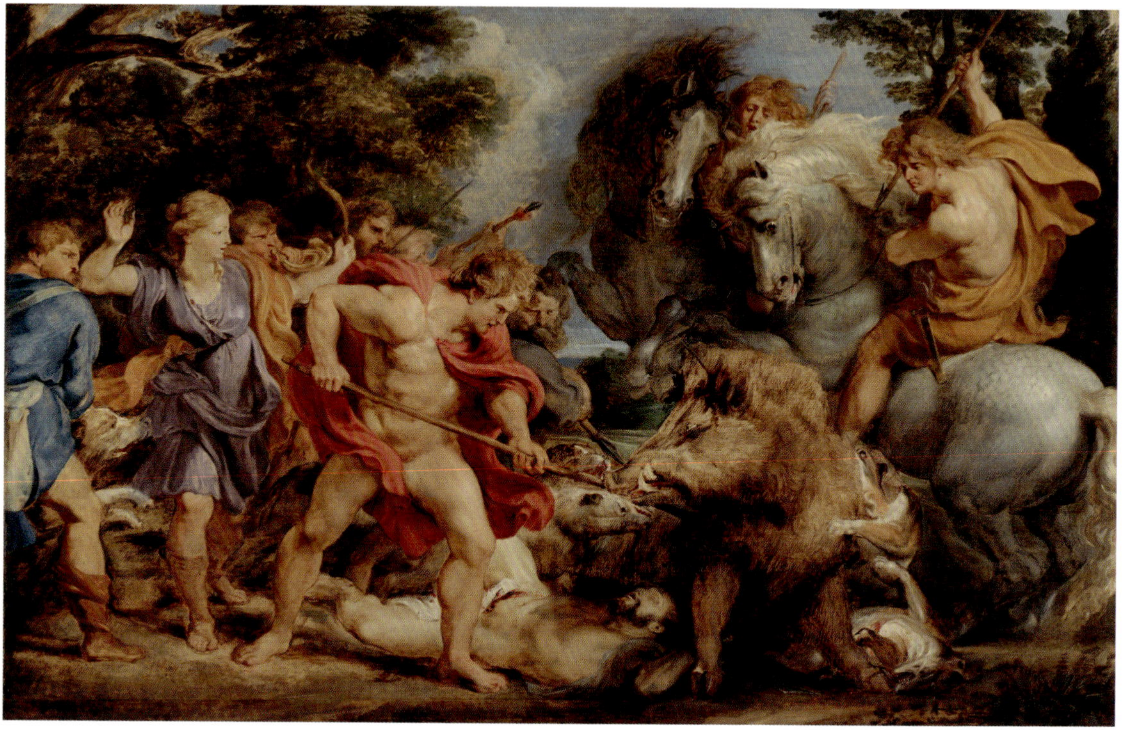

This thrilling confrontation between man and beast is Rubens's earliest hunt scene. The subject, rare in paintings made around 1600, is the climax of a tale told in Ovid's *Metamorphoses*, when the ancient Greek hero Meleager delivers the mortal spear thrust into the shoulder of the fearsome Calydonian boar. Rubens quotes well-known classical sculptures and reliefs he had studied in Italy, breathing new life into antique sources by combining them into a compelling, dynamic narrative. His descriptive brushwork, looser in the boar and more polished in the figure of Meleager, for example, contributes to the vividness of the scene. This oil sketch may have served to introduce patrons to Rubens's ideas for a new genre of hunt subjects focusing on mythological themes.

Peter Paul Rubens

Flemish, 1577–1640

The Entombment, circa 1612

Oil on canvas, 131.1 × 130.2 cm

(51⁵⁄₈ × 51¼ in.), 93.PA.9

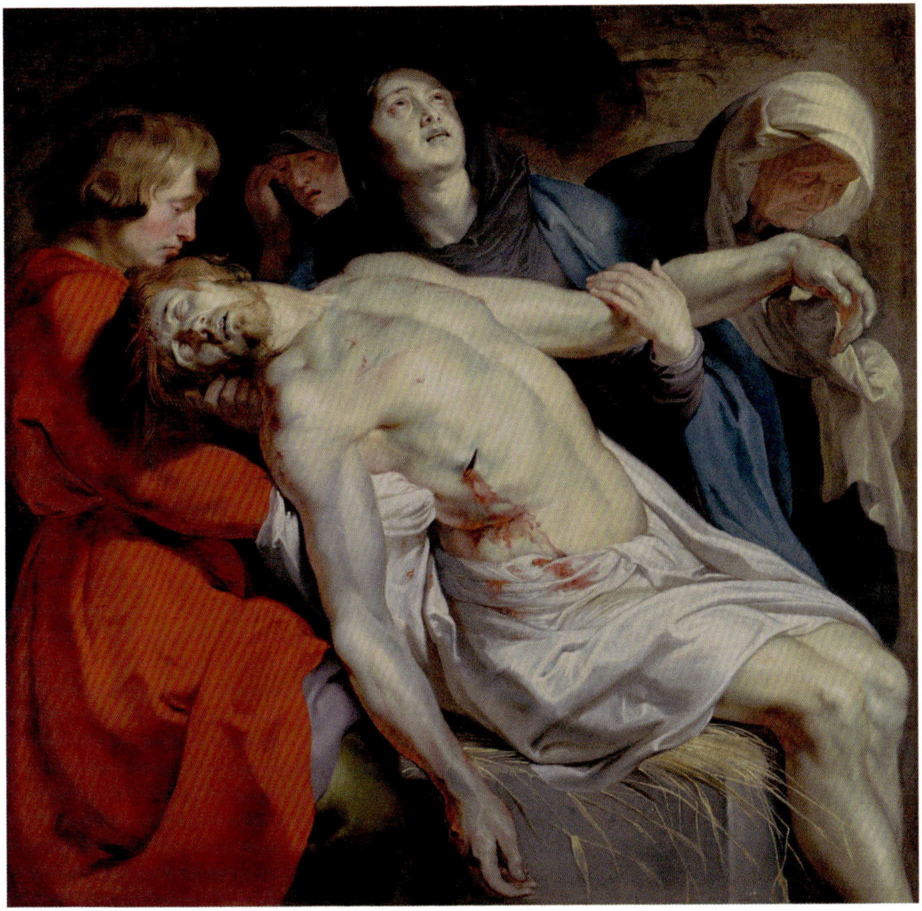

Rubens's dramatic religious paintings, characterized by imagery that engaged the emotions of the viewer, expressed the intensity of early seventeenth-century Counter-Reformation Catholicism in the Southern Netherlands. In this powerful altarpiece, the head of Christ, frozen in the agony of death, is turned to confront the observer. A pitiless light illuminates the scene, revealing even the depths of Christ's wound, which occupies the center of the canvas. His suffering and sacrifice are portrayed graphically by his battered flesh and the intense grief of the mourners. The slab under the body suggests an altar upon which the Eucharistic bread (symbolized by the wheat) and wine (symbolized by the blood) are placed during Catholic Mass.

Anthony van Dyck
Flemish, 1599–1641
Portrait of Agostino Pallavicini, circa 1621
Oil on canvas, 217.5 × 142.2 cm
(85 5/8 × 56 in.), 68.PA.2

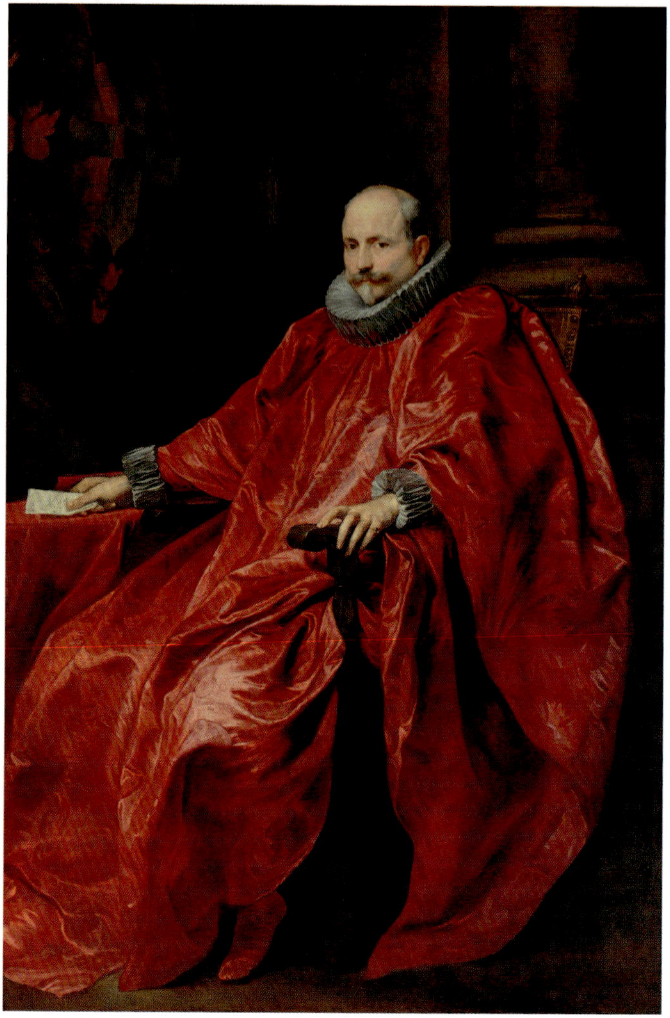

This splendid portrait was one of the first commissions Van Dyck received upon his arrival in the cultivated port city of Genoa in November 1621. It also marks the first in a group of monumental full-length likenesses by the artist that express the elegance and status of the Genoese aristocracy. The subject here, the senator Agostino Pallavicini (1577–1649), chose to be portrayed in the red robes (*robone*) of office that he had worn the previous spring to convey the felicitations of the Genoese state to the newly elected pope, Gregory XV (r. 1621–23). Van Dyck's likeness combines expressive brushwork inspired by Venetian Renaissance exemplars with a dignified characterization of the sitter. Above the cascade of shimmering scarlet silk damask, Pallavicini regards the viewer with aloofness.

Michael Sweerts

Flemish, 1618–1664

Head of a Woman, circa 1654

Oil on panel, 50.6 × 37.5 cm

(19 15/16 × 14 3/4 in.), 78.PB.259

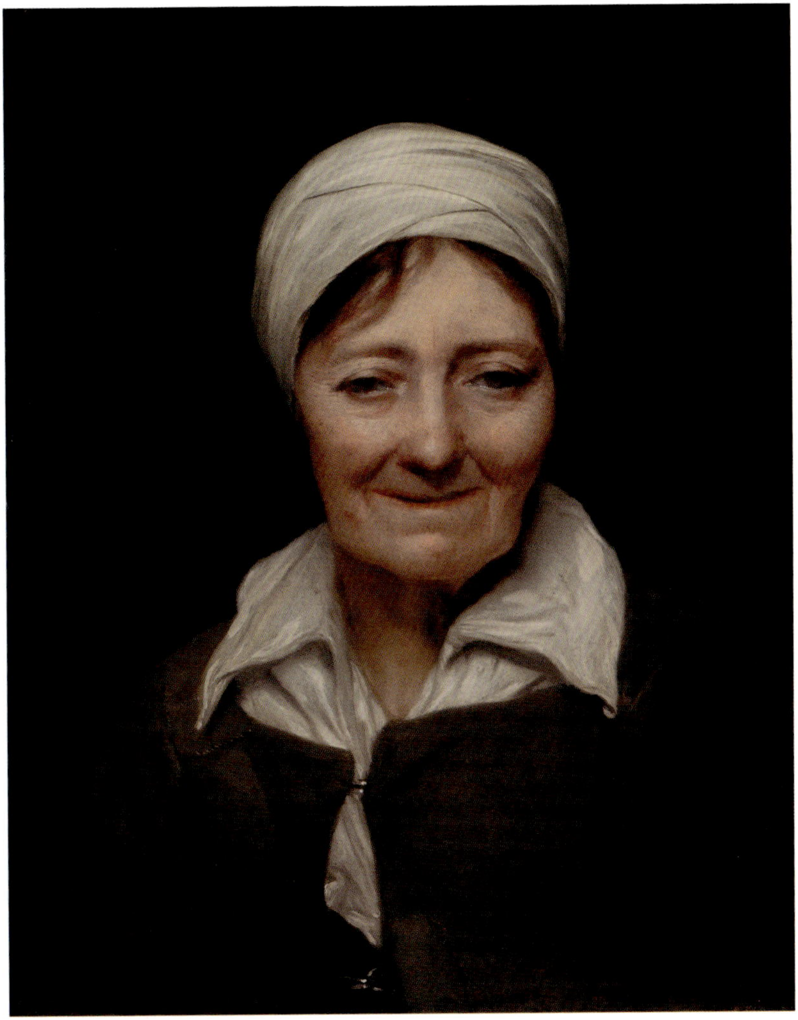

Sweerts brought his keen interest in human physiognomy and expression to the rendering of *tronies*, or character studies, a specific form practiced by artists throughout the Netherlands that focused primarily on a subject's youth and age. Here, he captures not only the distinctive facial features but also the congenial immediacy of a local woman dressed in a brown jacket over a white collared shirt. The unsparing light glints off the metal fastenings and reveals the stitched repairs on the front of her coat. Sweerts gently animated his subject by turning her shoulders and rendering her expression lines with textured strokes, imbuing his subject with both a relaxed frankness and a timeless dignity.

Jan Brueghel the Elder

Flemish, 1568–1625

The Entry of the Animals into Noah's Ark, 1613

Oil on panel, 54.6 × 83.8 cm (21½ × 33 in.), 92.PB.82

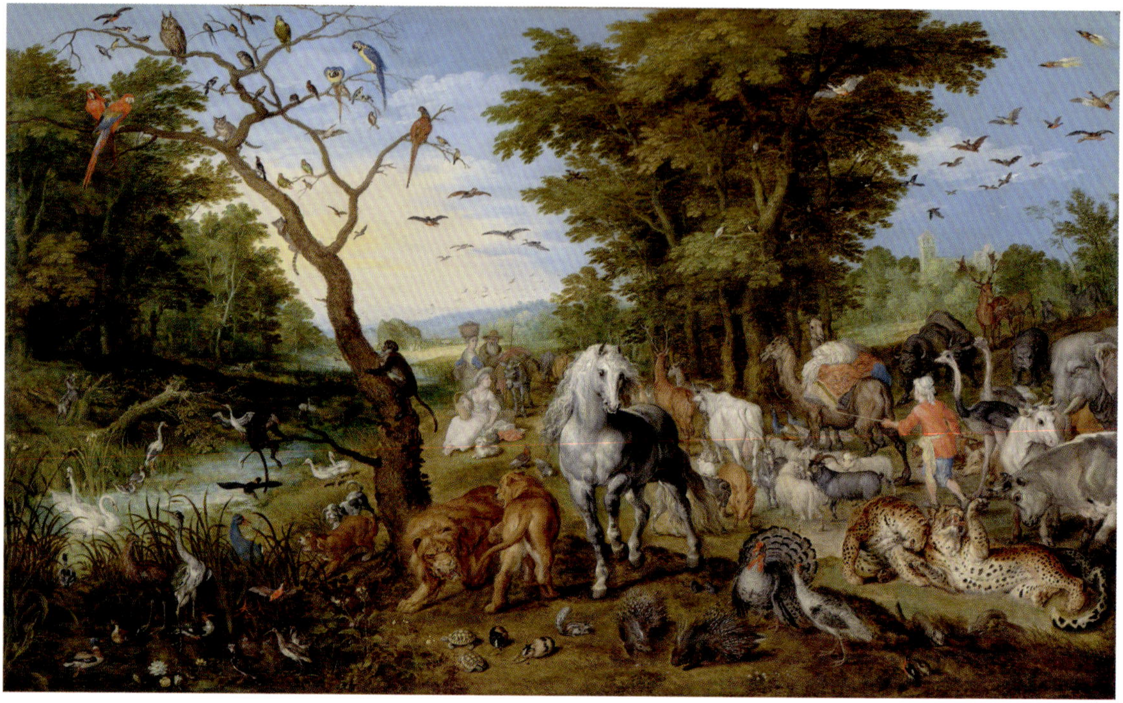

Around 1600 Brueghel developed a new genre of landscape painting centered on biblical themes of Paradise that celebrated God's creative power in the natural world. In this episode from the story of Noah's ark (Genesis 6–8), Brueghel combines rare species of birds and animals, including several from the so-called New World, with beasts already familiar to Europeans, delineating their characteristics with precise, spirited brushwork. His arrangement of animals by domain (air, water, earth) reflects the heightened interest at that time in natural history, while the feisty interactions between creatures recall late medieval visual traditions. The handsome gray stallion, lions, and leopards are based on works by his friend, countryman, and sometime collaborator Peter Paul Rubens.

Joachim Anthonisz. Wtewael

Dutch, 1566–1638

Mars and Venus Surprised by Vulcan, 1604–8

Oil on copper, 20.3 × 15.5 cm (8 × 6⅛ in.), 83.PC.274

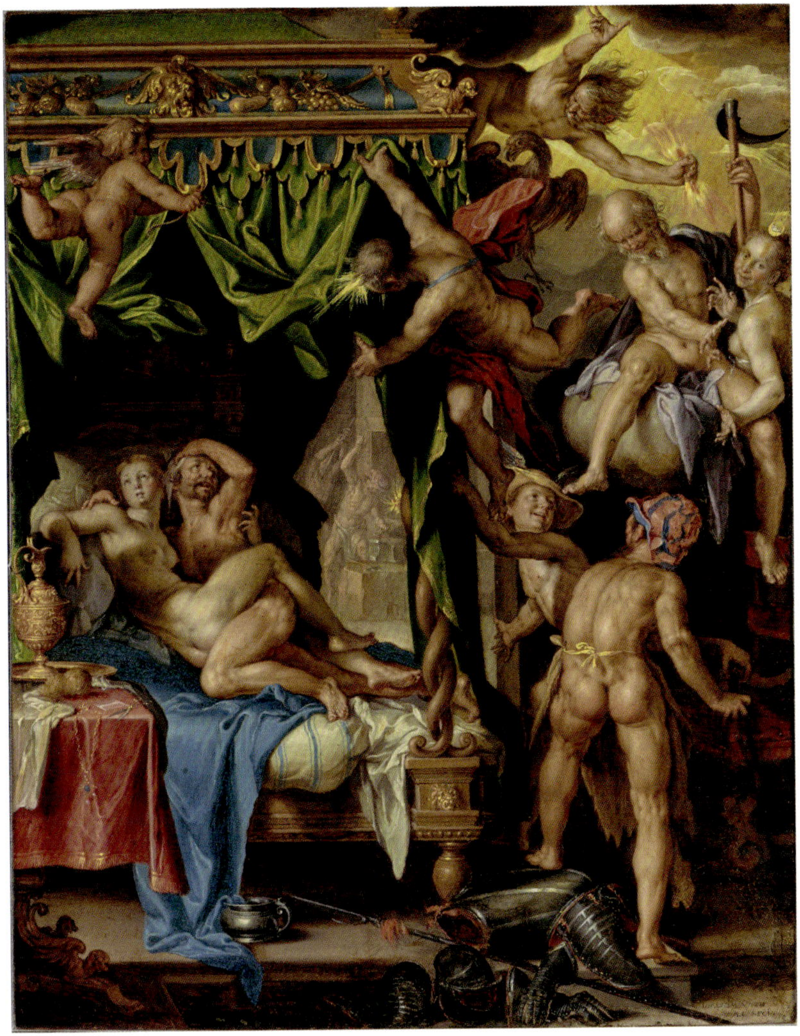

On this small copper panel, Wtewael deftly portrayed a moment of high drama in the lives of the gods, as described by the Roman poet Ovid in the *Metamorphoses* (4:171–89). When Vulcan, god of fire, caches his wife, Venus, goddess of love, having an affair with Mars, god of war, he traps the illicit lovers beneath an iron net, assembling the rest of the gods to witness their betrayal and mock the couple. Wtewael characterizes the deities who surround the luxurious canopied bed with a robust physicality. The classical literary source and erotic subject would have appealed to an erudite collector in the Netherlands, who would also have appreciated the prosaic humor of the prominently situated chamber pot.

Jacob van Ruisdael

Dutch, 1628/29–1682

Two Undershot Water Mills with an Open Sluice, 1653

Oil on canvas, 66.4 × 84.1 cm

(26⅛ × 33⅛ in.), 82.PA.18

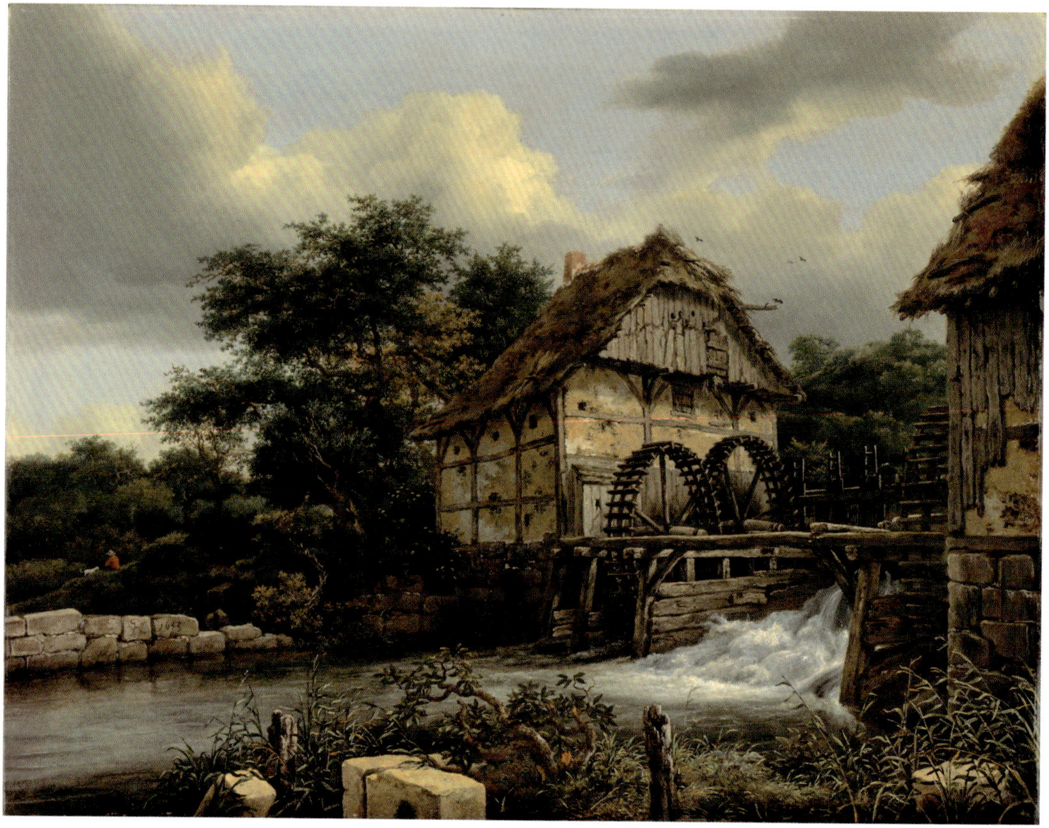

Ruisdael transformed the landscape tradition of the Netherlands by basing his portrayals of the natural world on firsthand observation. Through the careful selection, rearrangement, and invention of elements, he succeeded in making the windmill—a ubiquitous sight in the Dutch countryside—as well as the rarer water mill compelling subjects. The half-timbered undershot water mills he observed in the eastern provinces of the Netherlands, near the border with Germany, are the central motif of this canvas. The cascade rushing through the sluice represents the vigorous forces of nature that humans strive to control. By using a low viewpoint that situates the mills against dark clouds and a dense forest, the whole illuminated by cool sunlight, Ruisdael imbues a rural subject with drama.

Meindert Hobbema and Abraham Storck

Dutch, 1638–1709; Dutch, 1644–1708

A Wooded Landscape with Travelers on a Path through a Hamlet, circa 1665

Oil on canvas, 97.5 × 130.8 cm (38³/₈ × 51¹/₂ in.), 2002.17

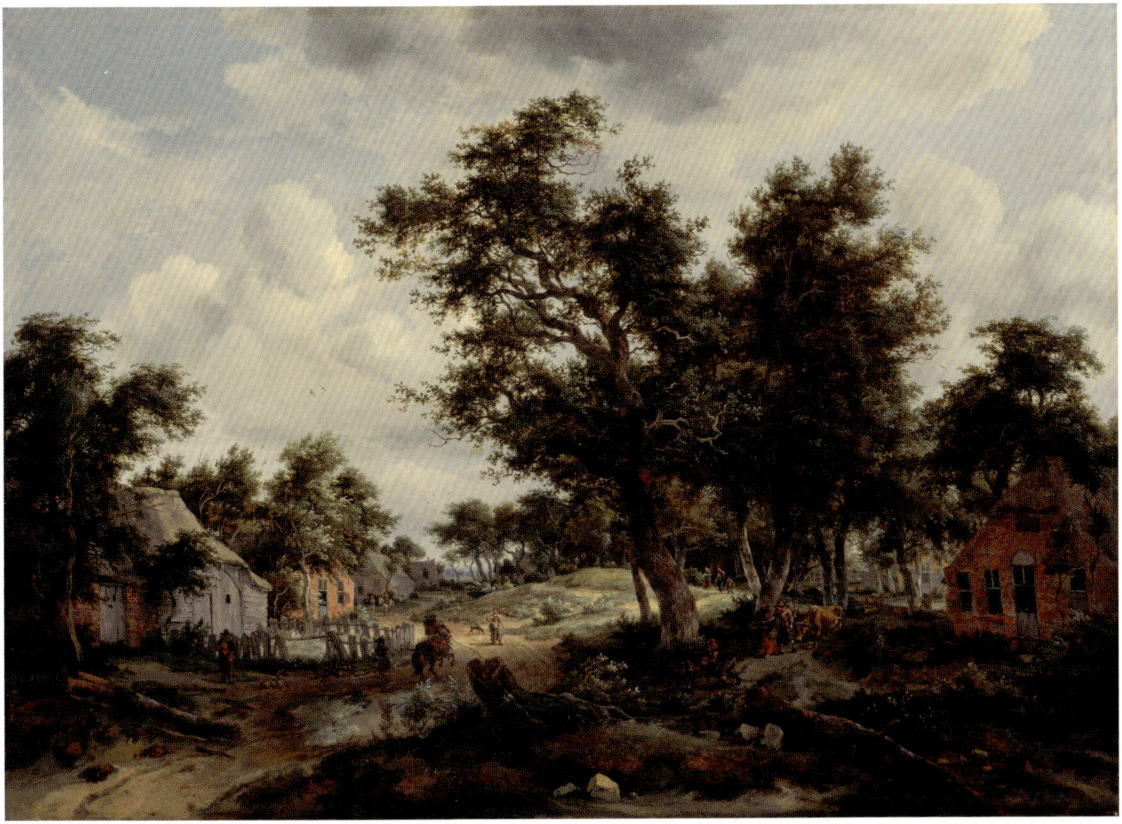

Hobbema here captures the languid atmospheric qualities of a breezy, sunny day in the eastern provinces of the Netherlands, near the border with Germany. Using a wide variety of brushwork, he expertly describes muddy soil, dry bark, crumbling brick, and diverse foliage. Hobbema, however, never painted outdoors, instead executing complex scenes like this one in his Amsterdam studio. Populated by an assortment of travelers, from gentry mounted on horseback to farmers journeying with their animals (the work of the Amsterdam painter Abraham Storck), the canvas features two separate vanishing points that lead the eye into the composition, a purposeful device intended to engage the viewer in a visual meander through the countryside.

Pieter de Hooch

Dutch, 1629–1684

A Woman Preparing Bread and Butter for a Boy, circa 1660–63

Oil on canvas, 68.6 × 53.3 cm (27 × 21 in.), 84.PA.47

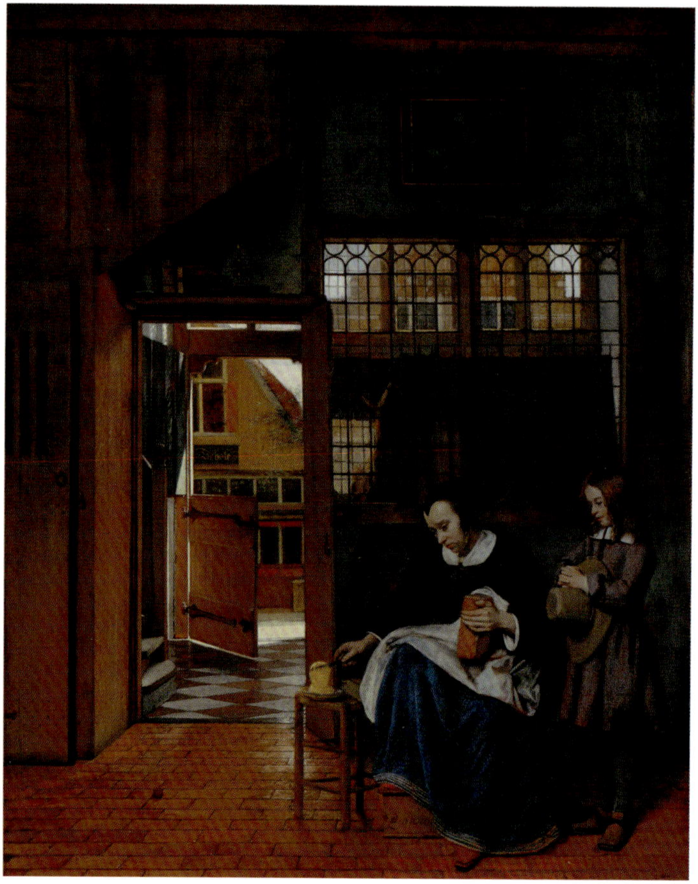

In the seventeenth-century Netherlands, a well-ordered household and the proper education of children were considered a reflection of the stability of the state. De Hooch specialized in scenes in which he innovatively used space and perspective to convey the tranquility and virtue of the domestic sphere. In this tidy home, a woman prepares a simple meal for a boy on his way to school, the latter visible through the open door. The meticulously constructed interior, with subtle lighting effects and views to other spaces, evokes the household as a realm of quiet order.

Gerard ter Borch

Dutch, 1617–1681

Horse Stable, circa 1654

Oil on panel, 45.4 × 53.5 cm

(17⁷⁄₈ × 21¹⁄₁₆ in.), 86.PB.631

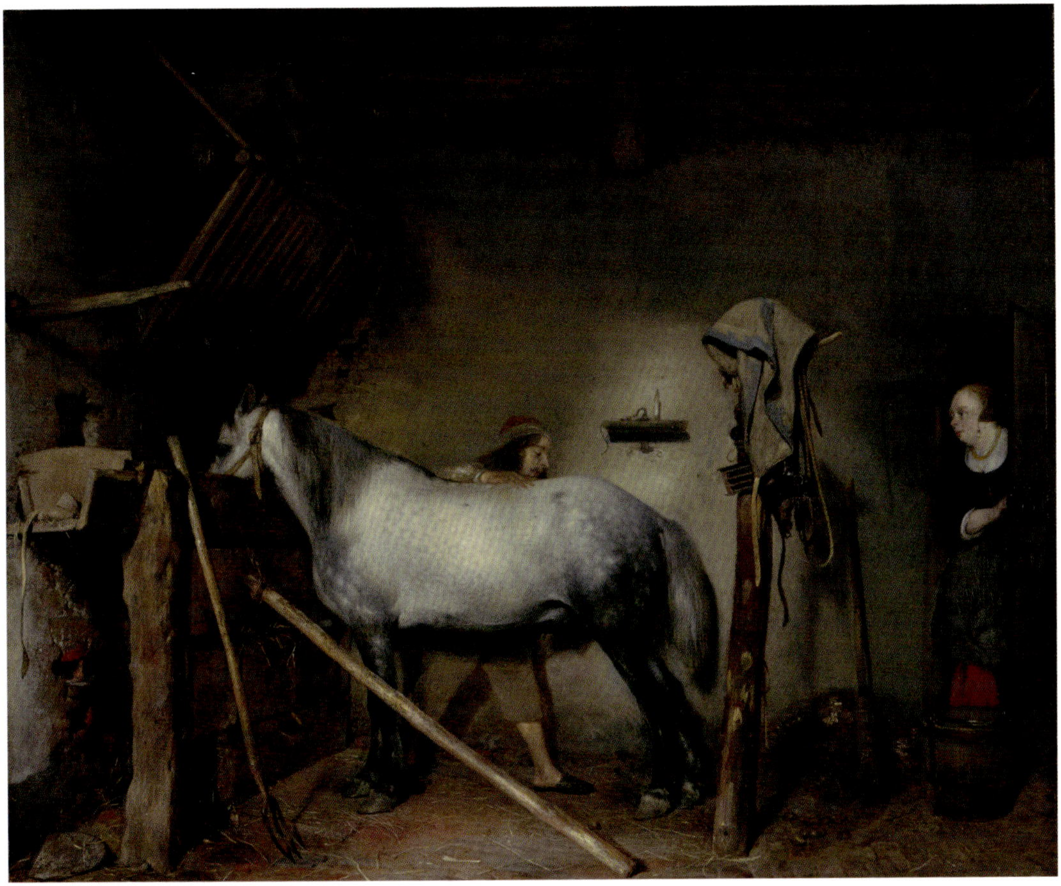

Light, perhaps from an open door, illuminates the inside of a stable, highlighting the glossy, dappled coat of a riding horse and the shelf on the wall behind it, which supports a candle. Ter Borch captures a fleeting moment of suspended action. At center, a man grooms his striking gray mount, an Appelschimmel, while it contentedly consumes its hay. At right, a woman emerges from the house, on the verge of interrupting the tranquility of the routine. Flecks of bright yellow and red on the wood floors and plaster walls animate the surfaces and heighten the suspense. Offering neither a typical equestrian portrait nor a familiar scene of everyday life, Ter Borch celebrates the profound humanity of the rural household.

Frans van Mieris the Elder

Dutch, 1635–1681

Pictura (An Allegory of Painting), 1661

Oil on copper, 12.7 × 8.9 cm (5 × 3½ in.), 82.PC.136

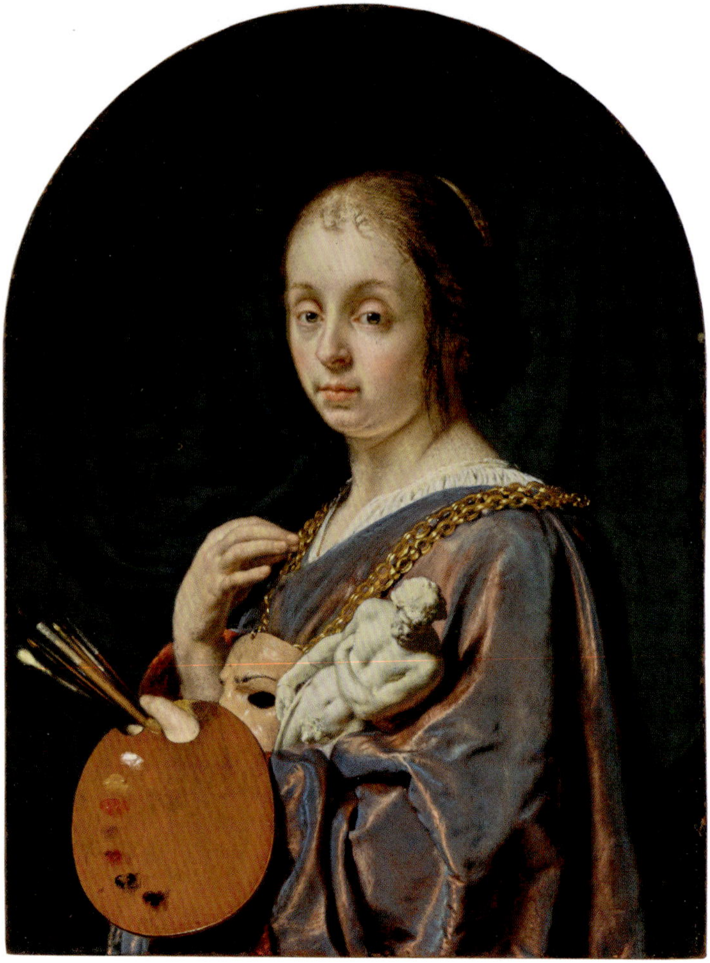

Van Mieris, renowned for the exceptional refinement and delicacy of his technique, celebrated his profession as a painter with this tiny allegory. The palette, brushes, and statue the woman holds identify her as Pictura, the personification of the art of painting. The mask she wears on a gold chain may be either an emblem of deceit or artifice (because the painter creates the illusion of reality) or a reference to the stage, and thus to the act of imitation that is central to the painter's vocation. Van Mieris conveyed the inspiration essential to his own artistic process in a personal way: his wife, Cunera, served as his model for Pictura.

Jan Steen

Dutch, 1626–1679

The Drawing Lesson, circa 1665

Oil on panel, 49.2 × 41.2 cm

(19 3/8 × 16 1/4 in.), 83.PB.388

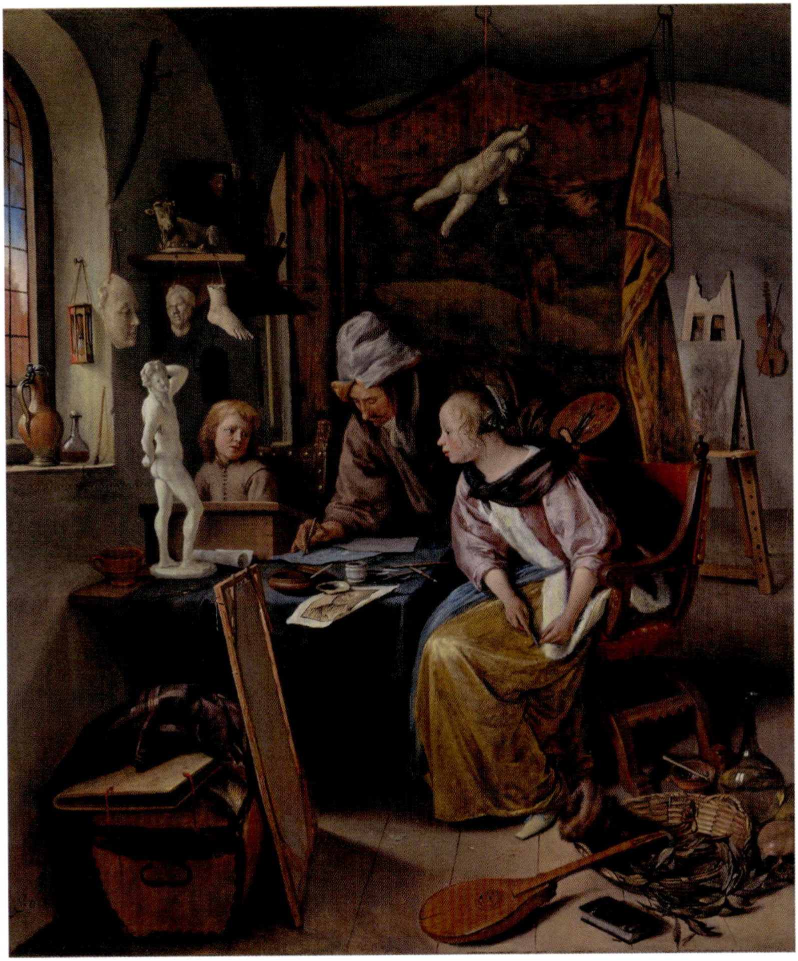

Inside a painter's studio, the master instructs two young pupils by correcting a drawing. Paying particular attention to the effects of the light shining through the large window, Steen describes the diverse materials essential to the artist's workshop and offers an allegory of the painter's art. Among the implements strewn on the table are quill pens, brushes, sticks of charcoal, and a woodcut depicting the head of a man. Plaster casts hang from a shelf that supports a sculpture of an ox, the symbol of Saint Luke, patron saint of painters. The laurel wreath, skull, wine bottle, fur muff, lute, and pipe piled in the lower right corner express the theme of *vanitas* (vanity), reminding viewers of the brevity of life and the fleeting nature of fame.

Cornelis Bega

Dutch, 1631/32–1664

The Alchemist, 1663

Oil on panel, 36.2 × 32.2 cm

(14¼ × 12¹¹⁄₁₆ in.), 84.PB.56

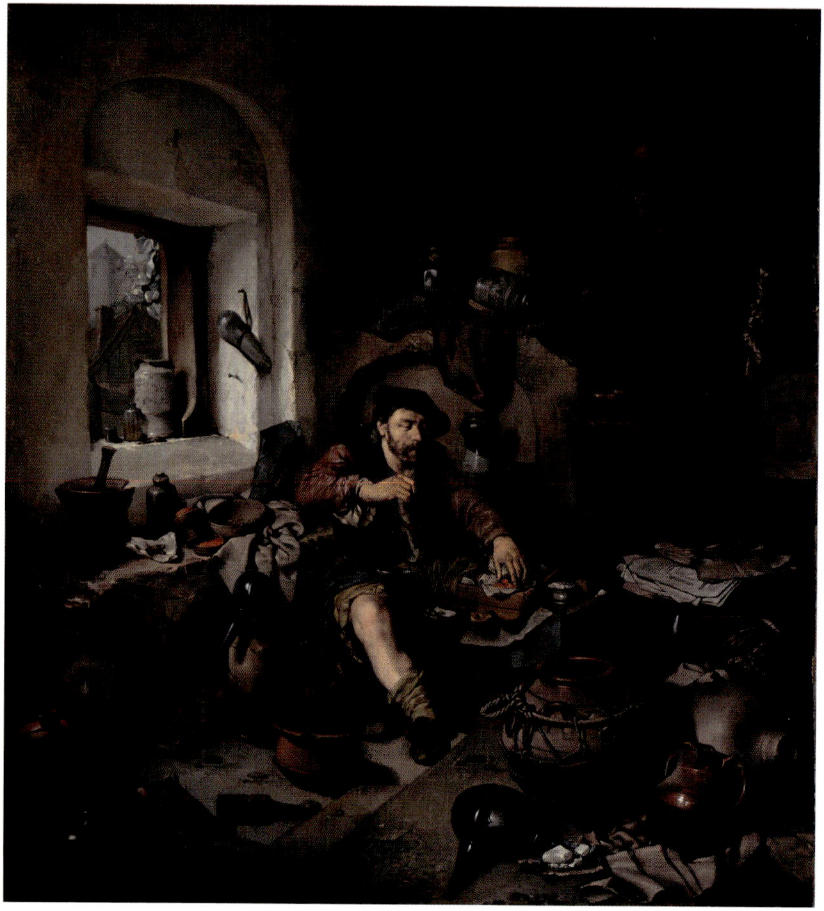

Bega specialized in scenes of dimly lit interiors, in which individuals might toil at mundane tasks, carouse, or, as here, pursue the idealistic rewards of alchemy, a pseudoscience through which people sought to transform base metals into precious silver and gold. The cool light of the moon pouring through the window illuminates the figure of the alchemist, clearly intent on his mission, and casts the forms of ceramic pots, crucibles, and other vessels into a monochromatic scene of violet and gray. The general disorder and decrepit nature of the room, along with the alchemist's dingy yellow stocking, convey the extent of the futility of his pursuit.

Gerrit Dou
Dutch, 1613–1675
Astronomer by Candlelight, late 1650s
Oil on panel, 32 × 21.2 cm (12 5/8 × 8 3/8 in.),
86.PB.732

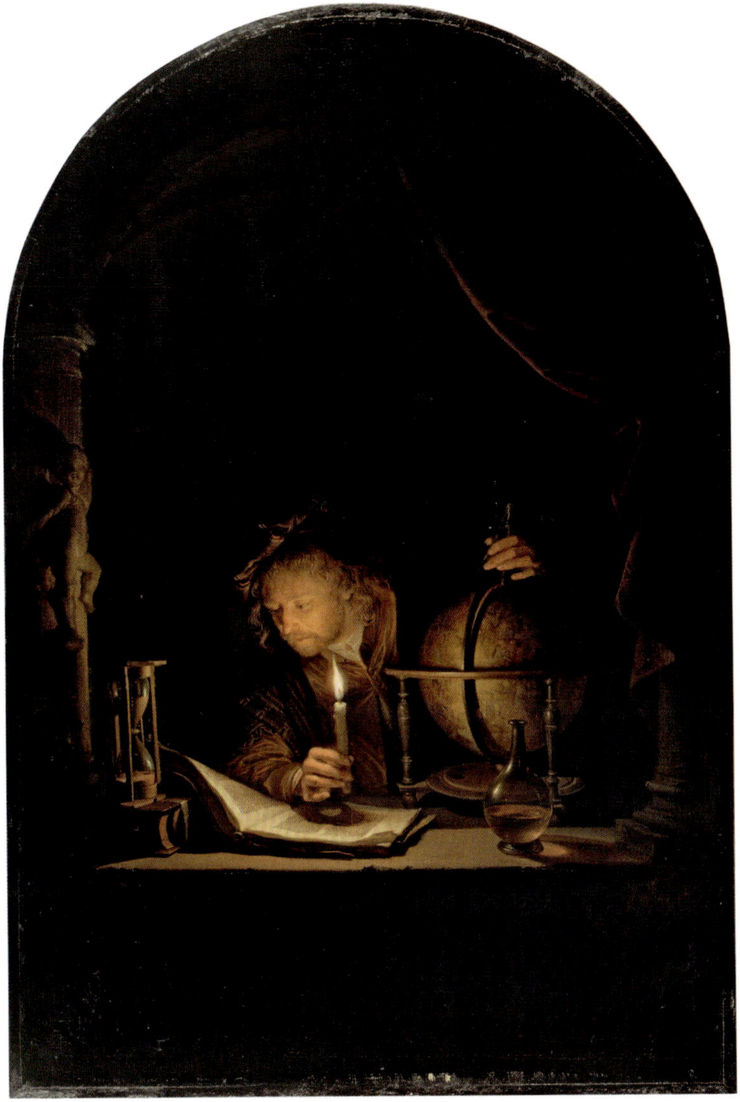

Rather than gazing up at the night sky, Dou's astronomer focuses on the text before him while using a quadrant to take a measurement on a celestial globe. The candle he holds illuminates the vaulted ceiling of his chamber, as well as a plum-colored curtain, tied back to reveal a decorated column that, together with the drape, frames the space in which he conducts his studies. The warm light reveals the astronomer's scholarly robes, the individually described tendrils of his hair and beard, and his rapt expression. At the time Dou executed this painting, the Netherlands had long been a center for scientific endeavors, especially astronomy. The image attests to the interest and mystery that surrounded the study of the heavens.

Rembrandt Harmensz. van Rijn
Dutch, 1606–1669
An Old Man in Military Costume,
circa 1630–31
Oil on panel, 65.7 × 51.8 cm
(25⁷/₈ × 20³/₈ in.), 78.PB.246

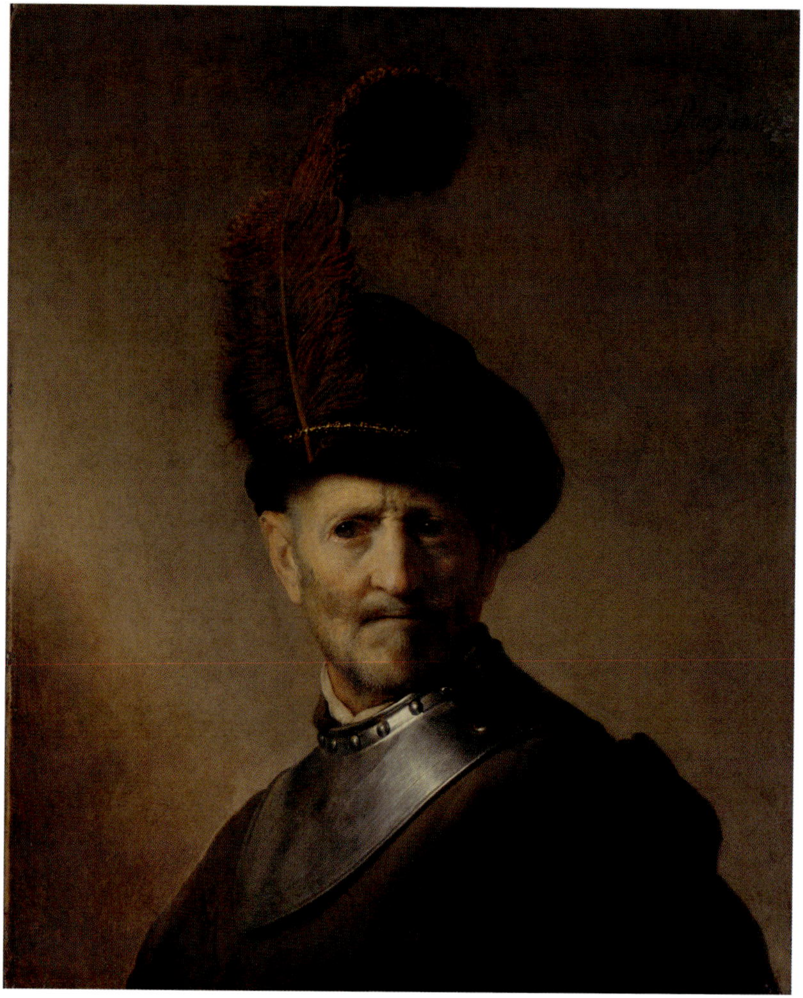

Rembrandt turned to a familiar model for this *tronie*, or character study, of a man dressed in a soldier's metal collar (gorget) and a striking plumed beret. Distinguished by finely wrinkled skin, a sparse mustache, and watery eyes, the subject appears to be listening to something beyond the frame of the picture. The composition demonstrates Rembrandt's skillful handling of textures—notably, the gleaming surface of the polished steel—and of the light falling across the figure and the plaster wall. The model's evocative visage evidently proved compelling to the artist, since he painted it over another *tronie* of a young man. The subject may relate to military themes popular at that time, during the Dutch struggle for independence from Spain.

Rembrandt Harmensz. van Rijn

Dutch, 1606–1669

The Abduction of Europa, 1632

Oil on panel, 64.6 × 78.7 cm (25 1/6 × 31 in.),

95.PB.7

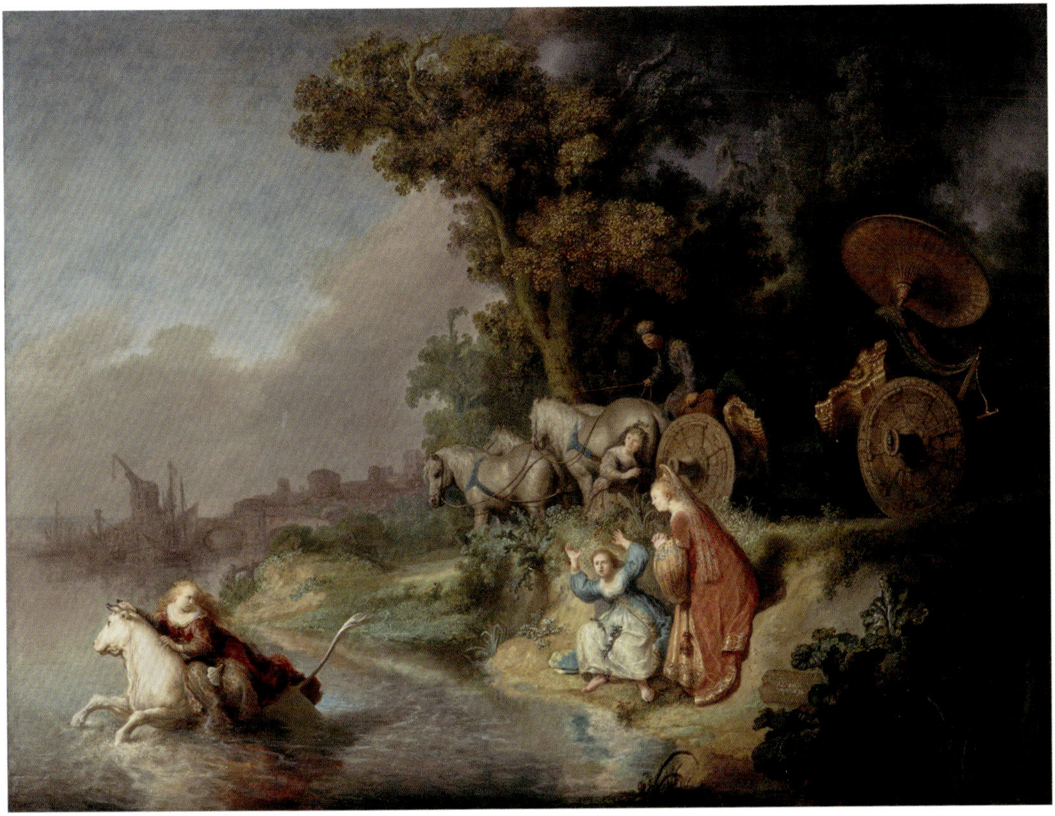

When Rembrandt turned to subjects from classical mythology in the early 1630s, he enriched these familiar narratives with vivid characterizations of human emotion. Here, the artist recounts a dramatic episode from Ovid's *Metamorphoses*, that of the abduction of Europa, princess of Tyre, by the god Jupiter in the guise of a white bull. The painting offers a virtuosic display of a variety of emotions. In fear and confusion, Europa tensely grips the bull's neck, while her companions meet her backward gaze with distress and a dawning comprehension of her fate. The looming screen of trees, one of the artist's earliest landscapes, sets a forbidding stage. Painted on a modest scale suitable for an Amsterdam canal house, Rembrandt conveys his eloquent narrative in a dazzling display of refined brushwork and brilliant color.

Rembrandt Harmensz. van Rijn

Dutch, 1606–1669

Saint Bartholomew, 1661

Oil on canvas, 86.7 × 75.6 cm

(34⅛ × 29¾ in.), 71.PA.15

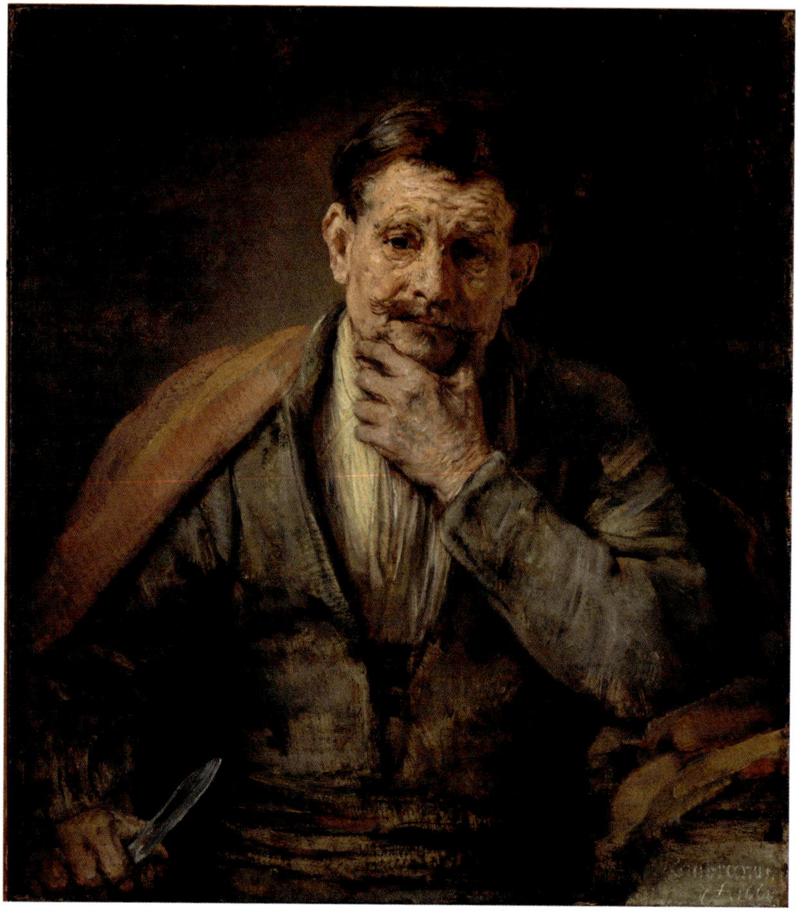

The unusual frontal pose of the figure in this work reflects Rembrandt's search for direct engagement with saints as both holy and human subjects. The descriptive brushwork, a hallmark of the artist's late "rough" manner, draws attention away from the more thinly painted torso and focuses instead on the saint's countenance and striking gray left hand. The individualized features of Bartholomew, who was martyred by being skinned alive, suggest that Rembrandt took inspiration from an acquaintance to execute this imposing characterization. Bartholomew holds a knife, an attribute of his martyrdom, and his pensive demeanor suggests a complex internal state.

Georges de La Tour

French, 1593–1652

The Musicians' Brawl, circa 1625–30

Oil on canvas, 85.7 × 141 cm

(33¾ × 55½ in.), 72.PA.28

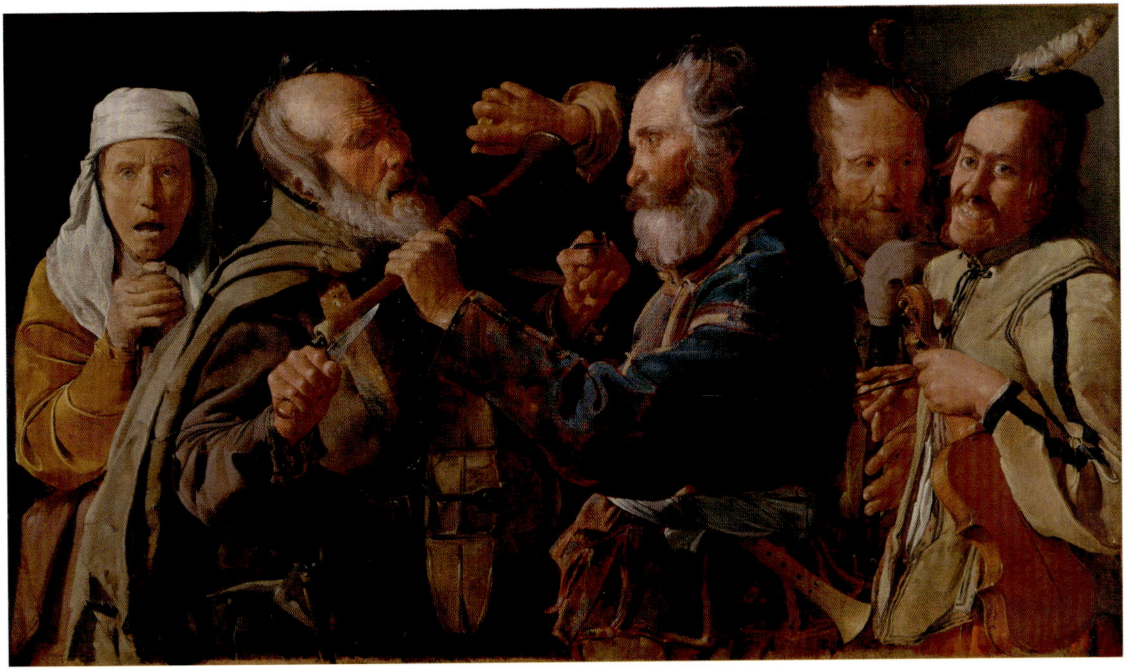

Two street musicians engage in a brawl, perhaps over a primely positioned street corner where both wish to perform. The man on the left, wearing a stringed hurdy-gurdy slung around his shoulders, defends himself with both a knife and the crank of his instrument. The man at center hits him with a shawm, a precursor to the oboe, and squeezes a lemon into his eyes to determine the legitimacy of his purported blindness. The figures are pushed up close to the viewer, adding to the immediacy of the scene. The cool palette, detached treatment of characters, and attention to unusual textures (such as the wrinkled skin of the aged beggar) made La Tour one of the most original and enigmatic painters of the seventeenth century.

Claude Lorrain (Claude Gellée)

French, 1604/5(?)–1682

Coast View with the Abduction of Europa, 1645(?)

Oil on canvas, 96.2 × 167.6 cm

(37 7/8 × 66 in.), 2007.32

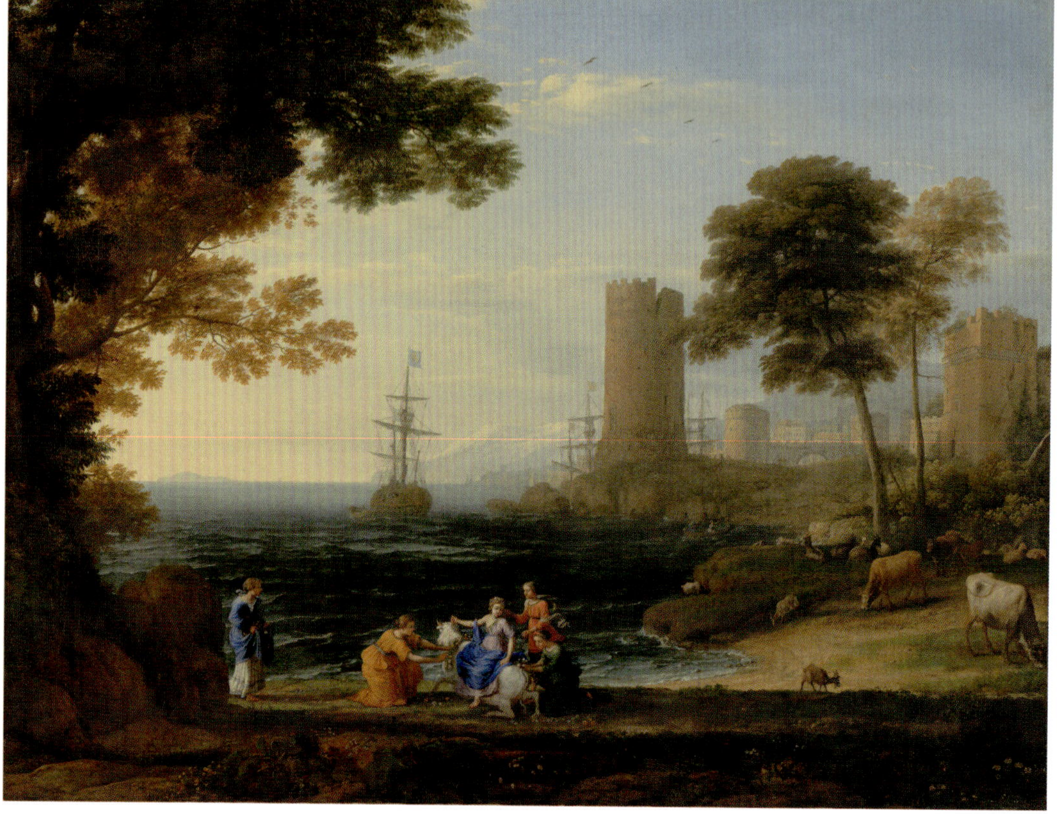

Considered one of art history's greatest landscape painters, Claude Lorrain transformed the genre with his refined "ideal" landscapes—that is, images of nature that surpassed nature's own beauty and harmony. His unrivaled command of light and atmosphere imbued subjects from classical poetry and biblical history with a lyricism that delighted his elite patrons and raised the status of landscape painting. Executed at the height of his career, this canvas is the most dramatic of Claude's five treatments of this subject, the abduction of Europa, princess of Tyre, by the Roman god Jupiter disguised as a magnificent bull. The scene captures the spirit of the tale, recounted in the poet Ovid's *Metamorphoses*, portraying the still-mirthful princess in the moments before Jupiter commits his dastardly deed.

Nicolas Poussin

French, 1594–1665

Landscape with a Calm, 1650–51

Oil on canvas, 97 × 131 cm

(38 3/16 × 51 9/16 in.), 97.PA.60

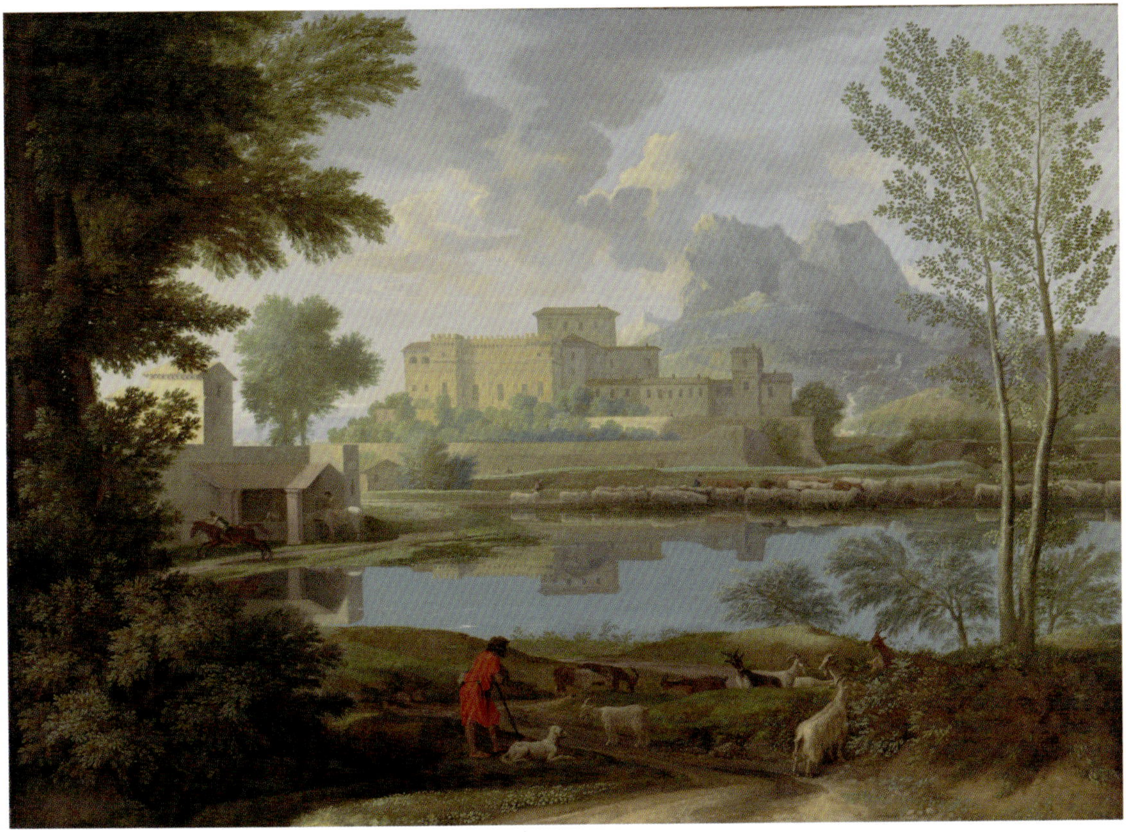

In the late 1640s and early 1650s, at the height of his artistic maturity, Poussin turned from historical narrative to landscape painting. This example does not illustrate a story but, rather, evokes a mood. The ordered composition and clear, golden light contribute to the painting's serenity, while glowing, gemlike colors enliven the benevolent depiction of nature. Poussin painted a pendant, or companion piece, to this work, *Landscape with a Storm*, that is today in the Musée des Beaux-Arts in Rouen, France. Together, the paintings' contrasting weather effects embody nature's changing and unpredictable relationship with humankind. Both pictures were executed for the Parisian merchant Jean Pointel, a friend of Poussin and a great collector of his landscape paintings.

Jan van Huysum

Dutch, 1682–1749

Vase of Flowers, 1722

Oil on panel, 80.3 × 61 cm ($31\frac{5}{8}$ × 24 in.), 82.PB.70

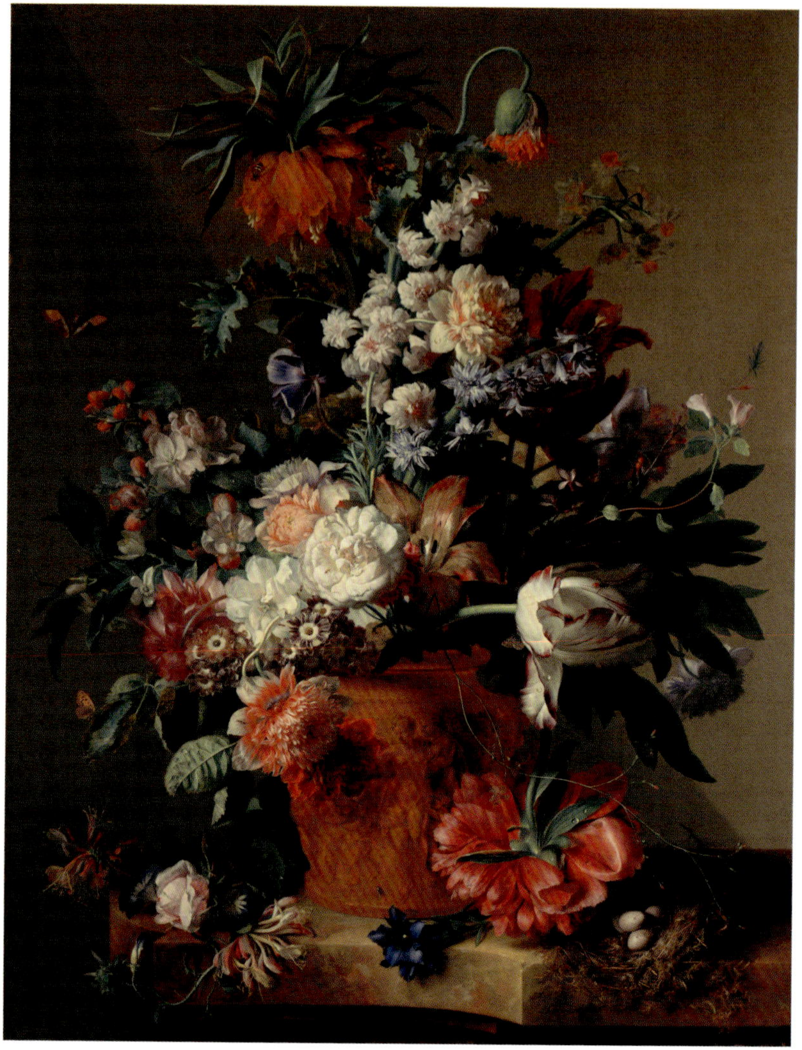

The Amsterdam-based Van Huysum was avidly interested in flowers, especially new varieties cultivated in the nearby city of Haarlem. He painted rare blooms directly from life and by referring to drawn studies. This bouquet features fashionable "double blooms" such as anemones and hyacinths, as well as the traditional and popular white rose and striped tulip. The arrangement combines flowers from different times of year, along with equally beautiful and short-lived insects and a bird's nest that is remarkable for the realism of its soft, mossy interior. The artist celebrated the decorative qualities of his subjects but also sought to use the ephemerality of flowers to provoke reflection on the transience of life and beauty. Although secretive about his technique, Van Huysum was a master of materials who worked painstakingly over long periods.

Jean-Siméon Chardin

French, 1699–1779

Still Life with Fish, Vegetables, Gougères, *Pots, and Cruets,* 1769

Oil on canvas, 68.6 × 58.4 cm (27 × 23 in.), 2003.13

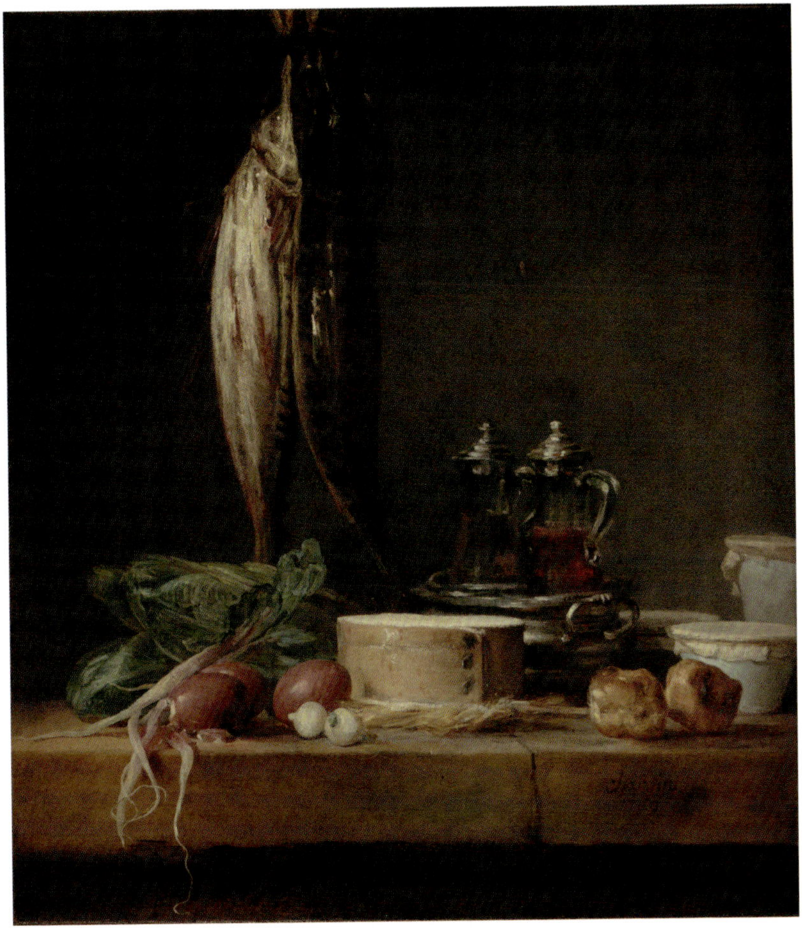

Among the greatest still-life painters in the history of art, Chardin carefully organized everyday household objects into complex compositions with an architectural balance and integrity. In this picture he skillfully renders various textures by using thick applications of opaque paint in some areas and thin glazes in others. The color harmonies are highly sophisticated, from the strongly complementary reds and greens in the beets at left to the subtler consonance of powder-blue ceramic pots against the warm hues of the pastry at right. This work is the artist's last signed and dated still life.

Jean-Antoine Watteau

French, 1684–1721

The Surprise, circa 1718–19

Oil on panel, 36.4 × 28.2 cm

(14 5/16 × 11 1/8 in.), 2017.72

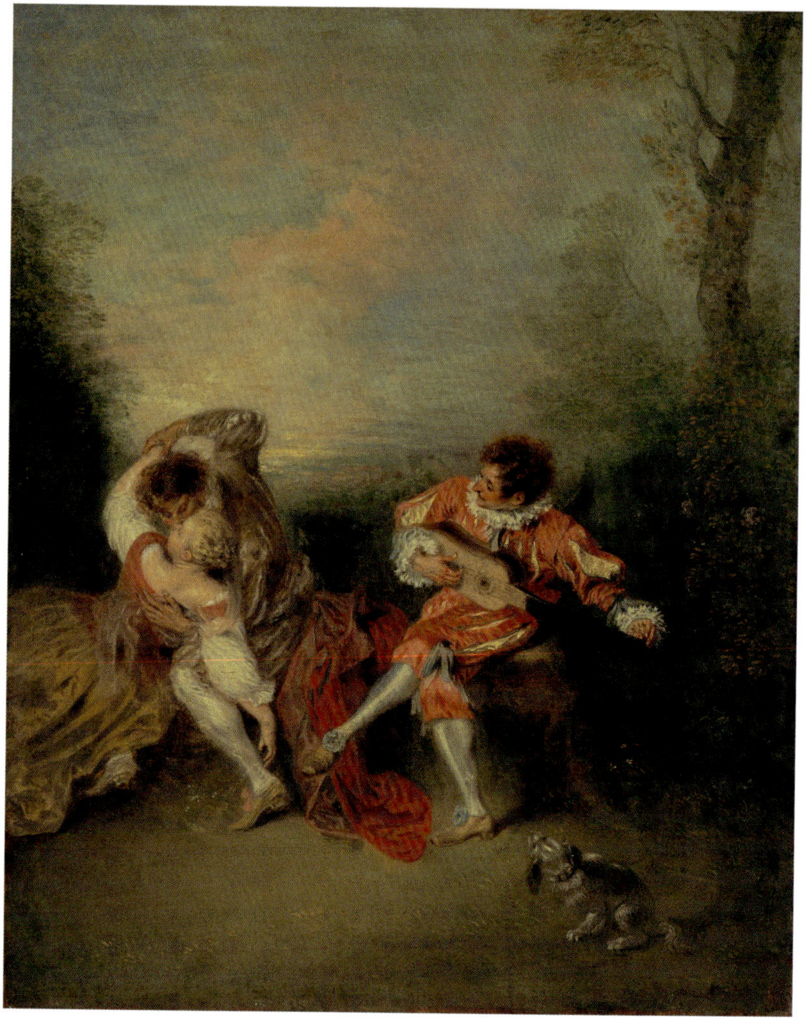

In a verdant park at sunset, a young woman abandons herself to her tousle-haired companion's embrace. They seem oblivious to the presence of a third figure sitting next to them on a rocky outcrop, tuning a guitar. It is Mezzetin, a stock figure from the theatrical tradition of the Italian commedia dell'arte. He gawks at the couple, and as such represents a poignant foil to their unbridled passion. The small dog at the bottom right seems to share the same sense of surprise and curiosity over the amorous scene he is witnessing. The small painting brings together many typical elements of Watteau's painterly poetics: the celebration of nature, music, and love in a peerless mixture of reality and artifice, humor and seriousness, melancholy and sensuality.

Nicolas Lancret

French, 1690–1743

Dance before a Fountain, by 1724

Oil on canvas, 97.8 × 130.8 cm

(38½ × 51½ in.), 2001.54

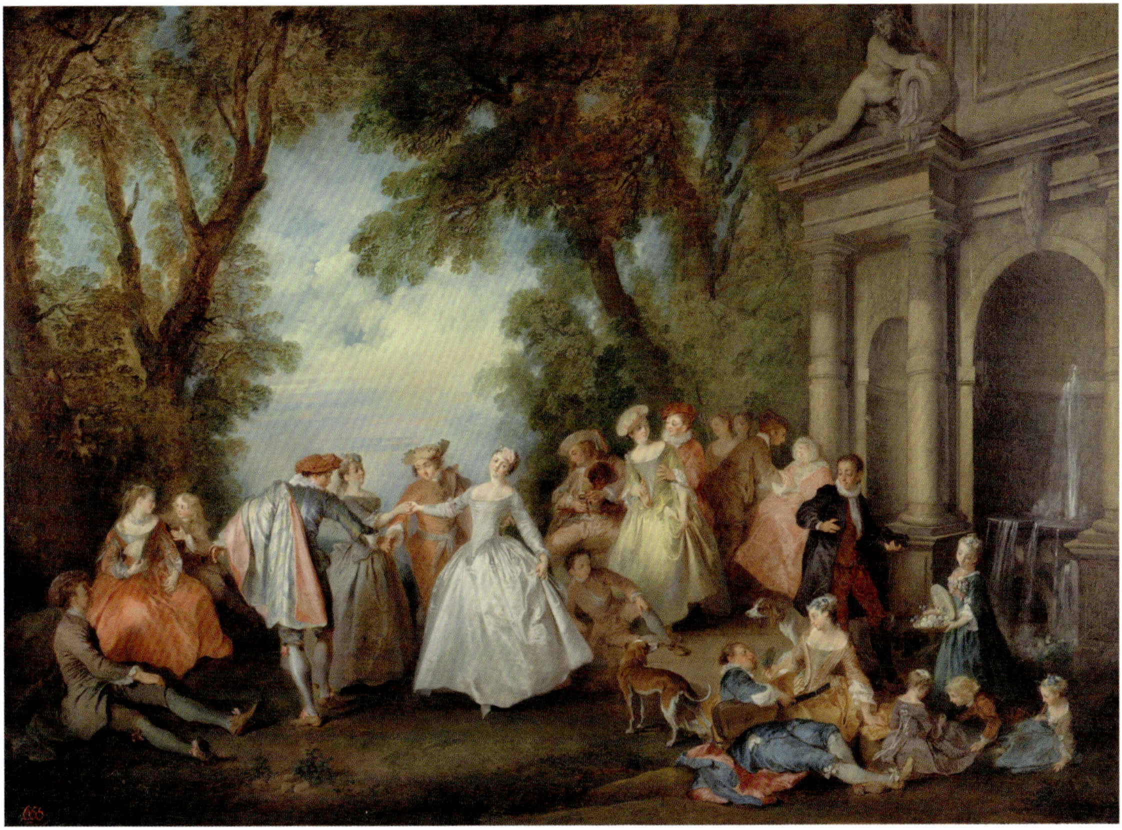

Influenced by his more famous mentor, Jean-Antoine Watteau (see p. 184), Lancret was a prolific painter of the genre known as the *fête galante*—pastoral landscapes populated by elegantly attired aristocrats strolling, dancing, and flirting. *Dance before a Fountain,* one of Lancret's most accomplished paintings, brilliantly exemplifies this archetypal product of the exuberant Rococo style. With a monumental fountain in a verdant landscape as a backdrop, two couples perform a country dance, while others engage in the arts of conversation and seduction. The shimmering colors of the figures' sumptuous costumes and the rhythmic interweaving of their various poses, gestures, and gazes create an effect of heady pleasure. Lancret counted King Louis XV of France (r. 1715–74) among his elite patrons.

Giovanni Battista Tiepolo
Italian, 1696–1770

Alexander the Great and Campaspe in the Studio of Apelles, circa 1740
Oil on canvas, 42.5 × 54 cm
(16¾ × 21¼ in.), 2000.6

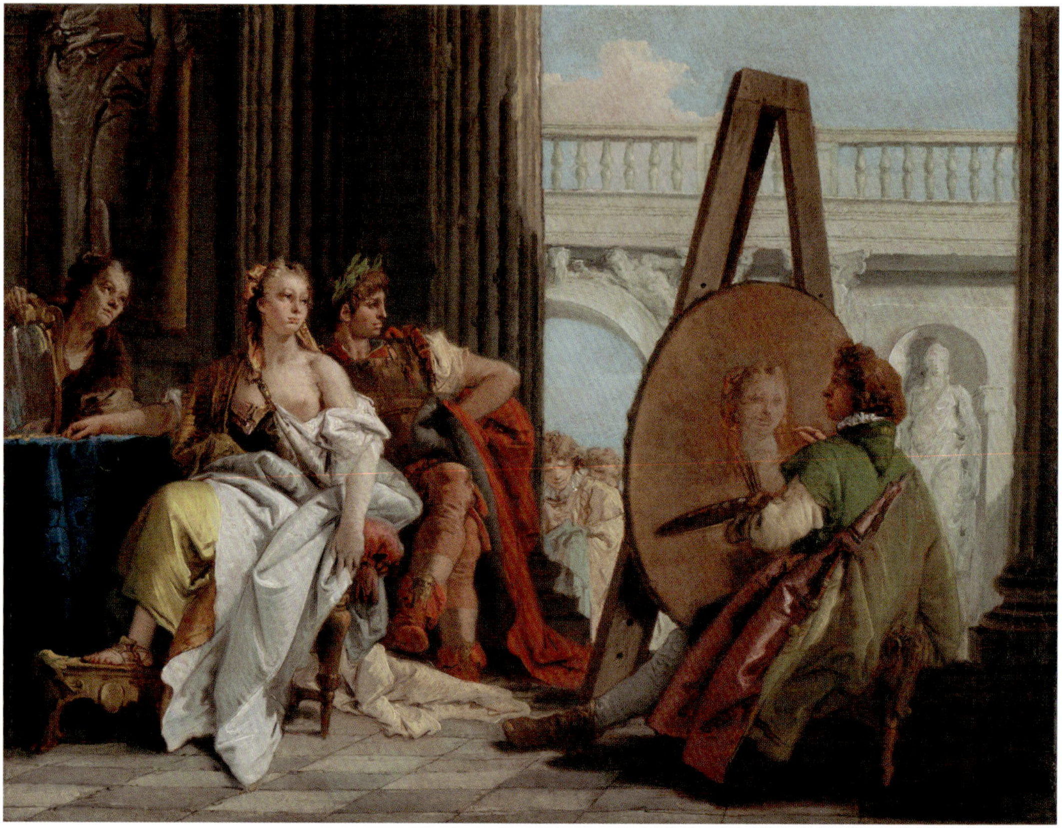

In a famous story taken from Pliny's *Natural History*, the Macedonian conqueror Alexander the Great (356–323 BCE) realizes that Apelles, the greatest painter in ancient Greece, has fallen in love with Campaspe, Alexander's mistress. Rather than respond in anger, Alexander graciously concedes to the couple's newfound love. Artists often invoked this story to reflect on the painter's command over powerful patrons. Tiepolo returned to the subject three times, changing the emotional tone considerably on each occasion. Here, he conveys the moment when Alexander sees through Apelles's attempts to restrain his passion for Campaspe. Tiepolo added even more drama to the story through lush, varied brushwork, unexpected shifts in scale, surprising contrasts of light and dark, and rich, saturated color.

Canaletto
(Giovanni Antonio Canal)
Italian, 1697–1768

The Grand Canal in Venice from Palazzo Flangini to Campo San Marcuola,
circa 1738
Oil on canvas, 47 × 77.8 cm
(18½ × 30⅝ in.), 2013.22

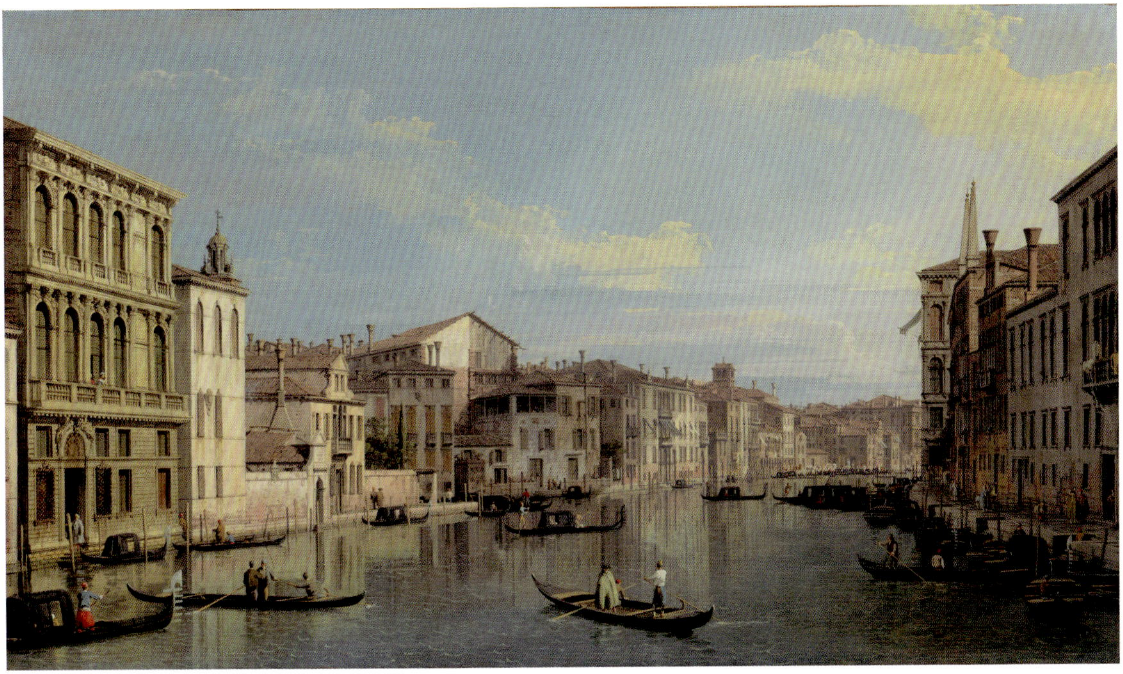

Canaletto was at the peak of his powers when he painted this view of sun-drenched Venetian palaces, their facades reflected in the shimmering water of the city's Grand Canal. With precise brushwork, he evokes the disfiguring effects of soot and crumbling stucco. The viewer's vantage point is seemingly from a boat in the middle of the waterway, immersed in the city's bustling activity. A bewigged nobleman stands in the doorway of Palazzo Flangini, at left, either about to board or having just alighted from a gondola moored at the steps. A *traghetto* carrying passengers across the water is seen departing from the embankment at right; another, with a standing passenger in a long greenish cloak, has already reached the radiant sunshine in the middle of the canal.

Anton Raphael Mengs

German, 1728–1779

Portrait of Friedrich Christian, Prince of Saxony, 1751

Oil on canvas, 155.7 × 110.8 cm ($61\frac{5}{16}$ × $43\frac{5}{8}$ in.), 2023.100

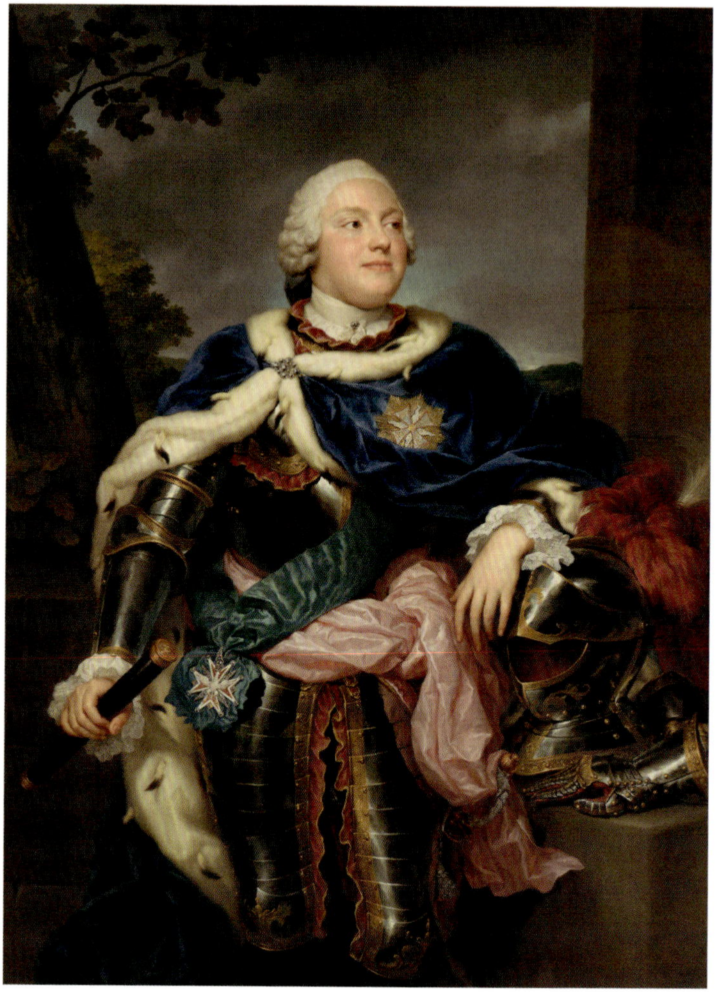

This splendid portrait captures the pink-cheeked optimism of a youthful prince whose future is filled with promise. The precocious Mengs was only twenty-three himself when he painted this likeness of Friedrich Christian (1722–1763), heir to the throne at the Saxon court in Dresden. Modeled after images of the prince's royal ancestors, the painting asserts Friedrich Christian's dynastic legitimacy while also conveying a sense of his lively mind and kindly temperament. It conceals his disability (likely cerebral palsy), which in reality would have prevented him from adopting the confident stance seen here. Friedrich Christian acceded to the throne in 1763 but died of smallpox only a few months into his reign.

Jean-Baptiste Greuze

French, 1725–1805

The Laundress, 1761

Oil on canvas, 40.6 × 33 cm (16 × 12⅞ in.),

83.PA.387

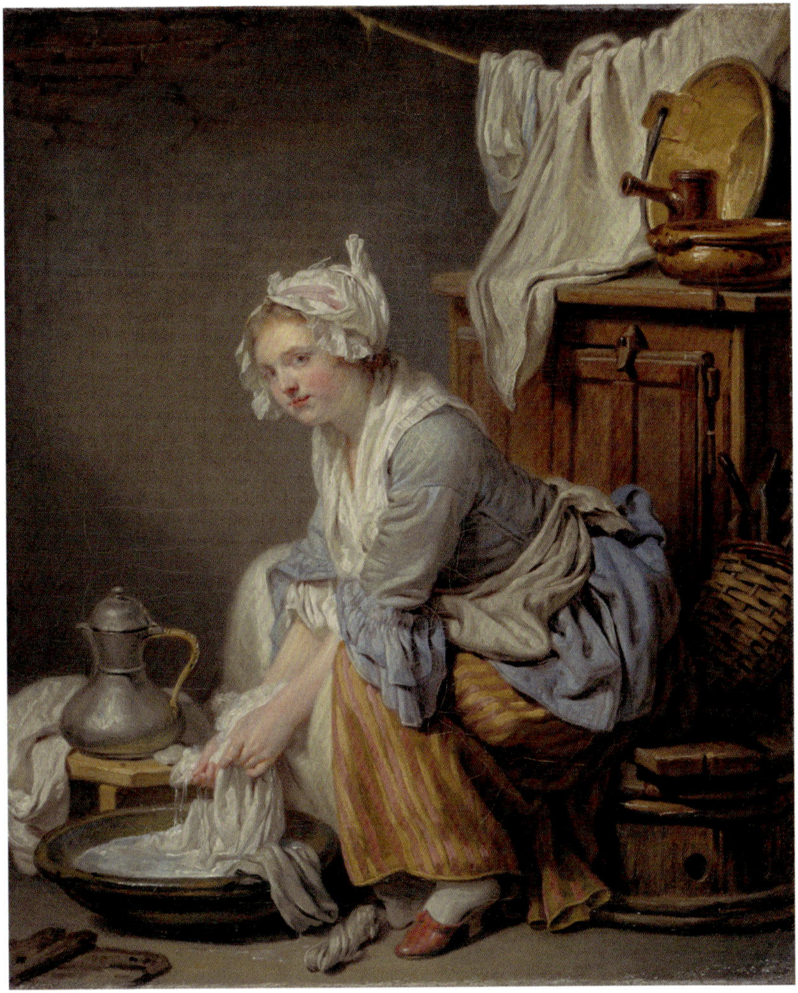

Greuze specialized in genre paintings, or images of daily life. Here, he describes a laundress's modest room and humble possessions with loving detail and a luxurious handling of paint. Washing linens was, however, an arduous, outdoor activity, so the interior setting, as well as the laundress's well-kept garments, delicate hands, and red shoe, does not document the lived reality of her profession. The painting drew on images of domestic servants by seventeenth-century Dutch and eighteenth-century French artists, as well as a form of contemporary popular literature called the *genre poissard*, which cast the laundress as a sexually charged figure. Greuze reimagined this working-class woman in a more sensual way, to satisfy the tastes of his elite clientele.

Johann Zoffany

German, 1733–1810

John, Fourteenth Lord Willoughby de Broke, and His Family in the Breakfast Room at Compton Verney, circa 1766

Oil on canvas, 101.9 × 127.3 cm (40 1/8 × 50 1/8 in.), 96.PA.312

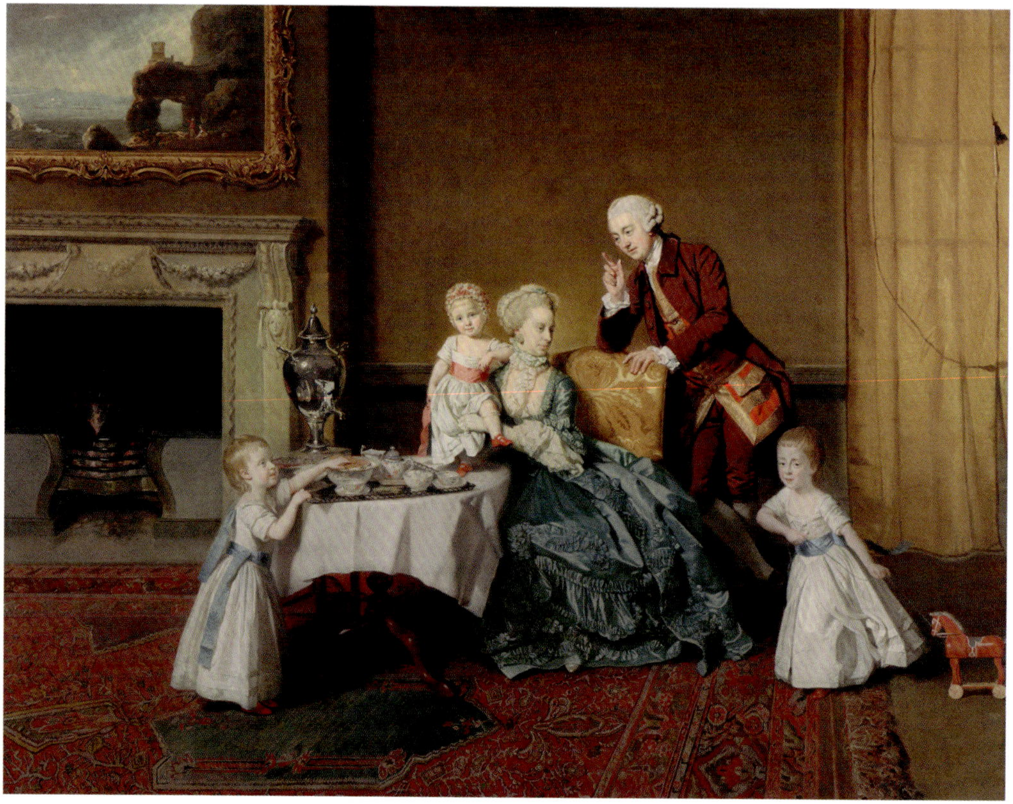

This painting of an English lord and lady with their children in the breakfast room of their ancestral home is a "conversation piece," a type of informal group portrait popular in eighteenth-century Britain. One of the finest practitioners of the genre, Zoffany vividly portrays the accoutrements of class—the fine costumes, imported Turkish rug and Chinese porcelain tea service, and silver urn—while describing an active and engaged family. Young George reaches for a piece of buttered toast as his father admonishes him; George's brother, John, enters the room pulling a toy horse, while his mother looks on, absently restraining her one-year-old daughter, Louisa. Zoffany's lustrous handling of paint combined with his meticulous illusionism mark this late painting as one of his finest.

Pietro Longhi

Italian, 1701–1785

The Painter in His Studio, circa 1741–44

Oil on canvas, 41 × 53.3 cm (16⅛ × 21 in.).

Purchased in part with funds realized from the sale of paintings donated by Burton Fredericksen and William Garred, 2011.20

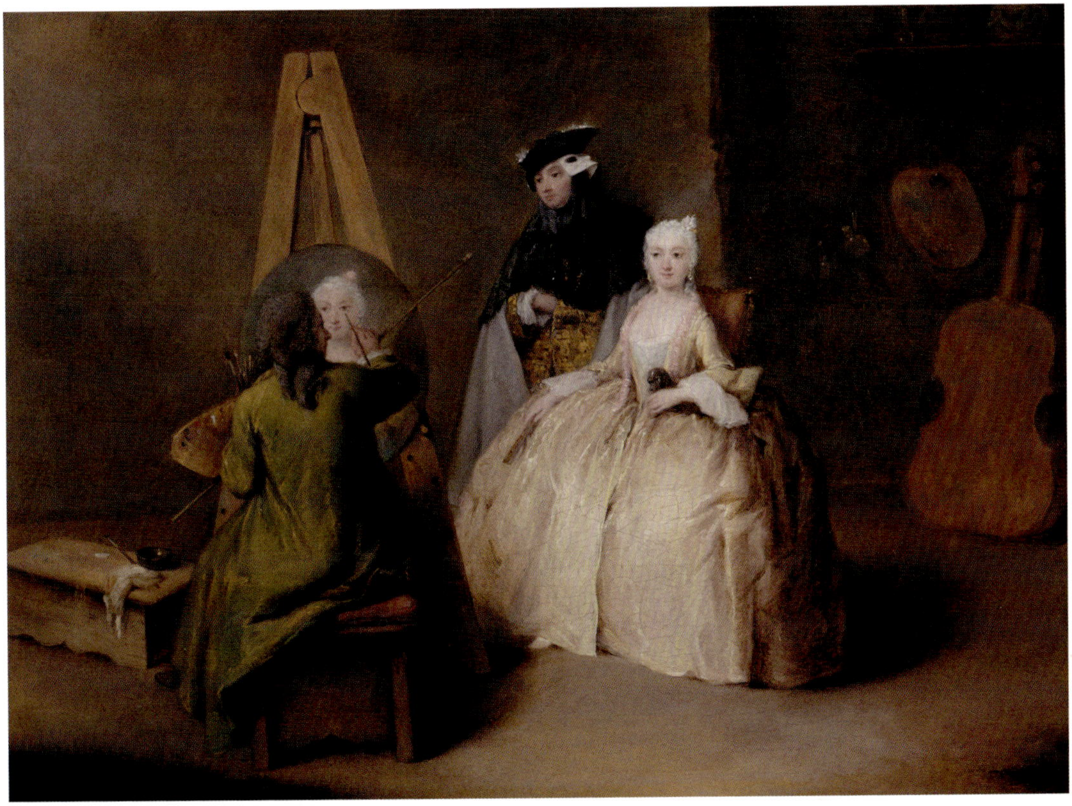

Longhi here conflates an allegory of the art of painting with an intimate scene of contemporary Venetian life. He invites us into a painter's studio, where the artist, surrounded by an array of tools and props, is executing a faithful likeness of a Venetian lady sitting for her portrait. Her costumed companion has removed his mask, which Venetians wore to remain incognito as they passed through crowds during the free-spirited months of Carnevale. Small, refined paintings like this one were especially popular as souvenirs for British travelers visiting Venice in the eighteenth century.

Thomas Gainsborough
British, 1727–1788
Portrait of James Christie, 1778
Oil on canvas, 127.6 × 102.2 cm
(50¼ × 40¼ in.), 70.PA.16

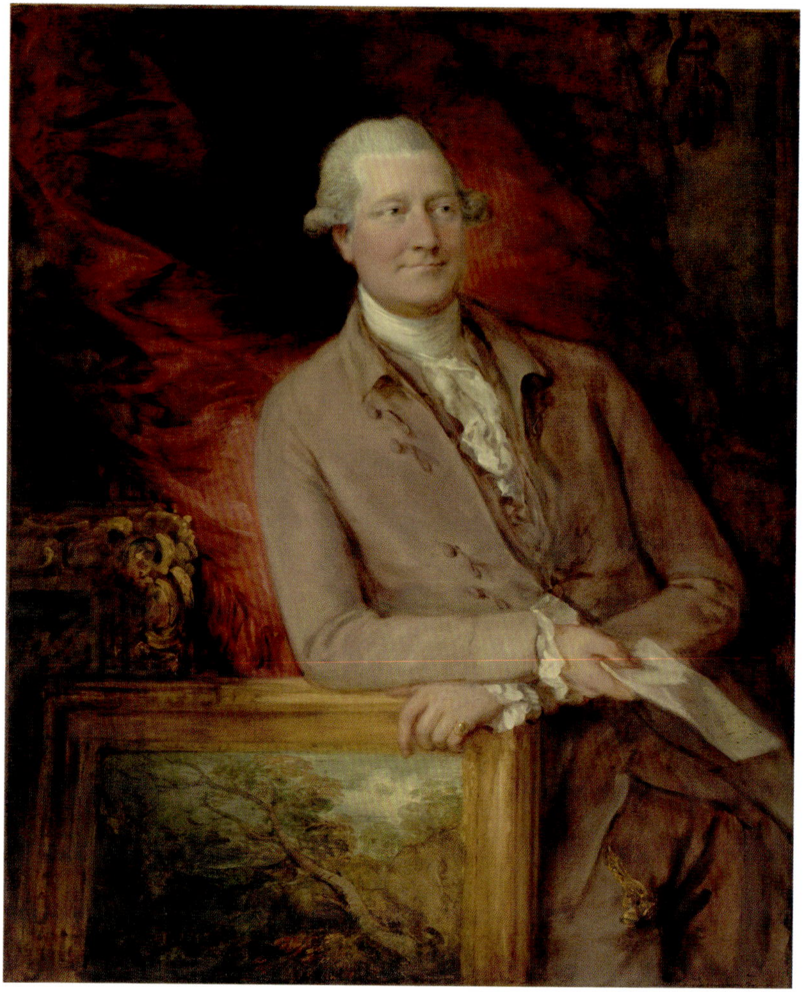

Gainsborough's portrait of James Christie (1730–1803) showcases the famous auctioneer's elegance and sophistication, with his powdered wig and signet ring. Handsome and quick-witted, Christie befriended numerous collectors and artists, Gainsborough among them. This portrait, an expression of mutual admiration between the two men, also served as a vehicle for mutual promotion: Gainsborough agreed to paint it on the condition that it would hang prominently in the saleroom of Christie's auction house, which still bears his name. Unusually for Gainsborough, the sitter is depicted indoors, leaning nonchalantly on the frame of a large landscape, undoubtedly another work by Gainsborough. This self-conscious reference highlights the artist's lifelong passion for landscape painting.

Sir Joshua Reynolds

British, 1723–1792

Portrait of Mai ("Omai"), circa 1776

Oil on canvas, 236 × 140 cm

(92 15/16 × 55 1/8 in.). Purchased jointly by the J. Paul Getty Trust and the Board of Trustees of the National Portrait Gallery, London, 2023. Support provided to NPG by the National Heritage Memorial Fund, Art Fund and other generous supporters, 2023.18

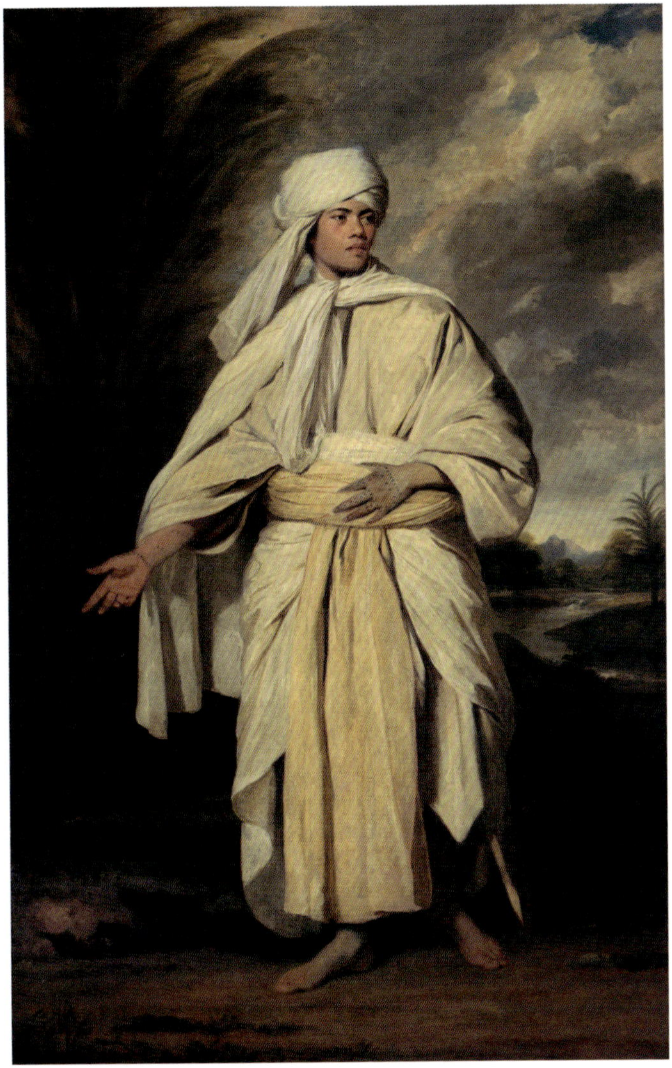

In 1774 a young man named Mai became the first Polynesian visitor to Great Britain. He had sailed from Tahiti with Captain James Cook, hoping to secure British military aid. Mai (or Omai, as he was known in England) aroused curiosity and admiration across British society. Reynolds depicts him standing barefoot before an idealized tropical landscape. The dynamic pose recalls that of the Apollo Belvedere, one of the most celebrated sculptures from classical antiquity, while Mai's turban and tattooed hands signal his non-European origin. Today, this painting, though magnificent, stands as a monument to the era's complicated history and troubling legacy of colonial incursion: behind its heroic presentation lies the story of a real individual whose life was profoundly affected by British imperialism.

Joseph Wright of Derby
British, 1734–1797
Two Boys with a Bladder, 1767
Oil on canvas, 92.7 × 73 cm
(36½ × 28¾ in.), 2020.20

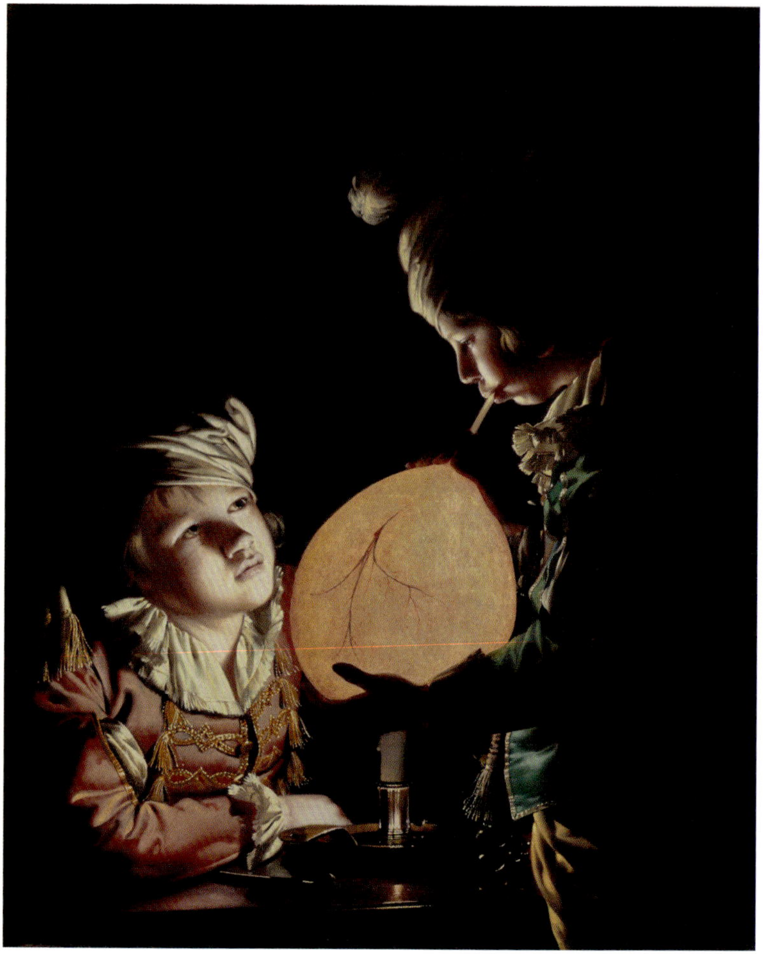

A single candle illuminates this striking nocturnal scene. At left, a sweet-faced boy leans forward in hushed excitement, looking up in wonder as his playmate, standing at right, blows air into an inflated bladder. The translucent toy at the center of the picture conceals the candle's flame, though its reflection glints in the boys' eyes. To increase the bladder's radiance, the artist adopted an experimental technique of applying silver within the paint layers on his canvas. This recently rediscovered painting, which belongs to a small group of distinctive "candlelight" pictures painted by Joseph Wright of Derby in the late 1760s, originally was part of a pair: its pendant is a similarly formatted picture of girls at play, now at Kenwood House, London.

Jean-Honoré Fragonard

French, 1732–1806

The Fountain of Love, circa 1785

Oil on canvas, 64.1 × 52.7 cm

(25¼ × 20¾ in.), 99.PA.30

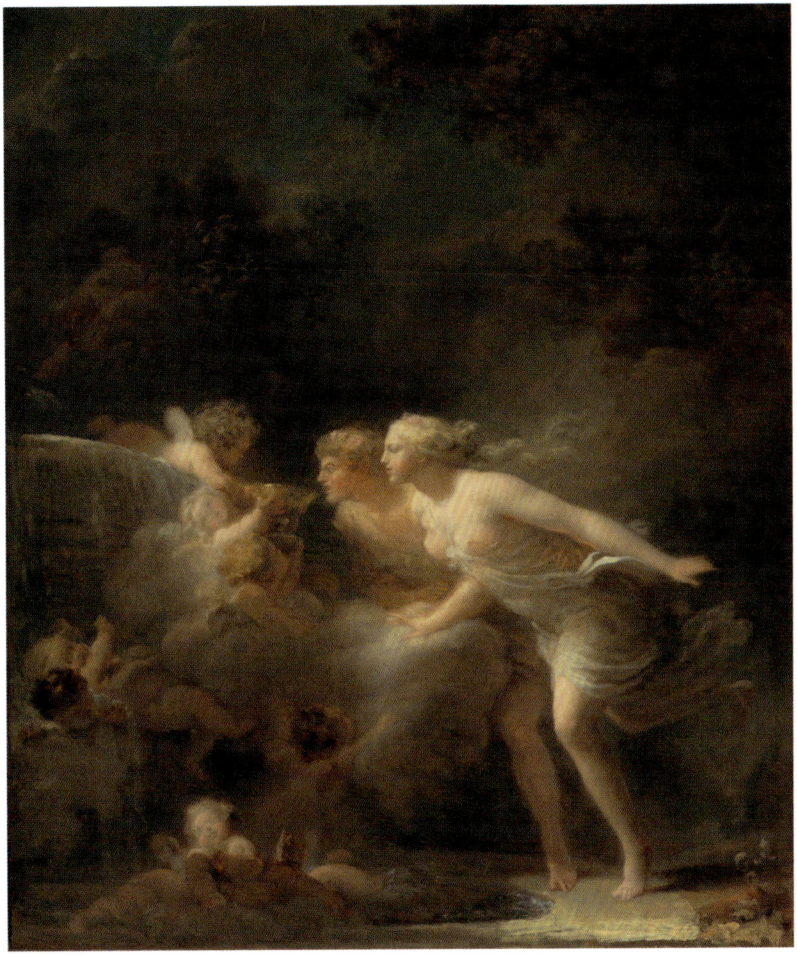

Fragonard, best known for sensuous, lighthearted images that epitomized the Rococo style, responded to the later Neoclassical movement with his own moonlit vision of antiquity. In *The Fountain of Love,* luminous effects and fluid brushwork bring a softness to the semiclad figures, all based on classical sculpture. The focal point of a poetic allegory of the progress of love, the fountain brings forth blissful waters from which couples drink and fall in love. During the eighteenth century, artists treated the theme as an everyday genre subject, with lovers in contemporary dress engaged in flirtation. Here, however, Fragonard returns the allegory to its classical origins, imbuing it with an intoxicating sense of new love's thrilling urgency.

Élisabeth Louise Vigée Le Brun

French, 1755–1842

The Vicomtesse de Vaudreuil, 1785

Oil on panel, 83.2 × 64.8 cm

(32¾ × 25½ in.), 85.PB.443

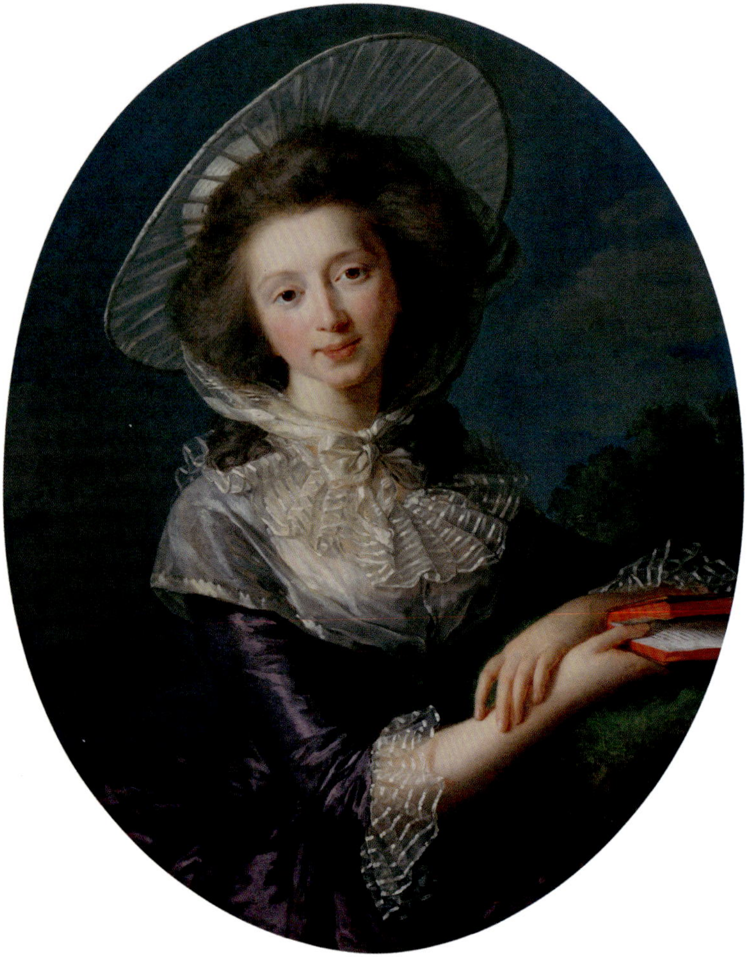

One of the first female artists to be admitted to the French Royal Academy, Vigée Le Brun was portrait painter to Queen Marie-Antoinette until the French Revolution. Royal patronage thrust her into illustrious society across Europe, making her the highest-paid woman painter at the time. In this portrait of the noblewoman Victoire-Pauline de Riquet de Camaran (1764–1834), Vigée Le Brun emphasizes the sitter's elegant, refined persona. In keeping with Enlightenment ideals, the viscountess has her thumb in a book, as if interrupted while reading. Engaging the viewer with a gentle smile, she boasts the latest fashions. Her violet satin *robe à l'anglaise*, topped with a linen fichu (shawl) and lace-trimmed collar and sleeves, highlight the artist's skill in rendering various fabrics.

Francisco de Goya (Francisco José de Goya y Lucientes)
Spanish, 1746–1828
Portrait of the Marquesa de Santiago, 1804
Oil on canvas, 209.9 × 126.7 cm (82⅝ × 49⅞ in.), 83.PA.12

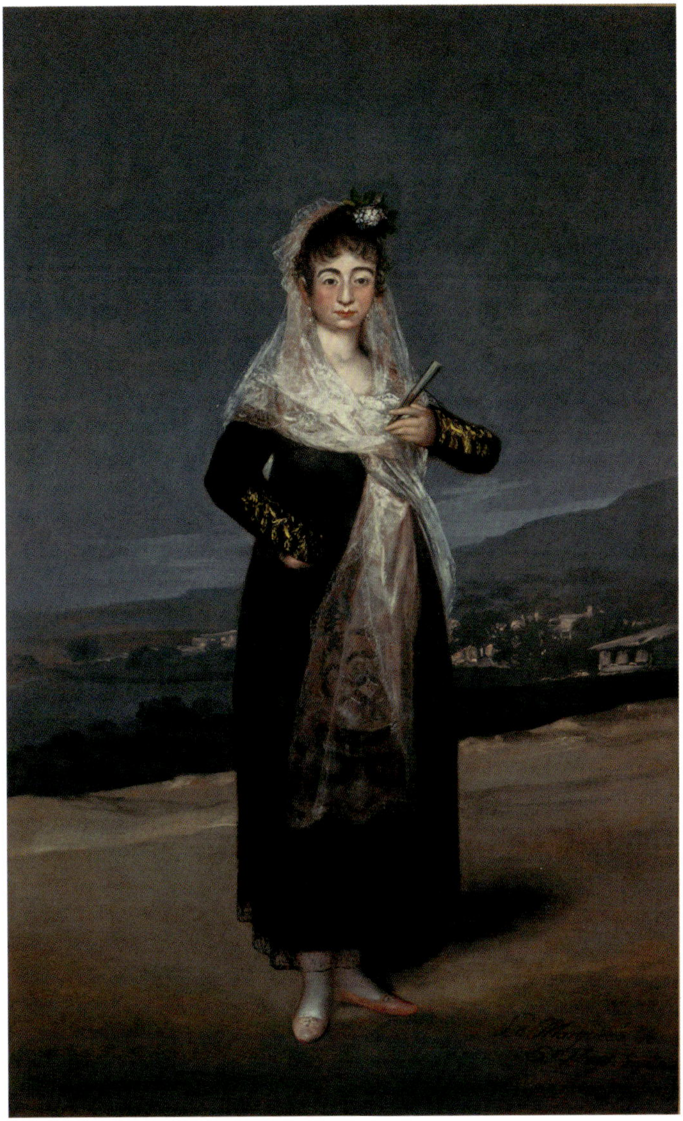

By the early 1800s Goya was the leading painter of the Spanish royal family, aristocracy, and liberal intelligentsia. This bold portrait depicts a wealthy noblewoman known for her independent spirit and quick wit. She faces the viewer with one hand assertively placed against her hip and the other holding a fan. Distinguished by a white lace mantilla (shawl), gold-braided sleeves, black lace skirt, and dainty coral-colored shoes, the marchioness's attire was highly fashionable, but Goya refused to idealize his subject, depicting her with extraordinary frankness.

Louis-Léopold Boilly

French, 1761–1845

Entrance to the Jardin Turc, 1812

Oil on canvas, 73.3 × 91.4 cm

(28⅞ × 36 in.), 2010.11

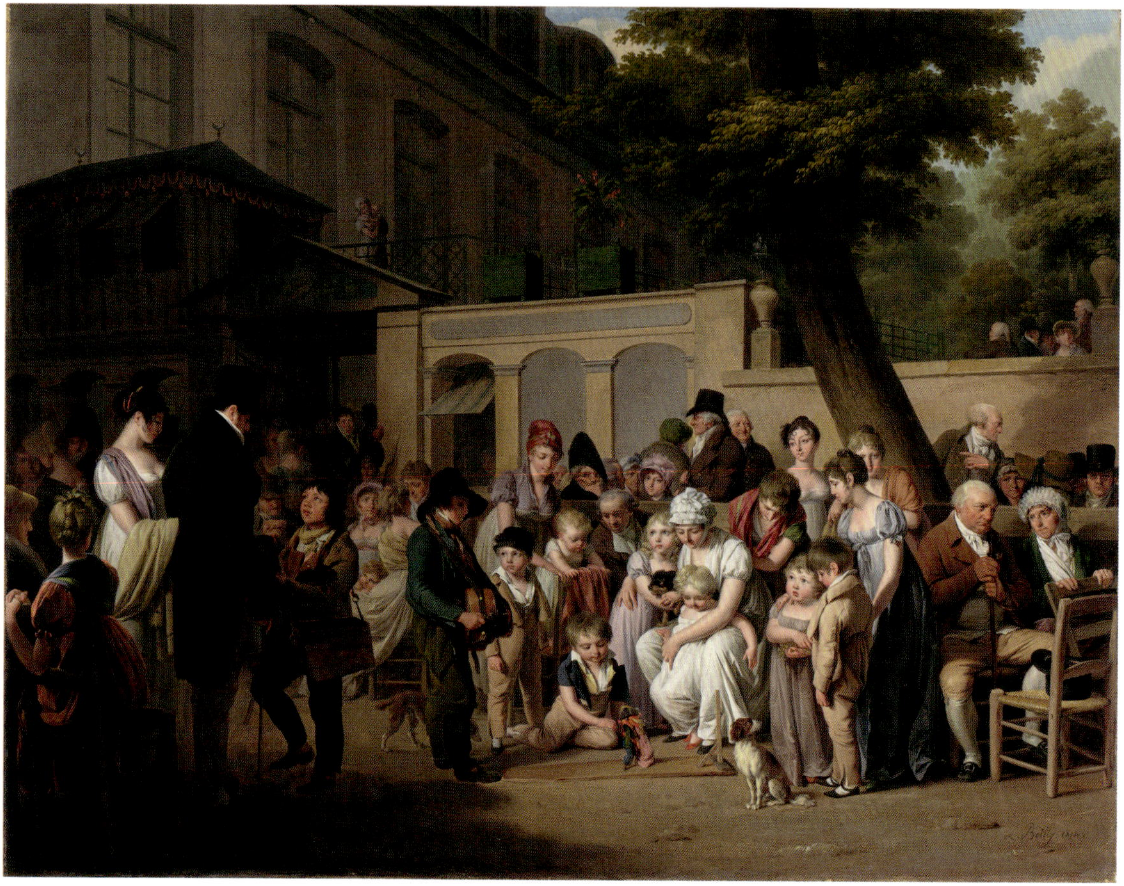

This charming scene of public leisure was calculated to flatter Boilly's contemporary audience. The setting is the Jardin Turc (Turkish Garden), a fashionable Parisian café and pleasure garden. Well-to-do patrons sit contentedly inside while all manner of social types mingle on the boulevard. Two child performers solicit particular attention, one holding a marmot and the other playing a hurdy-gurdy while dancing marionettes with his leg. Among several figures engaging the viewer with a direct look is Boilly himself, in spectacles and a top hat at far right. Although the painting's high degree of technical polish hearkens back to earlier traditions of Dutch painting, the artist's interest in the urban spectacle of modern Paris anticipates the work of the Impressionists later in the nineteenth century.

Jacques-Louis David

French, 1748–1825

Suzanne Le Peletier de Saint-Fargeau, 1804

Oil on canvas, 60.3 × 49.5 cm (23¾ × 19½ in.), 97.PA.36

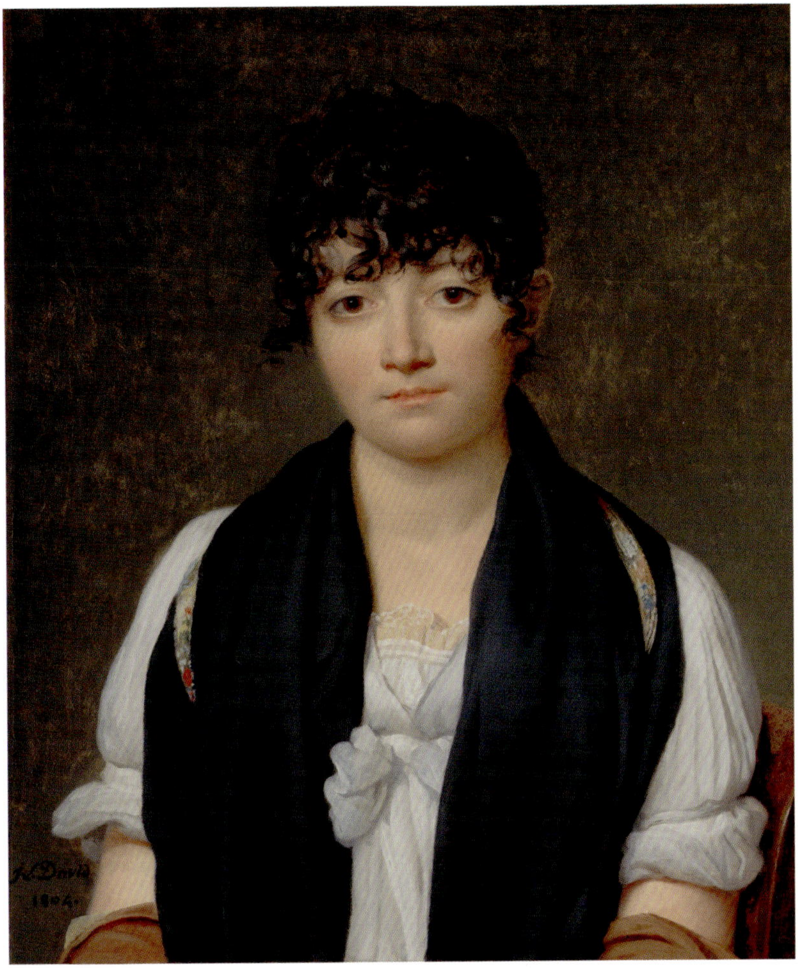

Despite the demanding obligations of his new post as Napoleon's First Painter, David accepted a commission to paint this intimate portrait of Suzanne Le Peletier (1782–1829), the daughter of a revolutionary martyr whom the French nation had officially adopted as a "daughter of the state." She is eminently stylish, with her tight, glossy ringlets, black cashmere stole, high-waisted empire dress, and elbow-length gloves, but there is also a disarming hint of vulnerability in her calm, soft gaze. The portrait was likely painted on the occasion of her engagement and intended primarily for her fiancé.

Jacques-Louis David

French, 1748–1825

The Farewell of Telemachus and Eucharis, 1818

Oil on canvas, 88.3 × 103.2 cm (34¾ × 40⅝ in.), 87.PA.27

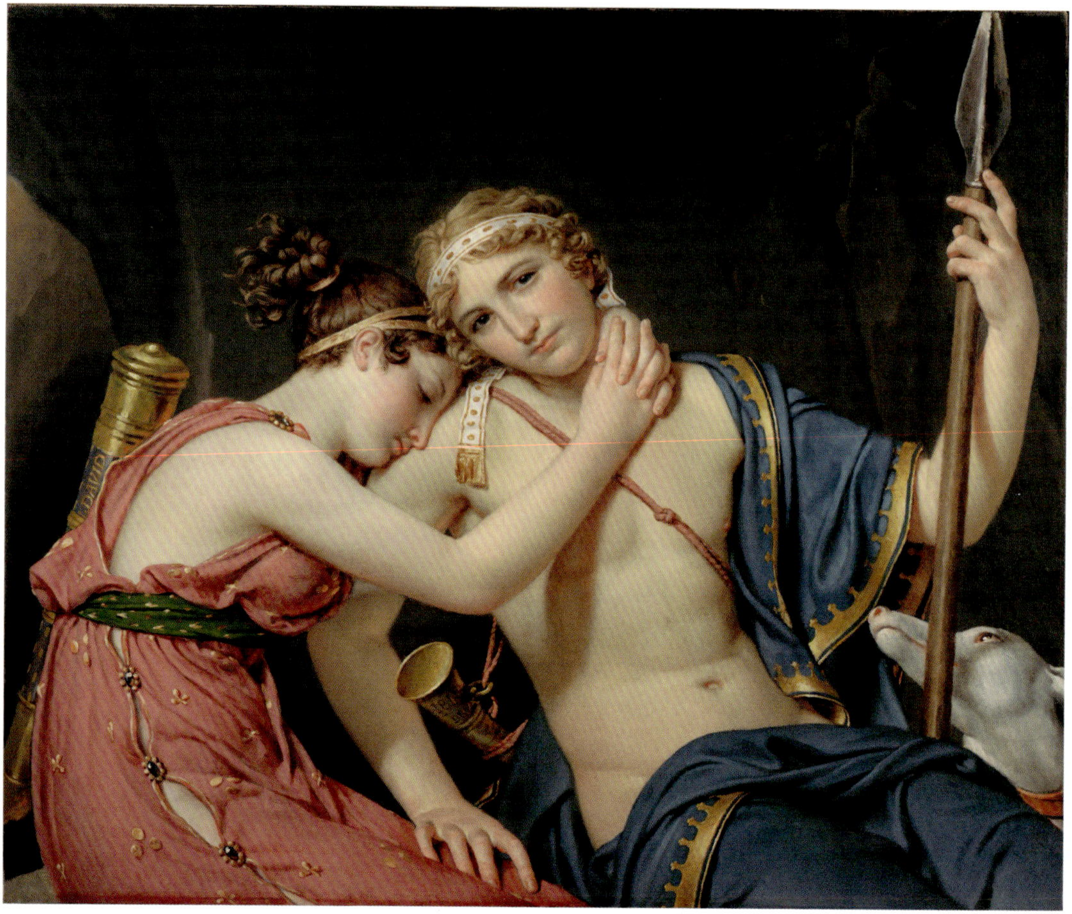

During the final decade of his life, which he spent in voluntary exile in Brussels, David created a series of innovative paintings of classical mythological subjects involving erotic entanglements. In *The Farewell,* based on a scene from the ancient Greek epic *The Odyssey*, filial duty compels the hero Telemachus to abandon his lover, the nymph Eucharis, to search for his missing father, Odysseus. The elegantly interlacing figures of the two lovers showcase David's characteristic perfection of line and form, here combined with Flemish-inspired color harmonies of reds, blues, and cool flesh tones.

Théodore Géricault

French, 1791–1824

Study of the Model Joseph, circa 1818–19

Oil on canvas, 47 × 38.7 cm

(18½ × 15¼ in.), 85.PA.407

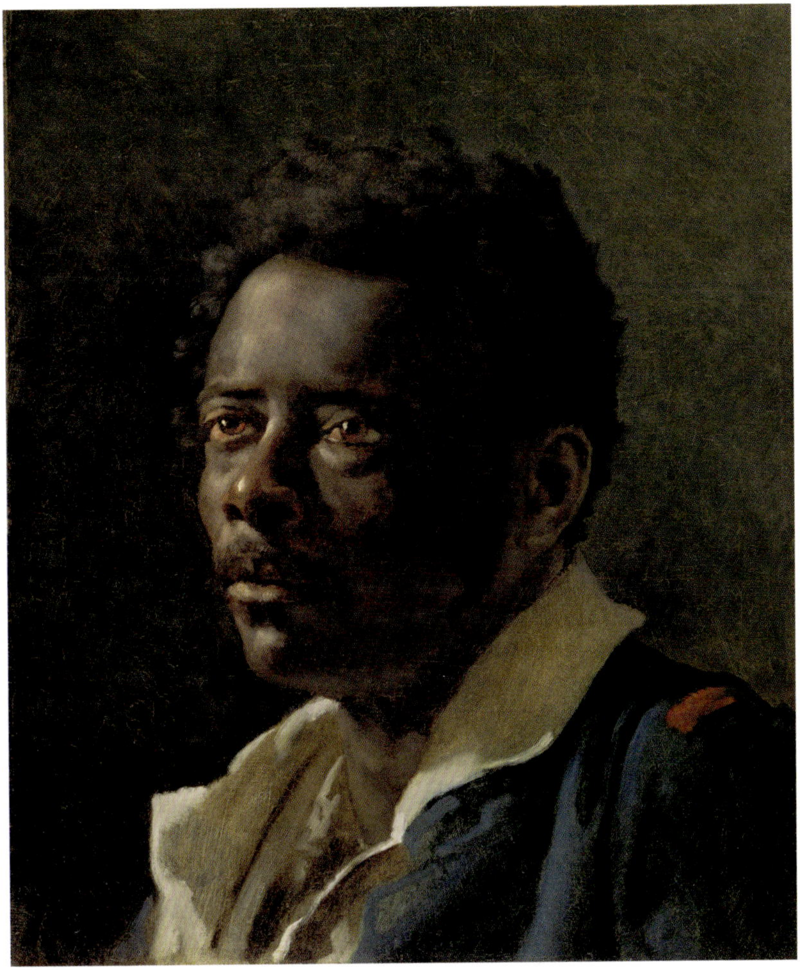

Géricault painted this moving *tête d'étude*, or head study, as part of the intensive preparations he undertook to create his famous large-scale masterpiece, *The Raft of the Medusa* (Paris, Musée du Louvre). It depicts a man known as Joseph, whose full name has not come down to us. Born in Saint-Domingue (modern Haiti), Joseph emigrated to France, where he found employment as an acrobat before being recruited as a model by Géricault. Joseph became renowned in the studios of Paris and eventually won a competitive position as a model at the École des Beaux-Arts, France's premier art school.

Caspar David Friedrich

German, 1774–1840

A Walk at Dusk, circa 1830–35

Oil on canvas, 33.2 × 43.2 cm

(13 1/16 × 17 in.), 93.PA.14

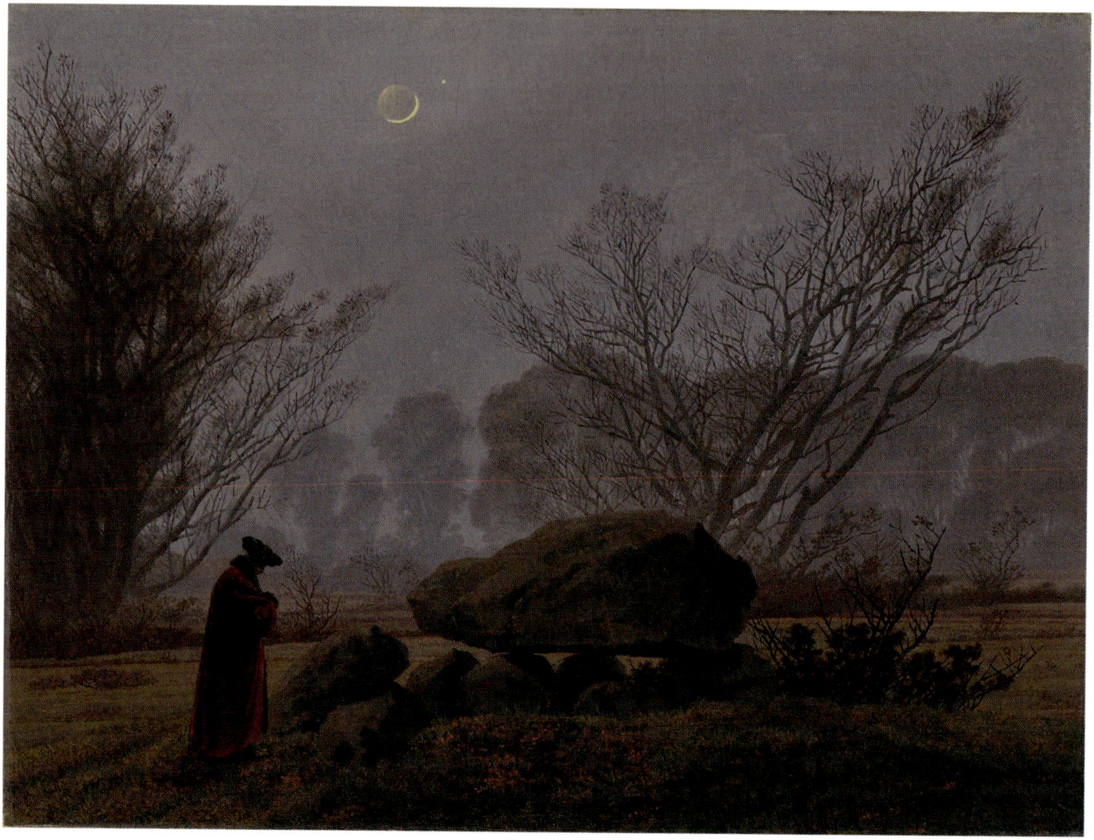

In Friedrich's exalted and highly spiritual conception of landscape painting, nature symbolized the most profound human experiences and feelings. Among the last canvases he completed before suffering a debilitating stroke, *A Walk at Dusk* shows a solitary figure in scholar's dress contemplating death in the form of an ancient megalithic tomb. It is winter, and leafless trees loom like specters, but the waxing moon above—a recurring motif for the artist—carries a promise of rebirth.

Joseph Mallord William Turner

British, 1775–1851

Modern Rome–Campo Vaccino, 1839

Oil on canvas, 91.8 × 122.6 cm

(36⅛ × 48¼ in.), 2011.6

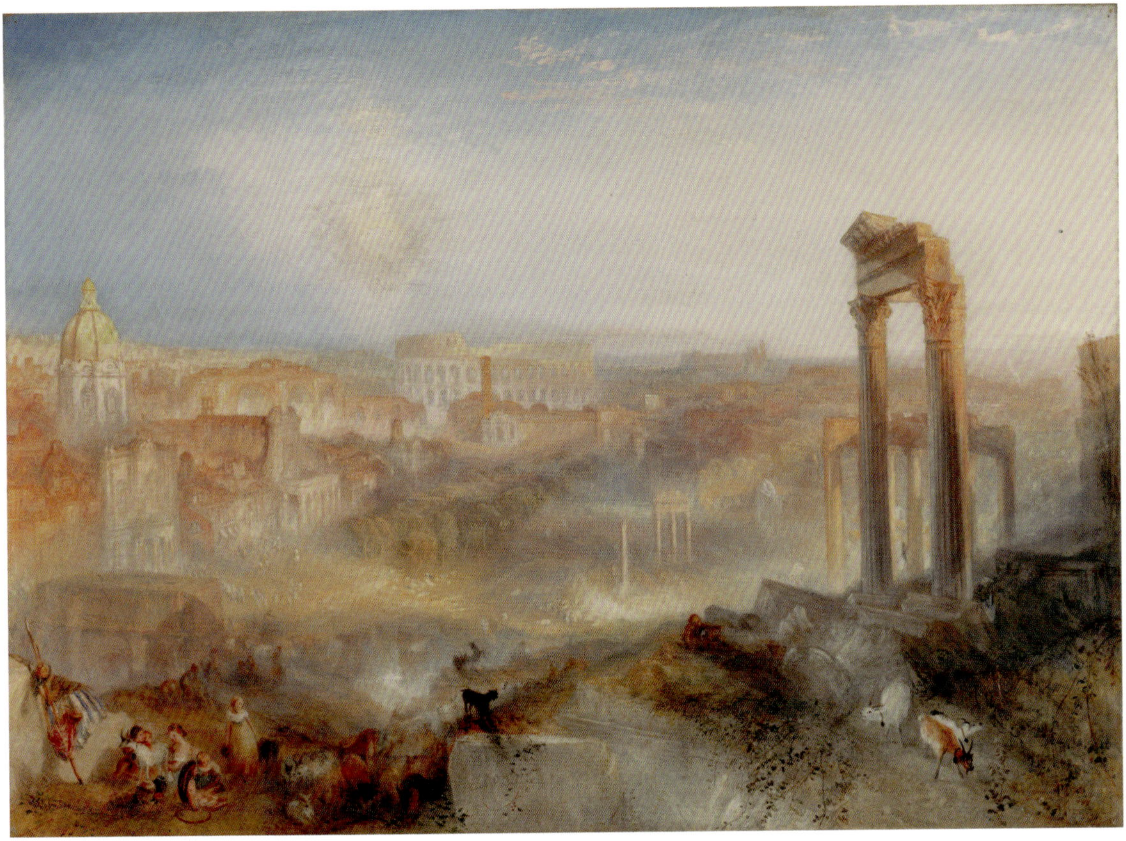

Turner's dazzling use of color may have attracted ridicule in his day, but the brilliant palette of his paintings undoubtedly helped set them apart. This painting was inspired in part by a line from Lord Byron's epic poem *Childe Harold's Pilgrimage* (1818), describing the city of Rome: "The Moon is up and yet it is not night; / The Sun as yet divides the Day with her." As in the poem, a moon rises over the Colosseum at left while the sun sets behind the Capitoline Hill at right, bathing the Baroque churches and antique monuments that surround the Roman Forum in an iridescent light. Amid the city's bygone splendors, its modern inhabitants carry on with their lives, herding goats, taking part in a religious procession, and laying out laundry to dry.

Jean-François Millet
French, 1814–1875
Portrait of Louise-Antoinette Feuardent,
1841
Oil on canvas, 73.3 × 60 cm
(28⁷⁄₈ × 23⁵⁄₈ in.), 95.PA.67

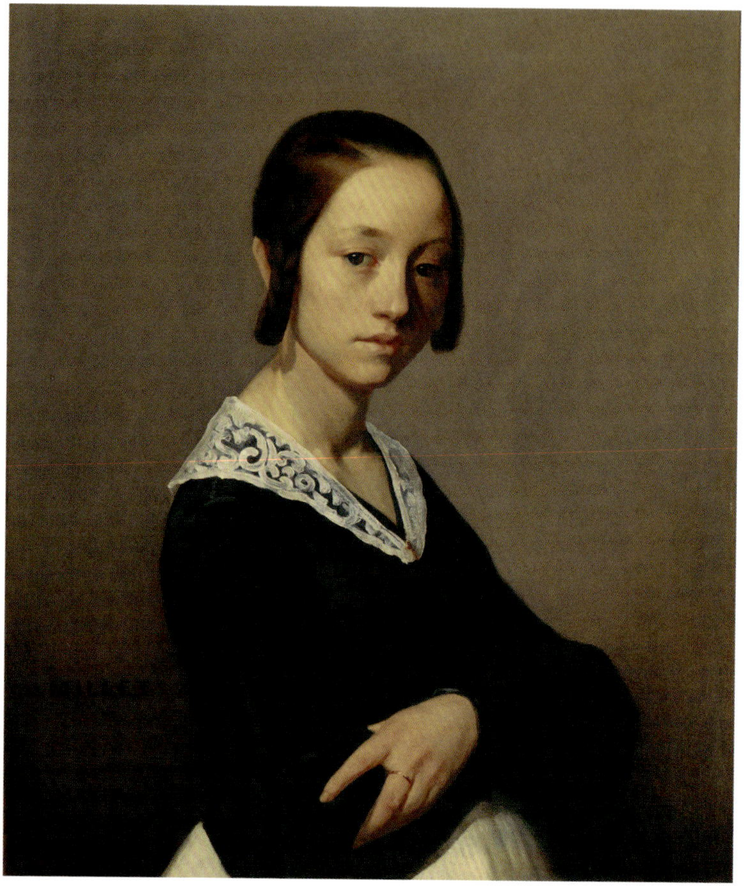

A strong gaze counters the sitter's modest pose in this beautifully restrained portrait. It depicts the twenty-two-year-old Louise-Antoinette Casini (1818–1907), a widow who had just married Millet's close friend Félix-Bienaimé Feuardent (1819–1907), a bookseller in Cherbourg, in the artist's native Normandy. Posing for Millet shortly after the marriage, the ring on her finger prominently displayed, Madame Feuardent would go on to bear eleven children, one of whom would marry the artist's eldest daughter, Marie, in 1871. By that point, Millet had achieved international fame as a painter of peasant life in such works as *Man with a Hoe* (see p. 205), his humble beginnings as a provincial portraitist long behind him.

Jean-François Millet

French, 1814–1875

Man with a Hoe, 1860–62

Oil on canvas, 81.9 × 100.3 cm

(32¼ × 39½ in.), 85.PA.114

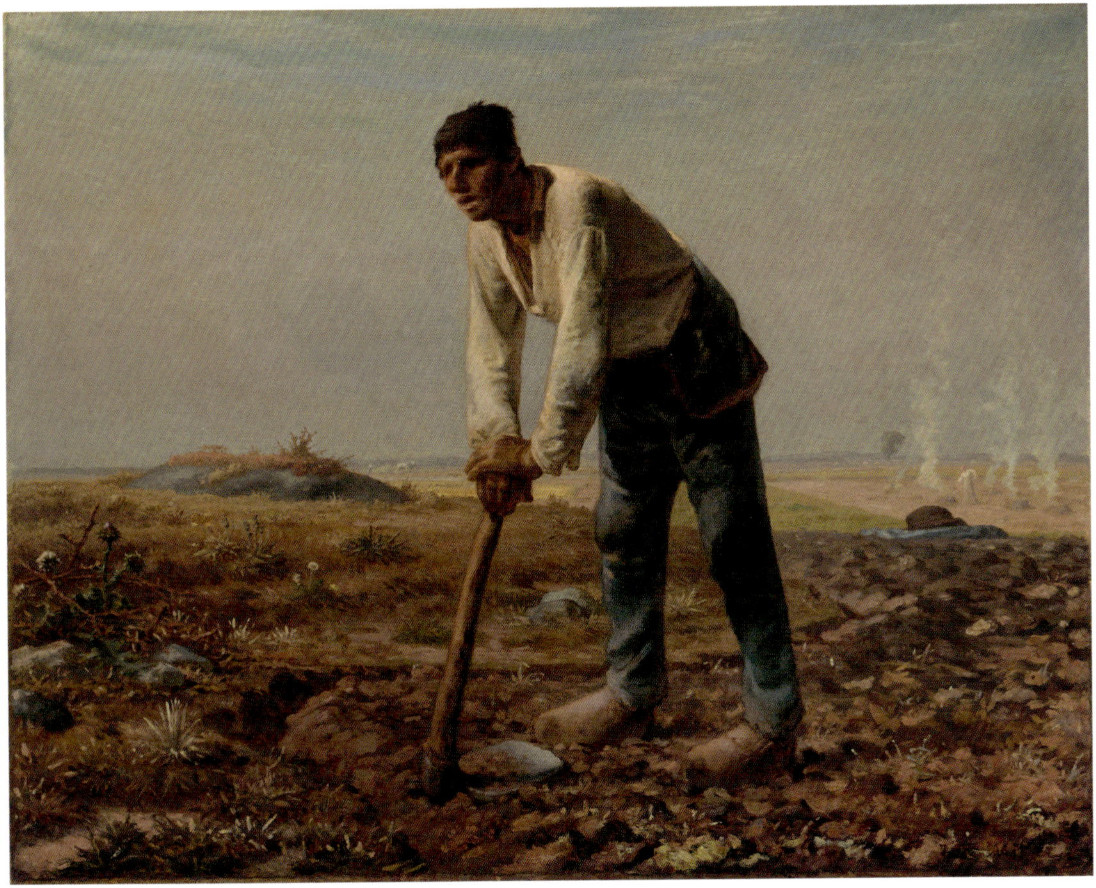

Leaning heavily upon his crude tool, an exhausted laborer who has been tilling rocky, weed-choked terrain looks up to catch his breath. Stooped and weary yet looming above the horizon, this imposing figure embodied, for Millet, a hard biblical truth about the human condition: "Thou shalt eat thy bread in the sweat of thy brow" (Genesis 3:19). Scandalized critics at the time, however, saw the painting as an ugly nadir in modern realism, describing the figure as a "cretin" and denouncing Millet for making a spectacle of human degradation. Some went so far as to compare Millet's everyman to Martin Dumollard, a notorious serial killer whose trial and execution had riveted France in 1862.

Édouard Manet

French, 1832–1883

Portrait of Madame Brunet, circa 1861–63, reworked by 1867

Oil on canvas, 132.4 × 100 cm (52⅛ × 39⅜ in.), 2011.53

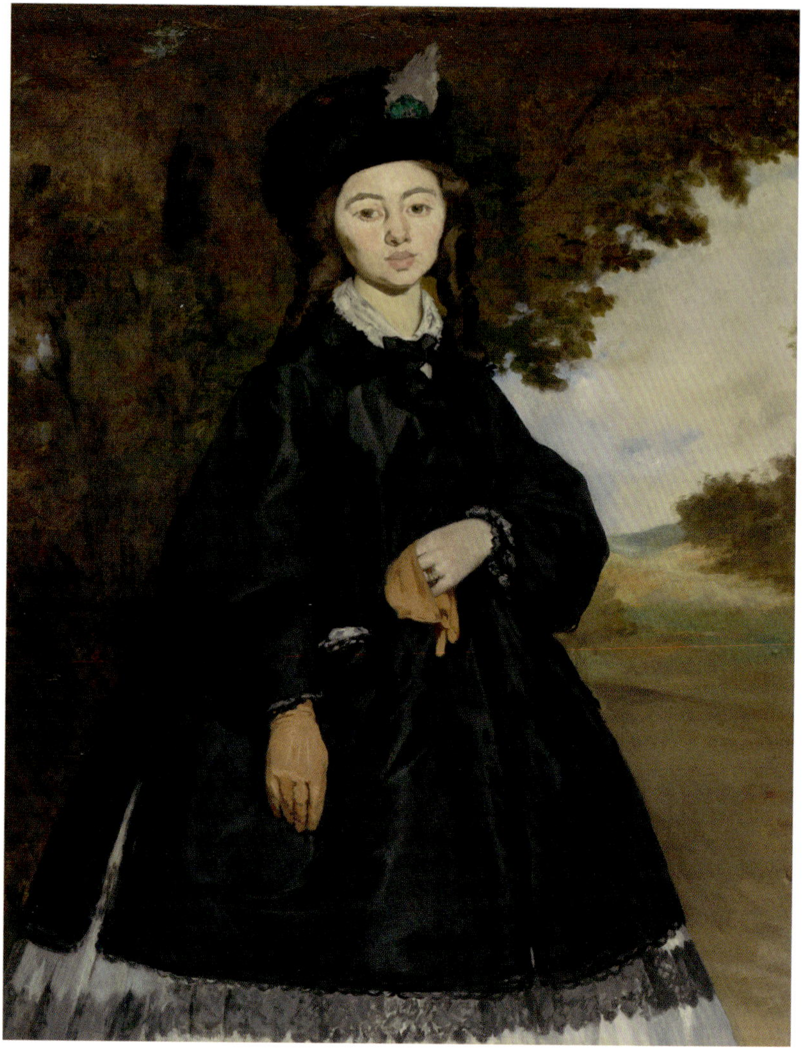

This portrait's bold brushwork, stark contrasts of light and dark, and forthright presentation reflect Manet's passion for seventeenth-century Spanish painting and his impatience with the established portrait conventions of his day. The woman depicted, Caroline Brunet (née de Pène; 1837–1878), the wife of an artist friend, is said to have tearfully rejected the painting on account of its perceived ugliness. Retaining it in his studio, Manet eventually cut off the bottom portion of the canvas, reducing it from a full-length to a three-quarter-length portrait. He then displayed it in a solo exhibition that he mounted in Paris in 1867—a defiant show of independence opposing the official survey of French painting that had been organized as part of the World's Fair that year.

Édouard Manet

French, 1832–1883

Jeanne (Spring), 1881

Oil on canvas, 74 × 51.5 cm (29⅛ × 20¼ in.), 2014.62

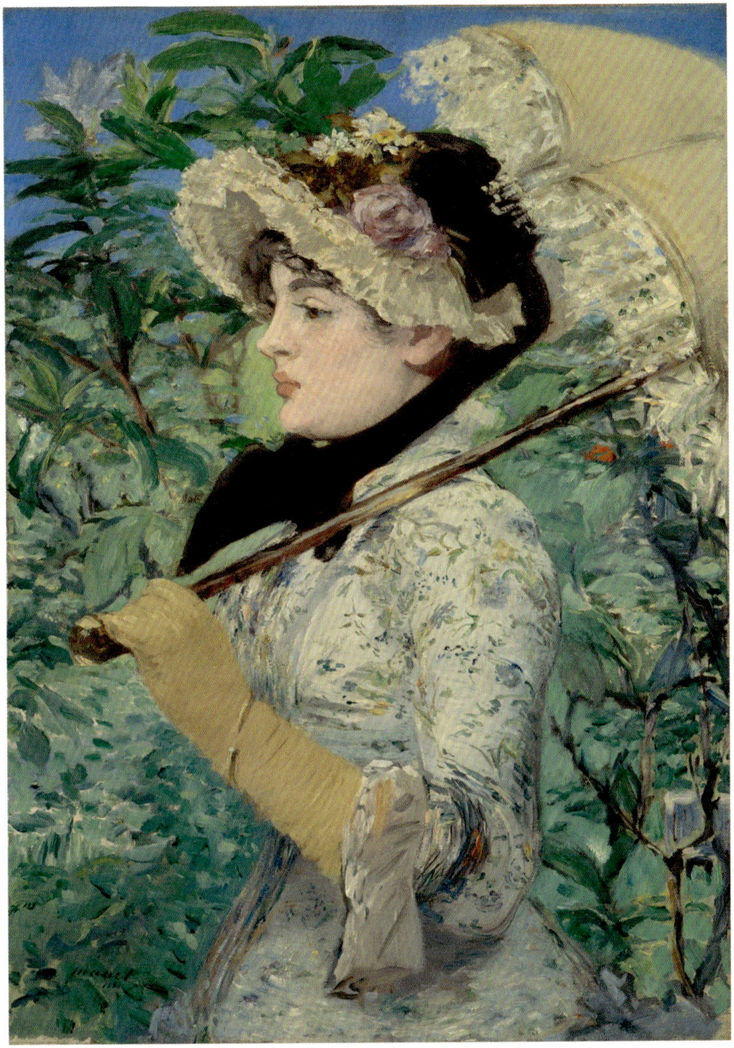

This half-length portrait of the actress and model Jeanne Demarsy as the embodiment of Spring was the first in an unfinished series of paintings of the seasons that Manet undertook in the last two years of his life. Presented in profile against a background of rhododendrons, Jeanne typifies the chic Parisienne (Parisian woman) in her white dress with floral accents, camel-colored gloves, ruffled bonnet, and dainty parasol—a springtime ensemble that Manet, a connoisseur of women's fashion, is said to have selected himself. The painting's charming model, vibrant palette, and luscious, painterly handling made it one of the few resounding public and critical successes of Manet's career when he exhibited it in Paris in 1882.

Édouard Manet

French, 1832–1883

The Rue Mosnier with Flags, 1878

Oil on canvas, 65.4 × 80 cm

(25¾ × 31½ in.), 89.PA.71

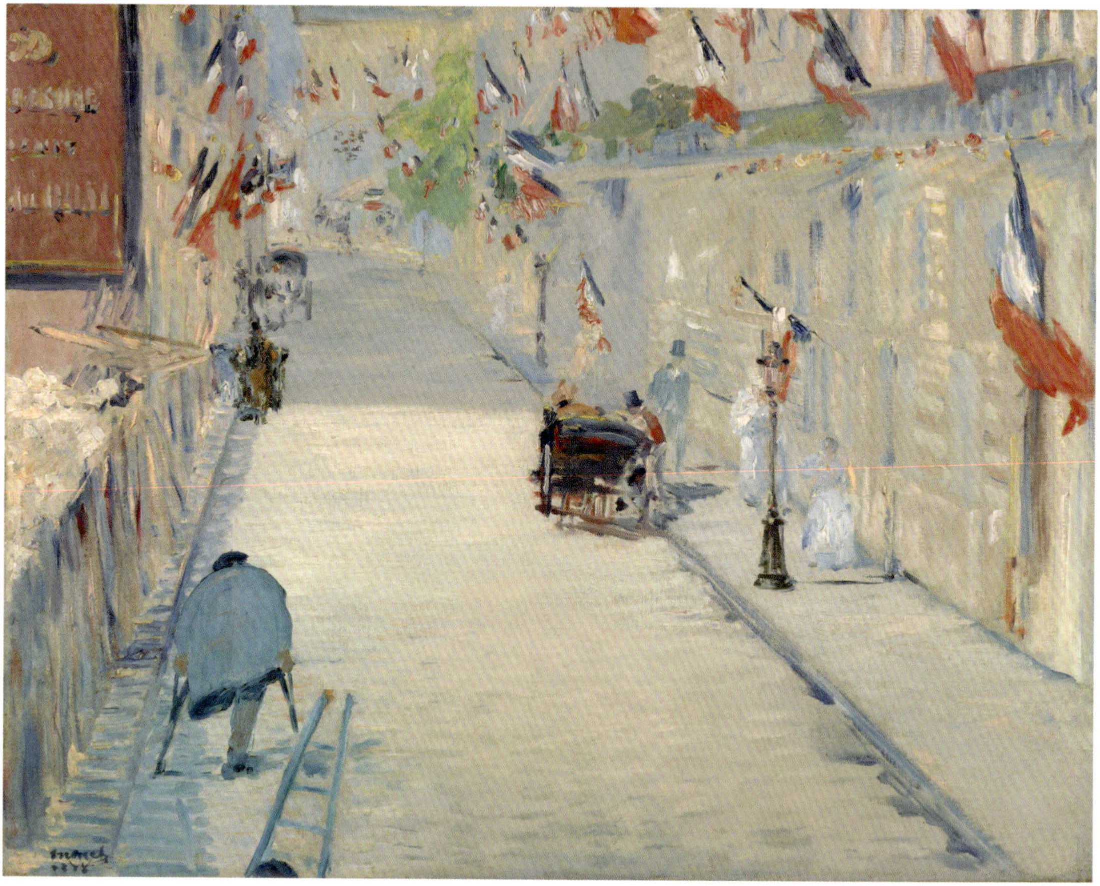

Manet's studio window looked onto the rue Mosnier, a newly built street in Paris in the redeveloped area around the Saint-Lazare train station. Here, the street is bedecked with flags for a national holiday—June 30, 1878—meant to celebrate France's triumphant recovery from the traumas of the Franco-Prussian War and ensuing revolutionary uprising known as the Paris Commune (1870–71). Manet's painting, however, is more ironic than celebratory, despite the brilliant sunshine and lively Impressionist brushwork. By juxtaposing a one-legged veteran in a worker's smock hobbling past a pile of construction rubble on the left with the bourgeois pedestrians and elegant apartment facades on the right, Manet underscored the social divisions and inequities that persisted in modern Paris.

Gustave Caillebotte

French, 1848–1894

Young Man at His Window, 1876

Oil on canvas, 116 × 81 cm

(45 11/16 × 31 7/8 in.), 2021.67

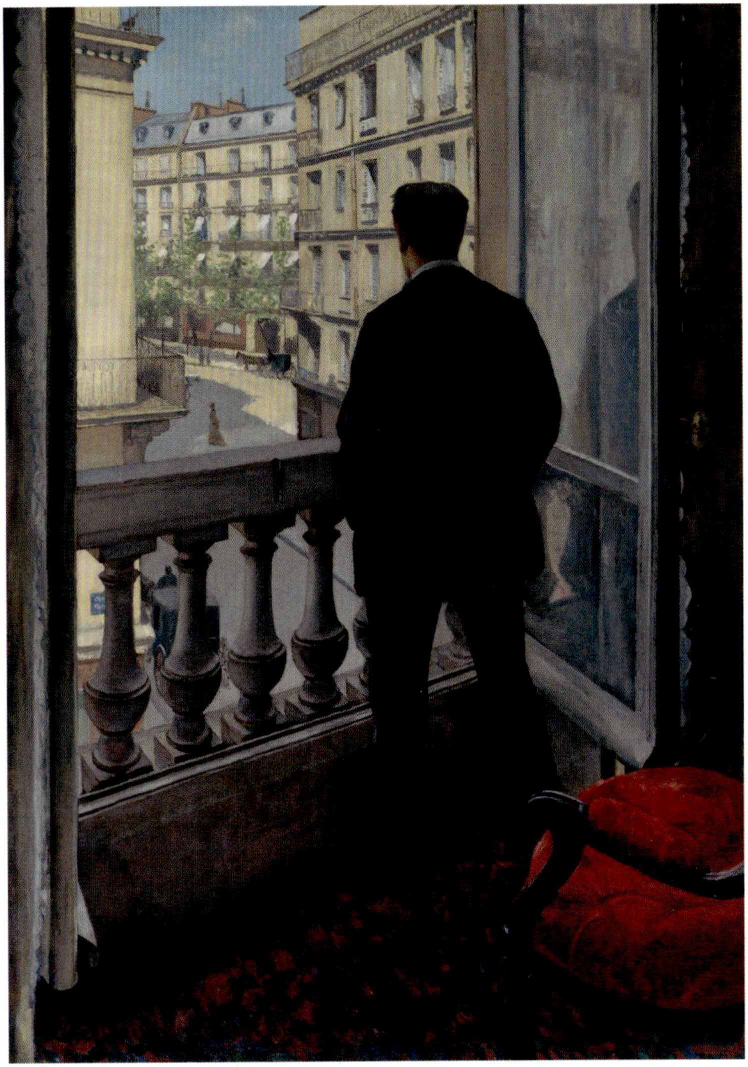

With his back to the viewer and his hands in his pockets, the artist's brother René stands at the third-story window of their affluent family's Paris mansion, surveying the sunlit streetscape below. The picture's forceful perspective pinpoints the object of his gaze: a solitary woman walking along the boulevard. Elevated and detached, the young man's view is commanding and proprietary: this is *his* window, as the title specifies. Caillebotte's own visual mastery is implied in the painting's sharp detail and complex perspective. A highly original conjunction of domestic interior and street scene, the work marked Caillebotte's memorable public debut in 1876, at the Impressionists' second group exhibition in Paris.

Pierre-Auguste Renoir
French, 1841–1919
The Promenade, 1870
Oil on canvas, 81.3 × 64.8 cm
(32 × 25½ in.), 89.PA.41

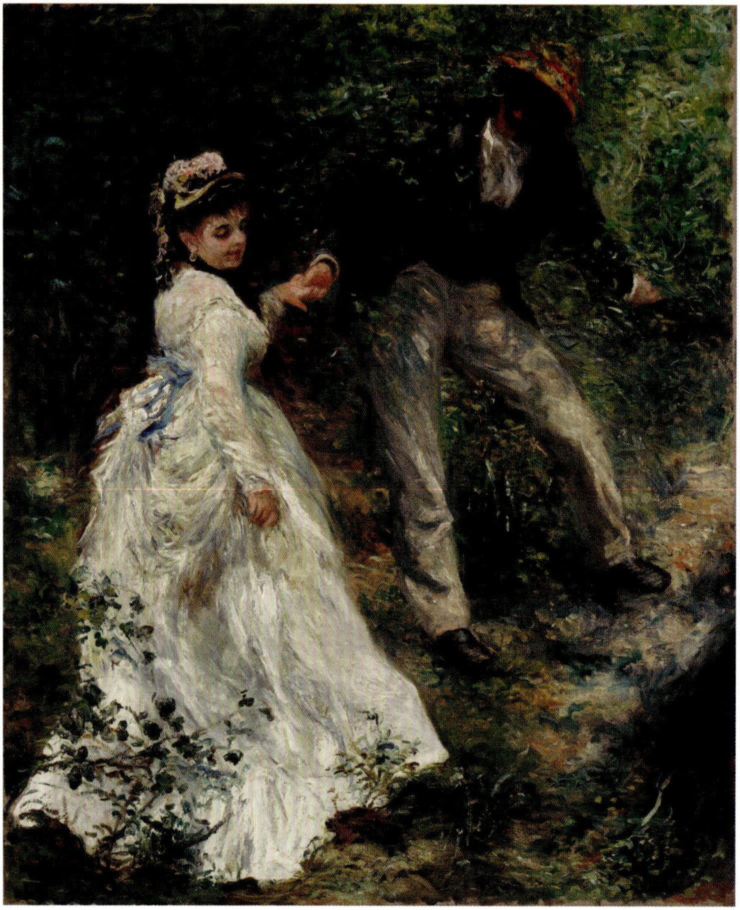

Renoir's unapologetically sensual art often treats themes of romance and courtship. Here, a swarthy young man, holding back undergrowth in a show of gallantry, leads a young woman into the shaded privacy of a wood. Brilliantly conveying the dappled effect of sunlight filtered through foliage, this painting is among the first in which Renoir depicted large-scale figures in an outdoor setting with the flickering, broken brushstrokes of the new Impressionist technique, which he had been developing in close dialogue with fellow painter Claude Monet (see pp. 211, 212).

Claude Monet

French, 1840–1926

Sunrise (Marine), 1872 or 1873

Oil on canvas, 50.2 × 61 cm (19¾ × 24 in.),

98.PA.164

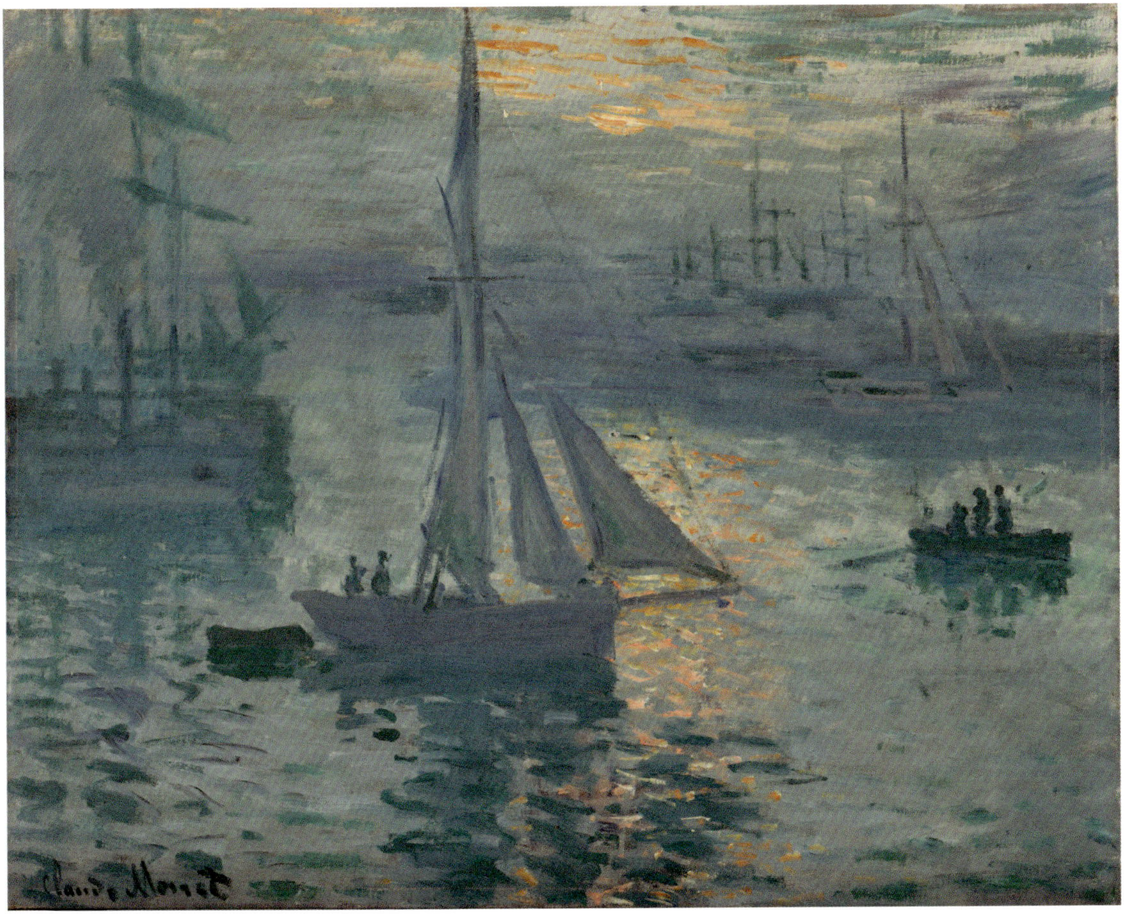

Monet's paintings of the northern French harbor of Le Havre in the early 1870s marked the birth of Impressionism in the popular imagination. In this remarkably well-preserved example, the painter concentrated on capturing the effect of early morning light, diffused by fog and smoke, shimmering on the water. The rapid, sketchlike execution of such works shocked contemporary art critics, who considered them unfinished "impressions" rather than full-fledged pictures.

Claude Monet

French, 1840–1926

Wheatstacks, Snow Effect, Morning, 1891

Oil on canvas, 64.8 × 100.3 cm

(25½ × 39½ in.), 95.PA.63

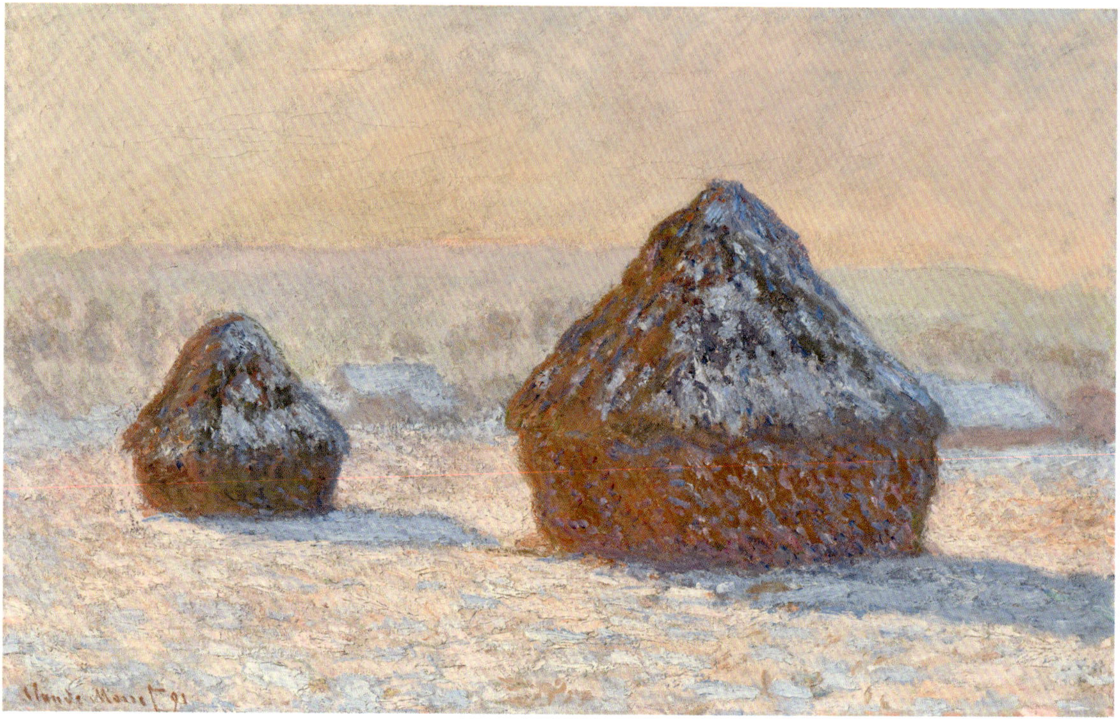

In the fall of 1890, Monet, the pioneer of Impressionism in the 1870s, embarked on his most ambitious project to date. Once again, he introduced an important innovation, that of painting a single motif in a concerted series of pictures that expressed a wide range of light and weather effects. The stacks of harvested wheat that punctuated the fields near his property in Giverny, northwest of Paris, were the subject of his first series. Here, Monet employed thick brushstrokes to describe the crusty, frozen ground, imposing wheat stacks, and long, blue shadows cast by the cold morning light. This virtuoso work is the result of both direct observation outdoors and extended effort in the studio.

Edgar Degas

French, 1834–1917

After the Bath, circa 1895

Oil on canvas, 65.7 × 82.2 cm

(25 7/8 × 32 3/8 in.), 2001.20

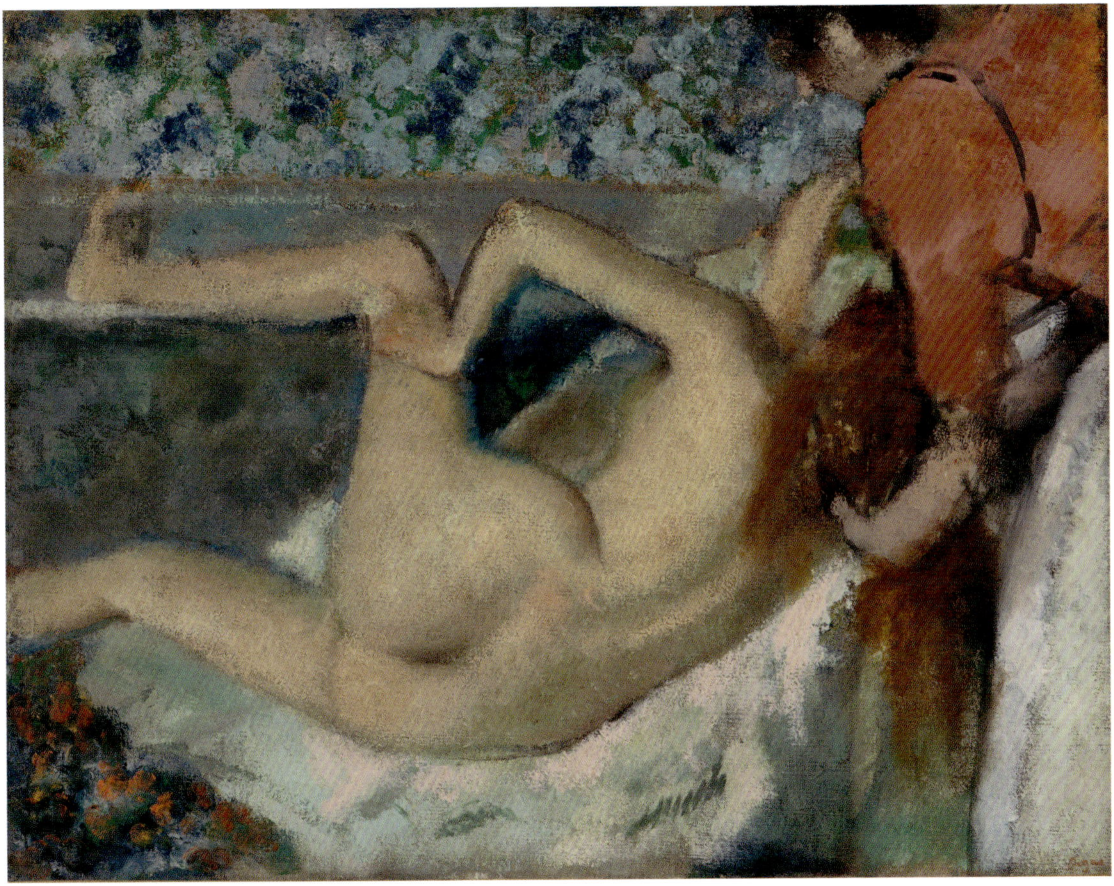

The female nude was a primary vehicle for Degas's relentless artistic experiments during much of his long career. Posing a radical challenge to convention, *After the Bath* resists any straightforward narrative reading, for the woman's awkward stance is highly implausible for the mundane scenario suggested by the title. One is reminded instead of the rigorous sessions to which Degas notoriously subjected his hired models in the studio. Angular, disjointed, and turned away from the viewer, the chastened nude also frustrates any vulgar expectations of eroticism. Rather than offer up for the viewer's pleasure a voluptuous rendering of the female body, Degas's painting emphasizes the tactile properties of paint itself, both body and background subsumed into an aggressively manipulated and richly textured surface.

Paul Gauguin

French, 1848–1903

Arii Matamoe (The Royal End), 1892

Oil on coarse fabric, 45.1 × 74.3 cm

(17¾ × 29¼ in.), 2008.5

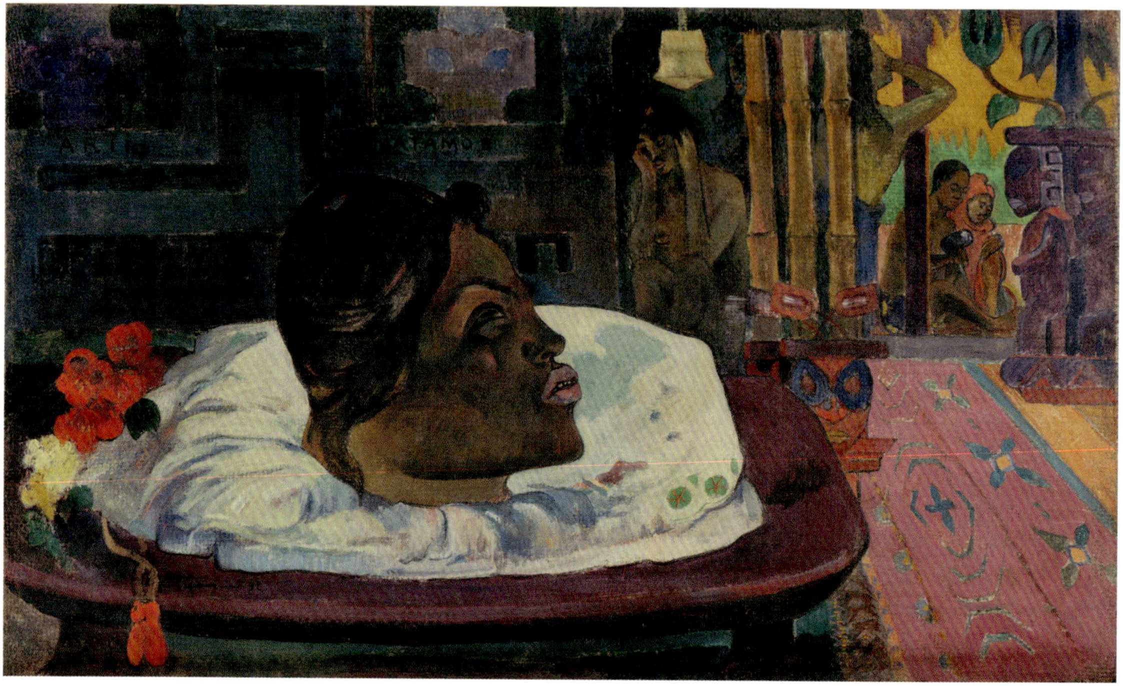

Painted during Gauguin's first trip to Tahiti, *Arii Matamoe (The Royal End)* breaks decisively from the dream of an easy, sensual life in the tropics. Presenting a severed head watched over by mourning and guardian figures in a richly ornamented hut, the painting evokes the Polynesian funerary rites that the artist had read about in ethnographic literature. Simultaneously, it resonates with Gauguin's rueful meditations on the passing of traditional Tahitian culture that were occasioned by the death of Pomare V, the last king of Tahiti, in 1881. Ultimately addressed to Gauguin's European audience, *Arii Matamoe* also reflects his generation's obsession with Orpheus and Saint John the Baptist, whose severed heads served as poetic symbols for the archetype of the martyred artist, with which Gauguin identified.

Paul Cézanne

French, 1839–1906

Young Italian Woman at a Table,

circa 1895–1900

Oil on canvas, 92.1 × 73.5 cm

(36¼ × 28 15/16 in.), 99.PA.40

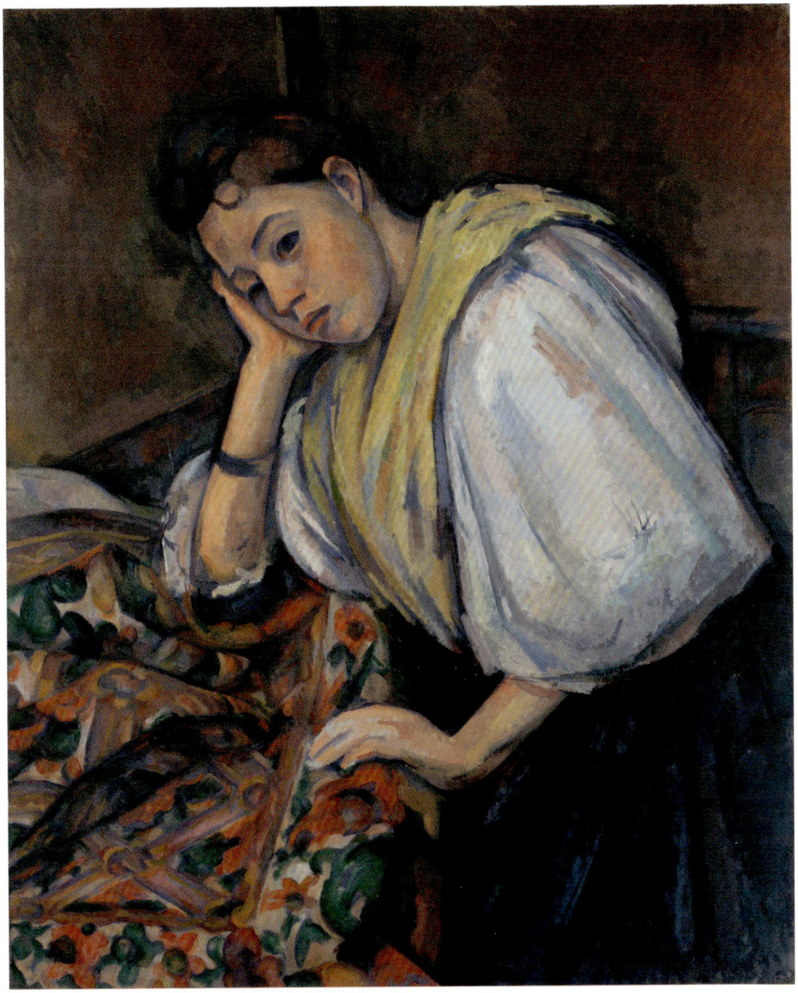

Cézanne's radical approach to painting, often combining multiple viewpoints in atemporal and ambiguous spaces, is renowned for having laid the foundations for Cubist abstraction. Here, in a monumentalizing figure painting that is modern in form but not in content, Cézanne represents an unidentified model wearing dress typical of the southern French region of Provence, with voluminous sleeves and an ample yellow kerchief. Leaning on her elbow with her head in her hand, she brings to mind a long art historical tradition of pensive, melancholy figures, but her radically simplified features imbue the work with a certain psychological impenetrability.

Paul Cézanne

French, 1839–1906

Still Life with Apples, 1893–94

Oil on canvas, 65.4 × 81.6 cm

(25¾ × 32⅛ in.), 96.PA.8

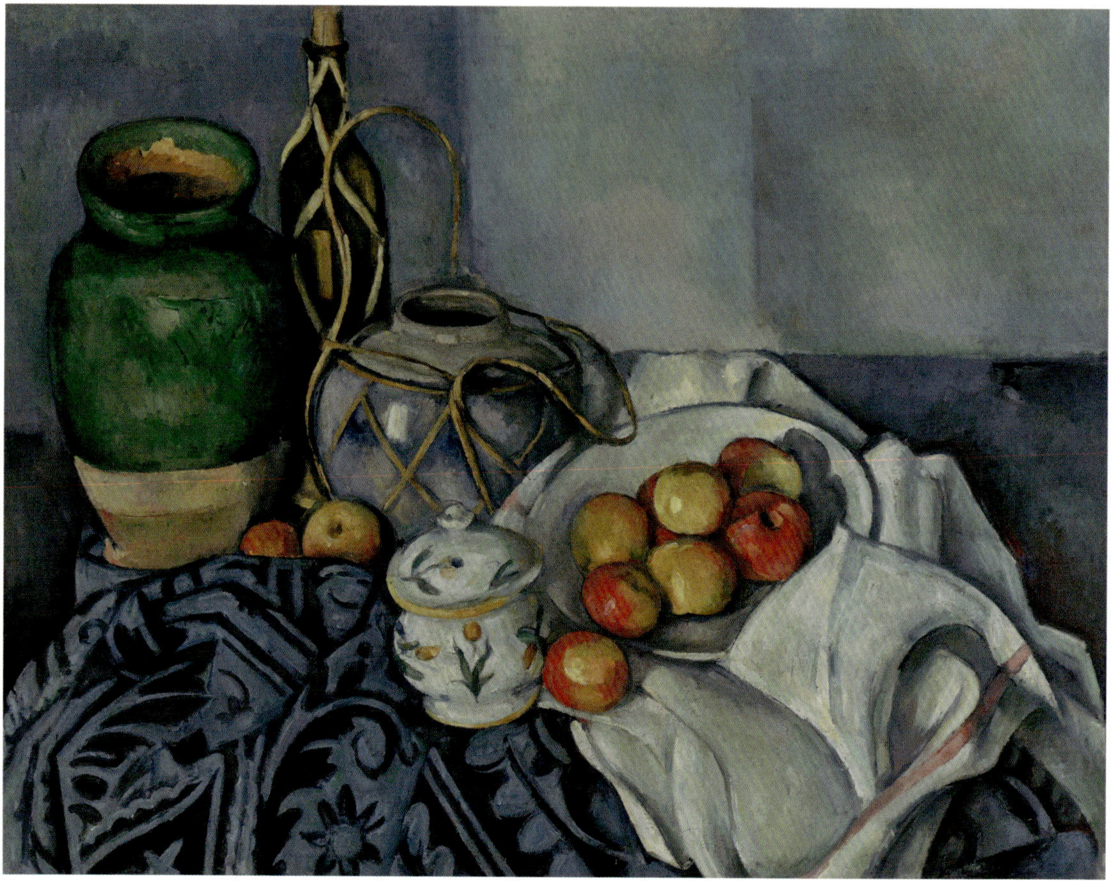

This grand, sumptuous composition presents familiar objects from Cézanne's studio in Provence. The solidly planted grouping of green-glazed vase, rum bottle, and ginger pot creates a sense of stability that is countered by the looping rattan netting, swelling folds of the draperies, and off-kilter placement of the sugar pot and plate of apples. There is nothing haphazard in this tightly orchestrated arrangement, but ambiguities persist. What viewing angle is implied by the rims of the vase and ginger pot? Can we read the dark blue wedge at right as a horizontal tabletop? Do the vertical lines in the upper register indicate the corners of a room or the crisp folds of a cloth backdrop? Cézanne's art continually tests our visual habits and assumptions.

Vincent van Gogh

Dutch, 1853–1890

Irises, 1889

Oil on canvas, 74.3 × 94.3 cm

(29¼ × 37⅛ in.), 90.PA.20

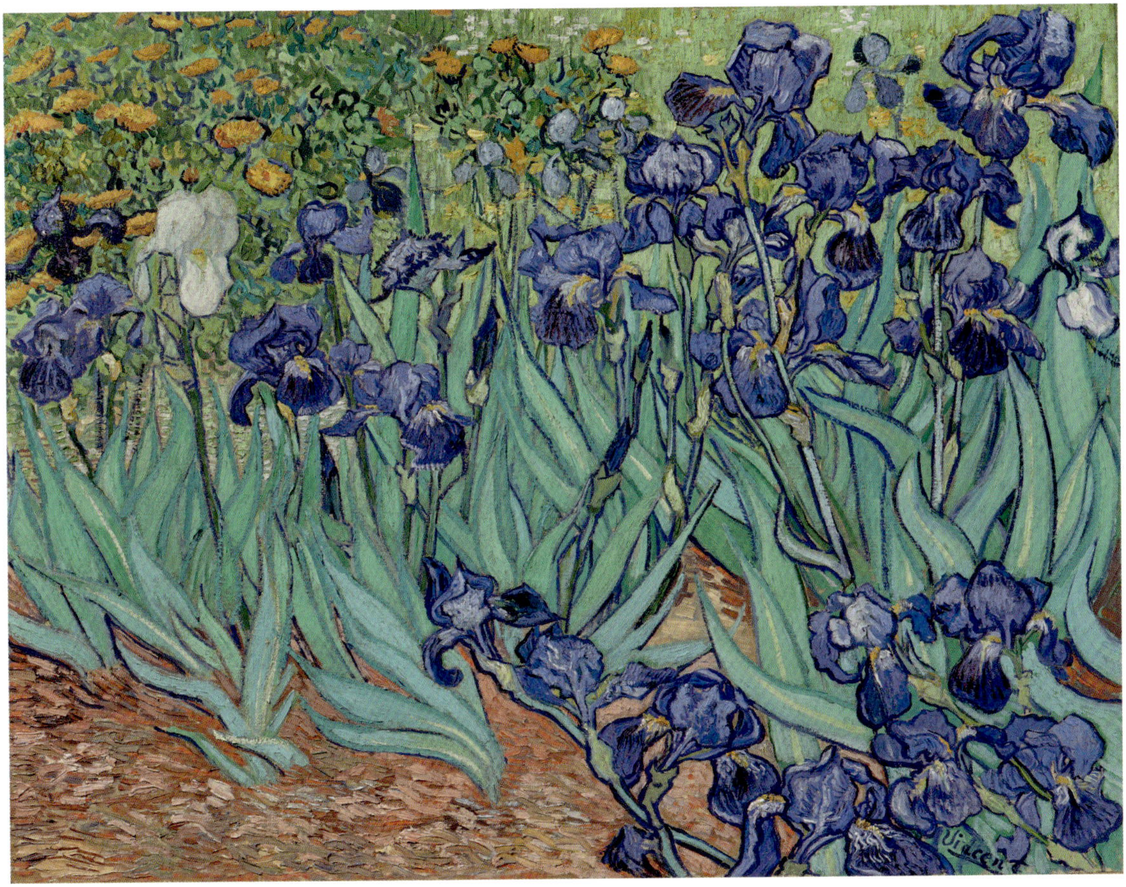

A severe mental-health crisis prompted Van Gogh to admit himself to the hospital of Saint-Paul-de-Mausole in Saint-Rémy-de-Provence, in the south of France. His recuperation involved making paintings of the hospital garden, *Irises* chief among them. The close study of nature was the foundation of Van Gogh's art, as his precise delineation of individual flowers suggests, but he also brought to that study an astonishing degree of subjective intensity. One feels this fervor in the painting's strong colors, thickly applied paint, and powerful, decorative rhythms, all of which convey the artist's impassioned sense of nature's surging vitality.

Giovanni Segantini

Italian, 1858–1899

Spring in the Alps, 1897

Oil on canvas, 116 × 227 cm

(45 11/16 × 89 3/8 in.), 2019.3

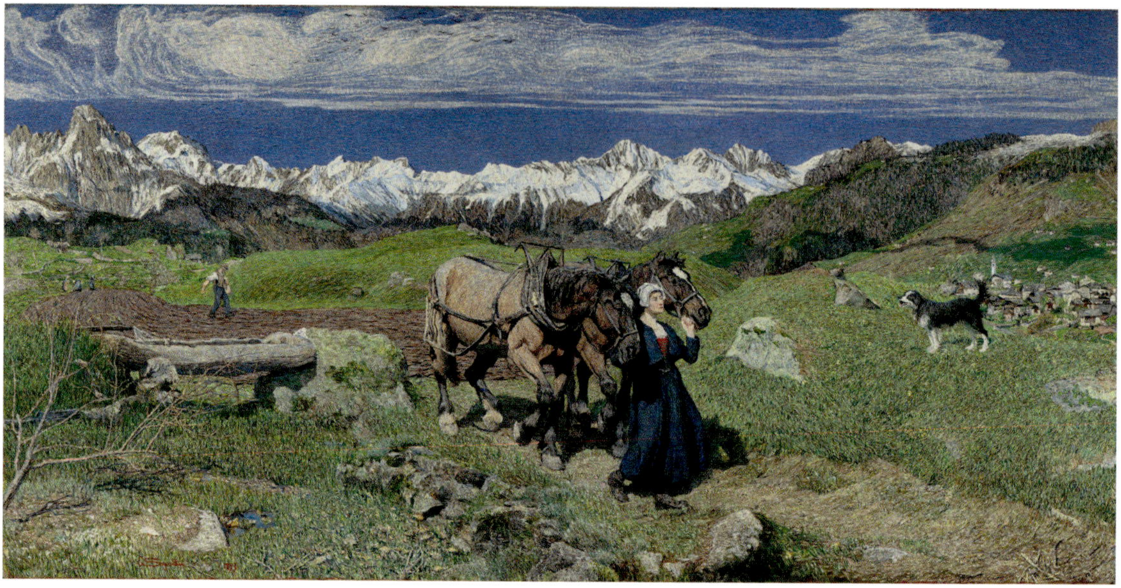

Executed at the peak of Segantini's short career, *Spring in the Alps* celebrates the cyclical revitalization of nature. It features a panoramic Swiss landscape animated by a solemn peasant leading two draft horses, a burly sower, and a bushy-tailed mountain dog. Densely layered and rhythmic strokes of bright color capture the crisp, brilliant atmosphere of the scene and create a highly tactile, almost tapestry-like surface. The painting has a noteworthy Californian provenance, having been commissioned directly from the artist in 1897 by Jacob Stern, a San Francisco collector and director of Levi Strauss and Co.

James Ensor

Belgian, 1860–1949

Christ's Entry into Brussels in 1889,

1888–early 1890s

Oil on canvas, 252.6 × 431 cm

($99\frac{7}{16} \times 169\frac{11}{16}$ in.), 87.PA.96

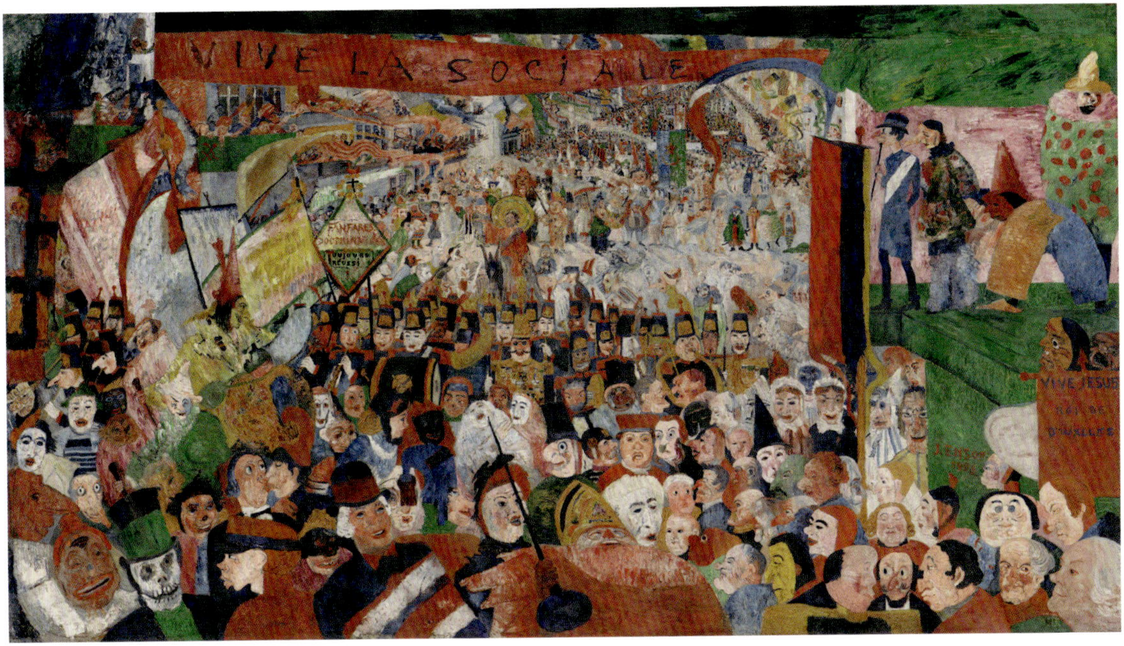

Flouting convention with its thick paint, raw colors, and crude caricatures, Ensor's enormous painting restaged the traditional biblical subject of Christ's entry into Jerusalem to satirize the Belgian society of his day. Paying little heed to Jesus on his donkey—a thinly veiled portrait of Ensor himself—the carnivalesque crowd surges down a gigantic boulevard in a procession led by buffoonish representatives of the church, military, and bourgeoisie. Slogans on jostling banners and flags evoke official civic and religious events as well as mass political demonstrations. Though intended for the 1889 exhibition of the Brussels-based artists' association Les XX, Ensor's masterpiece was not finished in time to be included. It remained in the artist's home and studio for decades before its first public showing in 1929.

Edvard Munch

Norwegian, 1863–1944

Starry Night, 1893

Oil on canvas, 135.9 × 140.3 cm

(53½ × 55¼ in.), 84.PA.681

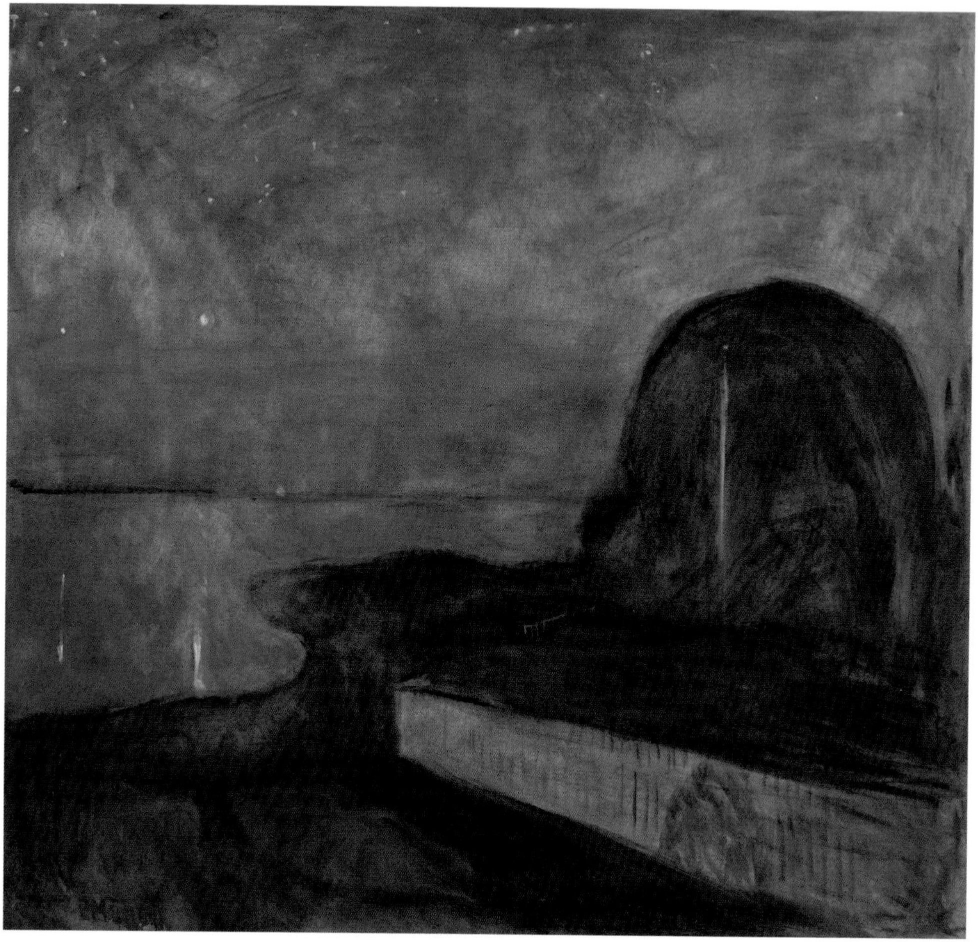

This moody landscape presents a view from the Grand Hotel in Åsgårdstrand, a resort town south of Oslo, Norway. Steeped in personal memories for Munch, Åsgårdstrand was the setting for the spiritual and sexual dramas that inspired many of his career-defining works. Here, the artist radically simplified and stylized the scene, subordinating reality to a lyrical vision in which stars pulsate in the night sky and trees and shore fuse in one sinuous, flowing line. Introducing a note of psychic disturbance is a looming shadow on the white fence, which vaguely recalls Munch's iconic images of fatefully entwined lovers.

Vilhelm Hammershøi

Danish, 1864–1916

Interior with an Easel, Bredgade 25, 1912

Oil on canvas, 78.7 × 70.5 cm

(31 × 27¾ in.), 2018.59

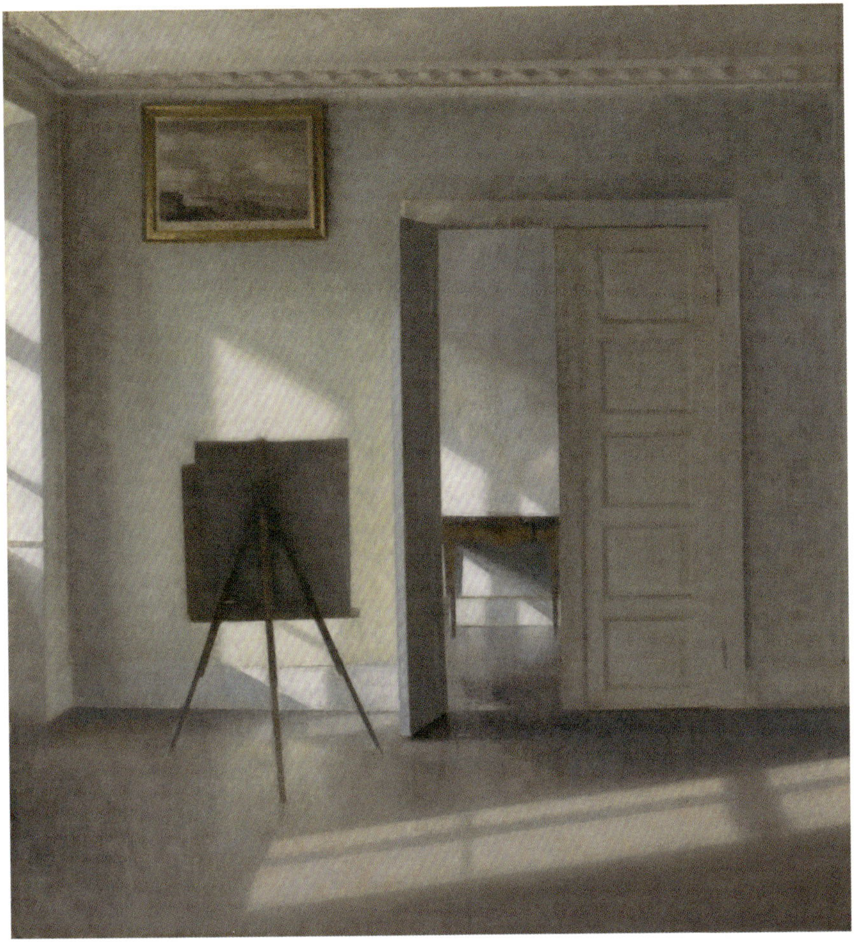

Hammershøi is renowned for his austere, meditative depictions of his Copenhagen apartments, which doubled as his studios. Here, at Bredgade 25, the painter's final address, the impression of stillness and silence is palpable, the only action being the play of cold Nordic light falling across the sparsely furnished space. A shimmering weave of thin, textured brushstrokes in subtly modulated tints of gray softens the geometric rigor of the composition and creates a sense of atmosphere, helping to transform the everyday subject into something strangely poetic.

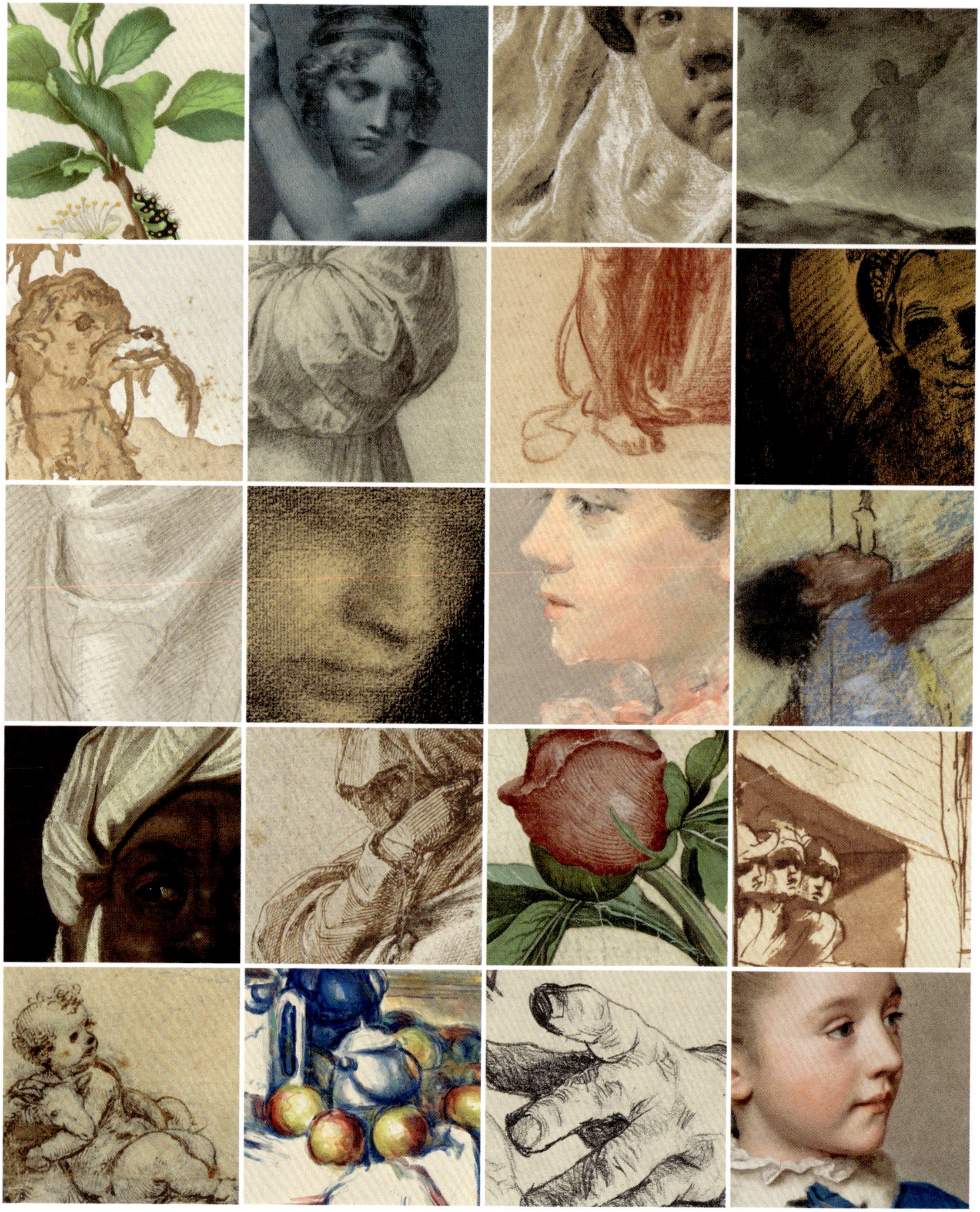

Drawings

Drawing is perhaps the most universal, spontaneous, and direct of all art forms, and the only one practiced by most people, if only at a rudimentary level. The Getty Museum began to build its collection of drawings in July 1981, five years after the death of J. Paul Getty, when it acquired Rembrandt van Rijn's red-chalk study *Nude Woman with a Snake* (p. 237). A year later the Department of Drawings was established. The collection now comprises more than one thousand sheets, including two sketchbooks, that together represent most of the main schools of Western European drawing from the fourteenth to the early twentieth century, exemplified by works of outstanding quality and condition.

With few exceptions, the great artists of the past—painters, sculptors, printmakers, and architects alike—employed drawing as an integral part of the creative process, embracing a wide variety of techniques, including metalpoint, graphite, pen and ink (often used in conjunction with wash), colored chalk, watercolor, and pastel. Drawing is often used to help artists explore ideas prior to their realization in the more durable media of paint or stone, yet it can also be an end in itself. While the Museum's collection of drawings historically centered on masterpieces by canonical Western artists such as Michelangelo Buonarroti (p. 228), Raphael (p. 229), and Paul Cézanne (p. 269), recent acquisitions have expanded the Museum's holdings by female artists, with important sheets by Lavinia Fontana, Maria Sibylla Merian (p. 241), and Rosa Bonheur (p. 259). Drawings after the nude model have always been considered a fundamental step in an artist's training. Either as preparatory sketches for larger compositions or as independent works, such studies are particularly well represented in Getty's collection, including Rembrandt's *Nude Woman with a Snake* and Pierre-Paul Prud'hon's *Study of a Female Nude* (p. 254). The collection also boasts high-quality examples in the genre of pastel—normally drawn on paper or vellum—such as the beloved *Portrait of Maria Frederike van Reede-Athlone at Seven Years of Age* by Jean-Étienne Liotard (p. 250).

Visitors to the Getty Museum can always see a selection of drawings from the collection in exhibitions based on theme, subject, medium, or artist shown in our dedicated galleries. The complete collection of drawings is available online, and for works not on view, our study room is open by appointment.

Martin Schongauer

German, circa 1450/53–1491

Studies of Peonies, circa 1472–73

Opaque and translucent watercolor,

25.7 × 33 cm (10⅛ × 13 in.), 92.GC.80

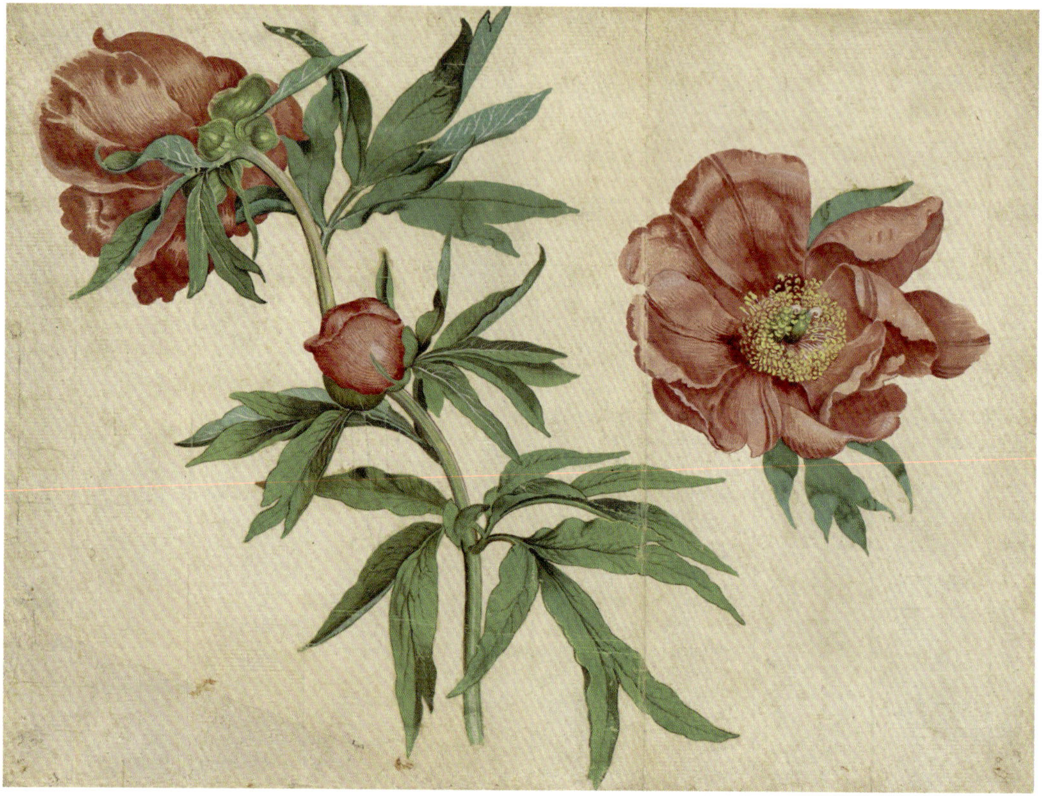

This drawing of three life-size peony flowers (*Paeonia officinalis* L.) is among the earliest manifestations of the movement toward the realistic depiction of nature in Northern Renaissance art. At left is a leafy stem with a blossom, seen from its underside, and a tightly closed bud. A separate study of a fully opened flower with delicately drawn stamens and pistils floats independently at right. Schongauer used this large sheet as the model for some of the flowers in his great altarpiece *The Madonna of the Rose Garden*, painted in 1473 for the Dominican church in Colmar, Germany. His meticulously rendered watercolor constitutes a crucial precedent for Albrecht Dürer's nature studies of the early sixteenth century, for example, *Stag Beetle* (see p. 225).

Albrecht Dürer

German, 1471–1528

Stag Beetle, 1505

Opaque and translucent watercolor,

14.2 × 11.4 cm (5 9/16 × 4 1/2 in.), 83.GC.214

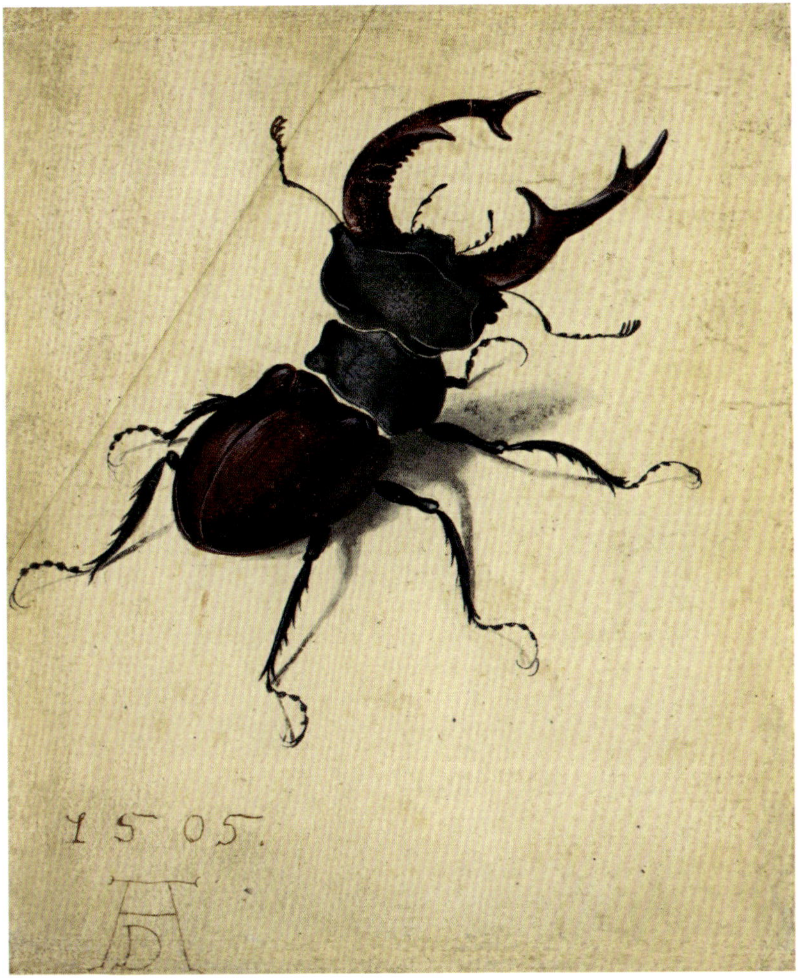

In the 1490s the German Renaissance artist Albrecht Dürer explored his surroundings in detailed watercolor landscapes and nature studies. Here, he depicted a male stag beetle (*Lucanus cervus* L.), carefully differentiating between the smooth texture of the abdomen and the rough surfaces of the head and thorax. To animate his insect, drawn from direct observation, Dürer added shadows on the plain ground of the paper, as if the beetle were crawling across it. Since its acquisition in 1983, the drawing has become emblematic of the Museum's collection.

Filippino Lippi

Italian, circa 1457–1504

Standing Saint, circa 1482

Metalpoint heightened with white opaque watercolor on gray prepared paper, 27.1 × 17.5 cm (10$\frac{11}{16}$ × 6$\frac{7}{8}$ in.), 91.GG.33

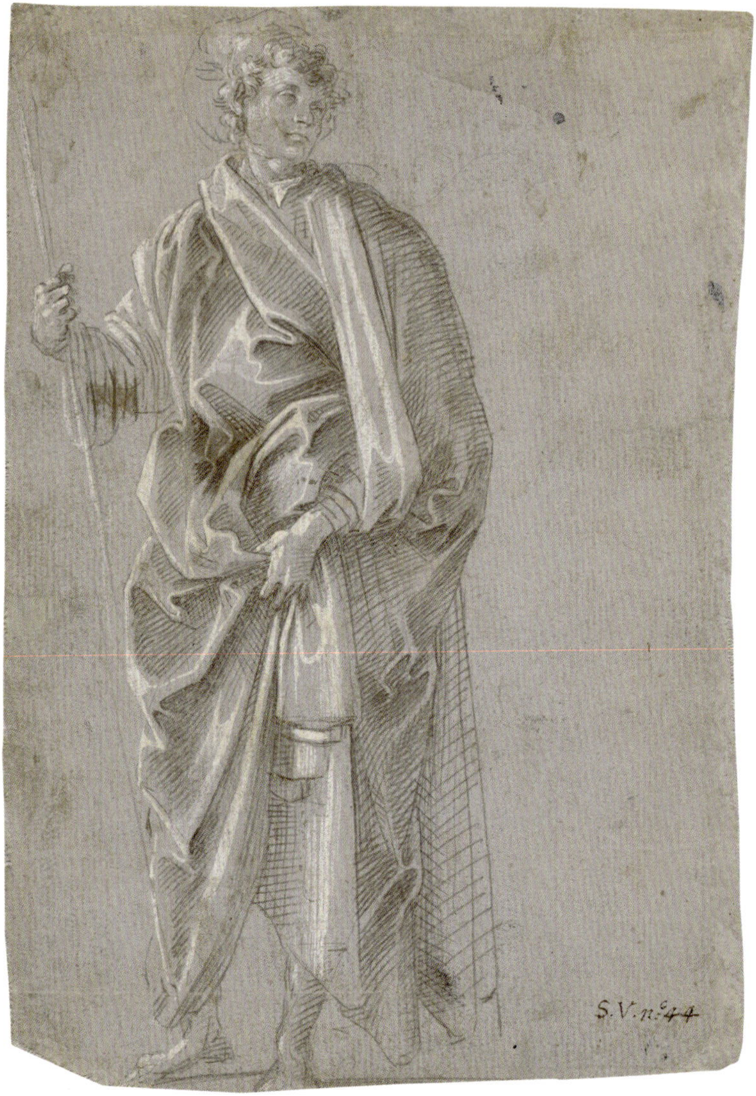

Son of the artist Filippo Lippi (ca. 1406–1469) and an apprentice of Sandro Botticelli (ca. 1445–1510), Filippino was renowned for his drawings. On this sheet he sketched a heavily draped figure holding a pole, concentrating specifically on the fall of light and shade on the complex folds of cloth. Several figures of standing draped saints in Lippi's painted work maintain similar poses, suggesting that drawings such as this one were kept in the studio and used as reference material. For this study Lippi used the technique of metalpoint, in which the artist draws with a metal stylus on a sheet of paper prepared with a slightly rough surface. The technique was popular in the fifteenth century but fell out of use as chalk became more widely available.

Leonardo da Vinci

Italian, 1452–1519

Studies for the Christ Child with a Lamb,

circa 1503–6

Pen and brown ink and black chalk,

21 × 14.2 cm (8¼ × 5⁹⁄₁₆ in.), 86.GG.725

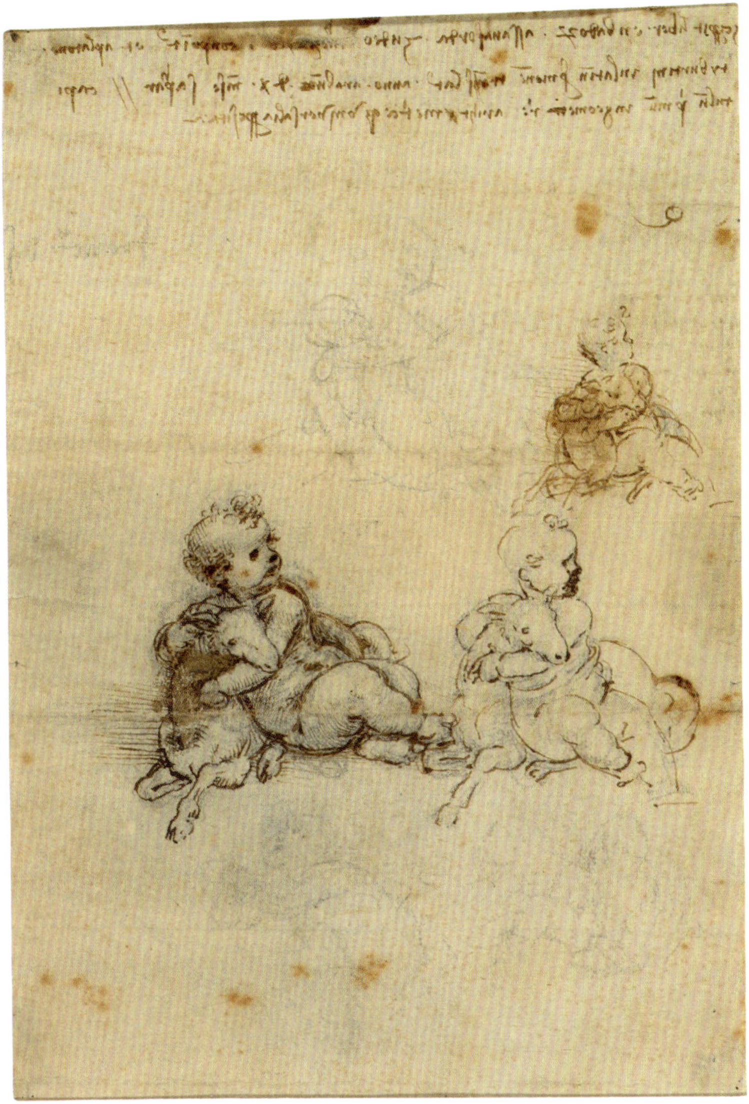

This sheet exemplifies the type of exploratory drawing pioneered by Leonardo, in which the polymath wrestled with artistic and engineering problems through sketches and notes poured onto the page. Multiple black-chalk studies consider the Christ child and lamb from various angles and in different poses. The artist then worked up the most successful sketches in pen and ink.

Similar figural groups appear in several paintings produced by Leonardo at this time. At the top of the sheet the artist made a note to himself—in his characteristic mirror writing—to consult a treatise on geometry by the early mathematician Abraham Savasorda (1070–1136).

Michelangelo Buonarroti
Italian, 1475–1564
Study of a Mourning Woman,
circa 1500–1505
Pen and brown ink heightened with
white opaque watercolor, 26 × 16.5 cm
(10¼ × 6½ in.), 2017.78

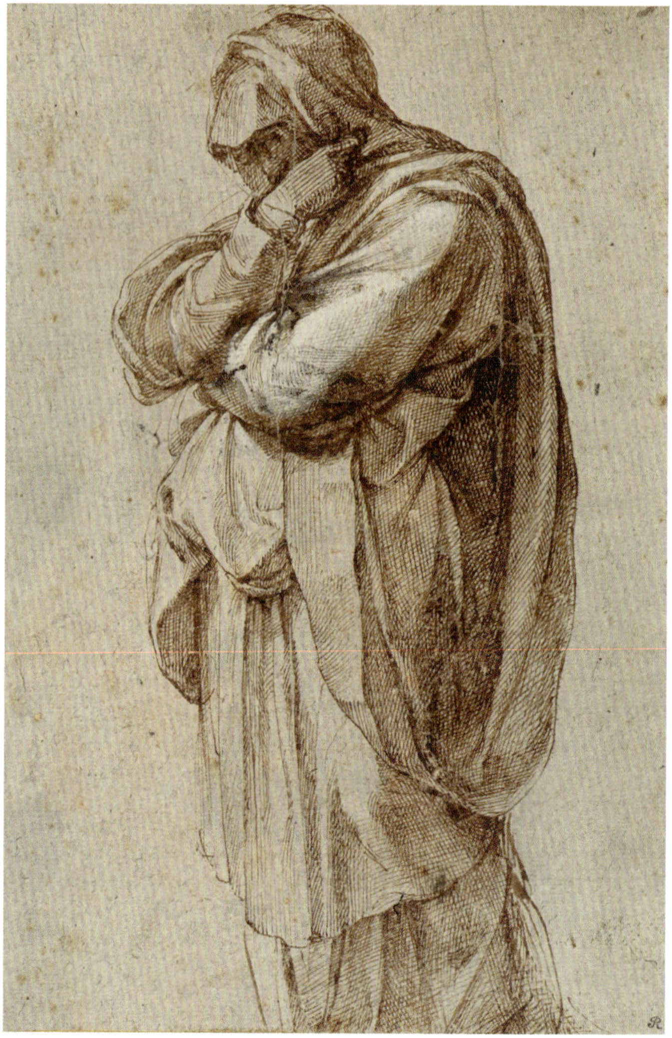

This powerful drawing features a mourning figure, her face partially hidden and her arms wrapped tightly around her upper torso. The whole body is shrouded in heavy drapery. Michelangelo made the work at a pivotal moment early in his career when, already renowned as a sculptor, he became increasingly celebrated as a painter. The weight and solidity of the figure suggest a sculptor's conception of three-dimensional space, translated into graphic form through dense hatching and cross-hatching and judicious white heightening. Previously unknown to scholars, the drawing came to light in a library album at Castle Howard in Yorkshire, England, in 1995. It is unclear whether the sheet was made as an independent drawing or as a study for a painting, although copies drawn by Michelangelo's contemporaries attest to its early fame.

Raphael (Raffaello Sanzio)

Italian, 1483–1520

Saint Paul Rending His Garments,

circa 1515–16

Metalpoint heightened with white opaque watercolor on violet-gray prepared paper, 23 × 10.3 cm (9 1/16 × 4 1/16 in.), 84.GG.919

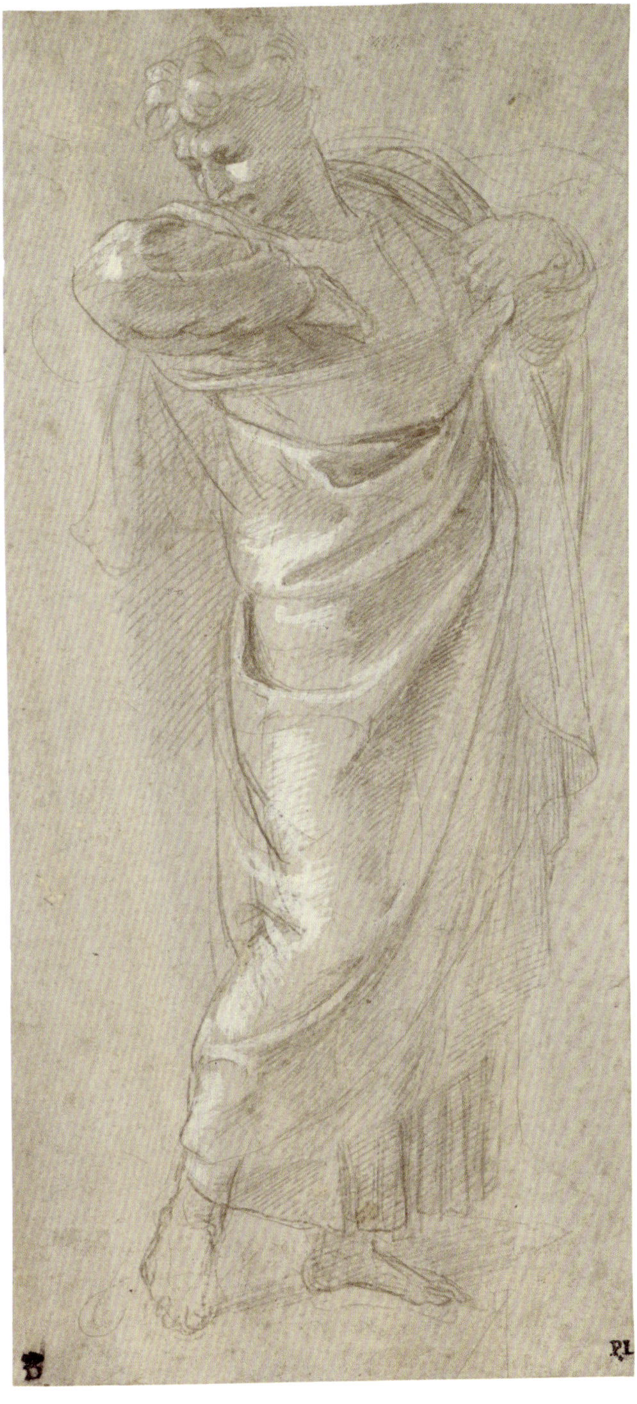

This study by Raphael was made in preparation for the figure of Saint Paul in *The Sacrifice of Lystra*, one of a series of ten tapestries that Pope Leo X (r. 1513–21) commissioned to decorate the lower walls of the Sistine Chapel in the Vatican. The scene recounts how Saint Paul, angered at the people of Lystra for preparing an idolatrous sacrifice, violently tore at his garments. Here, the convincingly rendered twisting of the saint's body in space demonstrates Raphael's facility with the challenging metalpoint technique, while thick white highlights bring solidity to the figure.

Andrea del Sarto

Italian, 1486–1530

Study for the Head of Saint Joseph,

circa 1526–27

Red and black chalks, 37.5 × 22.6 cm

(14¾ × 8⅞ in.), 2017.73

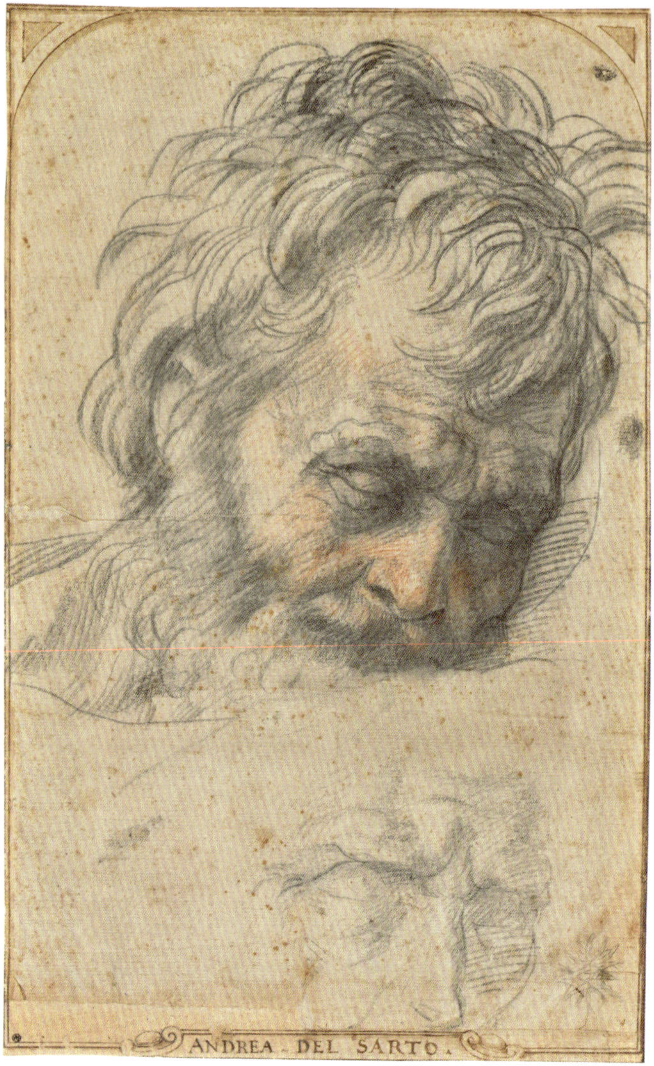

One of Andrea del Sarto's largest, most impressive drawings, this sheet studies the sleeping Saint Joseph for the artist's painting *Bracci Holy Family* (Florence, Palazzo Pitti). Disregarding Joseph's chin, obscured in the painting by his left arm, Andrea instead focused on the upper portion of the face. For the realistically rendered gray hair, the artist created patches of shadow by adding strokes of black chalk to previously rubbed areas of chalk.

A brief subsidiary study lower on the page explores the possibility of raising Joseph's head slightly and showing him awake. The ruled-line mount and inscription were added to the drawing by the famous artist-biographer Giorgio Vasari (1511–1574), who was Andrea's pupil and the first owner of this sheet.

Hans Holbein the Younger
German, 1497/98–1543
Portrait of a Scholar or Cleric,
circa 1532–35

Black and red chalks and pen and brush and black ink on pink prepared paper, 21.9 × 18.5 cm ($8\frac{5}{8} \times 7\frac{1}{4}$ in.), 84.GG.93

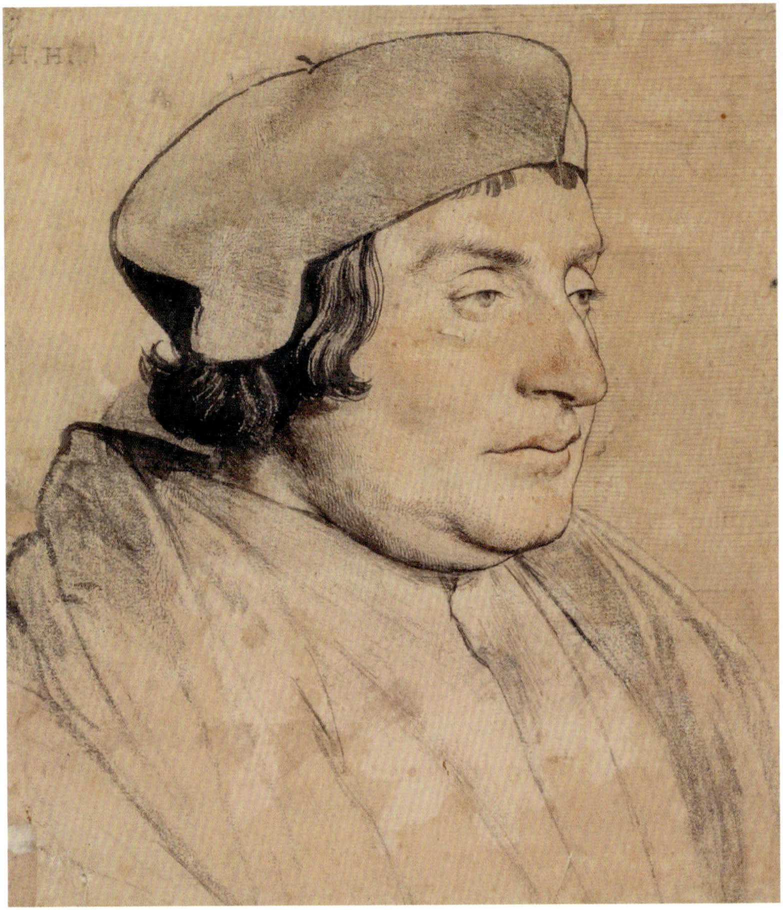

The distinctive hat worn by the unidentified sitter in this drawing suggests that he is either a cleric or a scholar. Holbein probably made the portrait during his second English period (1532–43), when he served as painter to King Henry VIII (1491–1547), so the sitter may have been connected with Henry's Tudor court. Holbein sketched the contours of the man's face in black chalk and then deftly went over them in black ink. The face is softly modeled in red chalk, using the natural pink of the paper as a middle tone. Beyond the face, the handling is broad and painterly, as seen in the hair and robe. Holbein was attuned to the unique features of each of his sitters, which he rendered with unparalleled precision and objectivity.

Federico Zuccaro

Italian, circa 1541–1609

Taddeo Decorating the Facade of the Palazzo Mattei, circa 1595

Pen and brown ink and brown wash over black chalk with touches of red chalk, 25 × 42.2 cm ($9\frac{7}{8} \times 16\frac{5}{8}$ in.), 99.GA.6.19

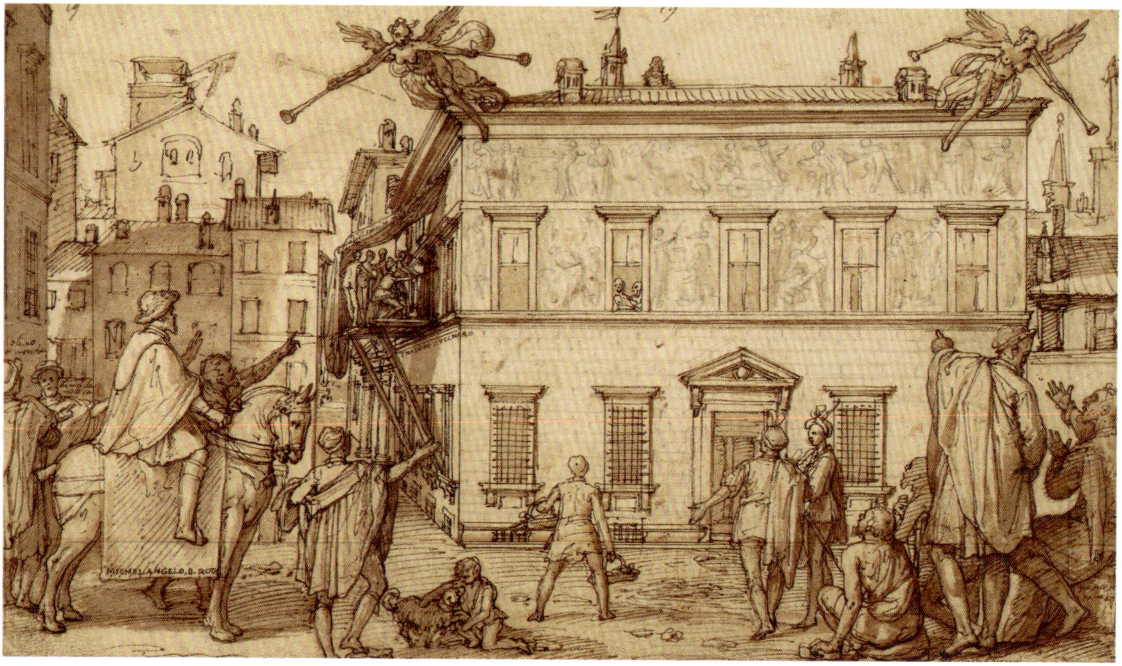

During the 1590s Federico Zuccaro made a series of twenty drawings depicting the early life of his deceased older brother and teacher, Taddeo (1529–1566). These drawings, all in the Museum's collection, are a moving tribute to Taddeo's artistic toils and triumphs, culminating with this scene of him decorating the now-destroyed facade of the Palazzo Mattei in Rome. Taddeo stands painting on a scaffold at upper left; the mythological Three Graces and personifications of Spirit and Pride stand with him, while allegories of Fame fly above. Marveling at his work are the greatest painters of Rome in Taddeo's lifetime: Michelangelo, on a horse at the left, with his servant Urbino; Girolamo Siciolante; and Daniele da Volterra. At right is the artist-biographer Giorgio Vasari, shown discussing the facade with another painter, Francesco Salviati.

Bartholomaeus Spranger

Flemish, 1546–1611
The Holy Family with Saint Joseph Holding the Rose, circa 1591
Pen and brown ink and brown wash over black chalk, heightened with white opaque watercolor, on blue paper, incised for transfer, 22.2 × 16.3 cm ($8^{3}/_{4}$ × $6^{7}/_{16}$ in.), 2023.11

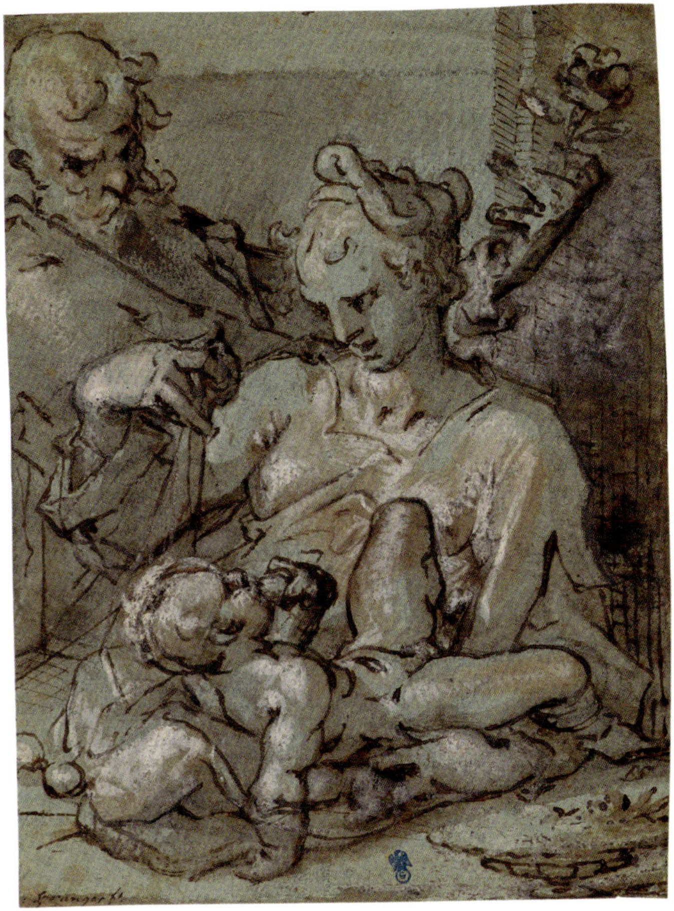

Spranger began his international career in papal Rome before joining the court of Holy Roman Emperor Rudolf II (1552–1612) in Prague. This drawing of the Holy Family is one of fewer than one hundred sheets by Spranger to survive. In the center of the composition, the Virgin Mary gazes adoringly at the child Jesus resting on a pillow, while Saint Joseph stands behind the pair, holding up a rose. With its muscular figures in contrived poses, rendered in sharp pen strokes, the drawing is highly characteristic of Spranger's Mannerist style. The artist made the drawing as a model for a print: he sent it to Antwerp to be engraved by Pieter de Jode (1570–1634). The incision marks on the sheet attest that the design was transferred directly onto a copperplate.

Peter Paul Rubens

Flemish, 1577–1640

Head Study for Balthazar, circa 1609–11

Oil on paper, laid on panel, 54 × 39.3 cm (21¼ × 15½ in.), 2018.48

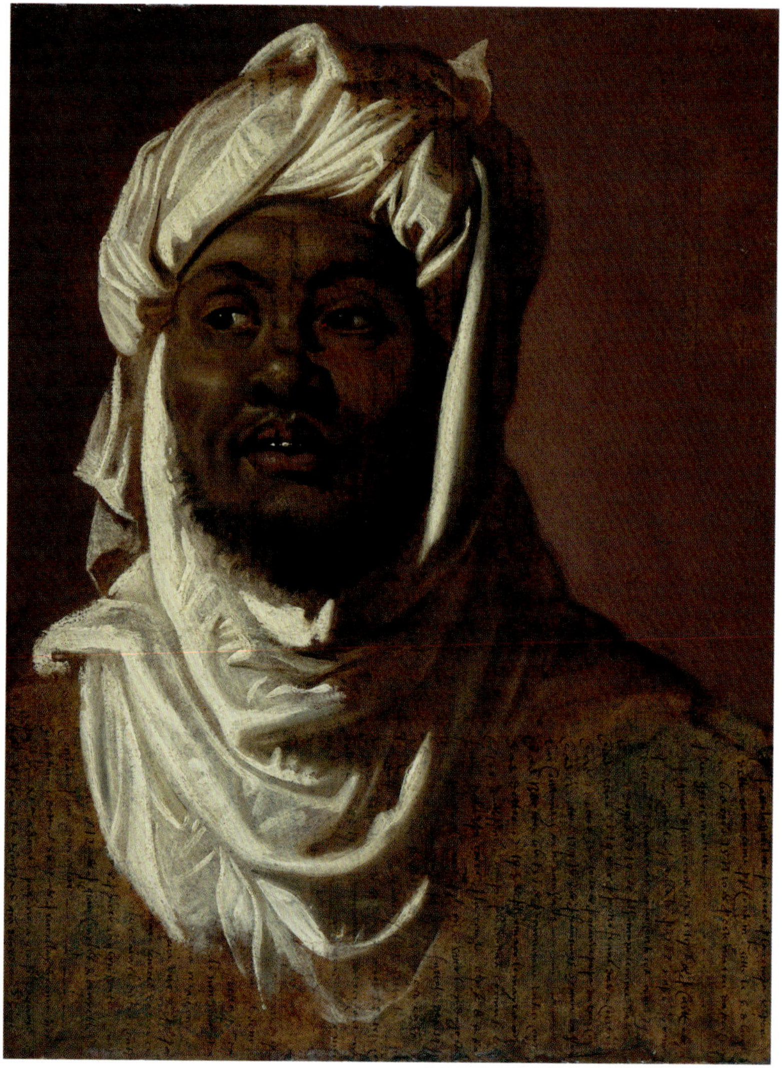

Before Rubens completed his large-scale painting *The Adoration of the Magi* (Madrid, Museo Nacional del Prado), he made this oil sketch for the central figure of Balthazar, the Black African king. Unlike a portrait, an independent work recording the likeness and status of an individual, this head study was made to explore the fall of light across the face. Grayish-white highlights on the left cheek, nose, and temple bring the face, with its deep brown complexion, into relief. An elaborate white turban draped around the head and neck further enhances a powerful three-dimensional presence. The partly open mouth evokes a fleeting moment and lends a sense of spontaneity. It is likely that Rubens enlisted a household servant or perhaps even an enslaved person in Antwerp as a model for the biblical character.

Peter Paul Rubens

Flemish, 1577–1640

Man in Korean Costume, circa 1617

Black and red chalks, 38.4 × 23.5 cm (15⅛ × 9¼ in.), 83.GB.384

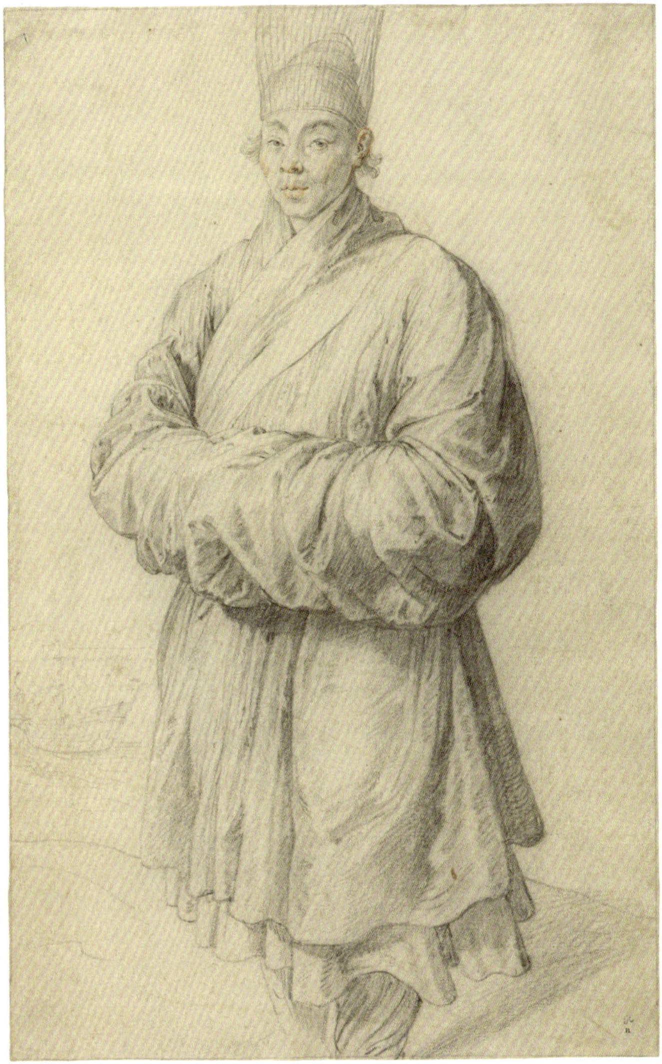

Rubens made this figure study in preparation for *The Miracles of Saint Francis Xavier*, a large altarpiece commissioned by the Jesuits in Antwerp to glorify the Catholic order's missionary work in Asia. With a meticulous handling of black chalk, the artist offers a naturalistic portrayal of the man's voluminous robes and transparent horsehair headdress. A compelling depiction by a European artist of an East Asian subject, the drawing is thought to be the earliest representation of Korean costume in Europe. The sheet has attracted attention since the time it was made; the figure has been variably associated with a Siamese priest, a formerly enslaved Korean man who traveled to Italy, and a Chinese merchant working in the Netherlands.

Anthony van Dyck
Flemish, 1599–1641
The Entombment, 1617–18
Pen and brown ink and brown and red wash over black and chalks, heightened with white opaque watercolor, 25.4 × 21.9 cm (10 × 8⅝ in.), 85.GG.97

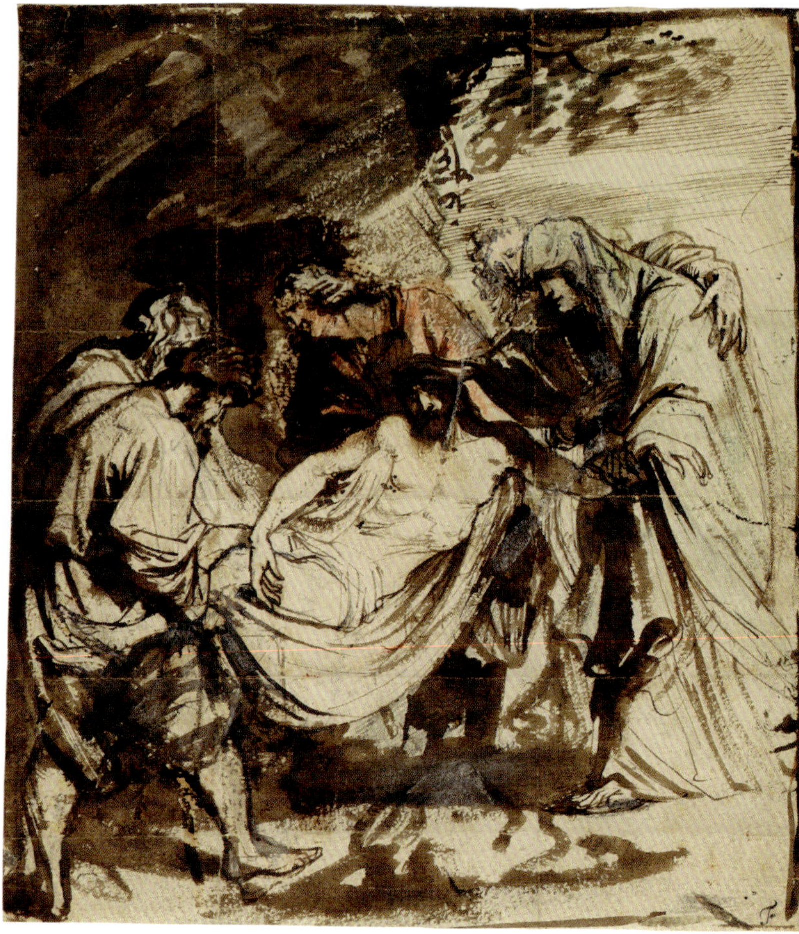

To create this poignant depiction of Christ being carried to his tomb, the young Van Dyck turned to Italy for inspiration. Looking to a copy of the *Entombment* (now Paris, Musée du Louvre) by the Venetian Renaissance master Titian (see p. 150), he exchanged the Italian artist's sweeping horizontal composition for a vertical format, resulting in a more tightly integrated, somber scene. Van Dyck set extremely fine pen lines, visible on Christ's torso, in contrast to gestural, tenebrous strokes of brown wash that, together with the grieving Virgin Mary holding the arm of her dead son, heighten the sense of anguished mourning. Van Dyck might have made this drawing as a preparatory study for a painting that was either abandoned or did not survive.

Rembrandt Harmensz. van Rijn

Dutch, 1606–1669

Nude Woman with a Snake, circa 1637

Red chalk with white opaque watercolor,

24.7 × 13.7 cm (9 11/16 × 5 7/16 in.), 81.GB.27

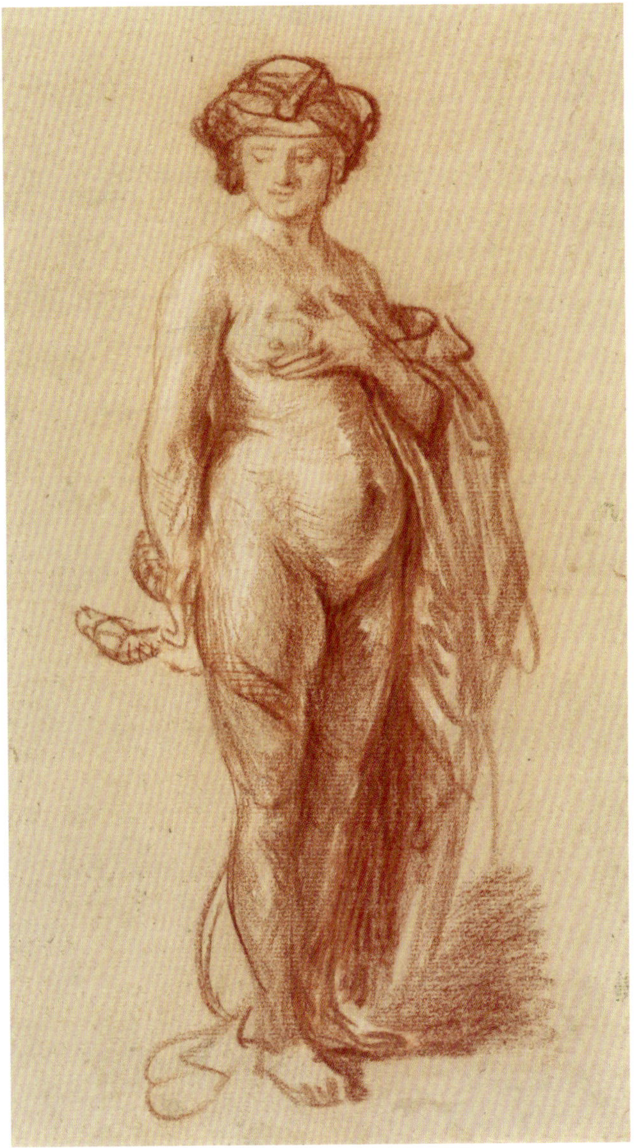

The first drawing to enter J. Paul Getty's collection, this unidealized nude is also Rembrandt's only surviving red-chalk study of a female figure. The large snake coiled around her leg and the gesture of squeezing her breast suggests that the artist envisaged the model as a biblical or historical character. Whether she is Eve or Cleopatra, her downward gaze and slight smirk convey an act of contemplation. Rembrandt enhanced the chromatic brilliance of the red chalk by applying white opaque watercolor underneath it, particularly visible in her right arm and torso. The fine modeling of the body stands in great contrast to the virtuoso passages of freely sketched drapery.

Guercino
(Giovanni Francesco Barbieri)
Italian, 1591–1666
Spectators Hiding behind a Barricade,
circa 1630
Pen and brown ink with brush and
brown wash, 17.2 × 24.7 cm (6.8 × 9.7 in.),
2024.13.1

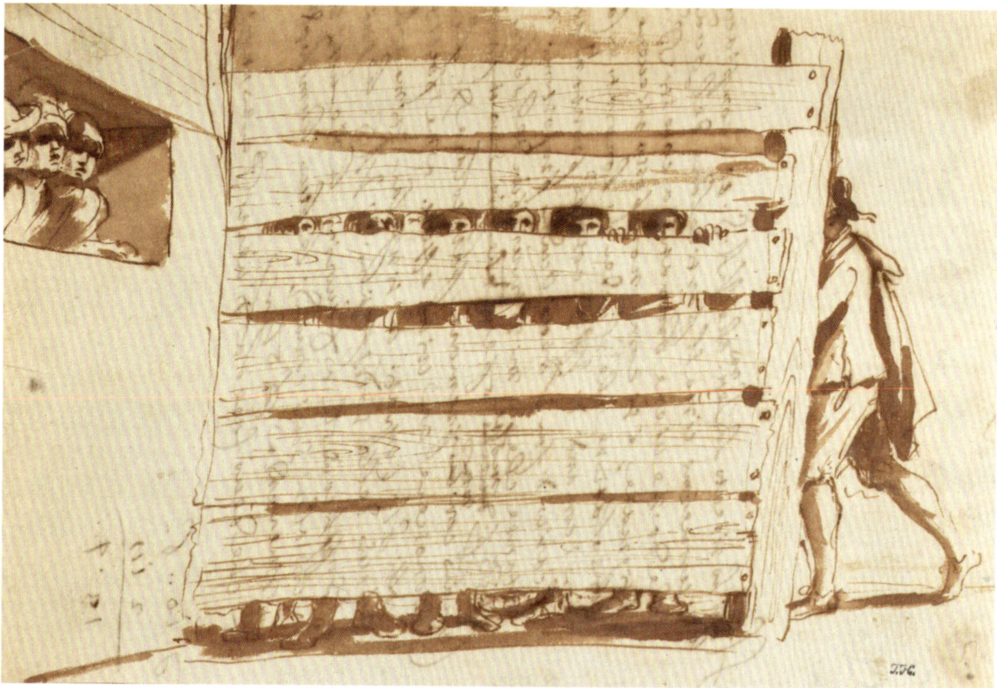

Spectators peer through a wooden barricade and out of a small, high window. There is no indication of what they are hiding or seeking protection from, but the drawing may record the sidelines of an Italian bull run, or *palio*, a form of bareback horseracing that takes place on urban streets. While Guercino made his reputation as a celebrated painter of religious altarpieces, all carefully prepared through dozens of drawings, he also recorded the world around him in poignant or humorous sketches such as this one. It was drawn on the back of a letter, and the artist, whether consciously or not, seems to have used the brown ink of the writing, which shows through the paper, to lend texture to the barricade slats.

Jacob Jordaens

Flemish, 1593–1678

A Merry Company, circa 1644

Watercolor over black chalk, heightened with white opaque watercolor, 21.9 × 23.8 cm (8 5/8 × 9 3/8 in.), 2000.59

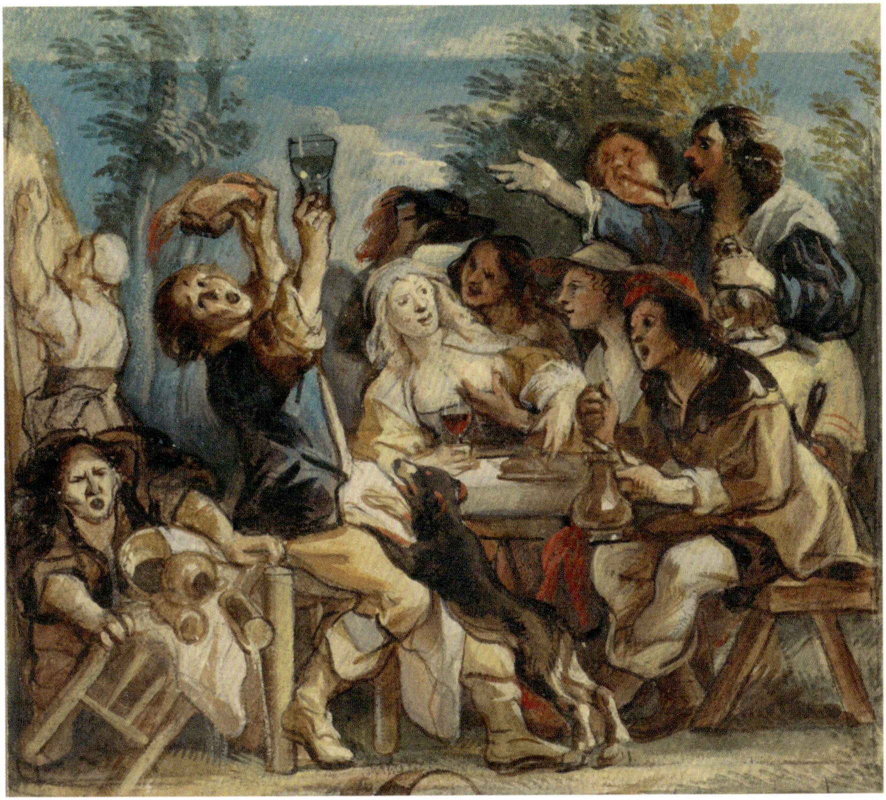

A rowdy group gathered outside a tavern finds delight in wine and song. Infused with Jordaens's characteristic exuberance and humor, this raucous scene was likely inspired by a popular proverb of the 1600s: "Ill gained, ill spent." The revelry unfolds around a table, where money easily gained is also easily spent on alcohol and female company. In the background, a watchful server records the party's expenses. Jordaens used watercolor to create a rich finish that reflects the earthy humor of the composition, and broken, angular lines imbue the figures with movement and depth. The artist returned to this theme in a series of tapestries illustrating eight famous proverbs, as well as in a painting. While all the works share common elements, the nature of their association is not clear.

Claude Mellan

French, 1598–1688

Portrait of Nicolas-Claude Fabri de Peiresc, 1636

Black chalk, 14.5 × 11 cm (5 11/16 × 4 5/16 in.), 2019.11

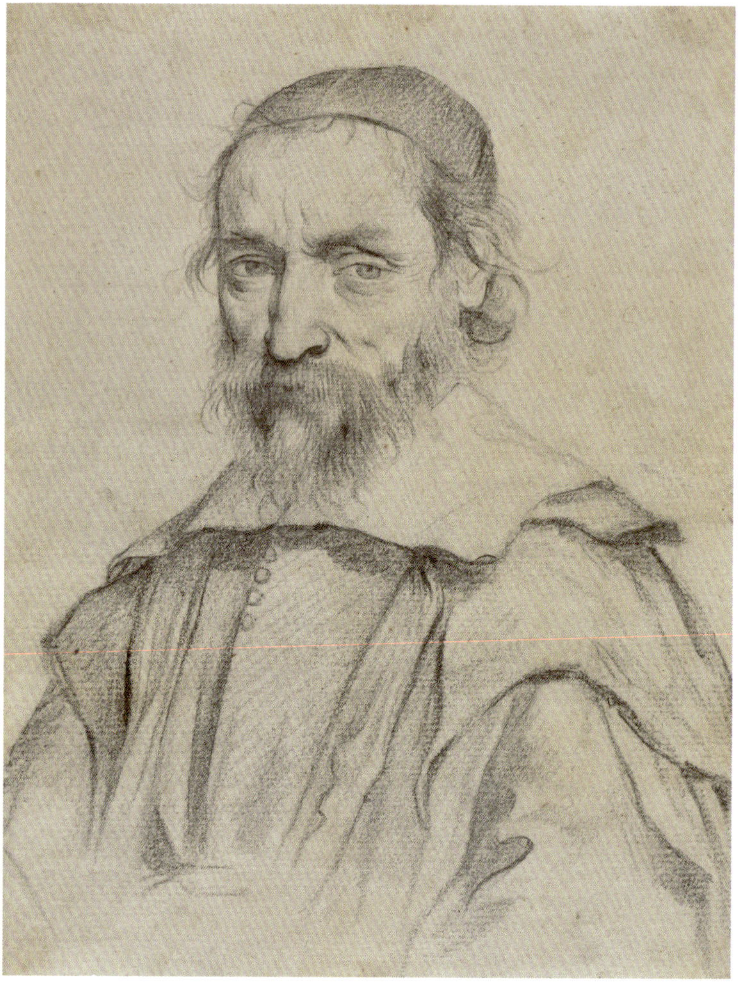

A French collector and polymath whose areas of expertise ranged from archaeology to zoology, Nicolas-Claude Fabri de Peiresc (1580–1637) was a friend and patron of Mellan, arguably the greatest French printmaker of the seventeenth century. This portrait dates to 1636, when Mellan visited Peiresc, then in failing health. Physically frail and careworn but fiercely—indeed, almost alarmingly—present, Peiresc looks back at us from Mellan's tiny sheet with all the blazing intensity of his formidable intellect. Here is an exacting portrait of a remarkable mind. The chalk design served as the basis for an engraved portrait, published after Peiresc's death.

Maria Sibylla Merian

German, active in the Netherlands, 1647–1717

Metamorphosis of a Small Emperor Moth on a Damson Plum, 1679

Plate 13 of *The Caterpillar Book*

Translucent and opaque watercolor over a counterproof print on parchment, 18.7 × 14.9 cm (7³/₈ × 5⁷/₈ in.), 2020.10

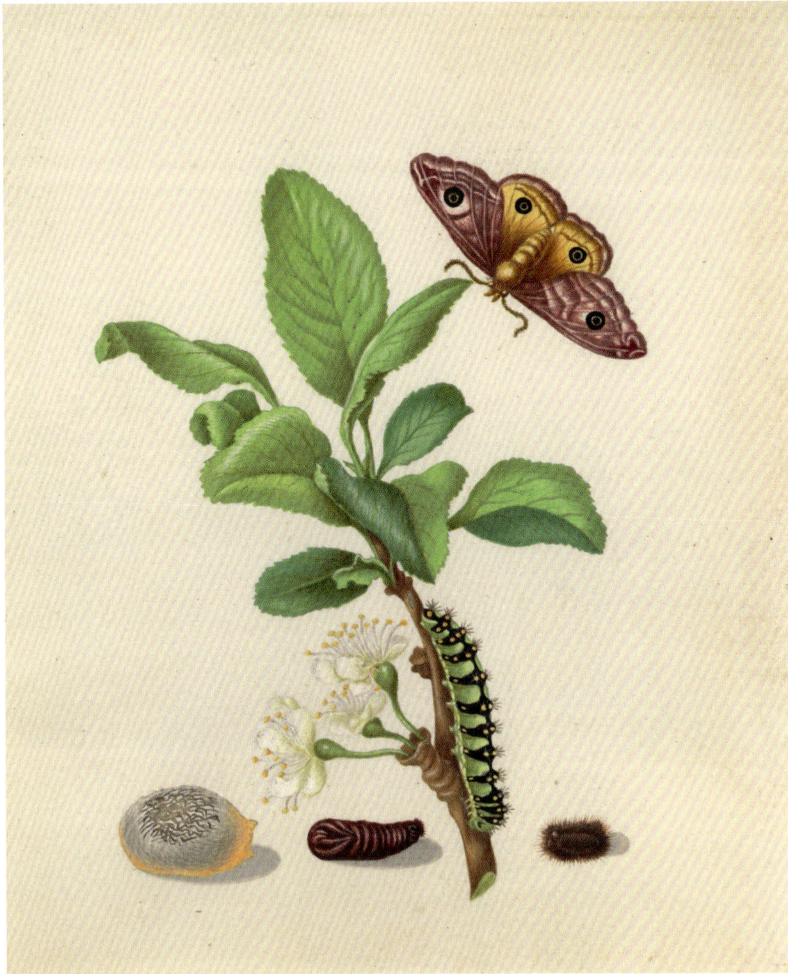

In this colorful illustration that entwines the life cycle of a male emperor moth with its food source, Merian makes the complicated process of insect metamorphosis both easier to understand and delightful to observe. A mature caterpillar crawls down a branch, past blossoms and curling leaves. Cast shadows suggest sunlight pouring in from the left, which also illuminates the silk casing of the cocoon, the pupa, and the freshly emerged caterpillar at the bottom of the sheet. Placed on a sharp diagonal near the leafy branch, the purple-and-yellow moth with black markings appears suspended in air. Merian was, because of her gender, barred from a university education and the privilege of using oil paint, but she nevertheless laid the groundwork for modern entomology and ecology.

Claude Lorrain (Claude Gellée)

French, 1604/5(?)–1682

Figures in a Landscape before a Harbor, late 1630s

Pen and brown ink and brown wash with red and yellow chalks, heightened with white opaque watercolor, on blue paper, 23.8 × 33.8 cm (9 3/8 × 13 5/16 in.), 82.GA.80

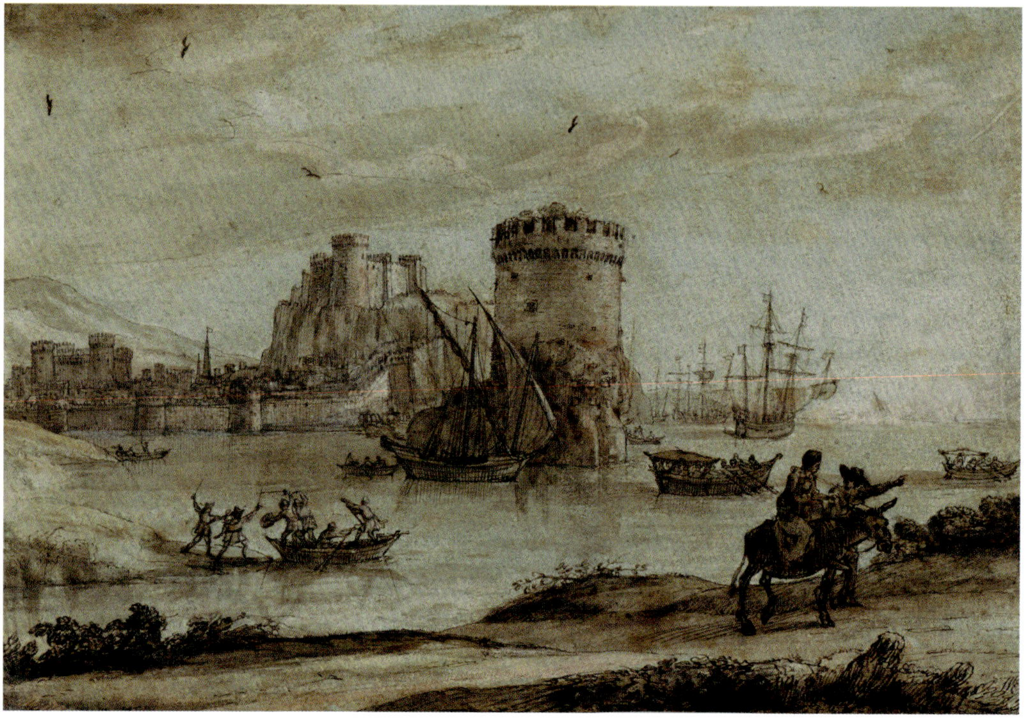

A prolific draftsman, Claude Lorrain sought to capture the brilliant effects of light in his landscape drawings, as he did in his celebrated paintings (see p. 180). In this lively harbor scene, filled with imaginative architecture and figures, Claude utilized inky brown washes on blue paper to produce atmospheric effects, from soft reflections on the water to hanging mist. While many of the artist's compositions illustrated literary or historical subjects, this drawing appears to present a view of an active port. Despite the unclear narrative, Claude imbues the sheet with drama, including a group of fighting brigands landing on the shore. The drawing relates to a painting of the same subject that was commissioned by the French ambassador in Rome.

Cornelis Vroom

Dutch, 1590/92–1661

Mountain Landscape with a Distant View Behind, circa 1635–40

Pen and brown ink on laid paper,

20 × 31.1 cm ($7\frac{7}{8}$ × $12\frac{1}{4}$ in.), 2020.16

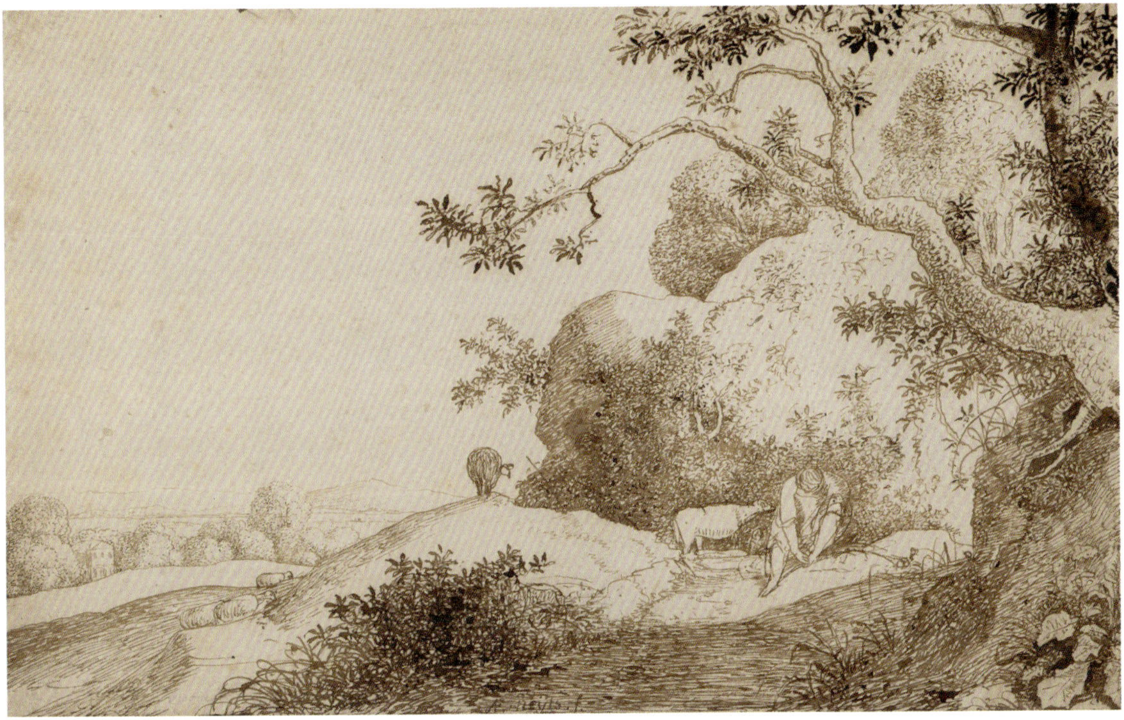

In this tranquil view of a rocky hillside before a distant river, an overhanging tree leans toward a shepherd whose flock is scattered across a rugged terrain. The landscape bears little resemblance to the Dutch countryside around Haarlem, where Vroom worked and resided for much of his life, suggesting that the scene is imaginary rather than documentary. Vroom used zigzagging pen strokes, dashes, and dots to create brilliant light effects, which he enhanced further by layering the terrain asymmetrically across a vast distance. The result is a luminous and highly finished work of art. An earlier collector evidently mistook the drawing to be the work of Vroom's Flemish contemporary Aegidius Neyts (1618–1687) and added an erroneous attribution at bottom center.

Aelbert Cuyp

Dutch, 1620–1691

Panoramic View of Dordrecht and the River Maas, circa 1645–52

Brush and brown ink with gray wash and ocher watercolor over black chalk, with selectively applied gum glaze, 15.9 × 50.5 cm (6¼ × 19⅞ in.), 2017.74

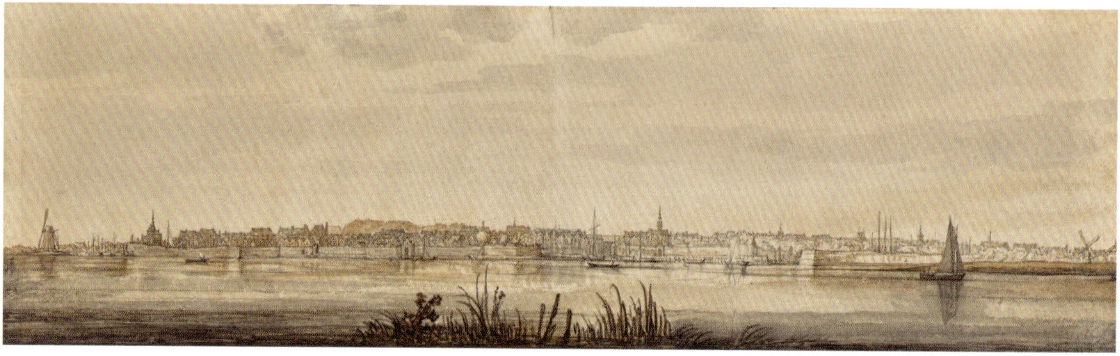

This majestic panorama depicts Cuyp's native city of Dordrecht along the River Maas, from the windmills outside the North Dike Harbor to the New Harbor's northern entrance. Over precise and descriptive strokes of black chalk, the artist enlivens his cityscape with watercolor washes. In the foreground, tufts of vegetation darkened by the sparing application of gum arabic enhance the perceived distance from the city. The detailed topography over the delicate reflection of the large expanse of water imparts an extraordinary richness to the composition. Although made as a highly finished work of art, the sheet relates to Cuyp's painting of Dordrecht that dates to 1647.

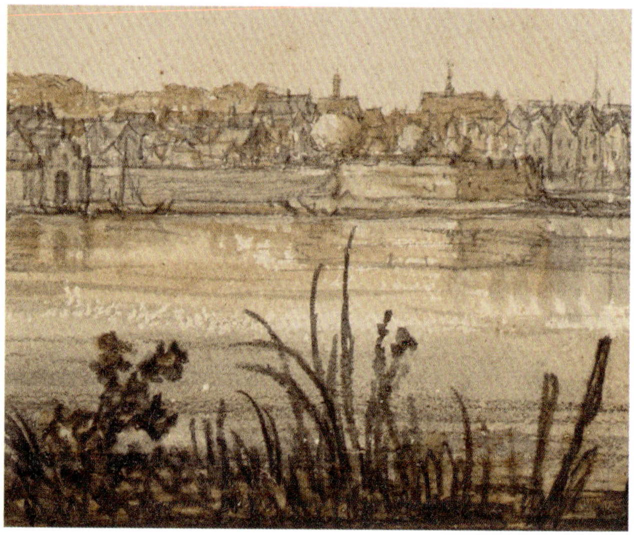

Detail view

Samuel van Hoogstraten

Dutch, 1627–1678

The Crucifixion, circa 1650

Pen and brown ink with gray wash and red chalk, heightened with white opaque watercolor; corrections in white opaque watercolor, 24.5 × 25.1 cm (9⁵/₈ × 9⁷/₈ in.), 2020.39

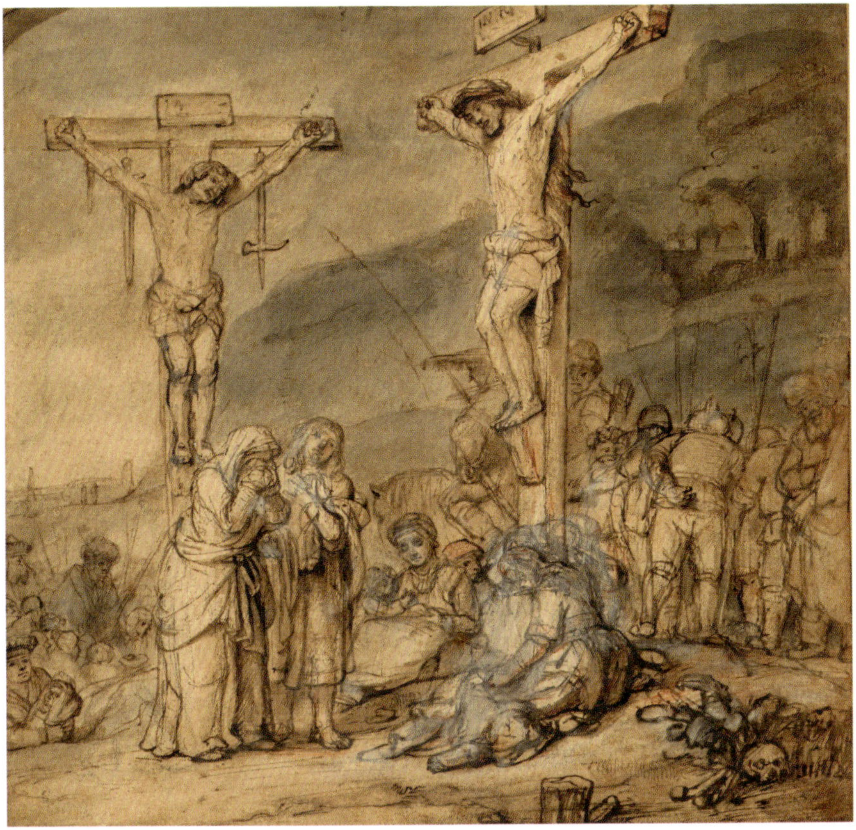

Van Hoogstraten, a gifted pupil of Rembrandt (see p. 237), employed a rich array of techniques and media to create this emotionally charged drawing. The effect is less of an exploratory sketch than of a finished work of art, filled with stirring detail. Christ hangs on the cross at right, blood streaming from his hands and feet, as the mourning Mary Magdalene, the Virgin Mary, and John the Evangelist gather beneath him. The artist contrasted their sorrow with the indifference displayed by the group of soldiers at right, whose backs are turned to the viewer, gambling over Christ's garments. The drawing shows traces of having had a rounded frame at the top, which would have given the impression of a small devotional painting.

Gian Lorenzo Bernini

Italian, 1598–1680

Design for a Fountain, with a Marine God Clutching a Dolphin, 1652–53

Black chalk, 34.9 × 23.8 cm

(13 11/16 × 9 3/8 in.), 87.GB.142

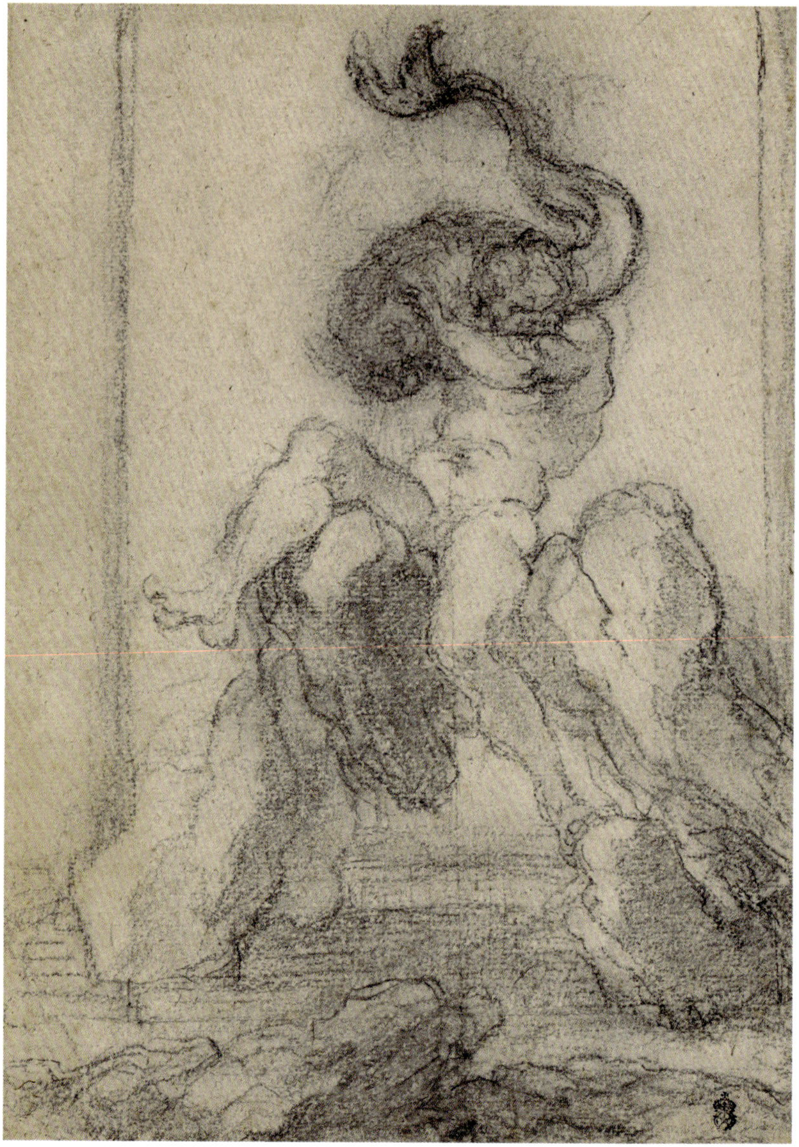

Bernini was an architect and a painter, as well as the most successful Italian sculptor of his day. This powerfully evocative design is for the fountain of Neptune designed to embellish a niche at the palace of Duke Francesco I d'Este (1610–1658) at Sassuolo, Italy. Swiftly drawn in a vibrant black-chalk technique, the sheet exhibits a dynamism that echoes the drama of the deity-versus-dolphin subject matter. Bernini's assistant, Antonio Raggi (1624–1686), referred to this design to execute the stucco fountain.

Jean-Antoine Watteau

French, 1684–1721

Two Studies of a Flutist and One of the Head of a Boy, 1718

Red, black, and white chalks,

21.4 × 33.6 cm (8 7/16 × 13 3/16 in.), 88.GB.3

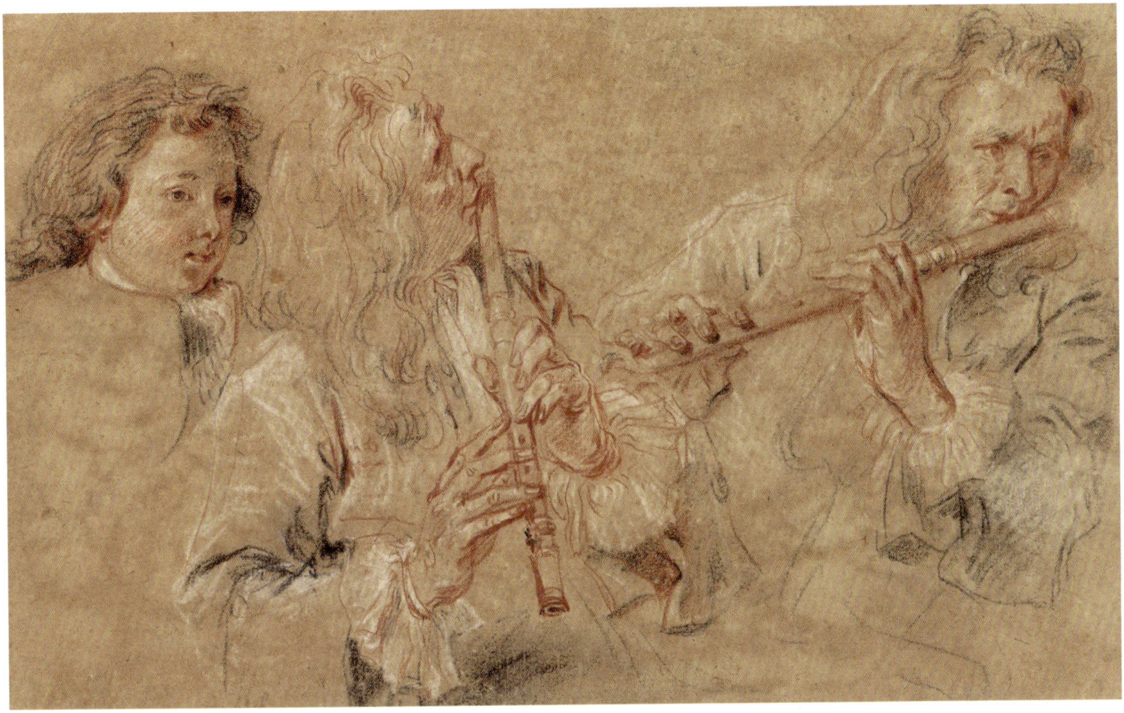

One of the most influential and gifted draftsmen of the French Rococo period, Watteau was a master of the technique known as *trois crayons*, which involved the use of red, black, and white chalks. In this drawing he expertly employed various media to suggest texture and convey compelling details, such as the shape of the musician's long, tapered fingers and the waves of his hair. Watteau observed the flute player from life and captured his expression of keen concentration from two angles as he blows into his instrument through pursed lips. The head of a boy appears at left, as if listening to the music across the lyrical sheet of sketches.

Rosalba Carriera
Italian, 1673/75–1757
A Muse, mid-1720s
Pastel on blue paper, 31 × 26 cm
(12 $\frac{3}{16}$ × 10 $\frac{1}{4}$ in.), 2003.17

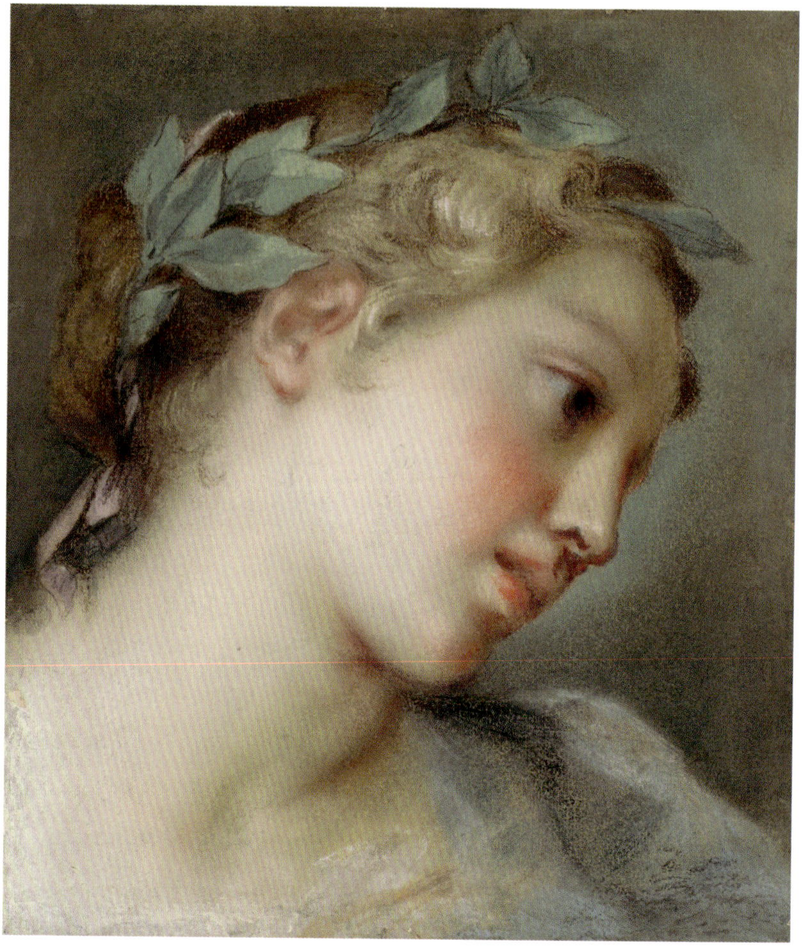

While few women in the early modern era had the opportunity to work as professional artists, the Venetian Rosalba Carriera defied the odds to become one of the leading pastelists of her time. Here, a young woman, her head slightly tilted, wears a laurel wreath that identifies her as one of the nine Muses, daughters of the Greek god Zeus, who provided inspiration in the arts, literature, and science. Rosalba rendered the head skillfully using a combination of wet and dry pastel and allowing the blue color of the paper to serve as an undertone. Such idealized representations of women in allegorical and mythological guises were extremely popular in the eighteenth century. This drawing, for example, was once in the prestigious collection of Augustus III, elector of Saxony and king of Poland from 1733 to 1763.

Giovanni Battista Piazzetta

Italian, 1682–1754

A Boy Holding a Pear (Giacomo Piazzetta?), circa 1737

Black and white chalks on blue paper (now discolored), 39.2 × 30.9 cm ($15^{7}/_{16}$ × $12^{3}/_{16}$ in.), 86.GB.677

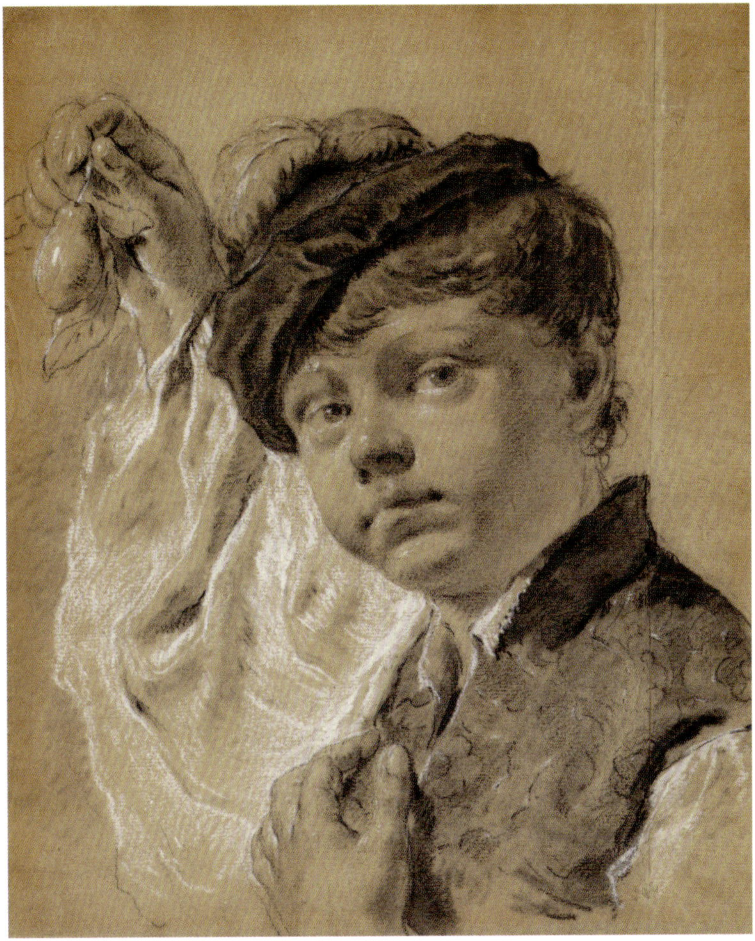

In this spirited drawing, a young boy dressed in a beautiful brocade vest, full-sleeved shirt, and feathered cap holds up a pear. The same sitter appears in a number of works by Piazzetta and has been tentatively identified as the artist's son, Giacomo. The drawing seems to have been made as an independent work of art; such sheets were widely collected in Venice at the time. Piazzetta applied chalk with varying degrees of pressure so as to juxtapose lightly shaded areas with rich, velvety patches. White-chalk highlights—most visible in the billowing sleeve—help to further model form. Blue fibers in the paper show that the sheet was once fully blue, yielding different tonal balances to those observable now. The paper likely lost its color within decades of being made.

Jean-Étienne Liotard

Swiss, 1702–1789

Portrait of Maria Frederike van Reede-Arhlone at Seven Years of Age, 1755–56

Pastel on vellum, 54.9 × 44.8 cm

($21\frac{5}{8} \times 17\frac{5}{8}$ in.), 83.PC.273

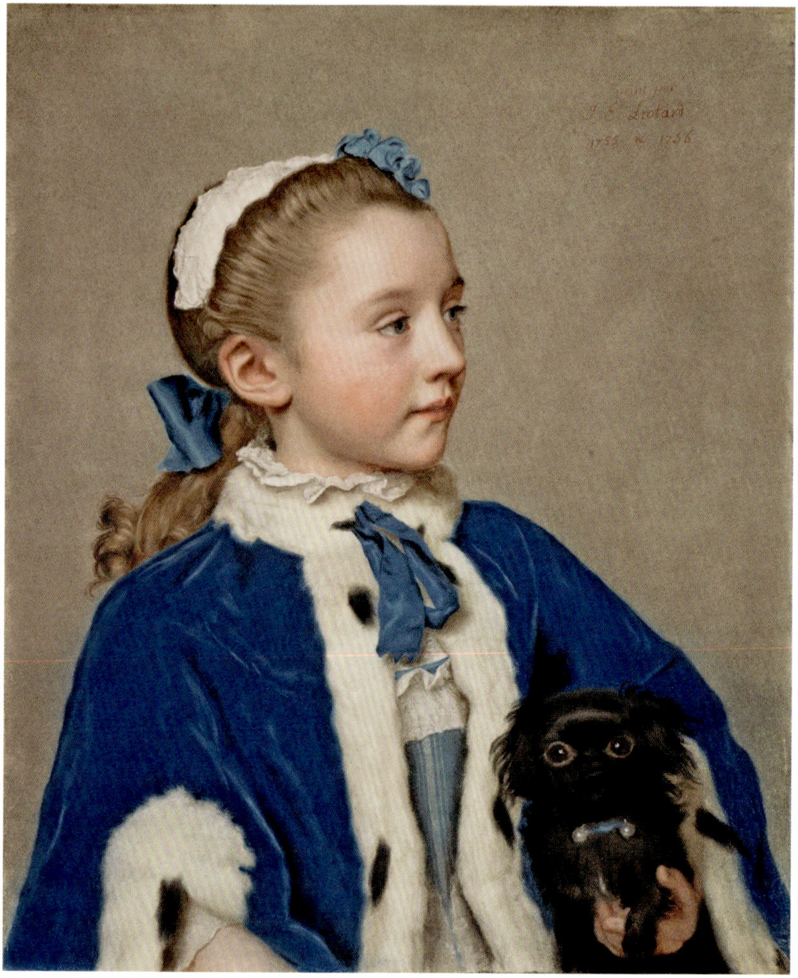

Liotard captured Maria Frederike, the seven-year-old daughter of an aristocratic Dutch family, with startling naturalism. Lost in thought, she is composed yet shy in comparison to her small dog, which stares out at the viewer with unabashed curiosity. The warmth of the girl's blond hair and rosy complexion differ from the vibrant blue of her ermine-trimmed dress. Liotard developed remarkable technical skills in the challenging medium of pastel. Brilliantly describing surfaces and defining volume through subtle gradations of color, he depicted forms, textures, and the play of light with great immediacy. Here, he employs these abilities to evoke both the physicality and the psychology of his young subject.

Adélaïde Labille-Guiard

French, 1749–1803

Portrait of Madame Charles Mitoire with Her Children, 1783

Pastel on blue paper, laid on canvas, 98.5 × 79 cm (38¾ × 31⅛ in.), 2021.37

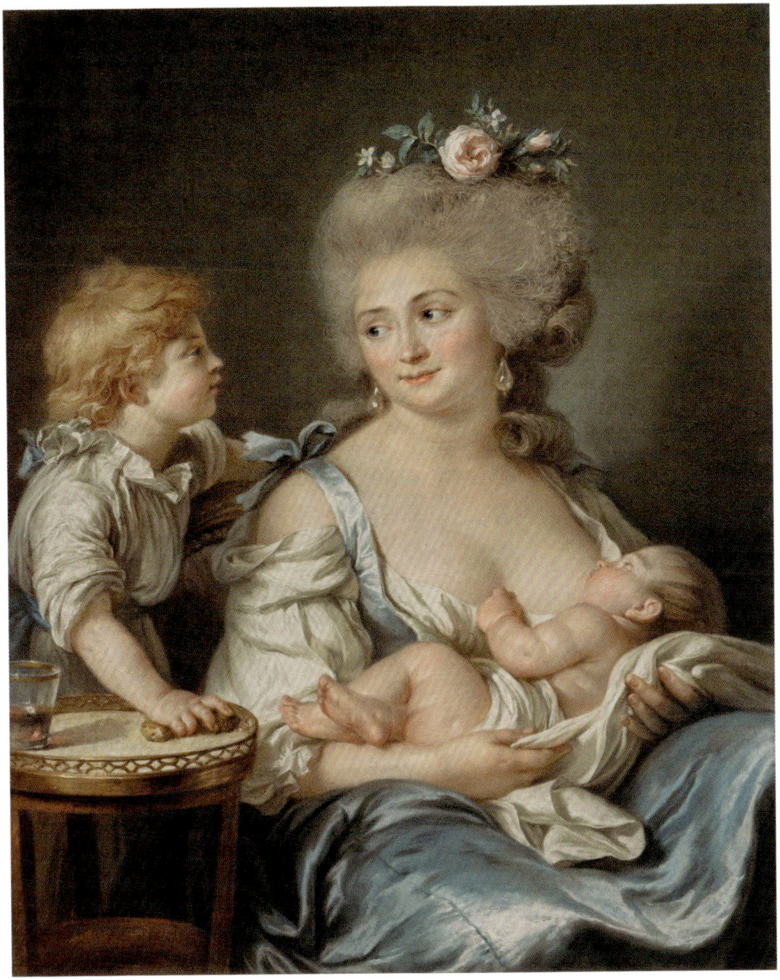

A successful portraitist, Labille-Guiard skillfully rendered the vitality of her royal and aristocratic patrons. In this large pastel, the artist portrayed the fashionable Madame Mitoire (1760–1842) in an intimate moment with her children. Applying pastels both wet with a brush and dry with a stick, Labille-Guiard depicted the distinct textures of her sitter's pale blue satin gown and powdered coiffure piled with roses and orange blossoms, as well as the soft, dimpled skin of the infant in her arms. This image of a nursing mother was striking for eighteenth-century Parisian viewers when the portrait was first exhibited in 1783.

Giovanni Domenico Tiepolo

Italian, 1727–1804

The Punchinello Riding a Camel at the Head of a Caravan, late 1790s

Brush and brown ink over black chalk, 35.6 × 47.4 cm (14 × 18 11/16 in.), 2017.81

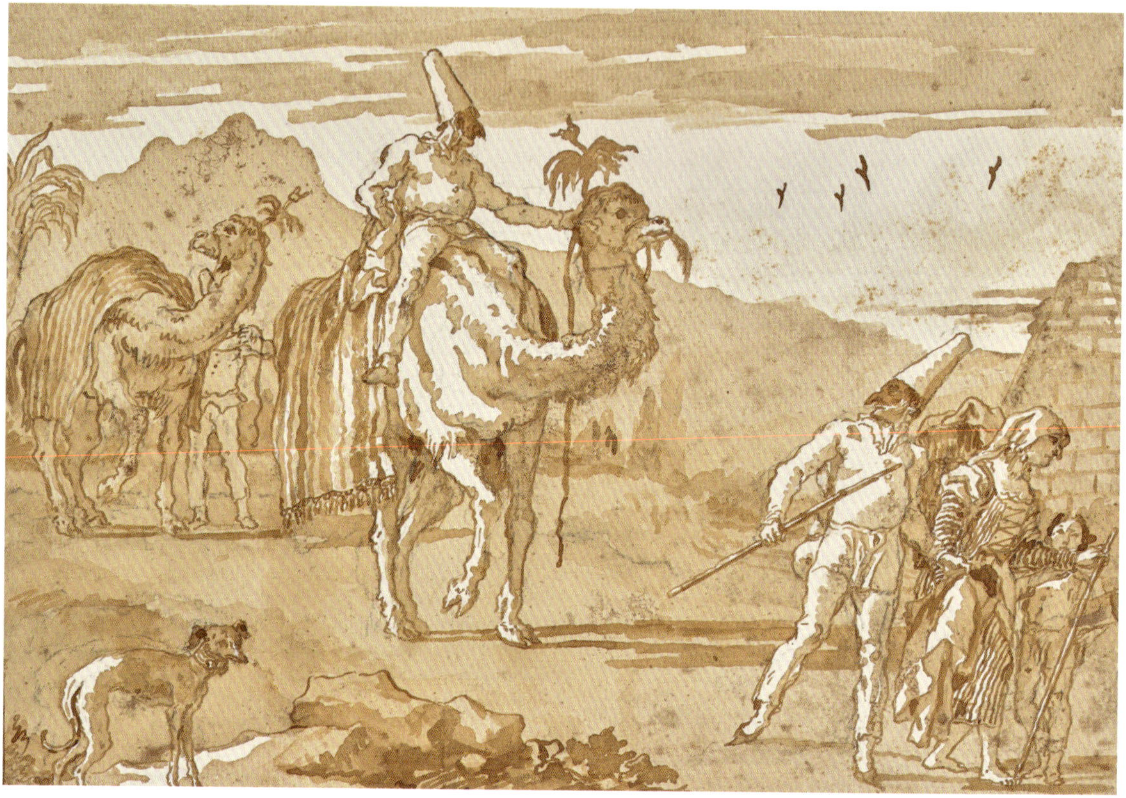

Son of the celebrated eighteenth-century Venetian painter Giovanni Battista Tiepolo (see p. 186), Giovanni Domenico achieved fame in his own right with several large series of drawings. This sheet is one of 104 from *Divertimenti per li Ragazzi* (Entertainments for Children), a now-dispersed album illustrating the life and death of Punchinello, the sly, lazy antihero from the commedia dell'arte, a traditional form of Italian theater. Golden ink and brilliant white paper, selectively left blank for highlights, create the impression of an arid, sun-soaked landscape. The vainglorious Punchinello, seated atop a dromedary, proudly leads a caravan of camels. His companion at right looks back as he ushers along a basket-laden woman and her small child. Meanwhile, a dog at left looks out at the viewer as if in disbelief at this procession of fools.

Francisco de Goya (Francisco José de Goya y Lucientes)

Spanish, 1746–1828

The Eagle Hunter, circa 1812–20

Brush and brown ink with brown wash, 20 × 14 cm (7⅞ × 5½ in.), 2017.76

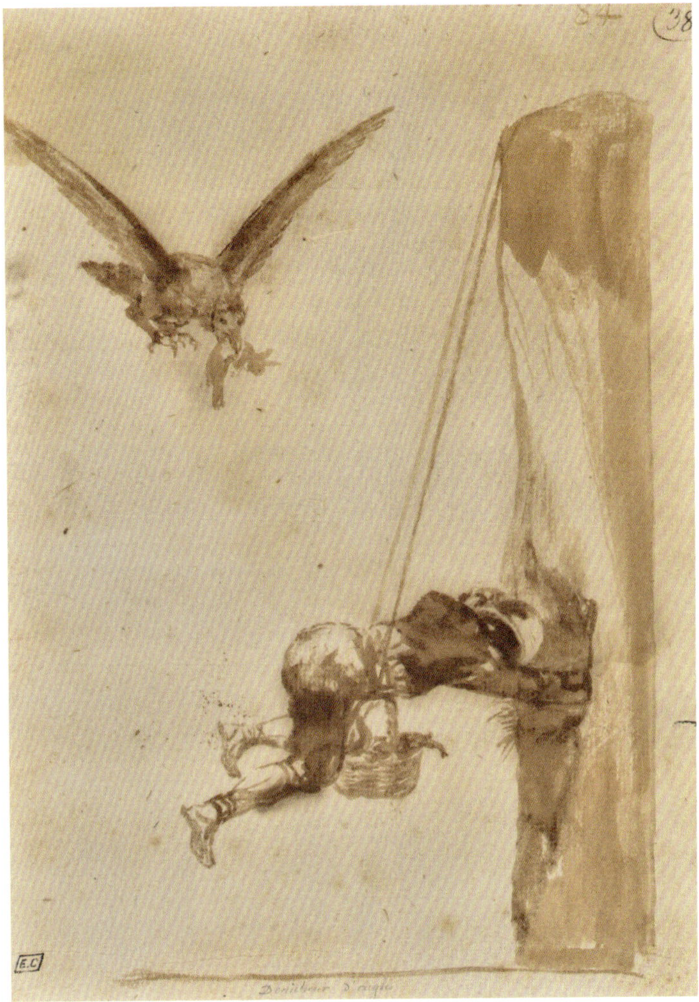

Bold line work, gradations of wash, and striking use of the blank paper compellingly render eagle hunting as a brutal and slightly comic task. The hunter dangles from a precipice by a thin rope around his waist, with only a cooking pot on his head to protect him. Hovering midair while plucking the young birds from a nest, the hunter remains completely unaware of his impending doom: with sharp talons outstretched, the mother eagle returns. The scene could illustrate the proverb "He who would take will himself be taken." Goya drew the composition with common writing ink on inexpensive Spanish paper—materials he was forced to use during the Napoleonic occupation of Spain (1808–14). Like the subject, the medium and support bear the imprint of desperation.

Pierre-Paul Prud'hon

French, 1758–1823

Study of a Female Nude, circa 1800

Black and white chalks with stumping on blue paper, 60.4 × 31.8 cm ($23\frac{3}{4}$ × $12\frac{1}{2}$ in.), 99.GB.49

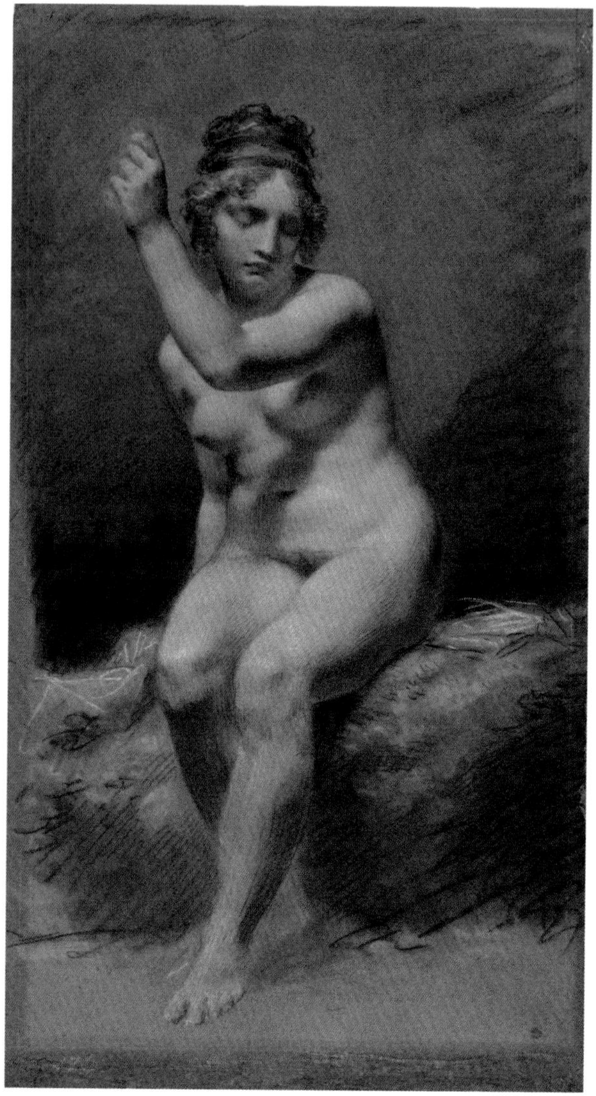

This drawing is a striking example of an *académie*, or a study of a nude model posed in the studio. Prud'hon demonstrated his classical understanding of the female body in this intimate study, in which the figure strikes a refined pose in imitation of antique sculpture. Far from statuary, however, Prud'hon's figure is brought to life through a blend of tiny strokes of white chalk and smoky passages of stumped (rubbed or smudged) black chalk. Her dreamy, downturned gaze and the soft play of shadows across her flesh impart an aura of sensuality.

Jean-Auguste-Dominique Ingres

French, 1780–1867

Portrait of Lord Grantham, 1816

Graphite, 40.5 × 28.2 cm ($15\frac{15}{16} \times 11\frac{1}{8}$ in.), 82.GD.106

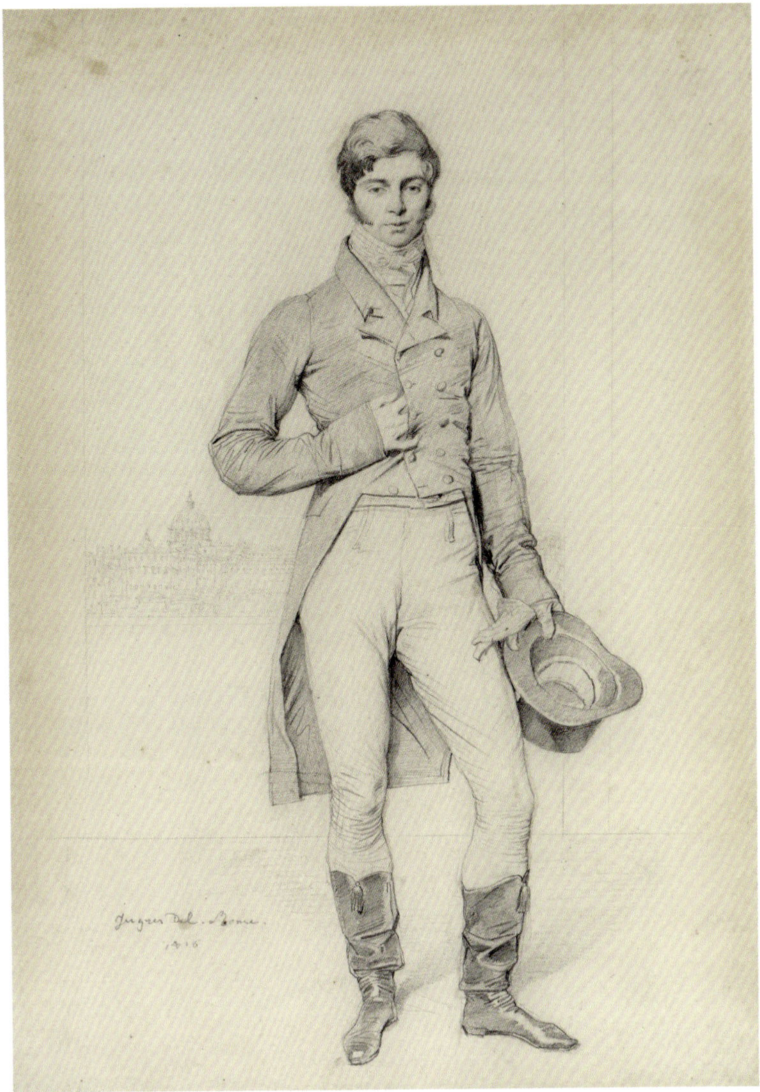

Thomas Robinson, 3rd Baron Grantham and later Earl de Grey, was thirty-five when Ingres drew this refined portrait of him in graphite. The artist chose a pose that combined the informality of youth and the self-assurance of his subject's aristocratic origins. Grantham, who commissioned this portrait himself, stands confidently against a distant view of Saint Peter's Basilica in Rome, an important site for travelers on the so-called Grand Tour to see the major cultural landmarks of Europe, and one that the artist often included in portraits. Ingres made this drawing when he was a struggling young artist in Rome, earning his living by drawing portraits of wealthy visitors to the city.

William Blake
British, 1757–1827
Satan Exulting over Eve, 1795

Color print with watercolor and pen and black ink over graphite, 42.5 × 53.5 cm (16¾ × 21¹⁄₁₆ in.), 84.GC.49

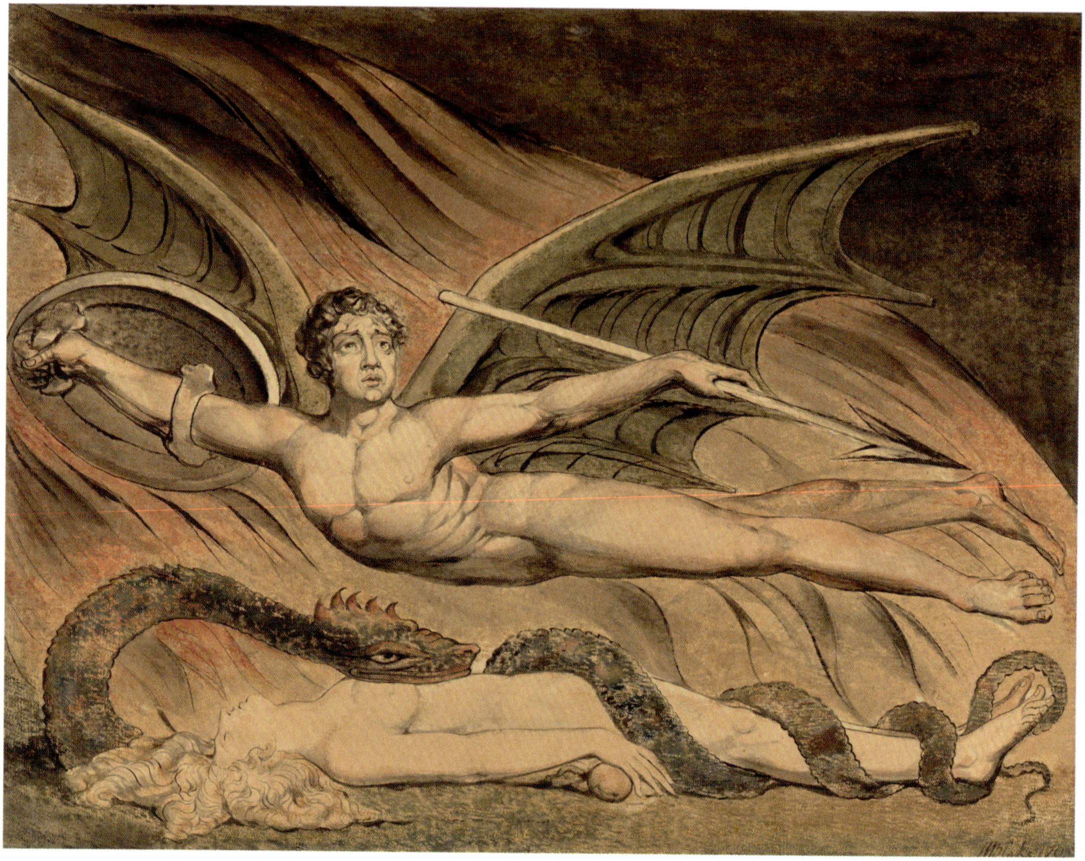

Satan hovers in malevolent glory over Eve, whose body is entwined by the serpent from the Garden of Eden. Though the characters are taken from the Bible, this composition sprang entirely from Blake's imagination. The poet, painter, and print-maker made this work using an experimental process. He first painted his design on thick cardboard, then placed a damp sheet of paper on top and ran the two through a rolling press, transferring the wet paint onto the paper. Finally he heavily reworked the impression in watercolor and reinforced the outlines in pen and ink. The printed areas—the mossy ground, scaled body of the serpent, and Eve's golden locks—can clearly be distinguished from the painted ones by their distinctive webbed surface patterns.

Richard Parkes Bonington
British, 1802–1828
Riva degli Schiavoni, from near San Biagio, Venice, 1826

Watercolor over graphite with opaque watercolor, 18.4 × 17.1 cm (7¼ × 6¾ in.), 2015.51

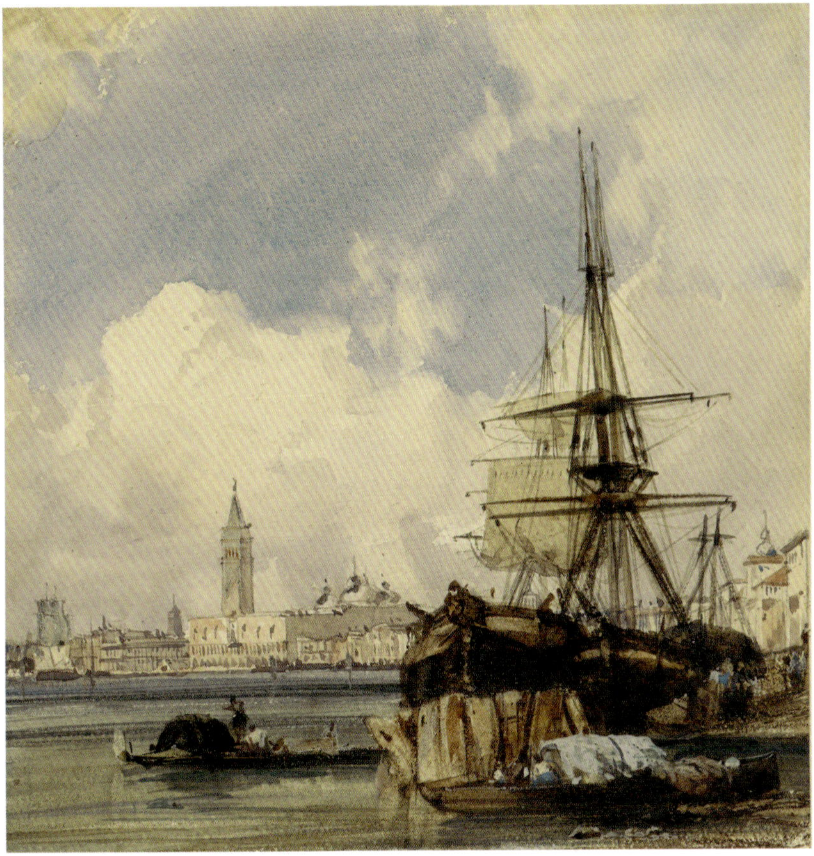

This jewel-like watercolor captures the atmospheric effects of light and water for which Venice is still so famous. With the distinctive Palazzo Ducale and belltower of San Marco visible in the distance, the composition represents a view from the Venetian waterfront, close to the Church of San Biagio and not far from the public gardens. By relegating the city's famous architecture to the background and instead positioning several large ships in the foreground, Bonington highlighted the maritime roots of Venice's power. He made this watercolor on his only trip to the city, at age twenty-three. The artist's views of Venice in watercolor or oil, created for exhibition and sale, were highly popular, but his promising career was cut short by his death from tuberculosis at age twenty-five.

Eugène Delacroix

French, 1798–1863

The Education of Achilles, 1862

Pastel, 30.6 × 41.9 cm (12¹/₁₆ × 16¹/₂ in.),

86.GG.728

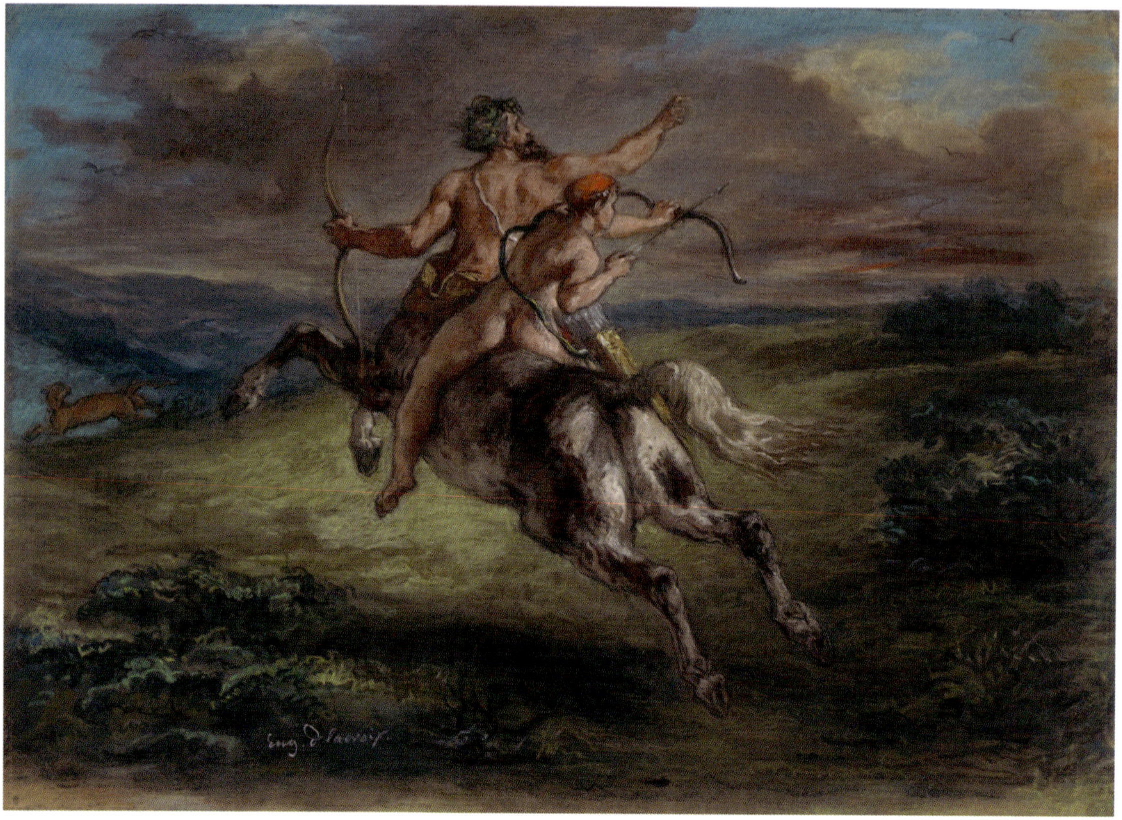

A leading artist of the Romantic movement in France, Delacroix often drew from literary subjects and his knowledge of antiquity to create his dramatic compositions. The subject of this pastel, taken from Greek mythology, is the hero Achilles learning to hunt from the centaur (human-horse hybrid) Chiron. Delacroix's vigorous touch energizes the figures as they gallop through the landscape. The rich palette of dark greens, blues, and browns in the untamed landscape are varied by light flesh tones and reds. Delacroix made this pastel as a gift for a friend, the writer and artist George Sand (1804–1876), who had expressed her admiration for a painting he had made of the same subject.

Rosa Bonheur
French, 1822–1899
Charcoal Burners (Les charbonniers),
1880s–90s

Charcoal and white chalk, stumping and lifting, on gray-green paper, 49.5 × 64.3 cm ($19\frac{1}{2} \times 25\frac{5}{16}$ in.). Gift of Daniel and Sophie Thierry in honor of Lee Hendrix, 2016.106

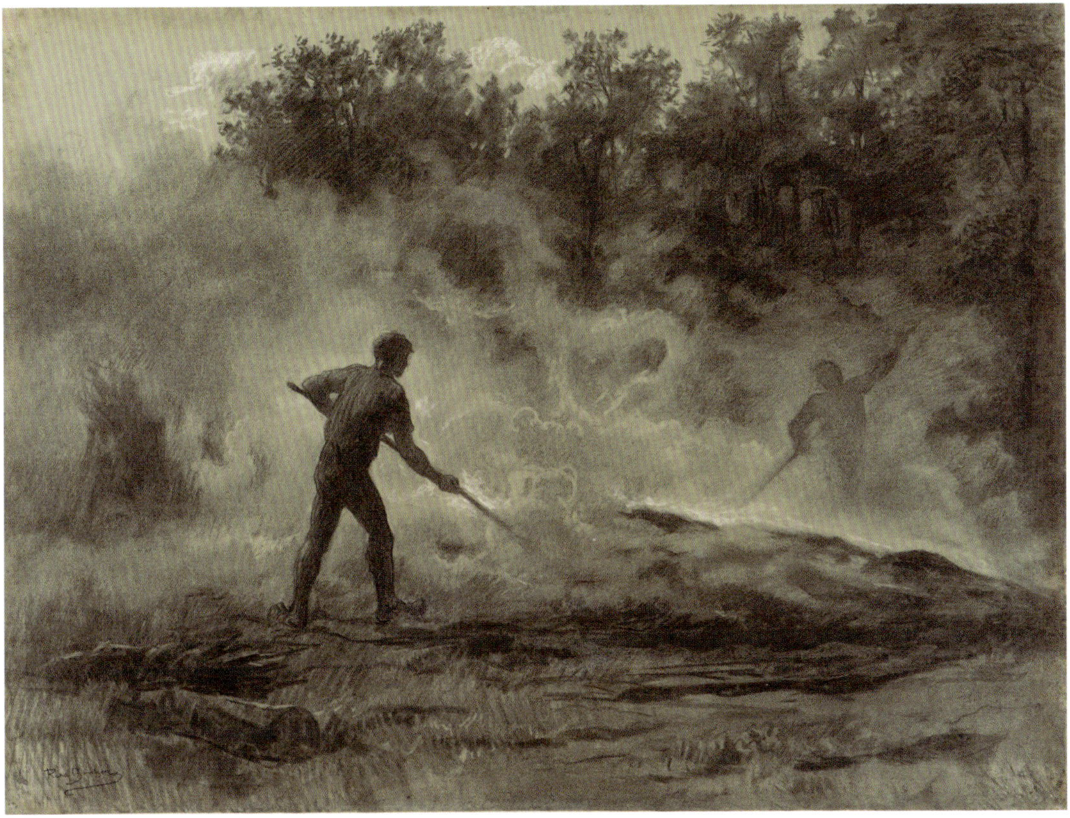

One of the most successful women artists of the nineteenth century, Bonheur was celebrated for her naturalistic depictions of rural life. In this large, atmospheric drawing, she represented two charcoal burners at work near her home at the edge of the Forest of Fontainebleau. One of the men appears only as a shadowy silhouette, nearly disappearing amid soft plumes of smoke. Charcoal burners traveled to Fontainebleau each spring, settling in huts in the forest and attending to the outdoor kilns at all hours. Bonheur expertly blended and manipulated the charcoal on the sheet to produce a depiction of the powdery media itself. The gray-green paper helps accentuate the contrast between the dark landscape and the clouds of smoke accented with white chalk.

Honoré Daumier
French, 1808–1879
A Criminal Case, circa 1865

Translucent and opaque watercolor with pen and brown ink over black chalk, 38.5 × 32.8 cm (15⅛ × 12$^{13}/_{16}$ in.), 89.GA.33

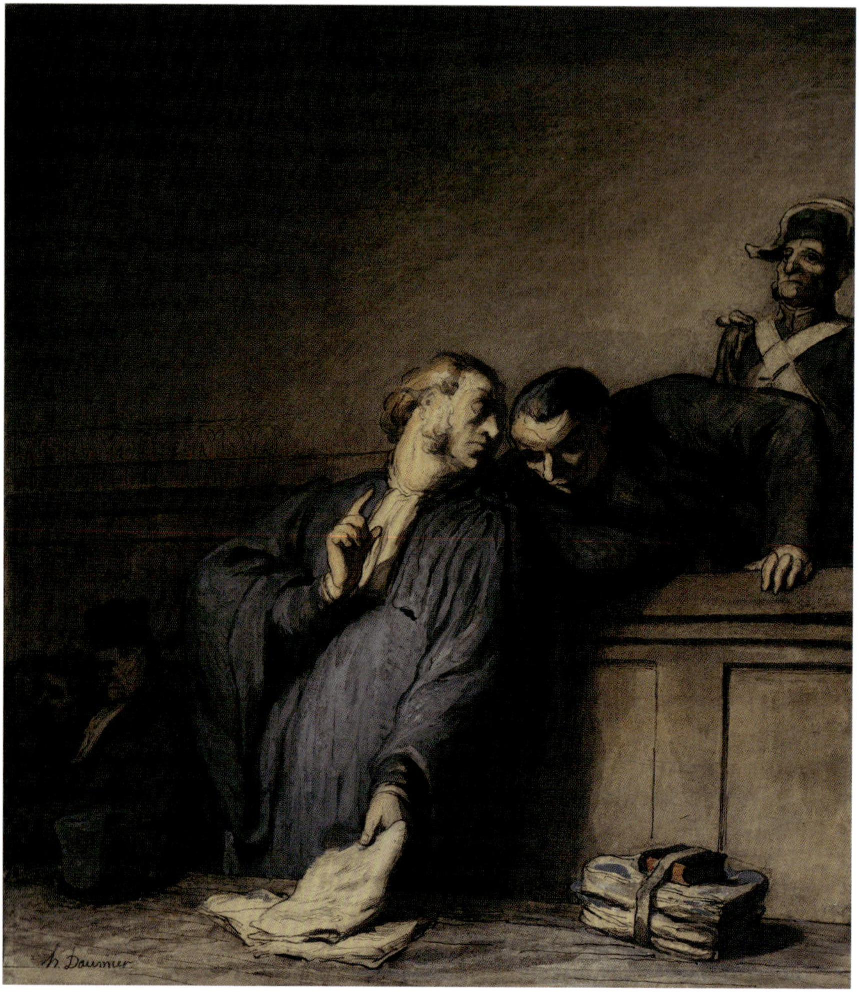

At a young age, Daumier worked as a messenger for the Paris courts, where he was exposed to the complexities and inequities of the legal system that would go on to inform his often satirical works of art. Here, he skillfully employed watercolor to illustrate the foibles of the French judicial system. The monumentality of the figures and theatrical depiction of light heighten the drama of a court proceeding. The strong compositional diagonal draws attention to the accused criminal, who leans over to consult with his elegantly robed lawyer. An impassive guard stands behind them, oblivious to their conversation.

Adolph von Menzel
German, 1815–1905
Study for Heinrich von Kleist's "Broken Jug," circa 1877

Graphite, 24.8 × 37.5 cm (9¾ × 14¾ in.).
Gift of Dr. Richard A. Simms in honor of Lee Hendrix, 2016.80

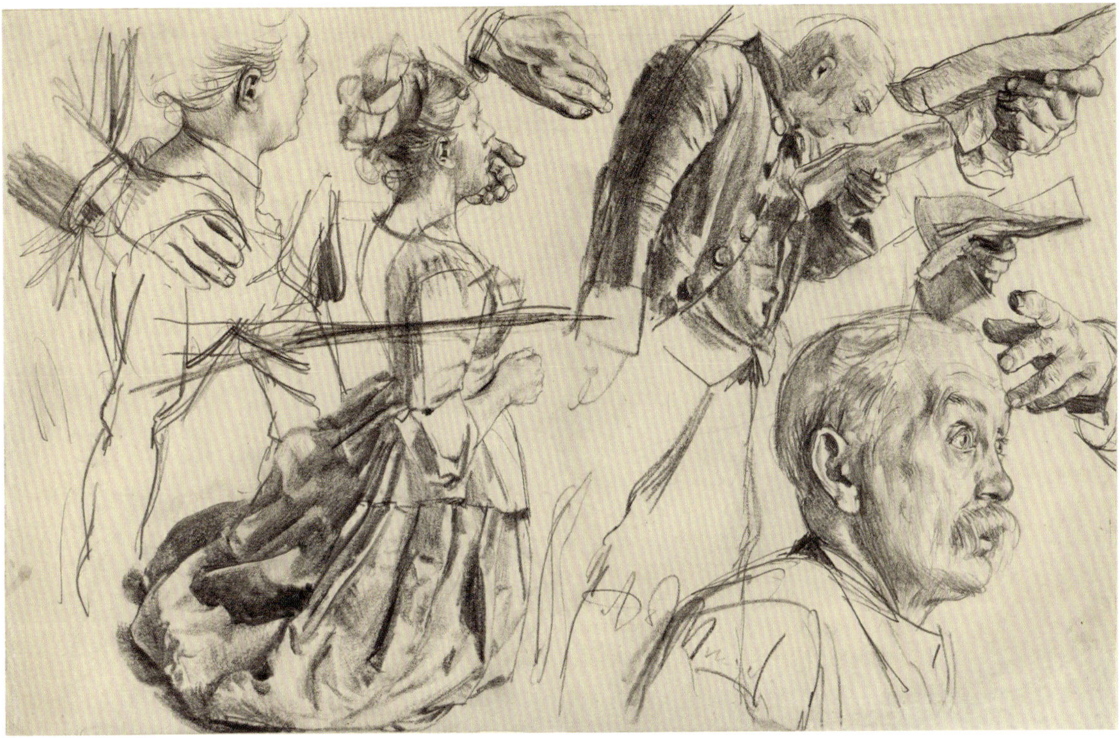

A kneeling woman, an elder scrutinizing a document, the gaunt face of a man with his eyebrows raised in shock, and hands in various poses—these studies were drawn by the German Realist artist Adolph Menzel in preparation for a wood engraving. Published in 1877, the print was part of a set illustrating the playwright Heinrich von Kleist's popular comedy *The Broken Jug* (1806). The play, which explores themes of love and corruption, revolves around a trial in a village court over the destruction of an old jug and the virtue of a young woman called Eve. Here, Menzel explores details related to the climactic scene where the characters learn that the presiding judge destroyed the piece of pottery—and might have also taken Eve's virginity.

Edgar Degas

French, 1834–1917

Miss Lala at the Fernando Circus, 1879

Pastel on blue paper (now discolored), squared in black chalk, 46.4 × 30 cm ($18\frac{1}{4} \times 11\frac{3}{4}$ in.), 2004.93

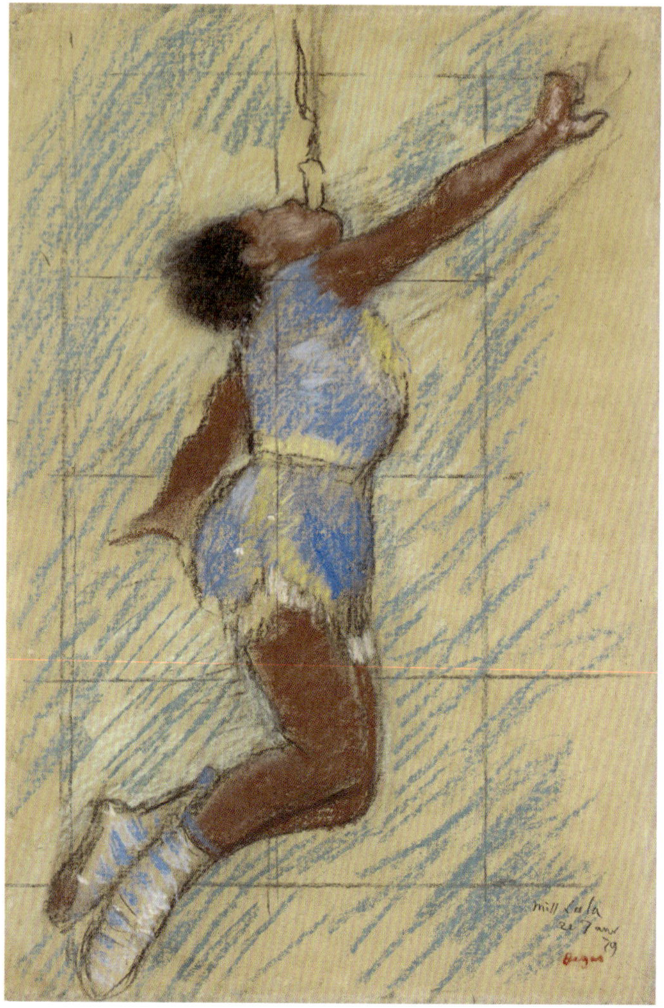

Miss Lala's acrobatic feats created a sensation when she performed in Paris at the Fernando Circus in 1879. In this pastel drawing, Degas depicted her during one of her signature acts, in which she was pulled to the ceiling by a rope held in her clenched teeth. One of several studies made for a painting, this work shows Degas exploring and refining Miss Lala's pose; he initially drew her right arm at a lower angle and made alterations to her right hand, chin, thighs, and feet. He also experimented with his pastel technique, layering the colors purple, blue, and yellow to capture her iridescent costume and smudging the black pastel to represent her hair. The diagonal blue lines surrounding her body help emphasize the movement of her soaring form.

Edward Burne-Jones

British, 1833–1898

Study for Perseus, circa 1882

Brown essence (thinned oil paint) and opaque watercolor over white chalk, on brown paper, 57.8 × 44.5 cm ($22\frac{3}{4} \times 17\frac{1}{2}$ in.), 2023.16

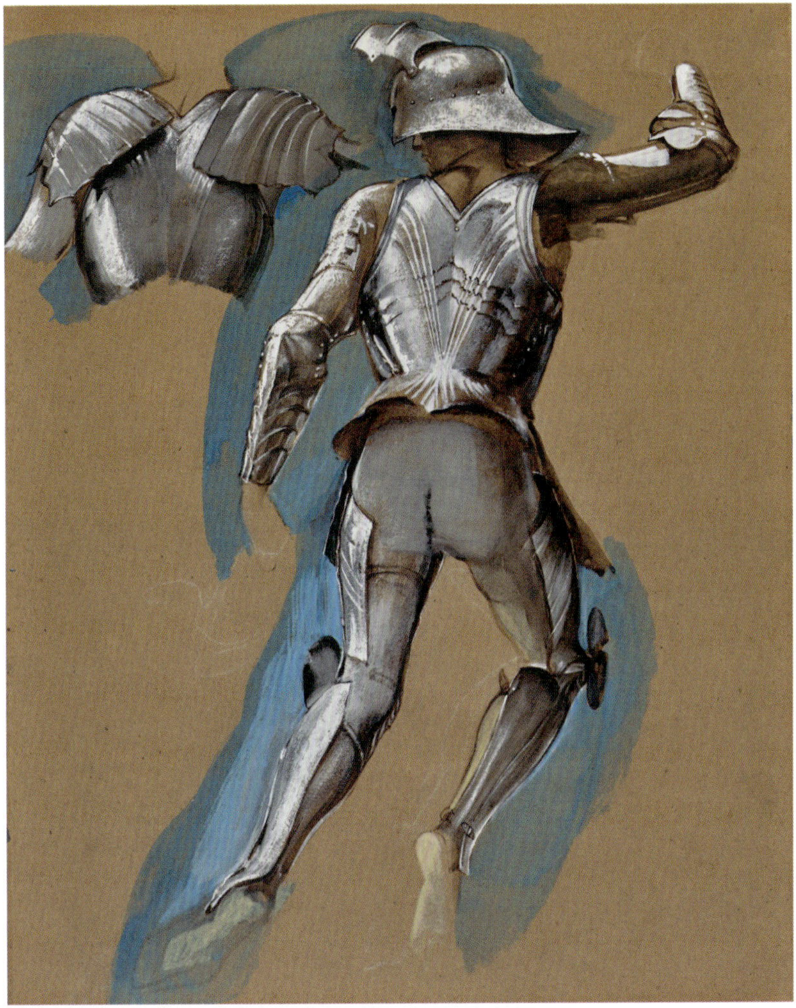

The Pre-Raphaelite painter Edward Burne-Jones made this large-scale drawing of a man dressed in armor in preparation for a partially realized, site-specific ensemble of paintings. The cycle, known as the Perseus Series, was commissioned by the rising young conservative politician Arthur Balfour (1848–1930) for his house in London. The study depicts Perseus, the Greek mythological hero, in a highly dynamic pose, with his right arm raised and legs bent as if flying. Burne-Jones skillfully applied white over gray opaque watercolor to convey the sheen and shimmer of the polished armor. Attesting to his keen attention to detail, the artist also executed a secondary study of the backplate and spaulders in the upper left of the sheet.

Georges Seurat

French, 1859–1891

Madame Seurat, the Artist's Mother,

circa 1882–83

Conté crayon, 30.5 × 23.3 cm

(12 × 9 3/16 in.), 2002.51

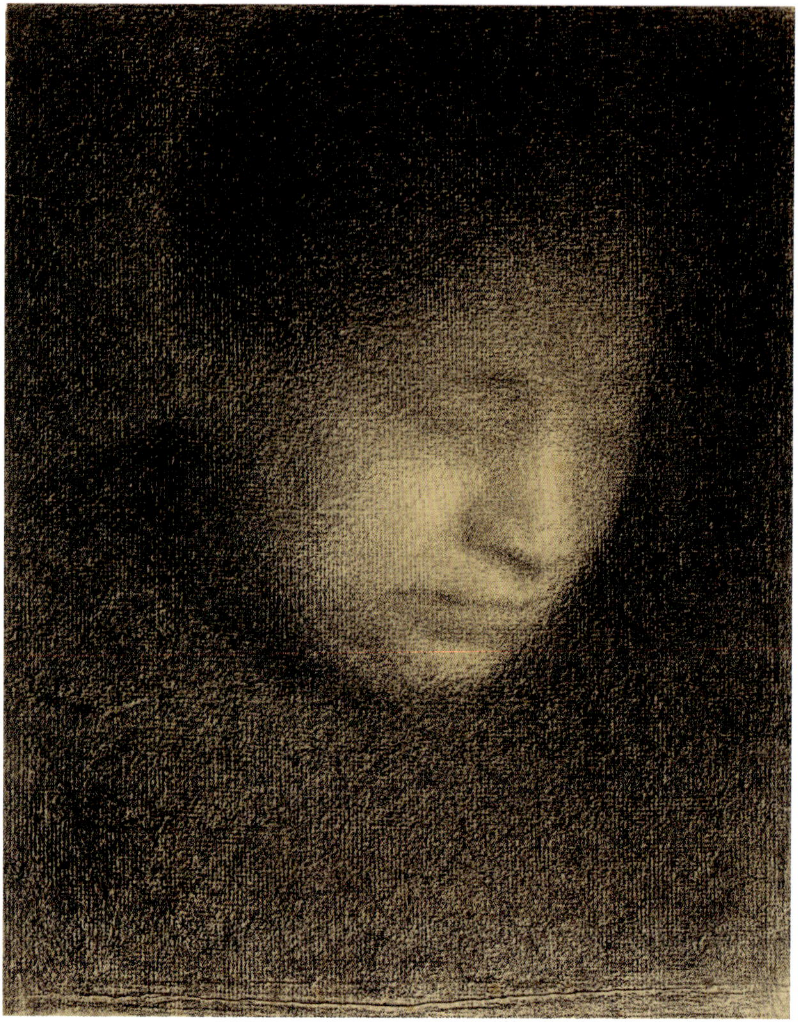

Though Seurat created many portraits of his mother, none has the same arresting sense of calm and simplicity of this intimate study. He filled almost the entire sheet with Madame Seurat's face, her downcast eyes suggesting that she is engaged in a quiet activity such as reading or embroidery. The portrait was modeled without lines, allowing the shadowy form to emerge from the darkness through the subtle interplay of the dark tones of conté crayon and the prominent laid texture of the bare paper. Seurat gave the drawing to his mother, who in turn presented it to her son's friend and fellow Neo-Impressionist painter Lucien Pissarro (1863–1944) after Seurat's premature death in 1891.

Odilon Redon

French, 1840–1916

Apparition, circa 1880–90

Charcoal, powdered charcoal,
and yellow pastel with stumping,
52.5 × 37.3 cm (20⁵⁄₈ × 14⁵⁄₈ in.), 2013.38

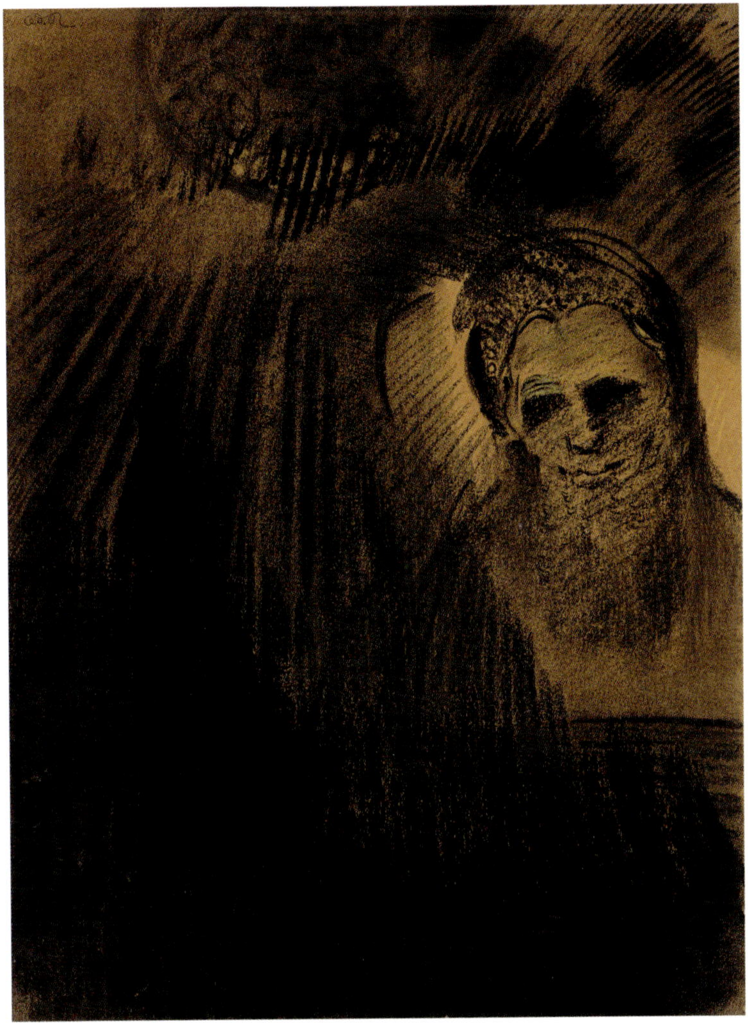

Redon endured a lonely childhood, and both the dreams and nightmares he experienced in his youth would go on to inform his artwork. Using a variety of black media, ranging from the opaque to the vaporous, Redon rendered this eerie apparition of a bearded head, smiling benignly with its gaze cast downward. The eyes appear as dark shadows, with no suggestion of anatomy, foregrounding the dreamlike, ambiguous quality of the subject. Sharp, staccato lines radiating around the figure and the velvety pastel heighten the dramatic depiction of an imaginary realm. Like many of Redon's works from this period, *Apparition* resists alignment with a specific literary or religious subject.

Vincent van Gogh
Dutch, 1853–1890
Portrait of Joseph Roulin, 1888
Reed and quill pens and brown ink over black chalk, 32.1 × 24.4 cm (12⅝ × 9⅝ in.), 85.GA.299

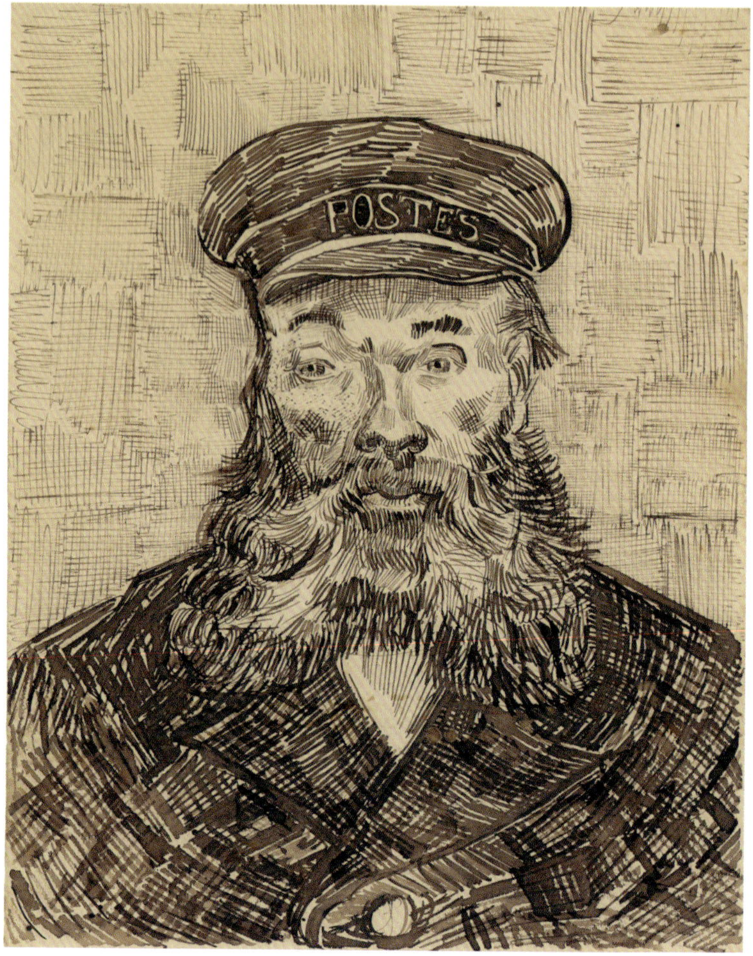

Joseph Roulin was a postal worker with whom Van Gogh became friends during his stay in Arles, in the south of France, from 1888 to 1889. The artist wrote that the postman's physical appearance and beliefs reminded him of the ancient philosopher Socrates: he was "neither embittered, nor happy, nor always irreproachably just." Van Gogh's presentation of Roulin finds bold expression in the close-up, frontal pose and intense gaze. The artist used two different pens and various techniques to animate his subject and achieve a remarkable range of textures. Dark, thick lines rendered with reed pen delineate Roulin's cap, beard, and coat, while the background, drawn with a quill, contains a patchwork of nervous, intersecting lines that reinforces the sitter's energy.

Eva Gonzalès

French, 1849–1883

The Maid of Honor (La Demoiselle d'Honneur), 1879

Pastel on canvas, 45 × 37 cm

(17$\frac{11}{16}$ × 14$\frac{9}{16}$ in.), 2024.12

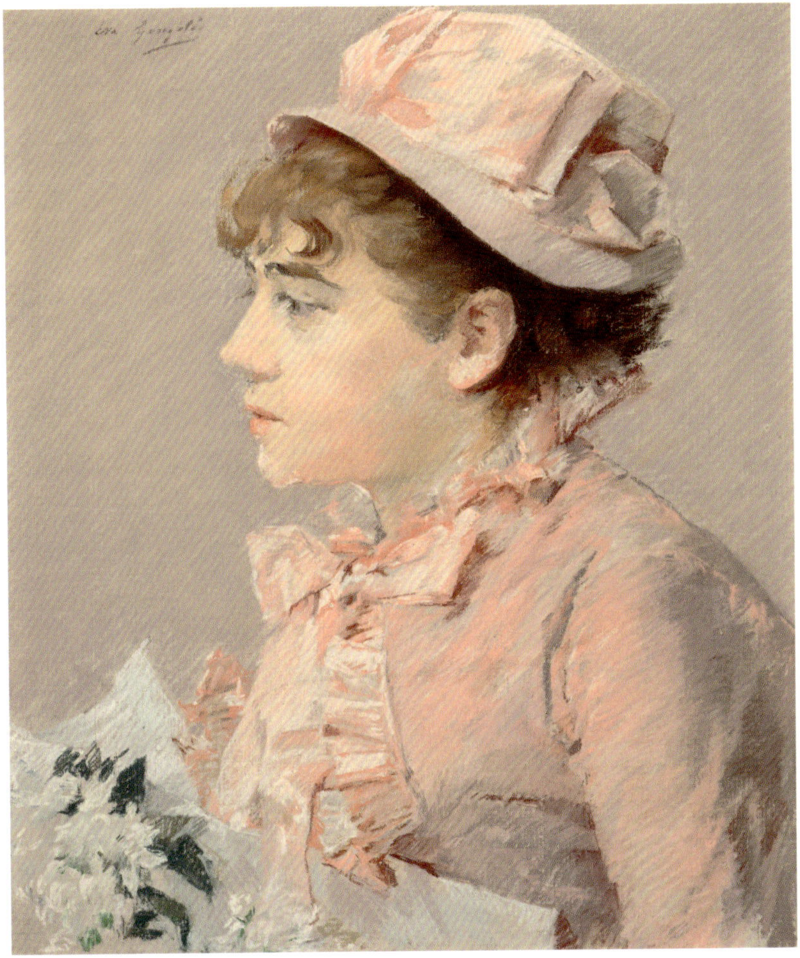

Associated with the Impressionist movement in France, Gonzalès focused primarily on portraits and scenes of domestic life. In this delicate drawing, she represents a young woman in a fashionable pink bonnet holding a bouquet of soft white flowers. Having recently married, the artist made a series of pastels around this time related to themes of matrimony, including this portrait of an unidentified maid of honor. Celebrated for her remarkable expertise in layering and blending the powdery medium of pastel, Gonzalès expertly portrayed the details of the woman's ruffled dress while capturing her refined features in profile.

Piet Mondrian

Dutch, 1872–1944

Landscape near Arnhem, 1903

Watercolor over graphite, heightened with white opaque watercolor,

53.5 × 71.5 cm (21 1/16 × 28 1/8 in.), 2020.43

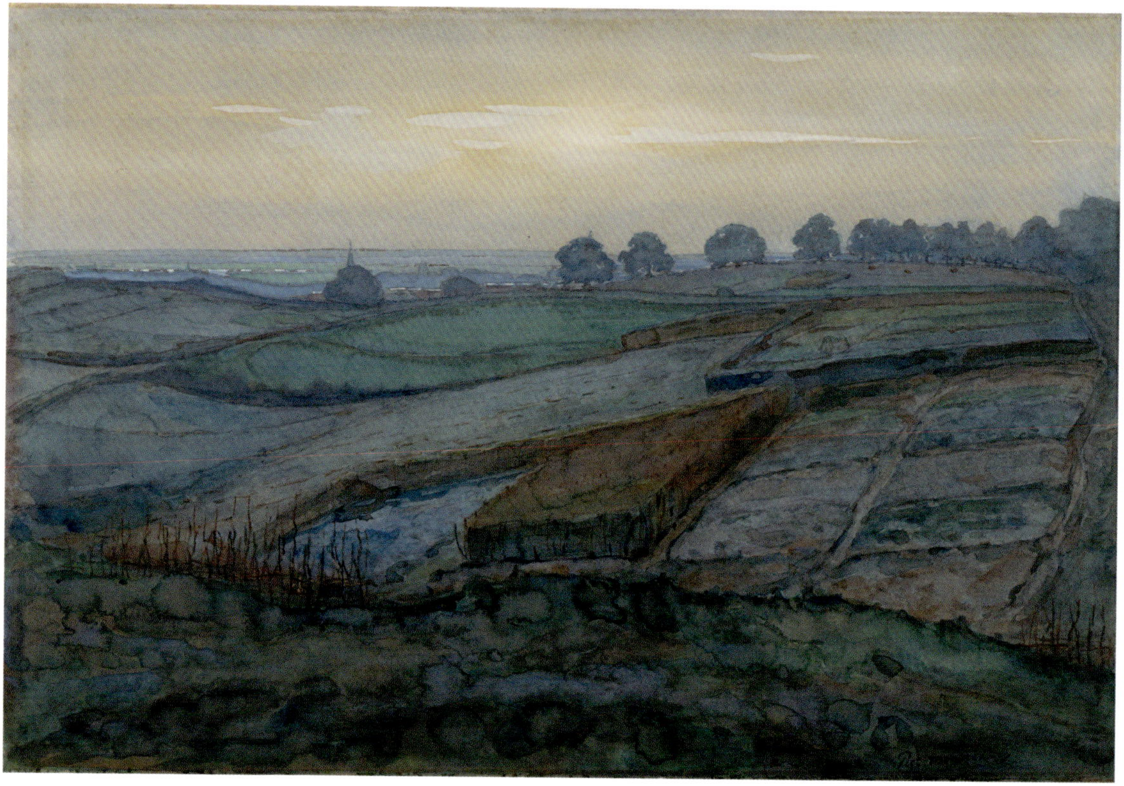

Early in his career, Mondrian championed the tranquility of his native Dutch countryside. Here, the city of Arnhem, including the distinctive steeple of the Church of Saint Martin, can be seen in the hazy distance at left. The high horizon line, elaborately worked surface, and pattern of light and dark planes of color are characteristic of the landscapes Mondrian made around 1900. Applying blue and green translucent and opaque watercolors in a "wet-into-wet" layering technique, he used aqueous tidelines to create a dreamlike view. The first work by Mondrian to enter the Getty collection, *Landscape near Arnhem* testifies to the artist's unwavering interest in the abstract foundations of nature.

Paul Cézanne

French, 1839–1906

Still Life, circa 1900–1906

Watercolor over graphite, 48 × 63.1 cm

(18 15/16 × 24 7/8 in.), 83.GC.221

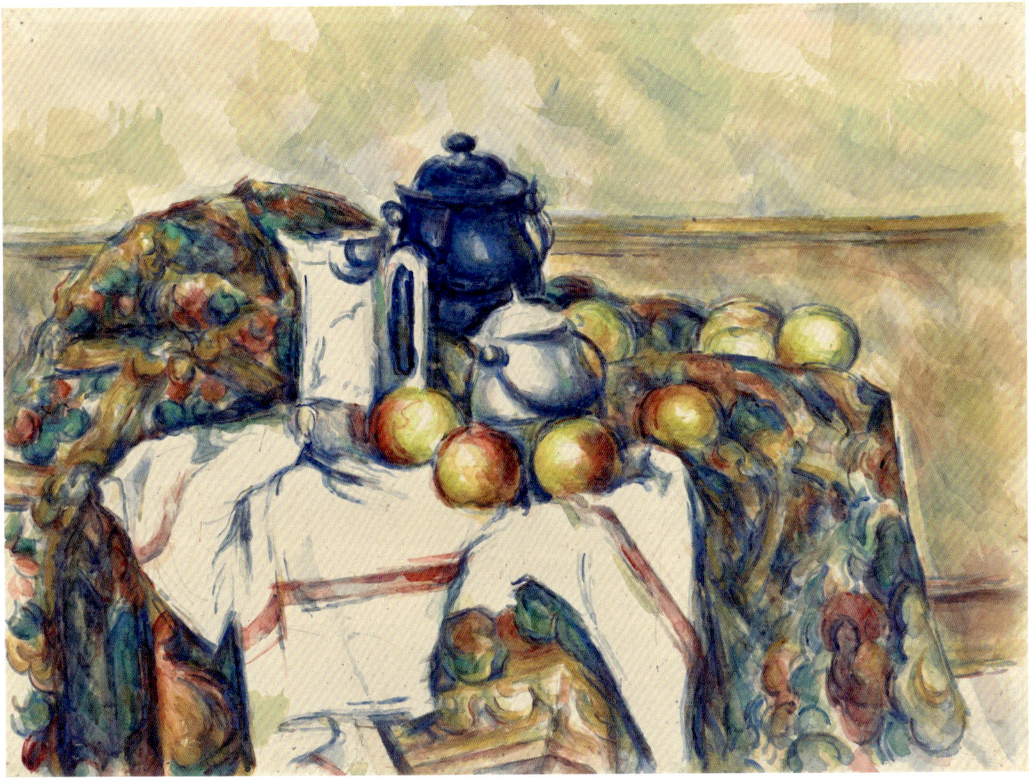

This vivid depiction of a bountiful table is one of Cézanne's largest, most finished watercolors. Still life was a principal theme throughout his career. Using a repertoire of everyday objects such as fruit and jugs, he experimented with relationships of form, color, and pattern. Although the groupings seem casual, Cézanne is known to have taken great care with these arrangements, sometimes spending hours positioning the simple objects. Here, using layers of translucent watercolor the artist placed small patches of color next to one another to build complex forms. The contrast between the colored washes and the untouched passages of white paper evokes the plasticity of substance.

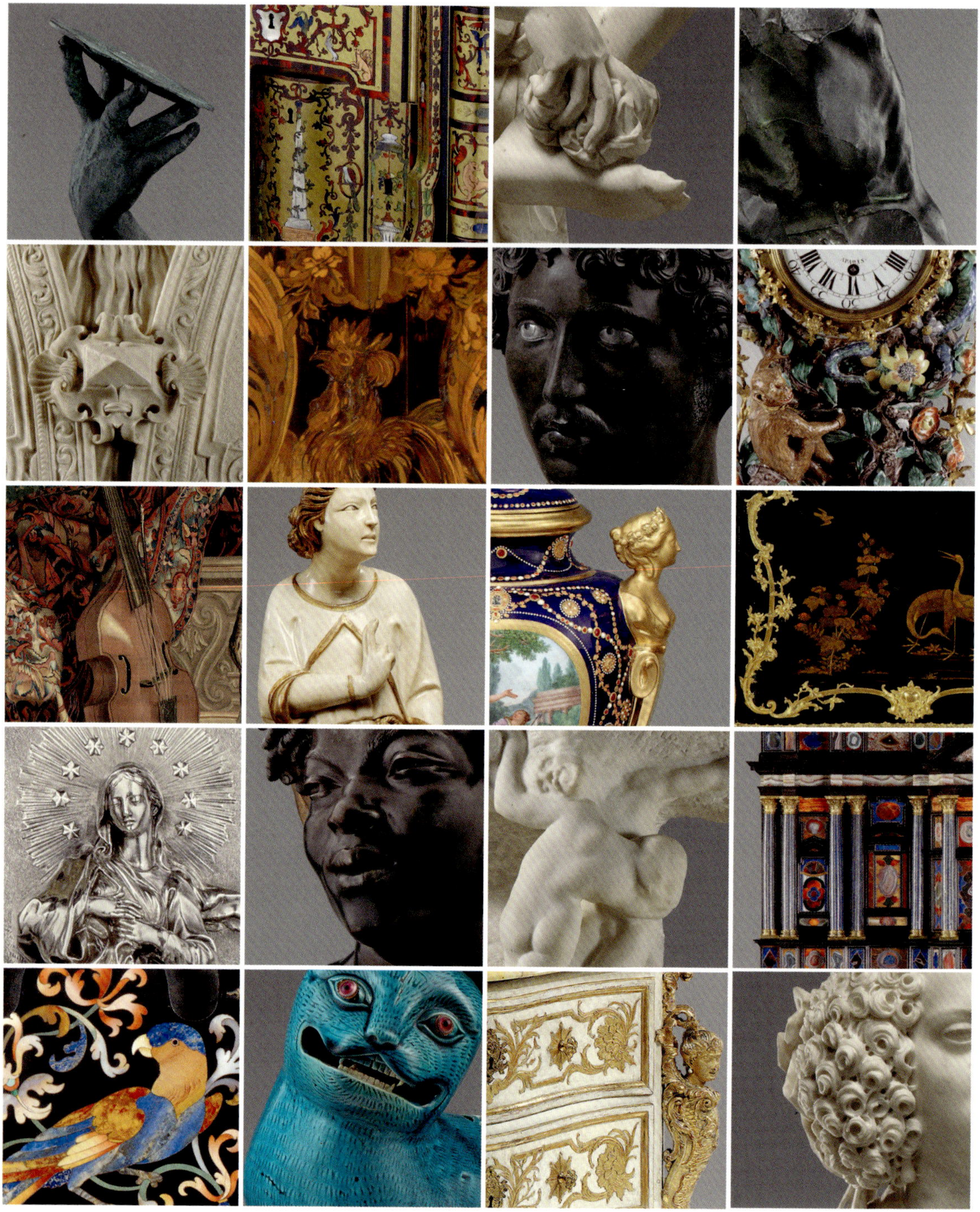

Sculpture and Decorative Arts

J. Paul Getty began collecting eighteenth-century French decorative arts in the 1930s. By the time he opened a small museum in his home in Malibu in 1954, he had acquired about thirty objects, including the unique double desk by the cabinetmaker Bernard II van Risenburgh (p. 313). With the prospect of filling a much larger museum, which was to open in 1974, Getty began to acquire more actively and continued to do so until his death in 1976, adding many significant works with French royal and noble provenances. Gradually, the goal of forming a representative collection of French decorative arts from the early years of Louis XIV's reign (1643–1715) to the end of Louis XVI's reign (1774–92) was realized: these holdings now count among the finest in the world. With the creation of the J. Paul Getty Trust in 1982, acquisitions of decorative arts expanded to include objects made in other European countries before 1900. The collection has since been enriched with refined Renaissance ceramics and glass; a significant selection of medieval and Renaissance stained glass; a small number of objects in silver, gold, and other precious metals; singular examples of ivory carving; and Italian furniture from the sixteenth through the nineteenth century.

First established in the early 1980s, the European sculpture collection, comprising works from the twelfth through the early twentieth century, represents a wide range of artists and media. Italian and Netherlandish Renaissance and Baroque bronzes, French eighteenth-century terracottas and marbles, Italian and British Neoclassical marbles, and French and Italian bronzes and marbles of the early 1900s predominate and include masterpieces by such renowned European sculptors as Giambologna, Adriaen de Vries, Gian Lorenzo Bernini, La Roldana, Francis Harwood, Jean-Antoine Houdon, Antonio Canova, Auguste Rodin, and Camille Claudel. All these artists are represented by exemplary works illustrated in the following pages.

Since 1997, with the opening of the Getty Center, the much expanded and more diverse collection of sculpture and decorative arts has been displayed to full advantage in galleries arranged in historical sequence. Exhibited together with the paintings collection, these works showcase the many extraordinary achievements of European artists and craftspeople from the Middle Ages through the early twentieth century. New acquisitions are added regularly.

In 2005 the Getty Museum acquired a group of twenty-eight twentieth-century American and European sculptures, donated by the Fran and Ray Stark Revocable Trust. These sculptures are installed throughout the Getty Center site, mostly out of doors, where they have been integrated into the environment and complement the Richard Meier–designed architecture. The Fran and Ray Stark Sculpture Collection includes works by the century's foremost sculptors, such as Alexander Calder (p. 349), Alberto Giacometti, Barbara Hepworth (p. 348), Ellsworth Kelly, Roy Lichtenstein, Aristide Maillol, Joan Miró, Henry Moore, and Isamu Noguchi. Supplementing holdings from earlier centuries, these modern masterworks further support Getty's aim of presenting to the public sculpture and decorative arts of the highest aesthetic quality, historical interest, and rarity.

Christ in Majesty

French (Limoges school), probably 1188

Engraved and gilt copper,

champlevé enamel, colored glass,

45.6 × 21.1 × 4.7 cm (17 7/8 × 8 1/4 × 1 13/16 in.),

2007.6

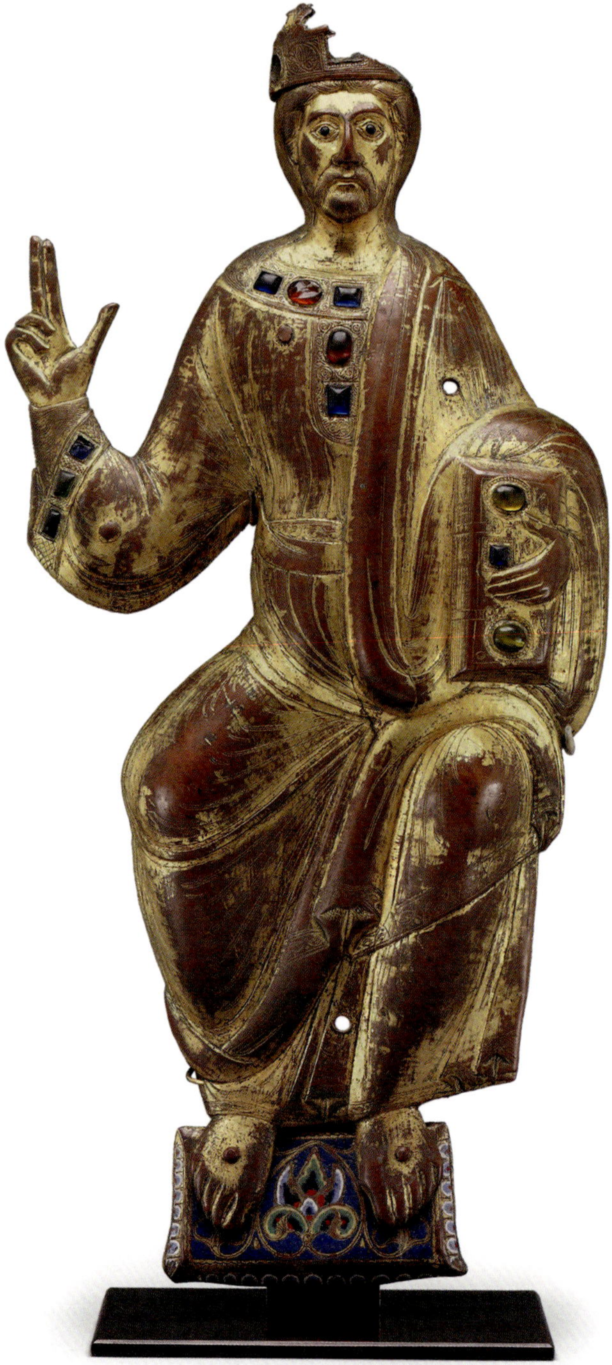

Created from a single sheet of copper and gilded, this relief was produced in Limoges, France, an important center of enamel production during the Middle Ages and the Renaissance. In this early example, Christ's facial features are delicately modeled, and his long hair is skillfully engraved; the eyes, tunic, and Bible are inset with colored glass; and the feet rest on an enamel plaque. The seated pose, with the right hand raised in blessing and the left hand holding a Bible, is typical of an iconographic type known as Christ in Majesty that goes back to the Byzantine tradition. This figure was probably the centerpiece of an elaborate altar frontal made for the Cathedral of Saint Martin in Ourense, Spain, that would have been surrounded by other reliefs representing saints.

Giovanni di Balduccio

Italian, circa 1300–after 1349

The Annunciation, circa 1333–34

Marble with traces of polychromy, Mary: 78.5 × 24 × 19 cm ($30\frac{7}{8} \times 9\frac{7}{16} \times 7\frac{1}{2}$ in.);

Gabriel: 75 × 22.5 × 20 cm ($29\frac{1}{2} \times 8\frac{7}{8} \times 7\frac{7}{8}$ in.), 2019.117

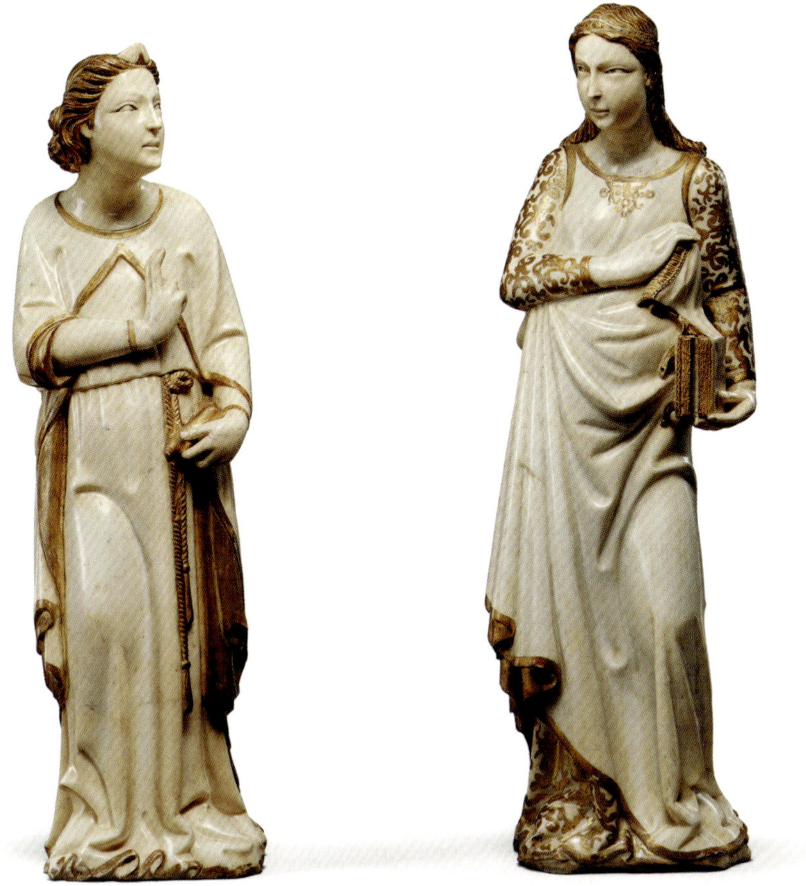

The Annunciation depicts the moment, in Christian belief, when the archangel Gabriel announces to the Virgin Mary that she will become the mother of Jesus. Here, Gabriel's (left) backward-flowing hair indicates his sudden arrival as he makes a sign of benediction. Surprised, Mary (right) observes the angel through almond-shaped eyes. Clutching her prayer book, she bends one knee, creating a delicate cascade of folds in her robe. These statues count among the masterpieces of Giovanni di Balduccio, a leading sculptor of the fourteenth-century Italian Gothic style. Giovanni carved the figures in the round in highly polished white marble highlighted with colored and gilt paint. The pair originally was displayed in a now-destroyed pontifical chapel in Bologna, Italy, which was decorated with paintings by the artist Giotto (ca. 1267–1337).

Desiderio da Settignano
Italian, circa 1430–1464
Bust of a Young Boy, circa 1460–64
Marble, 25 × 24.5 × 14 cm
($9\frac{13}{16} \times 9\frac{5}{8} \times 5\frac{1}{2}$ in.), 2018.5

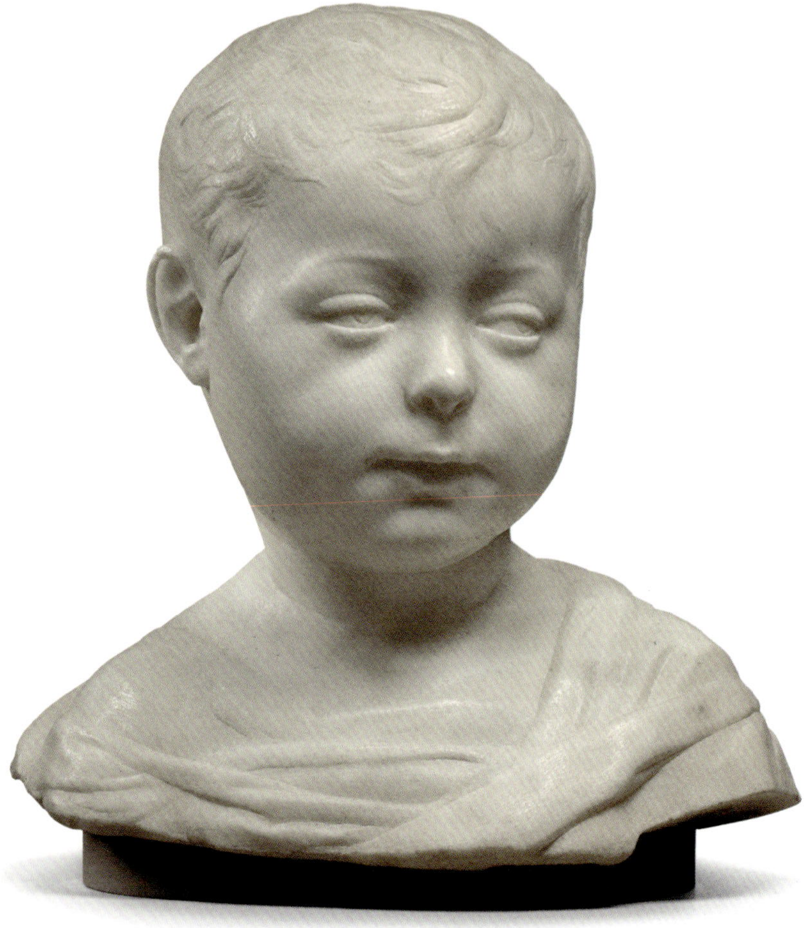

This boy's gaze is thoughtful, with his eyes half-closed and his lips hinting at a smile. Skillfully carved, the marble evokes the subject's youthful features—smooth cheeks, chubby neck, and silky locks. The refined textures and subtlety of expression exemplify Desiderio's style and accomplishment. Busts of young boys became an important genre in fifteenth-century Florence, when childhood was recognized as a distinct and auspicious stage of life. Noble patrons who commissioned these works envisioned their children as future leaders of the republic.

Veit Stoss

German, 1447–1533

Corpus Christi, circa 1510–15

Probably pearwood, 34.5 × 33 × 6.5 cm

(13⁹⁄₁₆ × 13 × 2⁹⁄₁₆ in.), 2019.94

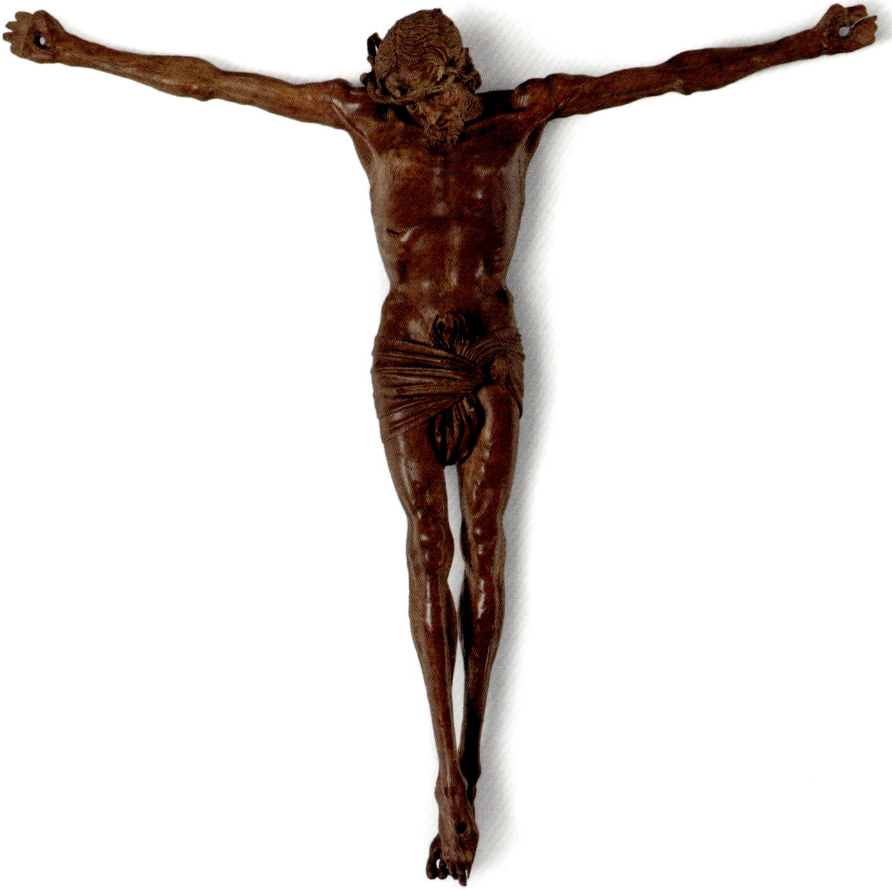

Corpus Christi, which means "body of Christ" in Latin, shows Christ nailed to a cross at his hands and feet, wearing the woven crown of thorns. Its small size and carefully carved details indicate that the statuette was intended for private devotion, to be held in the hands of the patron during worship. Its sculptor, Veit Stoss, excelled at carving both small-scale and monumental wooden statues. He counts among the leading artists of his generation working in Germany (he was also active in Poland). Stoss rendered the anatomy of Christ's body hanging on the cross with great realism, as well as the elaborate folds of the drapery, the highly detailed tendrils of the hair and beard, and the dramatic expression of suffering.

Antico (Pier Jacopo Alari-Bonacolsi)

Italian, circa 1455–1528

Bust of a Young Man, circa 1520

Bronze with silver eyes,

54.7 × 45 × 22.3 cm (21½ × 17¾ × 8¾ in.),

86.SB.688

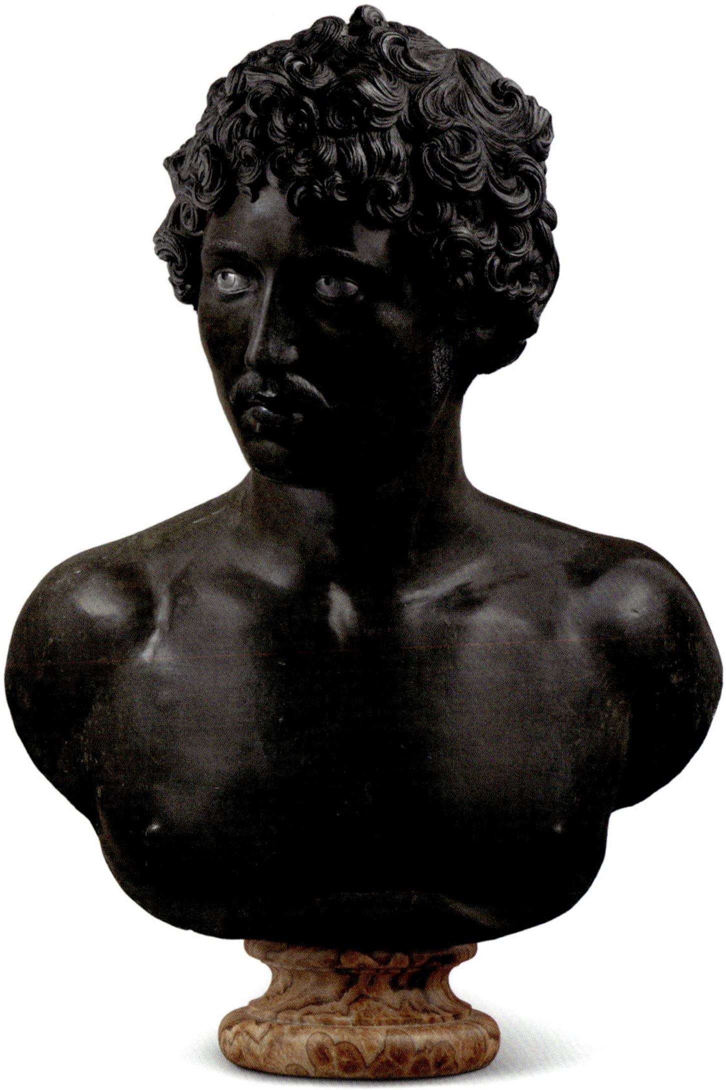

Trained as a goldsmith, Pier Jacopo Alari-Bonacolsi became the principal sculptor at the court of Mantua in the late fifteenth and early sixteenth century. He was considered an expert in antiquities and excelled in their restoration, and he also executed many bronze reductions and variants of famous antique sculptures, earning himself the nickname "Antico." The Getty Museum's bronze is one of only seven known busts generally accepted as being made by him. It derives from a first-century Roman marble bust now in the museum of the Hispanic Society of America, New York. The use of silver for the eyes emulates a frequent practice of antiquity.

Ewer

Italian (Murano), late fifteenth or early sixteenth century
Free-blown colorless (slightly purple) glass with gold leaf and enamel decoration, H: 27.2 cm (10¹¹⁄₁₆ in.), 84.DK.512

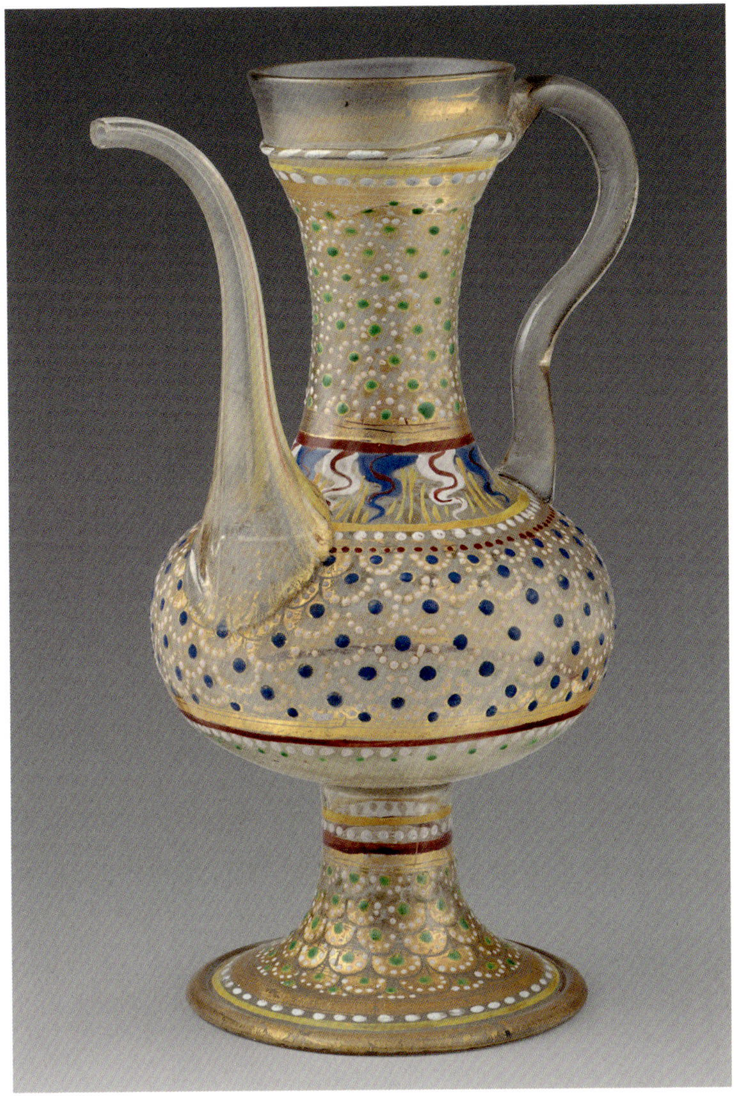

Venice, Italy, has been an important center for the production of glass since the Middle Ages, with the industry concentrated then, as now, on the island of Murano. The craft flourished during the Renaissance, and this ewer is a prime example of the elaborate, lavish vessels for which the city became famous. The complex form, with a long spout and curved handle, is based on ancient Middle Eastern models. An enamellist decorated the surface with a scalloped pattern of small gilt dots enclosing a larger colored dot, a design typical of Venetian luxury glass of the period. This ewer is distinctive for the flame- or raylike pattern around the neck, which may reference the insignia of the followers of Saint Bernard of Siena.

Heraldic Panel with the Arms of the Eberler Family

Swiss (possibly Basel), circa 1490

Flashed pot-metal, colorless glass, vitreous paint, and silver stain; lead came, 44 × 31 × 1 cm (17⁵⁄₁₆ × 12³⁄₁₆ × ³⁄₈ in.), 2003.47

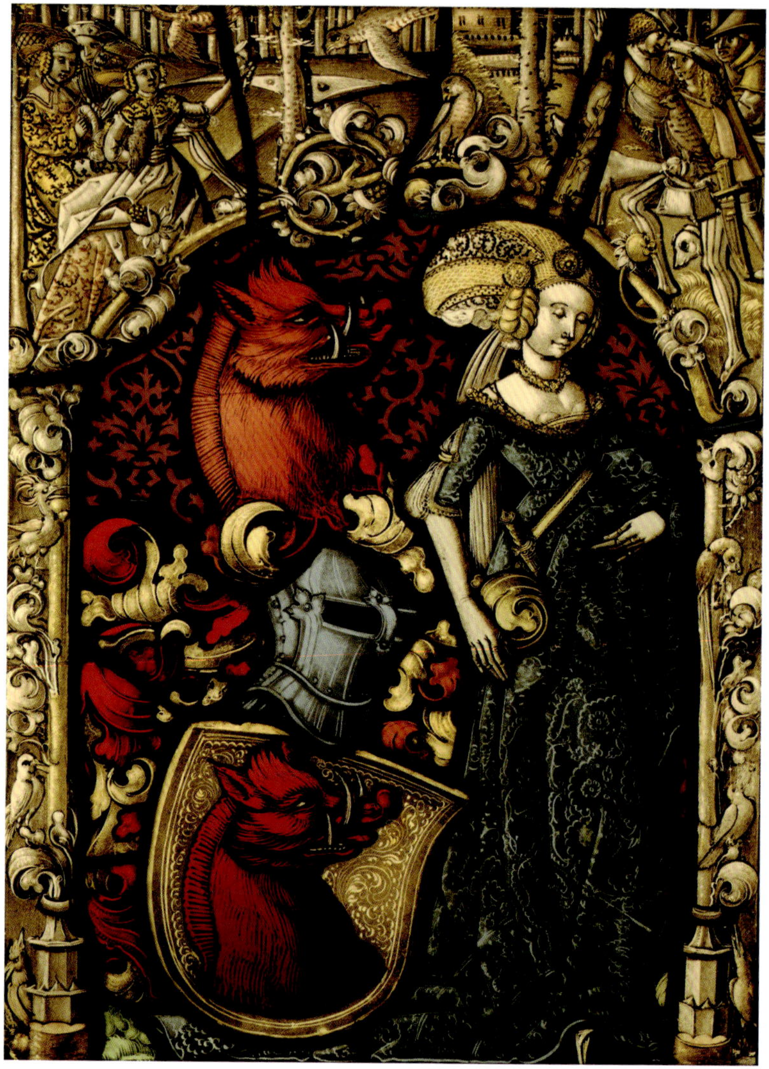

Different artists, technicians, and craftspeople were involved in designing, cutting, painting, and assembling the separate elements of a stained-glass panel. This piece is a particularly sophisticated example, with its richly detailed imagery meticulously executed to the highest level of refinement. The panel features the coat of arms of the wealthy Eberler family of Basel, Switzerland, comprising a shield and a crest (the motif on top of a helmet) bearing red boars' heads. The elegantly dressed woman is known in heraldic imagery as a supporter—that is, a figure, animal, or object that appears to hold a coat of arms upright. These elements are set beneath an arbor incorporating a variety of birds and a lively image of falconry, a prominent leisure activity of the upper class.

Armorial Dish with the Flaying of Marsyas

Italian, mid-1520s

Nicola da Urbino (Nicola di Gabriele Sbraghe [or Sbraga]), Italian, circa 1480–1537/38

Tin-glazed earthenware, Diam: 41.4 cm (16 5/16 in.), 84.DE.117

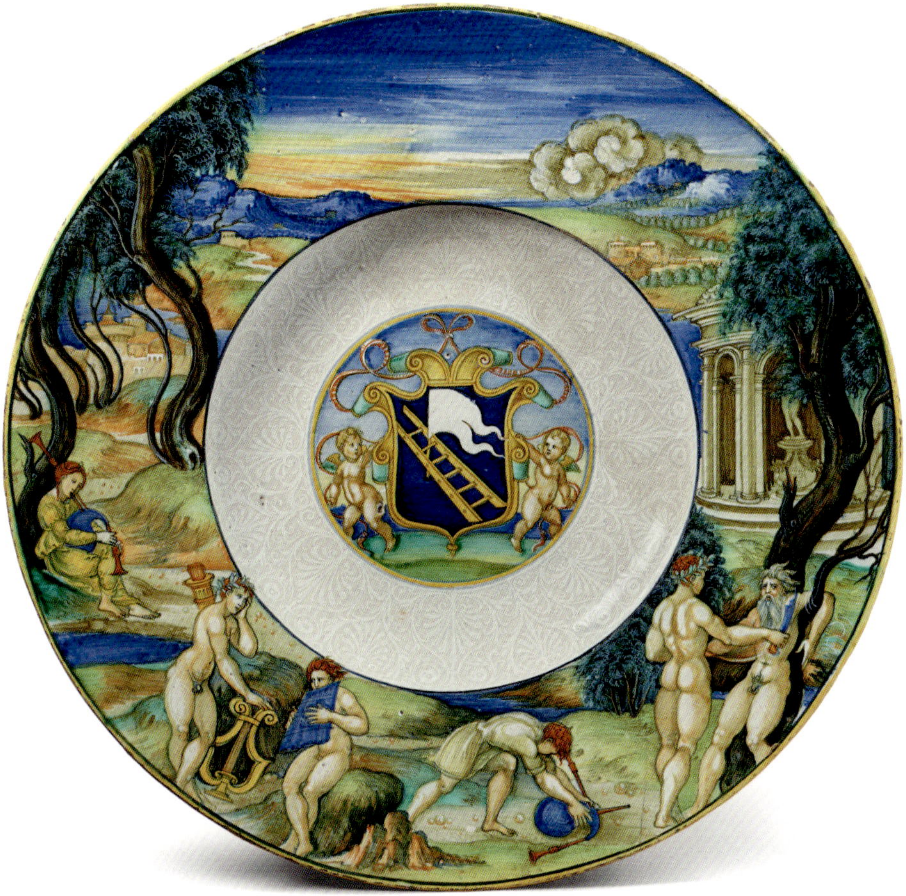

Italian tin-glazed earthenware, called maiolica, developed into a supremely pictorial art form during the sixteenth century, displaying some of the same narrative techniques as contemporary fresco and oil painting. Indeed, narrative, or *istoriato*, ceramics—in which most or all of the surface features scenes from historical, literary, mythological, or religious texts—is a high point of Renaissance art. The Flaying of Marsyas is one of the myths recounted in the *Metamorphoses* by Ovid (43 BCE–17 CE). It tells the story of Marsyas, a satyr (an acolyte of the wine god Dionysos) who challenges the god Apollo to a musical contest. Apollo is declared the winner and takes the cruel revenge of peeling away Marsyas's skin while he is still alive, seen at the lower right edge of the plate.

Benvenuto Cellini

Italian, 1500–1571

Satyr, circa 1543–45

Bronze, 56.8 × 8.9 × 8.4 cm

(22 3/8 × 3 1/2 × 3 3/8 in.), 85.SB.69

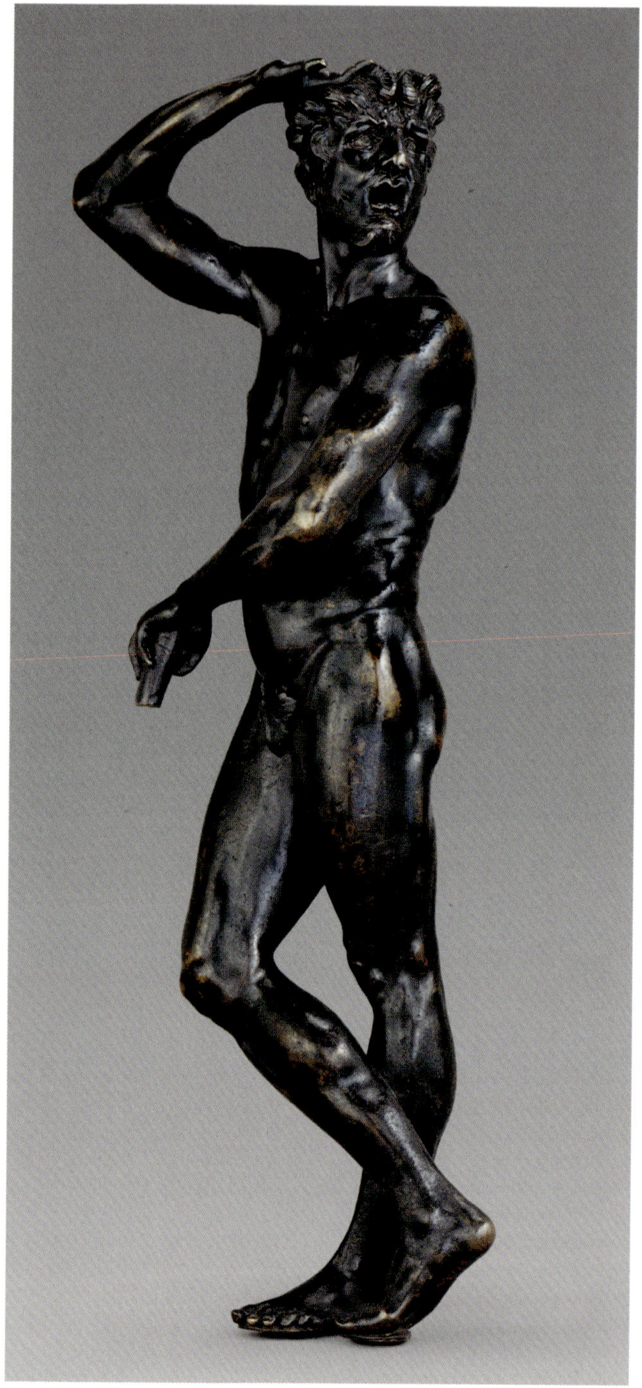

Cellini, a leading sixteenth-century Italian sculptor and goldsmith, traveled to Fontainebleau in 1540 to work for the French king Francis I (1494–1547). Among the artist's major commissions was the Porte Dorée, or Golden Door, a monumental entryway to the palace. The project called for a bronze overdoor relief (now Paris, Musée du Louvre) depicting the nymph thought to reside in the Forest of Fontainebleau. The door was meant to be supported on both sides by menacing satyrs (followers of the god of wine), crowned by winged personifications of Victory. Cellini made this small satyr together with its companion piece (London, Royal Collection) to test the skills of the local founders before casting the full-scale statues. The project, however, remained unfinished when the artist left France in 1545.

Giambologna
(Jean de Boulogne)

Flemish, active in Italy, 1529–1608
Female Figure (Possibly Venus), 1571–73
Marble, 114 × 34 × 47 cm
(44 7/8 × 13 3/8 × 18 1/2 in.), 82.SA.37

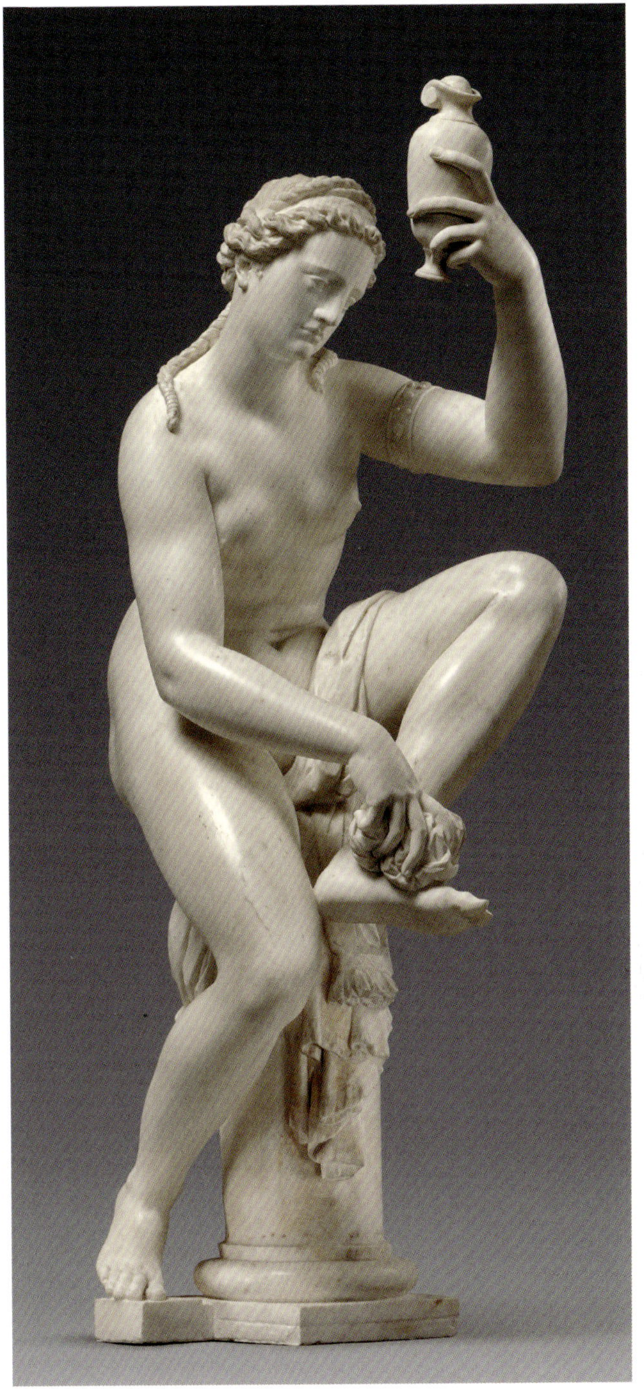

Giambologna was court artist to the powerful Medici family of Florence and a leading sculptor of the second half of the sixteenth century. Proficient in both marble and bronze, he excelled especially in his explorations of the serpentine figure, sinuous sculptures that demand to be looked at from every point of view. Here, the figure's pose conforms to an ideal, artificial spiral achieved through the graceful but complicated twisting of limbs, which is characteristic of the style known as Mannerism. Giambologna's carving skills are evident in the way he successfully contrasted the elegant contours of the figure's smooth, attenuated body and expressionless face with the intricately carved, classicizing coiffure, drapery, and armband.

Johann Gregor van der Schardt
Dutch, circa 1530–1581
Mercury, circa 1570–80
Bronze, 114.9 × 86.4 × 38.1 cm
(45¼ × 34 × 15 in.), 95.SB.8

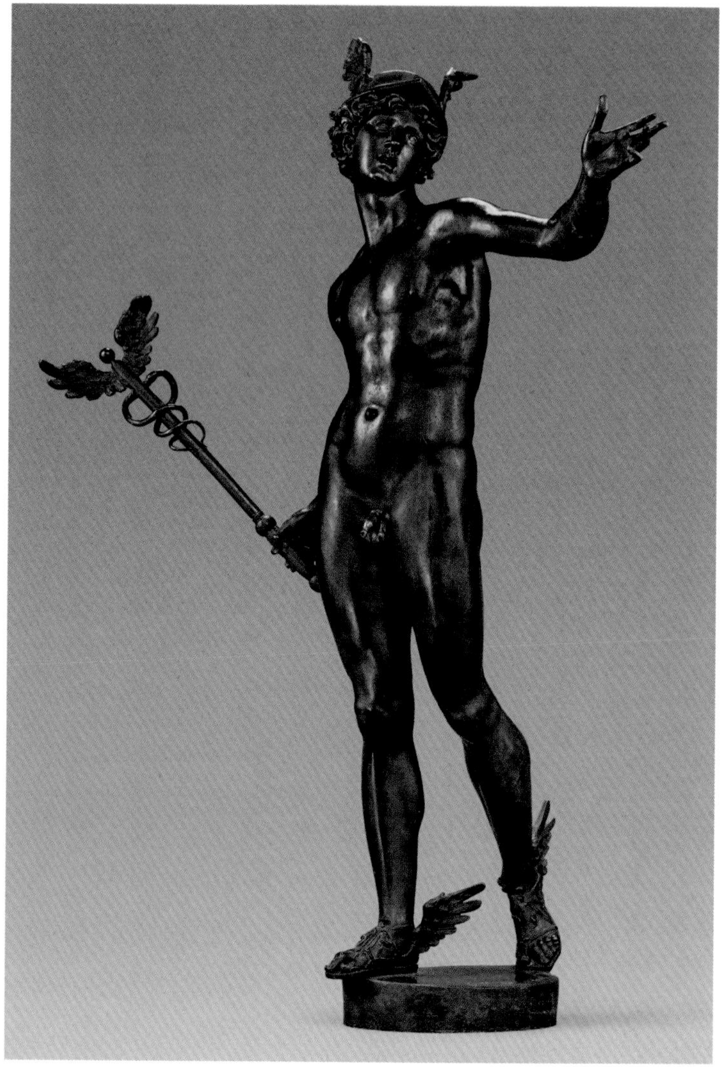

Van der Schardt was one of the first sculptors to introduce the Italian Mannerist style to Northern Europe when he entered the service of Emperor Maximilian II (r. 1564–76) in Vienna. In this bronze, he depicted the divine messenger Mercury, identifiable by his winged sandals, hat, and caduceus (a wand with two serpents twined around it), as an athletic youth. While the pose derives from the famous ancient statue *Apollo Belvedere,* which the artist would have seen during a visit to Rome, the elegant gesture, elongated limbs, and asymmetry of the body reflect the influence of Mannerism. This *Mercury* can be traced to the famous collection of a Nuremberg patrician, Paul Praun (1548–1616), who owned numerous terracotta and bronze figures by the artist.

Pilgrim Flask

Italian (Medici manufactory), 1580s
Soft-paste porcelain with underglaze blue decoration, 26.4 × 18.7 × 4.8 cm ($10\frac{3}{8} \times 7\frac{3}{8} \times 1\frac{7}{8}$ in.), 86.DE.630

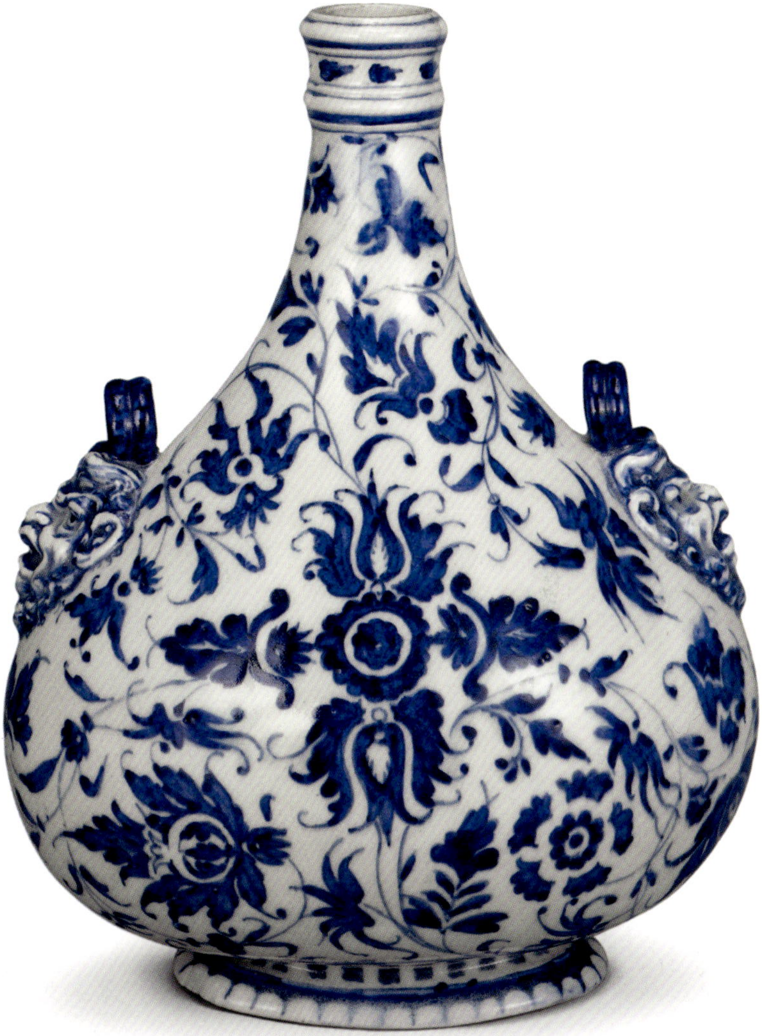

The fourteenth century witnessed the first imports of Chinese porcelain to Europe, where the rarity and beauty of these translucent white ceramics with richly colored surfaces made them highly prized and much emulated. The first porcelain-like ware produced in Europe, known as soft-paste porcelain, was made in the late sixteenth century at the manufactory of the powerful Medici family in Florence. This flask is one of about sixty Medici porcelain pieces known to survive. The arabesque patterns and stylized floral decoration derive from wares produced in Iznik, Turkey, around 1500. Flasks of this kind replicate vessels used by pilgrims to carry drinking water during their long journeys. This elaborate piece, however, would not have been used as a container but, rather, cherished as a display item.

Trilobed Basin with Moses Striking Water from the Rock

Italian (Urbino), circa 1600

Workshop of Francesco Patanazzi (d. 1616). Tin-glazed earthenware, H: 22 cm (8 5/8 in.); max. W: 50 cm (19 3/4 in.), 2024.31

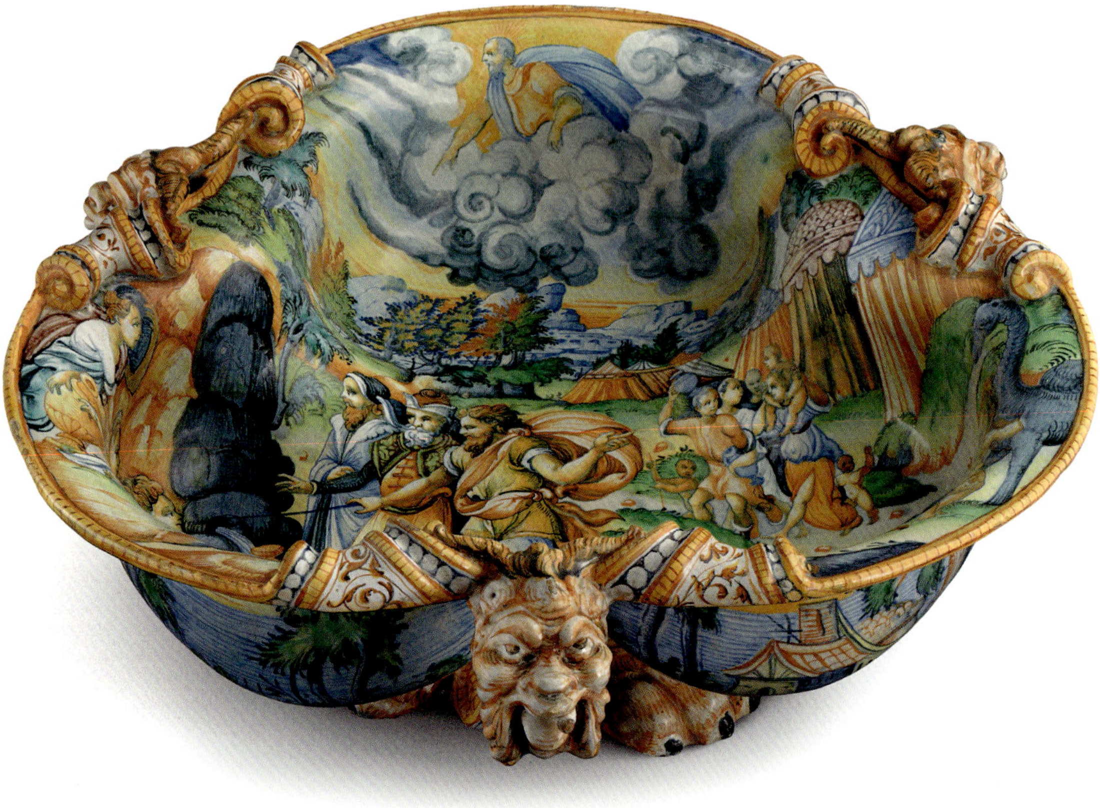

Deep, trilobed basins such as this example were used by noble families as beverage coolers during important events. They were largely produced in Urbino, Italy, starting in the late Renaissance, and the Patanazzi family workshop was among their leading producers. The scene on this example depicts Moses Striking Water from the Rock, a story from the biblical book of Exodus. Yahweh emerges from the clouds, pointing to the place from which Moses, who wears a long robe, strikes a rock with a long stick, causing water to gush forth. This basin was part of a service commissioned by Princess Isabella della Rovere (1552–1619) as a gift for Catalina de Zuñiga y Sandoval (1555–1628), wife of the viceroy of Naples.

The Borghese-Windsor Cabinet

Cabinet: Italian, circa 1620; stand: French, before 1821
Cabinet: fir, walnut, and chestnut veneered with tropical hardwoods and set with lapis lazuli, jasper, agate, amethyst, and other hardstones; gilt bronze; silver; silver gilt, 178 × 126 × 54 cm (70 1/16 × 49 5/8 × 21 1/4 in.); stand: beech, mahogany, and oak, ebonized and veneered with ebony; ebony columns; lacquered brass; mirror glass, 84 × 153.5 × 65.5 cm (33 1/16 × 60 7/16 × 25 13/16 in.), 2016.66

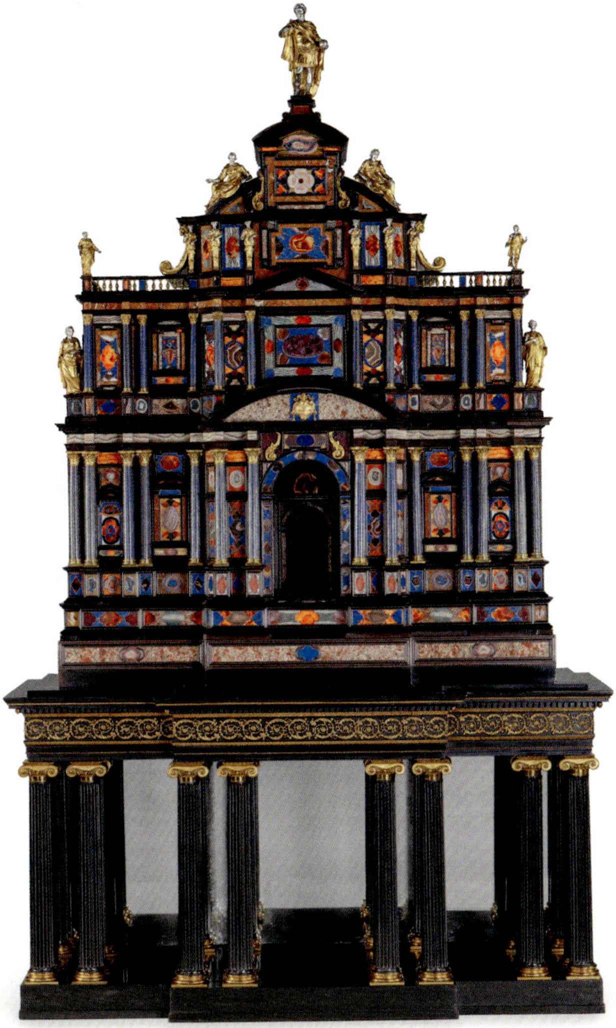

This cabinet, called a *stipo* or *studiolo* in Italian, is exceptional for its large size and sumptuous decoration. Its form resembles the exterior of a Baroque church, furnished with gilt-bronze and silver statuettes and richly patterned with copious amounts of lapis lazuli, jasper, agate, and amethyst, all expensive hardstones (*pietre dure*) that are notoriously difficult to carve. Such showpiece cabinets—especially intriguing for their multiple secret drawers—were the most prominent display furniture in Europe in the 1600s. This one first belonged to the noble Borghese family in Rome. Acquired by King George IV (1762–1830) in 1827, it remained in the British Royal Collection, first in Windsor Castle and then in Buckingham Palace, until 1959, when it was sold with the belongings of Queen Mary (1867–1953).

Display Cabinet

German (Augsburg), circa 1630
Several carvings by Albert Jansz. Vinckenbrinck (ca. 1604–1664/65). Ebony and other tropical and European woods, porphyry, gemstones, marble, pewter, ivory, bone, tortoiseshell, enamel, mirror glass, brass, and painted stone, 73 × 57.9 × 59.1 cm
(28¾ × 22¹³⁄₁₆ × 23¼ in.), 89.DA.28

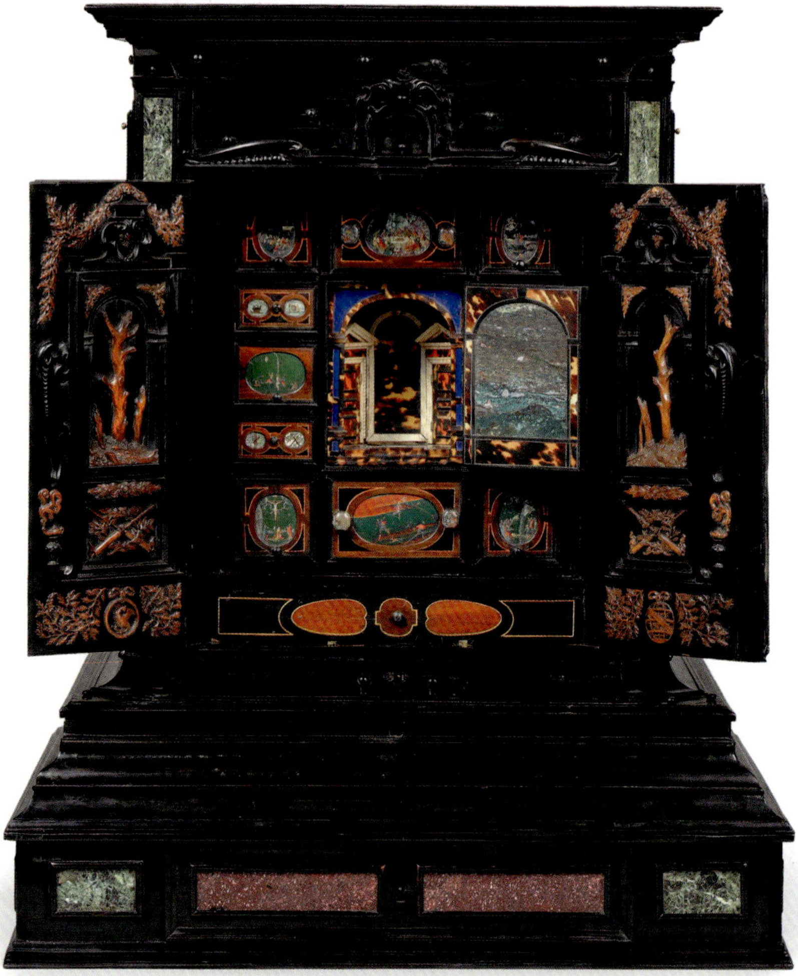

The desire to collect wondrous objects, whether naturally occurring or humanmade, goes back to antiquity. In the Renaissance—a period that witnessed the revival of ancient customs and the exploration by Europeans of many parts of the globe previously unknown to them—collecting marvelous objects became a popular pastime among royal and wealthy individuals. Cabinets such as this one were used to store and display an owner's collection of artistic and natural phenomena. The cabinet itself is a marvel: all four sides open to reveal a surprisingly complex series of drawers and compartments that are richly decorated in a variety of materials and techniques, depicting biblical, allegorical, historical, and mythological subjects.

Adriaen de Vries
Dutch, circa 1556–1626
Juggling Man, circa 1615
Bronze, 76.8 × 51.8 × 21.9 cm
(30¼ × 20⅜ × 8⅝ in.), 90.SB.44

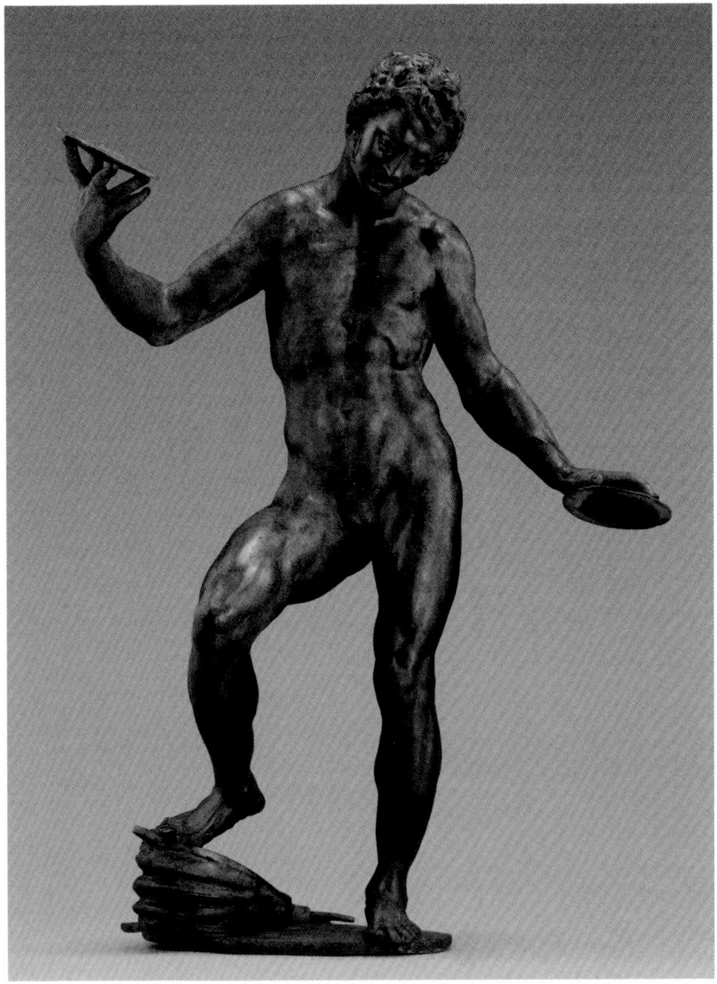

The perfectly balanced composition; the elegant curve of the body, caught in a precarious equilibrium; the naturalistic treatment of the musculature; and details of the hair, hands, and feet of this sculpture are all characteristic of the work of De Vries. The dynamic *Juggling Man*, represented balancing on a foot organ while holding cymbals for juggling, was inspired by the ancient Greek marble *Dancing Faun* in the collection of the Medici family (now Florence, Gallerie degli Uffizi). While in Florence, the artist trained with Giambologna, the most important Italian sculptor of the second half of the 1500s (see p. 281). De Vries, who excelled in bronze casting, served as the court sculptor to the Hapsburg emperor Rudolf II (r. 1576–1612) and was celebrated throughout Europe.

Attributed to Pietro Tacca

Italian, 1577–1640

Belvedere Antinous, circa 1630

Bronze, 64.6 × 28.4 × 20.3 cm

(25 7/16 × 11 3/16 × 8 in.), 2014.40

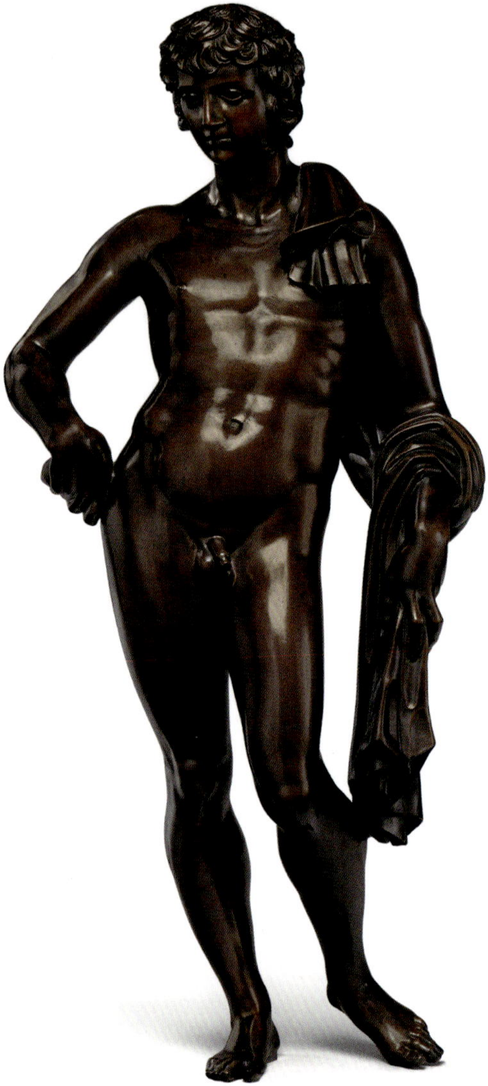

The composition of this bronze is based on the ancient Roman marble statue known as the *Belvedere Antinous,* considered to be one of the most beautiful surviving antique statues. The French king Louis XIV (1638–1715) acquired this statue from the estate of the courtier Louis Hesselin (1600–1662), who most likely purchased it during one of his trips to Italy in the 1630s. The "N.4" engraved on the right ankle is the inventory number of the French royal collection. Tacca, an artist at the service of the Medici grand dukes, was the leading sculptor in Italy at the time. After inheriting the studio of his mentor, Giambologna (see p. 281), Tacca played a critical role in maintaining the preeminence of Florence as the center for bronze casting in Europe.

Gian Lorenzo Bernini

Italian, 1598–1680

Bust of Pope Paul V, 1621

Marble, 78 × 65 × 29 cm

(30 11/16 × 25 9/16 × 11 7/16 in.), 2015.22

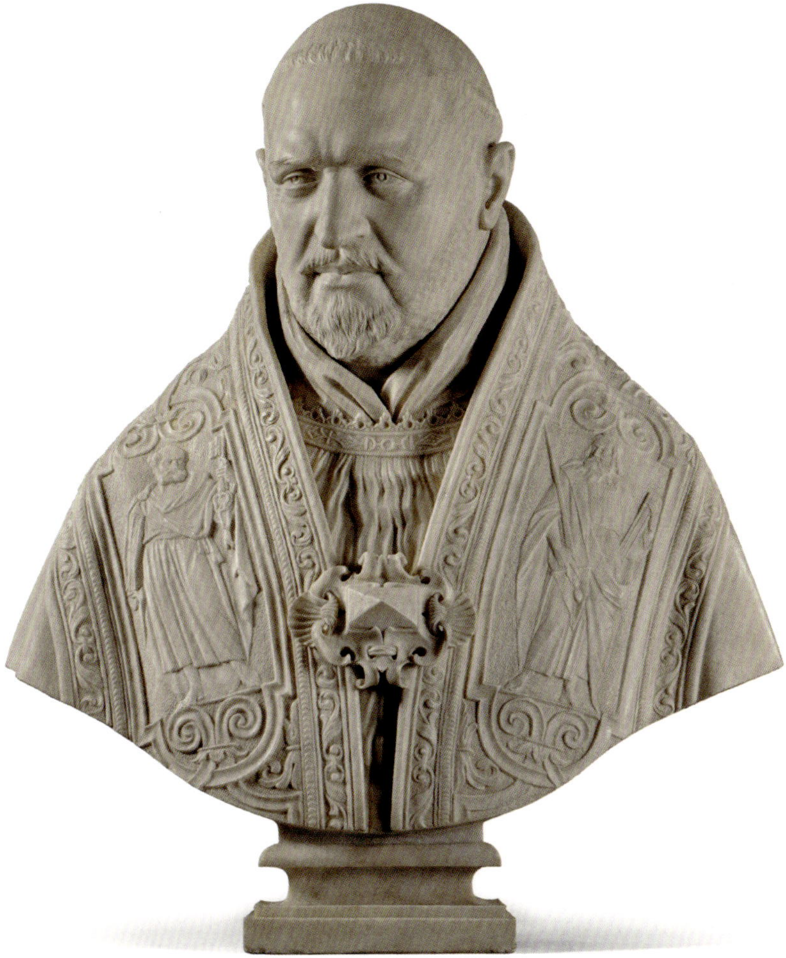

This life-size posthumous portrait of Pope Paul V Borghese (1552–1621) was commissioned from Bernini by the pope's nephew, Cardinal Scipione Borghese (1577–1633). The pope wears the traditional cope of his office, decorated with images of the two patron saints of Rome, the apostles Peter, holding keys, and Paul, holding the sword of his martyrdom. His hair is cut in the "tonsure of Saint Peter," which signified the renunciation of worldly fashion. The greatest of all Baroque sculptors, Bernini imbued his subject with a powerful liveliness that, together with the subtle surface treatment, is characteristic of his exceptional skills in carving marble. This masterpiece was kept in the Villa Borghese in Rome until 1893 and then sold. Its whereabouts remained unknown until its rediscovery in late 2014.

Attributed to Alessandro Algardi

Italian, 1598–1654

Bust of Maria Cerri Capranica, circa 1640

Marble, 90 × 61.2 × 29 cm

(35 7/16 × 24 1/8 × 11 7/16 in.), 2000.72

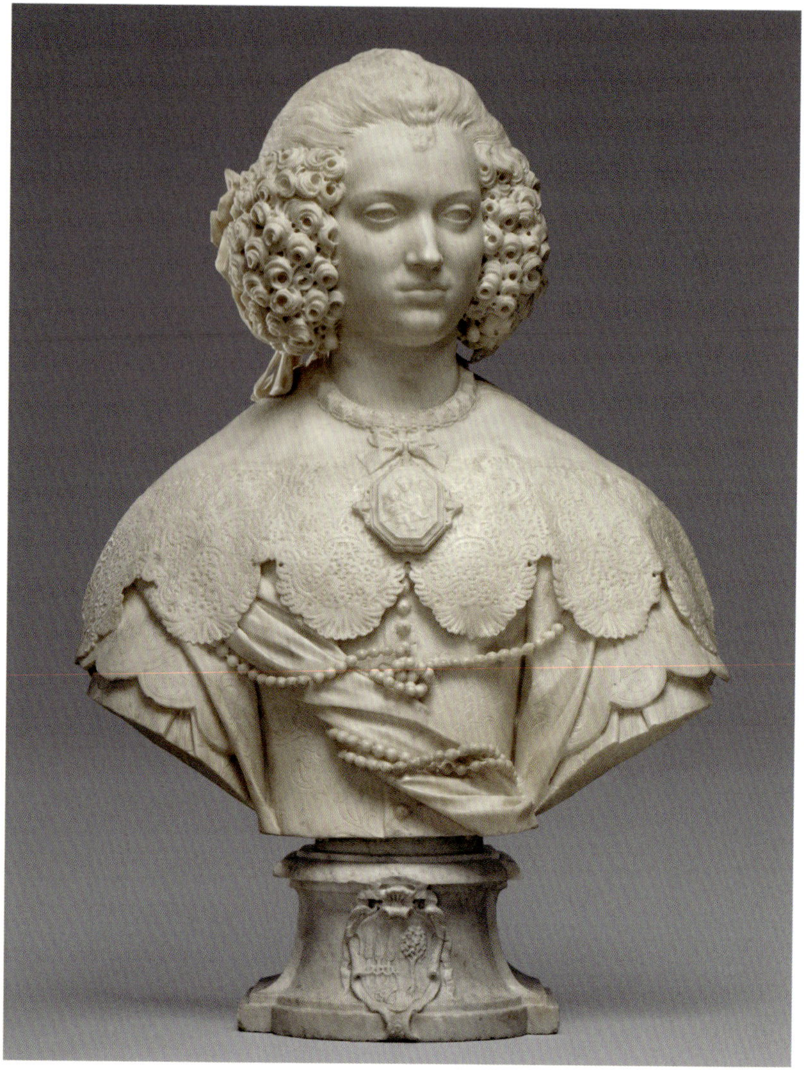

The subject of this portrait bust, the Italian noblewoman Maria Cerri, married Bartolomeo Capranica in 1637. As both their coats of arms appear on the base of the sculpture, the bust must have been made between the time of Maria's marriage and her death in 1643, at the age of twenty-five. The sculptor here combined a penetrating character study with a virtuoso display of marble carving. In the sinuous string of beads, stiff lace, and curly ringlets of hair, the artist seemingly transformed the stone into a variety of materials. At the same time, in the subtle carving of her features, the artist managed to invest his subject with a powerful and stately psychological presence. All these qualities are characteristic of Alessandro Algardi, a leading sculptor in Baroque-period Rome.

Side Table
Italian (Rome), circa 1670

Design attributed to Johann Paul Schor (Austrian, active in Italy, 1615–1674). Gessoed and gilt wood, 142.1 × 224.8 × 84.9 cm ($55\frac{15}{16} \times 88\frac{1}{2} \times 33\frac{7}{16}$ in.), 86.DA.7

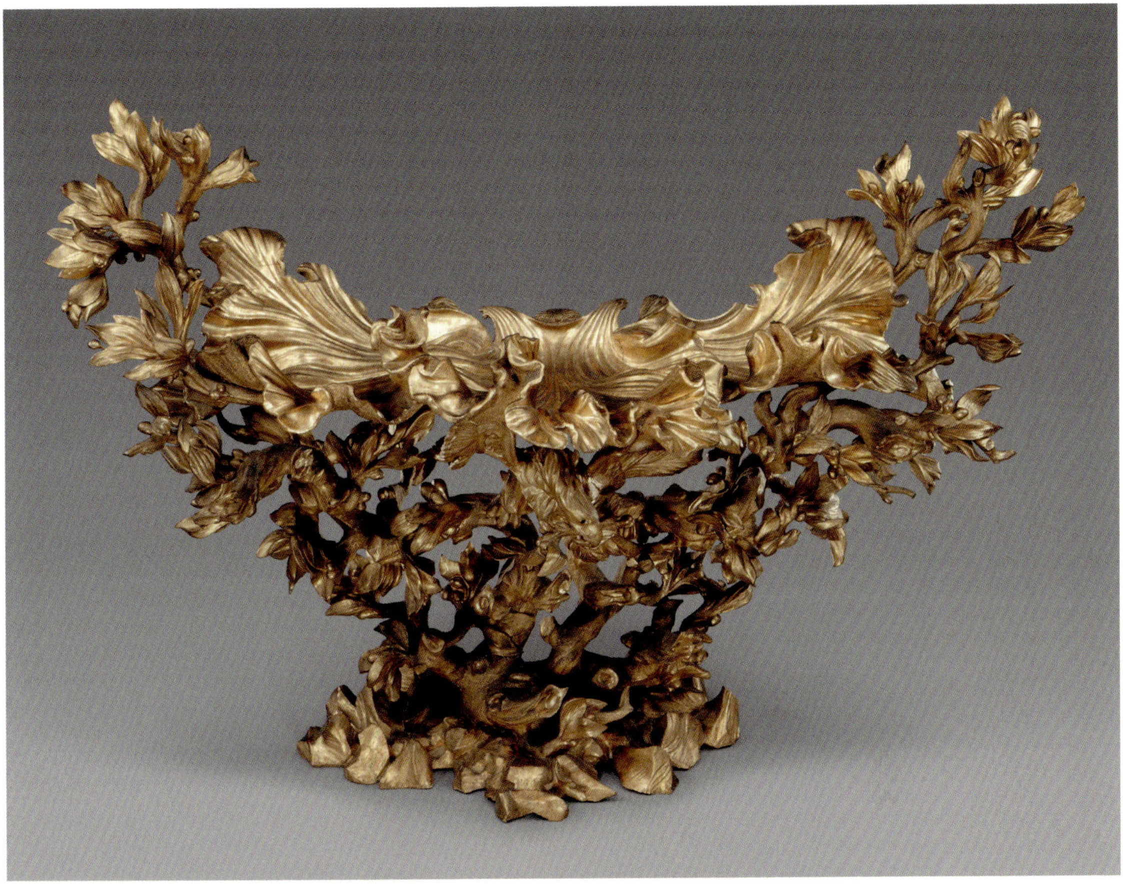

This remarkable table is unique in the history of Italian furniture: its top is an undulating sculpture of carved wood rather than a functional surface, suggesting that it might have started out as something other than a table. Schor, a sculptor, painter, and designer from Austria, moved to Rome in the mid-seventeenth century and was hired by Gian Lorenzo Bernini (see p. 289) to devise the coach used by Queen Christina of Sweden (1626–1689) for her entry into Rome in 1655. In addition to coaches and ecclesiastical furniture, Schor created garden settings and festival decorations that blurred the boundaries between nature and artifice, furniture and sculpture, monument and ephemera. The merging of these elements is characteristic of the spectacular artwork produced under the spell of Bernini in seventeenth-century Rome.

Cabinet on Stand

French, Paris, circa 1675–80
Attributed to André-Charles Boulle (1642–1732, master before 1666).
Oak veneered with various woods, pewter, brass, tortoiseshell, painted horn, and natural and green-stained ivory; drawers of snakewood and oak; figures of gessoed and gilt white oak; gilt-bronze mounts; mirror glass, 229.9 × 151.2 × 66.7 cm ($90\frac{1}{2} \times 59\frac{1}{2} \times 26\frac{1}{4}$ in.), 77.DA.1

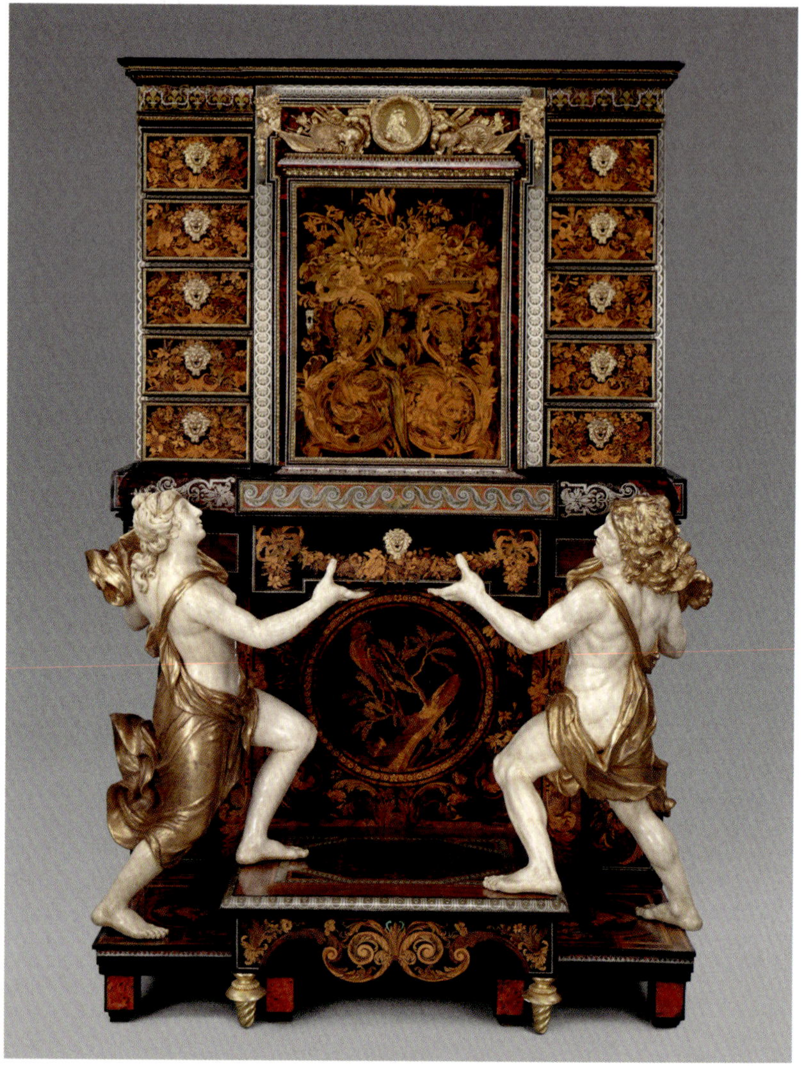

This monumental cabinet celebrates the military victories of the French king Louis XIV (1638–1715). His portrait appears in a bronze medallion above the central door, surrounded by military trophies. The main marquetry panel shows the cockerel of France standing triumphant over both the eagle of the Holy Roman Empire and the lion of Spain and the Spanish Netherlands, symbols referring to the Treaties of Peace of Nijmegen (1678–79), which concluded the French wars against the Dutch, Spanish, and imperial armies. Supporting the cabinet are two large figures from Greek mythology, the hero Herakles and Hippolyta, queen of the Amazons, representatives of strength and bravery in war. As the piece does not appear in the inventories of the king's possessions, it may have served as a royal gift.

Writing Table

French (Paris), circa 1670–75
Oak veneered with ivory, blue-painted horn, ebony, rosewood, and amaranth; drawer of walnut; gilt-bronze moldings; brass and iron fittings; modern velvet,
63.5 × 48.6 × 35.5 cm (25 × 19⅛ × 14 in.),
83.DA.21

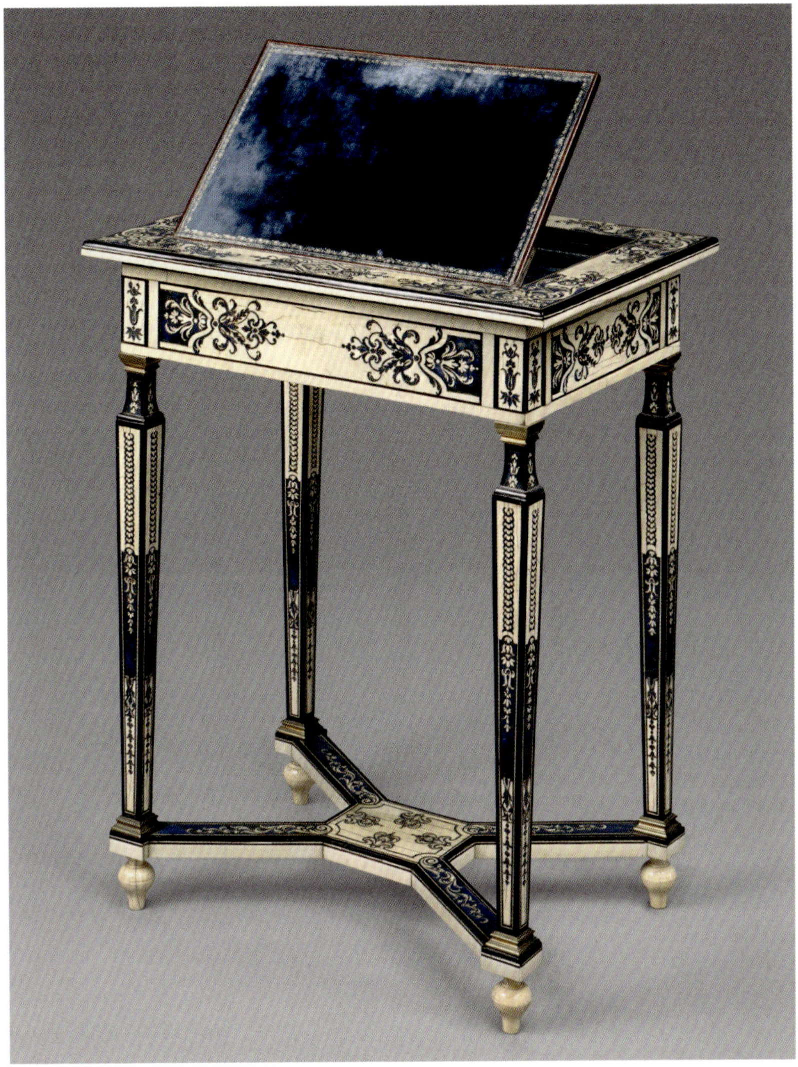

This table is described in great detail in a posthumous inventory of the possessions of the French king Louis XIV (1638–1715) in 1720. It was probably made for the Trianon de Porcelaine, an ensemble of five pavilions decorated with blue-and-white ceramic tiles built in 1670 for the king's mistress, Madame de Montespan (1640–1707), on the grounds of the palace at Versailles. The table's marquetry of ivory and horn, painted blue underneath, would have followed the pavilions' color scheme, imitating blue-and-white Chinese porcelain, a very fashionable and highly prized material. The Trianon de Porcelaine was demolished in 1687.

Writing Table

French (Paris), circa 1680
Attributed to Pierre Golle (ca. 1620–1684, master before 1656). White oak and fruitwood veneered with brass, pewter, tortoiseshell, and various woods; drawers of oak and ebony; gilt wood; gilt-bronze mounts, 76.8 × 42 × 36.2 cm (30¼ × 16½ × 14¼ in.), 82.DA.34

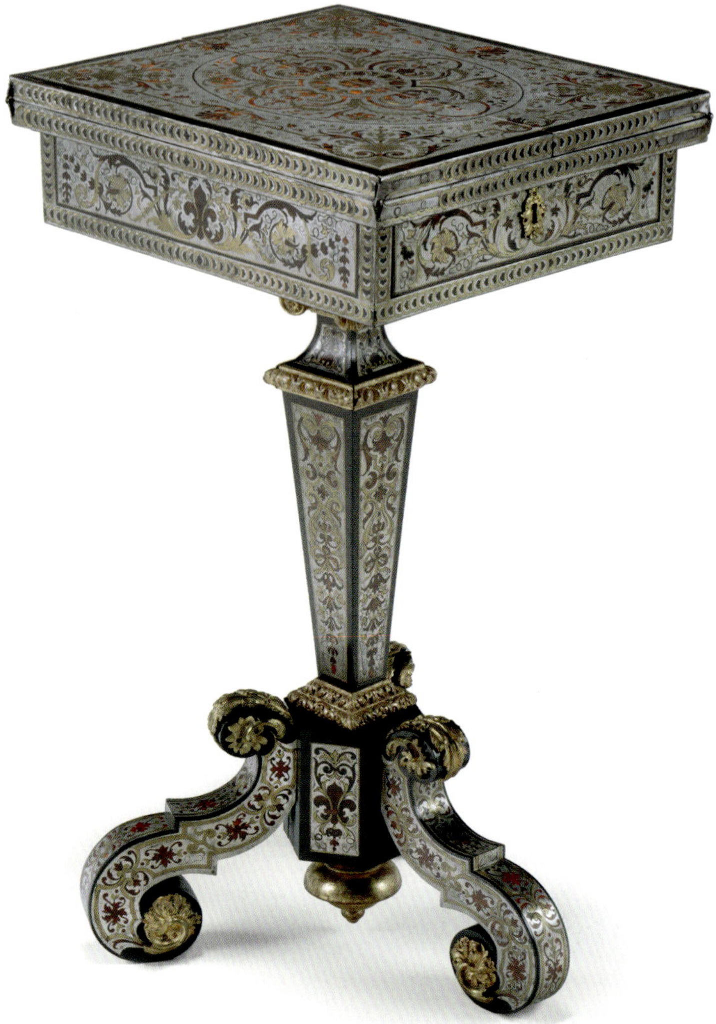

Four large dolphins (*dauphins* in French) and five fleurs-de-lis (a French royal symbol), all in tortoiseshell, are incorporated into the elaborate decorative veneer on this table. These emblems were used by the Grand Dauphin (1661–1711), eldest son of the French king Louis XIV (1638–1715), for whom this table was possibly made. It was originally intended as a support for writing; a small drawer at the front is fitted with compartments for writing equipment. The top, when opened, reveals a central panel of marquetry with an image of three women taking tea or coffee beneath a canopy. This scene closely resembles an engraving for a tabletop by the French designer Daniel Marot (1661–1752) and is probably a replacement added in the early eighteenth century.

Coffer on Stand

French (Paris), circa 1684–89
Attributed to André-Charles Boulle (1642–1732, master before 1666).
Oak and walnut veneered with cypress, ebony, padauk, rosewood, brass, pewter, blue-painted horn, and black- and red-painted tortoiseshell; gilt-bronze mounts; mirror glass, 156.6 × 89.9 × 55.8 cm (61⅝ × 35⅜ × 22 in.), 82.DA.109.1

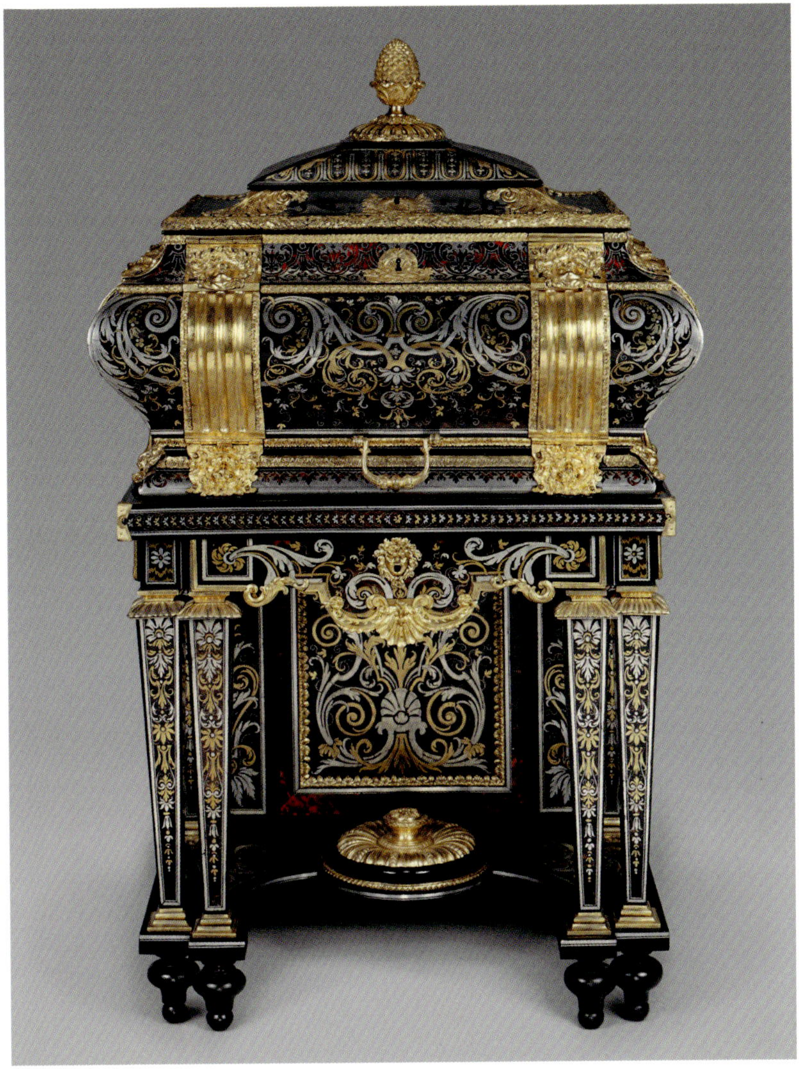

This coffer (chest) and its pendant (also in the Getty Museum) are said to have been made by the royal cabinetmaker André-Charles Boulle at a time when he was producing numerous pieces of furniture for the Grand Dauphin (1661–1711), eldest son of the French king Louis XIV (1638–1715). A coffer of similar form by Boulle is listed in the inventory of the Grand Dauphin's possessions in 1689. This coffer is decorated using a technique known as *première partie* marquetry, a pattern of brass and pewter inlays on a tortoiseshell ground. Such coffers were intended to hold jewelry and other precious objects. The large gilt-bronze straps at the front and sides can be let down to reveal small drawers.

Desk with Writing Stand
French (Paris), circa 1692–1700
Fir veneered with brass, copper, silver, ebony, bone, horn (painted, some laid on gold foil), mother-of-pearl, and tortoiseshell; drawers of beech, oak, and walnut; silvered-bronze mounts; silk velvet; steel key, 89.6 × 89 × 51 cm (35¼ × 35 × 20 in.), 87.DA.77 and 2009.6

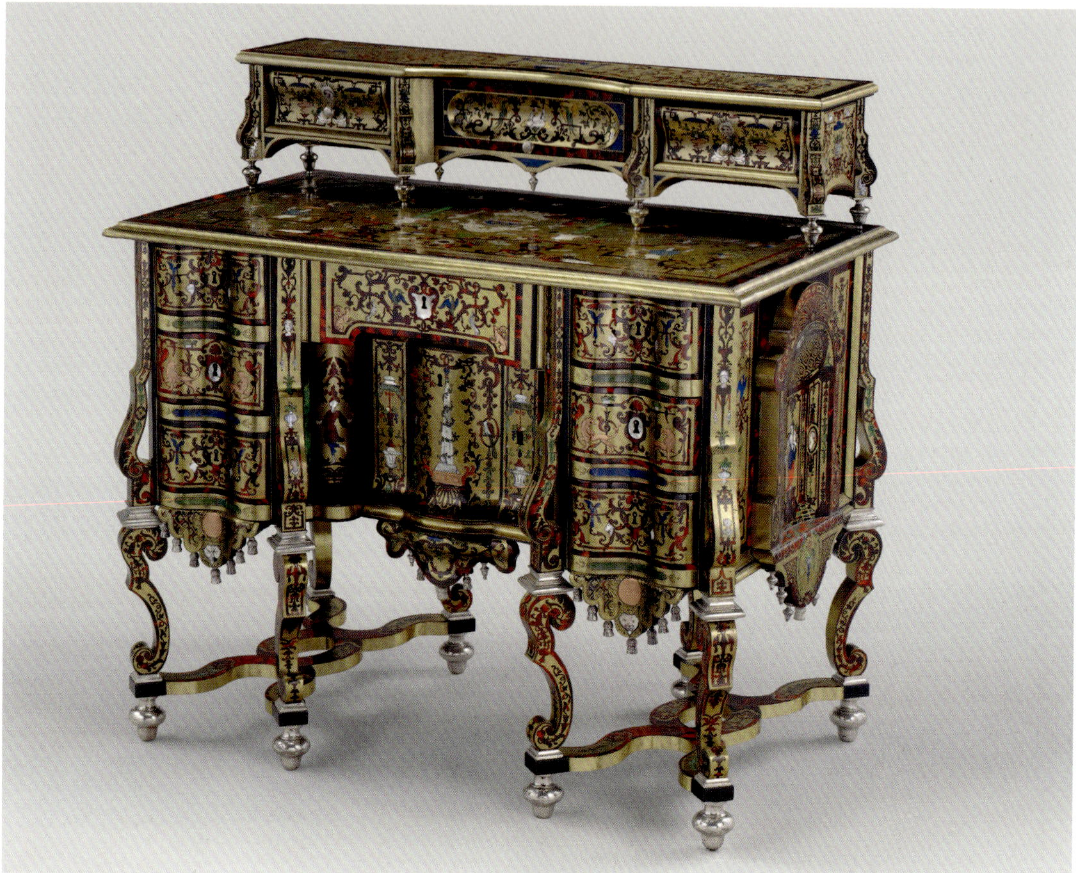

Nearly the entire surface of this delicate desk, designed as a showpiece rather than for actual use, is covered with a colorful veneer of various materials, including brass, tortoiseshell, copper, pewter, ebony, ivory, mother-of-pearl, and horn painted in different colors. These media are fashioned into an elaborate array of decorative motifs, including reclining figures, birds, animals, cupids, and vases of fruits and flowers. The desk was made for Maximilian Emanuel (1662–1726), elector of Bavaria, whose monogram and electoral crown decorate the original steel key used to unlock the desk's main drawer. It is listed in an inventory of his possessions in 1704.

Night Clock

Italian (Florence), 1704–5

Case and hardstone mosaics by Giovanni Battista Foggini (1652–1725) and Leonard van der Vinne (active mid-1660s–1713); bronze figures attributed to Massimiliano Soldani-Benzi (1656–1740); mechanism by Francesco Papillion (active ca. 1700). Ebony; gilt bronze; semiprecious stones, including chalcedony, jasper, lapis lazuli, and *verde d'Arno*, 95 × 63 × 28 cm ($37^{3}/_{8}$ × $24^{13}/_{16}$ × 11 in.), 97.DB.37

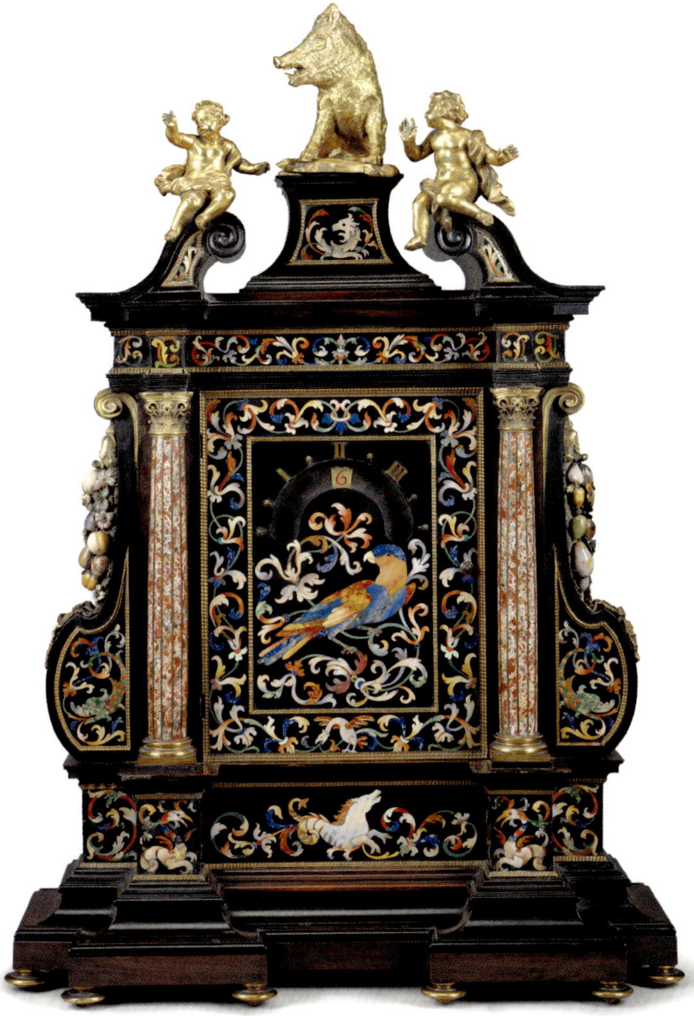

Popular in seventeenth-century Italy, night clocks were equipped with a small oil lamp that illuminated the dial from behind and made numbers visible in a dark bedroom. This piece takes the form of a Baroque altar, with the "altarpiece" housing the face of the clock. Combining rare materials, innovative forms, and fine sculpture, the clock was a collaborative effort. Foggini, court sculptor to Cosimo III (1642–1723), grand duke of Tuscany, and director of the Medici craft workshops, was responsible for developing the sculpted hardstone decoration. The cabinetmaker Van der Vinne specialized in masterful marquetry of floral patterns. Soldani-Benzi, then the finest bronze caster in Europe, probably made the clock's bronze boar, modeling it after a Hellenistic marble at the Gallerie degli Uffizi, Florence.

La Roldana (Luisa Roldán)
Spanish, 1652–1706
Saint Ginés de la Jara, circa 1692
Gilt and polychrome wood (pine and cedar) with glass eyes, 175.9 × 92 × 74 cm ($69\frac{1}{4} \times 36\frac{3}{16} \times 29\frac{1}{8}$ in.), 85.SD.161

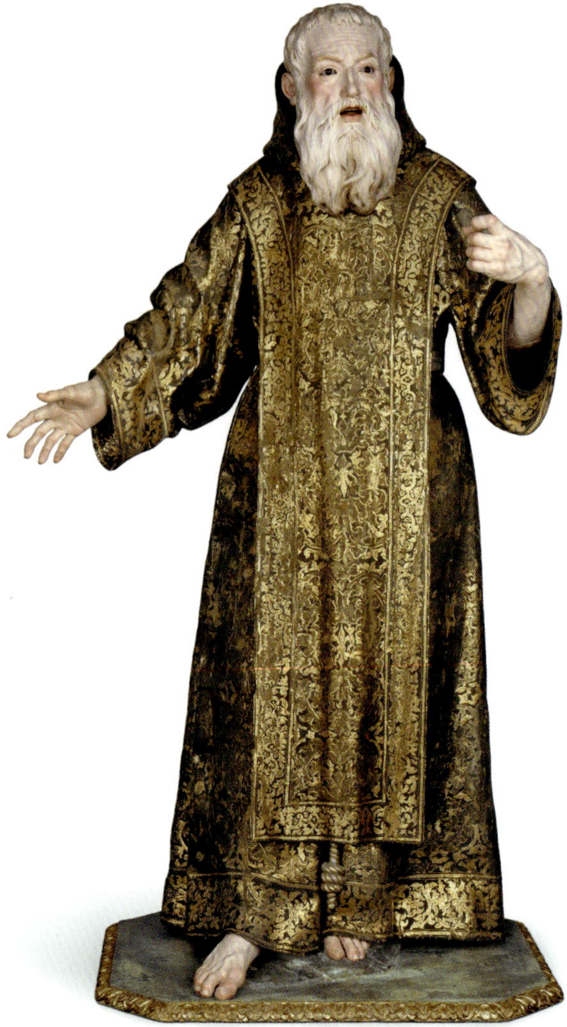

Luisa Roldán, called La Roldana, was the first woman sculptor recorded in Spain, where she was court sculptor to King Charles II (1661–1700). This figure was polychromed by her brother-in-law, Tomás de Los Arcos (1661–?), who used the Spanish technique of *estofado* to replicate in wood the rich brocade of ecclesiastical vestments. The process involves covering areas in gold leaf, painting over them with brown paint, and then incising the painted surface with a stylus to reveal the gold underneath. The sumptuous robe together with the lively gesture, open mouth, shining eyes, rosy cheeks, and bluish veins on the hands and feet achieve strikingly lifelike results. Reinforcing the emotional experience of the Catholic faithful, such heightened realism in devotional statues typified Spanish Baroque art during the Counter-Reformation.

Lidded Bowl

Porcelain: Japanese (Arita), circa 1700; mounts: French (Paris), circa 1717–22

Porcelain, underglaze blue, polychrome enamel decoration, and gilding; silver mounts, 27.9 × 34 × 27.6 cm (11 × 13 3/8 × 10 7/8 in.), 79.DI.123

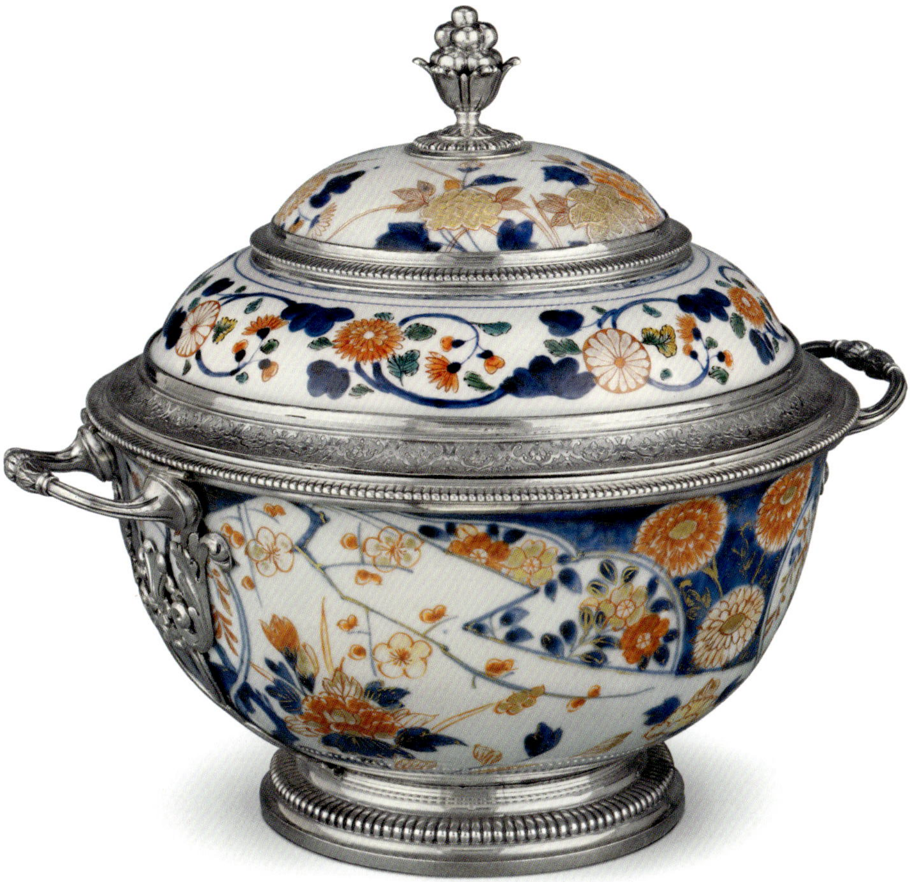

Japanese porcelain decorated with dense patterns in blue, red, and gold was made for export beginning in the late seventeenth century. Although produced in Arita, this porcelain is referred to as Imari ware in reference to the port in western Japan from which it was sent to the harbor in Nagasaki for shipment abroad. In this example, the Japanese porcelain was set in silver mounts in France to form a lidded bowl with elaborate handles, appealing to European tastes. It is made of three separate pieces of similarly decorated porcelain: a bowl and a lid formed by joining an inverted plate to the domed lid of a smaller bowl. Such assemblages demonstrate the inventiveness of French craftspeople in adapting Asian ceramics for European patrons.

Château de Monceaux: Month of December

French (Gobelins manufactory), before 1712

Designed by Charles Le Brun (1619–1690). Wool and silk, 317.5 × 330.8 cm (125 × 130¼ in.), 85.DD.309

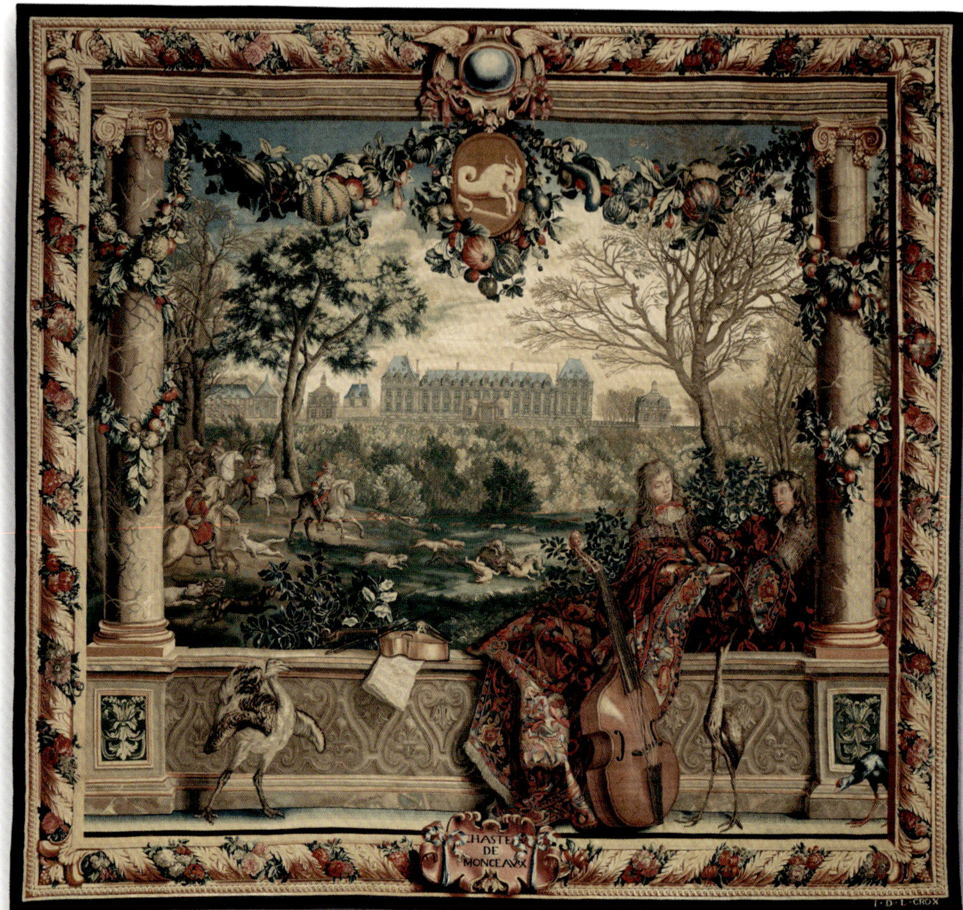

This tapestry is one in a series of twelve illustrating the months of the year. Each work in the set portrays a royal residence; the French king Louis XIV (1638–1715) engaged in one of his daily activities; and a selection of the monarch's riches. Here, the month of December is represented by the Château de Monceaux, shown in the background behind a scene of the king hunting for boar. In the foreground appear a rare Middle Eastern carpet, musical instruments, and birds from the royal menagerie. The series was conceived by Charles Le Brun for production at the royal workshop of the Gobelins, where seven complete sets, woven with gold thread, were made for the French Crown between 1668 and 1711.

Screen

French (Savonnerie manufactory), circa 1714–40
Wool and linen; cotton twill gimp; wooden interior frame; modern velvet lining, 273.6 × 193.2 cm (107¾ × 76⅛ in.), 83.DD.260.1

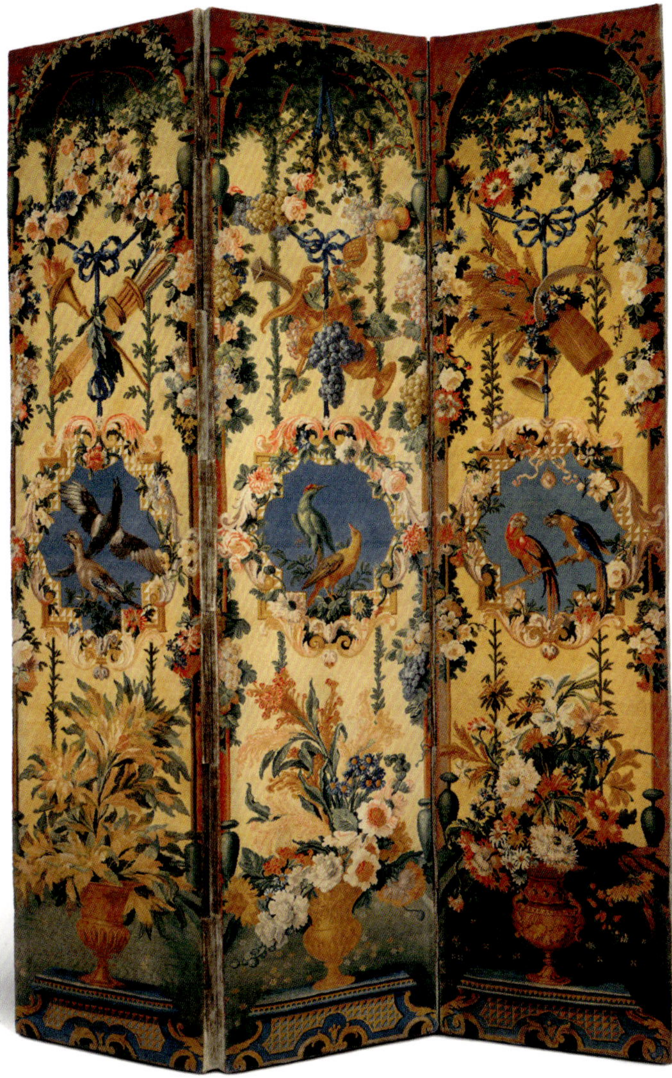

This three-paneled screen was made in the Savonnerie manufactory, which produced carpets, screens, and upholstery covers exclusively for the French Crown. Jean-Baptiste Belin de Fontenay (1653–1715) and Alexandre-François Desportes (1661–1743) provided the cartoons (preparatory painted or drawn designs) for this screen, one of the two largest models for folding screens. This example retains its original brilliant coloring, notable for the deep yellow background that was first introduced in 1686. Such tall screens were used to furnish the anterooms of royal apartments, and this series was particularly popular with the French king Louis XV (1710–1774).

Turkey
German (Meissen manufactory),
circa 1733
Model by Johann Joachim Kändler
(1706–1775). Porcelain, at base:
53.5 × 51 × 20 cm (21 1/16 × 20 1/16 × 7 7/8 in.),
2002.48

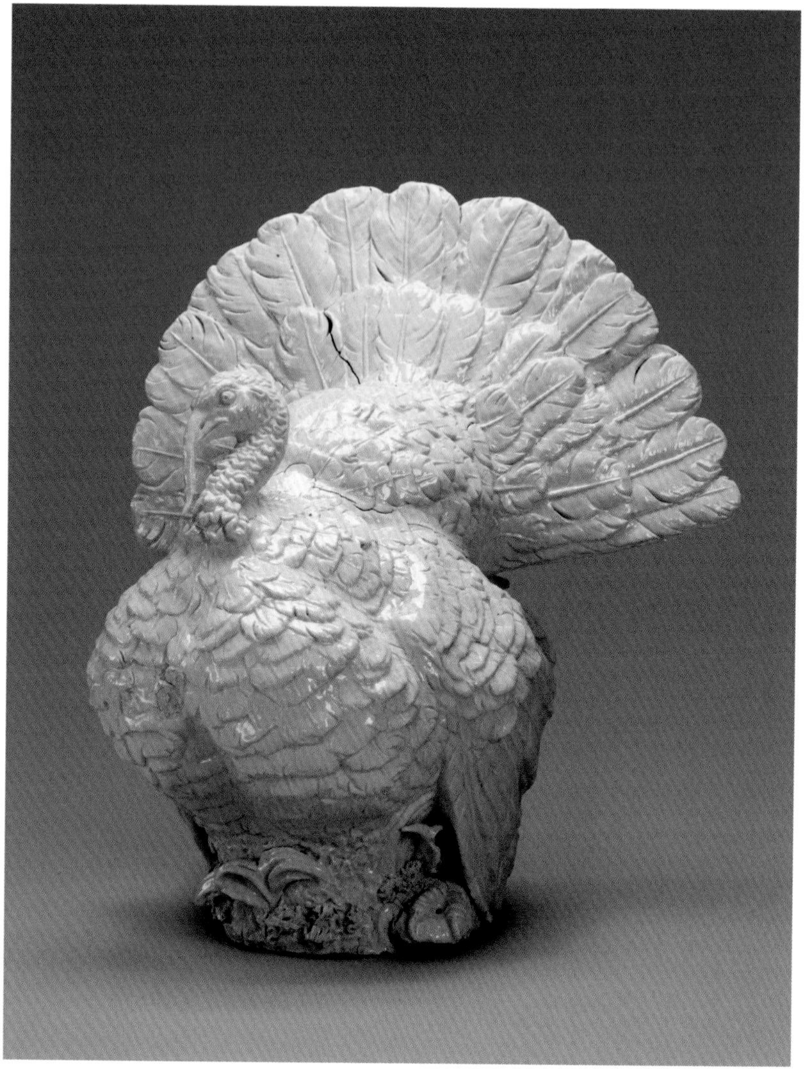

In 1710 the Meissen porcelain manufactory in Germany became the first European establishment to produce true hard-paste porcelain like that made in China. Twenty years later, Frederick Augustus I (1670–1733), also known as Augustus the Strong, elector of Saxony, commissioned a series of large porcelain animal sculptures from the manufactory. The production of life-size porcelain sculptures had never before been attempted in Europe. Devising a suitable porcelain recipe and learning how to construct, glaze, and fire the pieces presented significant challenges for the firm. Those models that emerged from the kiln intact exhibited cracks that made a final firing with enamel colors impossible. This turkey is one of eight made at Meissen for this extraordinary royal commission.

Box

French (Saint-Cloud manufactory), 1730–40
Soft-paste porcelain with glaze and enamel, 9.1 × 10.2 × 8.9 cm ($3\frac{9}{16}$ × 4 × $3\frac{1}{2}$ in.). Gift of MaryLou Boone, 2019.135

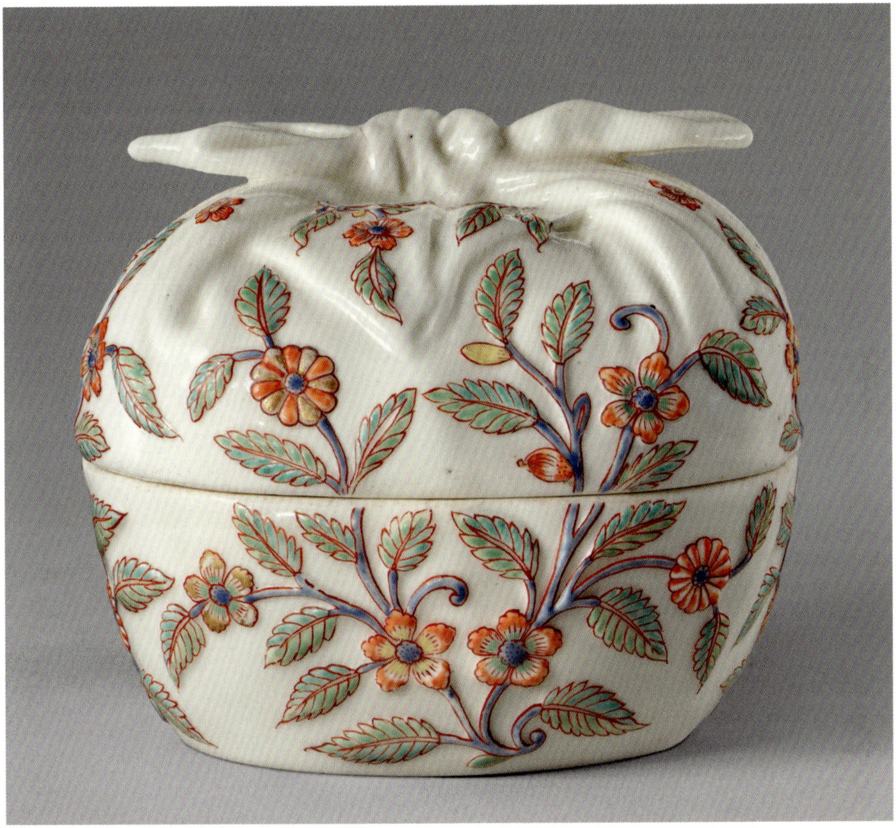

This small box is imaginatively conceived to look like a piece of fabric that has been wrapped around an object, gathered at the top, and tied with a double knot. The stylized branches of the decoration, leafy and in bloom, are slightly raised, giving the illusion of embroidery. The way the floral pattern extends over the joint between the base and the lid is characteristic of continuous designs found on East Asian ceramics and lacquer. While designed to hold small items, the box was likely treasured mainly for its delightful form and decoration. It is the only known piece of this shape and is a particularly sophisticated example of polychrome ware made at the Saint-Cloud porcelain manufactory outside Paris.

Francesco Natale Juvarra
Italian, 1673–1759
Plaque Representing the Virgin of the Immaculate Conception, 1730–40
Silver, gilt bronze, and lapis lazuli,
69.7 × 52.1 cm (27 7/16 × 20 1/2 in.), 85.SE.127

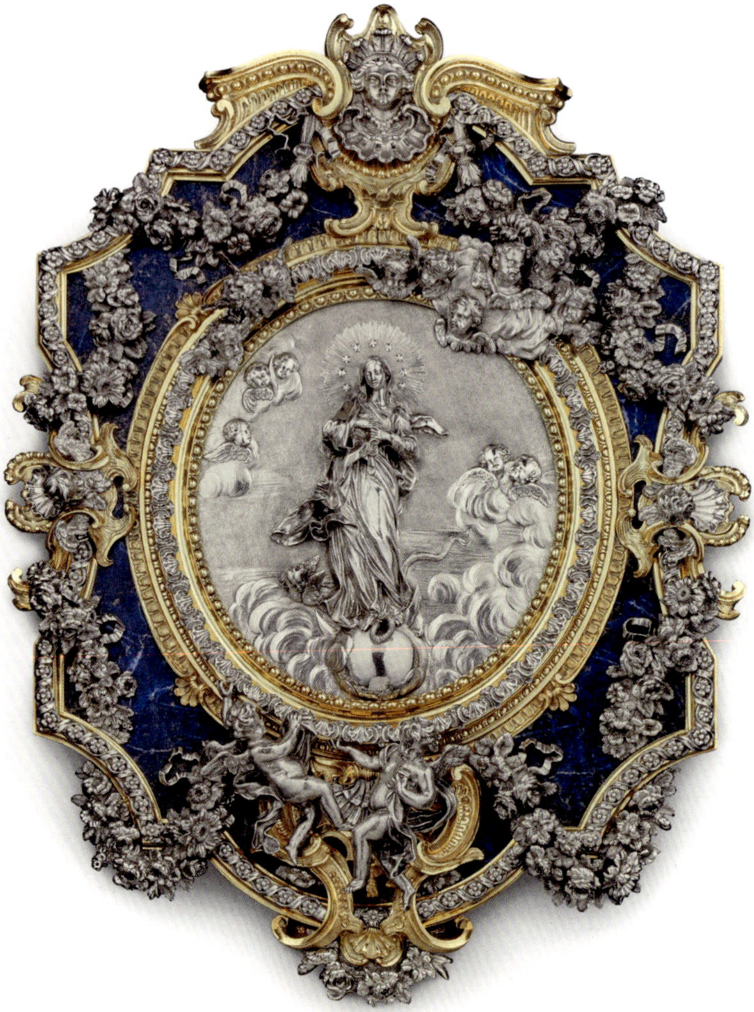

Surrounded by a lush golden frame inset with deep blue lapis lazuli, the silver Virgin Mary stands on a globe, symbol of her dominion with Christ, while under her feet she tramples a snake, understood as a sign of the Immaculate Conception. Cherub heads rise in low relief from the arabesques of clouds. An exuberant array of silver figurative, floral, and patterned elements enlivens the gilt-bronze frame's complex shape, giving it a jewel-like splendor. Juvarra, son of the goldsmith Pietro and brother of the architect Filippo, established a reputation as a maker of fine liturgical metalwork. His wall plaques, altar frontals, and chalices once graced the interiors of many Roman and Sicilian churches.

Pair of Potpourri Bowls

Porcelain: Japanese, circa 1660–80;
mount: French, circa 1750
Hard-paste porcelain, celadon ground color, and polychrome enamel decoration; gilt-bronze mounts,
15.2 × 18.7 × 16.5 cm (6 × 7 3/8 × 6 1/2 in.),
77.DI.90

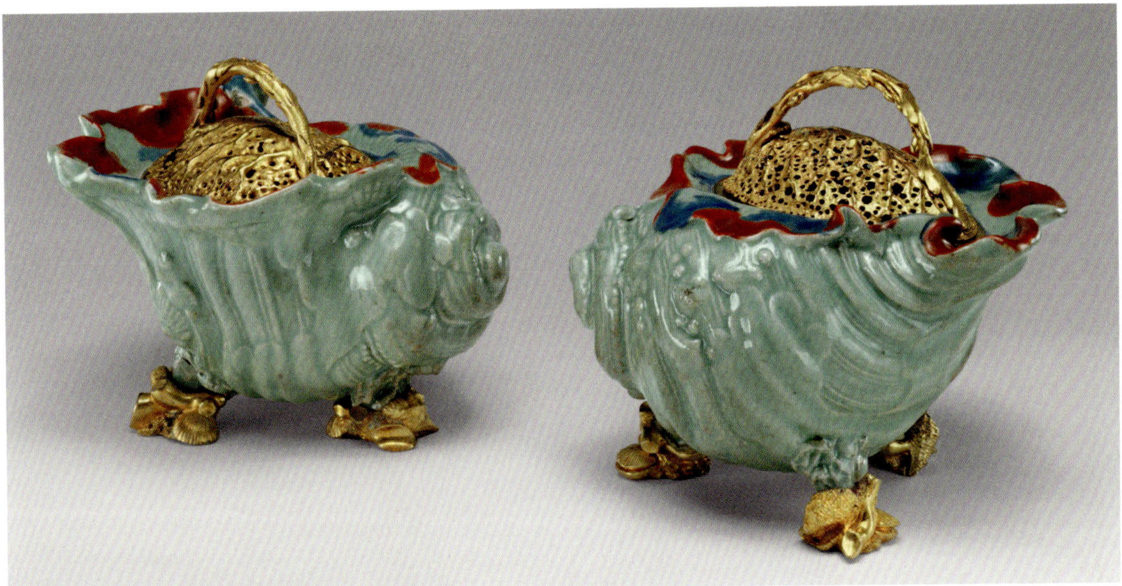

These shell-shaped porcelain bowls were made in Japan and probably intended for export to the West. In Paris they were fitted with gilt-bronze feet and lids in the form of coral, shells, and seaweed. Each lid is perforated to allow the scent of potpourri to escape. Such fanciful combinations of Asian porcelain with French gilt-bronze mounts were one of the primary trades of eighteenth-century *marchands merciers*, Parisian dealers in luxury goods, who would purchase the porcelain pieces and then commission local craftspeople to provide inventive embellishments in precious metals.

Wall Clock

French (Paris and Chantilly manufactory), circa 1740
Clock movement by Charles Voisin (1685–1761, master 1710). Soft-paste porcelain with polychrome enamel decoration; gilt bronze; enameled metal; glass, 74.9 × 35.6 × 11.1 cm ($29\frac{1}{2}$ × 14 × $4\frac{3}{8}$ in.), 81.DB.81

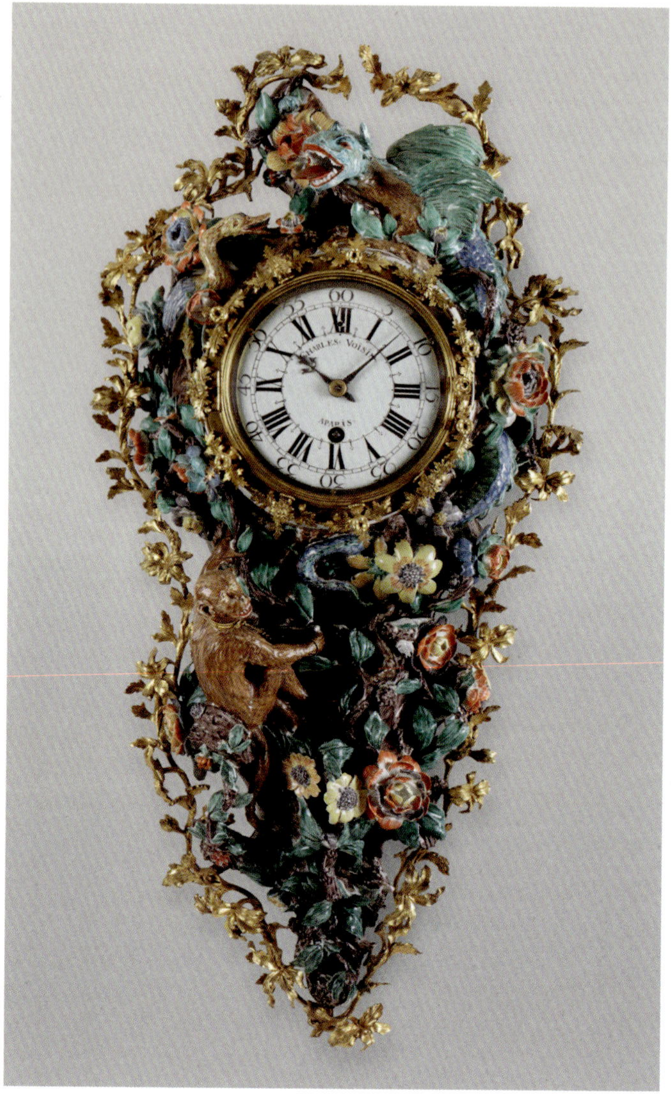

The porcelain decoration of this clock case features a variety of brightly colored flowers and whimsical elements such as a dragon, a goose, and a monkey. It was made at the Chantilly porcelain manufactory, established about 1725 by the prince of Condé. He owned a large collection of Japanese porcelain, which the factory used as models for its productions, developing its own imaginative interpretation of East Asian motifs. Intended for bed alcoves, clocks of this type were fitted with a chord that, when pulled, caused the bell to repeat the strike for the last hour and quarter hour. This clever design was useful in the dark, because one could hear the chiming bell and know the time without lighting a candle.

Box

Italian (Naples), circa 1735
Attributed to Giuseppe Sarao (active ca. 1725–45). Tortoiseshell, mother-of-pearl, gold, 15.9 × 26 × 21 cm (6¼ × 10¼ × 8¼ in.).
Gift of Ann and Gordon Getty, 2023.94

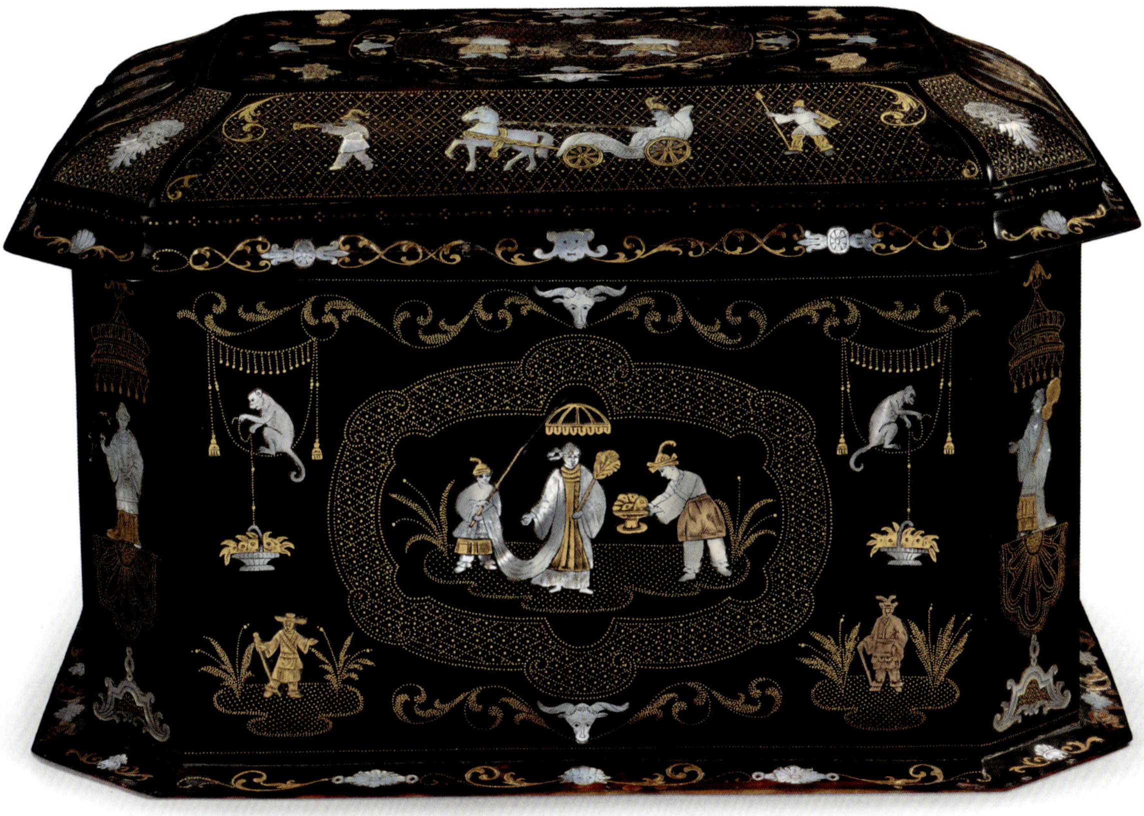

This box is a prime example of piqué work. *Piqué* refers to objects made of tortoiseshell inlaid with elaborate designs consisting of tiny gold pins, small pieces of engraved gold, and other precious materials, primarily mother-of-pearl. The process combines the mottled translucency of tortoiseshell with the iridescence of mother-of-pearl and the sparkle of gold to create extraordinary and precious objects for elite collectors. The technique reached its height in Naples, Italy, during the first half of the 1700s. This piece is an outstanding example attributed to Giuseppe Sarao, the most famous and accomplished Neapolitan artist working in this tradition.

Armchair

French, circa 1735–40
Gessoed and gilt beech; modern silk upholstery, 110.5 × 76.6 × 83.7 cm ($43\frac{1}{2} \times 30\frac{1}{8} \times 32\frac{7}{8}$ in.), 82.DA.95

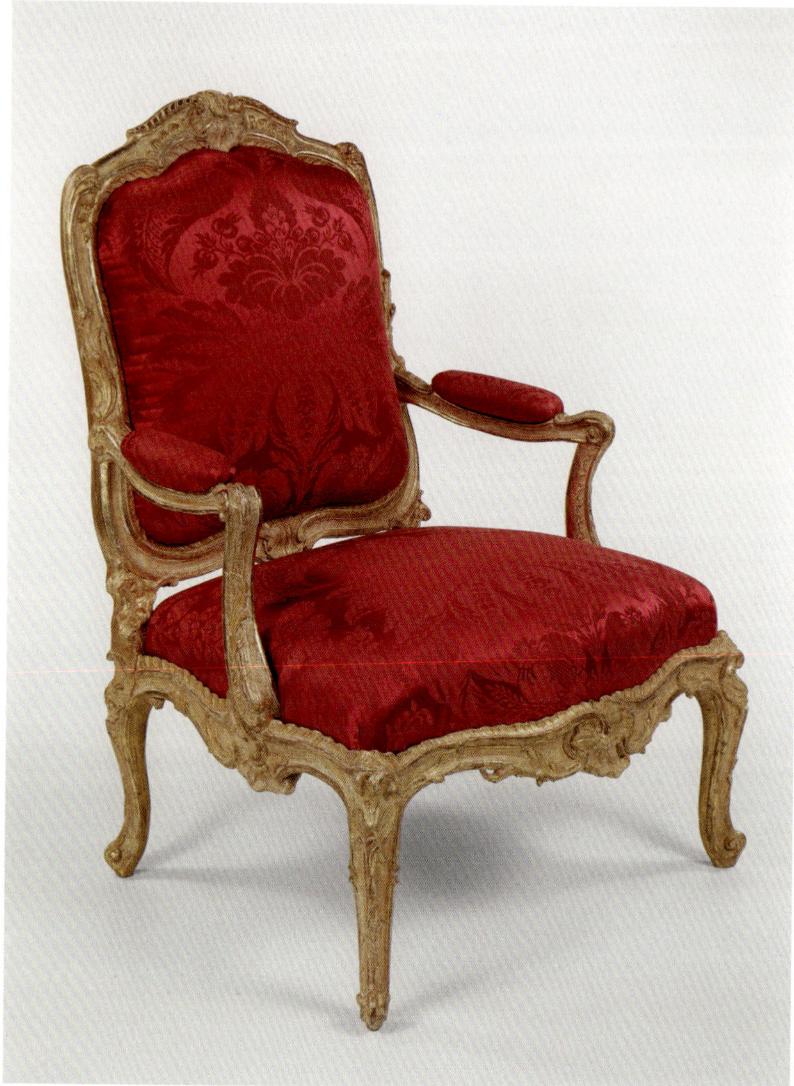

This armchair of the early Rococo period has fine carvings representing leaves, flowers, and scrolls. The wood frame still retains its original gilt surface, an unusual survival for furniture from the eighteenth century. With its flat, slightly sloping backrest and trapezoidal seat with a curved front, the form of this armchair is called *à la reine* (a "queen's" armchair) and was made to accommodate the voluminous skirts of women's dresses. The comfortably padded back, seat, and arms were easily removable to change the fabric according to the season: heavy damask or tapestry in the winter and lighter-colored silk in the spring.

Cartonnier with _Serre-Papier_, _Bout de Bureau_, and Clock

French (Paris), cabinet, circa 1740; clock, 1746
Cabinet by Bernard II van Risenburgh (ca. 1697–ca. 1766, master before 1730); clock movement by Étienne II Le Noir (1699–1778, master 1717); dial enameled by Jacques Decla (active 1742–64). White oak and poplar veneered with amaranth, cherry, and alder and painted with European lacquer; lacquered-bronze figures; gilt-bronze mounts; enameled-metal clock dial; glass; brass and iron hardware and lock; restorations in mahogany, 192 × 103 × 41 cm (75$^{5}/_{8}$ × 40$^{9}/_{16}$ × 16$^{1}/_{8}$ in.), 83.DA.280

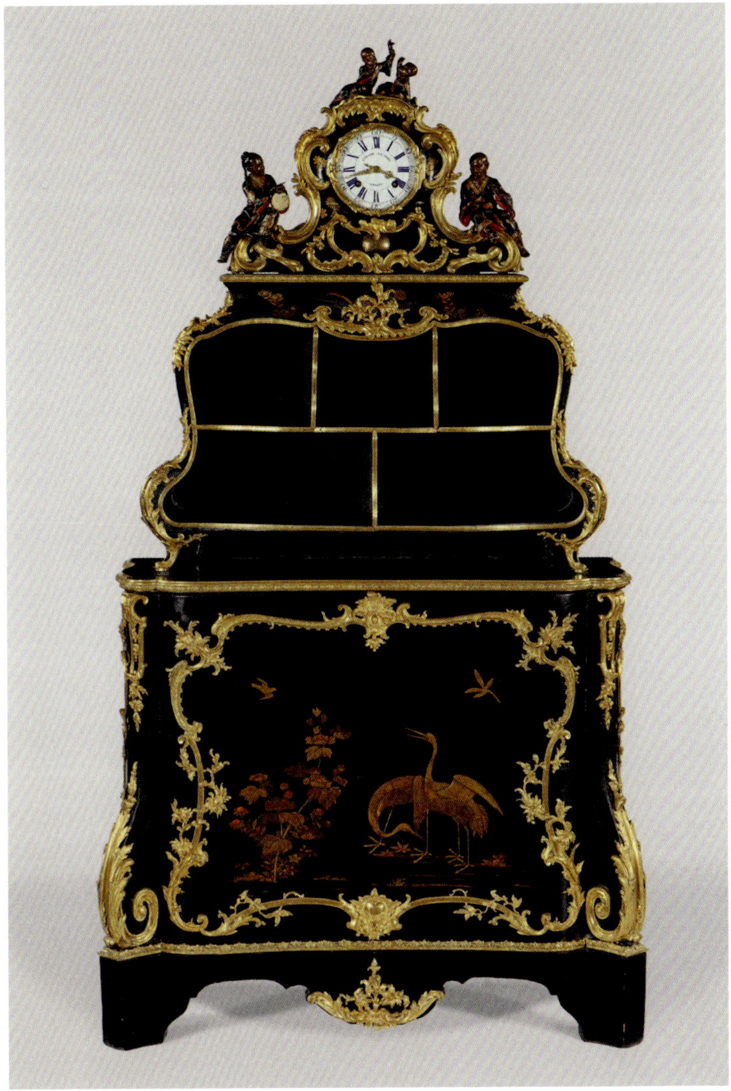

This *cartonnier*, or file cabinet, is composed of three parts: at the top is a clock set with four lacquered-bronze figures. It rests on a *serre-papier*, a cupboard with five open shelves, each of which was originally fitted with a filling box. These joined pieces are set above a *bout de bureau*, a low, shallow cabinet with a locking door on each short end. The ensemble was designed to be placed next to a matching desk. All surfaces are painted with black lacquer in imitation of East Asian techniques, as Japanese lacquer was popular in Europe at this time. Motifs like the cranes, small birds, and dragonfly on the front were also inspired by East Asian art, though here arranged in dense, symmetrical compositions according to European taste.

Decorative Bronze
French (Paris), 1738–1739
Surface by Étienne-Simon Martin (1703–1770) and Guillaume Martin (1689–1749). Painted, varnished, and gilt bronze; silver; bronze or brass screws (possibly gilded), 22.8 × 11.5 × 15.2 cm (9 × 4½ × 6 in.), 88.DH.127.2

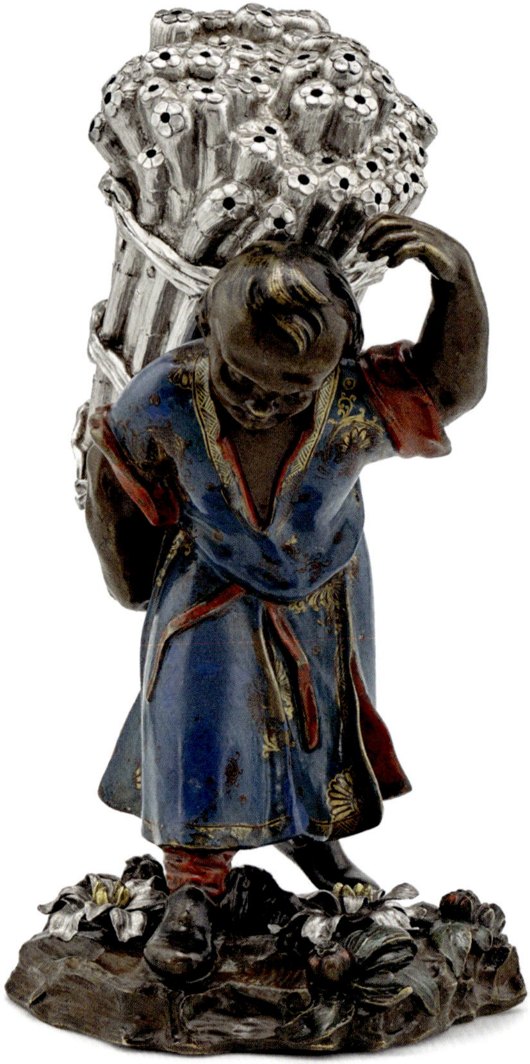

This bronze is one of a pair showing boys carrying bundles of sugarcane (made of silver). These unusual and inventive pieces masquerading as sugar casters (shakers) probably were not intended to be functional, given their size and unwieldiness. The figures are painted with a veneer that imitates the look of East Asian lacquer, demonstrating the eighteenth-century passion for chinoiserie, a term referring to objects made in a "Chinese manner." They may have belonged to Madame de Pompadour (1721–1764), mistress of King Louis XV, as this pair or a similar set is mentioned in the daily record book of the Parisian art dealer Lazare Duvaux for the month of September 1752, in which they are described as being cleaned.

Commode

German (Munich), circa 1745
Carving attributed to Joachim Dietrich (1690–1753). Gessoed, painted, and gilt pine; gilt-bronze mounts; *jaune rosé de Brignoles* marble top, 83.2 × 126.4 × 61.9 cm ($32\frac{3}{4} \times 49\frac{3}{4} \times 24\frac{3}{8}$ in.), 72.DA.63.1

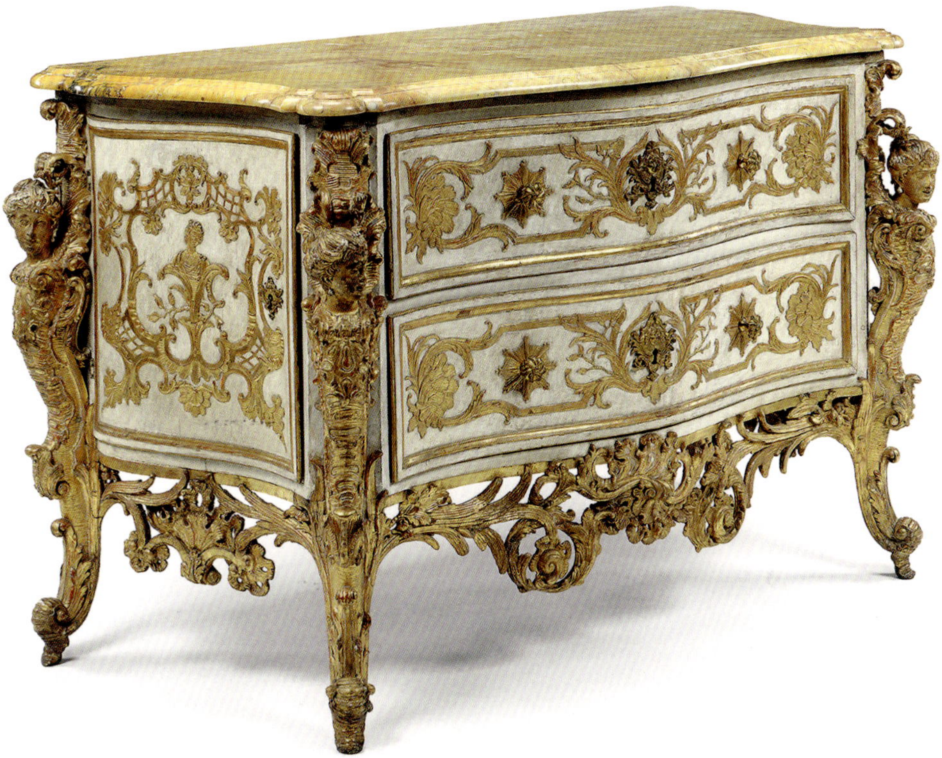

The design of both this ornately carved German commode (chest of drawers) and its mate (also in the Getty collection) was influenced by the engravings of François de Cuvilliés (1698–1768), architect for the electors of Bavaria and one of the leading interpreters of the Rococo style in Southern Germany. The combination of white painted surfaces and gilt pierced elements probably reflects the interior decoration of the room for which it was originally designed. The commode offers a contrast to French examples of the period, which would have featured gilt-bronze mounts, whereas the German maker has used carved and gilt wood.

Corner Cabinet

French (Paris), cabinet, circa 1744–55; clock, 1744
Jacques Dubois (1694–1763, master 1742); clock movement by Étienne Le Noir II (1699–1778, master 1717); dial enameled by Antoine-Nicolas Martinière (1706–1784, master 1720). Painted, varnished, and gilt bronze; silver; bronze or brass screws (possibly gilded), 289.5 × 129.5 × 72 cm (114 × 51 × 28 3/8 in.), 79.DA.66

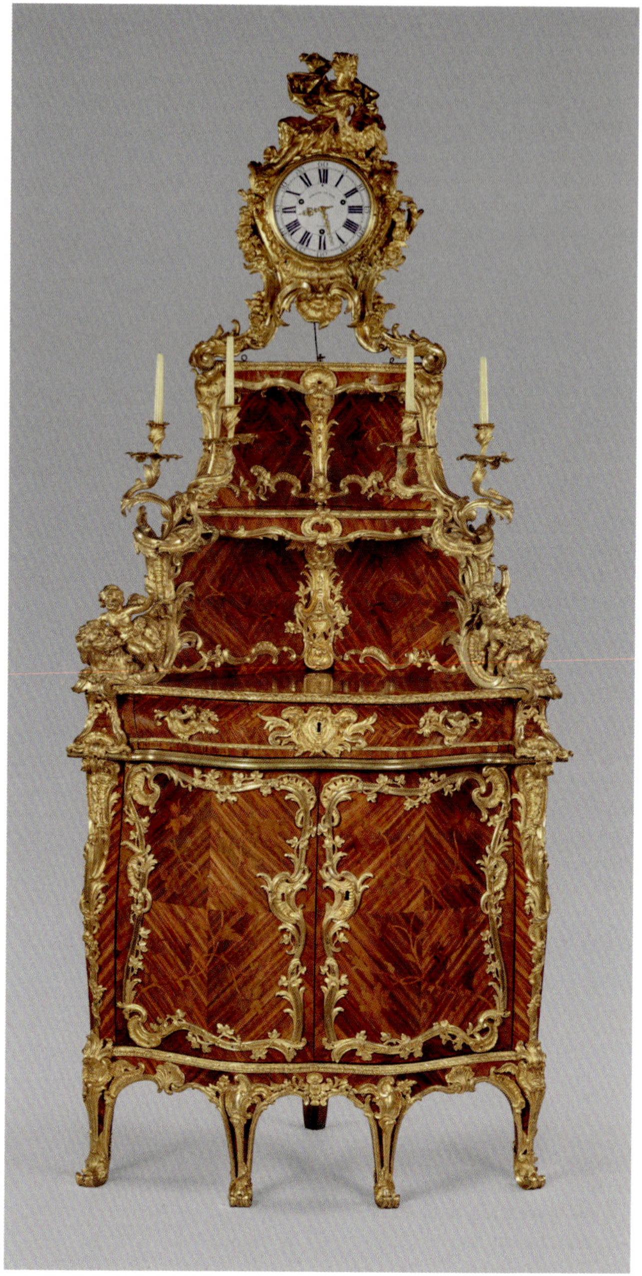

The design for this unique corner cabinet is based on a drawing by the French architect and ornament designer Nicolas Pineau (1684–1754), an early exponent of the Rococo style. However, the cupboard's large scale and exuberant gilt-bronze mounts reflect Eastern European rather than French taste. The piece was made in Paris for a Polish general, Count Jan Klemens Branicki (1689–1771), and delivered to him in Warsaw. An inventory of his possessions recounts that this corner cabinet was placed in a grand reception room of his residence opposite a large ceramic stove, the design of which it probably echoed.

Double Desk

French (Paris), circa 1750
Bernard II van Risenburgh (b. after 1696–ca. 1766, master before 1730). White oak veneered with tulipwood, kingwood, and bloodwood; drawers of mahogany; gilt-bronze mounts; gilt-bronze and iron hardware and locks; stained leather, 107.8 × 158.7 × 84.7 cm (42 7/16 × 62 1/2 × 33 3/8 in.), 70.DA.87

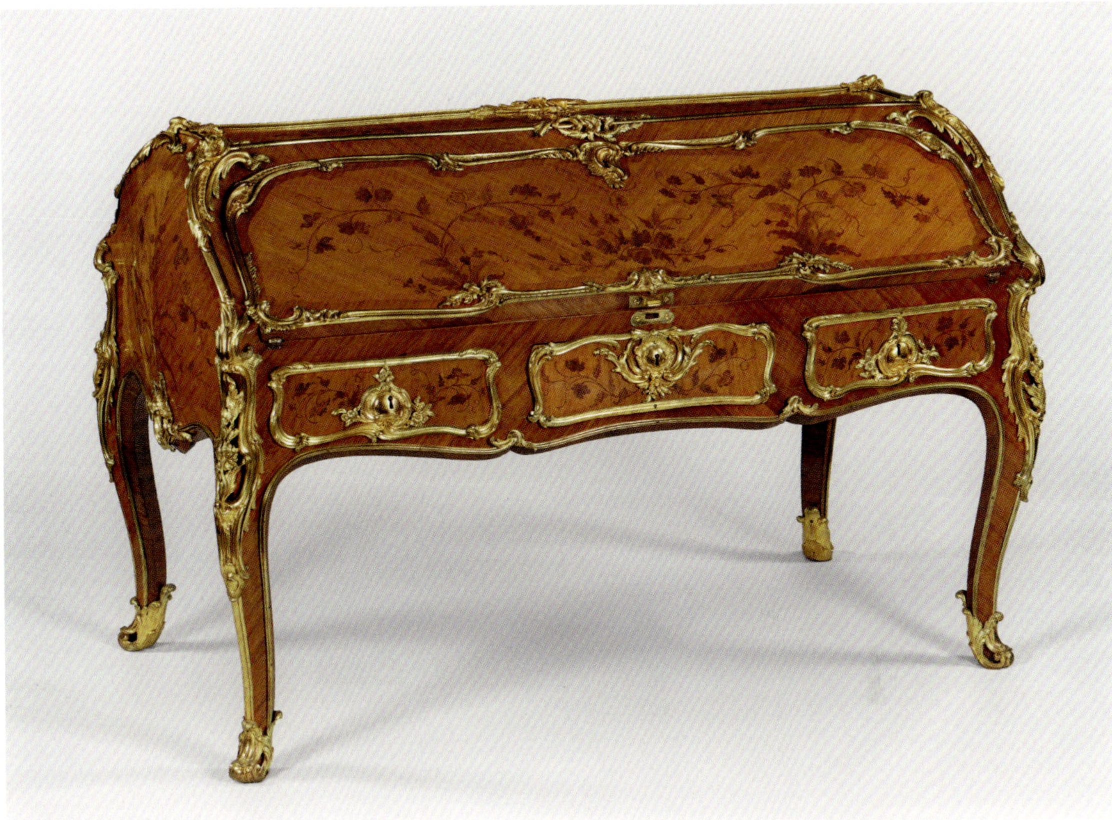

The double form of this desk is unique. The upper angled sections of both long sides conceal large panels that can be opened and lowered to form writing surfaces, revealing drawers and pigeonholes inside. The marquetry design on the desk is dominated by patterns of floral vines that seem to sprout from the sculptural gilt-bronze mounts. The piece was probably made for François Balthazar Dangé du Fay, a *fermier général* (a type of tax collector), since such a desk is described in an inventory made after his death in 1777. It is one of the most important works of decorative art acquired by J. Paul Getty himself.

Box

Italian (Turin), circa 1748–51

Attributed to Pietro Piffetti (1701–1777).

Walnut veneered with tortoiseshell, mother-of-pearl, ivory, bone, unidentified wood, and possibly horn; gilt bronze, 20.3 × 26 × 17.1 cm (8 × 10¼ × 6¾ in.).

Gift of Ann and Gordon Getty, 2023.93

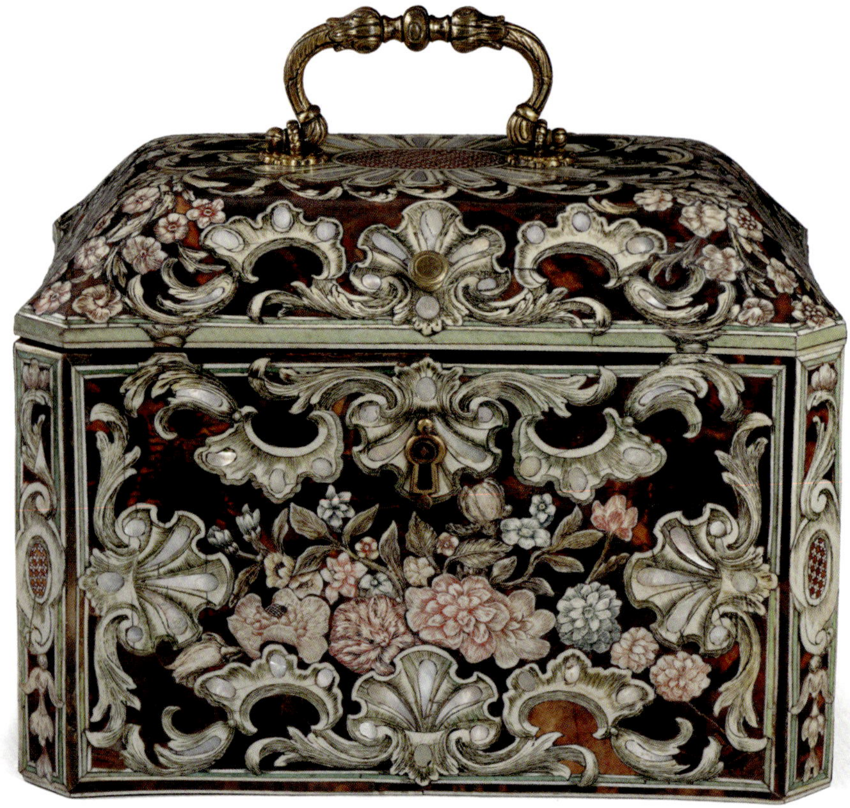

Piffetti was the leading cabinetmaker in Italy in the eighteenth century and one of the most accomplished of his time. He excelled in complex marquetry designs, in which tortoiseshell, mother-of-pearl, and engraved and colored ivory were incorporated into lush decorative veneers, as seen on this box. The abundance of various small-scale decorative motifs; the contrasts in texture, color, and iridescence; and the flowing lines of this work are characteristic of the florid Rococo style in Italy. Such an elaborately ornamented box was an object of extreme luxury and, being lockable, would have been used to house equally precious items such as documents or letters, or even additional containers made of valuable materials like lacquer or porcelain.

Compound Microscope and Case

French (Paris), circa 1751
Micrometric stage invented by Michel-Ferdinand d'Albert d'Ailly, 5th duke of Chaulnes (French, 1714–1769); gilt-bronze mounts attributed to Jacques Caffieri (French, 1678–1755, master 1714). Microscope: gilt bronze; glass and mirror glass; enamel; shagreen, 48 × 28 × 20.5 cm (18 7/8 × 11 × 8 1/16 in.); case: wood; tooled and gilt leather; brass; interior lined with velvet, silver braid, and lace; slides of various natural specimens; brass implements, 66 × 34.9 × 27 cm (26 × 13 3/4 × 10 5/8 in.), 86.DH.694

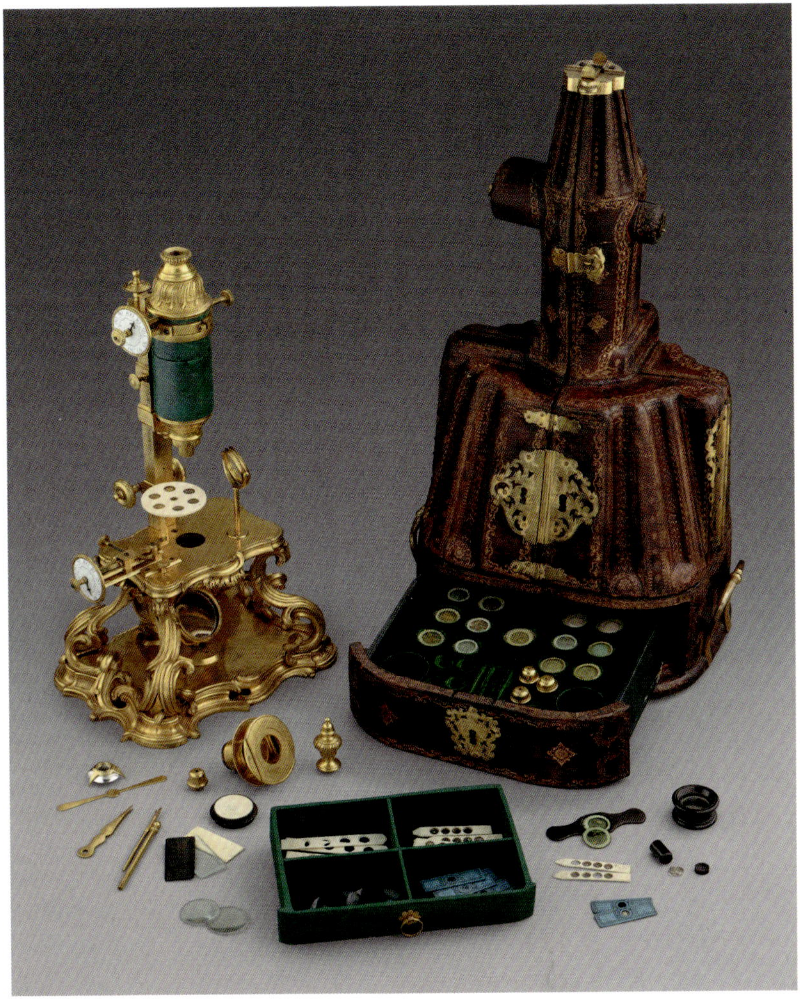

This elaborate microscope demonstrates the close affinity of the arts and sciences in eighteenth-century France. While the style of the gilt-bronze stand adhered to the era's prevailing tastes for the extravagant Rococo style, the instrument also incorporated a micrometric stage, a cutting-edge technological invention that allowed for the precise measurement of specimens. Doubtless made for an aristocratic amateur scientist, it is nearly identical to one that belonged to the French king Louis XV (1710–1774). As with so many of the instruments designed for the circle of noble dilettante scientists associated with both the court and the French Académie des Sciences, this microscope and its original tooled-leather case reflect the consummate skill of the numerous artisans and engineers involved in their making.

La Machine d'Argent

French (Paris), 1754

François-Thomas Germain (1726–1791, master 1748). Silver, 21 × 36.8 × 23.2 cm (8¼ × 14½ × 9⅛ in.), 2005.43

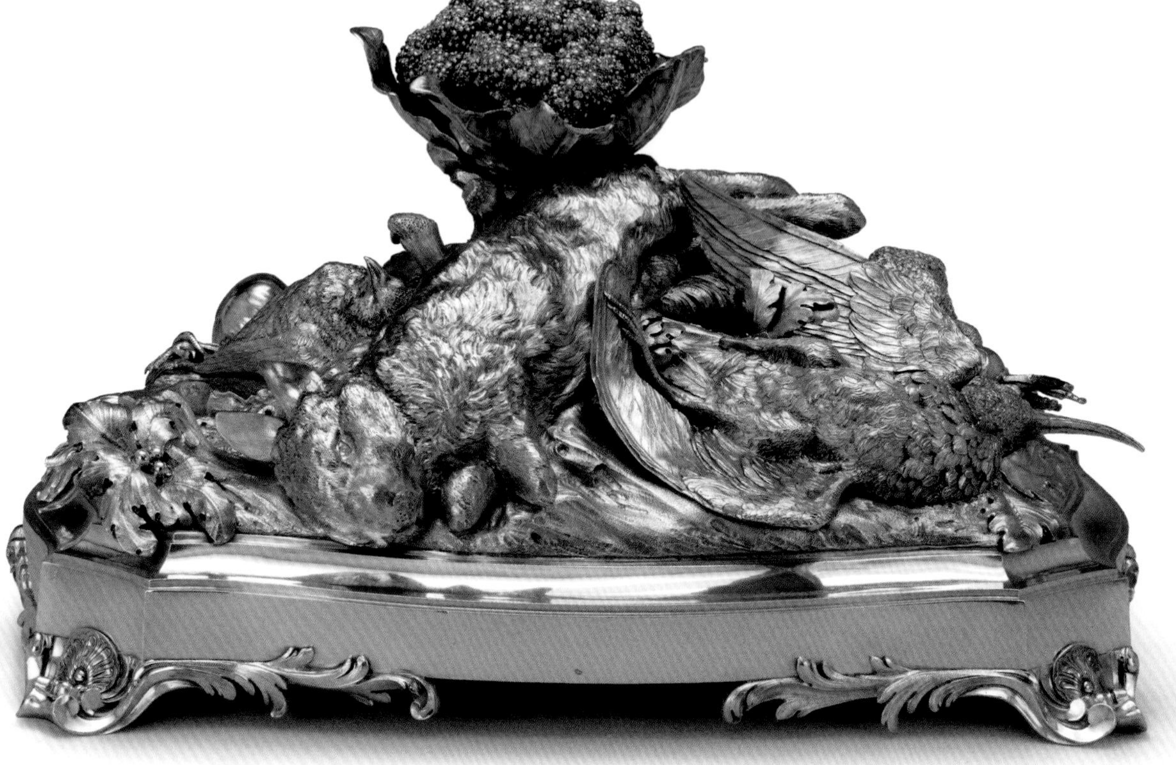

This unique still-life sculpture epitomizes the technical sophistication achieved by French silversmiths during the eighteenth century. The composition represents a rabbit and two game birds, along with a variety of vegetables. It was made in the tradition of silver centerpieces for dining tables. The subject refers to painted depictions of dead game and the ingredients for *oille-en-pôt*, a rich meat-and-vegetable stew popular at the time.

The sculptor-silversmith Germain rendered his subject with great naturalism, rivaling real life in the texture of the rabbit's fur, the birds' feathers, the smooth onion skin, and the rough, beaded head of cauliflower. The title of the work, *La Machine d'Argent* (literally, "The Silver Machine"), was understood to imply "a work of genius" rather than the modern connotation of a mechanism.

Wall Light

French (Paris), 1756
François-Thomas Germain
(1726–1791, master 1748). Gilt
bronze, 89.2 × 56.8 × 40.3 cm
(35 1/8 × 22 3/8 × 15 7/8 in.), 81.DF.96.2.2

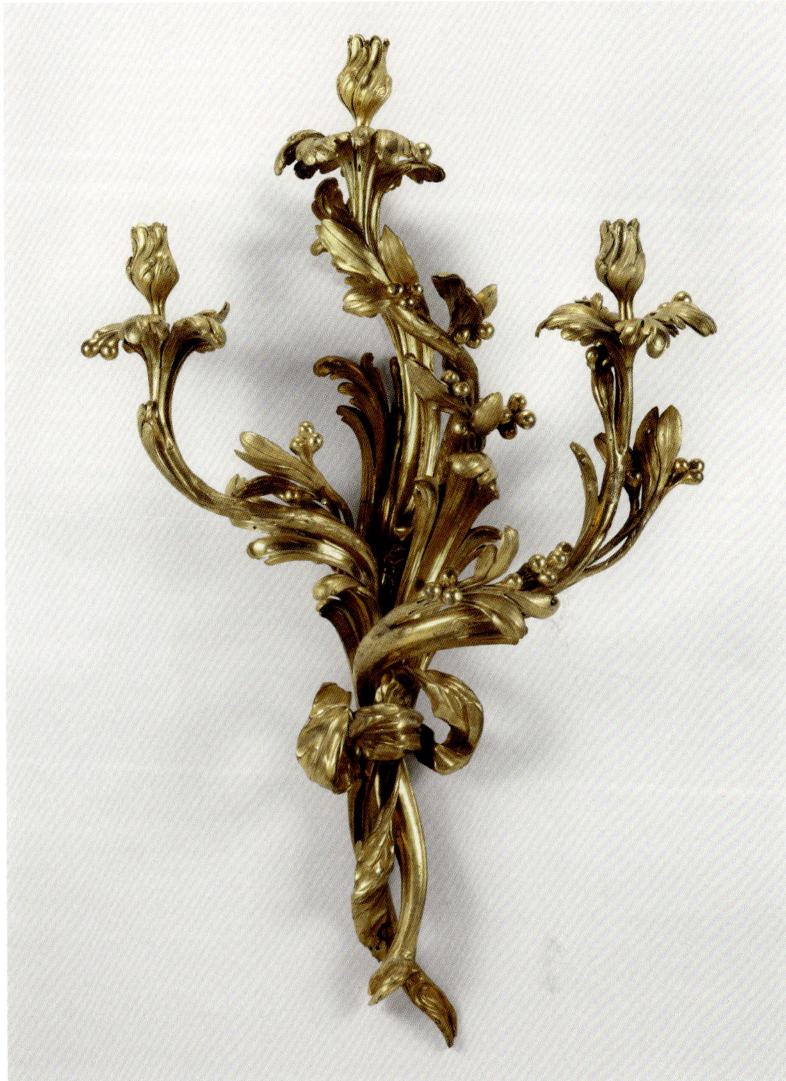

Signed by François-Thomas Germain, silversmith to the French king, this large wall light is from a set of eight made for a series of formal reception rooms built for the duc d'Orléans at the Palais-Royal in Paris (four are in the Getty Museum). Their refinement of execution and detail are comparable to what Germain was able to achieve in silver. Each is in the form of three laurel branches tied at the base by a ribbon. Laurel branches have been used as a symbol of victory and fame since the time of the ancient Greeks and Romans. Later in the eighteenth century the wall lights were acquired by King Louis XVI (1754–1793), and four were hung in rooms used by his wife, Marie-Antoinette (1755–1793), in the Château de Compiègne.

Writing and Toilette Table

French (Paris), circa 1760–70
Jean-François Oeben (1721–1763, master 1761) and workshop. White oak veneered with various stained woods; leather; silk; gilt-bronze mounts, 71.1 × 80 × 42.8 cm (28 × 31½ × 16⅞ in.), 71.DA.103

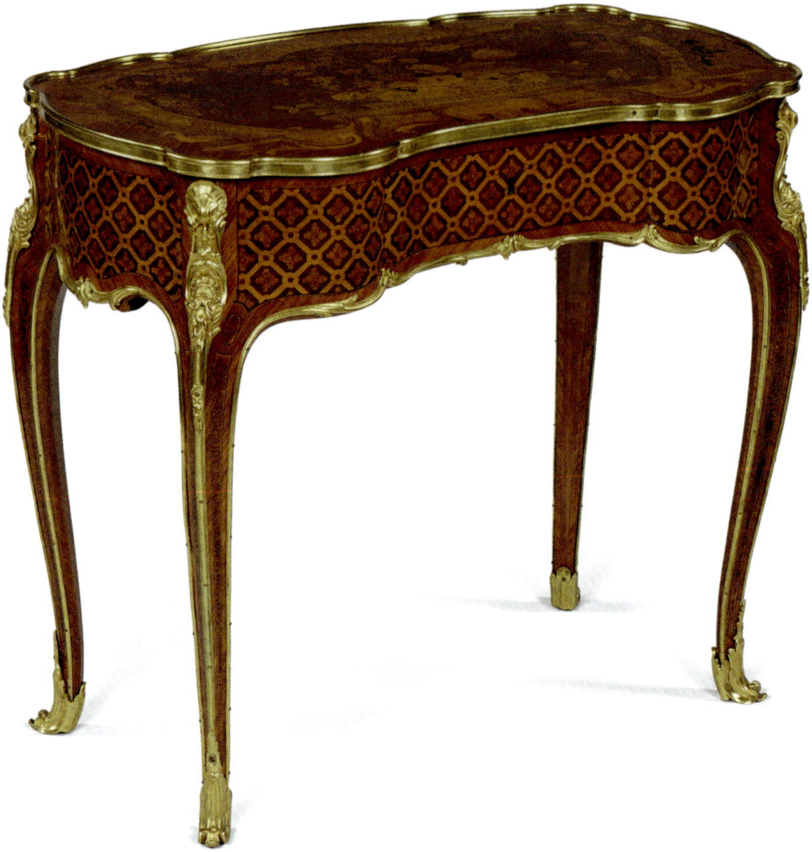

This type of mechanical table was invented by the royal *ébéniste* (cabinetmaker) Jean-François Oeben. Thanks to an elaborate mechanism, the tabletop slides back, revealing a drawer covered with a sliding lid veneered with marquetry. By pressing a button, the sliding lid releases, showing silk-lined compartments that once held writing materials and various containers of beauty products used during the morning toilette. The fine floral marquetry on the top is characteristic of the work of Oeben. After his death in 1763, his widow, Françoise Marguerite Vandercruse (1731–1775), continued the workshop, which was later taken over by Jean-Henri Riesener (1734–1806).

Reading and Writing Stand

German (Neuwied), circa 1760–65
Abraham Roentgen (1711–1793).
Pine, oak, and walnut veneered
with rosewood, alder, palisander,
ivory, ebony, and mother-of-pearl;
gilt-metal fittings, 77.5 × 71.7 × 48.8 cm
(30½ × 28¼ × 19¼ in.), 85.DA.216

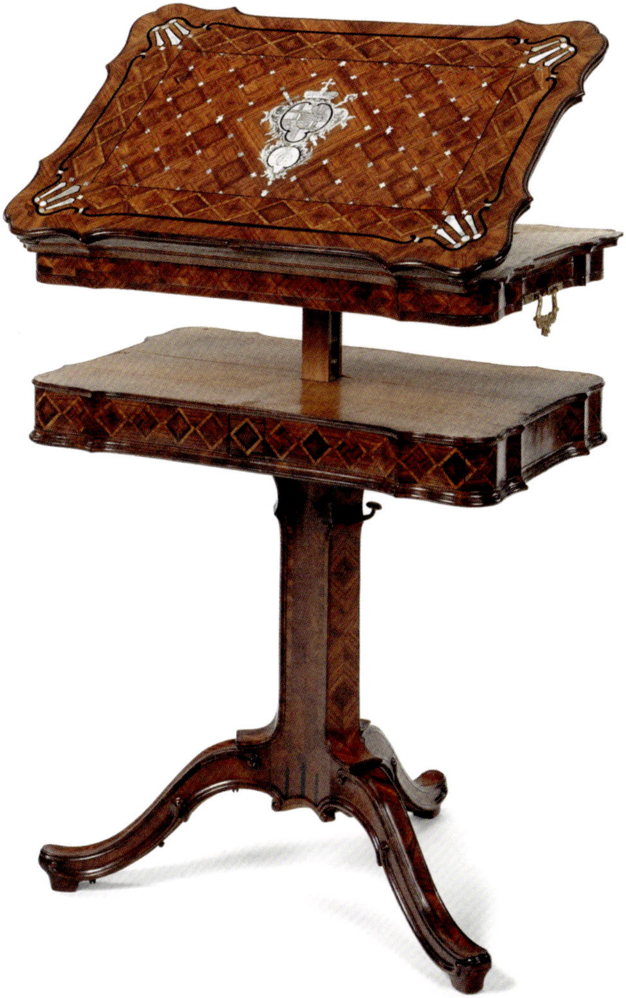

The top of this stand is inlaid with the coat of arms of Johann Philipp von Walderdorff (1701–1768), prince-archbishop and elector of Trier. Walderdorff was Roentgen's most important patron, and during the 1750s and 1760s, the latter delivered some twenty pieces of elaborate furniture for Walderdorff's palace. This stand is fitted with numerous concealed drawers that open at the press of a button or turn of a key.

Cat

Cat: China, circa 1700–1750; stool and cushion: France, circa 1750–55

Porcelain; gilt-bronze mount, 45 × 30 × 22 cm (17¹¹⁄₁₆ × 11¹³⁄₁₆ × 8¹¹⁄₁₆ in.), 2024.127

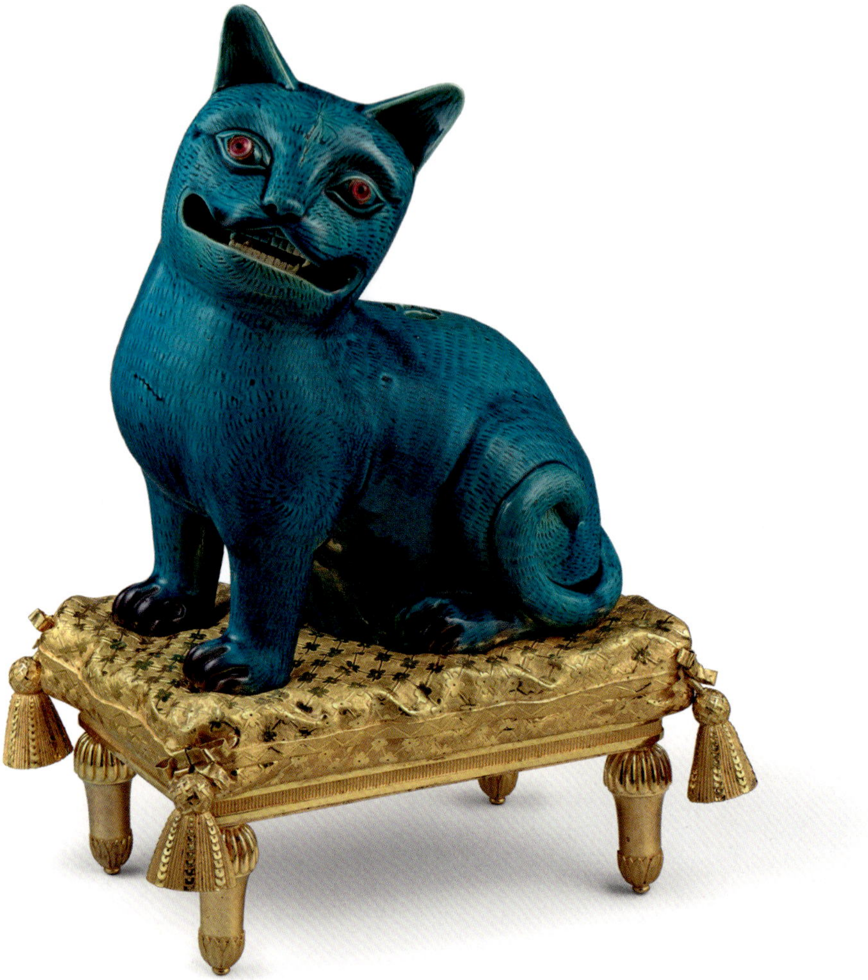

This blue porcelain cat was made in China to be exported to Europe in the mid-1700s. As a precious and curious object, it was mounted in France on a gilt-bronze cushion and stool. Embellishing ceramics with precious-metal mounts was a practice initiated by Parisian dealers of luxury arts, called *marchands merciers*. This cat belonged to one of the most important collectors of the eighteenth century, Randon de Boisset (1780–1776), who is said to have acquired the piece from the estate of Madame de Pompadour (1721–1764), mistress of King Louis XV, after her death. Cats of this sort and Asian ceramics were quite fashionable in Europe in the 1700s.

Lidded Potpourri Vase

French (Sèvres manufactory), circa 1760
Painting attributed to Charles-Nicolas Dodin (1734–1803). Soft-paste porcelain, pink and green ground colors, polychrome enamel decoration, and gilding, 37.5 × 34.8 × 17.3 cm (14³⁄₄ × 13¹¹⁄₁₆ × 6¹³⁄₁₆ in.), 75.DE.11

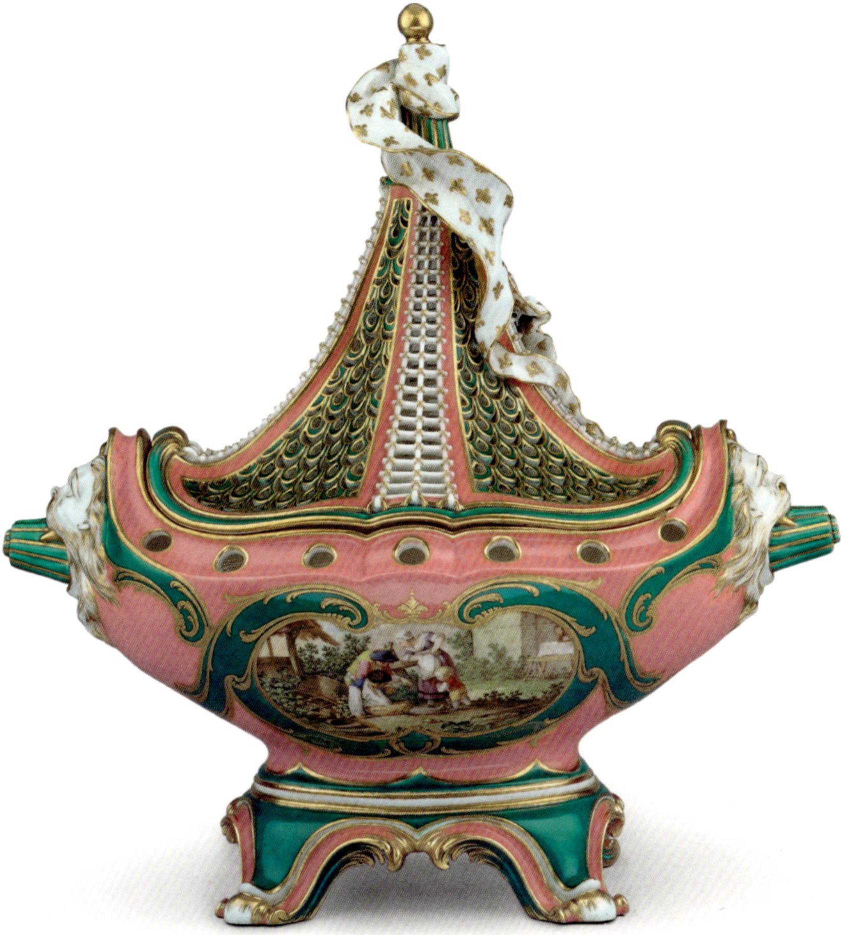

Boat-shaped potpourri containers such as this example are among the most famous innovations of the Sèvres porcelain manufactory, as well as some of the largest vessels produced there during the 1760s. The lids, elaborately shaped and pierced in imitation of a ship's rigging and furled sails, were extremely difficult to make; the multiple holes weakened the overall structure, and they often collapsed in the kiln. Consequently, only about twelve of these vases were ever completed, ten of which survive today. Charles-Nicolas Dodin, one of the most talented decorators at Sèvres, painted the rustic scene on the front of this ship, which he adapted from images found in Dutch and Flemish paintings of the 1600s.

Lidded Vase

French (Sèvres manufactory), 1768–69
Painting attributed to Jean-Baptiste-Étienne Genest (active 1752–89).
Soft-paste porcelain, *bleu Fallot* ground color, grisaille enamel decoration, and gilding; gilt-bronze mounts,
45.1 × 24.1 × 19.1 cm (17¾ × 9½ × 7½ in.),
86.DE.520.1

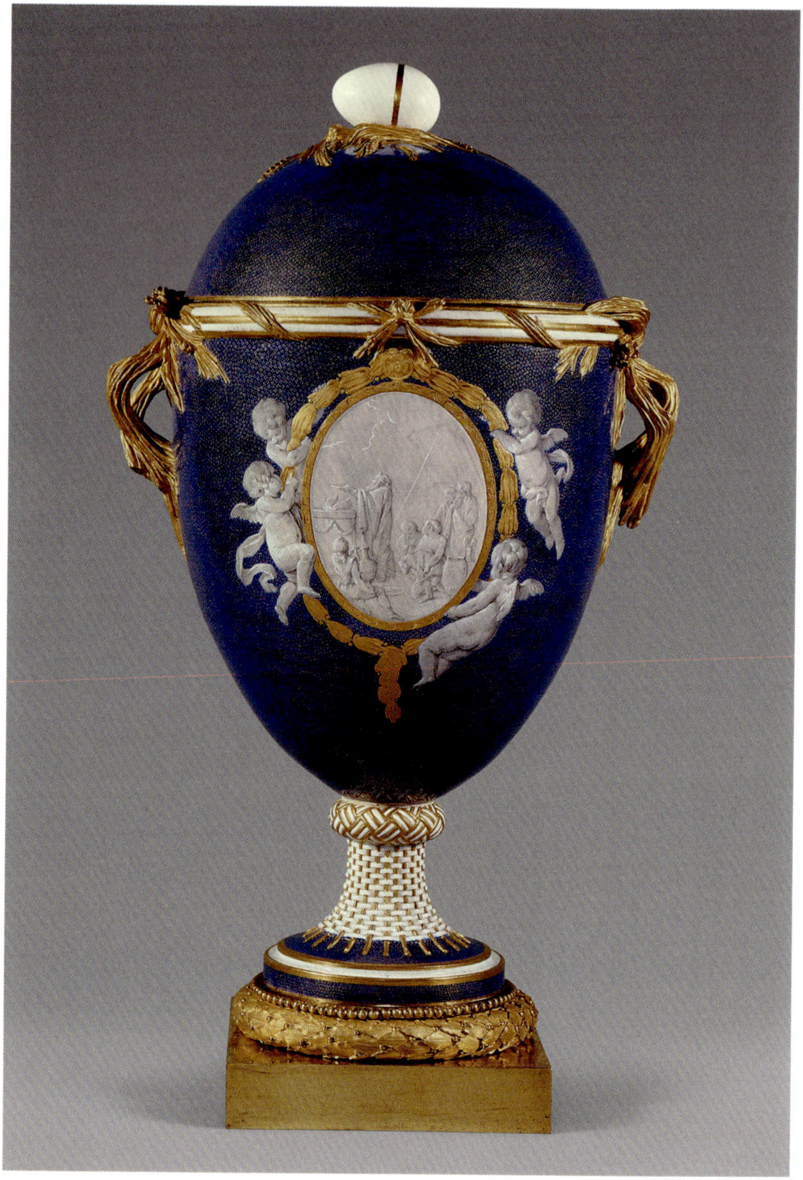

This ornamental vase is of a nearly unique form. The grisaille (grayscale) enameling and the pale blue ground strewn with gilt dots create a subtle finish that is markedly different from the strong, brightly colored decoration frequently employed at the Sèvres porcelain manufactory in the late eighteenth century.

Vase with Personification of Venice

Italian (Venice, Geminiano Cozzi manufactory), 1769
Hybrid soft-paste porcelain with underglaze blue decoration, H: 29.8 cm ($11\frac{3}{4}$ in.); Diam: 27.3 cm ($10\frac{3}{4}$ in.), 88.DE.9.2

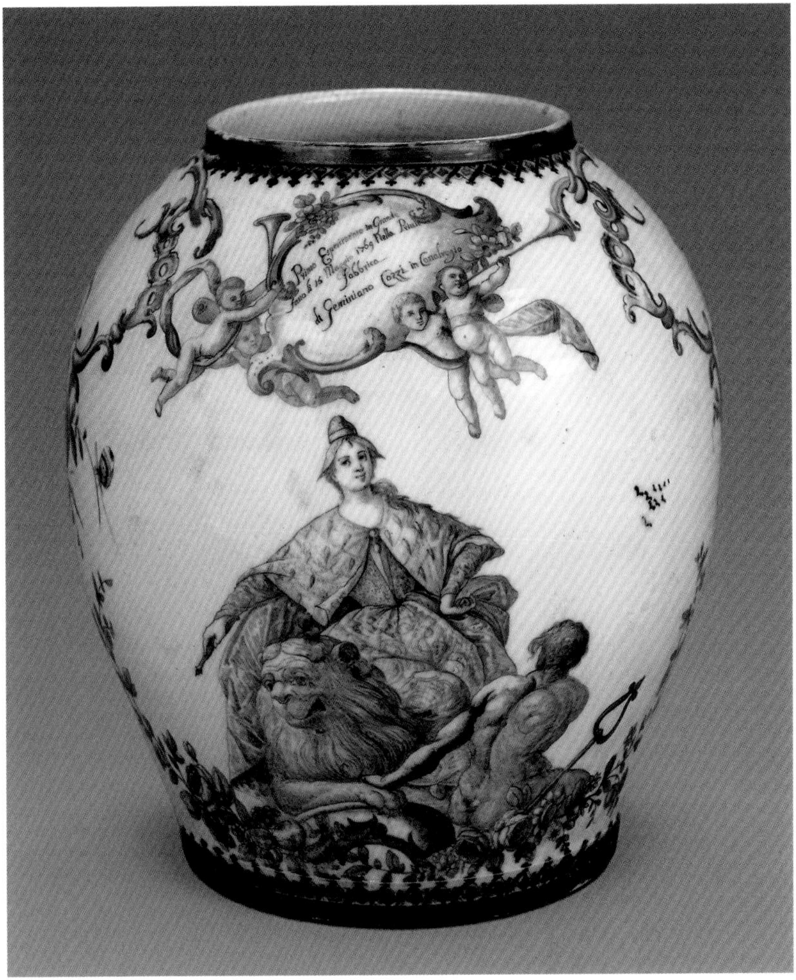

Produced in one of the leading Italian porcelain manufactories in the 1700s, this vase is remarkable for its large size, unusual shape, and delicately painted, sophisticated pictorial scheme. The decoration celebrates the beauty and sovereignty of the Venetian republic. The woman holding a scepter and wearing an ermine-trimmed cape represents Venice; she sits on a lion, an ancient symbol of the city. The elaborate inscription supported by trumpet-playing cherubs above her states that the vase is "the first large-scale experiment executed May 15, 1769, in the privileged factory of Geminiano Cozzi." Cozzi had founded his manufactory only a few years earlier, and this vase proudly proclaimed his success within the highly competitive and prestigious porcelain industry of that era.

Console Table

French, circa 1765–70
Attributed to Pierre Deumier (active 1760s). Silvered and gilt bronze; *bleu turquin* marble top; modern marbleized wood base, 83.5 × 129.5 × 52 cm (32 7/8 × 51 × 20 1/2 in.), 88.DF.118

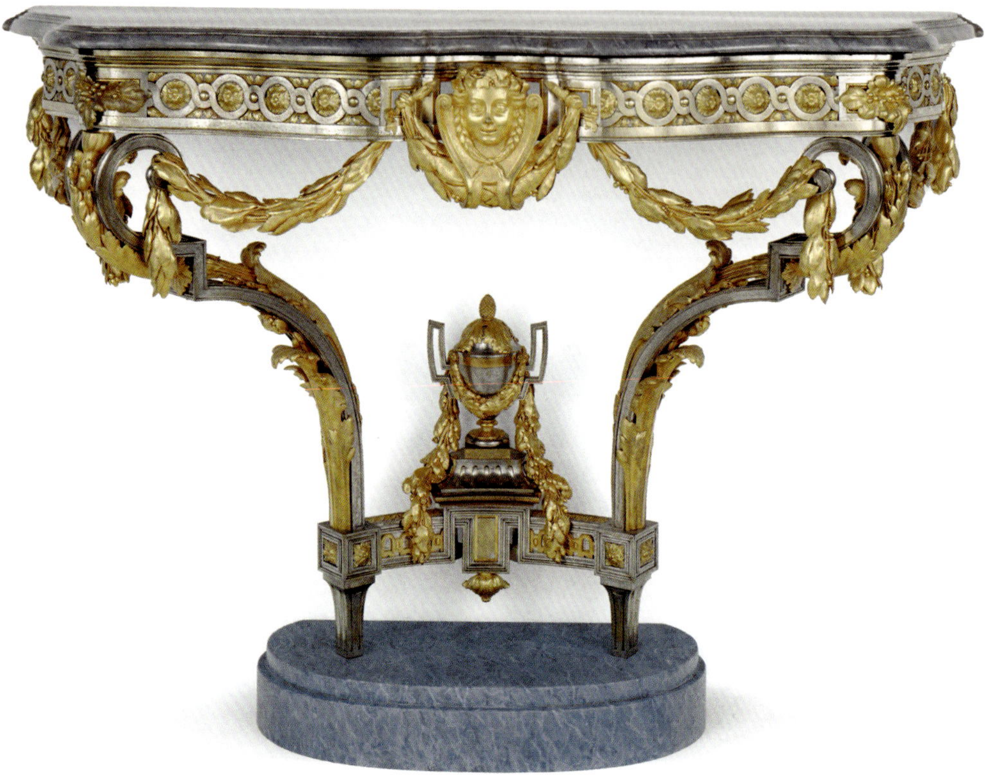

This unusual console table of both silvered and gilt bronze follows a type designed for the royal palace in Warsaw of Stanislas II Auguste, king of Poland (r. 1764–95). The French architect Victor Louis (1731–1807) was commissioned to renovate this residence according to the latest Neoclassical style, which was itself inspired by recent archaeological discoveries at Pompeii and Herculaneum in Italy. Louis was also responsible for designing some of the fitted furniture to coordinate with the new interiors. This table was probably cast according to his design by Pierre Deumier. It was no doubt Deumier's training as a locksmith that led him to forge the metal into many interlocking pieces.

Commode

French (Paris), 1769
Gilles Joubert (1689–1775). Oak veneered with kingwood, tulipwood, holly, bloodwood, and ebony; gilt-bronze mounts; *sarrancolin* marble top, 93.5 × 181 × 68.5 cm (36 13/16 × 71 1/4 × 27 in.), 55.DA.5

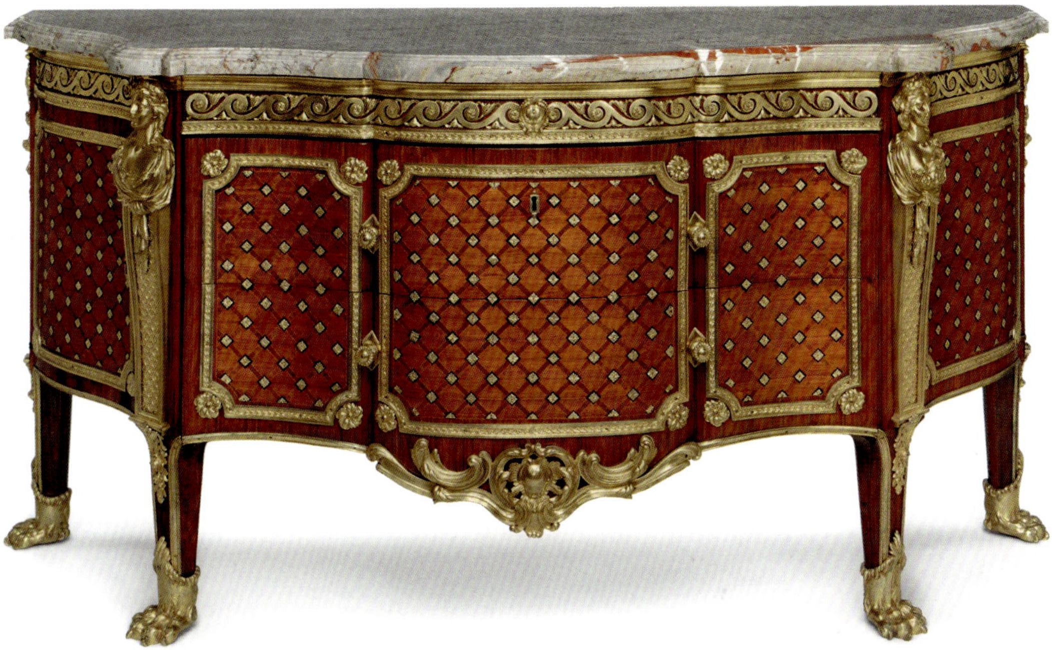

This commode (chest of drawers) is one of a pair made for the Versailles bedroom of Madame Louise (1737–1787), youngest daughter of King Louis XV. The extensive use of gilt-bronze decoration contributed to a sense of overall luxury that was suitable for a princess. The journal of the royal household's furnishings records the commode's delivery on August 18, 1769. It also includes the name of its maker—Gilles Joubert—its dimensions, a detailed description, and its inventory number, 2556.2, which is inscribed on the back. Joubert had a long career working for the royal household. When he delivered this commode, he held the title of royal cabinetmaker.

Francis Harwood
British, 1726/27–1783
Bust of a Man, 1758
Black stone (*pietra da paragone*); yellow Siena marble socle, 69.9 × 50.2 × 26.7 cm ($27\frac{1}{2}$ × $19\frac{3}{4}$ × $10\frac{1}{2}$ in.), 88.SA.114

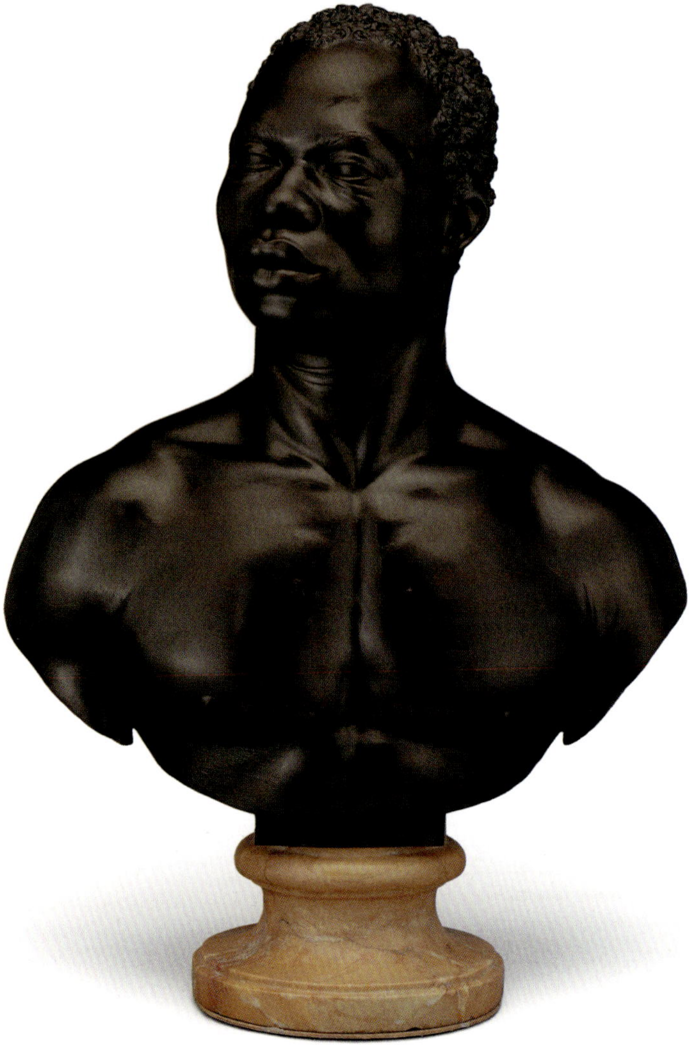

Harwood chose a black stone to render the sitter's skin tone. As in some ancient marble and bronze sculptures, the portrait ends in a wide arc below the man's chest. The artist may deliberately have used this elegant, rounded termination to evoke associations with ancient busts of notable men. Although the identity of the sitter is unknown, the scar on his face suggests that this portrait represents a specific individual. It may be one of the earliest sculpted portraits of a Black person by a European artist.

Joseph Nollekens

British, 1737–1823

Venus, 1773

Marble, 124 × 51 × 51 cm

(48 13/16 × 20 × 20 in.), 87.SA.106

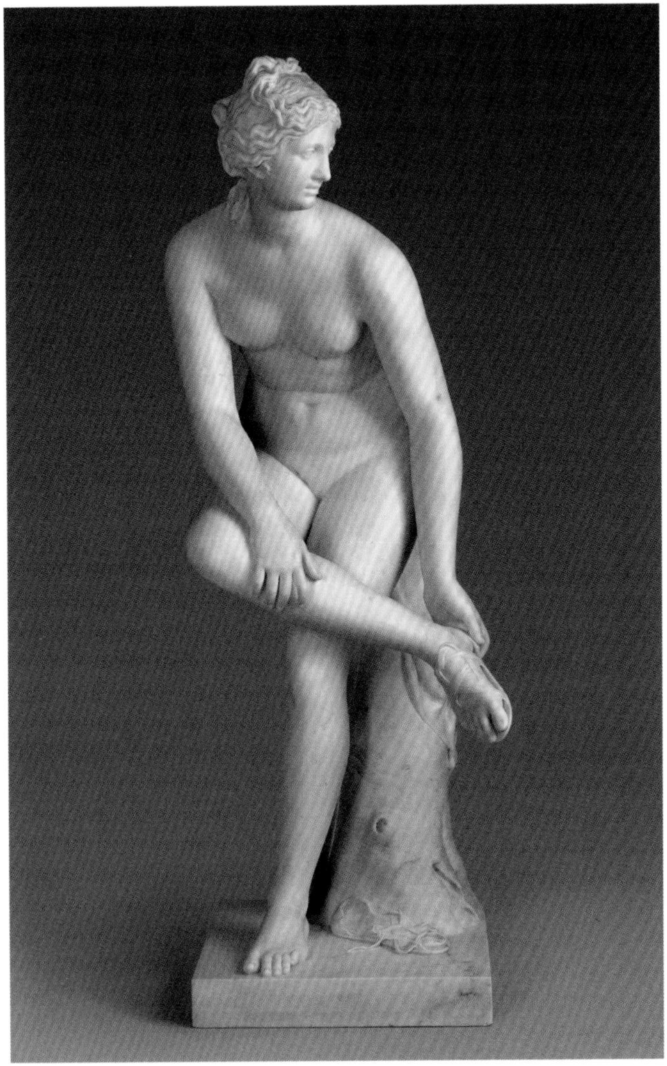

Nollekens studied in Rome from 1762 to 1770, and his style, a mannered classicism inflected by a coy charm, exhibits the influence of ancient and sixteenth-century Italian sculpture. Along with the figures of *Juno* and *Minerva*, this *Venus* was commissioned by Charles Watson-Wentworth (1730–1782), 2nd Marquess of Rockingham, to accompany an ancient marble statue of the Trojan hero Paris that this wealthy and keen English collector had already purchased. The four statues together represent the Judgment of Paris, the mythological story of the shepherd king who was empowered to decide which of three goddesses was the fairest. Nollekens chose to depict each goddess in a different state of undress. Venus, the winner of the contest, is nude except for the single sandal she is removing.

Clodion (Claude Michel)
French, 1738–1814
Offering to Priapus, circa 1775
Terracotta, 45.1 × 33.5 × 21.8 cm
(17¾ × 13³⁄₁₆ × 8⅝ in.), 85.SC.166

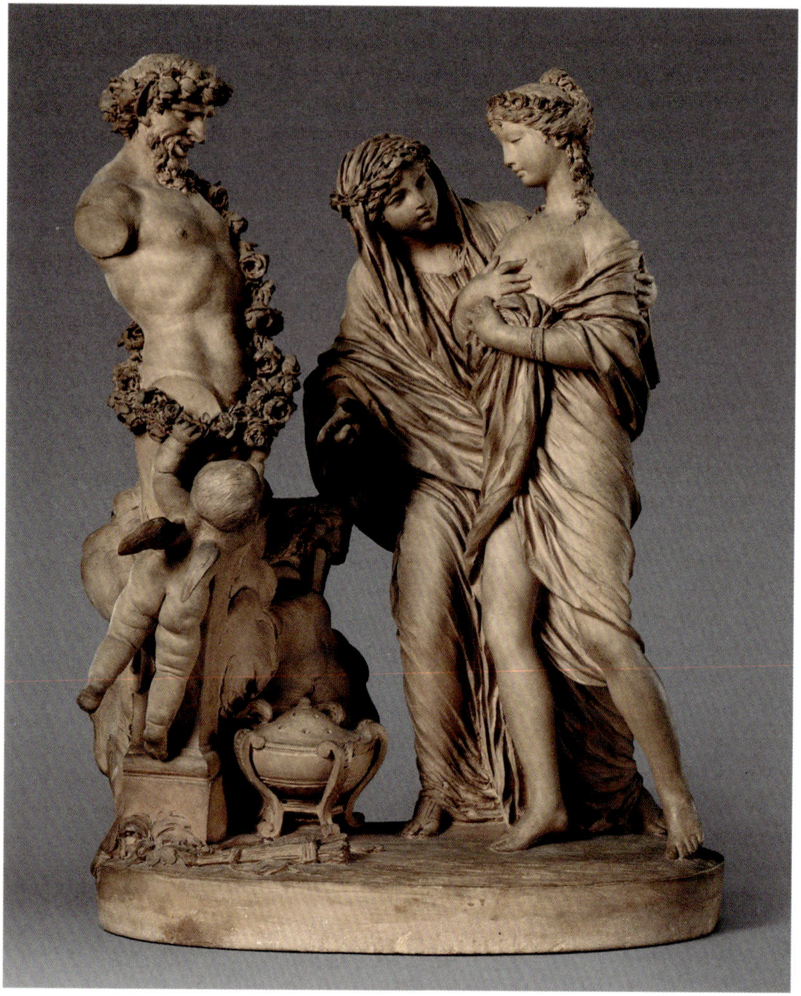

A woman dressed as a priestess leads a young girl toward a statue of Priapus, the ancient god of fertility. With distinctive goatlike ears, Priapus appears in the form of a herm, a column-like statue marking a territorial boundary. The smoking incense, the sacrificial tripod, and the presence of Cupid (shown arranging a garland around the herm) indicate that the girl is making an offering of her charms. Ancient mythology, for Clodion, provided a repertory of characters and settings with which to create playful and erotic works much appreciated by collectors. Through his technical brilliance and virtuoso handling of wet clay, he elevated terracotta sculpture as an art form in its own right, rather than merely a preparatory sketch or model for a sculpture in a more permanent material.

Mantel Clock

French (Paris), circa 1772
Case by Étienne Martincourt (d. after 1791, master 1762); clock movement by Étienne-Augustin Le Roy (1737–after 1792, master 1758). Gilt bronze, enameled metal, and glass, 71.1 × 59.7 × 32.4 cm (28 × 23½ × 12¾ in.), 73.DB.78

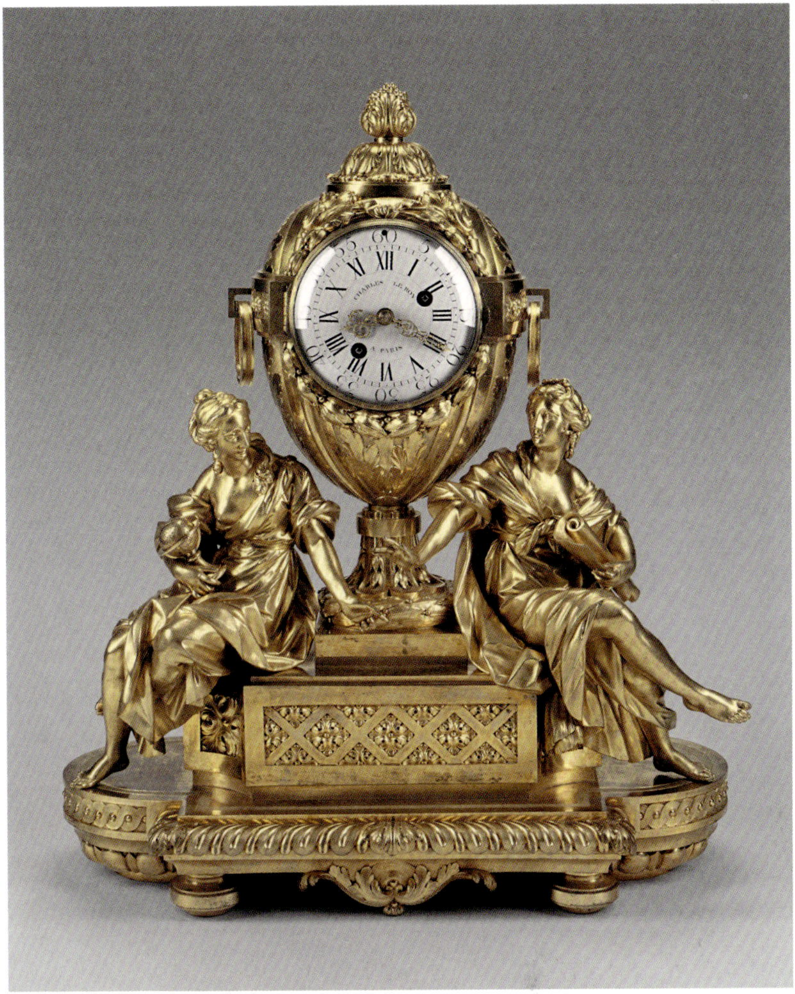

This remarkably fine clock features chasing, gilding, and burnishing of the highest quality. A Neoclassical-style urn, raised on a plinth and set on a platform, houses the clock's movement. The female figures sitting to either side have been identified as allegories of Astronomy and Geography. In 1790, this clock stood atop a mantelpiece in King Louis XVI's Council Room at the Palais des Tuileries in Paris. With its allegorical references to navigation and scientific reasoning, it referred to the astute decisions that the king and his council made in that very room as they devised strategies for France's naval and ground forces.

Secrétaire

French, Paris, circa 1775
Martin Carlin (ca. 1725/30–1785, master 1766).
Oak veneered with amaranth, tulipwood, ebony, holly, stained holly, incised with color mastics; set with soft-paste Sèvres porcelain plaques with *bleu céleste* ground color, polychrome enamel decoration, and gilding; gilt-bronze mounts; white marble top, 120 × 94 × 34 cm (47¼ × 37 × 13⅜ in.), 65.DA.2

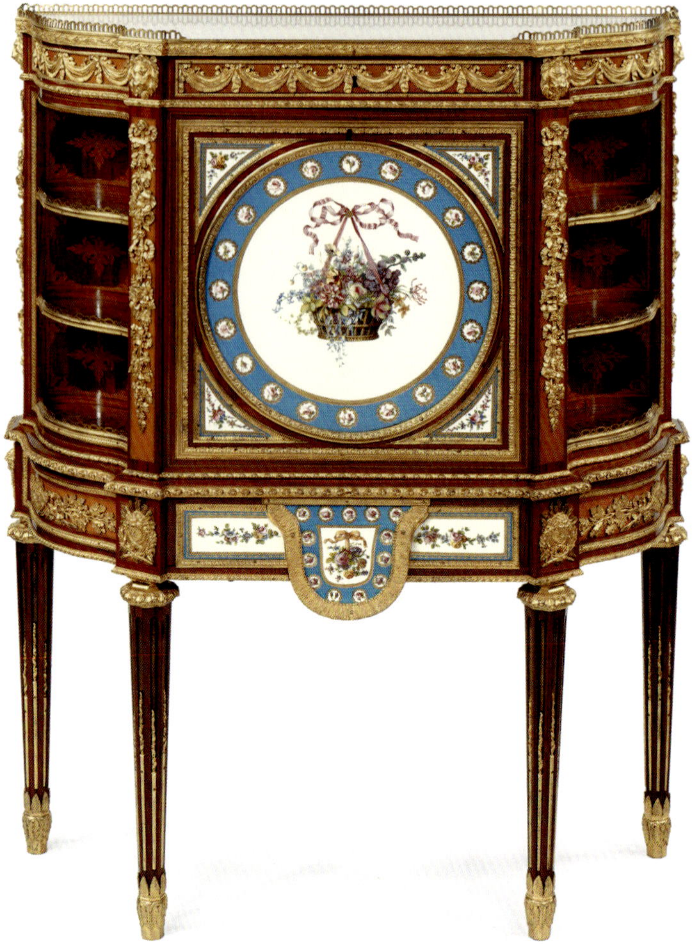

The front of this small *secrétaire* (a type of desk) opens to reveal a writing surface, as well as several drawers and cubbyholes, allowing its owner to both write and lock up private letters and documents. The exterior is fitted with delicate porcelain plaques, a specialty of the royal French porcelain manufactory at Sèvres. The large circular plaque is a technical tour de force of flower painting. The fashion for mounting costly porcelain plaques onto furniture was introduced by Parisian dealers of luxury goods in the 1760s, and Carlin, the maker of this desk, counted among the most skilled in the technique. J. Paul Getty appreciated such pieces of furniture; this *secrétaire* is one of two he purchased, along with two small tables and another writing desk bearing Sèvres plaques.

Bed *(Lit à la polonaise)*

French (Paris), circa 1775–80
Gilt and painted walnut; gilt iron; modern silk upholstery and *passementerie;* ostrich feathers, 302 × 226 × 179 cm (119 × 89 × 70½ in.), 94.DA.72

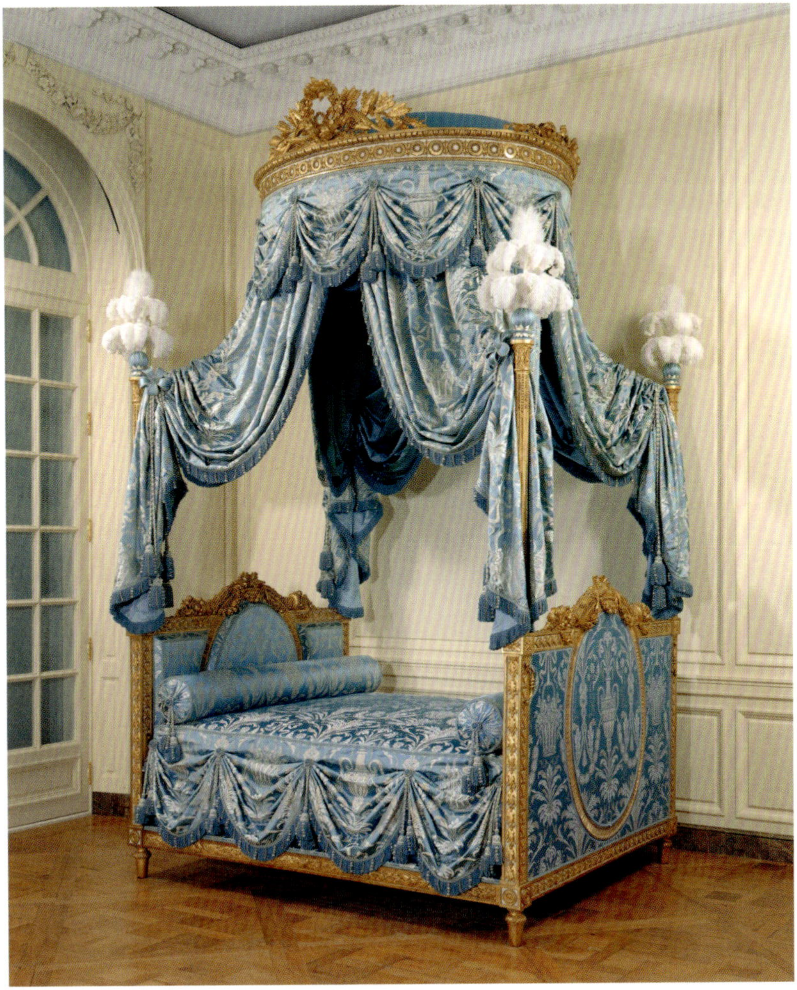

This type of grand, formal bed was meant to occupy a deep recess in the most important bedroom of a private residence, where visitors were received in the morning. It is not known who designed the bed, who executed the frame, or for whom it was made. The head- and footrails are carved in the form of cornucopia, each overflowing with fruit, flowers, sheaves of wheat, and nuts. A repeating pattern of oak leaves and acorns decorates the vertical posts. The modern upholstery and *passementerie* (fringes, cords, and tassels) follow the original designs of the *ornemaniste* (designer) Richard de Lalonde (active 1780–90), as well as historical photographs of the bed dating from the early twentieth century, when it still retained its original hangings.

Side Chair

French, 1780–81

Designed by Jacques Gondoin (1737–1818); carpentered by François-Toussaint Foliot (1748–ca. 1839); carved by Toussaint Foliot (ca. 1815–1798); gilded and painted by Marie-Catherine Renon (active late 1700s–early 1800s). Gessoed and gilt beech; modern silk upholstery, 88.9 × 53.3 × 50.8 cm (35 × 21 × 20 in.), 71.DA.93

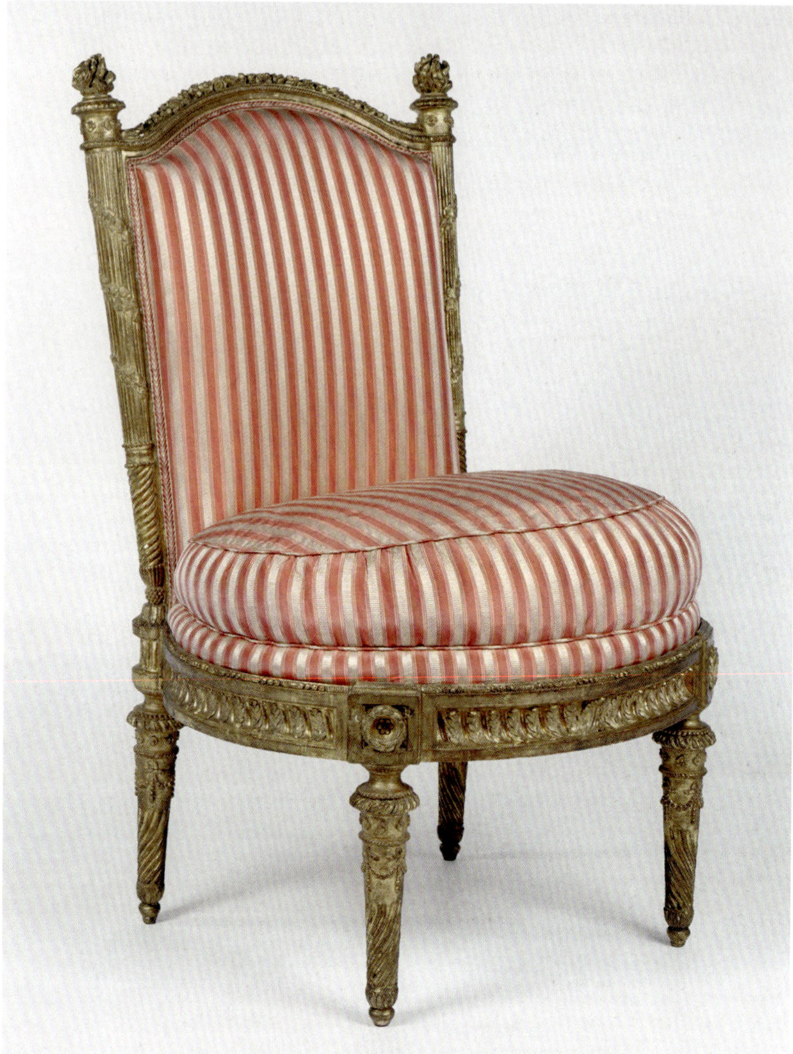

This chair is part of a unique set of eight made for Queen Marie-Antoinette (1755–1793) in 1780–81 to furnish the newly built Belvedere Pavilion. The pavilion was situated in the English gardens of the Petit Trianon, a small château located in the park of the palace at Versailles. The chairs' creation is exceptionally well documented: designed by the royal architect Gondoin in the fashionable Neoclassical style, they were built and carved by the famed Foliot workshop, then gilded and painted by Renon, widow of the royal painter and gilder. Originally, the carved wood was painted white and embellished with gilt decoration, and the silk upholstery was decorated with arabesques and flowers, which would have given the chairs a colorful appearance, characteristic of the newest tastes.

Garniture of Three Vases

French (Sèvres manufactory), 1781
Designed by Jacques-François Deparis (active 1746–97); at least one vase modeled by Étienne-Henry Bono (active 1754–81); reserves painted by Antoine Caton (active 1753–98); gilded by Étienne-Henri Le Guay père (active 1748–96); enamel jeweling by Philippe Parpette (active 1755–1806).

Soft-paste porcelain, *beau bleu* ground color, polychrome enamel decoration, enamel imitating jewels, gilding, and gold foil, vase 1 (left): 40.8 × 24.8 × 18.4 cm (16 1/16 × 9 3/4 × 7 1/4 in.); vase 2 (center): 47 × 27.6 × 19.4 cm (18 1/2 × 10 7/8 × 7 5/8 in.); vase 3 (right): 40.5 × 25.4 × 18.3 cm (15 15/16 × 10 × 7 3/16 in.), 84.DE.718.1–.3

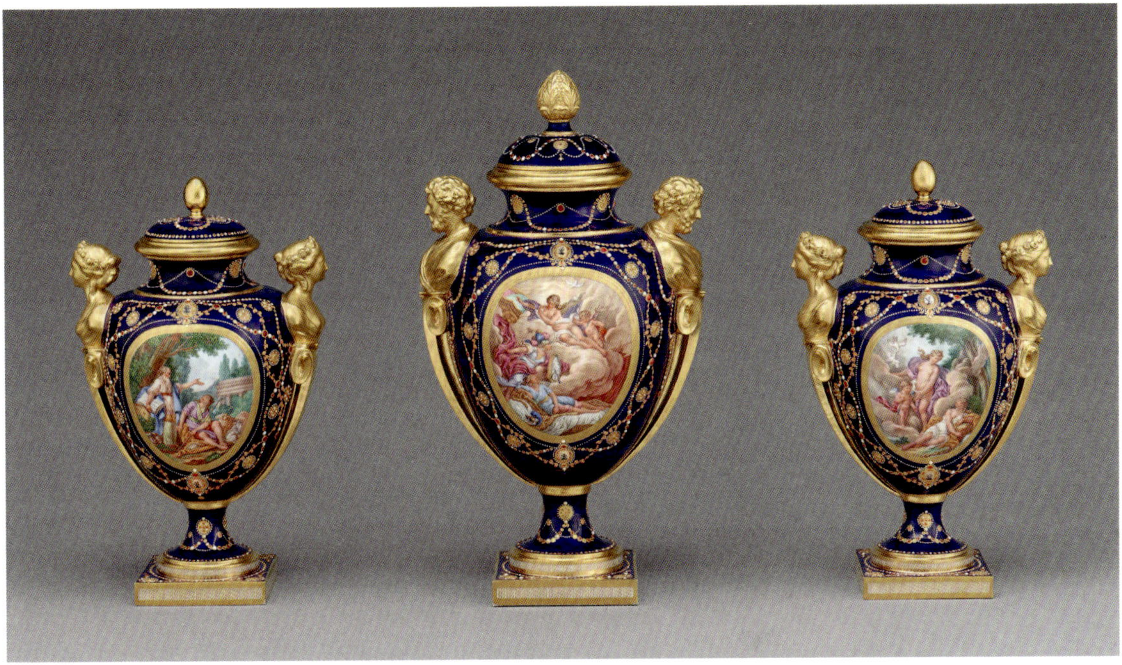

These lavish vases were purchased by the French king Louis XVI (1754–1793) in 1781 for his library in the palace at Versailles. They are of a type known as *vases des âges*, a shape produced at the royal porcelain manufactory at Sèvres in three sizes distinguished by their "handles": bearded male heads for the largest size (center); female heads for the middle size (left and right); and boys' heads for the small size (not represented in the Getty collection). These vases are rare examples of large-scale porcelain decorated with jeweled enameling, a process that involved applying patterned gold foil enameled with different colors to the surface, creating a jewel-like effect. The painted scenes are based on illustrations from one of Louis's favorite books, *The Adventures of Telemachus* (1699) by François Fénelon.

Cup and Saucer

French (Sèvres manufactory), circa 1782
Soft-paste porcelain, polychrome enamel, and gilding, cup: 6.8 × 6.9 × 9.7 cm (2 11/16 × 2 11/16 × 3 13/16 in.); saucer: 3.2 × 14 cm (1 1/4 × 5 1/2 in.), 2022.34

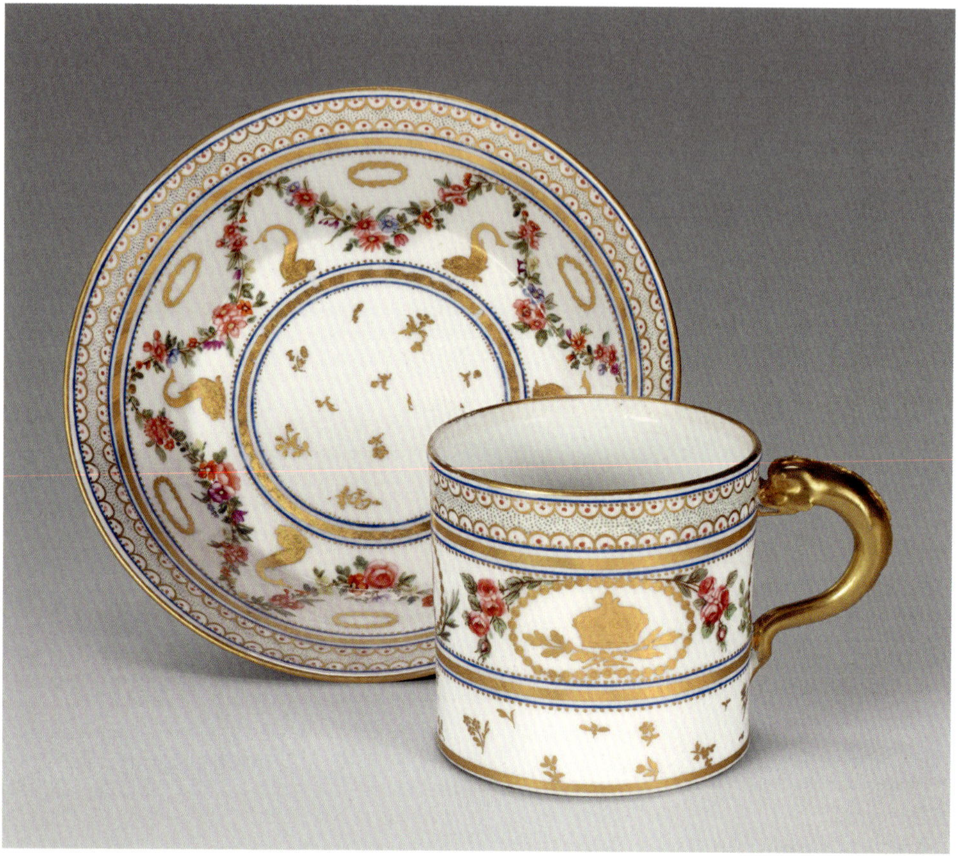

This cup and saucer commemorate the birth of the *dauphin*, the first son of King Louis XVI (1754–1793) and Queen Marie-Antoinette (1755–1793), on October 22, 1781. The heir to the French throne—the king's eldest son—was traditionally known as the *dauphin* since he was, from birth, the titular head of Dauphiné, a province in southeastern France. Since *dauphin* also means "dolphin" in French, a series of dolphins adorns the inside of the saucer, and the cup features a gilt dolphin at the front, a crown at each side, and a dolphin-shaped handle, a new type of decoration introduced by the royal porcelain manufactory at Sèvres to mark the occasion. The young *dauphin*, Louis Joseph, died a few years later, on June 4, 1789, just as the French Revolution was beginning.

Mantel Clock

French (Paris), circa 1785
Clock case attributed to Pierre-Philippe Thomire (1751–1843, master 1772); design attributed to Jean-Guillaume Moitte (1746–1810); rings enameled by Henri-François Dubuisson (active until ca. 1823, master 1769). Patinated bronze, gilt bronze, enameled metal, *vert Maurin des Alpes* marble, and white marble, 53 × 63.8 × 23.5 cm (20⅞ × 25⅛ × 9¼ in.), 82.DB.2

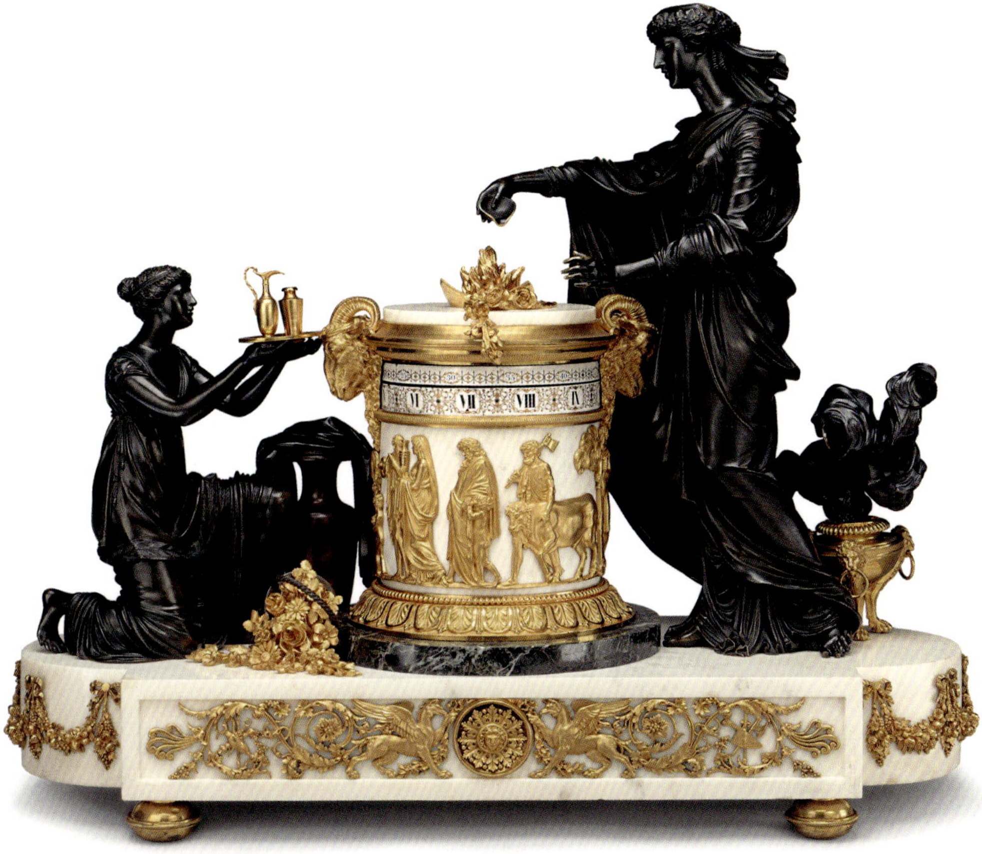

On a white marble base, two Vestal Virgins—so called because they are consecrated to the Roman goddess of the hearth, Vesta—tend to a flame and pour libations onto it in honor of the goddess. The white marble altar, decorated with a gilt-bronze relief depicting a sacrificial procession, contains the clock movement. A spray of gilt-bronze flowers overhanging the front edge of the altar serves as a pointer to the time, which may be read from the Roman numerals on the horizontally revolving hour and minute rings below. In this late-eighteenth-century model, all traditional semblance of a clock is gone, and the object takes the form of a piece of decorative sculpture, its basic function not obvious at first glance.

Jean-Antoine Houdon

French, 1741–1828

Bust of Marie-Sébastien-Charles-François Fontaine de Biré, 1785

Marble, overall with socle:

82.3 × 55 × 34.7 cm

(32 3/8 × 21 5/8 in. × 13 11/16 in.), 2003.102

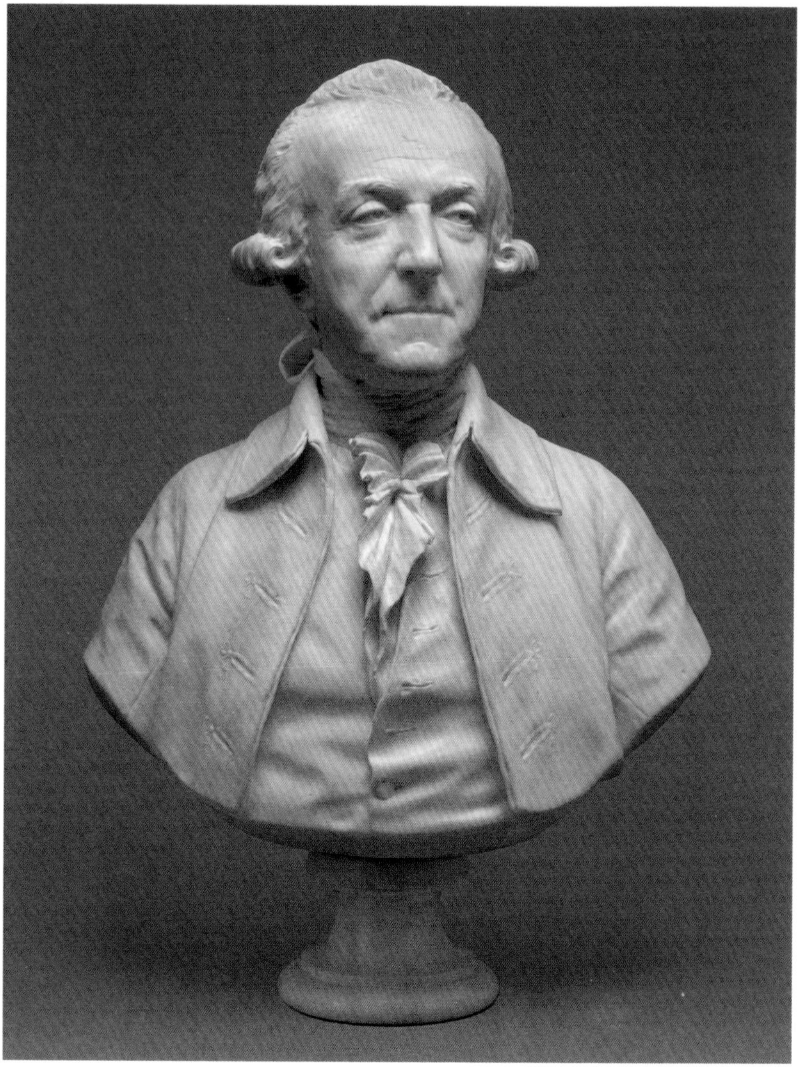

Houdon's bust of Monsieur de Biré (1727–1803) epitomizes the imperious image of a high-level public servant in late eighteenth-century France. It may have been commissioned to commemorate Biré's appointment in 1782 as a treasury official in the War Department in Paris. Houdon's sitter is elegantly restrained in his pose yet has a hint of a smile playing around his mouth. The fine wrinkles, slightly sagging flesh, and pupils of the eyes exemplify Houdon's breathtaking sculptural virtuosity. This bust takes its rightful place in the sculptor's celebrated pantheon of male portraits, which includes such French luminaries as King Louis XVI, the marquis de Lafayette, and Voltaire, as well as the Americans George Washington, Benjamin Franklin, and Thomas Jefferson.

Rolltop Desk
German, 1787–88
Attributed to David Roentgen (1743–1807); mounts by François Remond (1747–1812). Oak, fir, and Scots pine veneered with mahogany and maple burl; gilt-bronze mounts; steel fittings, 168.3 × 155.9 × 89.3 cm (66¼ × 61⅜ × 35$^{3}/_{16}$ in.), 72.DA.47

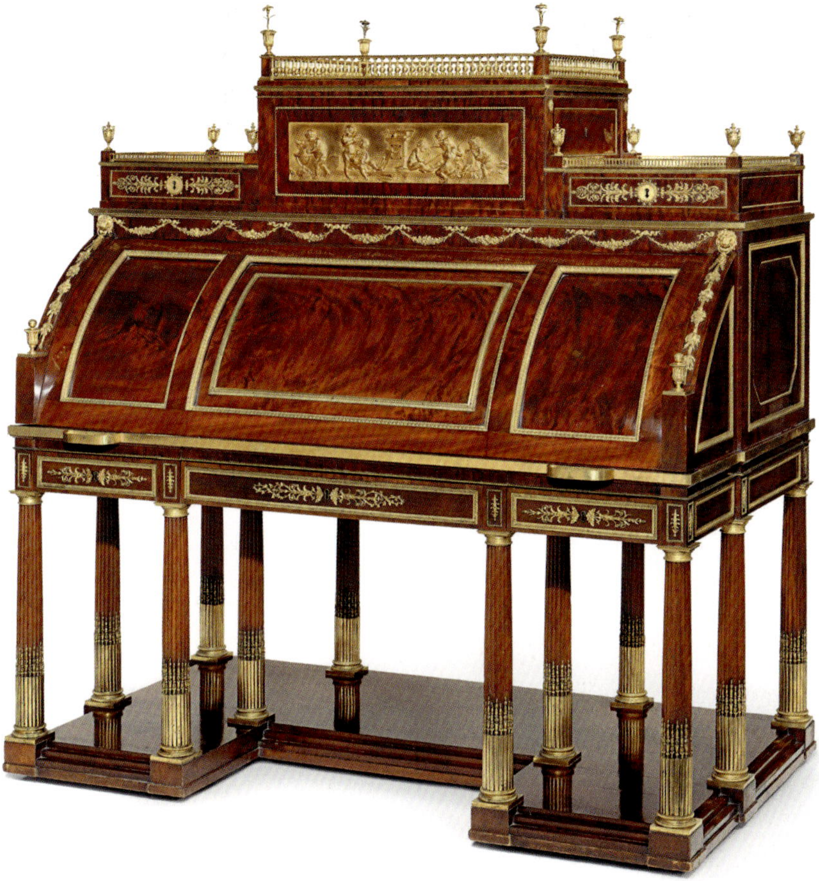

This monumental rolltop desk is characteristic of the distinctive Neoclassical style made famous by the German *ébéniste* (cabinetmaker) David Roentgen at his workshop in Neuwied. Standing on twelve fluted legs, the desk is decorated with exquisite hardwood veneers, as well as delicate gilt-bronze mounts made by the French gilder François Remond. The desk is fitted with numerous complex mechanical devices, a specialty of Roentgen's. When the writing surface is pulled out, a mechanism automatically draws back the rolltop, revealing the drawers and pigeonholes inside the desk. Behind the large gilt-bronze plaque at center is a folding stand for reading and writing with movable compartments that open at the turn of a key.

Cabinet

French (Paris), 1788
Jean Benneman (1748–?, master 1785).
Oak veneered with ebony, mahogany, and lacquer and set with seventeenth- and eighteenth-century *pietre dure* plaques; gilt-bronze mounts; *bleu turquin* marble top, 92.2 × 165.4 × 64.1 cm ($36^{5}/_{16}$ × $65^{1}/_{8}$ × $25^{1}/_{4}$ in.), 78.DA.361

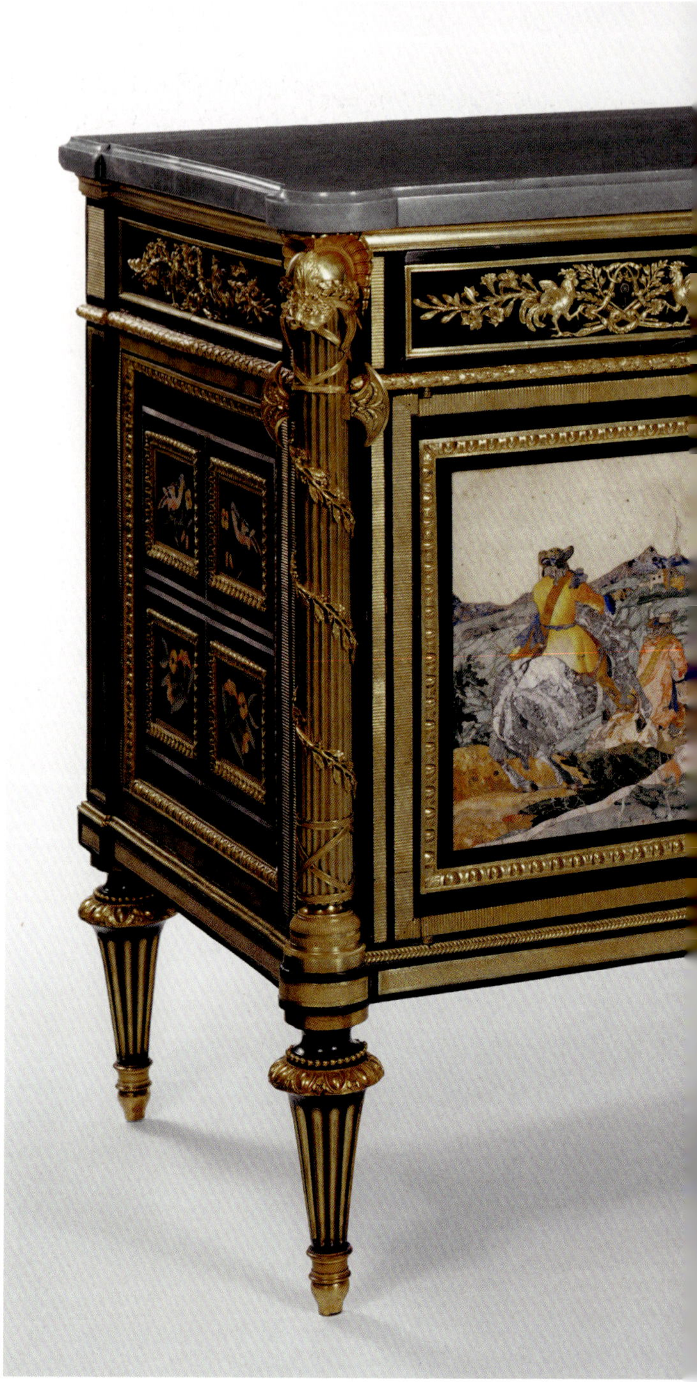

This cabinet was one of a pair delivered in 1788 to the Château de Saint-Cloud, intended for the bedroom of King Louis XVI (1754–1793). Surviving documents confirm that this cabinet was originally veneered with panels of Japanese lacquer, a fashionable but expensive imported material that was difficult to obtain, even for royal workshops such as the one operated by Benneman. Nevertheless, the preserved invoice lists the elaborately chased and gilt mounts as the most expensive part of the piece: elements including cockerels (a symbol of France) and military trophies that reference the Roman Empire emphasize the power and legitimacy of the king. In the early 1800s, the lacquer panels were replaced with hardstone plaques to match the new owner's taste.

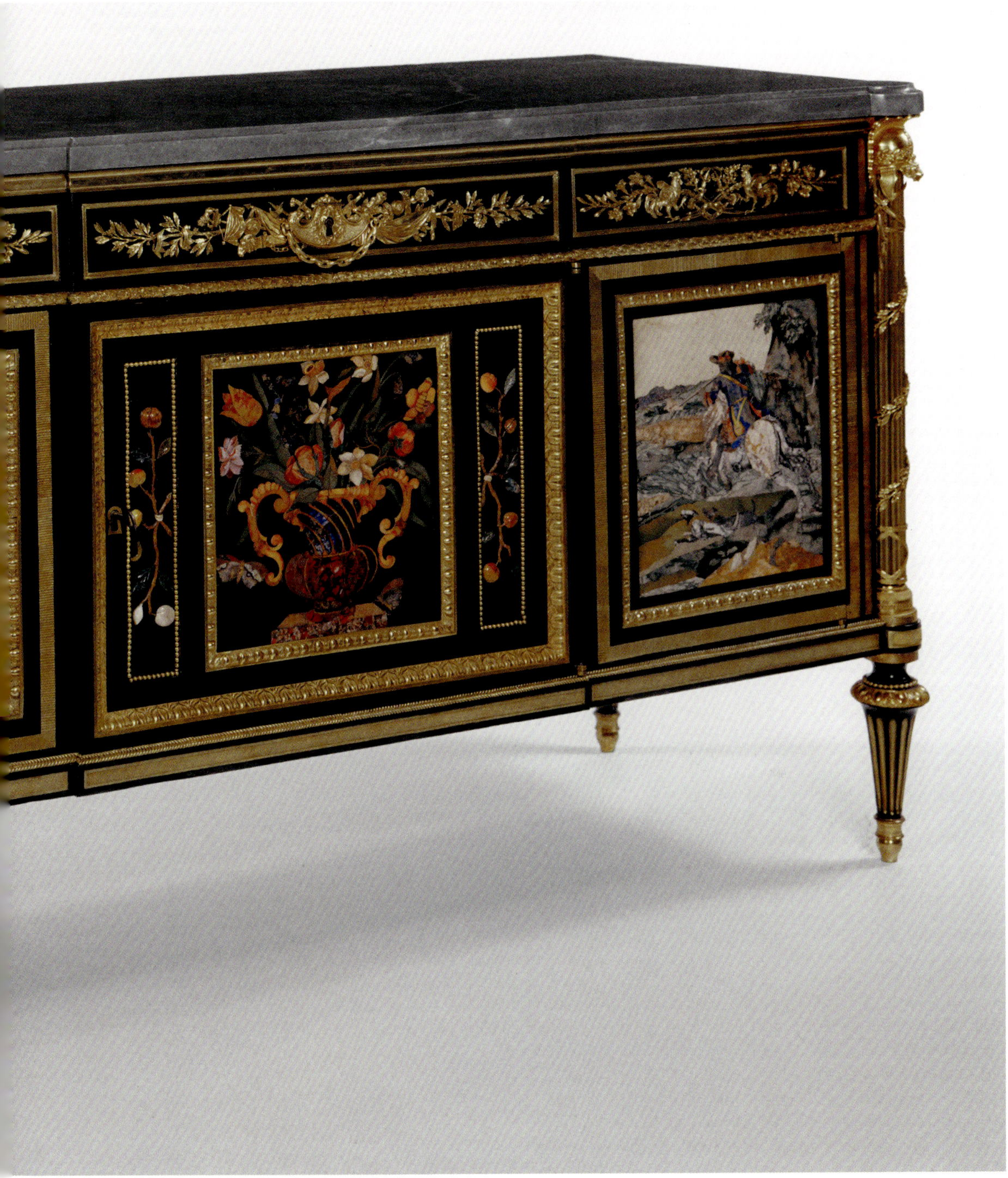

Table

Italian (possibly Naples), 1790s

Francesco Abbiati (active ca. 1780–ca. 1800). Oak, walnut, and poplar veneered with purplewood, satinwood, ebony, and various fruitwoods, 77.8 × 87.5 × 87.5 cm ($30\frac{5}{8} \times 34\frac{7}{16} \times 34\frac{7}{16}$ in.), 84.DA.77

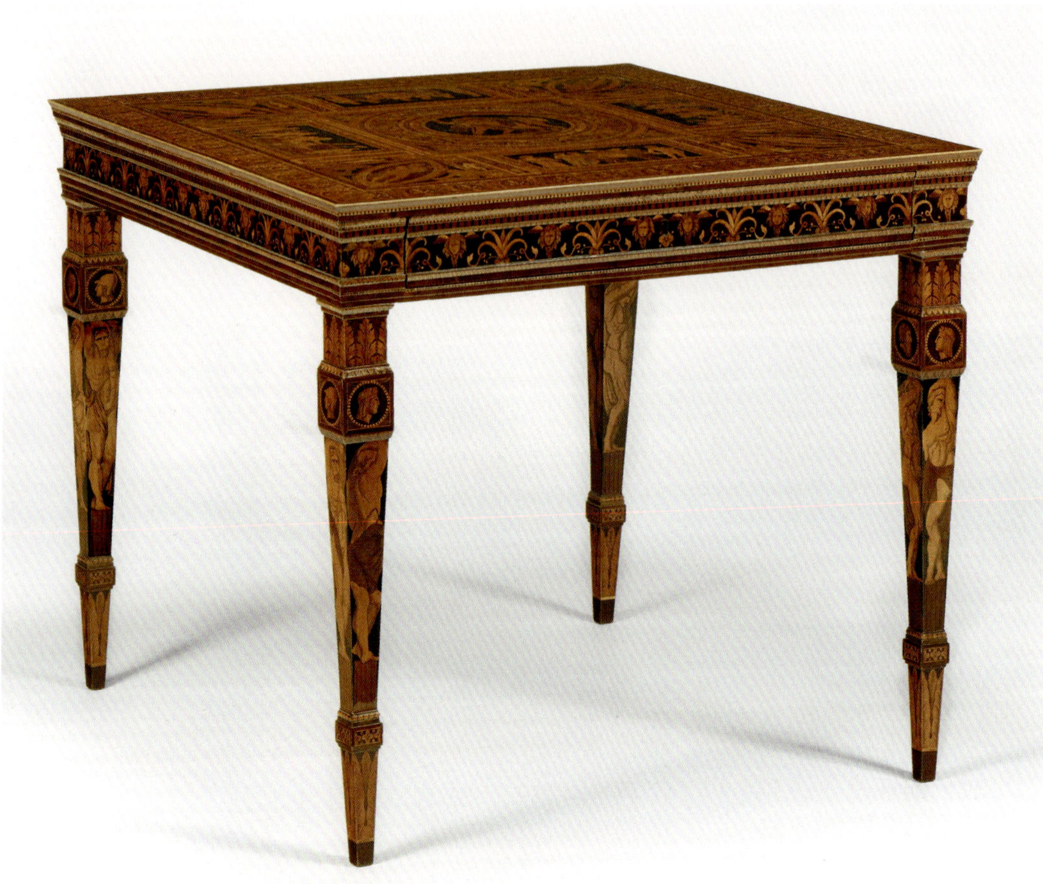

The cabinetmaker Francesco Abbiati is known especially for his elaborate marquetry designs using motifs derived from antiquity. Here, the tabletop shows scenes of classical subjects copied after engravings of a series of ancient Roman marble carvings in the Museo Pio-Clementino in the Vatican. The engravings were published in 1788 by Ennio Quirino Visconti (1751–1818) in his book on the collection in that museum, which was founded in 1771. Visconti was an expert in antique sculpture and the museum's director. In this remarkable table, produced a few years after publication of that volume, Abbiati veneered every surface with finely detailed classical motifs, including the legs, each of which inventively displays a male nude as if carved in the round.

Painted Wood Panel

French (Paris), 1790–95
Designed by Claude-Nicolas Ledoux (1736–1806); panel painted by Jean-Siméon Rousseau de la Rottière (1747–1820, master 1771) and Jules-Hughes Rousseau (1743–1806). Painted and gilt oak; painted and gilt plaster, H (with frame): 266.1 cm (104¾ in.); W (with frame): 71.4 cm (28⅛ in.), 98.DH.149.9

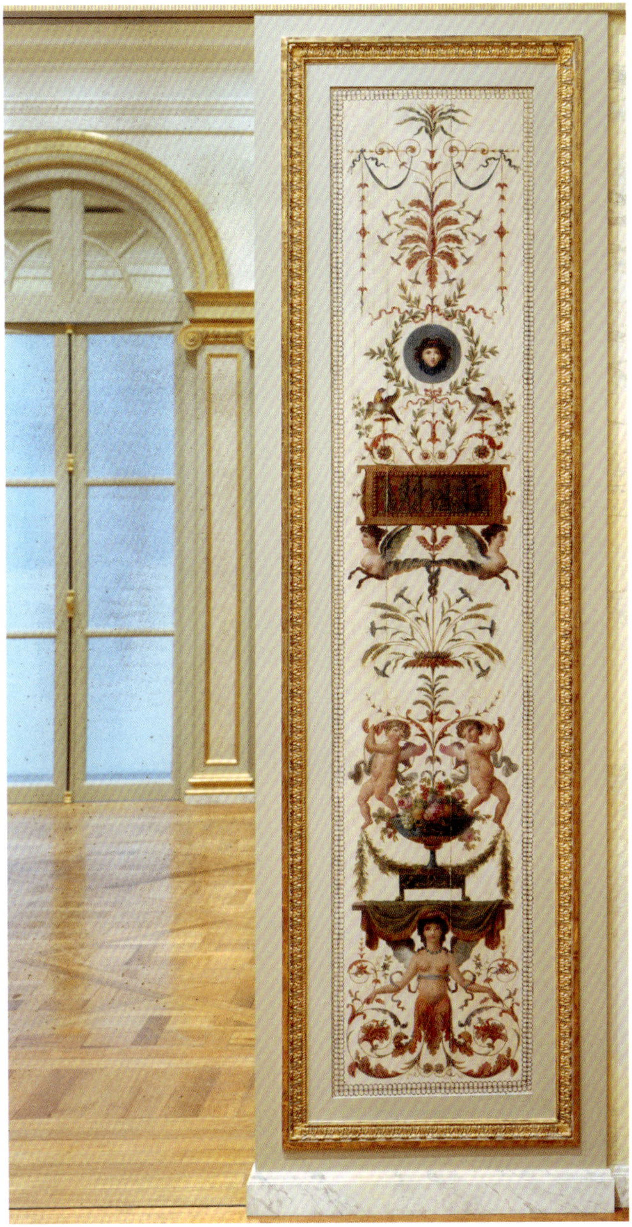

This panel formed part of the decoration of the *salon de compagnie* (formal reception room) in the Parisian townhouse of Jean-Baptiste Hosten (1713–1795), who derived his fortune from a sugar plantation in the French colony of Saint-Domingue (modern Haiti), where two hundred enslaved people worked. It was designed by Claude-Nicolas Ledoux, one of the most celebrated French architects of his generation. The ornamentation, which combines graceful arabesques and winged centaurs (human-horse hybrids) with palmettes and sphinxes, shows some of the finest decorative work of the late 1700s. Inspired by the art of ancient Rome, such designs are characteristic of the Neoclassical style, which was fashionable in Europe during that time.

Mantel Clock

French, circa 1790–1800
Clock movement by Nicolas-Alexandre Folin (ca. 1750–after 1815); enamel plaques by Georges-Adrien Merlet (born 1754; active 1780s). Gilt bronze; enameled metal; white marble base; glass and gilt-metal case, 45.7 × 27.6 × 14 cm (18 × $10\frac{7}{8}$ × $5\frac{1}{2}$ in.), 72.DB.57

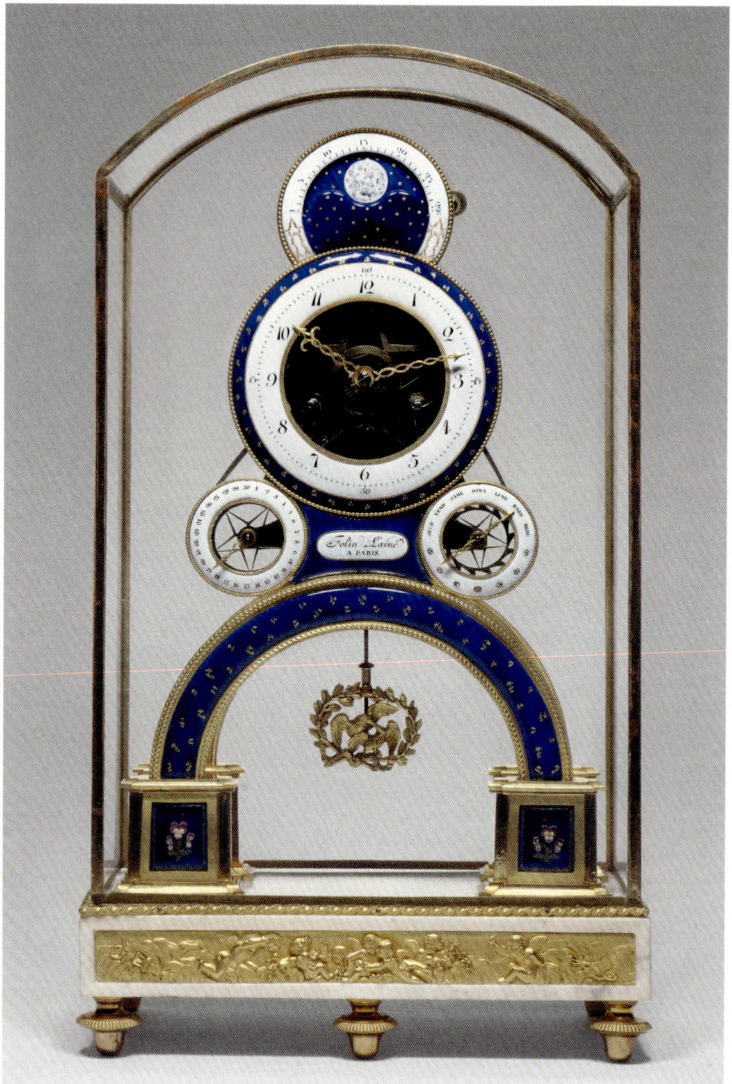

This type of mantel clock is known as a skeleton clock because of its exposed inner workings, allowing the viewer to marvel at the precise movements and interactions of its various mechanical parts. Four enameled dials display different information: the central dial tells the time; that at lower left, the day of the week; that at lower right, the day of the month; and that at the top, the current phase of the moon. This type of timepiece became fashionable at the end of the 1700s, at a time of growing interest in the sciences. The clock's movement is now seen as an object of beauty to be enjoyed and an example of scientific achievement to be admired.

Chandelier

French (Paris), circa 1818–19
Gérard-Jean Galle (1788–1846). Gilt bronze; enameled metal; glass,
H: 129.5 cm (51 in.); Diam: 96.5 cm (38 in.),
73.DH.76

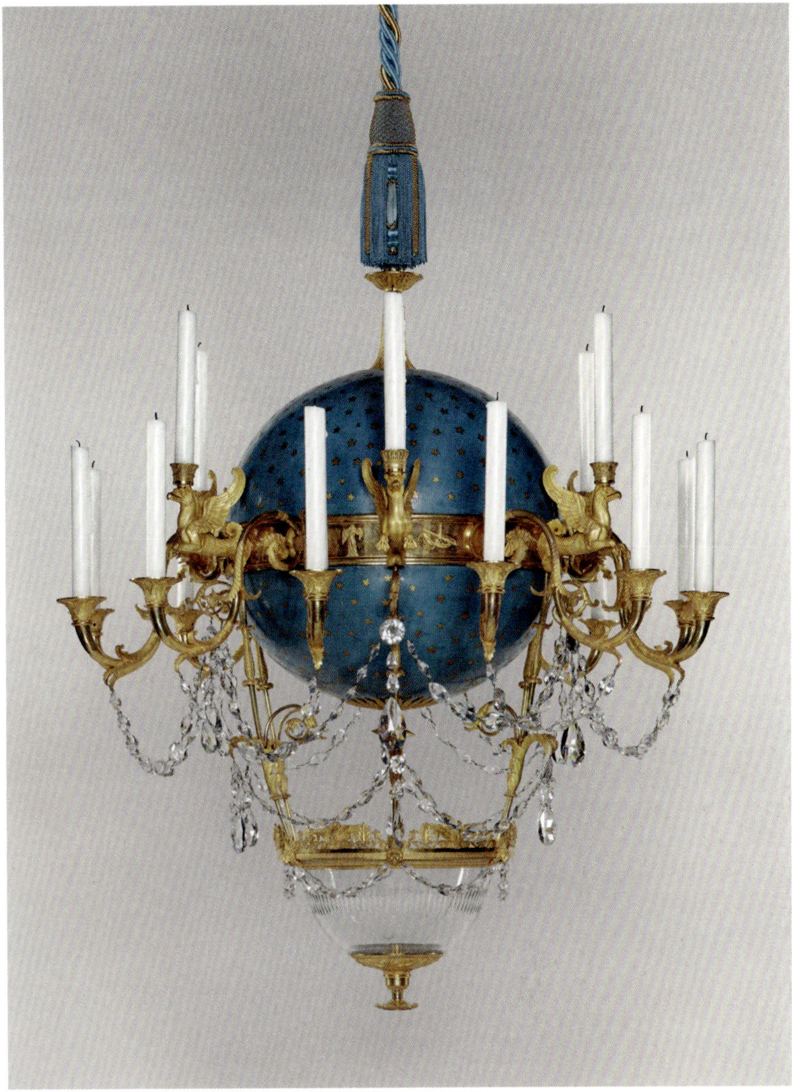

The design of this chandelier resembles a hot-air balloon, much like the one launched by the brothers Joseph-Michel and Jacques-Étienne Montgolfier from the grounds of the palace at Versailles in 1783. The large blue enameled globe at the center of the chandelier is painted with gold stars and encircled by a gilt-bronze band fitted with the signs of the zodiac; six of the eighteen candleholders are in the form of winged griffins (lion-eagle hybrids). When the chandelier was displayed in an 1819 Paris exhibition, Galle's description explained that the glass bowl suspended below was intended to contain goldfish swimming in water. The continuous movement of the fish was meant to give "agreeable recreation to the eye."

Antonio Canova

Italian, 1757–1822

Herm of a Vestal Virgin, 1821–22

Marble, 49.8 × 31.9 × 24.1 cm

(19 5/8 × 12 9/16 × 9 1/2 in.), 85.SA.353

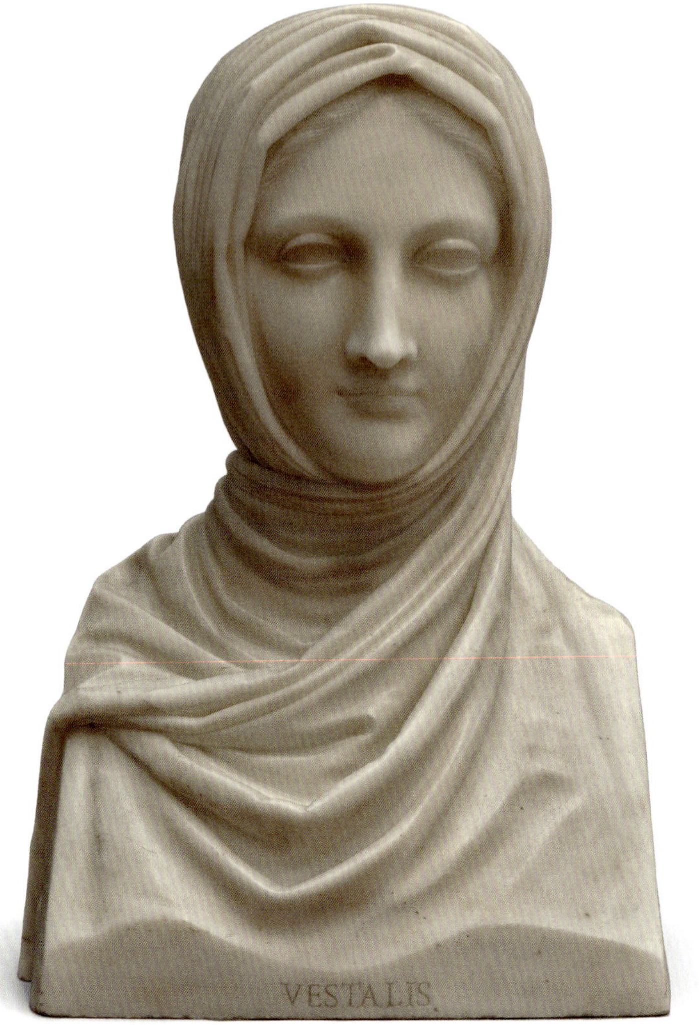

This herm (a squared stone pillar with a carved head) depicts a Vestal Virgin, a priestess consecrated to the Roman goddess of the hearth, Vesta. Canova is recorded to have carved three versions of the subject as part of a series of "ideal heads," as the artist described them, depicting mythological, historical, literary, and allegorical figures. Making multiple iterations allowed the sculptor to refine his portrayal of ideal female beauty. The notion of perfection was especially appropriate for the representation of a Vestal Virgin, for legend held that they were required to be pure of mind and body. This subject became popular in eighteenth- and nineteenth-century art following the excavation of the ancient Casa delle Vestali (House of the Vestals) at Pompeii, Italy.

Charles-Henri-Joseph Cordier
French, 1827–1905
Sudanese Man (Nègre du Soudan), 1856, and *Woman from the French Colonies (Câpresse des Colonies)*, 1861

Bronze, marble, onyx, and silvered and oxidized bronze; gilt and enameled ornaments; green porphyry socles, man: 99.1 × 61 × 35.6 cm (39 × 24 × 14 in.); woman: 94 × 58.4 × 33 cm (37 × 23 × 13 in.), 2022.31

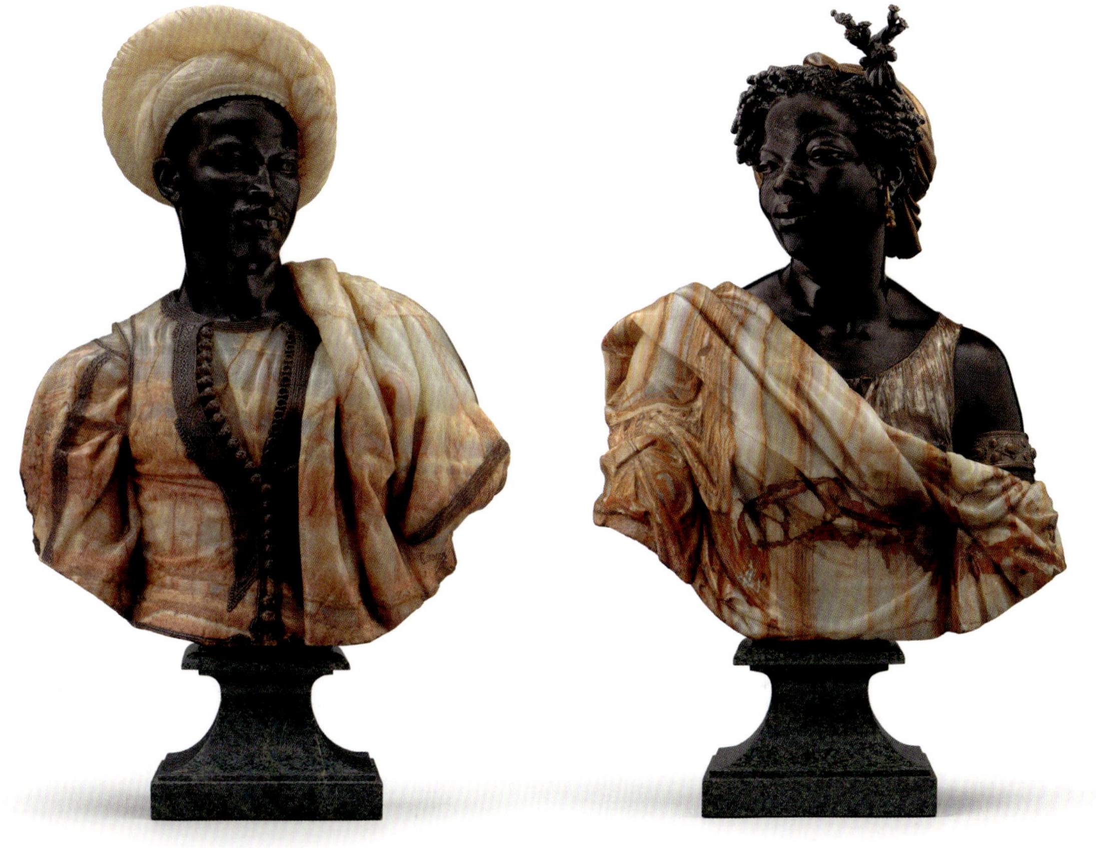

Cordier modeled *Sudanese Man* during a French governmental mission to Algeria in 1856. The sitter, a native of Sudan whose name is unrecorded, lived in Algiers and was a percussionist for religious festivities. Cordier likely portrayed the woman, whose identity also remains unknown, in Paris. The work's historic French title indicates that she was born to one Black and one biracial parent in the French colonies of the Antilles, a group of islands in the Caribbean. These naturalistic portraits combining numerous colorful, luxurious materials exemplify the sculptor's efforts to express his "idea of the universality of beauty." Cordier innovatively applied his artistic skills to the nascent field of ethnography, which at that time used racialized terms, as in these artworks' historic French titles.

Camille Claudel
French, 1864–1943
Torso of a Crouching Woman, modeled circa 1884–85, cast by 1913
Bronze, 35 × 27 × 26 cm
(13¾ × 10⅝ × 10¼ in.), 2018.32

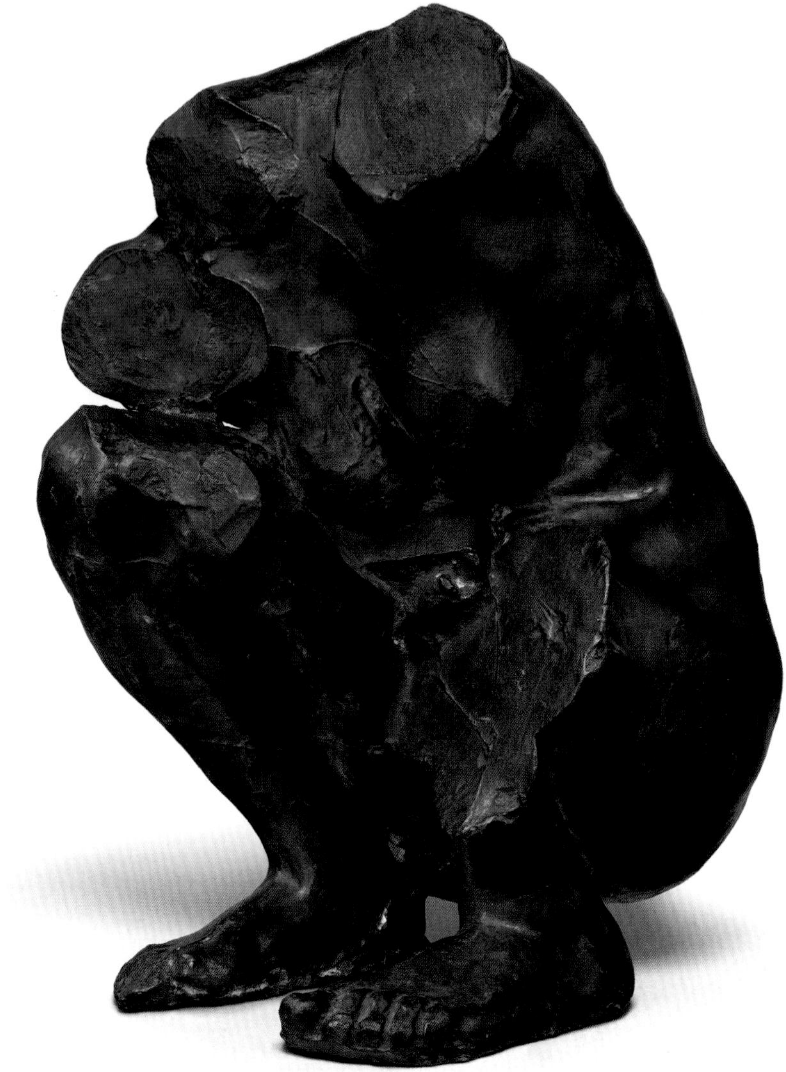

Pain, isolation, and even fear emanate from the contorted pose of this torso, its fragmentary nature reflecting the broken condition of the ancient Greek and Roman sculptures that inspired it. The figure suggests movement through the perfectly mastered balance of the body, with the weight resting firmly on the feet. The harmoniously modeled back presents a delicate study of anatomy, with a subtle illusion of bones and muscle underneath the skin. This sensual and powerful rendering of the human body is characteristic of Claudel's innovative contributions to sculpture at the turn of the twentieth century.

Auguste Rodin

French, 1840–1917

Christ and Mary Magdalene, 1908

Marble, 109.2 × 85.1 × 78.8 cm

(43 × 33½ × 31 in.), 2014.32

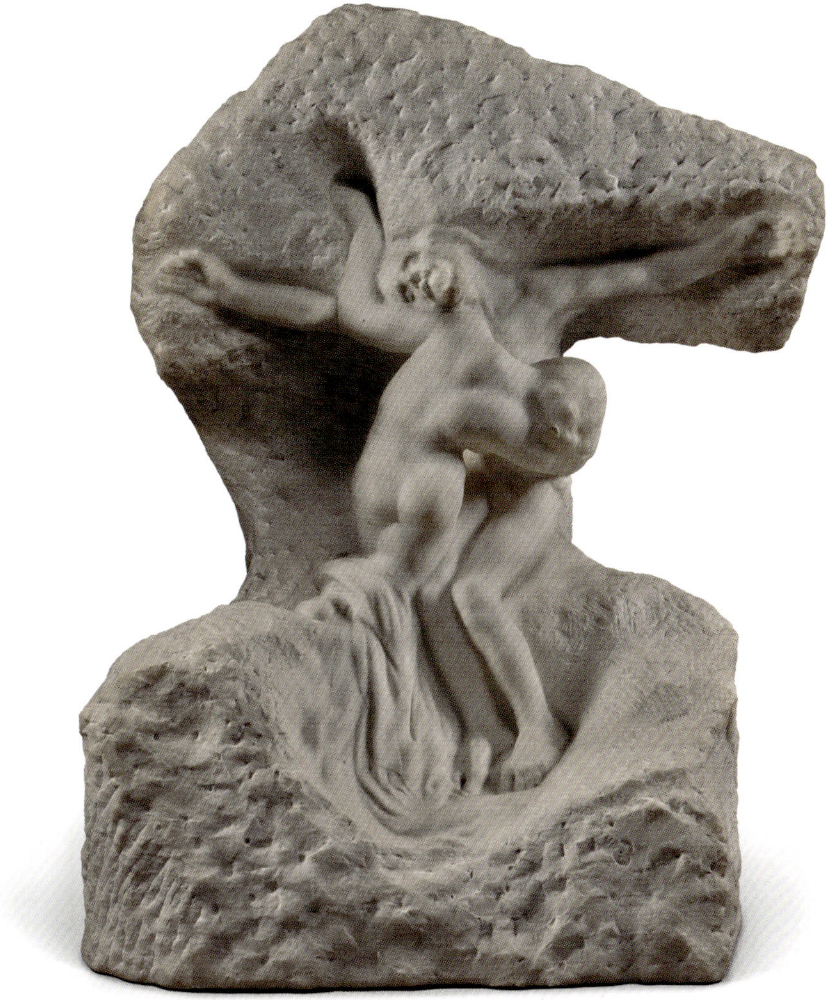

Nailed to a rocky cross, a dying bearded man is mourned by a naked woman kneeling in front of him. Rodin called this group *Christ and Mary Magdalene* but also *The Genius and Pity* and *Prometheus and the Oceanid*. The group's compelling strength stems from the contrast between the highly polished surfaces of the naked flesh and the surrounding rough-hewn marble. This ingenious use of the *non finito* (unfinished) technique reflects the impact that the sculptures of Michelangelo (see p. 228) had on Rodin during his trip to Italy in 1876. The Austrian businessman Karl Wittgenstein (1847–1913) commissioned this marble for his collection in Vienna. Unlike most of Rodin's works, *Christ and Mary Magdalene* was never cast in bronze, and only one other marble version exists, in the Museo Nacional Thyssen-Bornemisza, Madrid.

Barbara Hepworth

British, 1903–1975

Figure for Landscape, designed 1960, cast 1968

Bronze, overall: 271.8 × 132.1 × 71.1 cm (106 × 52 × 28 in.); base: 8.9 × 64.8 × 67.3 cm (3½ × 25½ × 26½ in.). Gift of Fran and Ray Stark, 2005.108

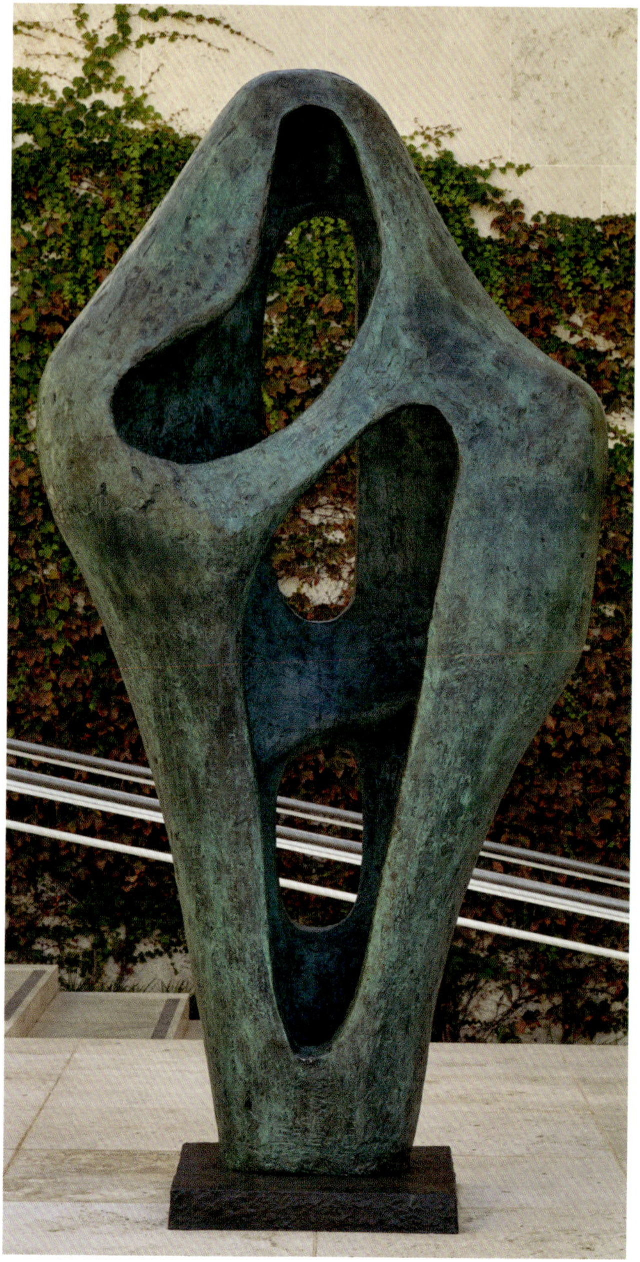

Hepworth is widely known as one of the first British sculptors to produce abstract, as opposed to figural or representational, works. She believed that art should be enjoyed for the sake of its shape—hence the decidedly freeform style of *Figure for Landscape*. As with many of Hepworth's sculptures, it was inspired by natural forms and conceived for an outdoor, public setting. The sculpture's concave inner space is a recurrent element in Hepworth's work and evokes maternal protectiveness. This space has also been said to echo the rhythmic and sloping qualities of an inlet or cove, while the large and majestic overall form is reminiscent of wave-worn Neolithic rocks.

Alexander Calder

American, 1898–1976

Spiny Top, Curly Bottom, 1963

Painted steel, 224.8 × 181 × 174 cm ($88\frac{1}{2} \times 71\frac{1}{4} \times 68\frac{1}{2}$ in.). Gift of Fran and Ray Stark, 2005.104.1

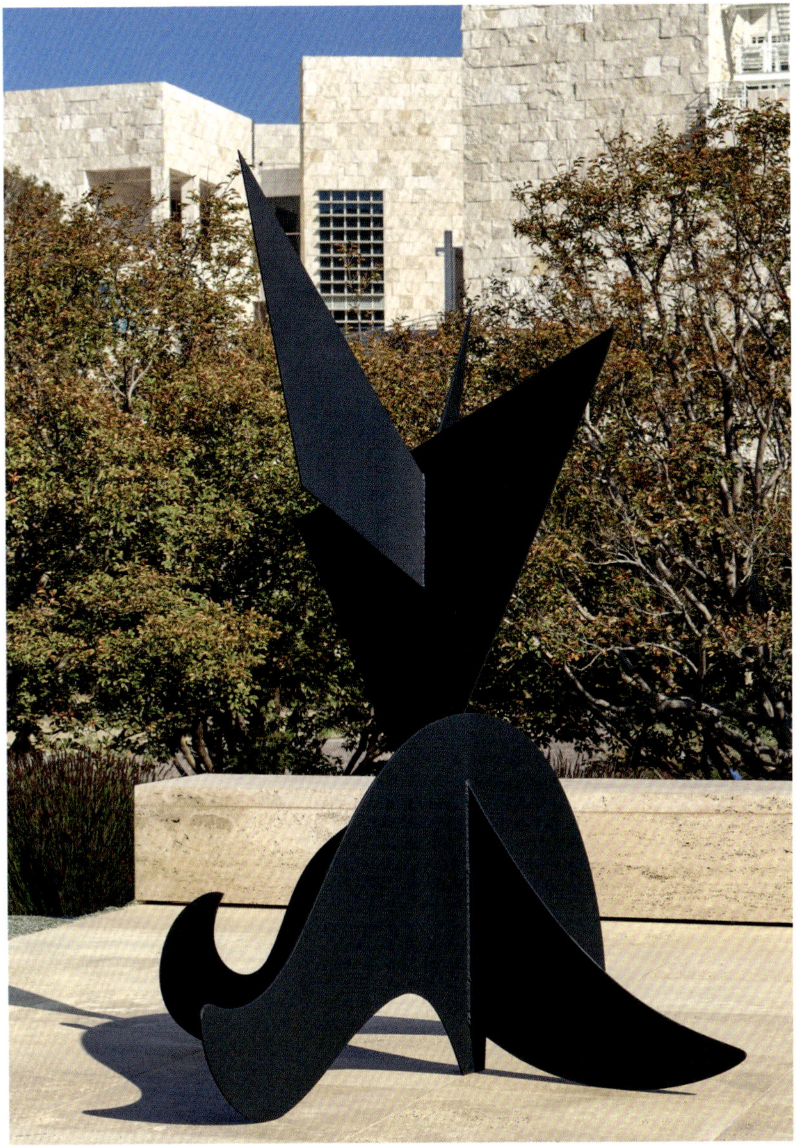

Calder made *Spiny Top, Curly Bottom* from five pieces of machine-cut steel, welded together and painted in the artist's trademark black. It is one of Calder's works called stabiles—completely stationary abstract forms. Though Calder is often admired for his mobiles, which are kinetic and easily set in motion by the wind, the stabiles are notable for their fixed solidity, without the need for a base or support. This strength, when considered in contrast to its refined elegance, is one of the most alluring aspects of the work.

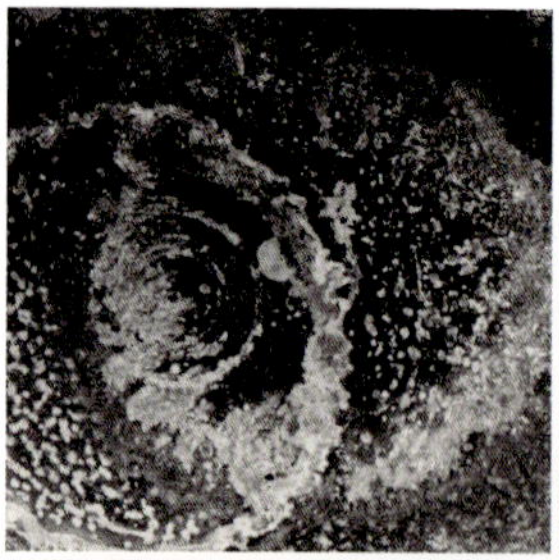
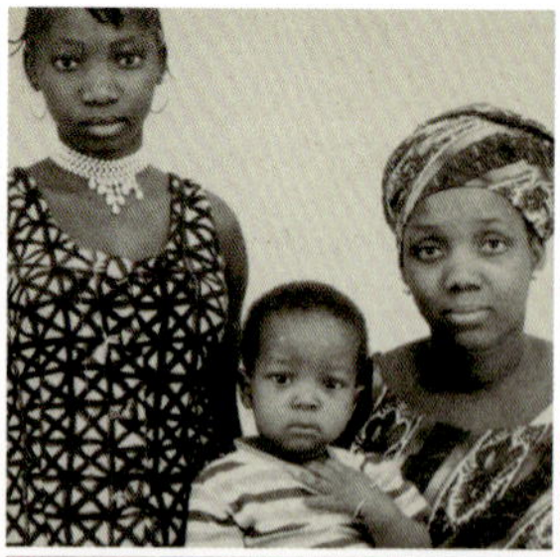
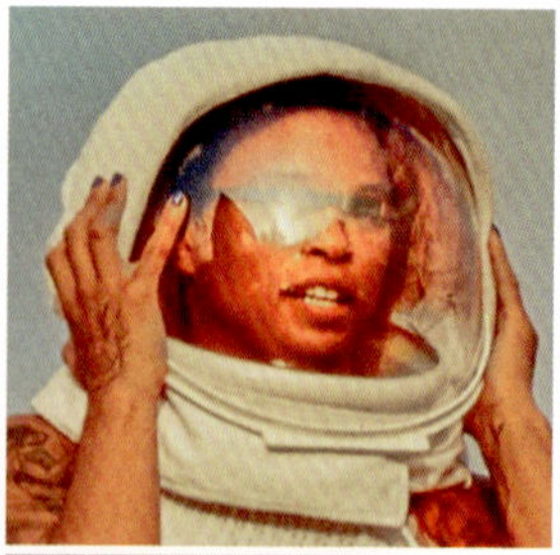
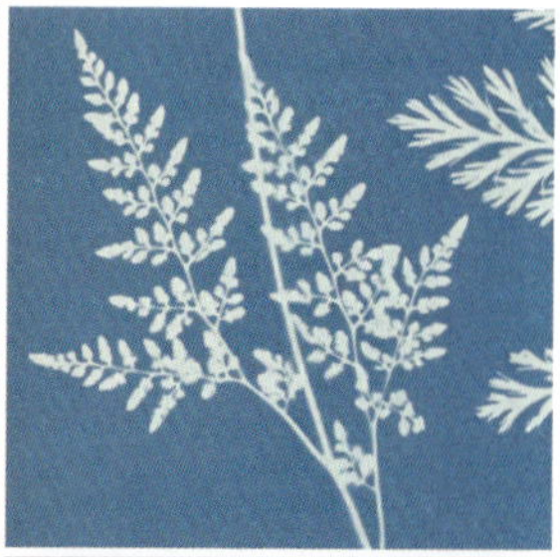
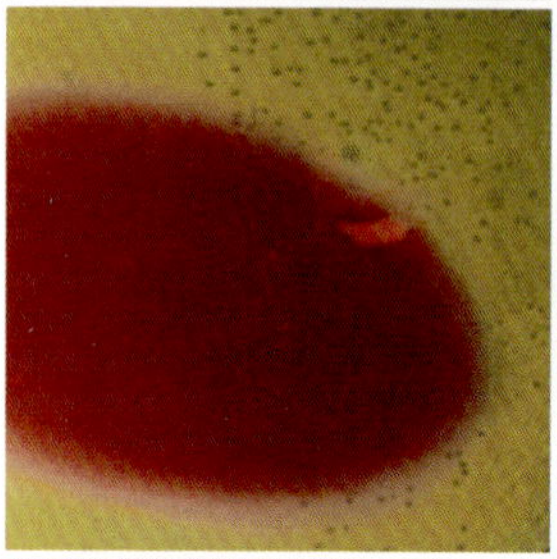
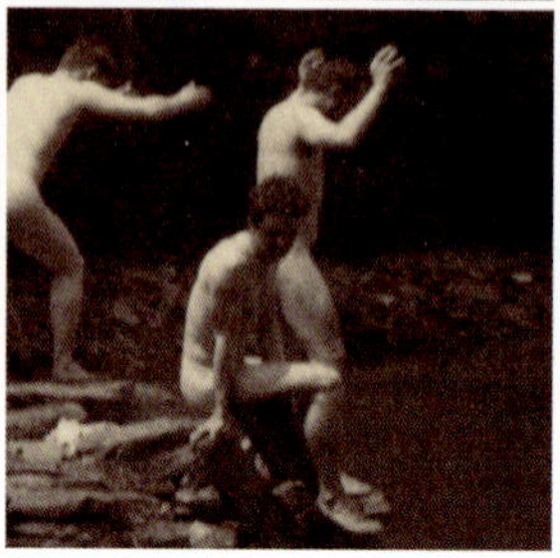
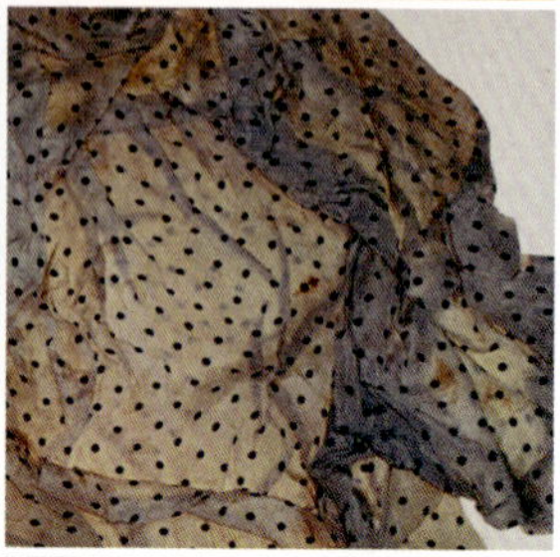
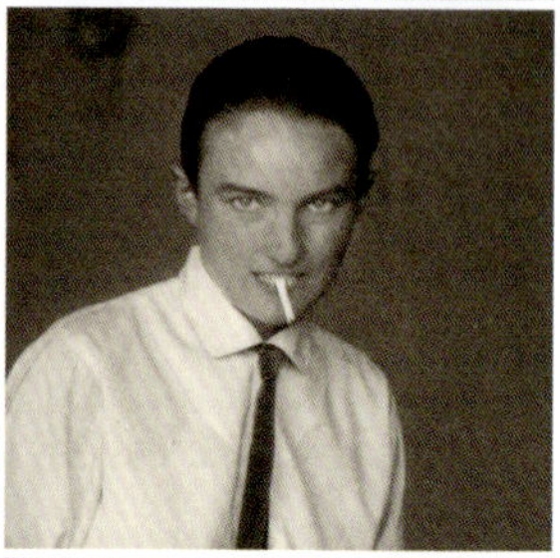
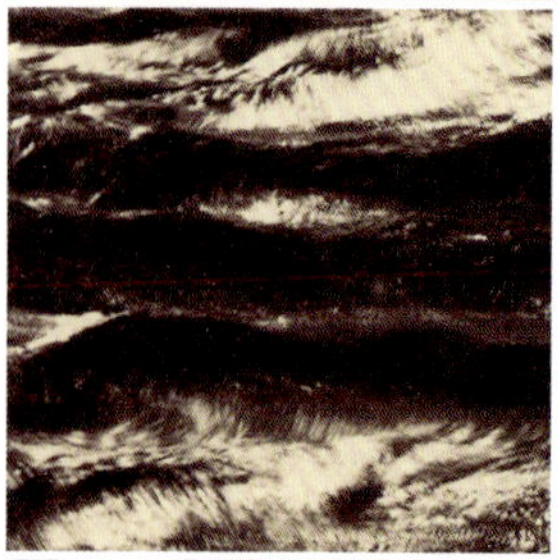
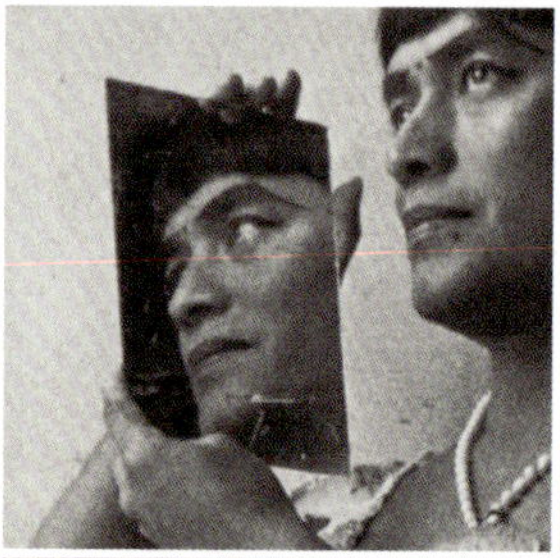
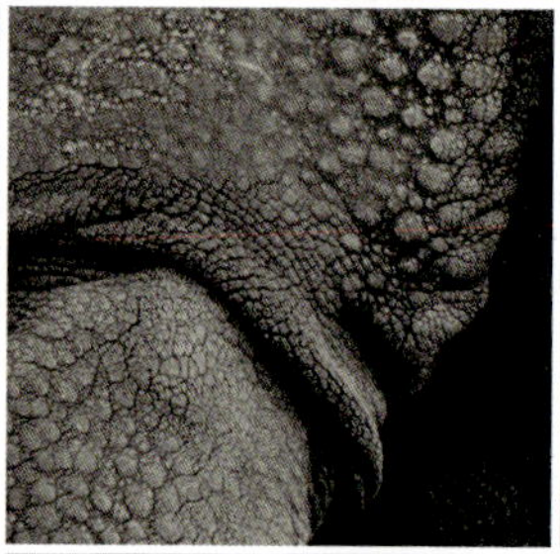
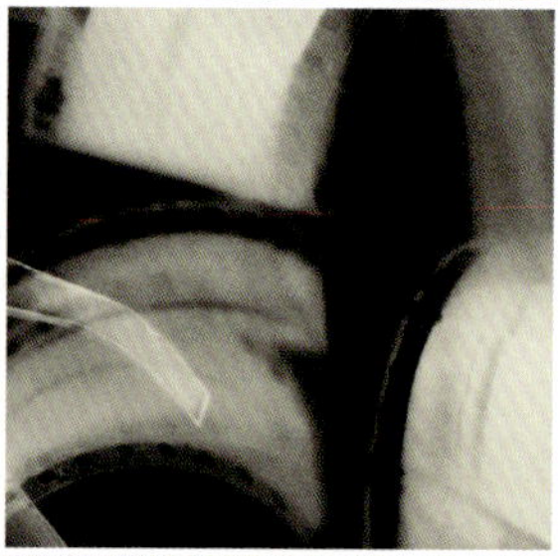
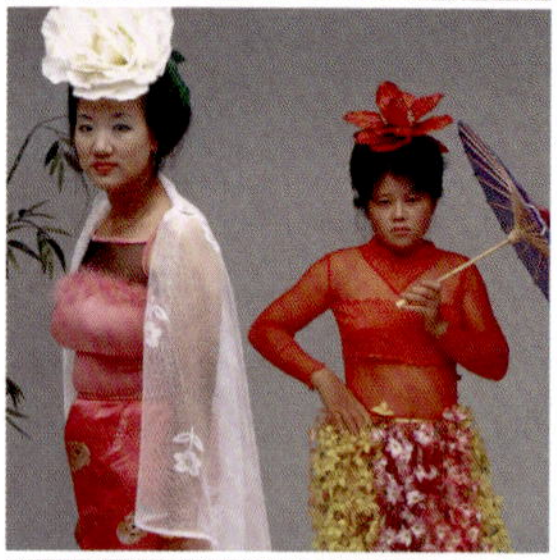
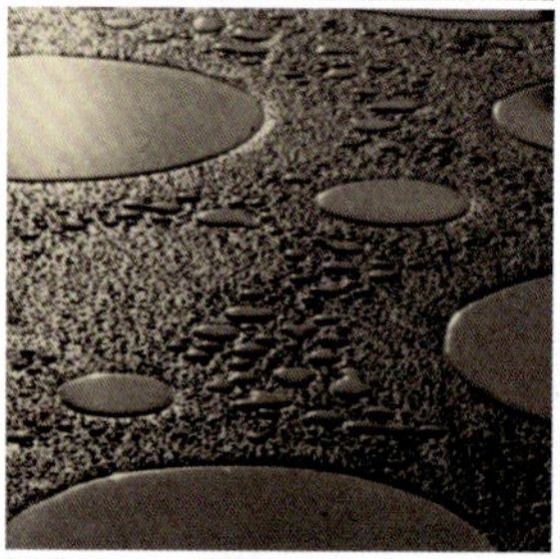
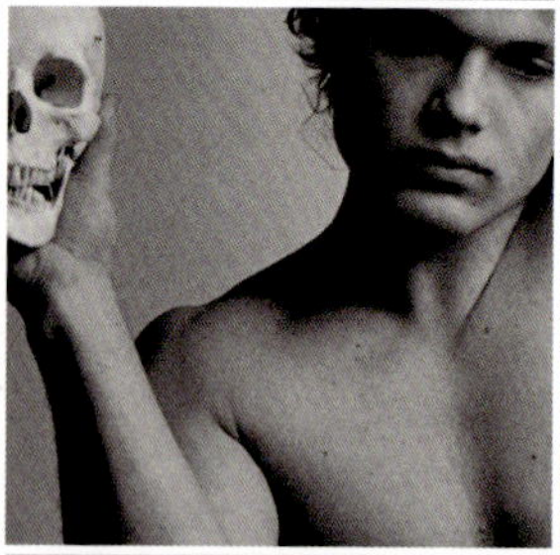
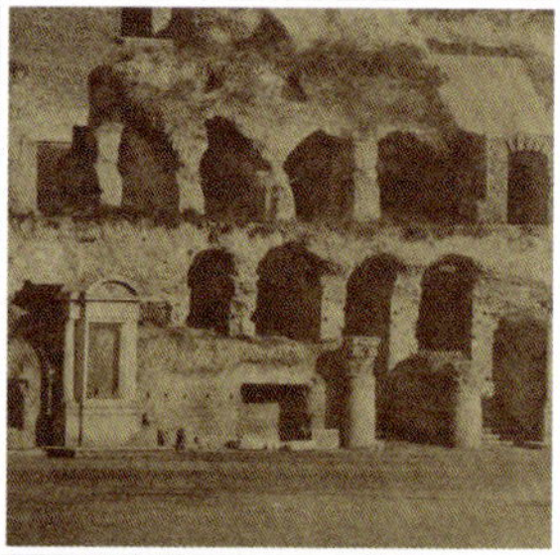
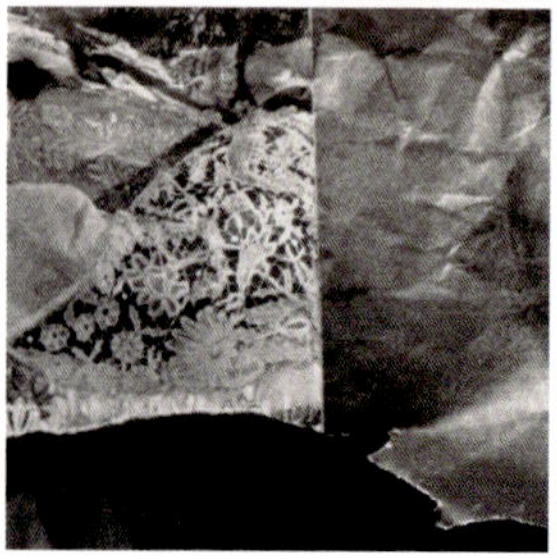
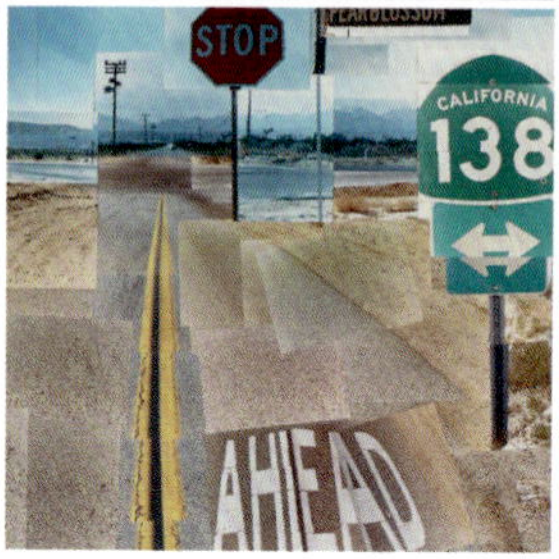
STOP
CALIFORNIA
138
AHEAD
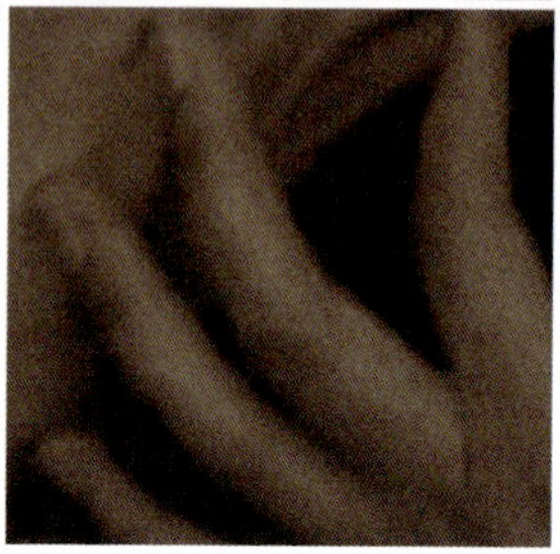
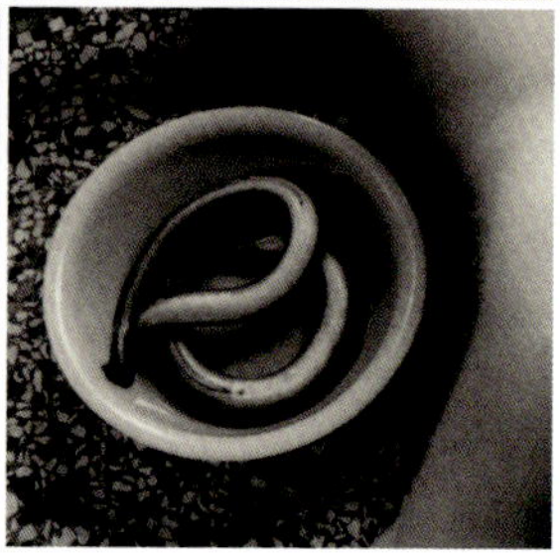

Photographs

In 1984 the Getty Museum announced its creation of a new curatorial department dedicated to photographs. Initial holdings included more than forty thousand objects from several international private collections, notably, those of Bruno Bischofberger, Arnold Crane, Georg Heusch, André Jammes, Volker Kahmen, and Samuel Wagstaff Jr. This dramatic initiative, which extended well beyond the collecting parameters favored by J. Paul Getty, immediately established the Museum as one of the world's leading centers for the collection and display of photography.

The founding collection was particularly strong in nineteenth- and early twentieth-century European and American photographs, starting with daguerreotypes and the medium's earliest experimental works of the 1830s. Several key historical figures, from Hippolyte Bayard to Julia Margaret Cameron to Man Ray, were also well represented with significant concentrations of works (see pp. 353, 363, 372). Over time, the department has broadened and deepened its holdings by canonical figures like Eugène Atget (p. 369), Manuel Álvarez Bravo, Imogen Cunningham (p. 374), Masahisa Fukase, Graciela Iturbide (p. 396), Gertrude Käsebier, Robert Mapplethorpe (p. 395), Irving Penn (p. 383), and Herb Ritts, among others. With support from the Getty Museum Photographs Council, launched in 2015, the department has further enriched the collection's breadth by acquiring contemporary works by un- or underrepresented artists, not only from the United States, but also from Argentina, Australia, Canada, Japan, Korea, Malaysia, and South Africa.

Forming a mosaic of more than 148,000 photographs that continues to evolve, the collection has been shaped by several generations of dedicated curators and has benefited from the generosity of numerous collectors and patrons. While the department continues to study and add historical works, the current acquisitions program emphasizes local and global artists who have been previously marginalized, including Japanese American photographers active on the West Coast prior to World War II; the Kamoinge collective of Black photographers that emerged in New York in the 1960s; and contemporary Latinx artists from Southern California. By focusing on photographers who explore the challenging issues that contemporary viewers face today while continuing to forge meaningful dialogues with the art of the past, Getty seeks to expand the "canon" and contribute to shaping new histories of photography for the twenty-first century.

William Henry Fox Talbot
British, 1800–1877

The Roofline of Lacock Abbey,
probably 1835–39
Salt-fixed photogenic negative,
11.2 × 11.9 cm (4 9/16 × 4 11/16 in.), 84.XM.478.9

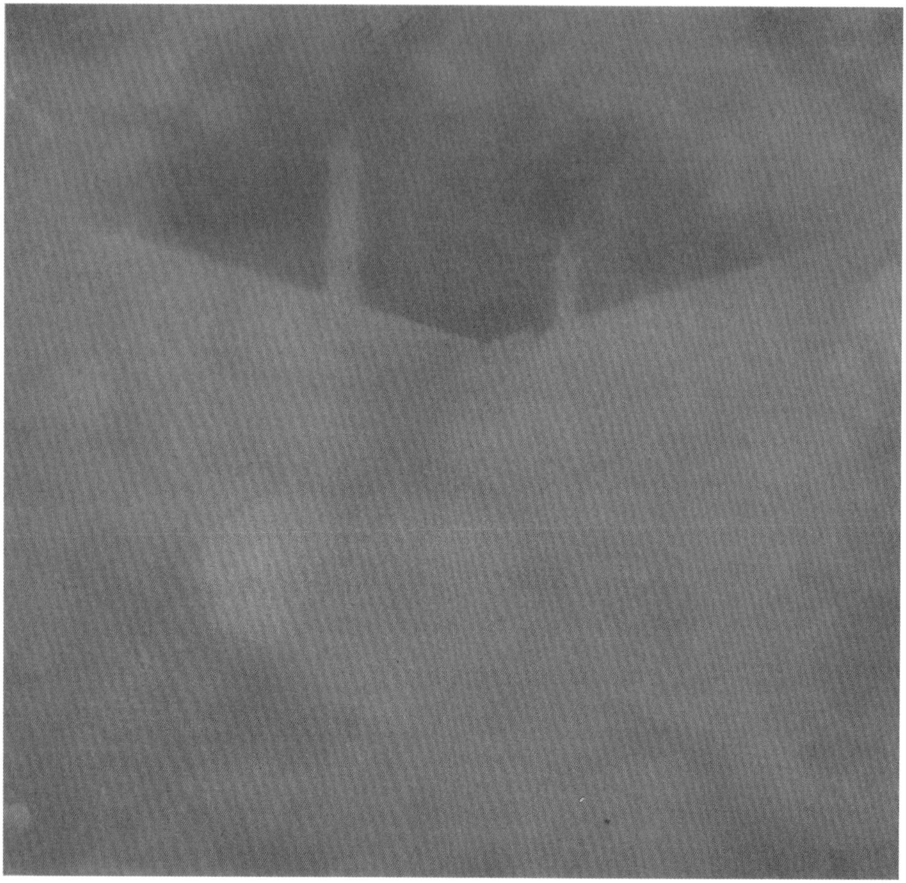

Talbot, one of the inventors of photography, began experimenting with light-sensitive materials on paper after growing frustrated with his drawing abilities. Building on the centuries-old concept of the camera obscura, an early optical device, he created small wood boxes with a simple lens that could hold a square sheet of paper. Dubbed "mouse traps" by his wife, the devices allowed him to make "solar pictures" with short exposure times. These photogenic drawings, which frequently featured his grand country home, Lacock Abbey, as a subject, reversed light and dark tones and appeared as mirror images of the actual scene. Talbot made his photographic discoveries public in January 1839, just weeks after Louis-Jacques-Mandé Daguerre (1787–1851) announced his method—daguerreotype—in Paris. Talbot would go on to develop the calotype, another successful negative-positive process.

Hippolyte Bayard
French, 1801–1887

"Bather" by Etienne-Maurice Falconet, Bust, Medallion, and Curtain, 1839
Direct positive print, 13.3 × 12.9 cm
(5¼ × 5 1/16 in.), 84.XM.261.2

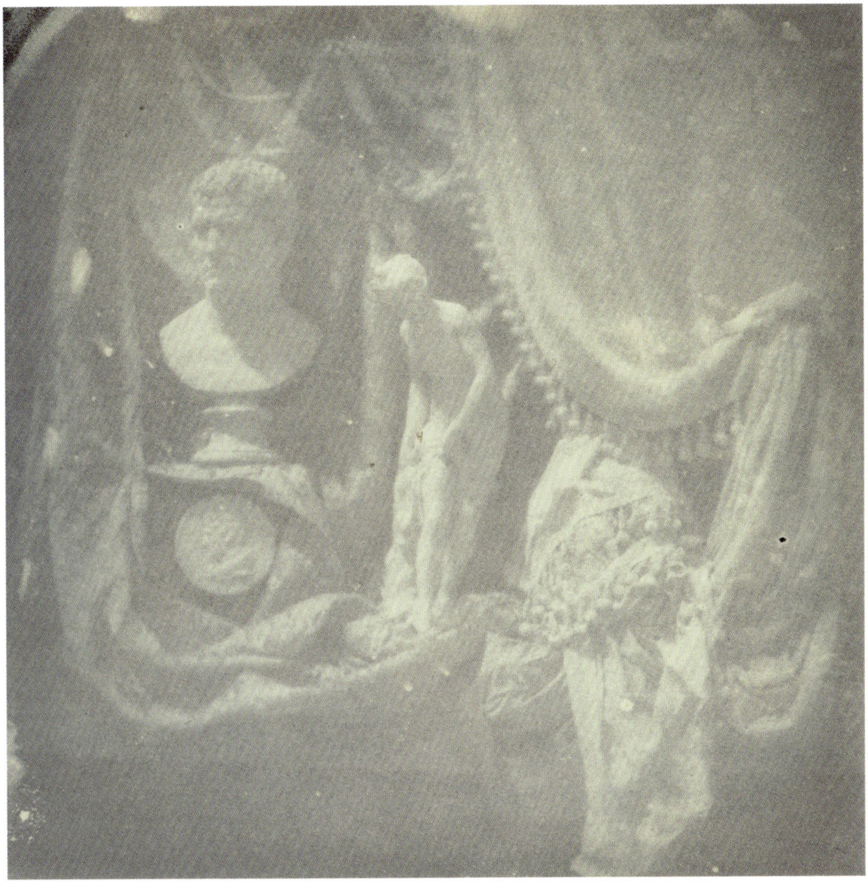

Bayard, a Parisian bureaucrat by profession, was one of the most important if lesser-known pioneers of photography. In a career spanning more than thirty years, he invented the direct-positive process and several other photographic techniques on paper. He could produce only one, unique image from each direct-positive exposure, similar to the daguerreotype. However, while Daguerre's process employed metal plates, Bayard advocated for using paper. Also an amateur painter, Bayard brought his artistic sensitivities to his photographic compositions and considered the new technology both a revolutionary tool for artists and an art form unto itself. Plaster sculptures feature often in his early work, as light bounced off their surfaces, and they naturally remained motionless through exposures of twenty minutes or longer, making them perfect photographic subjects.

Attributed to Théophile Gautier and Eugène Piot
French, 1811–1872; French, 1812–1890

Court of the Lions, 1840
Daguerreotype (quarter plate),
8.1 × 10.5 cm (3 3/16 × 4 1/8 in.); image:
7 × 9.1 cm (2 3/4 × 3 9/16 in.), 84.XT.265.29

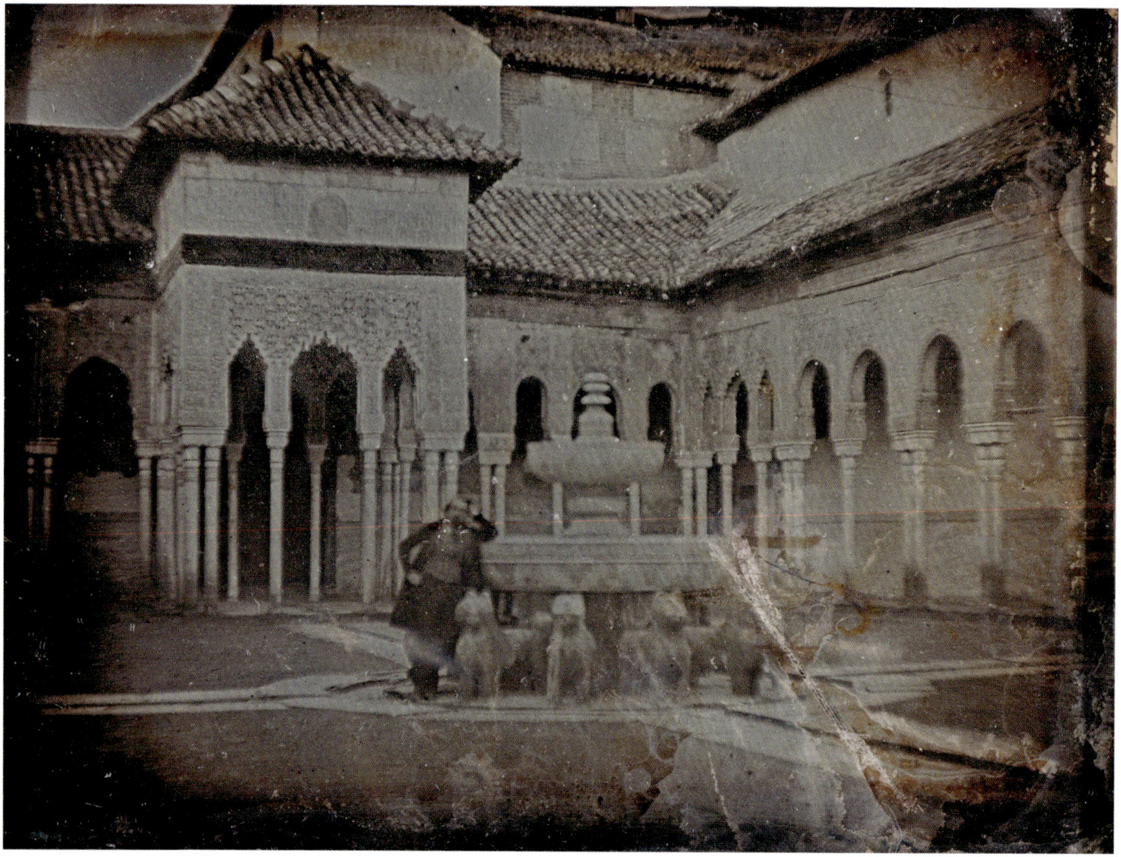

Gautier and Piot traveled to Spain in 1840, just months after the daguerreotype process had been introduced. The photographs they made of Spain's spectacular cultural riches, captured on light-sensitized metal plates, validated the promised potential of this revolutionary new technology. In his 1843 book *Voyage in Spain,* Gautier described the architecture of the Alhambra, rhapsodizing about the white rays of the moon crossing the yellow flame of a lamp as he and Piot slept in the palace's Hall of Two Sisters, just off the fabled Court of the Lions. The figure leaning against the fountain in this image—likely Piot or Gautier—would have had to hold still for the exposure over several minutes. In subsequent years, Piot photographed the monuments of other European countries on behalf of the French government.

Southworth & Hawes
American, active 1844–62

Early Operation Using Ether for Anesthesia, July 3, 1847
Daguerreotype (whole plate),
14.6 × 20 cm ($5\frac{3}{4} \times 7\frac{7}{8}$ in.), 84.XT.958

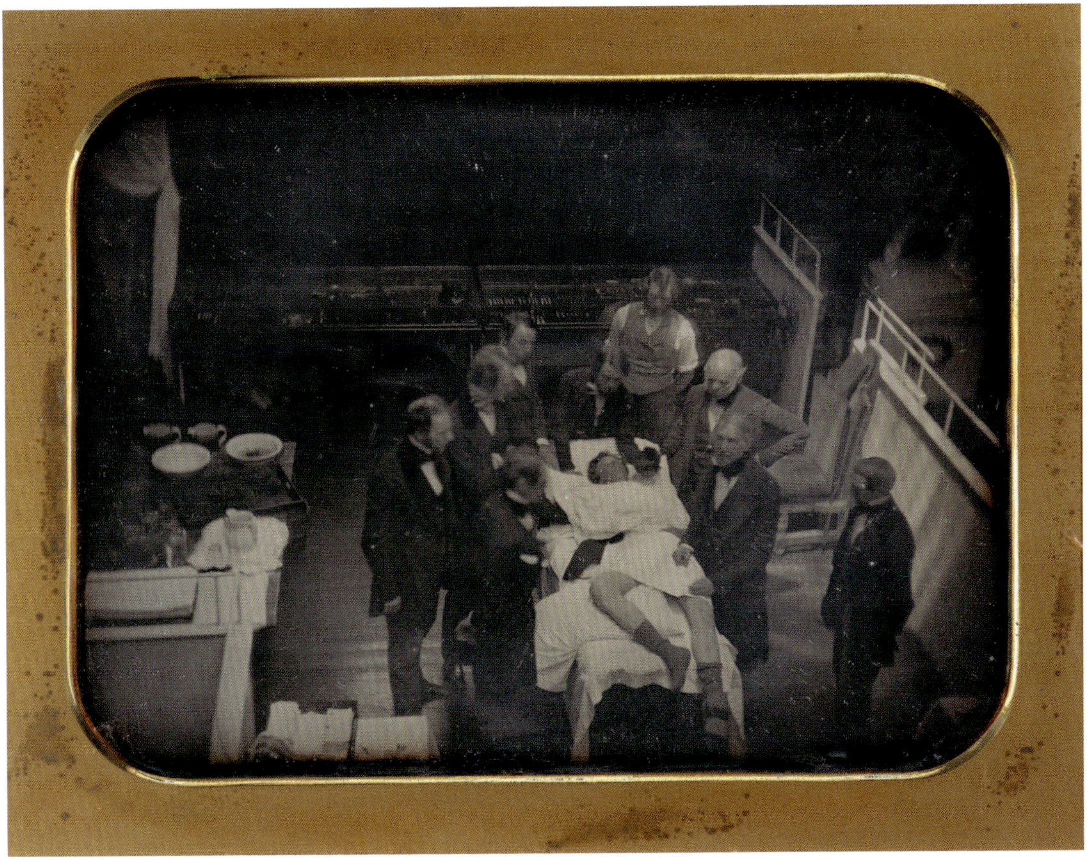

The rapid pace of innovation in the mid-nineteenth century was staggering. Trains crisscrossed continents, telegraphs relayed messages far and wide, and steam power sped the production and trade of goods. Photography—a similarly radical technology—enabled news and views of these advancements to be shared more easily, and with a striking immediacy. The use of ether as an anesthetic, with its life-changing potential to mitigate surgical pain, was such a momentous development that the Boston portrait studio of Southworth & Hawes was commissioned to photograph early demonstrations of its use. Here, doctors are posed carefully around an anesthetist and his listless patient. Taken only a few years after the introduction of photography in the United States, the image demonstrates the medium's capacity to craft as well as to capture historic events.

Count Jean-François-Charles-André Flachéron
French, 1813–1883

Coliseum, 1850
Waxed paper negative and salted paper print, negative: 25.3 × 33.6 cm ($9\frac{15}{16} \times 13\frac{1}{4}$ in.); positive: 24.8 × 33.3 cm ($9\frac{3}{4} \times 13\frac{1}{8}$ in.), 2015.34, 84.XP.677.43

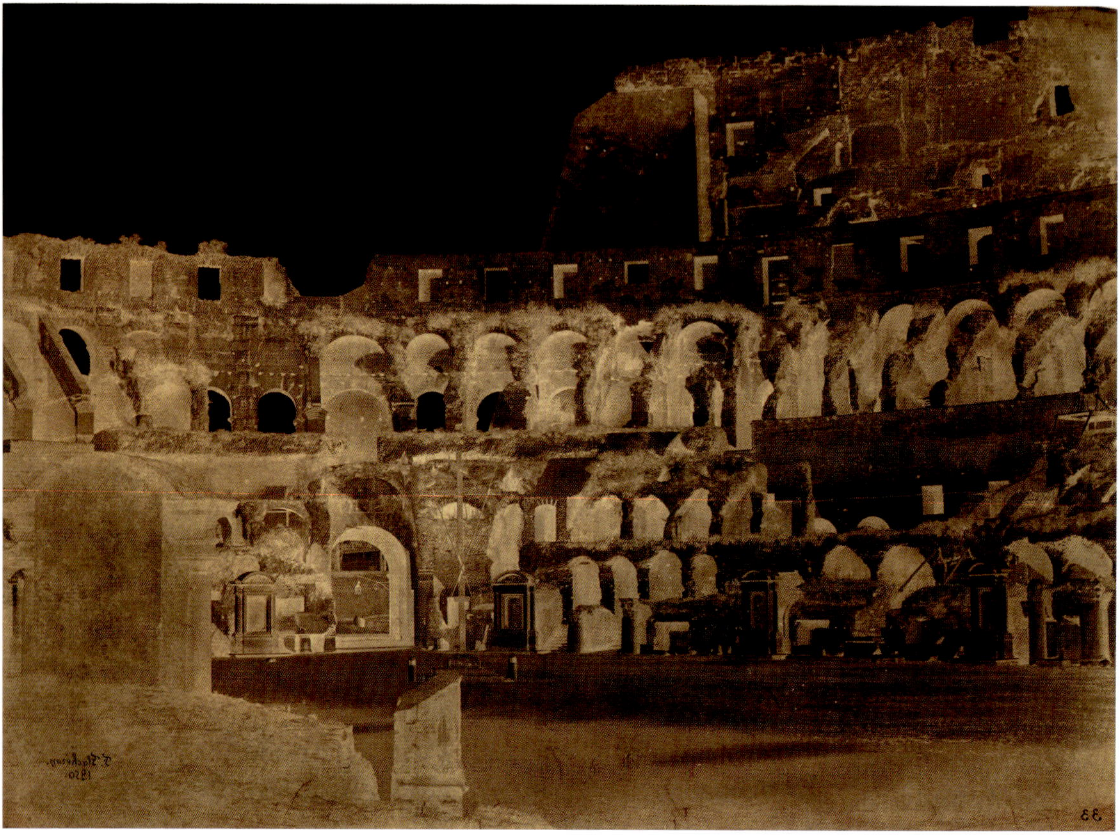

Flachéron joined his brother in Rome in 1839 after winning second place in the Prix de Rome, a prize for art students at the École des Beaux-Arts, Paris. He quickly took up painting landscapes for tourists, but in 1848 he shifted to making photographs of Roman architecture. His stunning images were popular with both souvenir seekers and people back in France. Flachéron's photographic process of choice was a variant of photographer Amélie Guillot-Saguez's (1810–1864) "Roman method," which worked well in the hot temperatures of Italy. He first applied a layer of beeswax to paper to make the exposed negative more transparent for printing, then retouched it to better balance the different areas. Processes like Flachéron's and William Henry Fox Talbot's (see p. 352) laid the foundation for the gelatin silver negative method that would be used throughout the twentieth century.

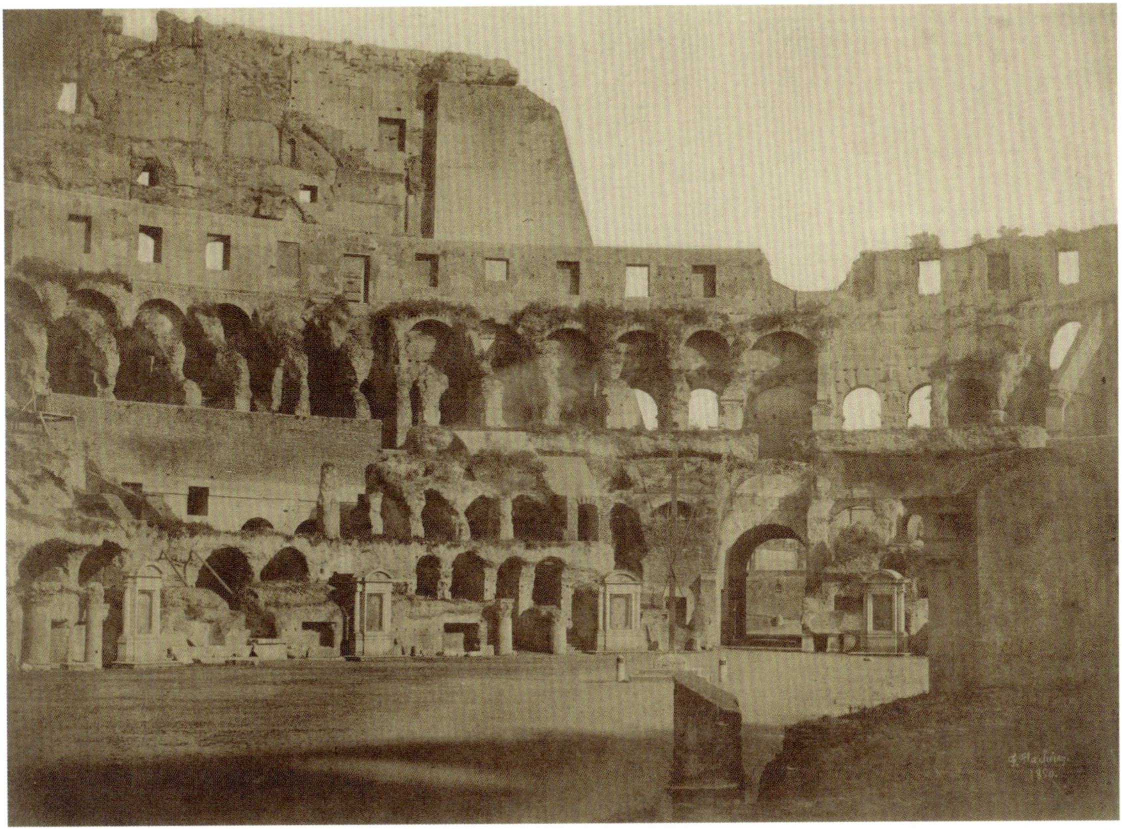

Unknown Photographer
Active United States
Edgar Allan Poe,
late May–early June 1849
Daguerreotype (half-plate), 12.2 × 8.9 cm
(4 13/16 × 3 1/2 in.), 84.XT.957

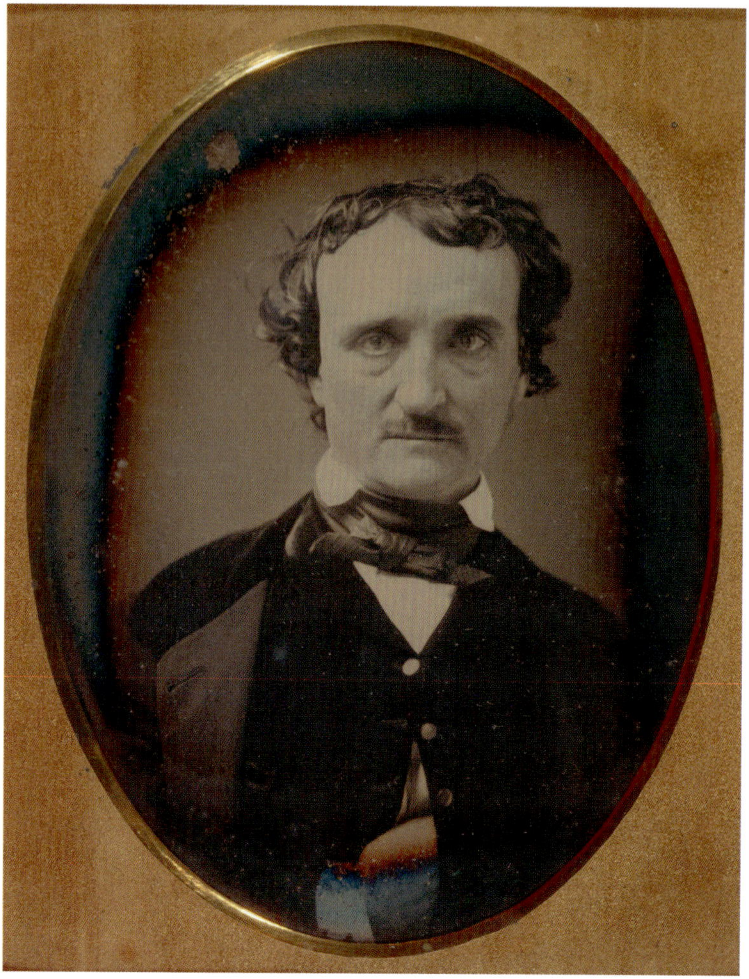

Portraits offer a powerful promise: to capture both surface appearance and a sitter's interior character. Here, the weary stare and disheveled appearance of author Edgar Allan Poe (1809–1849) channel the haunting quality of the stories for which he is known. While photographs capable of being printed in multiples would soon come to dominate the market, daguerreotype technology produced one-of-a-kind images on highly polished silver-plated copper, resulting in reflective pictures that, when held in the hand within the velvet or silk-lined cases that protect them, seem to appear and disappear like glimmering apparitions. Oxidization on this plate has seeped around the edges of its frame, encircling the writer with darkness. Poe died soon after this picture was taken, at only forty years old.

Unknown Photographer

Active United States

Portrait of a Young Man, likely late 1850s

Hand-colored ambrotype (one-ninth plate), 4.9 × 3.7 cm ($1\frac{15}{16} \times 1\frac{7}{16}$ in.), 84.XT.1568.36

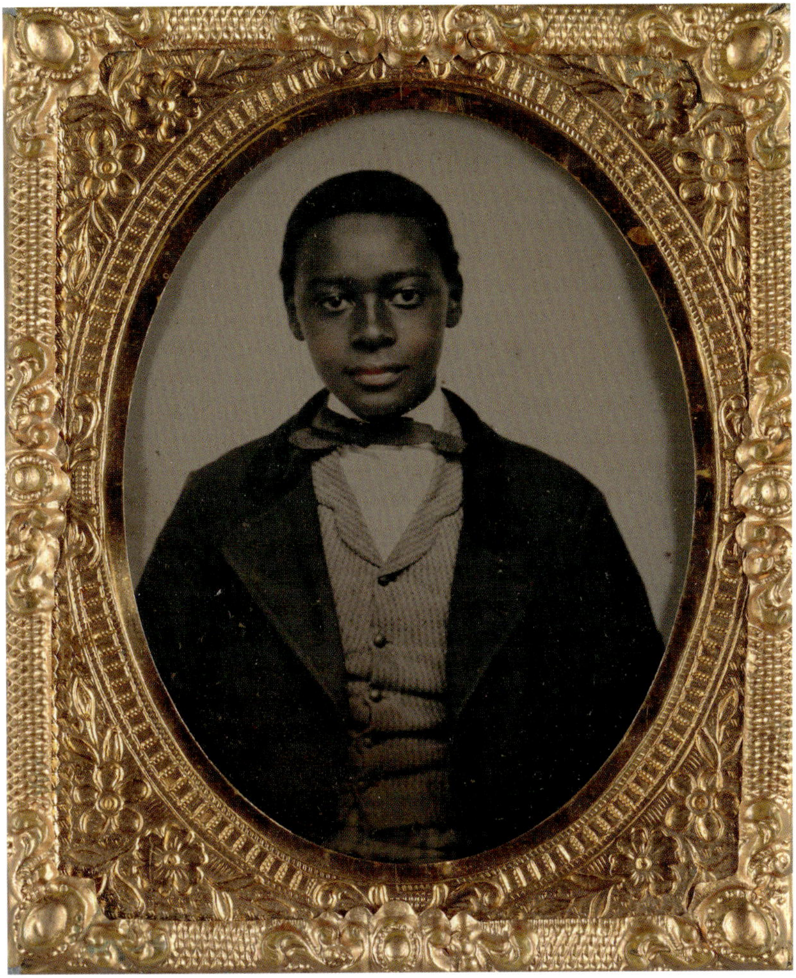

Delicate hand coloring enlivens this poignant portrait of youth. As photographic techniques improved in the mid-nineteenth century, greater numbers of people could afford to have their likenesses made, but for those who were not celebrities or politicians, having one's portrait taken would remain a special occasion until the advent of handheld cameras in the 1880s. Ambrotype techniques, popular in the 1850s, produced one-of-a-kind images on glass, their preciousness accentuated by velvet-lined cases, which protected them as they were passed from hand to hand among family and friends. Though details about this sitter's identity have been lost to time, he is at ease, nicely dressed, and surrounded by an ornate frame marked by the manufacturer as "superfine," accentuating both his presence and the portrait's power as a memento of affection.

Anna Atkins and Anne Dixon

British, 1799–1871; British, 1799–1864

Ceylon, 1853

From the album *Cyanotypes of British and Foreign Ferns*

Cyanotype, 25.4 × 19.4 cm (10 × 7⅝ in.), 84.XO.227.95

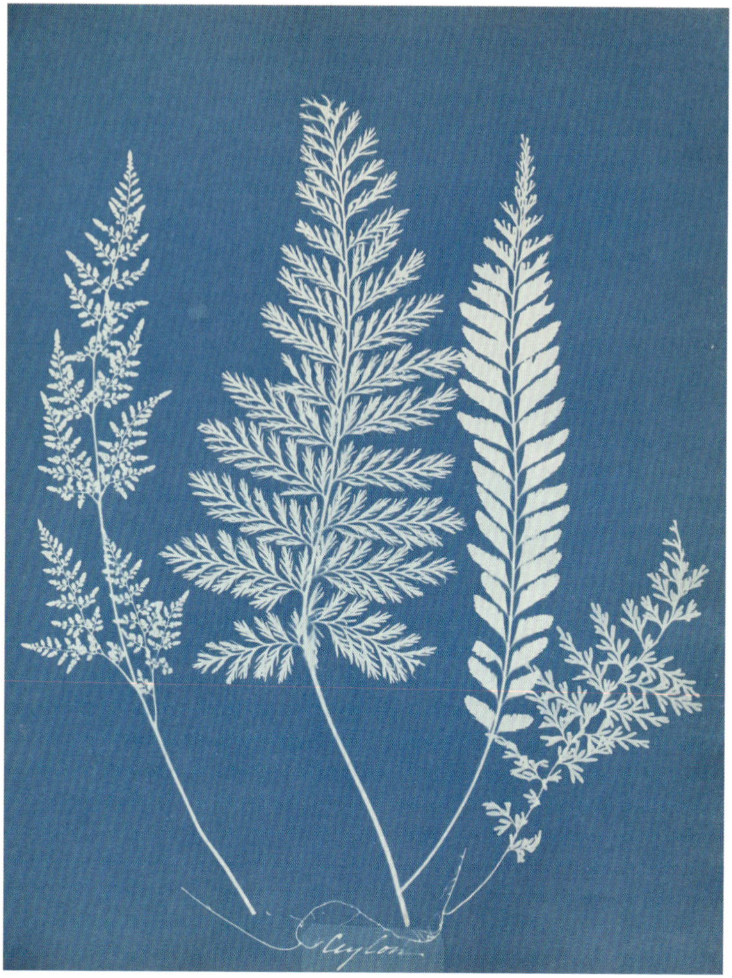

Atkins blazed a trail in science and photography, producing the first book to be illustrated with photographic images, *British Algae: Cyanotype Impressions* (1843–1853). Thanks to her chemist father's association with fellow Royal Society member Sir John Herschel (1792–1871), Atkins was privy to Herschel's cameraless cyanotype process soon after it came out, in 1842. By placing plant specimens directly on chemically treated paper that turned a vivid blue through light exposure, Atkins created hundreds of scientifically accurate visual records of her collection of botanical specimens. In 1853 she collaborated with fellow amateur botanist and friend Anne Dixon on an album focused on ferns. This photograph documents four distinct ferns from Ceylon (now Sri Lanka), then a British colony. Atkins's work emphasized the importance of preserving and protecting plant species.

Roger Fenton

British, 1819–1869

Dinornis elephantopus, circa 1857

Salted paper print, 38.1 × 30.3 cm (15 × 11 15/16 in.), 84.XP.452.3

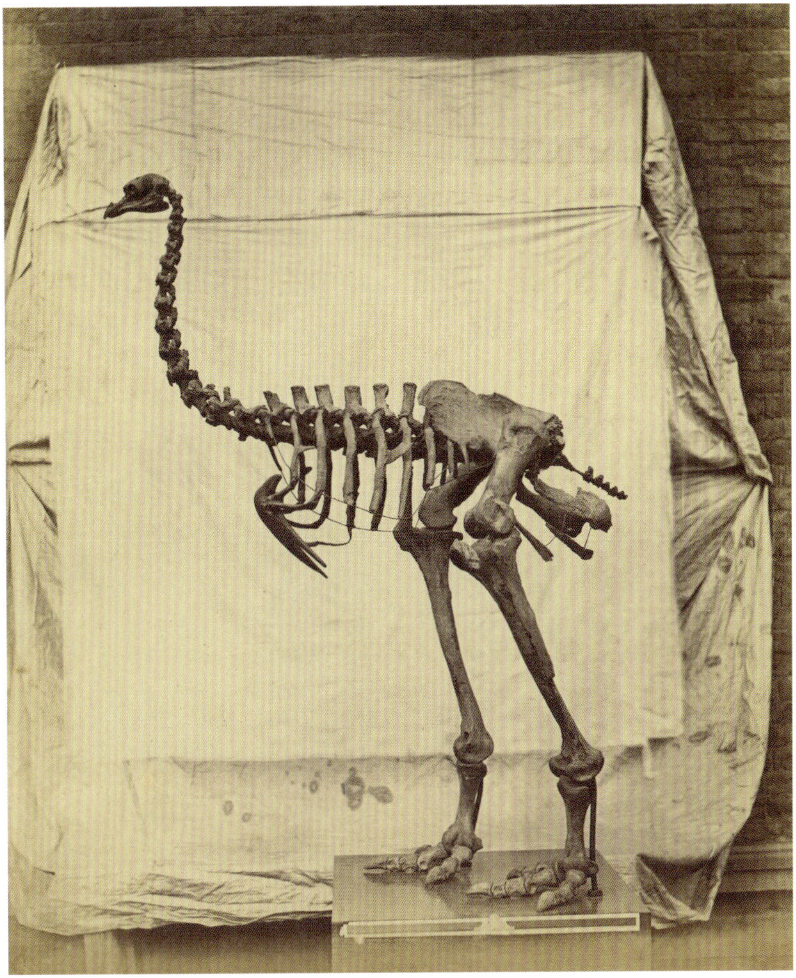

In 1854 the British Museum in London launched an innovative program of applying the relatively new medium of photography toward documenting its diverse collections, hiring Fenton to take on this ambitious project. He set up a studio on the museum's rooftop, where he developed novel methods of arranging and lighting his subjects, including this newly reconstructed skeleton of a heavy-footed moa, an extinct flightless bird native to New Zealand. Incorporating a white sheet to more clearly expose its structure, Fenton's photograph reveals the skeleton's scaffold support of thin wires, its many vertebrae, and its strange proportions, from a tiny head and long neck to wide hips and giant talons.

Adrien Tournachon

French, 1825–1903

Pierrot à la corbeille de fruits (Pierrot with a Basket of Fruit), 1854–55

Salted paper print, 27.9 × 20.3 cm (11 × 8 in.), 2023.15

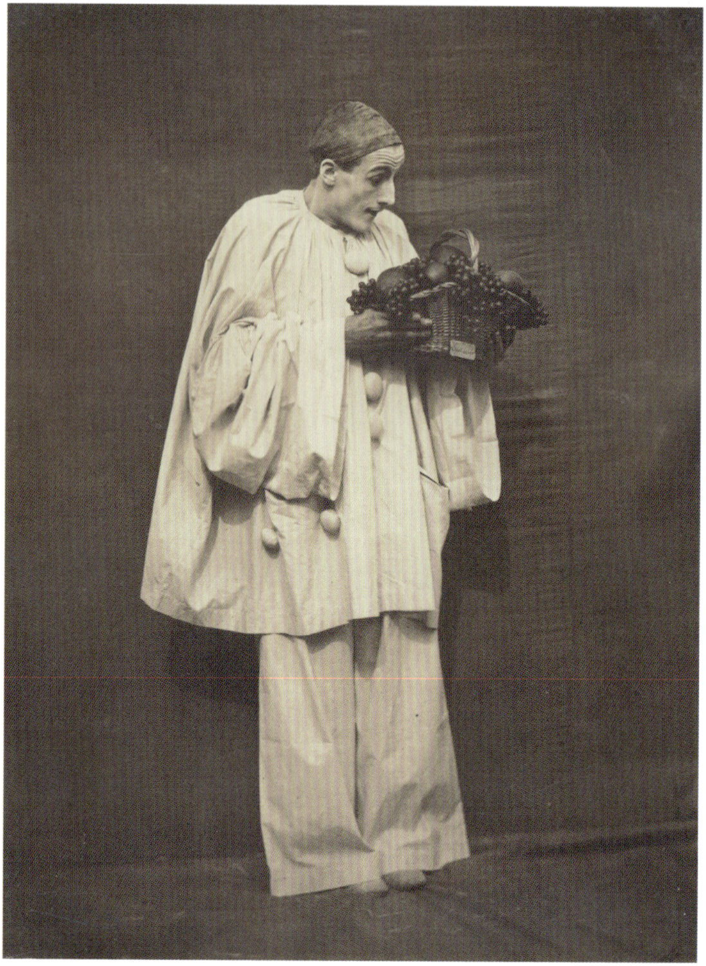

The brothers Adrien and Félix Tournachon (the latter known as Nadar) were collaborators and competitors in the nascent Parisian photography world of the 1850s. Adrien received support and guidance from his older brother in establishing a portrait studio on the boulevard des Capucines. There, he photographed the renowned pantomime artist Charles Deburau (1829–1873) as Pierrot, a stock character from the commedia dell'arte, a traditional form of Italian theater. Adrien captured Deburau in a series of expressive poses like this one, in which he gazes ravenously at a basket of fruit. Tournachon exhibited the Pierrot series at the 1855 World's Fair in Paris, winning a gold medal. These photographs were the last he produced with his brother's support before the two entered into a legal battle over the use of the name Nadar.

Julia Margaret Cameron

British, born India, 1815–1879

The Whisper of the Muse/Portrait of G. F. Watts, April 1865

Albumen silver print, 26 × 21.4 cm (10¼ × 8⁷⁄₁₆ in.), 84.XZ.186.96

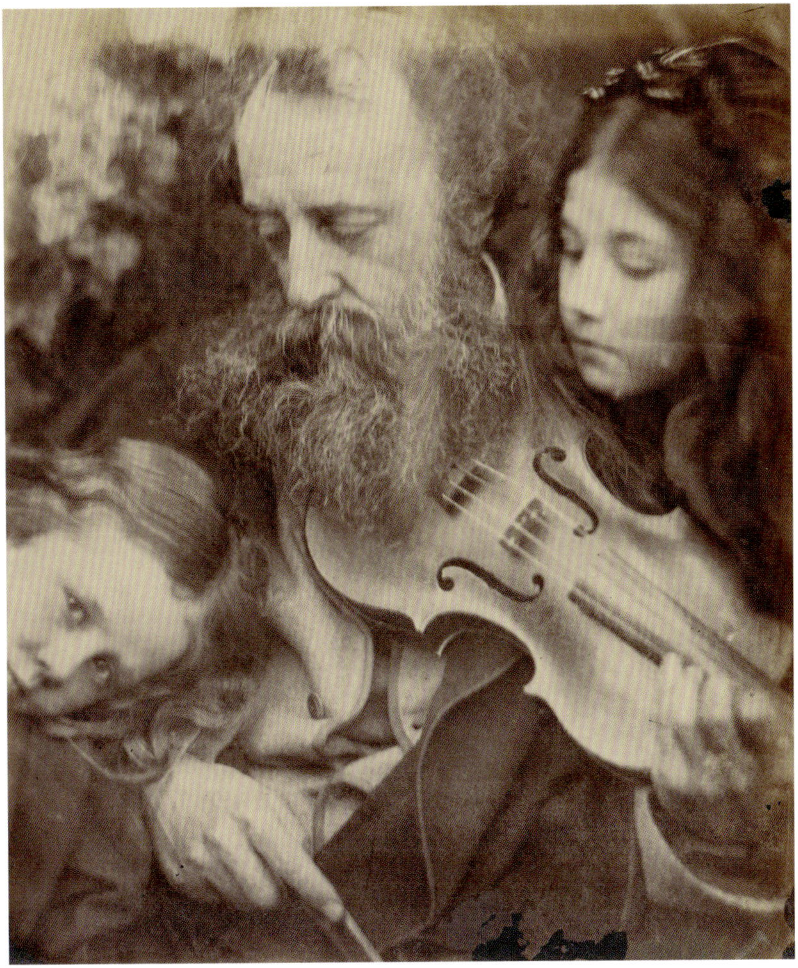

At her home on the Isle of Wight, in the English Channel, Cameron enlisted family, friends, and even the local fishmonger's daughter to pose in elaborate costumes as literary and religious figures. It was perhaps with Rembrandt van Rijn's 1661 painting *The Evangelist Matthew Inspired by the Angel* in mind that she presented her friend the painter George Frederick Watts (1817–1904) as a musician-prophet, a violin tucked under his bearded chin. Cameron's neighbor Elizabeth Keown (1859–?) along with another, unidentified girl pose as his muses. The composition's tight framing, the angles of the subjects' gazes, and the position of Watts's hand, combined with the contrast of light and dark tones, pull the viewer's attention in a dynamic circle. An inscription in Cameron's hand labels the image "a Triumph."

Gustave Le Gray

French, 1820–1884

Seascape with a Ship Leaving Port, 1857

Albumen silver print from glass negatives, 30.5 × 39.9 cm (12 × 15 11/16 in.), 84.XP.218.71

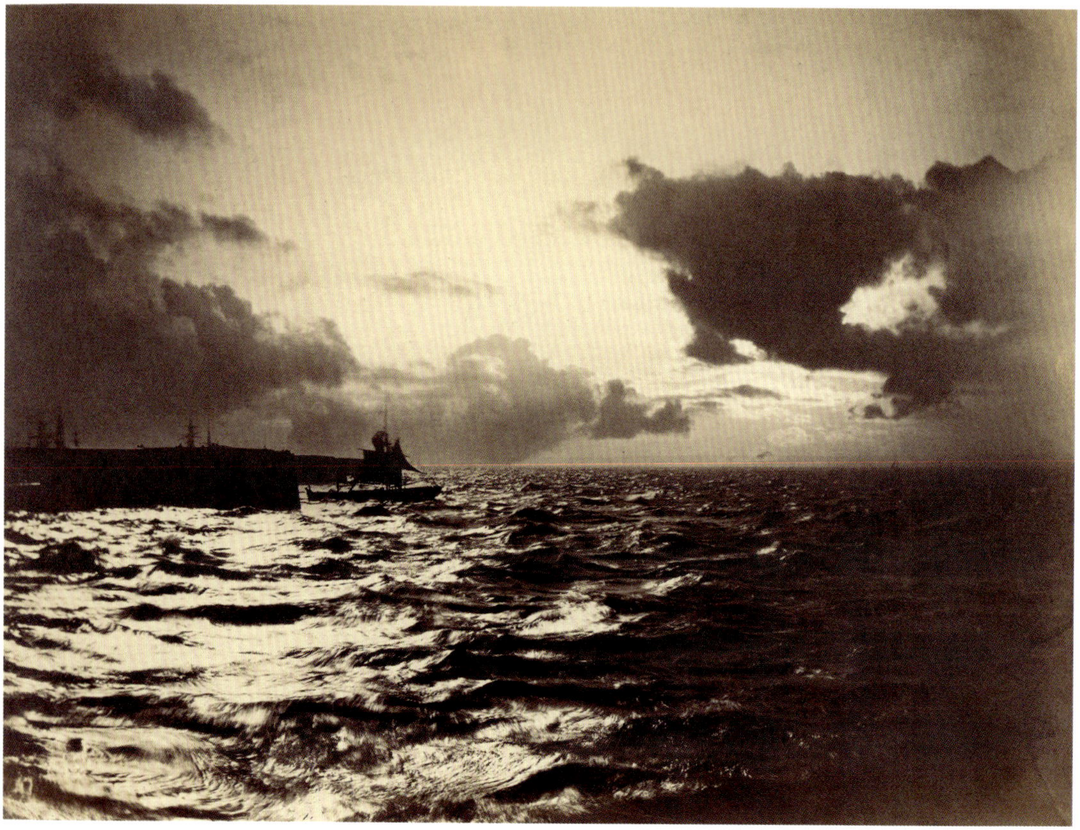

Around 1855 Le Gray began a series of photographic seascapes and maritime studies created at Sète, a Mediterranean port city southwest of Montpellier, France. The images proved both popular and financially profitable. Interestingly, he first exhibited them outside France, at the Photographic Society in London, in December 1856. Capturing motion, such as a bobbing boat or waves breaking on the rocks, was still a great challenge to photographers at that time, but Le Gray shortened his exposure times, enabling him to record the ever-moving sea. He overcame the different light intensities of water and sky by combining one negative in which the exposure was correct for one element, and a second that was exposed properly to capture the other. He then matched the negatives so expertly that it is difficult to detect the "seams."

Carleton Watkins

American, 1829–1916

Yosemite Valley from the Best General View, 1866

Albumen silver print, 41 × 52.2 cm (16⅛ × 20⁹⁄₁₆ in.), 85.XM.11.3

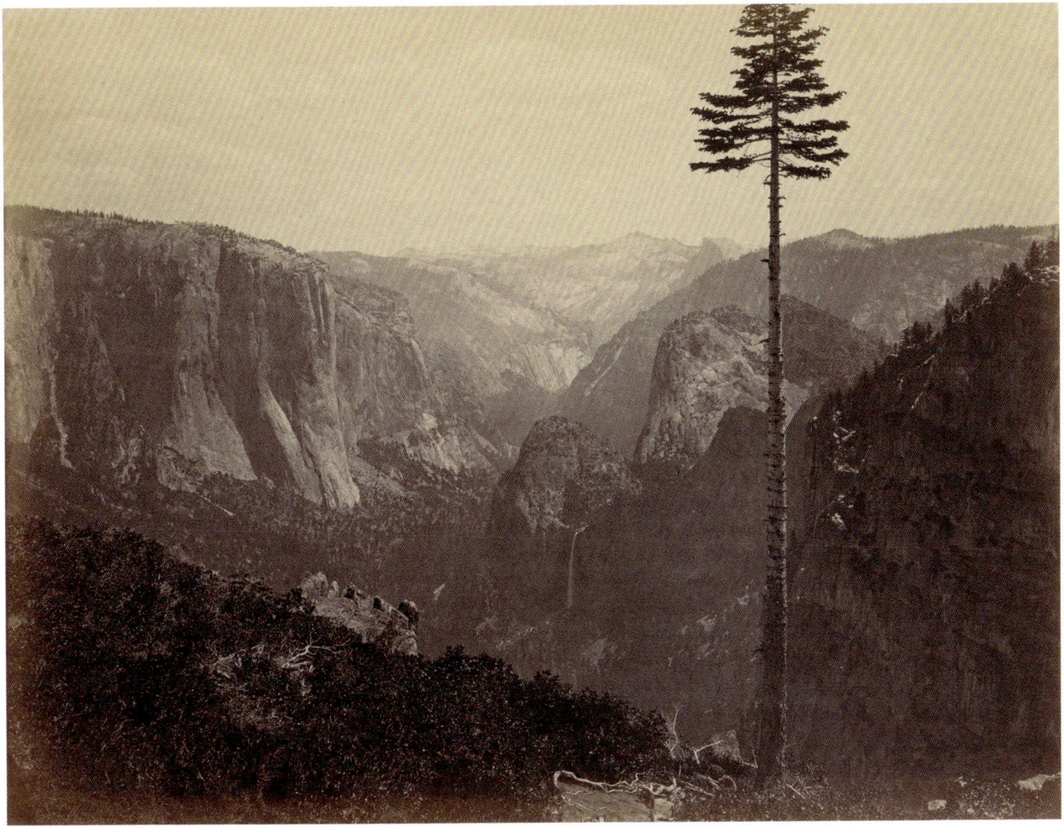

Watkins hauled thousands of pounds of photographic equipment through rugged terrain to make monumentally scaled glass negatives rich with scenic details. Here, his choice of viewpoint approaches the edge of a precipice, extending the viewer's attention far beyond Yosemite Falls to suggest the vastness of the landscape. Such carefully composed images of the expansive American West played a crucial role in shaping the nation's history, as they were used to help convince politicians to protect certain lands from development while laying the groundwork for the exploitation of natural resources found in others. While Watkins strove to depict the terrain as untouched wilderness, recent scholars have identified details that demonstrate the photographer's purposeful elision of Native inhabitants and their vigilant stewardship of the region.

Lala Deen Dayal

Indian, 1844–1905

Chachai Waterfall, Rewa[h], 1883–84; print, August 13, 1886

Albumen silver print, 26.5 × 19 cm (10 7/16 × 7 1/2 in.). Gift of Rowe Kaple in memory of Eloise Sager Bettge, 2016.135.24

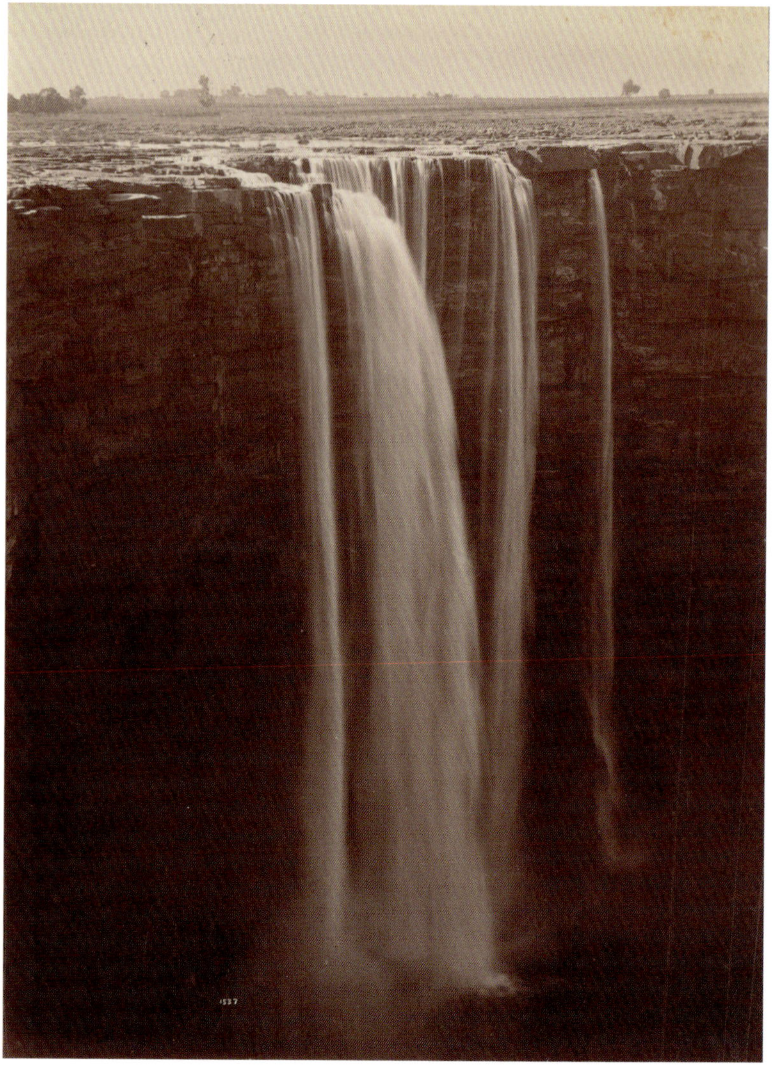

Striking images such as this one garnered Dayal the honorific Raja Musavir Jung Bahadur, or "bold warrior of photography," by his patron, the ruler of Hyderabad, in central India. Whether working for British clients eager to catalogue strategic locations in India and the spoils of colonial rule or for local dignitaries eager to signal their wealth and status, Dayal was adept at inspiring awe as he inventoried regional sites and societies. Dayal's studio employed large-format cameras that registered minute details of landscapes, architecture, and fine garments alike, imbuing natural wonders, iconic temples, ornate palaces, ceremonial events, and sumptuously styled sitters with an air of grandeur. Here, Dayal's dramatic framing draws attention to the graceful arc of the falls, the steep cliffs of which appear to dwarf the surrounding landscape.

Thomas Eakins

American, 1844–1916

Male Figures at the Site of "Swimming,"

1884

Albumen silver print, 9.3 × 12.1 cm

(3 11/16 × 4 13/16 in.), 84.XM.811.1

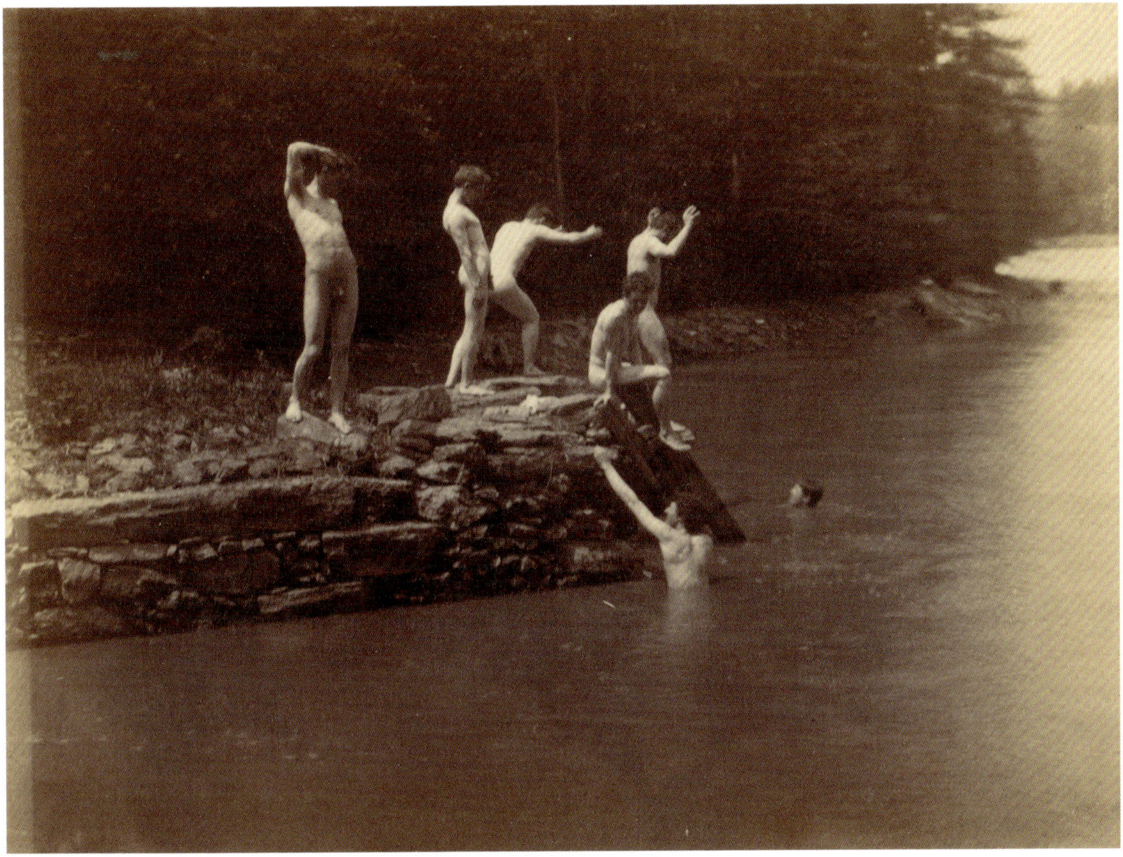

Although many nineteenth-century painters dabbled in photography, very few carried their experiments far enough to produce a significant body of work. One painter who did was Thomas Eakins, who took his first photographs in the late 1870s. Interested in the poses and gestures of nude figures, he made a series of studies of seven young men at Mill Creek, a location near Bryn Mawr, Pennsylvania. Male nudes were uncommon in photography, and Eakins was among the first American artists to experiment with the subject. His models were his students at the Pennsylvania Academy of the Fine Arts, which eventually dismissed him for this practice. Eakins's painting *Swimming* (1885), now in the collection of the Amon Carter Museum of American Art in Fort Worth, Texas, derives from this photograph and its variants.

Alphonse Bertillon

French, 1853–1914

Affaire Peugniez–Vue de la cuisine

(Peugniez Affair–View of the Kitchen),

June 5, 1898

Gelatin silver print, 17.1 × 23.1 cm

(6¾ × 9⅛ in.), 2019.22.41

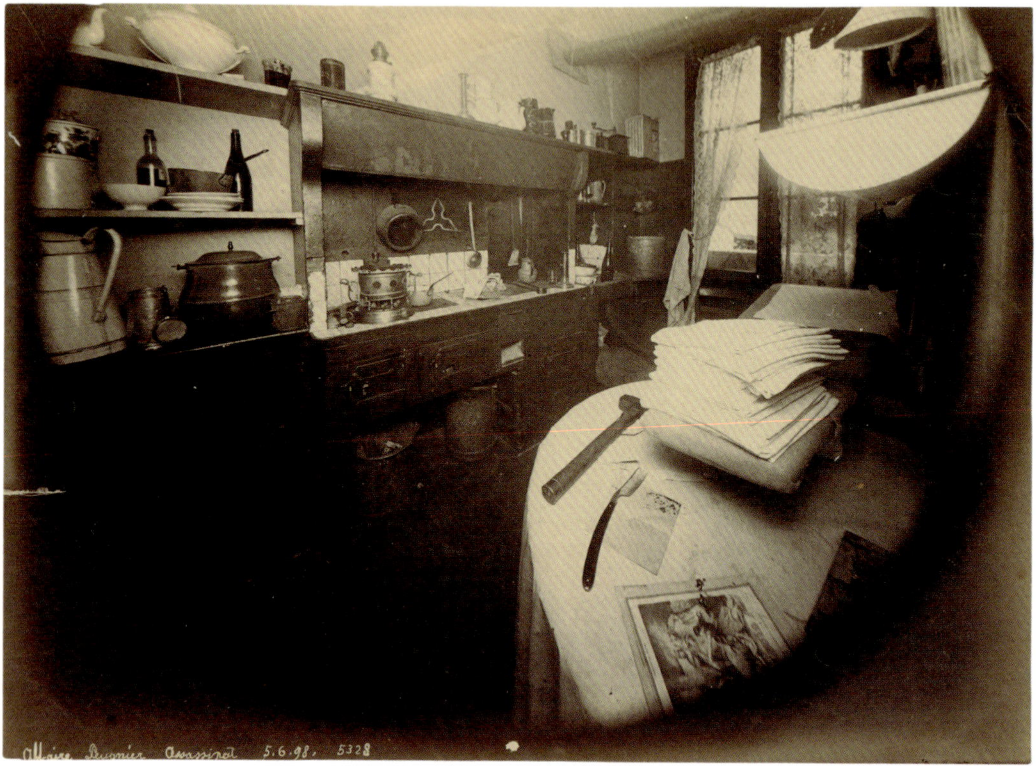

Best known for his influential system of criminal identification, which laid the foundations for the modern mugshot, Bertillon, a police officer, began pursuing crime-scene photography in 1890. Amid a crisis of public trust in the French courts, which had high acquittal rates, Bertillon recognized photography's potential to galvanize juries to convict. This view of a kitchen following a double murder demonstrates his distinctive approach to photographing crime scenes. Using a wide-angle lens, Bertillon leads the eye past a hammer and a razor on the kitchen table—likely placed there by the photographer himself—to a woman's body under the sink. While appearing purely evidentiary, Bertillon's photographs were carefully orchestrated for emotional impact, encouraging viewers to use their imaginations to reconstruct the criminal act.

Eugène Atget
French, 1857–1927
Boulevard de Strasbourg, 1912
Gelatin silver chloride print, 22.7 × 17.9 cm
($8\frac{15}{16} \times 7\frac{1}{16}$ in.), 2022.44.12

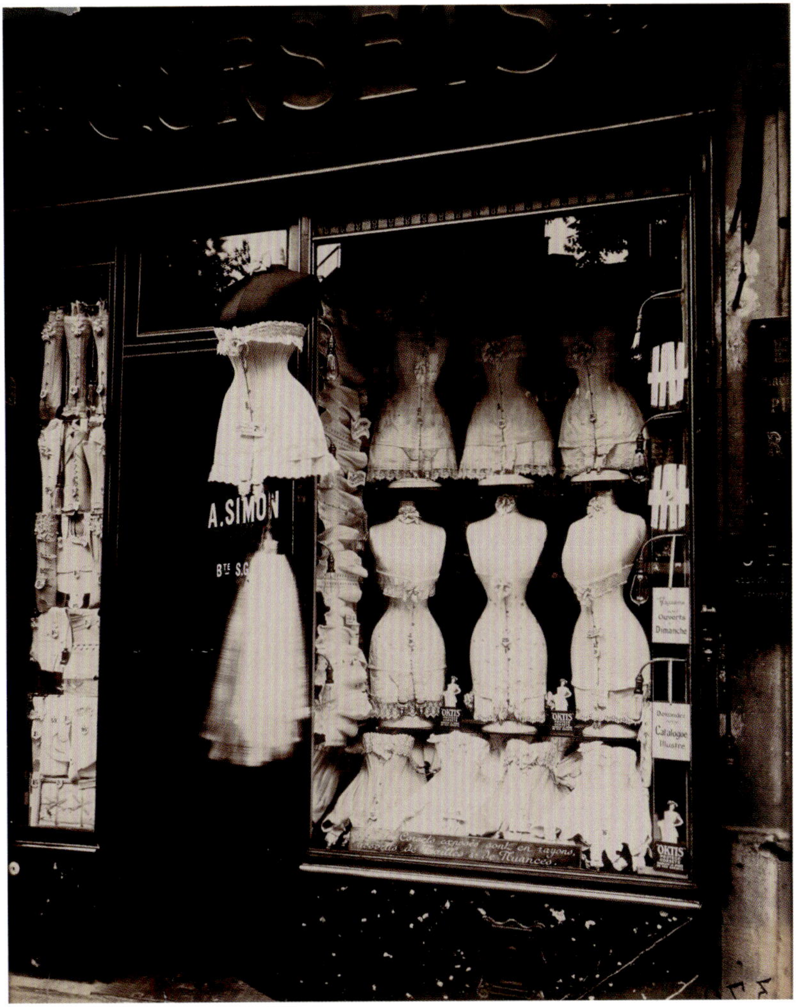

Atget occupies a central position in the history of photography as a strikingly original figure whose career bridged the nineteenth and twentieth centuries. In his obsessive visual documentation of Paris and its environs, which he marketed to municipal archives and working artists, he invented new approaches to street photography. The French Surrealists took a special interest in his work in the mid-1920s, admiring in particular his images of mannequins and consumer goods in shop windows. They reproduced Atget's iconic photograph of a corset shop on the boulevard de Strasbourg in their newspaper *The Surrealist Revolution* (June 15, 1926). It accompanied a text by the obscure Surrealist writer Marcel Noll, in which he recounted an erotic dream. Atget sold this print to the avant-garde poet and art critic Tristan Tzara (1896–1963).

Anne W. Brigman

American, 1869–1950

The Heart of the Storm, 1902; print, 1914

Gelatin silver print, 24.6 × 19.7 cm (9 11/16 × 7 3/4 in.). Gift of the Michael and Jane Wilson Collection, 94.XM.111

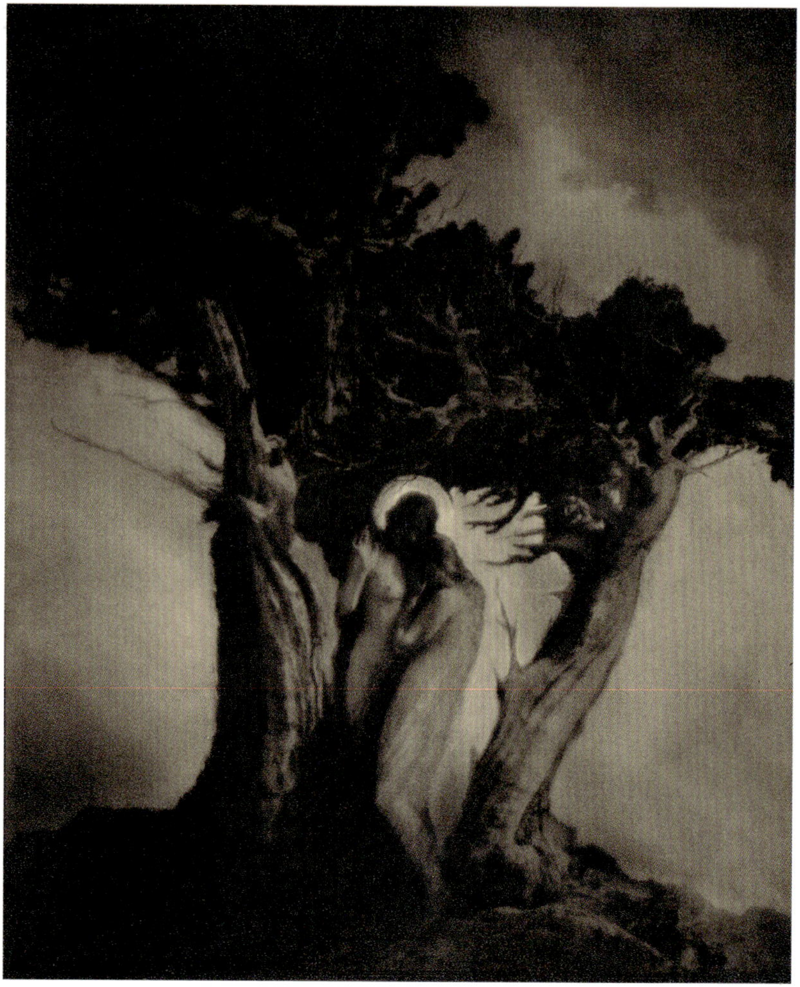

Originally trained as a painter, Brigman aligned herself with Pictorialism, an approach that celebrated photography's artistic potential by manipulating images into handcrafted works of art. She was the only member of Alfred Stieglitz's (see p. 371) influential art-photography group, Photo-Secession, to be based on the West Coast, and she often worked in the wilderness of the Sierra Nevada mountains. Using herself or female family members and friends as models, she staged evocative scenes of nude women in dramatic landscapes, then altered her negatives by hand to impart an atmospheric quality to her pictures. Here, Brigman created the halo above the head of the figure on the left and the translucent garment worn by the figure on the right by etching and drawing on the negative before printing.

Alfred Stieglitz

American, 1864–1946

Georgia O'Keeffe–Hands, 1918

Palladium print, 24.3 × 19.4 cm

(9 9/16 × 7 5/8 in.), 91.XM.63.6

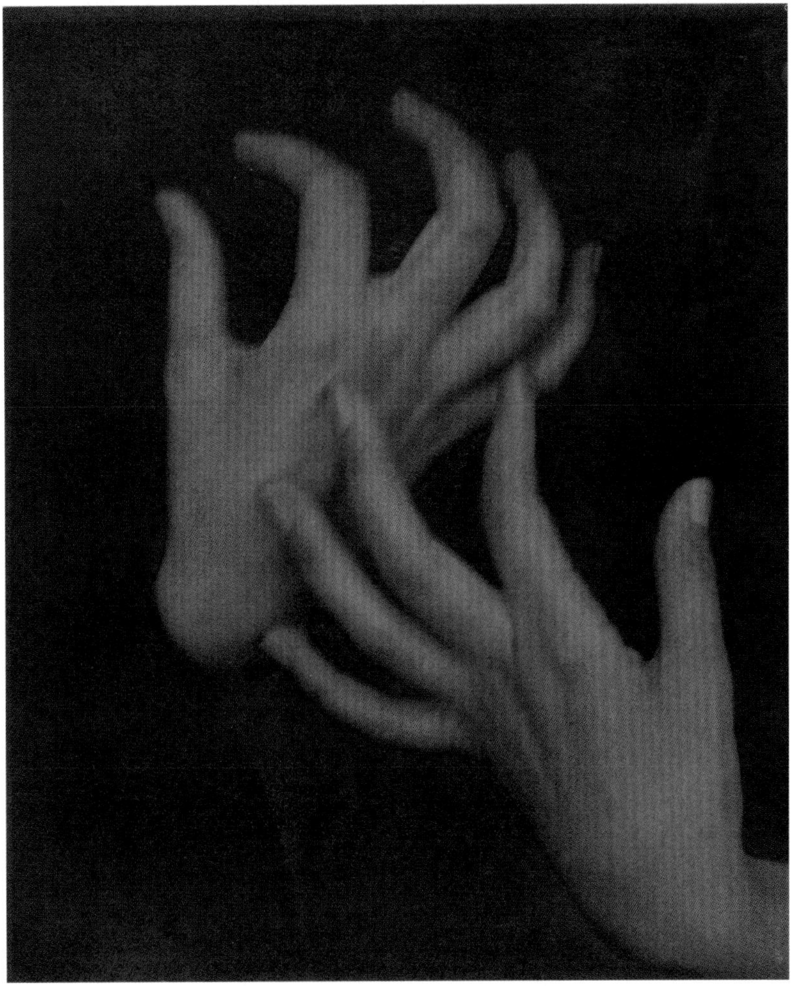

"My hands had always been admired since I was a little girl—but I never thought much about it," recalled Georgia O'Keeffe (1887–1986) when she looked at photographs Stieglitz had taken of her some sixty years prior. When the two artists met in 1916, O'Keefe was largely unknown while Stieglitz was one of the leading fine-art photographers and promoters of modern art in the United States. O'Keeffe soon became Stieglitz's lover and principal subject, and he photographed her over the course of their long relationship. The result is a remarkable composite portrait of her, comprising more than 325 photographs. In this closely framed picture, Stieglitz shows us only O'Keeffe's hands, her curled fingers evoking the abstract, organic shapes of her own drawings and paintings.

Man Ray

American, 1890–1976

Untitled Rayograph (Kiki and Filmstrips), 1922

Gelatin silver print, 23.8 × 17.8 cm (9 3/8 × 7 in.), 84.XM.1000.173

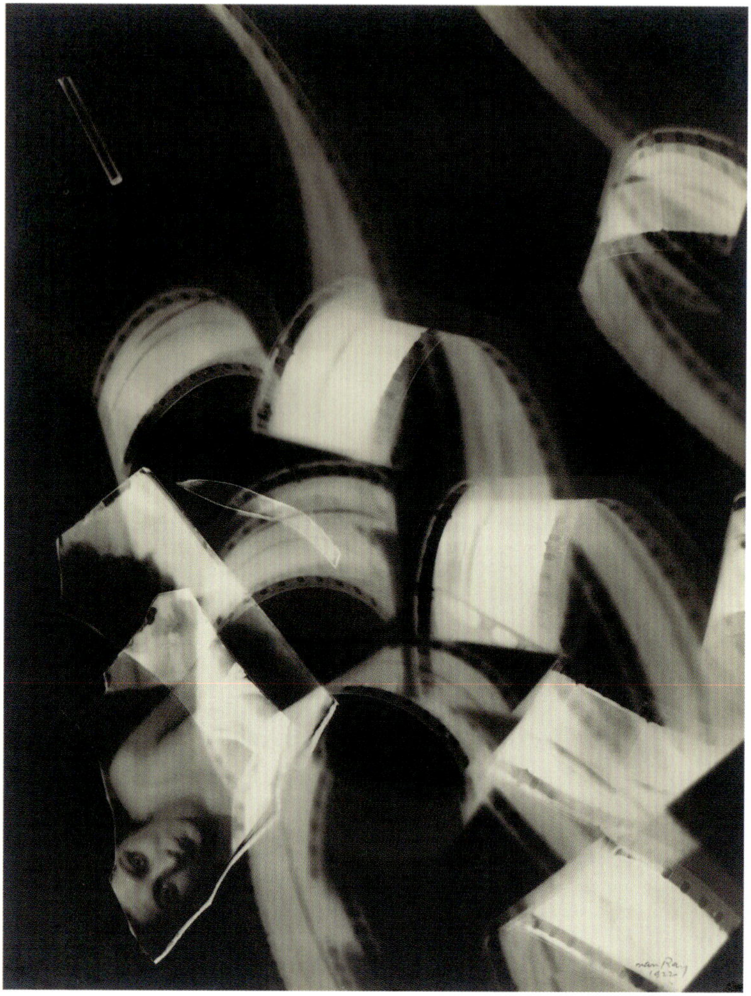

A photogram is a type of photograph in which objects are placed on photosensitive paper and then exposed to light. The process is as old as the photographic medium itself (see p. 360), but it was embraced with renewed enthusiasm in the twentieth century by Dada and Surrealist artists. Chief among them was Man Ray, who in 1921 began to make photograms—which he called "rayographs" after himself. This image appears almost accidental, as if the artist has dropped detritus from the studio floor directly onto the paper. Filmstrips tumble from above, and a glass negative of Alice Prin (1901–1953), better known as Kiki of Montparnasse, lies shattered at lower left. Here, Man Ray has symbolically thrown away the traditional instruments of photography in favor of a new approach to image making.

Shigemi Uyeda

American, born Japan, 1902–1980

Reflections on the Oil Ditch, circa 1925

Gelatin silver print, 33.5 × 26.5 cm

(13 3/16 × 10 7/16 in.), 2019.58.1

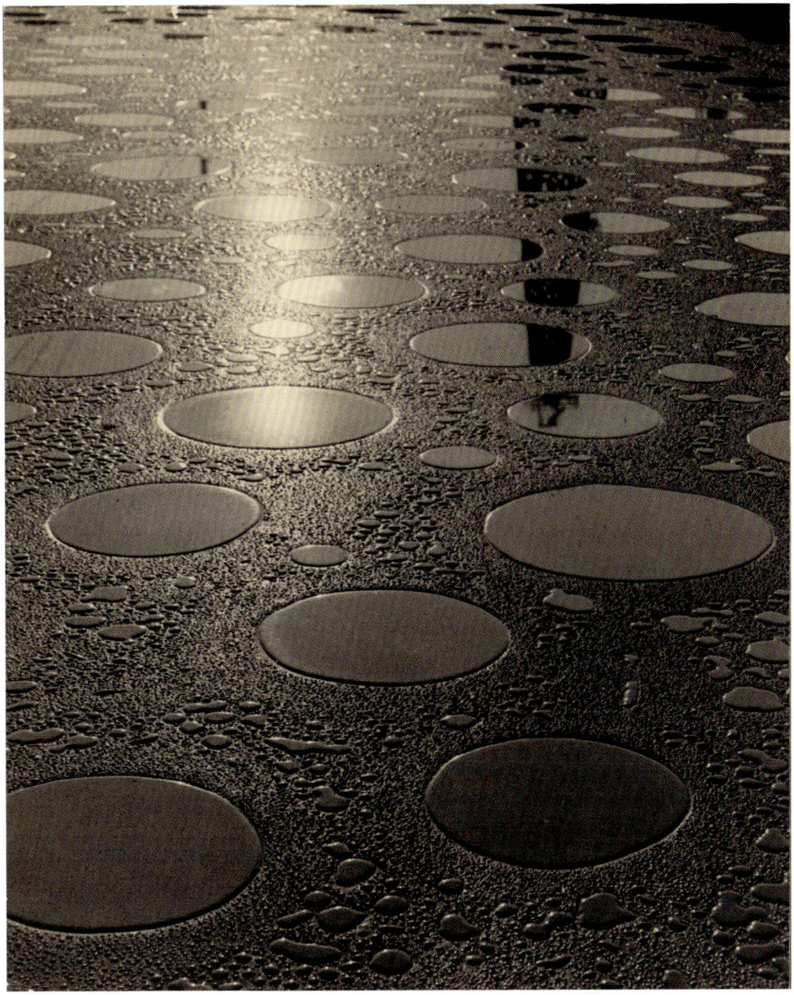

Uyeda was one of many young men who left Japan in the early twentieth century for employment in the United States. He arrived at age fifteen and worked as a farmer in Southern California for the rest of his life. He began photographing two years after his arrival and became involved with the Japanese Camera Pictorialists of California, a club based in the Little Tokyo neighborhood of Los Angeles that provided a sense of community and promoted photography through exhibitions, competitions, and publications. This image was made in Santa Fe Springs the morning after a light rainfall pooled on the surface of an oil ditch that had hardened in the cold. Uyeda cropped the image from a more expansive view, transforming it into a strikingly modernist composition.

Imogen Cunningham

American, 1883–1976

Flax, 1926

Gelatin silver print, 23.6 × 16.1 cm

(9¼ × 6⁵⁄₁₆ in.), 2019.93

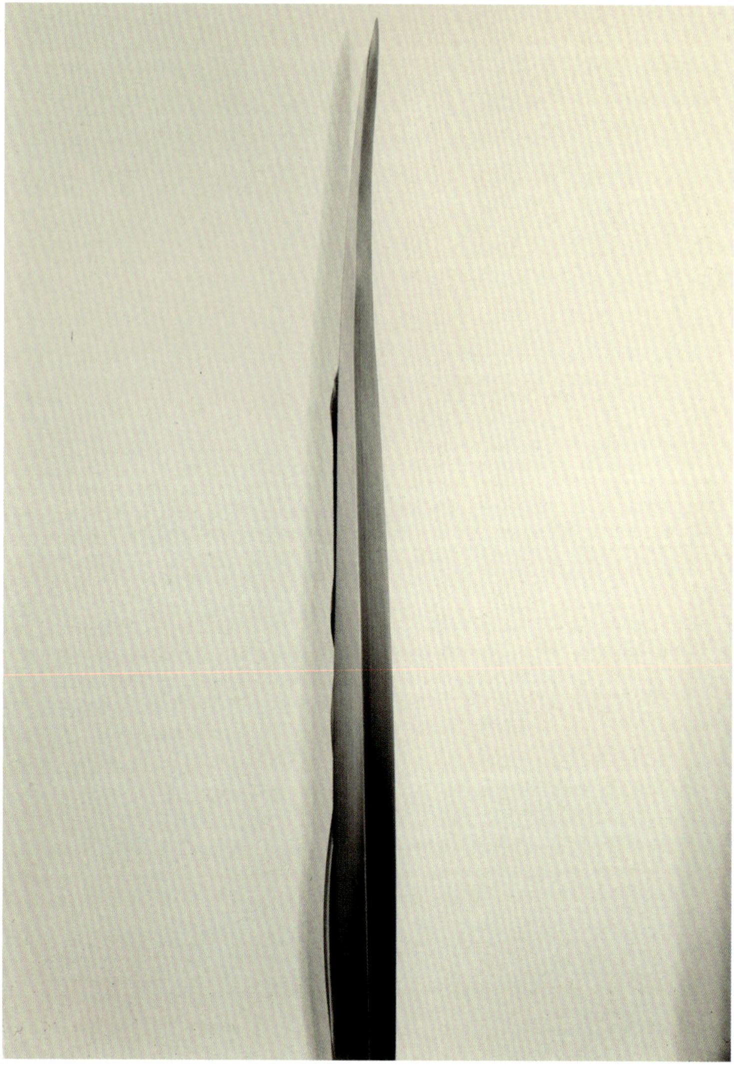

Cunningham enjoyed a long career as a photographer, creating a diverse and extensive body of work that underscores her vision and versatility. During the 1920s, the artist's garden became a creative refuge where she could experiment with her compositions and develop her artistic skills in a daily routine otherwise ruled by the demands of caring for three small children. Although she struggled to balance her family life and career, Cunningham gradually emerged as one of the most important and innovative American photographers. Unlike her celebrated pictures of magnolia blossoms or calla lilies, this starkly abstract image is not well known. It demonstrates the artist's exploration of advanced aesthetic concepts such as extreme simplicity, which would form the basis of the Minimalist art movement some twenty-five years later.

Edward Weston

American, 1886–1958

Bananas and Orange, April 1927

Gelatin silver print, 18.9 × 23.7 cm

(7 7/16 × 9 5/16 in.), 84.XM.860.4

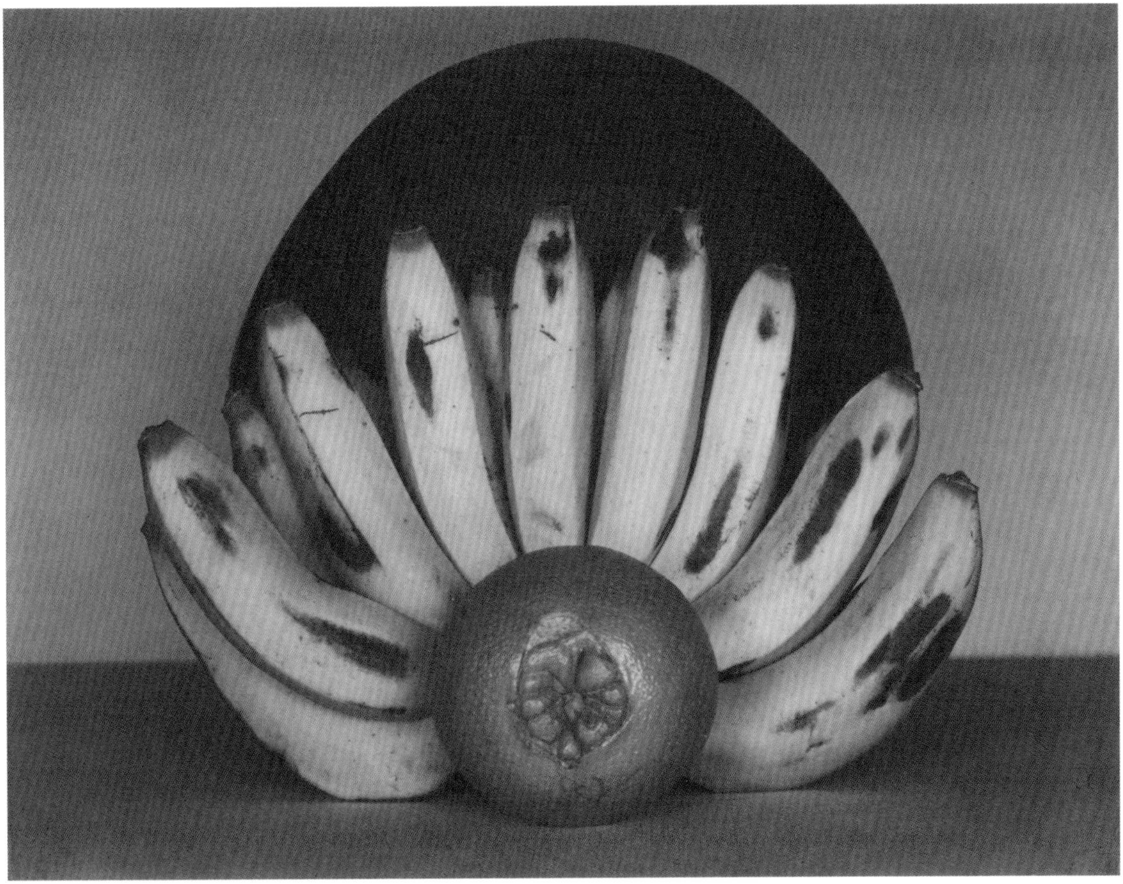

Weston was celebrated for his meticulously composed landscapes, still lifes, and studies of nude figures. After returning from a career-changing sojourn in Mexico City, he spent the latter part of the 1920s cultivating his growing interest in abstraction. This concentrated period in his studio practice was devoted to discovering the universal forms in all things. Weston's sculptural photographs elevate each subject, emphasizing its unique and imperfect characteristics to the point that it transcends its conventional purpose. In his words, "The camera should be used for a recording of life, for rendering the very substance and quintessence of the thing itself, whether it be polished steel or palpitating flesh."

August Sander

German, 1876–1964

Painter's Wife (Helene Abelen), 1926

Gelatin silver print, 22.9 × 16.4 cm

(9 × 6 7/16 in.), 84.XM.498.9

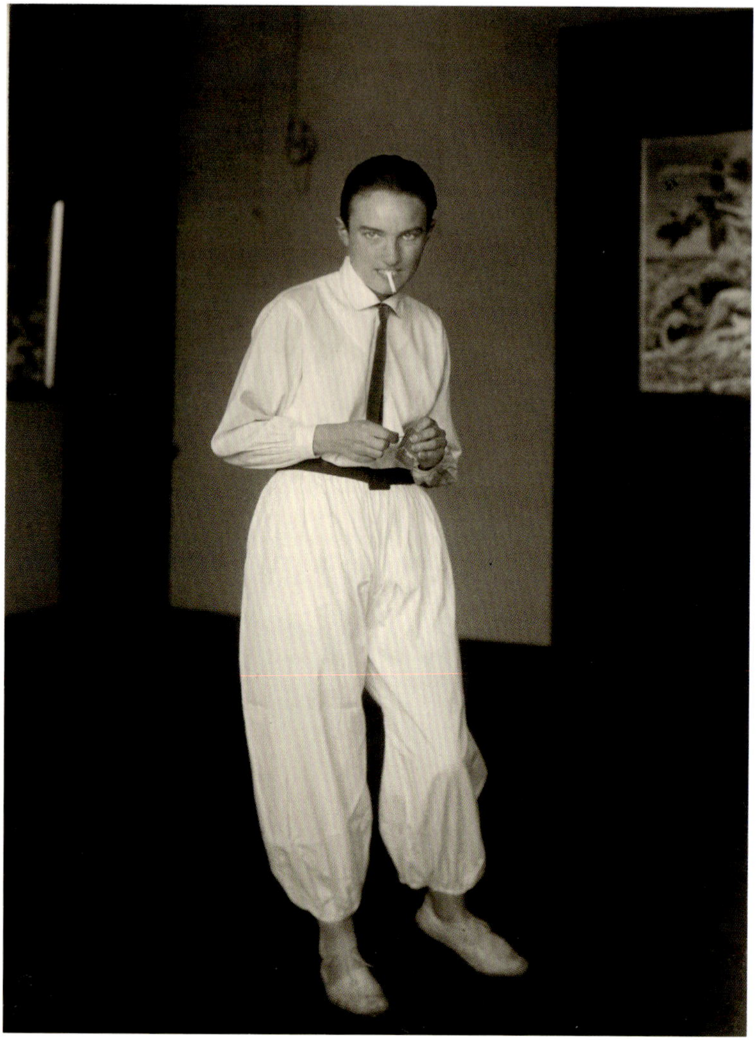

One of the most compelling photographers of the twentieth century, Sander dedicated five decades to compiling a collective portrait of the German people. Beginning with farmers, skilled tradespeople, women, and artists and ending with "the last people"—those who were ill or disabled, and death masks of those who had died—Sander arranged his portraits in portfolios that examined his sitters according to their class, profession, and association with the country or city. He created an overview of society based on the role of the individual within the context of the collective whole. Identified as "painter's wife," this woman is dressed in a crisp white shirt, thin necktie, and stylish culottes. With her slicked-back hair, cigarette clenched between her teeth, and defiant expression, she projects a quintessential image of the "new woman" of the Weimar Republic.

ringl + pit

German, active 1930–33

Hat and Gloves, 1930

Gelatin silver print, 37.8 × 24.8 cm

(14⁷⁄₈ × 9³⁄₄ in.), 84.XM.154.15

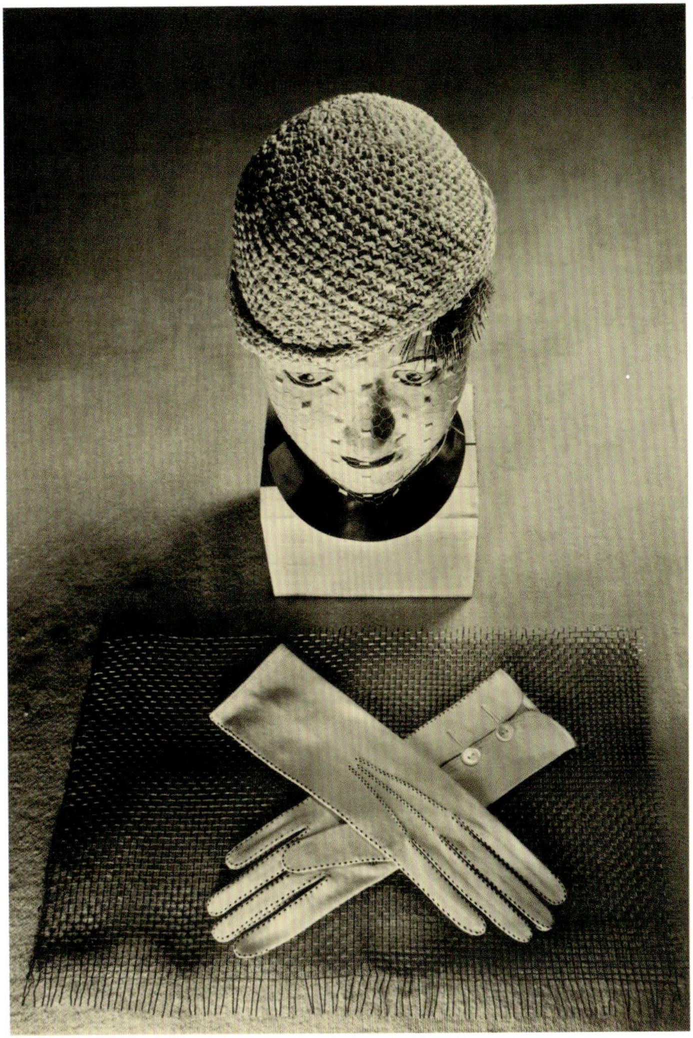

Ellen Auerbach (1906–2004) and Grete Stern (1904–1999) established the photography studio ringl + pit in Berlin in 1930. Auerbach and Stern met as private students of Walter Peterhans (1897–1960), a photography instructor affiliated with the influential Bauhaus school of art and design. In line with this training, ringl + pit embraced a highly rationalized style of photography. The studio specialized in advertisements, and its formally inventive, carefully constructed images wittily subverted the depiction of women in mainstream media. Here, Auerbach underscores the artifice of traditional markers of femininity. The hat and gloves are commodities for sale, but the disembodied mannequin acting as a "model," with its false hair and modestly crossed hands, comments on the commodification of women. Auerbach and Stern closed their studio and ended their collaboration when they were forced to flee Nazi Germany in 1933.

Lisette Model

American, born Austria, 1901–1983

Rhinoceros Resting on Its Side, 1933–38

Ferrotyped gelatin silver print,

28.7 × 22.2 cm (11 5/16 × 8 3/4 in.),

84.XM.153.16

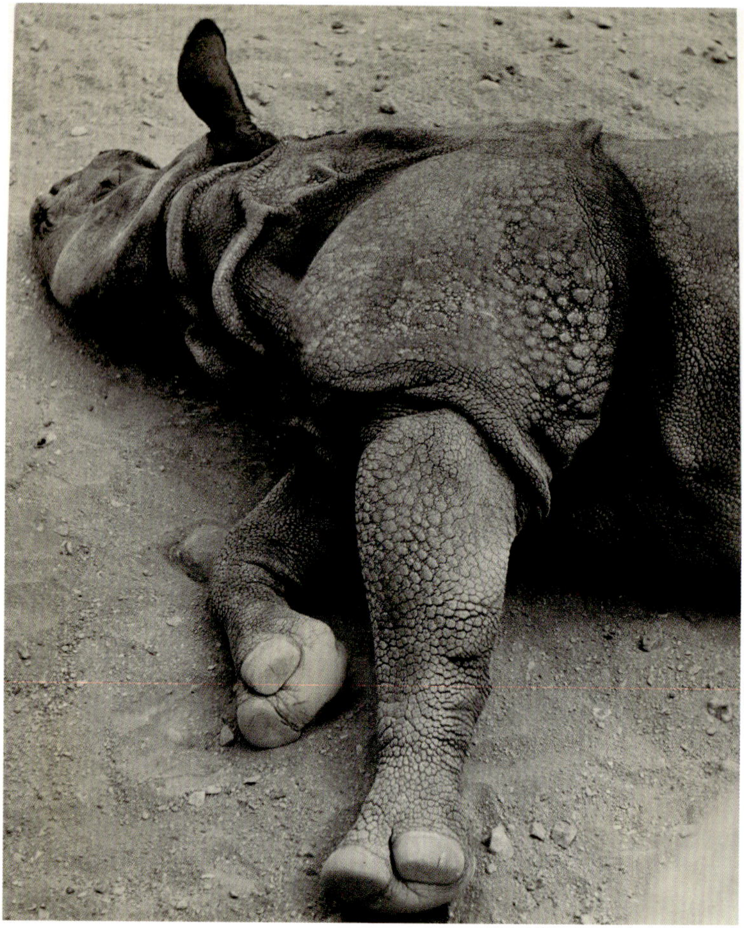

Model took up photography around 1933, trading in a career in music to pursue the visual arts. Her photograph of a rhinoceros, taken on a trip to the Vincennes Zoo in France, is one of her earliest works. Model excludes any traces of the animal's immediate surroundings in favor of a close study of its immense limbs and the intricate patterns of its textured skin. This treatment, likely achieved by enlarging and cropping the negative in the darkroom, would become a trademark of her later work as a documentary and street photographer. In photographs taken along the Promenade des Anglais in Nice, France, and in the Lower East Side neighborhood of New York City, Model privileged up-close, intimate views of her subjects that were at once direct and enigmatic.

Dora Maar

French, 1907–1997

Untitled (Fashion Photograph), 1936

Gelatin silver print, 19.6 × 16.6 cm

(7 11/16 × 6 9/16 in.), 84.XP.714.14

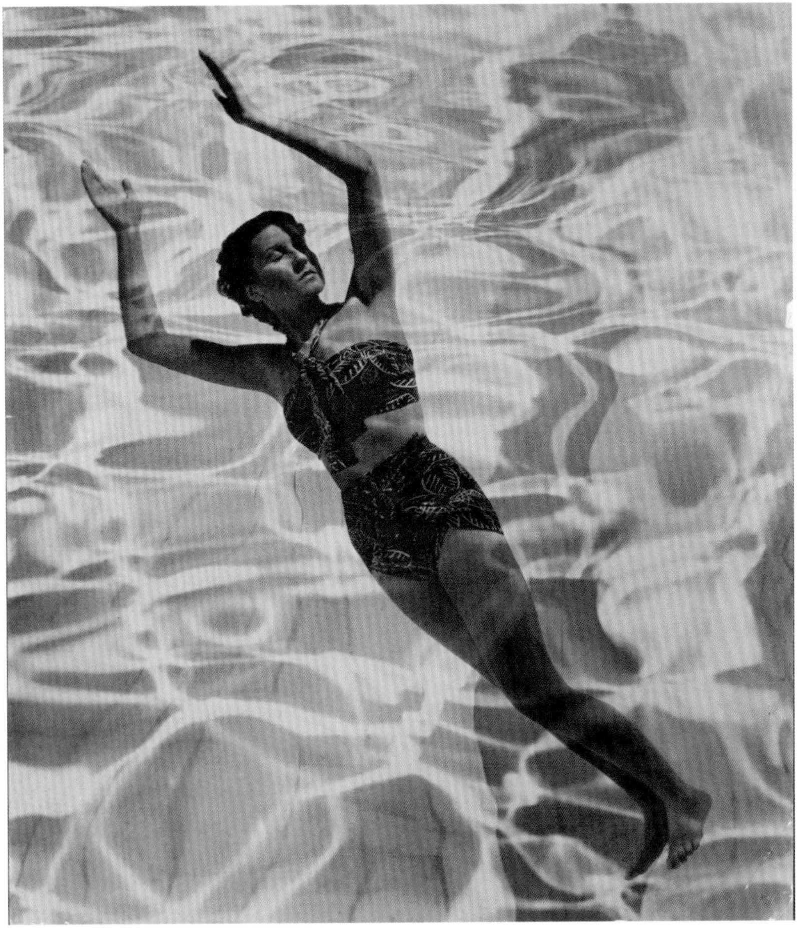

Maar, an established figure of the international Surrealist movement, made fashion and advertising photographs throughout the 1930s for magazines, fashion houses, and beauty companies. Having worked as an assistant to the fashion photographer Harry Ossip Meerson earlier in her career, she recognized the need to represent clothing and accessories clearly, posing her models against plain cloth backdrops in her studio. Yet Maar also brought her distinctive aesthetic to bear on this image of a model wearing a Jacques Heim–designed swimsuit, using double exposure to suspend the woman in a body of water that appears distorted and shifting. For Surrealist photographers such as Maar, commercial assignments and publications represented fertile spaces of experimentation that allowed them to explore the complex relationship between fantasy and reality.

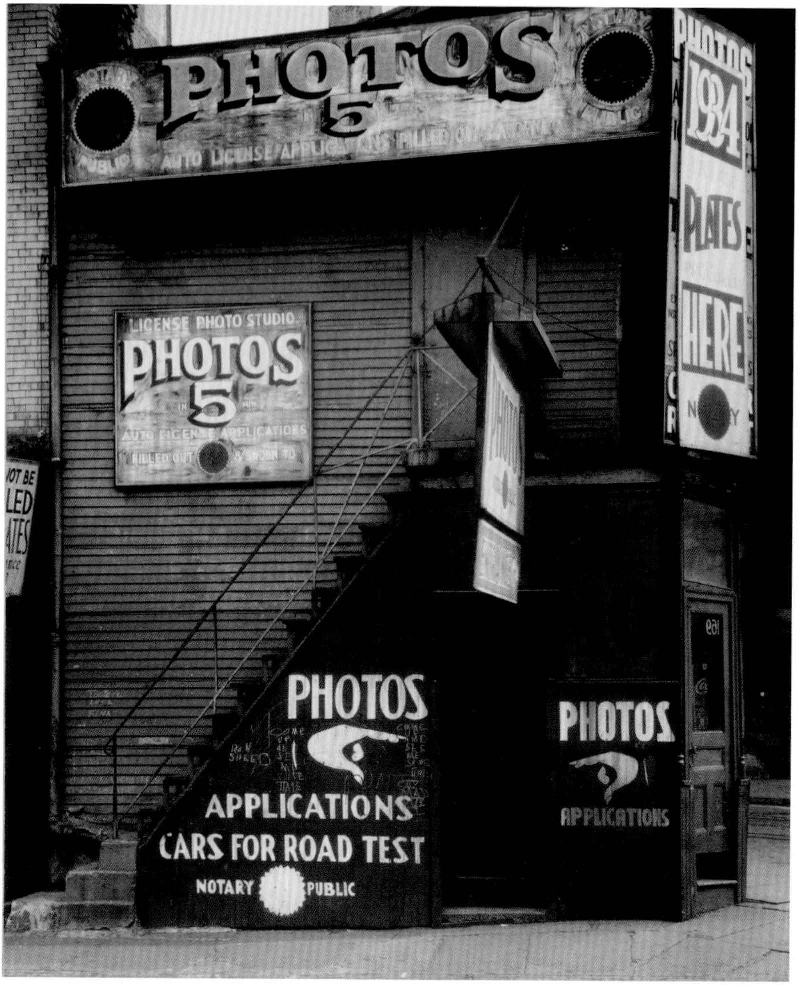

Walker Evans
American, 1903–1975
License Photo Studio, New York, 1934
Gelatin silver print, 18.3 × 14.4 cm
($7\frac{3}{16} \times 5\frac{11}{16}$ in.), 84.XM.956.456

Evans was a pioneering photographer renowned for his stark documentation of the American experience, particularly during the Great Depression. His interest in recording the quotidian aspects of life allowed him to capture various subjects, including objects of mass production, capitalism, and consumerism, while conveying the disparity between poverty and wealth. Here, Evans cultivates meaning from juxtaposed pictorial elements—the signs plastered on the walls, the imagery of hands pointing to the open doorway, and various small, inconspicuous details across and within the building. The repetition of the word "photos" creates a dynamic bombardment of information, emphasizing the photograph's self-referential elements. In a broader context, this photograph preserves the memory of objects and structures that eventually faded into obsolescence.

Dorothea Lange
American, 1895–1965
Human Erosion in California (Migrant Mother), March 1936
Gelatin silver print, 34.1 × 26.8 cm
($13\frac{7}{16} \times 10\frac{9}{16}$ in.), 98.XM.162

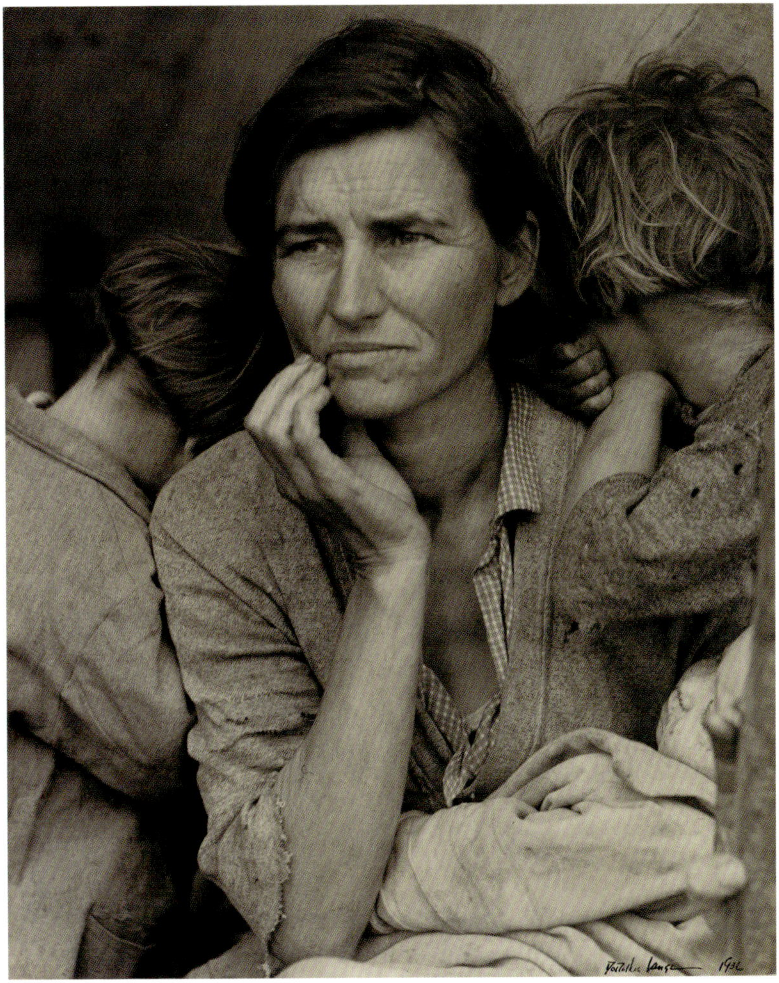

Lange made this austere portrait of the farm laborer Florence Owens and her children at a pea-pickers' camp in Nipomo, California, while working for the Resettlement Administration, a government agency that sought to raise public support for Depression-era economic relief programs. Foregrounding Owens's contemplative expression as she holds a sleeping baby in her lap, Lange's photograph recalls iconography of the Madonna and Child. Widely circulated in the press and featured in government campaigns, Lange's photograph rapidly came to symbolize the ravages of the Great Depression and catapulted Owens—then known only as "Migrant Mother" and presumed to be white—to unwanted national fame. In 1978, Owens, a member of the Cherokee Nation, appealed to magazines to remove the image from circulation, alleging that Lange had published the photograph without her consent.

Noboru Ueki

Japanese, 1905–1991

Untitled, circa 1948

Hand-colored gelatin silver print,

55.9 × 45.9 cm (22 × 18 1/16 in.), 2020.59.1

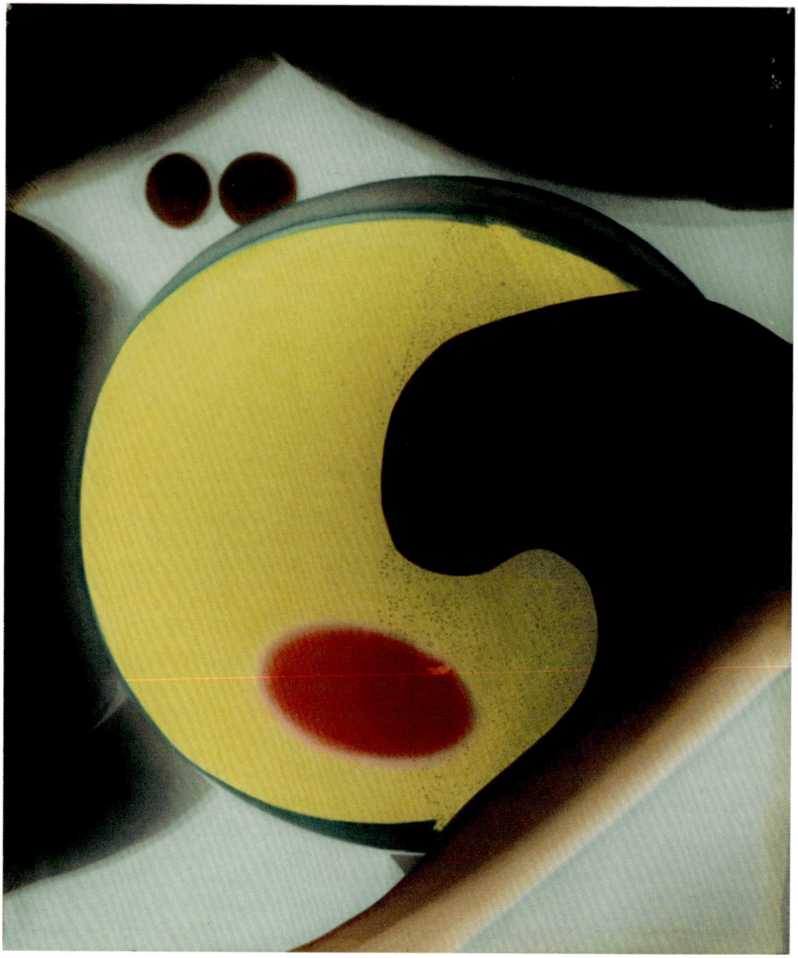

Trained as a portrait photographer, Ueki began experimenting with abstraction in the late 1930s amid a flourishing of avant-garde expression in the Kansai region of southern Japan. In the immediate aftermath of World War II, he turned to creating large-scale, hand-colored compositions that attracted immediate attention within Japanese photographic circles. Ueki described these photographs as still lifes inspired by Surrealist ideas of "deformation," which sought to defamiliarize the external world and plumb the depths of the unconscious mind. This arrangement of objects was likely photographed from above, with the highlights hand painted to create dense, dreamlike forms. Testifying to his deep interests in contemporary sculpture and painting, Ueki's photographs explore the associative potential of objects—a central concern of international Surrealism.

Irving Penn
American, 1917–2009
Marchande de Ballons (B), Paris
(Balloon Seller [B], Paris),
Paris, 1950; print, 1967
Platinum and palladium print,
40.6 × 32.4 cm (16 × 12¾ in.). Partial gift
of Irving Penn, 2008.1.243

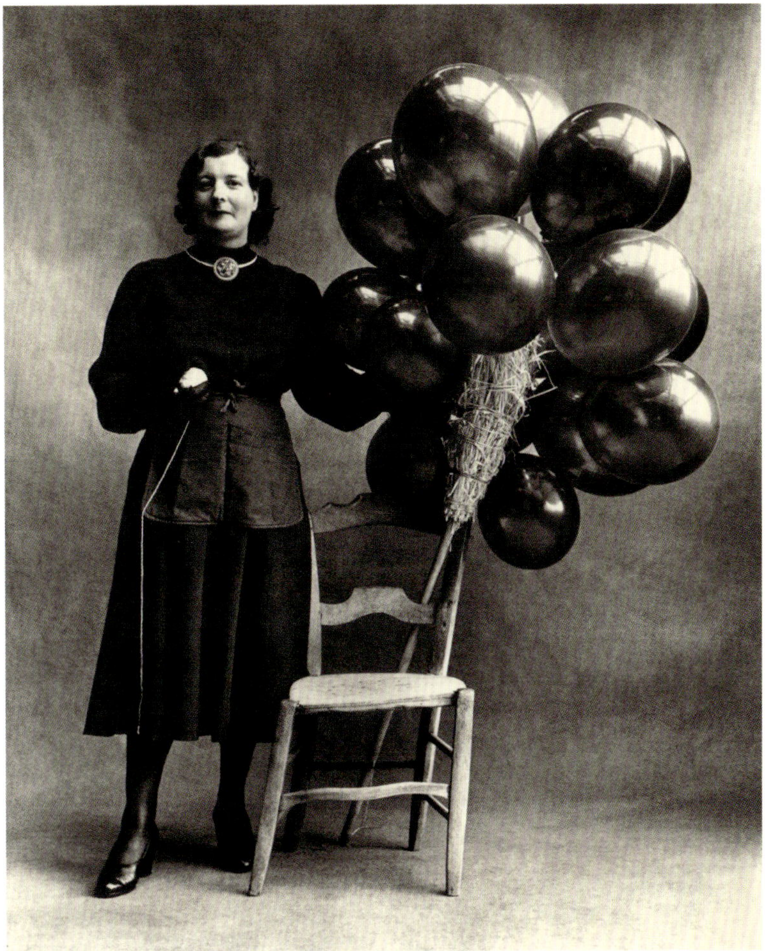

In a career that began at the premier fashion magazine *Vogue* in 1943 and spanned more than six decades, Penn created innovative fashion, still-life, and portrait studies. His photographs are defined by his stylistic trademarks of elegant simplicity and meticulous rigor. Penn began the body of work *Small Trades* while on assignment in Paris in the summer of 1950 and continued the project over the next year in London and New York. Based on the tradition of representing workers in popular print media, these full-length studies portray individuals dressed in their work clothes and carrying the tools of their trades. Penn preferred to work in studios with natural light, which in this image both illuminates the chicly dressed and coiffed balloon seller from the right and reflects off the surface of each balloon.

Minor White
American, 1908–1976
The Sound of One Hand Clapping, Pultneyville, New York, 1957; print, 1960

Gelatin silver print, 24.4 × 25 cm ($9^{11}/_{16} \times 9^{13}/_{16}$ in.). Purchased in part with funds provided by Daniel Greenberg, Susan Steinhauser, and the Greenberg Foundation, 2013.44.1

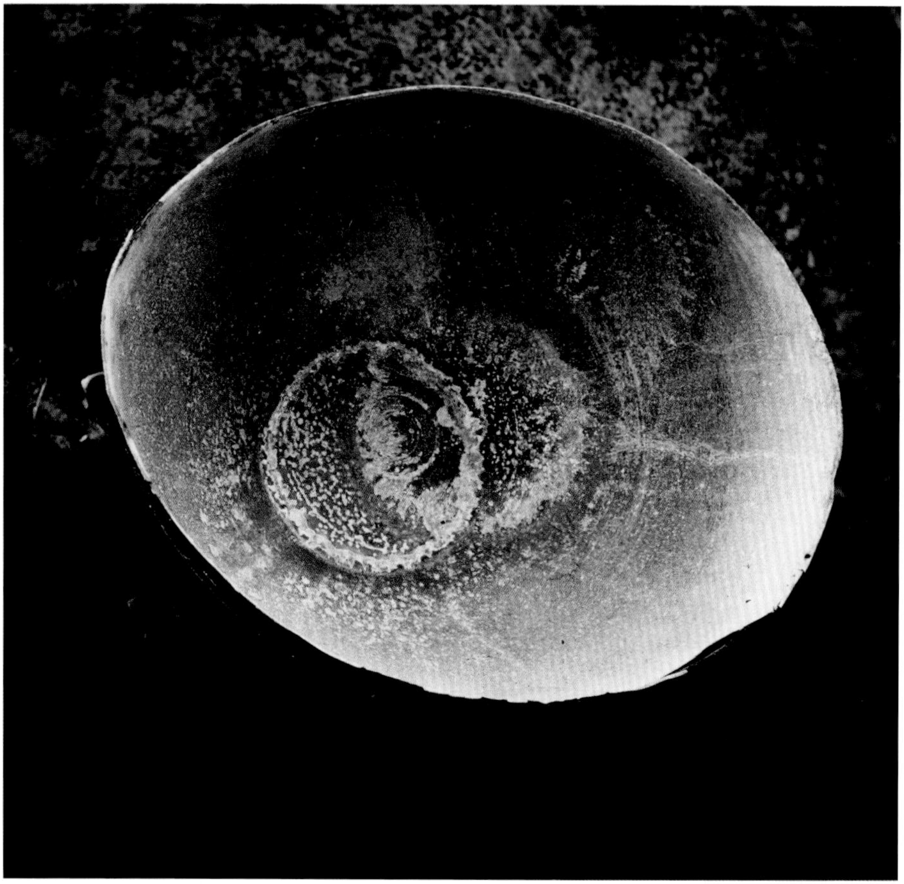

Throughout a nearly forty-year career, White pursued photography with great energy and purpose, endeavoring in various ways to extend the medium's expressive possibilities. Because one of White's goals was to photograph things not only for what they are but also for what they may suggest, his pictures teem with symbolic and metaphorical allusions. White was a student of Eastern religion, and while pondering the meaning of the Zen koan, or riddle, "What is the sound of one hand clapping?" he came upon an object resembling a Buddhist monk's begging bowl. The ringed marks inside the object, likely the result of exposure to inclement weather, underscore the overall circular dimensions of what was actually a discarded water tank.

Adger Cowans

American, born 1936

Fire Island, 1970

Gelatin silver print, 45.3 × 30.6 cm

(17 13/16 × 12 1/16 in.), 2021.12.5

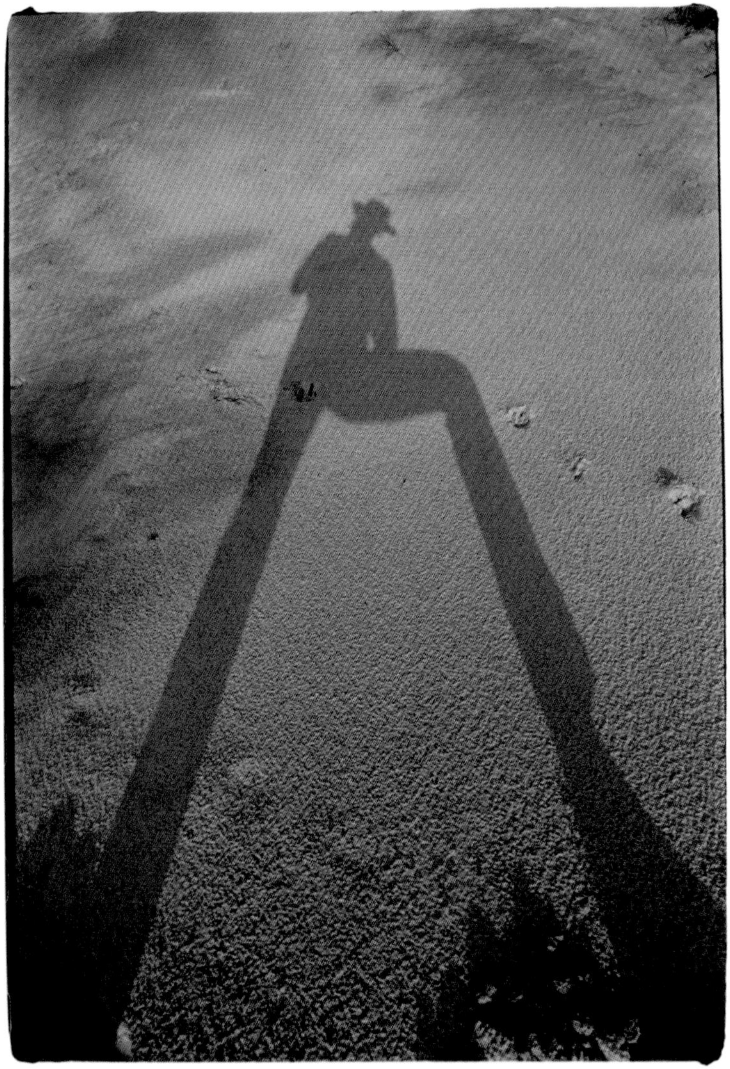

The artist's looming shadow fills the frame of this photograph so that he seems to tower over the landscape. The picture was made at a beach on Fire Island, New York, in 1970, a time when artists of color were rarely afforded space to show and share their work. Enterprising creatives like Cowans thus created opportunities for themselves. A vocal member of the Kamoinge Workshop, a collective of Black photographers founded in 1963, and AfriCOBRA, a group of artists committed to Black expression and advancement, Cowans works to record and foster Black empowerment through colorful paintings and dynamic photographs. Although North American beaches were long known as sites of segregation, Cowans's stride in this photograph is confident—he is unafraid to take up space and ready to make his mark.

Gordon Parks
American, 1912–2006
Flavio Amuses Smaller Brothers and Sisters, Rio de Janeiro, Brazil, 1961; print, 1960s–70s

Gelatin silver print, 13.6 × 19.7 cm ($5\frac{3}{8} \times 7\frac{3}{4}$ in.). Purchased with funds provided by the Photographs Council, 2015.18.9

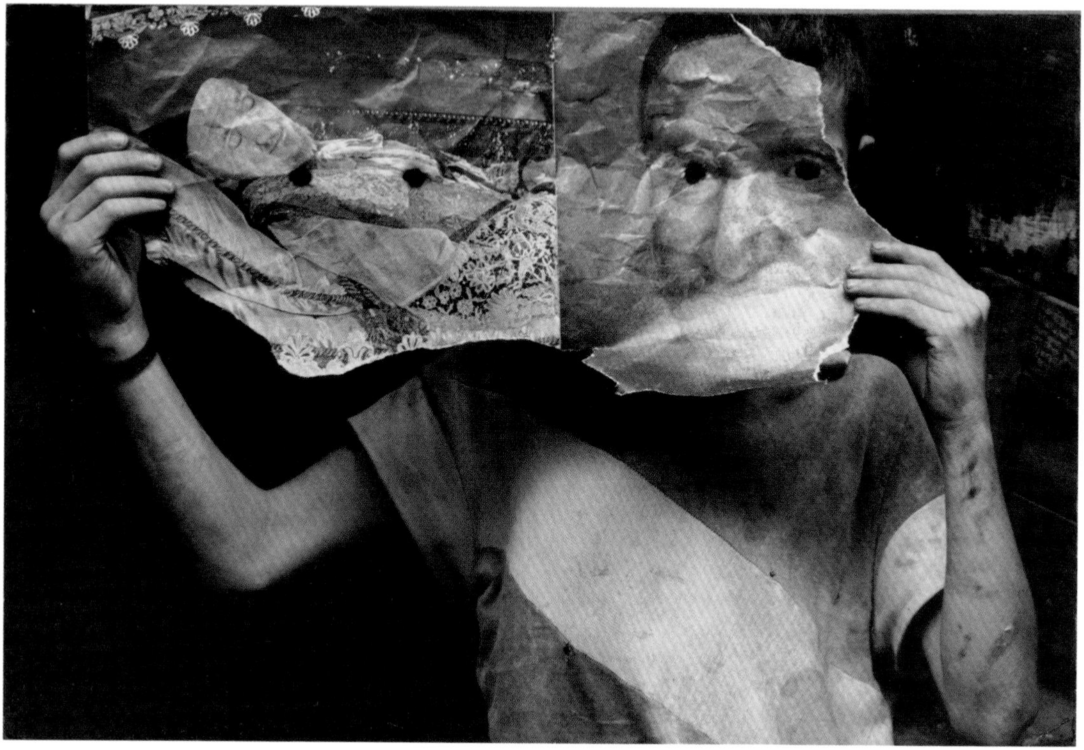

In 1961, *Life* magazine sent Parks to Rio de Janeiro to document the impact of poverty in Brazil. He returned with one of the most important photo-essays of his career, documenting the adversity that children faced in Rio's working-class neighborhoods. The subject of his story, twelve-year-old Flávio da Silva, spent his days caring for his seven younger siblings while suffering from malnourishment and an extreme case of asthma. Here, Flávio holds up a torn illustration of an older man and peers through two eye-shaped holes to amuse his siblings. By photographing the boy with this crude mask, Parks testifies to his resourcefulness and creativity while conveying the brutality of poverty, which has forced young Flávio to take on responsibilities beyond his years.

Gilles Peress

French, born 1946

Untitled, 1972

Gelatin silver print, 60.8 × 91.6 cm

(23 15/16 × 36 1/16 in.), 2021.71.3

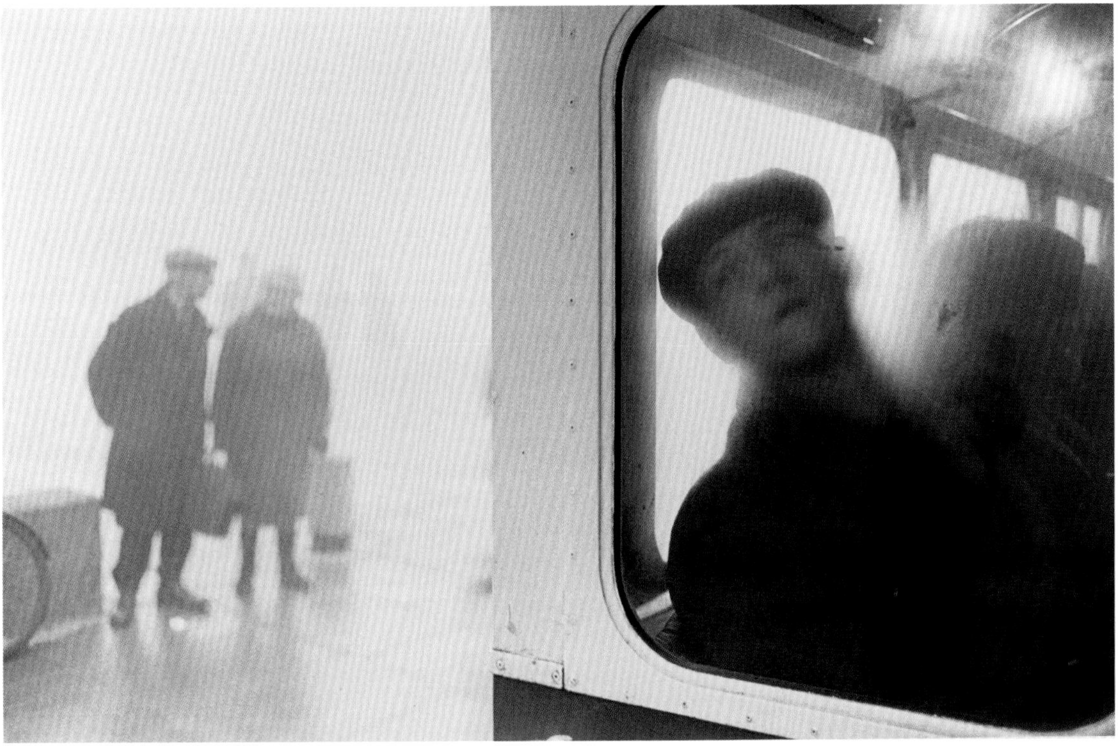

Peress has spent his professional life recording areas of strife and suffering around the world. He joined the celebrated cooperative Magnum Photos as a photojournalist in 1970 and traveled on his first assignment to Northern Ireland to document the Troubles, the decades-long, violent sectarian conflict between the country's predominantly Roman Catholic nationalists and Protestant unionists or loyalists. He returned to Northern Ireland nearly every year until the 1990s, generating a sprawling, multifaceted visual record. Peress captured not only scenes of bloodshed but also the monotony of daily life, as in this somber image of travelers in the Belfast city center, underscoring the excruciating passage of time as the Troubles continued with seemingly no end in sight.

Hiro

Japanese American, born China, 1930–2021

Black Evening Dress in Flight, New York, 1963; print, 1994

Dye imbibition print, 48.9 × 38.1 cm (19¼ × 15 in.). Purchased with funds provided by the Photographs Council, 2012.24.2

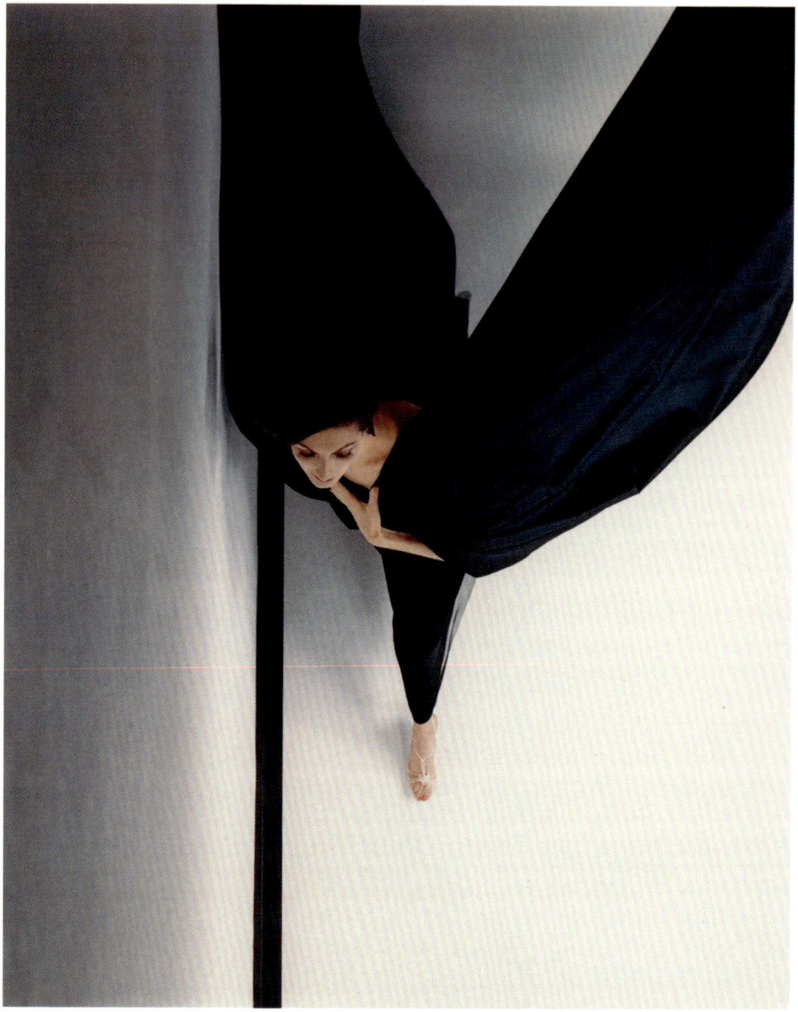

Impressed by photographs he saw in American magazines, Hiro left Japan for the United States in 1954 and eventually obtained an apprenticeship with the internationally renowned fashion photographer Richard Avedon (1923–2004). Avedon recognized Hiro's talent and recommended him to Alexey Brodovitch (1898–1971), art director at *Harper's Bazaar*. Brodovitch hired Hiro as a staff photographer for the magazine, a position he held from 1956 to 1975. Hiro quickly rose to prominence for his extraordinary fashion and still-life compositions, which often feature unusual juxtapositions and innovative lighting. Asked to photograph a shoe, for example, Hiro climbed through a hatch door onto the roof, so as to capture the model, her dress, and her shoe from an uncommon perspective. His innovations changed the face of photography and continue to influence the field today.

Malick Sidibé

Malian, 1936–2016

Untitled, 1975; framed, 2004

Gelatin silver print with glass, paint, cardboard, tape, and string, image: 12 × 7.5 cm (4 3/4 × 2 15/16 in.); frame: 18 × 12.7 × 1 cm (7 1/16 × 5 × 3/8 in.), 2010.26.1

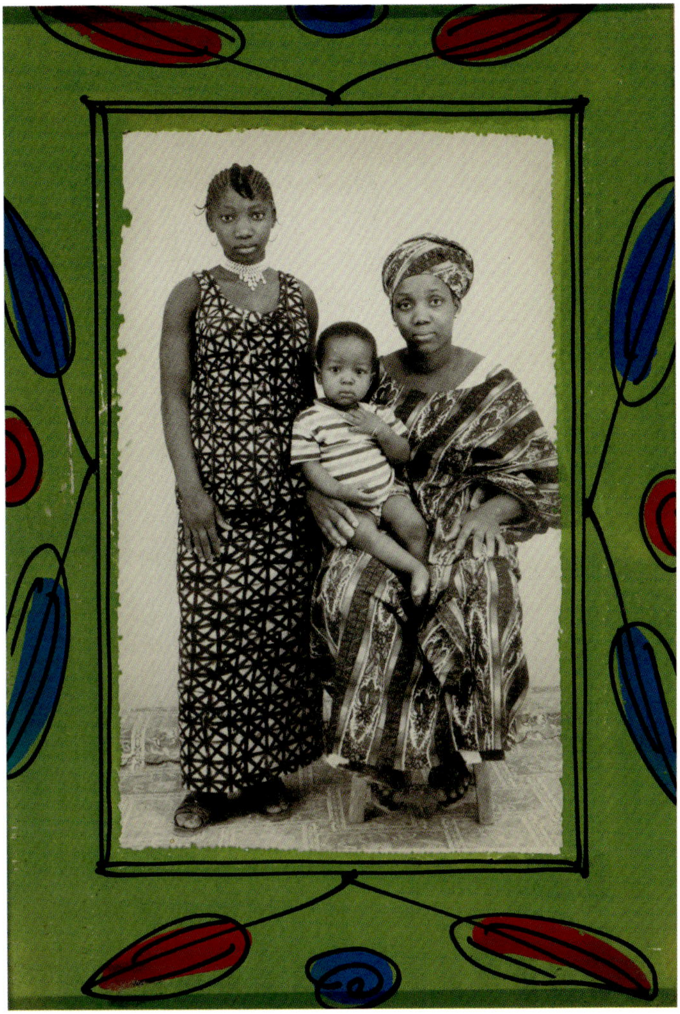

Sidibé opened Studio Malick in 1962, just two years after Mali achieved independence from French colonial rule, and at a time when few photography studios in the country's capital of Bamako were owned and operated by Africans. Clients went to Studio Malick to memorialize personal milestones, documenting in the process a period of rapid social and political change. Entering Sidibé's studio, sitters were offered a choice of backdrops, costumes, and props with which to accentuate aspects of their personalities or altogether reinvent themselves for the camera. Sidibé's clever eye for pose, pattern, and composition, combined with his renowned ability to put his sitters at ease, resulted in arrestingly beautiful portraits, like this one of a mother and her children. A neighboring frame maker, Checkna Touré, crafted the painted glass frame.

Jo Ann Callis
American, born 1940

Woman with Blonde Hair, 1977; print, 2016
Inkjet print, 68 × 53.4 cm (26¾ × 21 in.). Gift of the artist in honor of Judith Keller, 2017.84

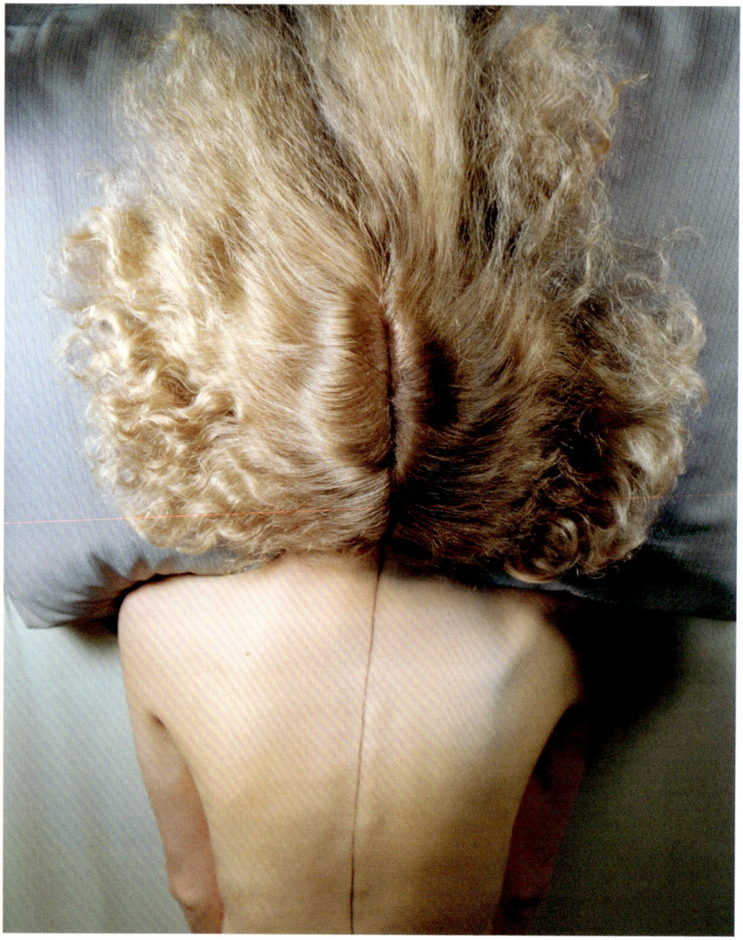

Born in Cincinnati, Ohio, and later relocating to Los Angeles in 1961, Callis was a pioneer in the staged-photography movement of the 1970s and 1980s. Her thoughtfully arranged scenes reveal the subtlety of the erotic imagination, serving as metaphors for feelings and experiences surrounding sexuality, sensuality, beauty, and power. In these provocative photographs, Callis plays with ideas of tactility to comment on the numerous societal pressures placed on women. Here, the artist has drawn an ink line along the part in the subject's hair and down her back, hinting at what lies below the frame and evoking a sense of sexual intimacy.

Francesca Woodman
American, 1958–1981

Untitled, 1978
From the series Eel
Gelatin silver print, 22 × 21.8 cm
(8 11/16 × 8 9/16 in.), 2023.65

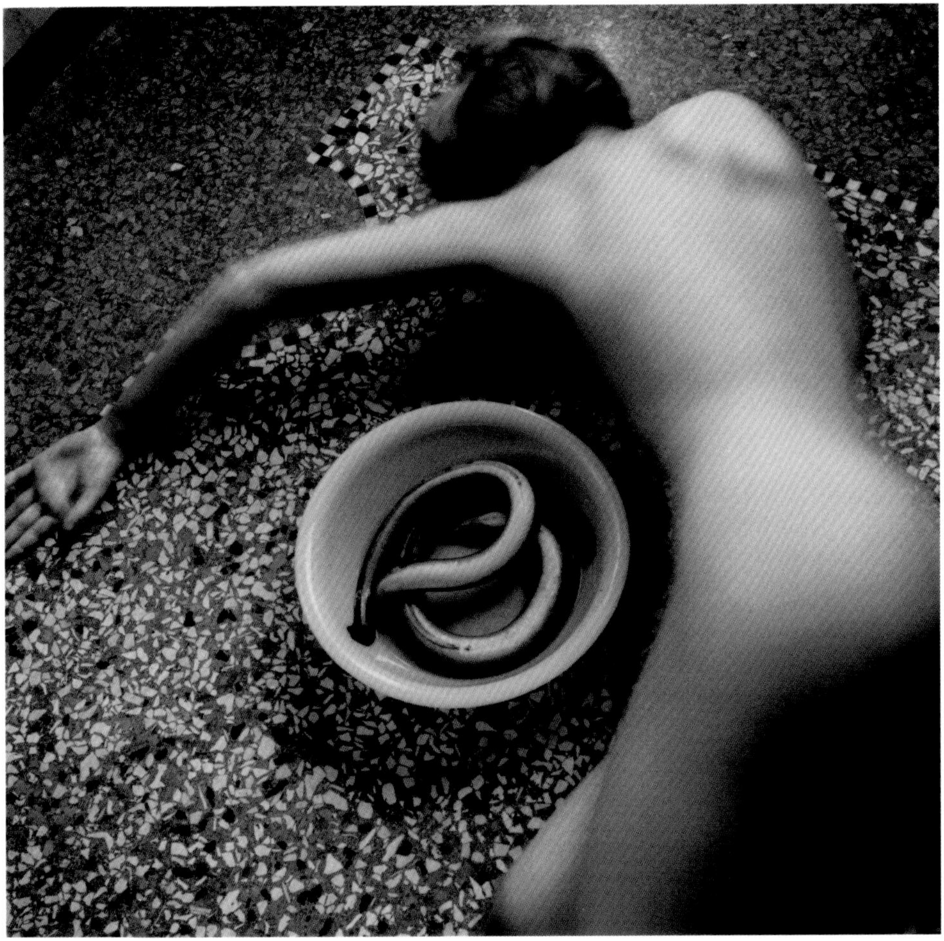

Throughout her short career, Woodman was heavily influenced by the Surrealist and Symbolist movements in art. Her photographs evoke dreamlike environments within limited spaces and frequently make use of her own body to explore themes of alienation and personal identity. Her precise use of composition was inspired by Italian art, architecture, and literature, absorbed during her years living in Italy. Here, Woodman lies naked on a mottled terrazzo floor in Venice, posing next to a bowl containing the coiled body of an eel. With her face obscured, limbs blurred, and sex ambiguous, the artist comments on the idea of the transformation and representation of the female form.

Tseng Kwong Chi
American, born Hong Kong, China, 1950–1990

Los Angeles, California, 1979
From the Expeditionary Self-Portrait Series (East Meets West)
Gelatin silver print, 38.1 × 38.3 cm (15 × 15 1/16 in.), 2023.103.1

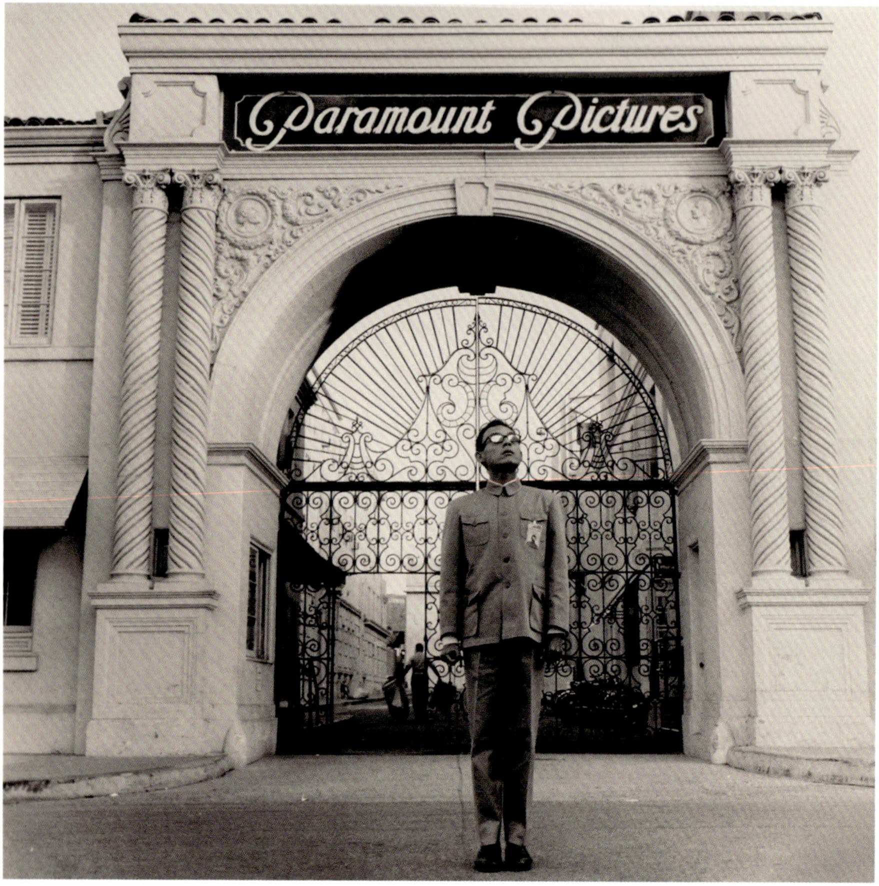

From the time he moved to the United States in 1979 until his death from AIDS-related illness eleven years later, Tseng created a vast body of photographic work, the most famous being the Expeditionary Series, also known as East Meets West. Donning sunglasses and a Zhongshan suit—now generally referred to as a "Mao suit"—Tseng photographed himself in the guise of a Chinese dignitary standing in front of iconic landmarks: the Eiffel Tower, the Roman Colosseum, Disneyland. This scene was created outside the gates of the Los Angeles film studio Paramount Pictures. As in nearly all his self-portraits, Tseng leaves visible the shutter-release cable, reminding the viewer that this is not a snapshot but a staged performance. With performativity thus established, Tseng subtly questions identity and cultural signifiers.

David Hockney
British, born 1937

Pearblossom Hwy., 11–18th April 1986, #2, 1986
Photocollage (chromogenic prints mounted on paper honeycomb panel), 181.6 × 271.8 cm (71½ × 107 in.), 97.XM.39

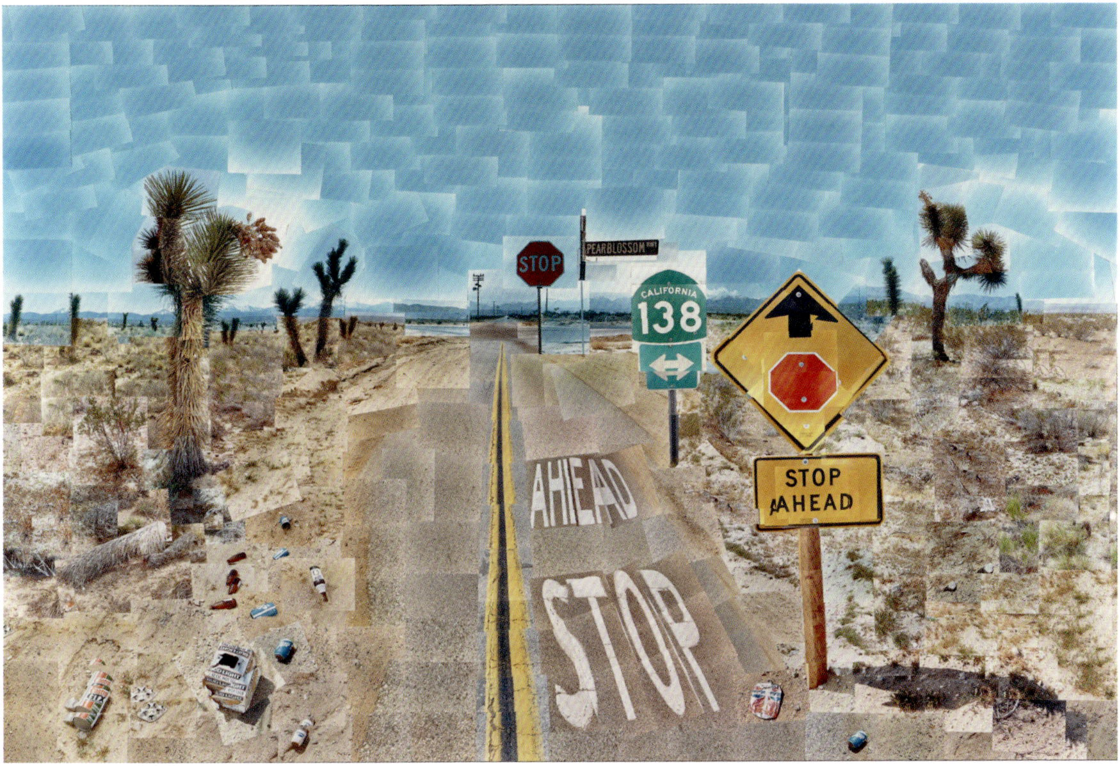

Convinced that the "decisive" moment captured in most photographs presents a static view, contrary to how we actually see, Hockney began exploring ways to invest photographs with a sense of time. He shot the almost eight hundred prints that comprise this collage in California's Antelope Valley over eight days. The resulting composition, which rivals the size of his paintings, encapsulates Hockney's understanding of photography as "drawing with a camera." By taking close-ups of individual objects that populate the desert landscape, he introduces multiple viewpoints that activate the scene and engage viewers, who are rewarded by spending time to register all the visual elements. The magazine *Vanity Fair* originally commissioned, but ultimately rejected, the work for a story about the monotony of the road, as experienced by the characters in Vladimir Nabokov's novel *Lolita* (1955).

Duane Michals
American, born 1932

All Things Mellow in the Mind, 1986
Gelatin silver print, sheet: 40.4 × 50.4 cm
(15 15/16 × 19 7/8 in.). Gift of Duane Michals,
2023.68.15

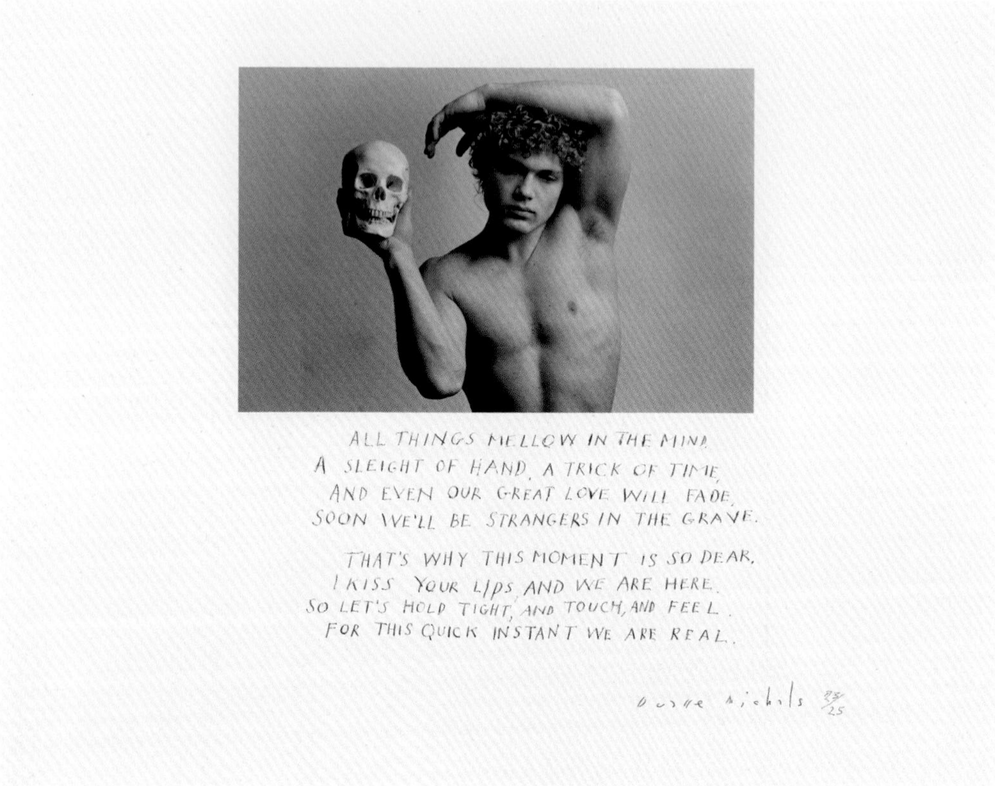

Michals, a prolific image maker, is widely considered to be a pioneer of staged photography. Influenced by cinema, his projects are driven by traditional narrative structures. He frequently arranges multiple prints into sequences and often annotates them with handwritten prose or poetry. The combination of text and image underscores the medium's ability to suggest what is outside the frame and cannot be seen. Here, Michals juxtaposes a skull, a symbol of death, with the model's athletic, nude body, posed to suggest sexual availability. The inscription beneath the image speaks to the ephemerality of life and love. The text calls on the viewer to recognize the passage of time and the inevitability of change, encouraging us to cherish the present moment before it is gone.

Robert Mapplethorpe
American, 1946–1989
Self-Portrait, 1988
Gelatin silver print, 58.9 × 48.3 cm (23 3/16 × 19 in.). Jointly acquired by the J. Paul Getty Trust and the Los Angeles County Museum of Art; partial gift of The Robert Mapplethorpe Foundation; partial purchase with funds provided by the J. Paul Getty Trust and the David Geffen Foundation, 2011.9.25

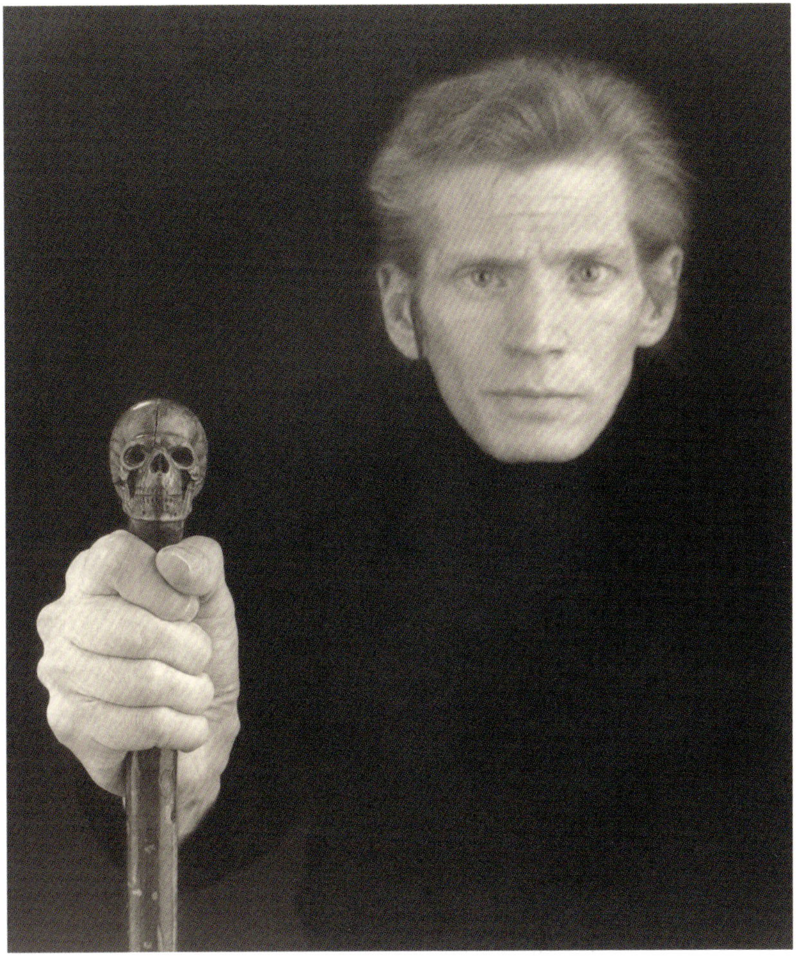

Mapplethorpe died of AIDS-related complications on March 12, 1989, at the age of forty-two. In 1988, while the disease wreaked havoc on his body, he used the camera to take artistic control over what was happening to him. In doing so, he joined artists such as Keith Haring (died at age thirty-one), Félix González-Torres (died at age thirty-eight), and David Wojnarowicz (died at age thirty-seven), all contemporaries of Mapplethorpe whose work also addressed the AIDS crisis. This photograph captures Mapplethorpe's face with signs of illness and fixed with an impassive expression. His head appears to float, and his hand grips a skull-topped cane, a symbol of his impending death. The composition features elements protruding from a tomblike darkness, and its brutal honesty makes this work one of Mapplethorpe's most powerful achievements.

Graciela Iturbide

Mexican, born 1942

Magnolia, Juchitán, Oaxaca, 1986; print, 2005

Gelatin silver print, 44.5 × 31.5 cm (17½ × 12⅜ in.). Gift of Susan Steinhauser and Daniel Greenberg, 2007.65.25

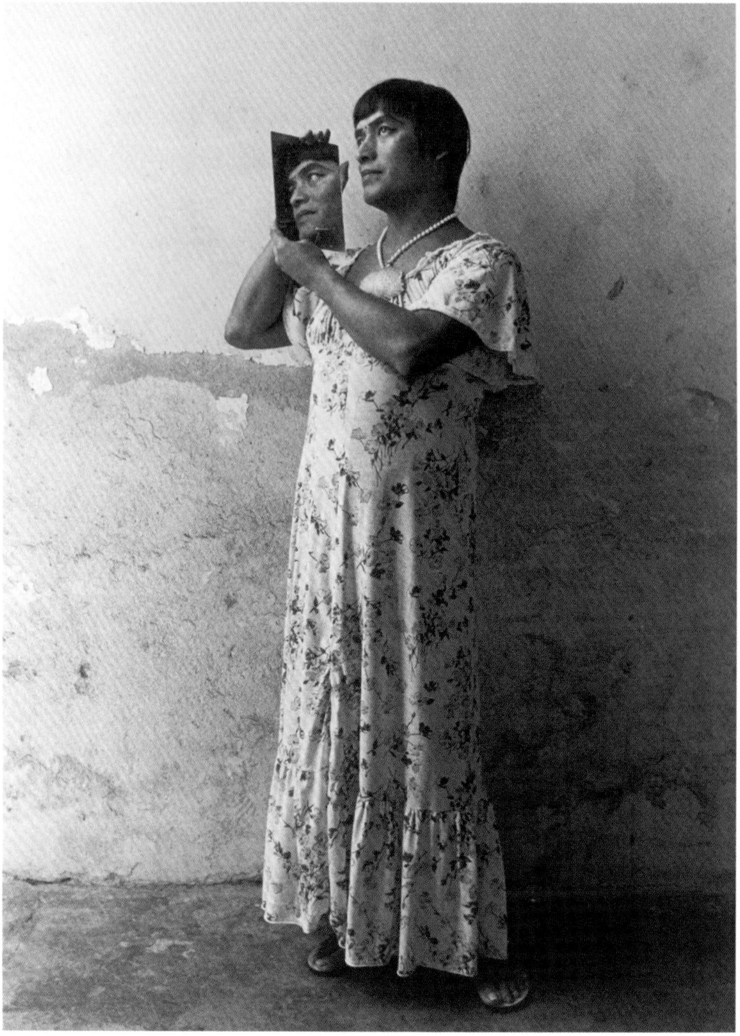

Born in Mexico City to an upper-class Catholic family, Iturbide had little exposure to Indigenous Mexican culture before she began studying under the celebrated Mexican photographer Manuel Álvarez Bravo (1902–2002) in the 1970s. Through later commissions for the Ethnographic Archive of the National Indigenous Institute of Mexico, she became well known for sensitive portraits made in close collaboration with her subjects. This photograph, taken during her 1986 stay in Juchitán de Zaragoza, depicts Magnolia, a person of the Zapotec third gender known as *muxe*. *Muxe* have been acknowledged in Mexico since before Spanish colonization and are celebrated in Zapotec culture. By the time Iturbide took this intimate, contemplative portrait of Magnolia holding a mirror, she had been photographing the town's inhabitants intermittently for seven years.

Nan Goldin

American, born 1953

Jimmy Paulette and Tabboo! Undressing, NYC, 1991

Silver-dye bleach print, 102 × 76 cm (40 3/16 × 29 15/16 in.). Purchased with funds provided by the Photographs Council, 2022.26

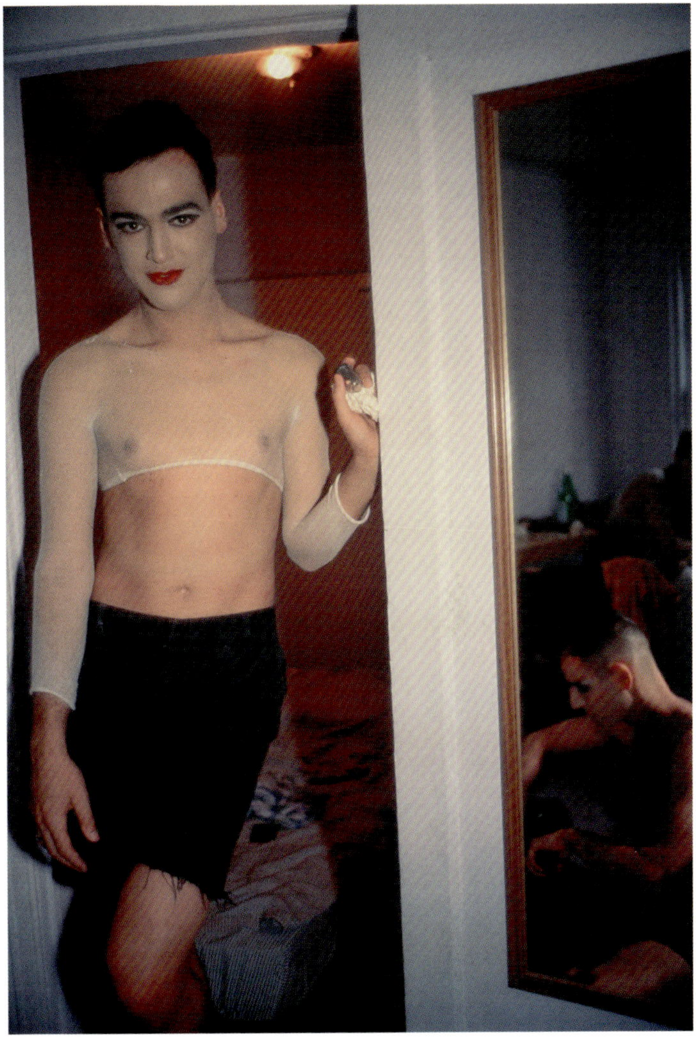

As one of the most influential photographers of our time, Goldin candidly chronicles the lives of her friends and lovers, many of whom live on the margins of mainstream society. For Goldin, photography is a form of salvation, one she strives to share. This image is from a series in which she captured the perils of drug addiction and the devastation of the HIV/AIDS epidemic, with a focus on queer kinship, in New York City from the 1970s to the 1990s. She pays homage to her friends by uplifting their individuality with dignity and empathy, rather than emphasizing aspects of their sexuality. This iconic photograph is one of several by Goldin that depict Jimmy Paulette and Tabboo!, two of her muses, within the vibrant New York drag scene.

Graciela Sacco
Argentinian, 1956–2017
Untitled #8, 1993
From the series Bocanada, 1993
Heliograph print, 71.5 × 45.4 cm
(28⅛ × 17⅞ in.). Purchased with funds
provided by the Photographs Council,
2016.3.4

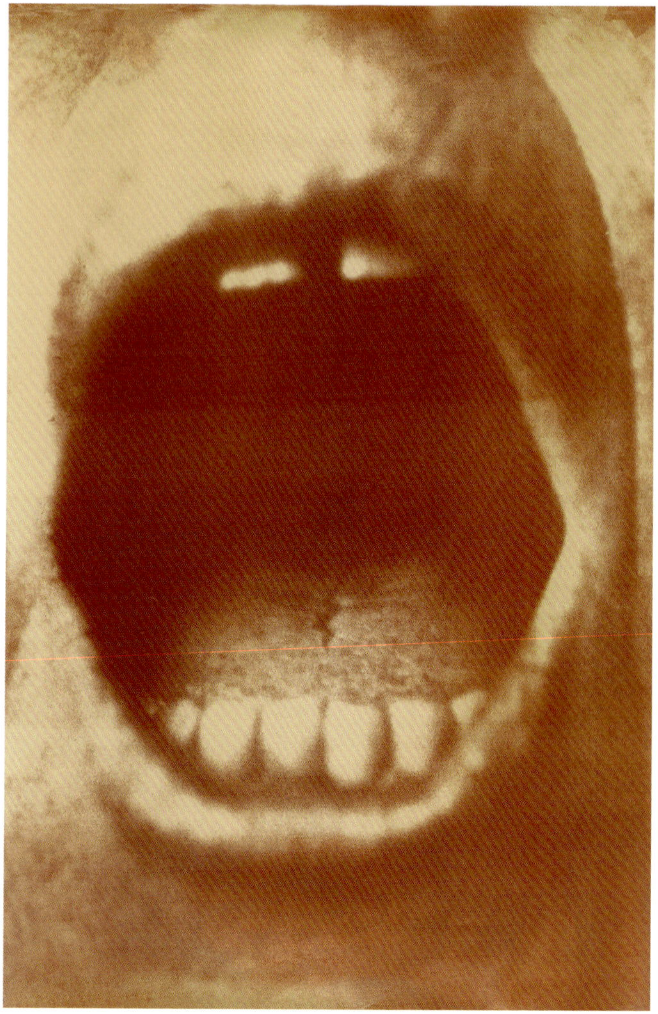

Sacco is known for works that reflect the social and political upheavals of her native Argentina. She often turned to early nineteenth-century processes like heliography—which involves the transfer of an image by placing it on any chemically treated surface that is then exposed to light—to make thousands of posters that were plastered in public places in cities throughout Argentina. These urban interventions encouraged chance encounters with passersby who came across these striking compositions and registered their call for urgent social change. Working with found photographs drawn from anonymous crowd scenes, Sacco often cropped and enlarged individual body parts for greater emphasis. Featuring an isolated view of an open mouth, this print illustrates the title of the series, which loosely translates to "empty mouth," as a way to call attention to hunger and poverty in Argentina and globally.

Shirin Neshat

Iranian, born 1957

Grace Under Duty, 1994

From the series Women of Allah, 1993–97

Gelatin silver print and ink, framed:

127.6 × 104.8 × 4.8 cm

(50¼ × 41¼ × 1⅞ in.), 2022.2

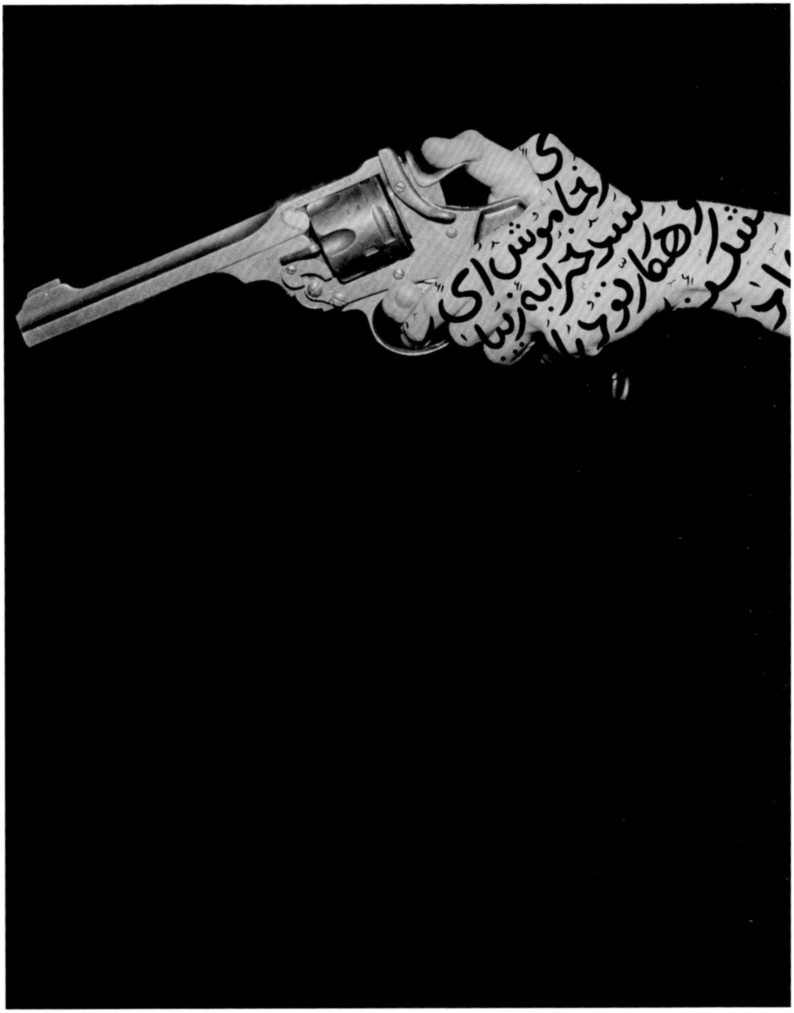

Neshat is known for photographs and films that intertwine the poetic with the political. She left her native Iran prior to the 1979 revolution, and her work often explores the difficult history of her country in relation to her personal experiences as an émigré Muslim woman now based in the United States. This photograph derives from her series Women of Allah (1993–97), in which she portrays gun-toting women to explore the martyrdom of women during the Iranian Revolution. In a spirit of protest, disruption, and confrontation, she incorporates Persian texts by feminist poets and authors, hand inscribing them onto the few parts of the female body that are allowed to be revealed in strict Muslim societies, primarily, the face, hands, and feet.

Laura Aguilar
American, 1959–2018
Nature Self-Portrait #2, 1996
Gelatin silver print, 35.6 × 48.4 cm
(14 × 19 in.). Purchased with funds provided
by the Photographs Council, 2019.19.2

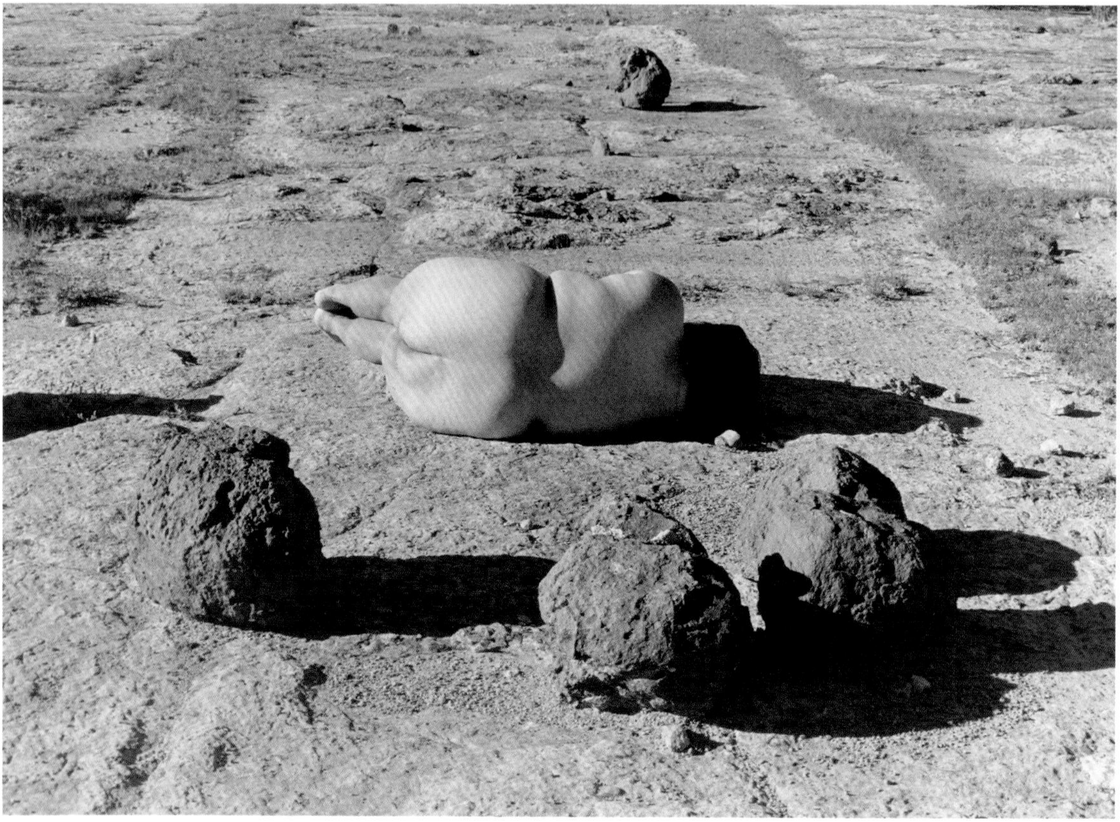

Over a thirty-year career, the Los Angeles–based artist Laura Aguilar made photographs that revealed the emotional and psychological texture of the various communities with which she identified. She regularly turned the camera lens on her own body as a way of reconciling deeply held insecurities about her weight. Her nude self-portraits in landscape settings reveal an interest in juxtaposing the fragile human form with the harsh conditions of the desert, often resulting in striking contrasts. This work is one of several in the series in which she lies amid boulders with her skin exposed, her body contorted to mimic the shape of the rocks. Blurring the distinction between human and nonhuman forms, these photographs suggest looking at the landscape of the American West in terms of a personal relationship.

Ming Smith

American, active since the 1960s

Aunt Stella, 1992

Gelatin silver print, 48 × 34.5 cm ($18\frac{7}{8} \times 13\frac{9}{16}$ in.). Purchased with funds provided by the Photographs Council, 2019.125.4

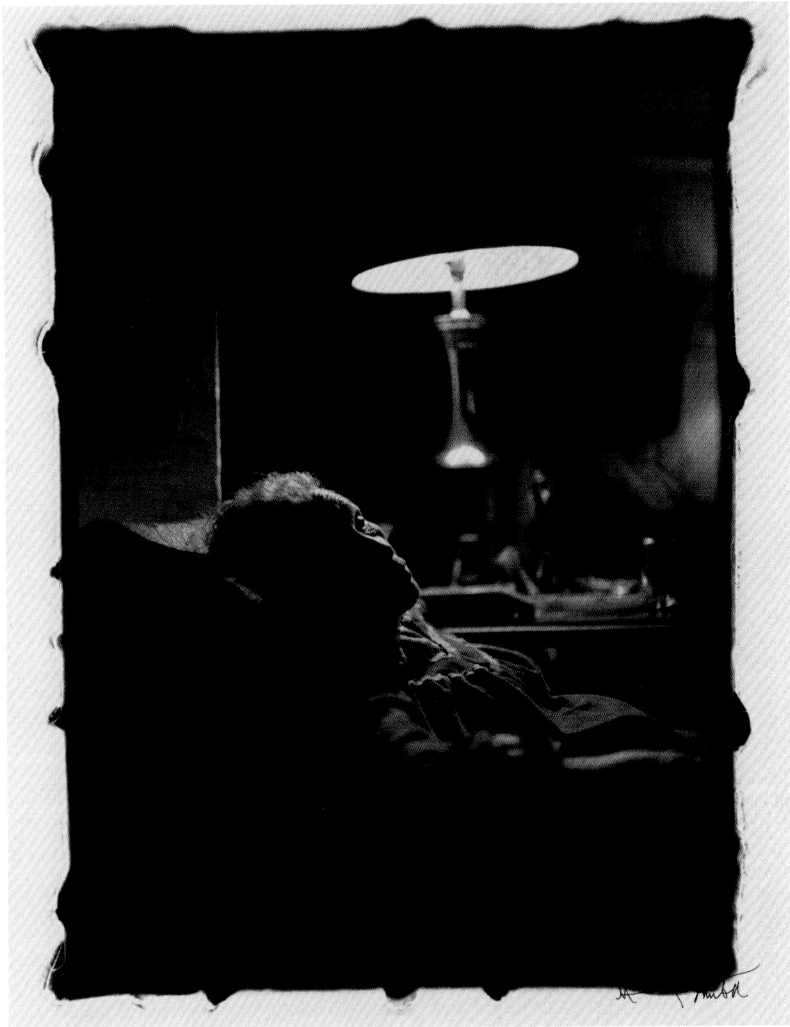

Inspired by the people and places of *The Pittsburgh Cycle*, a series of theatrical productions by the American playwright August Wilson (1945–2005) about the Black residents of that city's Hill District, Smith made a group of shadowy photographic images to comment on the long, dark history of Black marginalization. This portrait of the artist's aunt evokes the character Aunt Ester, a wise and powerful spiritual force in Wilson's plays. As Smith's elder gazes out of the frame, the edges of the photographic emulsion seem to pulse with her breath, the darkened corners of her room rendered as a rich metaphor for isolation and interiority.

Wang Qingsong
Chinese, born 1966
New Women, 2000
Chromogenic print, 120 × 220 cm
(47¼ × 86⅝ in.), 2009.18.2

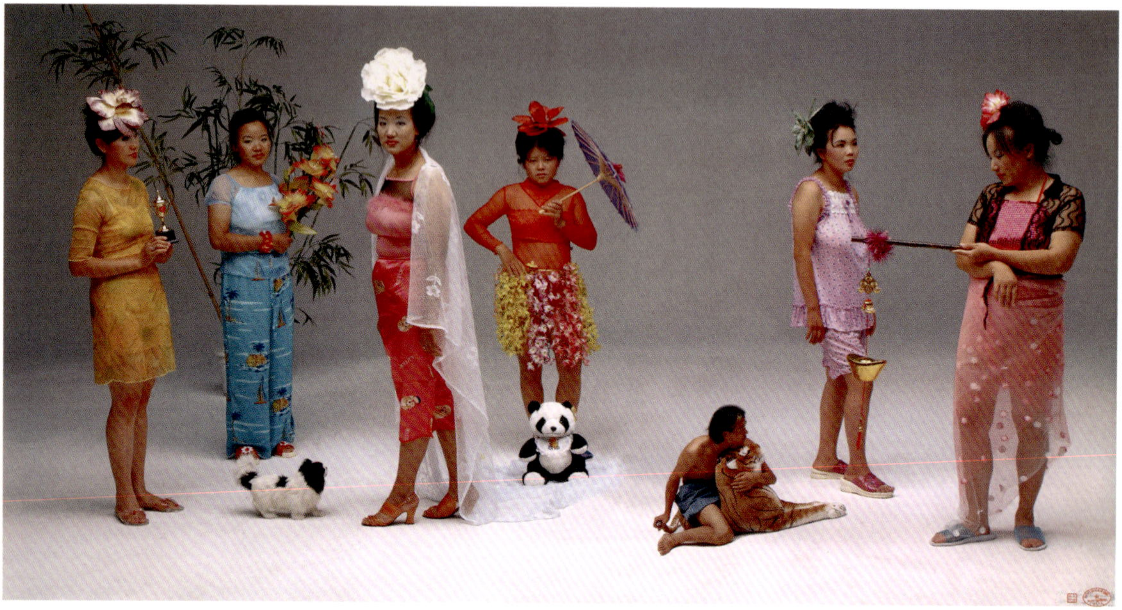

Initially trained as a painter, Wang turned to photography in the late 1990s when China's rapid economic rise coincided with an influx of Western cultural influences. His photographs from this period contend with the contradictions in Chinese society that simultaneously aim to adhere to traditional values while embracing a turn towards consumerism. This composition is based on the Tang dynasty (618–907) scroll painting *Court Ladies Adorning Their Hair with Flowers*, which depicts noblewomen and their maidservants amusing themselves in a garden. The staged scene is organized like a horizontal scroll painting, in which a narrative unfolds in a linear sequence. Costumes and props provide signs of contemporary life, while the scale of some figures was manipulated using early digital tools.

Uta Barth

American, born Germany, 1958

. . . and of time. (AOT 4), 2000

Chromogenic prints, each:

89.9 × 114.3 cm (35 × 45 in.), 2000.56

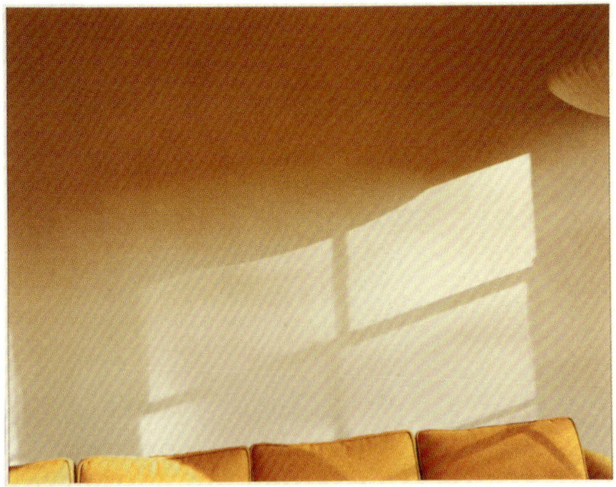

This work takes inspiration from the Getty Museum's *Wheatstacks, Snow Effect, Morning* (1891) by Claude Monet (see p. 212), a painting that demonstrates how light can affect a viewer's perception of a subject. Barth created a series of multipart photographs that study how daylight streaming through her living-room window alters the space. This diptych presents two subtle variations of the same scene, a sparsely appointed interior bathed in warm, soft light. In both images, the outline of a paned window cast against the wall floats over the yellow sofa like a specter. By relegating tangible objects to the edges of each composition, Barth emphasizes the negative space of the room while revealing how light can reorient perceptions of the familiar, transforming the spaces we inhabit into unconventional scenes.

Ishiuchi Miyako

Japanese, born 1947

ひろしま/*hiroshima #69 (Abe Hatsuko)*, 2007

Chromogenic print, 108 × 74 cm ($42\frac{1}{2} \times 29\frac{1}{8}$ in.), 2015.23.1

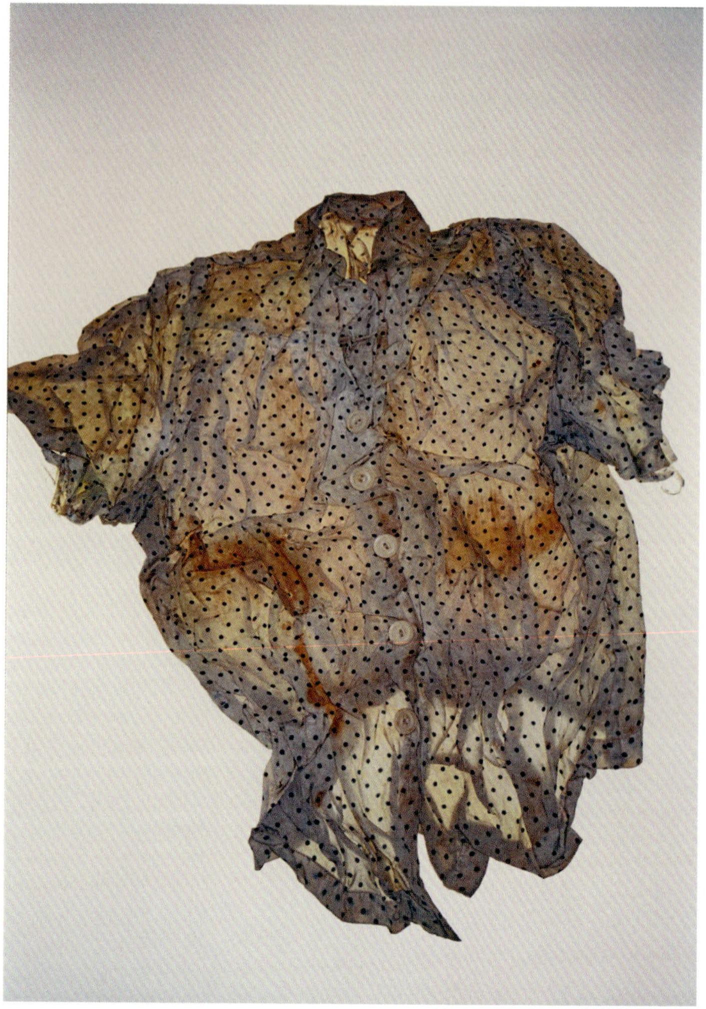

For more than fifteen years, Ishiuchi Miyako has photographed the personal belongings of survivors and victims of the atomic bombing of Hiroshima, Japan, now housed in the Hiroshima Peace Memorial Museum. Focusing on items of clothing worn by women on the day of the tragedy, she fosters a spiritual kinship with the garments, often speaking to them while photographing them. To create this image, she used a lightbox to illuminate each crease, seam, and stain of the blouse, imbuing the garment with a sense of presence while alluding to the blinding light of the atomic blast. Ishiuchi presents each piece of clothing as transcendent and floating in space—less a relic of history than a breathing being. She describes it as a way to invoke "the dead forever watching over the living."

Marco Breuer

German, born 1966

Spin (C-824), 2008

Chromogenic paper, 34.6 × 27 cm (13⅝ × 10⅝ in.). Purchased with funds provided by the Photographs Council, 2014.9.7

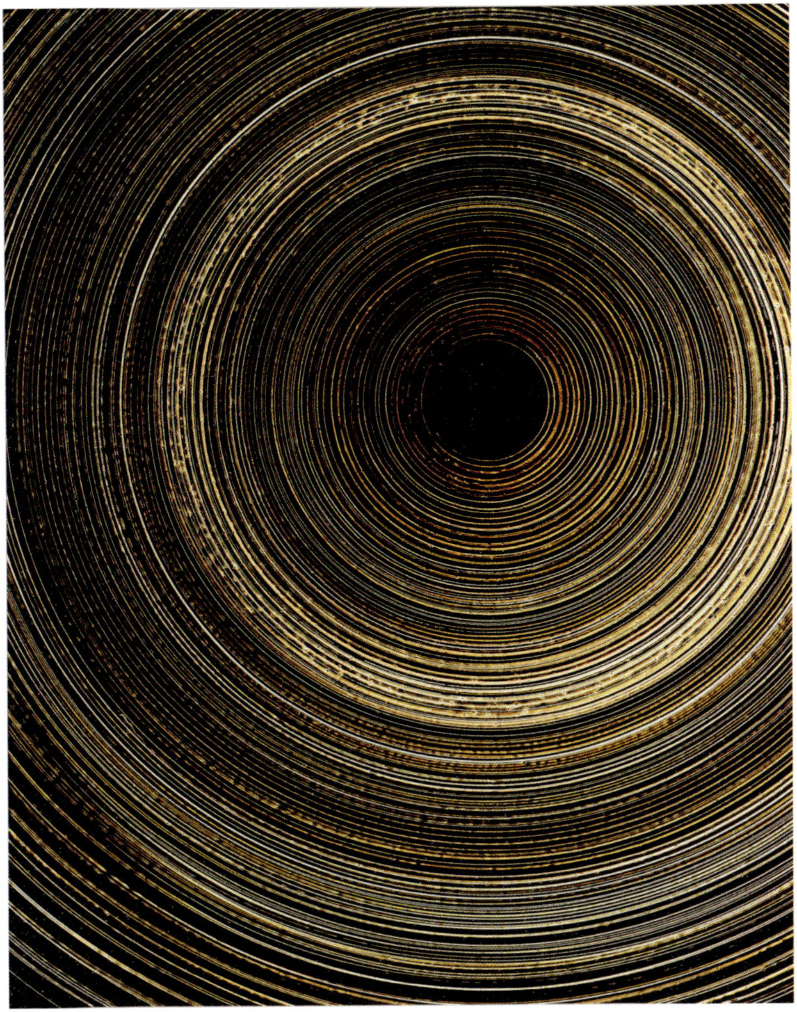

Breuer approaches the medium of photography as a method of investigation. In the early 1990s he eliminated cameras and film from his practice and began working directly with light-sensitive paper in the darkroom, abrading, burning, or scraping away the emulsion layer. Completely nonrepresentational, the resulting works have the immediacy of abstract drawings. However, because they are made on photographic paper and processed via traditional darkroom chemistry, either before or after Breuer's interventions, they are, materially speaking, "photographs." To make his Spin series, the artist modified a turntable with a razor blade to create a whirling vortex of concentric circles. The resulting images are as mesmerizing for the earthen tones excavated from the paper's emulsion as they are for the perfection of their execution.

Lieko Shiga
Japanese, born 1980
Portrait of Cultivation, 2009
Chromogenic print, 120 × 180 cm
(47¼ × 70⅞ in.). Purchased with funds
provided by the Photographs Council,
2015.1.4

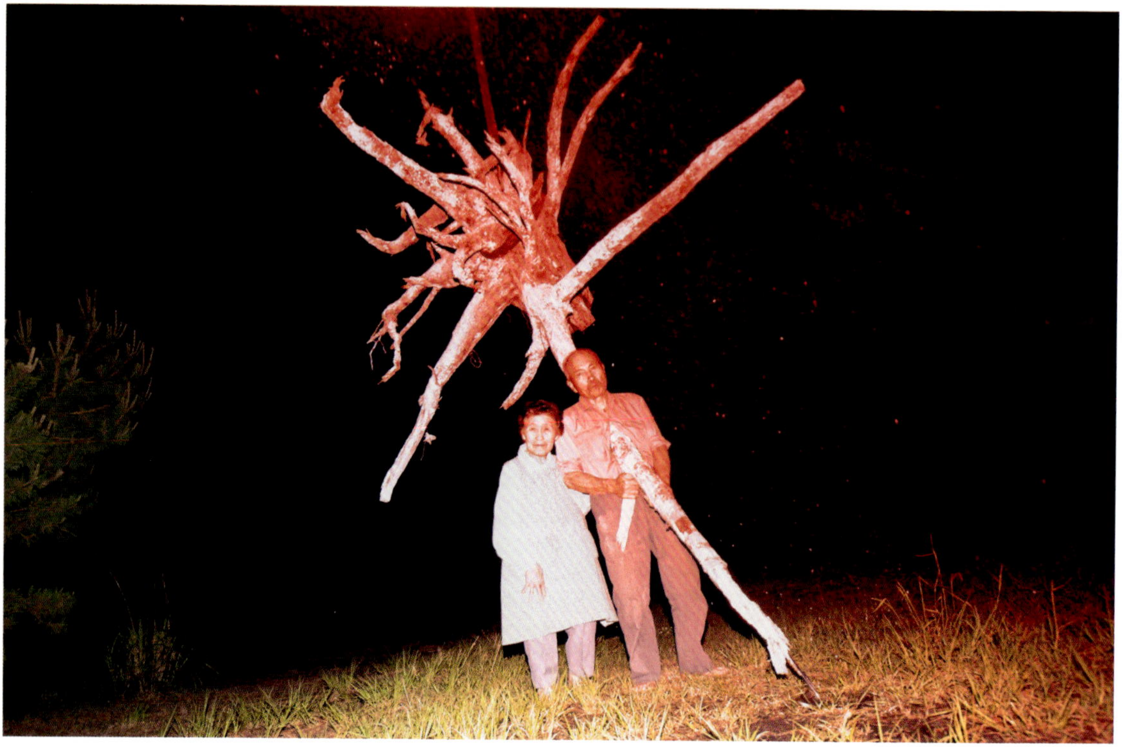

Shiga's photographs visualize the hidden relationships that underlie daily life. As the resident photographer of Kitakama, a small coastal community in northern Japan, Shiga works in collaboration with the individuals she photographs, drawing on their memories and personal histories to create her images. After interviewing her subjects, she arranges them in meticulously staged scenes, achieving hallucinatory effects through the use of colored filters, bright lighting, and double negatives. Here, a man bathed in an eerie red light links arms with his wife, unfazed by the pine roots piercing his chest. For Shiga, these roots convey the villagers' generational ties to the land. Upon first encountering the uprooted tree in the field nearby, Shiga recalls, "I just felt like I met his grandfather in front of my eyes."

Allison Rossiter
American, born 1953

Kilbourn Acme Kruxo, exact expiration date unknown, ca. 1940s, processed 2013, 2013
Gelatin silver print, 12.7 × 17.8 cm (5 × 7 in.).
Purchased with funds provided by the Photographs Council, 2013.76

Rossiter's approach to photography might be described as minimalist: she does not use a camera, film, or light. Since 2007 she has processed sheets of expired gelatin silver paper using photographic chemicals in the darkroom. She begins her work by collecting commercially manufactured papers dating from as far back as 1900 and concludes by immersing or dipping the paper in developer or pouring or pooling the developer onto the sheet, followed by stopping and fixing the print. Her actions resuscitate the expired papers, giving them new life simply through processing. She achieves a rich array of results, with some works suggesting the faint impressions of primitive mark making; others calling to mind mid-twentieth-century painterly abstractions; and still others—like this one—resembling landscapes.

Andrea Chung

American, born 1978

A Scene from Anthropocene no. 2, 2016

Cyanotypes, each: 57.2 × 76.2 cm (22 × 30 in.); overall: 116.8 × 152.4 cm (46 × 60 in.), 2021.20

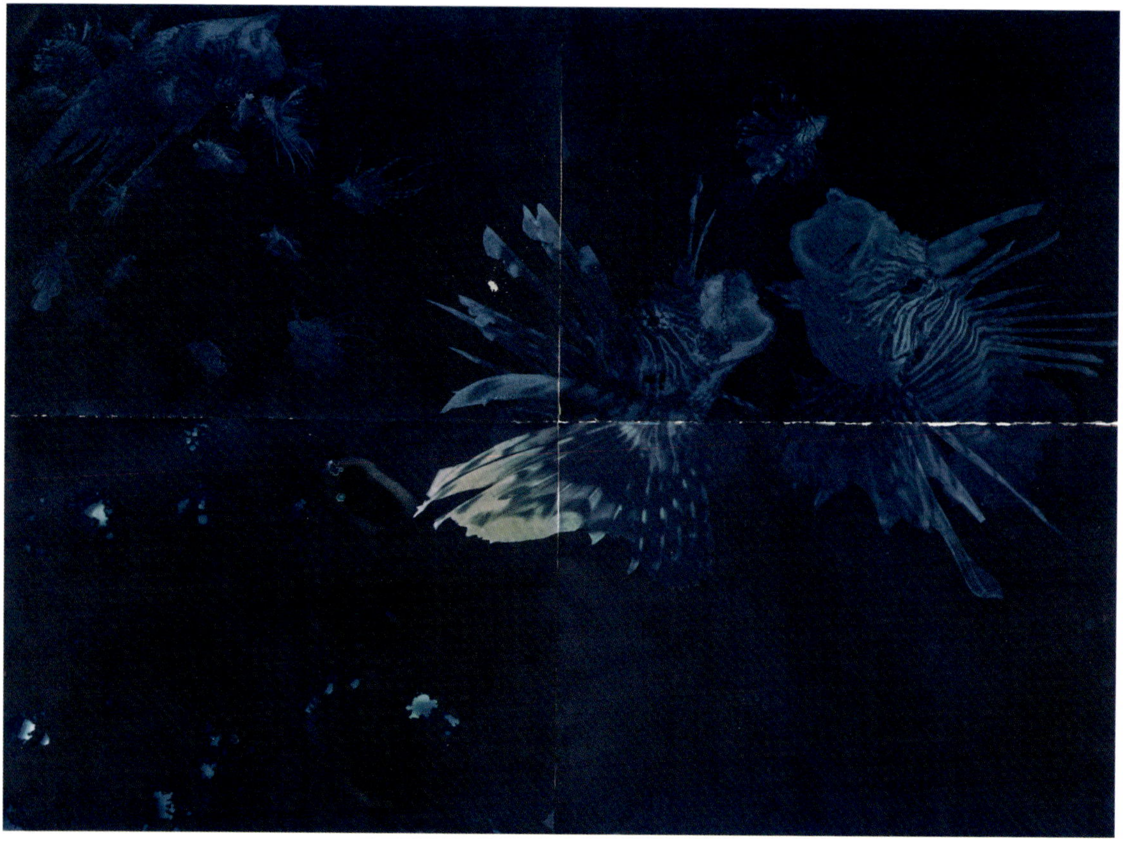

Chung works in a variety of media to highlight the legacies of European colonialism in the West Indies. As a Getty Museum staff member early in her career, she was exposed to the nineteenth-century cyanotypes of the British artist Anna Atkins (see p. 360) and was inspired to learn the technique and apply it to a series of underwater scenes. This lush cyanotype, printed on four sheets, depicts the beautiful but predatory lionfish, a non-native species from the Indo-Pacific that has thrived in the Caribbean Sea since being accidentally introduced in the early 1990s. They have decimated the marine ecosystem and endangered the local fishing industry. Chung portrays the lionfish as a potent visual metaphor for the destructive impact of centuries of colonization in the Caribbean.

Sky Hopinka
Ho-Chunk Nation member; descendant of the Pechanga Band of Luiseño people, born 1984

This is the changer, 2019
From the series The Land Describes Itself
Inkjet print, 32.6 × 32.6 cm
(12 13/16 × 12 13/16 in.). Purchased with funds provided by the Photographs Council, 2023.30.2

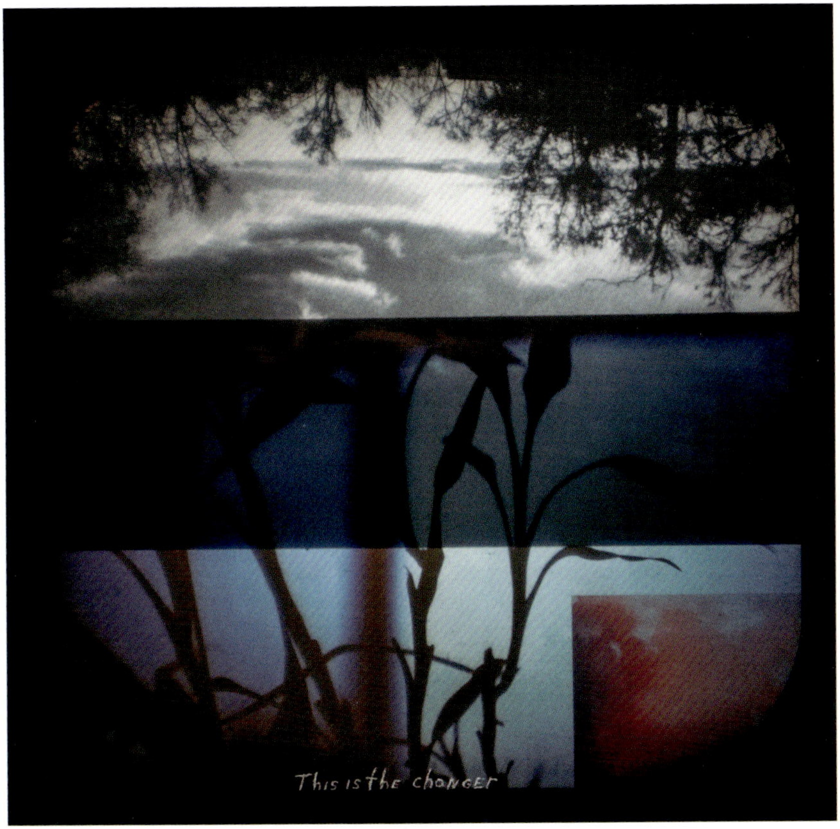

Hopinka is a multimedia artist known for films and photographs that foreground the relationship between Native communities, landscape, and language. This print is part of his series The Land Describes Itself. Hopinka begins by turning found images into transparencies before photographing the projections. He then assembles composite images that depict locations across vast geographies associated with his Indigenous heritage, tracing connections across personal, communal, and historical references. He scratches inscriptions into each print by hand. Hopinka reimagines the landscape genre by forgoing legibility of topography for a poetic, anticolonial reading of the land. His work provides a counternarrative to the dominant tradition of American landscape photography, which emphasizes the impulse to explore and discover.

Mickalene Thomas
American, born 1971
Jet Blue #23, 2021
Collage (chromogenic print, mixed-media paper, acrylic paint, rhinestones, and fiberglass mesh on museum board, mounted to Dibond), framed: 172 × 144 cm ($67^{11}/_{16}$ × $56^{11}/_{16}$ in.)
Purchased with funds provided by the Photographs Council, 2022.13

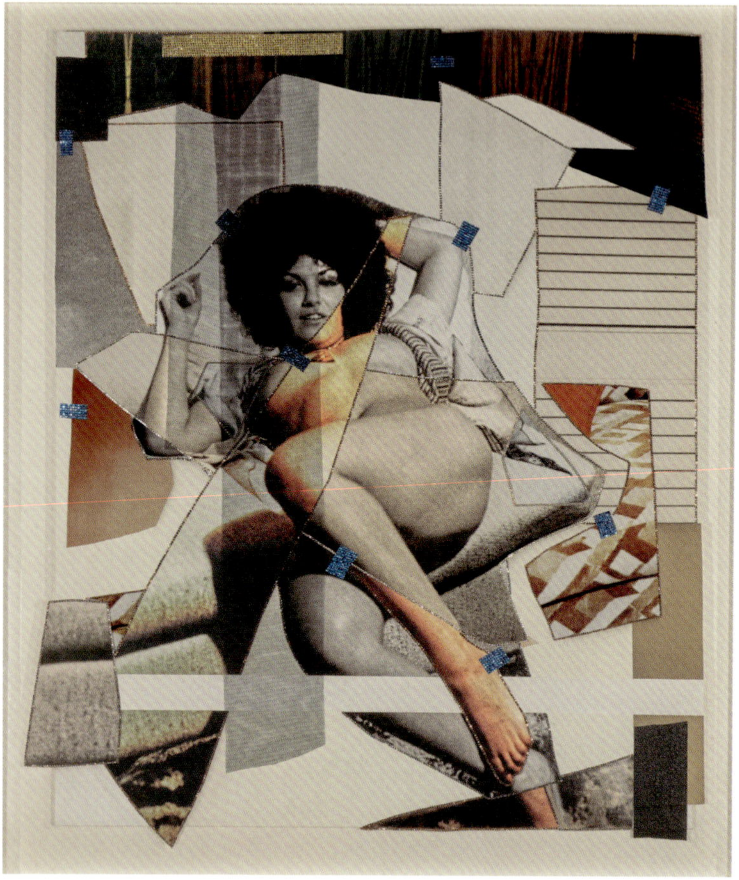

Thomas is known for her multimedia works that celebrate the sexuality and agency of Black women. To create her series Jet Blue, she mined the pinup calendars produced by *Jet* magazine in the 1970s and 1980s. Intrigued by the seductively posed women gracing the centerfolds, Thomas rephotographed and enlarged the images, recasting these women as the central figures of large-scale collages. While the calendars featured closely cropped views that emphasized the models' physicality, Thomas's collages reimagine her protagonists in vivid, kaleidoscopic environments that embrace the aesthetics of 1970s kitsch. Here, a nude woman lounges in a richly decorated interior replete with dark wood paneling, an orange-and-brown patterned sofa, and a zebra-print rug.

Tourmaline

American, born 1983

Summer Azure, 2020; print 2021

Dye sublimation print, 74.9 × 76.2 cm

(29½ × 30 in.), 2021.35

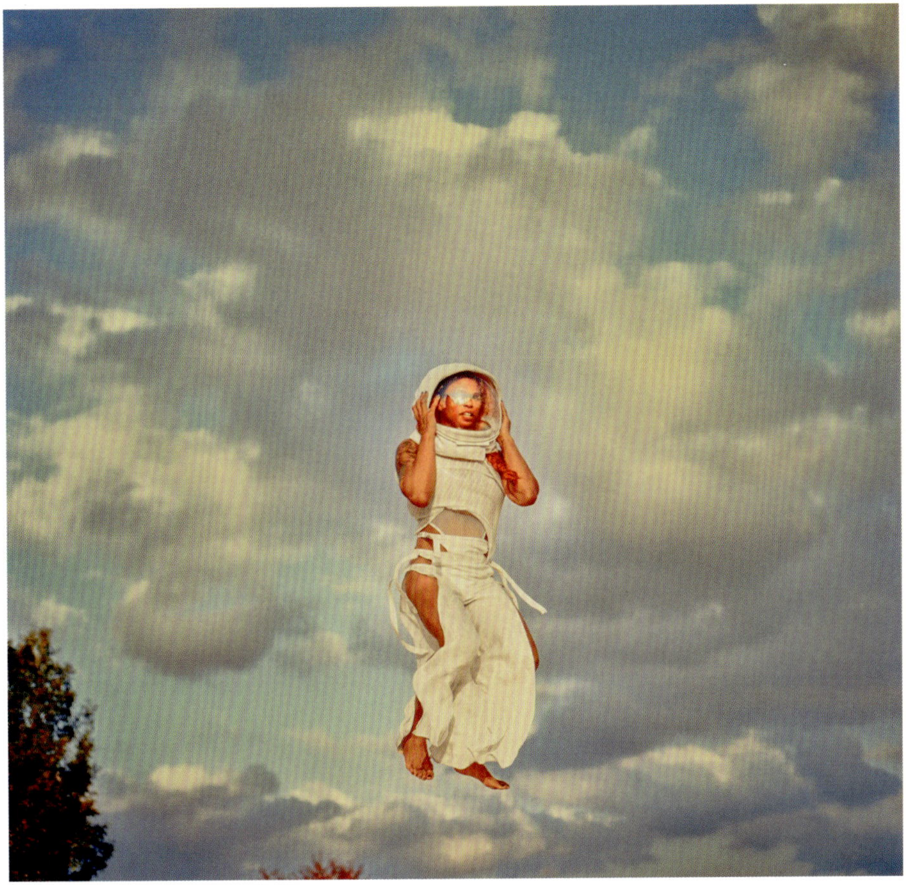

An activist and artist, Tourmaline aims with her work to highlight the overlooked histories and cultural achievements of the Black, queer, and transgender communities with which she identifies. Her photographs foreground queer agency and often embrace aesthetics associated with Afrofuturism, a movement in literature and art that explores the intersection of African diasporic cultures with science fiction. *Summer Azure* conjures a dreamlike moment of liberation from the everyday burdens and restrictions that circumscribe the Black and trans experience. Wearing a protective helmet, she levitates above the ground, disconnected from societal constrictions. By referencing imagined futures, she encourages audiences to reconsider the primacy of mainstream narratives and envision alternative possibilities.

Index of Makers

First edition 1986
Ninth edition 2026

Published by the J. Paul Getty Museum, Los Angeles
Getty Publications
1200 Getty Center Drive, Suite 500
Los Angeles, CA 90049-1682
getty.edu/publications

Timothy Potts and Elizabeth Morrison, *Editors*
Ruth Evans Lane and Darryl Oliver, *Project Editors*
Marcie Muscat, *Manuscript Editor*
Jon Grizzle, *Designer*
Michelle Deemer, *Production*
Danielle Brink, *Image Acquisition and Rights*
Diane Franco, *Typesetter*

Distributed in the United States and Canada by the University of Chicago Press

Distributed outside the United States and Canada by Yale University Press, London

Printed in China

Library of Congress Cataloging-in-Publication Data
Names: J. Paul Getty Museum author issuing body | Potts, Timothy F. writer of foreword writer of introduction
Title: The J. Paul Getty Museum handbook of the collection
Description: Ninth edition. | Los Angeles : J. Paul Getty Museum, 2026. | Includes index. | Summary: "This latest edition of the Getty handbook offers a fascinating look at objects in the J. Paul Getty Museum's collection"—Provided by publisher.
Identifiers: LCCN 2025018649 | ISBN 9798887120065 paperback
Subjects: LCSH: J. Paul Getty Museum—Catalogs | Art—California—Los Angeles—Catalogs | LCGFT: Catalogs | Collection catalogs
Classification: LCC N582.M25 A251 2026 | DDC 708.194/94—dc23/eng/20250618
LC record available at https://lccn.loc.gov/2025018649

Front cover detail from: Vincent van Gogh, *Irises* (p. 217)
Back cover details from: Parmigianino, *Virgin and Child with Saint John the Baptist and Mary Magdalene* (p. 145); Albrecht Dürer, *Stag Beetle* (p. 225); Tourmaline, *Summer Azure* (p. 411); Giovanni di Balduccio, *The Annunciation* (p. 273); Engraved Ring with Herakles Pouring a Libation (p. 35); Cat (p. 320); Jan van Huysum, *Vase of Flowers* (p. 182); Saint Jerome Extracting a Thorn from a Lion's Paw (p. 108)
p. 2: Rembrandt Harmensz. van Rijn, *An Old Man in Military Costume* (p. 176)
p. 4: Pierre-Auguste Renoir, *The Promenade* (p. 210)
p. 8: Interior view of a North Pavilion gallery at the Getty Center

Illustration Credits
p. 9: USC Digital Library, Los Angeles Examiner Photographs Collection; p. 10: Institutional Archives, The Getty Research Institute, Los Angeles (2010.IA.04); pp. 12, 376: © J. Paul Getty Trust; p. 348: © Bowness, Hepworth Estate; p. 349: © 2025 Calder Foundation, New York / Artists Rights Society (ARS), New York; p. 372: © Man Ray 2015 Trust / Artists Rights Society (ARS), New York / ADAGP, Paris 2025; p. 373: © Family of Shigemi Uyeda; p. 374: © 2025 Imogen Cunningham Trust / www.ImogenCunningham.com; p. 375: © 2025 Center for Creative Photography, Arizona Board of Regents / Artists Rights Society (ARS), New York; p. 377: © ringl + pit, courtesy Robert Mann Gallery; p. 378: © Estate of Lisette Model, courtesy Baudoin Lebon / Keitelman; p. 379: © 2025 Artists Rights Society (ARS), New York / ADAGP, Paris; p. 382: © Estate of Noboru Ueki, courtesy MEM, Tokyo; p. 383: © 1978 The Irving Penn Foundation; p. 384: Reproduced with permission of the Minor White Archive, Princeton University Art Museum / © Trustees of Princeton University; p. 385: © Adger Cowans, courtesy Bruce Silverstein Gallery; p. 386: © The Gordon Parks Foundation; p. 387: © Gilles Peress; p. 388: © Hiro; p. 389: © Estate of Malick Sidibé; p. 390: © Jo Ann Callis, courtesy of ROSEGALLERY; p. 391: © Woodman Family Foundation / Artists Rights Society (ARS), New York; p. 392: © Muna Tseng Dance Projects Inc.; p. 393: © 1986 David Hockney; p. 394: © Duane Michals; p. 395: © Robert Mapplethorpe Foundation; p. 396: © Graciela Iturbide; p. 397: © Nan Goldin; p. 398: © Estate of Graciela Sacco; p. 399: © Shirin Neshat, courtesy of the artist and Gladstone Gallery; p. 400: © Laura Aguilar Trust of 2016; p. 401: © Ming Smith; p. 402: © Wang Qingsong; p. 403: © Uta Barth; p. 404: © Ishiuchi Miyako; p. 405: © Marco Breuer; p. 406: © Lieko Shiga; p. 407: © Alison Rossiter; p. 408: © Andrea Chung; p. 409: © Sky Hopinka; p. 410: © Mickalene Thomas; p. 411: © Tourmaline.

Authorized Product Safety Representative in the European Union: Easy Access System Europe, Mustamäe tee 50, 10621 Tallinn, Estonia, gspr.requests@easyproject.com